'This entertaining first volume of diaries, which takes Violet from the age of 17 to 27, reveals her as a fluent writer with a good sense of place and an acute but pitiless power of observation ... Admirably edited'   David Gilmour, *Evening Standard*

'[Mark Pottle's] editorship has been meticulous and his contribution greatly enhances an enjoyable and instructive book. May further instalments follow shortly'   Philip Ziegler, *Daily Telegraph*

'We are given an incomparable glimpse of life at the summit when Britain was still the world's only superpower'   John Grigg, *Spectator*

'One must admire Violet Bonham Carter. She was a clever and spirited woman, and her literary gifts are remarkable. With extraordinary vividness and verve, she can conjure up a scene or describe a character'   Selina Hastings, *Sunday Telegraph*

Mark Bonham Carter, elder son of Violet Bonham Carter, was a publisher before being elected Liberal MP for Torrington, North Devon, in a sensational by-election in 1958. He was later the first chairman of the Race Relations Board. He edited *The Autobiography of Margot Asquith*. He was created a life peer in 1986.

Mark Pottle took a first in History at Sheffield University and then went on to gain his doctorate at Wolfson College, Oxford in 1988. He has worked as a research assistant on volume eight of *The History of the University of Oxford* (published in 1994) and since 1992 has been a research fellow at Wolfson College.

LANTERN SLIDES

The Diaries and Letters of
Violet Bonham Carter
1904–1914

Edited by

Mark Bonham Carter
&
Mark Pottle

'How strange it would be & how frightening
if one could see isolated scenes of one's life in
advance, like lantern-slides, without knowing
where they were or when, what led up to
them or what followed.'

Diary, Tuesday 27 December 1910, Omdurman

A PHOENIX GIANT PAPERBACK

First published in Great Britain by
Weidenfeld & Nicolson in 1996.
This paperback edition published in 1997 by
Phoenix, a division of Orion Books Ltd,
Orion House, 5 Upper Saint Martin's Lane,
London WC2H 9EA

A CIP catalogue record for this book is available
from the British Library

ISBN 1 85799 860 X

Typeset by Selwood Systems, Midsomer Norton
Printed and bound in Great Britain by
Butler & Tanner Ltd, Frome and London

Dedicated to the memory of
Mark Bonham Carter

CONTENTS

ILLUSTRATIONS

[1] Hon. Jamie Neidpath and Mrs Guy Charteris
[2] Lord Kilbracken
[3] Lady Judith Swire
[4] PA News
[5] Hulton Deutsch Collection

PREFACE

This volume owes its existence to the vision of Mark Bonham Carter, who died in Southern Italy on 4 September 1994. He was both the owner of the bulk of the papers presented here, and the elder son of their author, Violet Bonham Carter. I first began working with him on his mother's papers in October 1991, and in the three years before his death I came greatly to admire him. He was both intellectual and aesthetic, and combined sharpness of wit with compassionate understanding. I remember him most for his tremendous sense of style, a manner that was at once understated and unmistakable; without seeming dated, it recalled the grandeur of an earlier era. Many of these qualities belonged also to his mother. Like her, he was a steadfast Liberal who became a life peer. He would make a rich subject for biographical study in his own right. It is a tribute to his understanding of publishing, and of modern British history, that this volume has survived his death. It now stands as a testament to the creative energy of the last years of his life.

It also marks the devotion of his family, who in the difficult period following his death rallied to give renewed life to his original idea: Leslie Bonham Carter, and her children Jane, Virginia and Eliza, have each given essential support. They have been seconded by Raymond Bonham Carter, whose involvement in all aspects of the research has been unstinting since it first began. Special acknowledgement must also be made of the contribution of Elena Bonham Carter, whose understanding of Violet's character has been an invaluable reference point. Without this family support I could not have completed the work that was begun with Mark Bonham Carter in October 1991. The great kindness and hospitality of all of the abovementioned has been one of life's windfalls.

It was Mark Bonham Carter's intention that Violet and her contemporaries be allowed to speak for themselves, and I have ensured that the ratio of diaries and letters to editorial commentary reflects this, with more than four-fifths of the space being devoted to the former. The aim has been a balanced portrait of an individual, against a background of the times. And it should be remembered that these were times very different to our own. The attitudes of Violet and her contemporaries towards race, class and gender are to be read in context.

It is hoped that this work has biographical as well as broad historical significance. Whatever success there has been in realizing this aim is due in large measure to Dr Michael Brock, lately Warden of Nuffield College. Dr Brock's erudition, experience, and charm have guided every stage of the work, and are reflected in it. His advice has never been more highly valued than in the period since Mark Bonham Carter's untimely death. I am also deeply indebted to Mrs Eleanor Brock, who has made telling comments on successive drafts. Their contribution to this work has been a great one.

The volume also owes its existence to the generous support of a number of institutions, and I wish to express gratitude to the trustees of three foundations. The Joseph Rowntree Reform Trust provided the essential early funds that allowed preliminary research into the Violet Bonham Carter MSS to take place. The Leverhulme Trust made possible the extensive research into diaries and correspondence on which this volume is based. And The Wolfson Foundation provided the means whereby the unworked ore of source material could be refined, and fashioned into something of wider interest and importance. The warden and fellows of Nuffield College, Oxford, kindly made available research and administrative facilities. I am also thankful to the president and fellows of Wolfson College, Oxford, who have generously provided the infrastructure without which the research and editing could not have been undertaken. Thanks are also due to all of the members and to the staff of both colleges, who have made a greater contribution to this work than can be adequately acknowledged.

For their generous permission to use copyright material, I thank: the Marquess of Aberdeen; Mr Milton Gendel; the Rt. Hon. Lord Kilbracken; the Earl of Oxford and Asquith; the Marquess of Reading; Mary Rous; George Trevelyan.

For their support in applications for funding, and for their encouragement of the research, thanks are made to Lord Blake; Lord Bullock; Sir Raymond Hoffenberg; Lois Jefferson; Barbara Rashbass; Sir Rex Richards; Lord Wolfson of Marylebone. Many of Violet's friends and family have unselfishly given of their hospitality, advice and encouragement, including: Tim Bonham Carter, Charles Brand, Kate Fleming, the late Lord and Lady Grimond, Grizelda Grimond, John Grimond, Magnus and Laura Grimond, Laura Phillips, Mary Rous, John Rous, Sir Adam Ridley, Cressida Ridley. A host of individuals have responded kindly to what must sometimes have seemed troublesome queries, and a number of others have offered the most constructive advice, and for their thoughtfulness gratitude is expressed to Simon Bailey, Piers Brendon, Sir James Birrell, Beth Crutch, Cecilia Dick, Mike Edge, Lady Freyberg, Annabel Freyberg, Christina Freyberg, Caroline Fryer, Sir Martin Gilbert, Lord Gladwyn, John Grigg, Henry Hardy, Charlotte Havilland, Robin Jessel, Cassia Joll, John Jolliffe, Professor Diane B. Kunz, Anne Langslow, Judy Longworth, Peter McDonald, Lady Eliza Leslie Melville, Nigel Nicolson, Robert O'Neill, Isabelle Phan, Miranda Seymour, Margaret Skellern, Jon Sutherland. Comments made by Mark Curthoys, Brian Harrison, David

Langslow, and Jane Birkett have been especially helpful. The staff of the following libraries, archives, and educational establishments have given valuable assistance: Balliol College Library, Oxford; the Bodleian Library; British Library Newspaper Library, Colindale; Churchill Archives Centre, Churchill College, Cambridge; Hampshire Record Office; Hertfordshire Record Office; Harry Ransom Humanities Research Center, Texas; King's College Library, Cambridge; New College Library Oxford; Nuffield College Library, Oxford; Oxford University Archives; Oxford University Computing Service; Wolfson College Library, Oxford. For their assistance with the practicalities of book production, thanks are made to: Jackson and Dennett, bookbinders (Oxford); Photocraft Ltd., Hampstead; The Composing Room Ltd. (photography), London.

The involvement of a number of individuals in the final stages of drafting accelerated the work towards its conclusion. Lady Judith Swire unravelled difficult biographical notes, gave invaluable advice in character identification, and provided a wonderful illustration of Violet's 'life and times' in the photograph of the Castle Ashby house party. Lord Kilbracken offered critical editorial advice and the benefit of personal knowledge of Violet, as well as of Hugh Godley (his father). Lord Jenkins of Hillhead, in addition to writing a masterly introduction, made wise comments on a close reading of the script. Peter James further tightened and improved the text with an immaculate piece of copy-editing. And Ion Trewin has been everything one would hope for in a publisher, nurturing an idea into a reality with assurance and a sense of style.

This work has been improved by many hands and many minds. I have not been able to identify them all here, but to all of them I am deeply grateful, and to none more so than my family and friends. Any faults in this publication lie at my door.

Wolfson College, Oxford   Mark Pottle

EDITORIAL NOTE

This volume comprises almost 200,000 words, of which roughly three-quarters are source material (diaries and letters) and the remainder editorial text. The diary entries, comprising almost 93,000 words, have been selected from twelve diaries covering the years 1904–1914, which between them contain around 200,000 words. There is no diary for 1908, scant entries only for the first nine months of 1904, and also for the years 1906–7, 1909 and 1913–14. The correspondence included here comprises nearly 54,000 words. The selections have been made from more than 1,800 letters – probably more than half a million words in total. The correspondence that exists is fairly evenly distributed over the period, with a concentration around the years 1905–09.

The basic principle employed in the selection of material has been that it should illuminate, in an interesting and balanced way, 'life and times'. Letters and diary entries have been selected on the basis of their biographical and historical significance. Care has been taken, too, to make the published material an accurate reflection of the source as a whole. While it has proved impossible to include every word on any given theme, an attempt has been made to present a fair and representative sample. These transcriptions of the original documents are faithful to the source, with the inevitable concessions to intelligibility. Where errors in spelling, grammar and punctuation were likely to confuse the sense, they have been silently corrected. Exceptions have been made in order to retain some sense of the individuality of the authors, and the context in which they wrote. Like many of her generation, Violet made frequent use of the dash as a kind of halfway house between a full stop and a comma. It has not been changed as it gives some indication of the speed with which Violet wrote, and the pace of her ideas. For the same reason the ampersand has been kept – Violet almost never used 'and'. She also wrote the past tense of 'eat' as 'eat', and not as 'ate': in which she was like Virginia Woolf, and this mannerism has been retained.

The author's deletions have mostly been adhered to – 'whose remissness ~~excels~~ surpasses' *becomes* 'whose remissness surpasses'. Exceptions to this rule are those instances where the deletion must be reversed if sense is to be made of the text: '... a Marquis ~~occupying~~ the whole of the opposite side' is transcribed '... a Marquis occupying the whole of the opposite side'.

Words (and parts of words) that have been added by the editor, because they are necessary to the sense, are enclosed in square brackets. Occasionally a word has been omitted where it confuses the sense: for example 'the' in 'I felt in the unaccountably foolish & frivolous spirits'. Omissions that occur in the middle of a sentence are marked by a three-point ellipsis. A four-point ellipsis marks an omission occurring at the end of a sentence or following that sentence and may include one or more ensuing paragraphs. Where a three-point ellipsis occurs at the start of a new line of text, it indicates the omission of the beginning of a paragraph.

An attempt has been made to identify all individuals appearing in the text, and to provide biographical information on them. Notes on the principal characters appear in an appendix ('Biographical notes'). Lesser characters are given a short note that in the main appears at the foot of the page on which they first appear. The index can be used to locate both forms of reference. Where there is neither a note in the appendix, nor a footnote, it can be assumed that nothing could be discovered for the individual in question. The effective dates of the volume, for the identification of individuals by title, are 1 January 1904 to 30 June 1914. For example, though John Campbell Gordon ultimately becomes the 1st Marquess of Aberdeen and Temair (1915), he was in this period the 7th Earl of Aberdeen, and is identified as such.

LIST OF CHRISTIAN NAMES, INITIALS AND NICKNAMES APPEARING IN THE TEXT

A. Archie Gordon
A.B./AJB Arthur James Balfour
A.W. Arnold Ward
Abbess, the Lady Aberdeen
Aggie Lady Agnes Jekyll
Alec/Alick Alexander Carmichael
Anatole Archie Gordon
Archie Archie Gordon
Arnie Arnold Ward
Arnold Arnold Ward
Artie Arthur Asquith
Aubrey Aubrey Herbert
Austen Austen Chamberlain
B. Bongie (Maurice Bonham Carter)
B.C./B-C Edgar Bonham Carter
Baffy Blanche Balfour
Barbara Barbara Jekyll
Barnie E[mily]. Barnard
Baronet, the Sir Timothy Simpson
Bart, the Sir Charles Tennant
Batterdogs Lord Battersea
Beb Herbert Asquith
Bencks/Benck Count Benckendorff
Beo Beo Campbell
Bertie Herbert Asquith
Bim Lord Compton
Bluetooth/Bluey H. T. Baker
Bogey Bogey Harris
Bongy/Bongie Maurice Bonham Carter
Bron Auberon Herbert
Bud, the Nellie Hozier
C. Cyril Asquith
C.B. Campbell-Bannerman
Cairene Carter, the Frederick Bonham
  Carter
Capable Scot, the Archie Gordon
Carrier, the Maurice Bonham Carter
Charles Charles Lister
Charlie Charlie Meade
Charty Lady Ribblesdale

Cheeseman James Currie
Cicely Cicely Horner
Cincie Cynthia Asquith
Cis/Cizzy Cyril Asquith
Clemmie Clementine Churchill
Con Lady (Constance) Manners
Connie Lady Constance Battersea
Conrad Conrad Russell
Cynthia Cynthia Asquith
Cys Cyril Asquith
D.D. Edith Lyttelton
Desecrater, the Olive Macleod
Doddie Lord Haddo
E.G. Edward Grey
Eczie Reginald McKenna
Ed. Edwin Montagu
Eddy/Eddie Eddie Marsh
Edgar Edgar Vincent
Edward Edward Horner
Ego Hugo Charteris
Eileen Lady Eileen Wellesley
Eliza Elizabeth Asquith
Erchie Archie Gordon
Ettie Lady Desborough
Evan Evan Charteris
Ewen Ewen Cameron
F.E. F. E. Smith
Felix Felix Cassel
Frances Lady Horner
Francie Frances Tennant
Fräu [prob.] Anne Heinsius
Geoffrey Geoffrey Howard
Goonie Lady Gwendeline Churchill
Grambo T. Graham Smith
Gugs Francis Weatherby
Guy Guy Charteris
H. Hugh Godley
H.H.A. H. H. Asquith
Harry Harry Graham
Haverer, the Hugh Godley

Heifer, the Lady Aberdeen
Helen Helen Vincent
Herbert Herbert Gladstone
Hersey Hersey Maltby
Hugh/Hughley Hugh Godley
Ishbel Lady Aberdeen
Jack Jack Tennant
Jasper Jasper Ridley
Jo/Joe Joseph Chamberlain
John John Manners
Jonah L. E. Jones
K./Katharine Katharine Asquith
K. of K. Lord Kitchener
Kakoo Kathleen Tennant
Kissa Clarissa Bramston
Lawso Frank Lawson
Ld B. Lord Battersea
Letty Lady Violet Manners
Lillah Lillah McCarthy
Linky Lord Hugh Cecil
Ll.G./L.G. David Lloyd George
Lord K. Lord Kitchener
Loulou Lewis Harcourt
Lousbags Loustau
Lucy Lucy Graham Smith
Lulu Lewis Harcourt
M. Margot Asquith
M.B.C. Maurice Bonham Carter
McK Reginald McKenna
Margot Margot Asquith
Mark Mark Horner
Martian Edgar Bonham Carter
Mary Mary Vesey (later Herbert)
Master, the the Master of Elibank
Maurice Maurice Baring
May May Tomlinson
Melcho Lady [Mary] Elcho
Micky/Mikky Roderick Meiklejohn

Monica Monica Grenfell
Mrs G. Mrs Grosvenor
Mrs Horner Lady Horner
Nash Vaughan Nash
Nellie Nellie Hozier
Neville Neville Lytton
O.S. H. H. Asquith
Oc Arthur Asquith
Old Haverer, the Arthur Godley
Olive Olive Macleod
Pamela/Pamsky Pamela McKenna
Prime, the H. H. Asquith
Professor, the Sir Walter A. Raleigh
Puffin/Puff Anthony Asquith
R./Raymond Raymond Asquith
Reggie Reginald Farrer
Roger Rogers Low
Rosamund Rosamund Grosvenor
Rufus Rufus Isaacs
Sassbags Aline Sassoon
Sedgar Sir Edgar Vincent
Simon Sir John Simon *or* Lord Lovat
Sligger Francis Urquhart
Swank Elizabeth Asquith
Sympne Sir John Simon
Tante Edwin Montagu
Tweeders Lord Tweedmouth
V./V.A. Violet Asquith
Venice Venetia Stanley
Vincent Vincent Astor
Viola Viola Tree
W. Winston Churchill
W.S. Willie Strutt
Warty [unidentified; at Balliol]
Waxworks/W.W. Sir Reginald Macleod
Winston Winston Churchill
Yak, the Dorothy Ward

Asquith family tree at March 1914

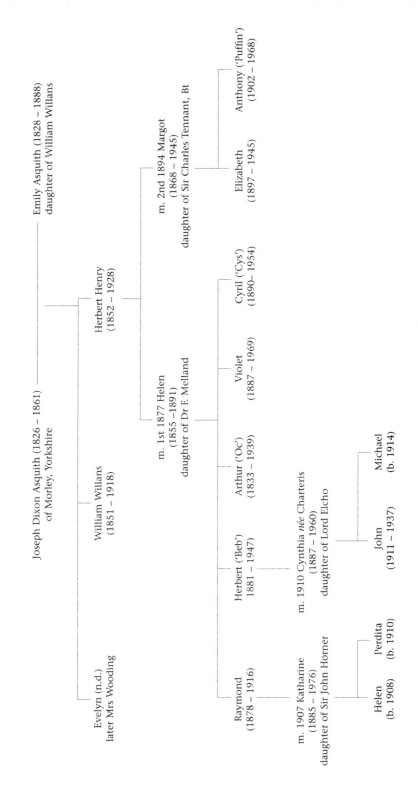

Tennant family tree (those mentioned in this book) at March 1914

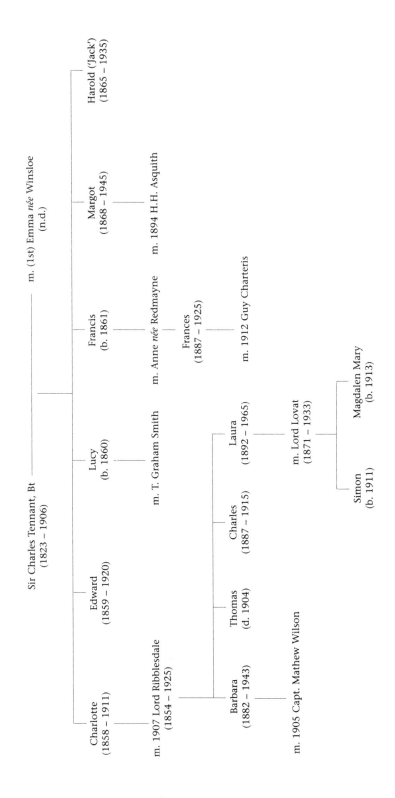

Sir Charles Tennant, Bt
(1823 – 1906)
m. (1st) Emma *née* Winsloe
(n.d.)

Charlotte
(1858 – 1911)
m. 1907 Lord Ribblesdale
(1854 – 1925)

Edward
(1859 – 1920)

Lucy
(b. 1860)
m. T. Graham Smith

Francis
(b. 1861)
m. Anne *née* Redmayne

Margot
(1868 – 1945)
m. 1894 H.H. Asquith

Harold ('Jack')
(1865 – 1935)

Barbara
(1882 – 1943)
m. 1905 Capt. Mathew Wilson

Thomas
(d. 1904)

Charles
(1887 – 1915)

Laura
(1892 – 1965)
m. Lord Lovat
(1871 – 1933)

Frances
(1887 – 1925)
m. 1912 Guy Charteris

Simon
(b. 1911)

Magdalen Mary
(b. 1913)

Introduction

Roy Jenkins

Violet Bonham Carter is best known to history as a daughter and was best known to me as a mother. As a result, despite her strong, almost eagle-swooping personality – she was, I think, the most effective woman orator I have ever heard – there is a danger of her being obscured in the trough of an intermediate generation. Against such a fate this admirably edited book of diaries and letters is a powerful corrective. Through it there flows the full self-confidence of patrician Edwardian Liberalism, accompanied by a certain emotional lushness which recalls a somewhat earlier age, a Pre-Raphaelite picture, a requiem by Saint-Saëns or a chapel by Burges or Butterfield.

Violet Asquith, as she was throughout the nine and a half years here covered, was born in 1887, the fourth child and only daughter by his first marriage of H. H. Asquith, whose rise from humble beginnings to a long premiership and, as some regarded him, 'the last of the Romans' in that office, epitomized 'the effortless superiority of the Balliol man' of that epoch. At the time of Violet's birth he was however only a spasmodically rising barrister who had rather rashly (because insecurely established) entered the House of Commons in the previous year. Her mother was the daughter of a Manchester doctor who, before her death from typhoid when Violet was four, was already finding oppressive (to her liking for modest domesticity) the speed of her husband's ascent in the great world. It would therefore be easy to dismiss Helen Asquith (the mother who had a singular beauty of profile, more so than Violet, although not ill-favoured, was ever to attain) as a dull incubus from whom Asquith, sharply though he grieved at the time, was lucky to have been relieved.

Yet the quality of Helen Asquith's five children makes it difficult to believe that she did not contribute a good deal to the genes. Before reading these diaries I had inclined to the view that Violet was a girl who had done well to keep up her end with four remarkable brothers, two of intellectual brilliance, all of exceptional charm and success of one sort or another. Now I see a different balance, that of four engaging young men, including the legendary (but like most legends somewhat overstated) Raymond, surrounding a sister who was the superior of all of them in purpose and personality.

It was an extraordinary comment on the epoch that whereas the boys were uniformly highly educated her instruction was distinctly casual. They were all at Winchester (where Asquith had not been), three of them at Balliol (where he had), and one at New College. Violet, by contrast, was left to governesses and finishing schools, although as the latter were in France and Germany she ended up a good linguist. But her other knowledge came more through osmosis than through education. What was even more extraordinary, however, was that, having herself been deprived of a university by the class and sex prejudices of Edwardian England, she proceeded to do exactly the same with her own daughters thirty years later, even though by then the 'unfashionableness' of Girton and Somerville was well on the ebb.

The further paradox was that although it was upper-class prejudice against institutional education for girls (the professional classes were much keener on using such university opportunities as developed around the turn of the century) of which she was the victim, there was not, as I well remember her elder son once pointing out to me, a drop of aristocratic blood in her veins. But by the time that the diary begins she was none the less firmly ensconced in an upper-class pattern of life and habit of mind, the latter sitting alongside fierce Liberal partisanship, but this in no way diluting the former. Partly, no doubt, this fashionable and even opulent way of life came with Violet's step-mother, the (fortunately) inimitable Margot Tennant, whom Asquith, causing a good number of raised eyebrows, had married in 1894, when he was forty-one, she thirty and Violet seven.

Margot was one of the many children of Sir Charles Tennant, known in the family and more widely by the not very distinguishing or distinguished sobriquet of 'the bart'. He had started not in rags but in moderate Glasgow commercial prosperity and he ended up in Grosvenor Square and vast riches. This did not exactly give Margot a more elevated lineage than Violet, but wealth, the smart marriages of her sisters (one to the Ribblesdale whom Sargent painted as a god in hunting clothes and one to a Lyttelton) and above all her own ability to capture lions with a mixture of exhibitionism and enticement made her the epitome of fast fashion. In my now thirty-year-old life of Asquith I tried to sum up her premarital haul in the following passage:

> Wherever she went she became the centre of attention. Her *forte*, especially on a first meeting, was the unexpected provocative remark. She told the Duke of Beaufort that his unique blue and buff hunting colours, although pretty for women, were unsporting for men; her reward was a portrait inscribed 'Hark Halloa!' She told Lord Randolph Churchill that he had 'resigned more out of temper than conviction', and was repaid with an invitation to meet and sit next

to the Prince of Wales at a supper party, which she attended wearing what most women present thought was her nightgown. She told General Booth (of the Salvation Army) that he did not believe in hell any more than she did, and then knelt with him, praying on the floor of the railway compartment in which they were travelling. She hinted to Lord Tennyson that she thought he was dirty and got him to give her a long reading from 'Maud' and 'The Princess'.

This was all more than a decade before Violet's diaries begin. In the meantime Margot had led Asquith (without much resistance, it must be said) into a life of balls and weekends at the grandest houses, although she herself had been somewhat tamed by the ten years being interspersed with still-births (as well as two live ones), neurasthenia and growing into middle age. But she had four decades to go as a maker of epigrams and enemies.

Such a step-mother of bright plumage and loud if discordant caw might have been expected to exercise a dominant influence on the life of the seventeen-year-old Violet. One of the surprises of the diaries is how little this was so. Apart from ensuring that a mixture of her husband's earnings, her father's subventions and (later) blithe over-spending jerked the family into a lavish standard of living, her acknowledged influence on Violet was almost nil. And the same thing went for the Asquith boys. As Margot wrote of them in her *Autobiography*: 'They rarely looked at you and never got up when anyone came into the room. If you had appeared downstairs in a ball-dress or a bathing-gown they would not have observed it and would certainly never have commented upon it if they had.'

Violet may have lounged less uncompromisingly but essentially her attitude to Margot was the same as that of her brothers. She was not hostile to her but did not really take her seriously, was indifferent to whether she was present or not, mentioned her remarkably infrequently in the diary, let her pronounce on matters like how to curtsey or dress or which was the best hotel, but would not dream of consulting her on any serious matter of the heart or politics. This note, as well as several of Violet's other attitudes and prejudices, is perfectly captured by an early description of the contrast between an unsuccessful Easter visit to Dinard (without Margot) and a subsequent confluence with her at the Paris Ritz:

What was our despair on arriving on a dank, damp grey morning to find a squalid, hideous, hotel-ridden sea-side hole, over-run with 3rd rate English & opulent Semites of the worst type. ... The links are reached by a *steam tram*. ...

Ten days later:

We have left Dinard! Oh the intense relief! The transition has been very sudden between the tapping masons, screeching housemaids, tepid water & swivelling looking-glasses & this *palace* where all what R[aymond] calls our carnal

appetitions are sinfully pandered to – where we bask in scented baths & sink
ankle deep in mossy carpets. We came here Wed. ... & found Margot here with
slight whooping-cough poor darling. She luckily rarely whoops except at night &
when she does we call it a crumb in the throat!

The style is very sophisticated for seventeen, and the note is one of tolerant
detachment.

Towards her father, on the other hand, Violet's attitude is one of almost
uncritical adoration. It was epitomized by a diary entry during the second
1910 general election: 'Father spoke marvellously at all meetings – his
fertility of word thought & arguments & the way he shakes the Kaleidoscope of the same case into a different combination every time is
amazing. His voice held out well & I think he was happy. ...' The hope
for his happiness is perhaps even more revealing than the undeviating
admiration. Here then, at the age of twenty-three, was the true Cordelia
who was to sustain him through the political vicissitudes which began in
1915 and were to be only temporarily relieved by the victory at Paisley
in 1920.

Her loyalty was unshakeable, but she had a natural gift for admiration
and could sometimes extend it in surprising directions. In the year following that unpromising Dinard expedition she was off again to the sea-
side. In Edwardian and early Georgian days when golf was more a game
of politics than of business, links, even along bleak shores, were the fatal
lure. Violet (although she once, according to her father, 'rather lost her
heart to the brindle-haired Labour leader' in a MacDonald/Asquith foursome at Lossiemouth) was a camp follower rather than a champion. But
she mostly followed famous camps, and in 1905 she was at Littlestone on
the sea edge of Romney Marsh, at the same time as Arthur Balfour and
both the Elchos, with Bishop Cosmo Gordon Lang, then of Stepney but
already with York and Canterbury in his sights, thrown in as I think
coincidental ballast. After two dinners with only Balfour (then Prime
Minister) and Lord and Lady Elcho (not bad for an eighteen-year-old) she
wrote: 'I can never remember feeling such joy in anyone's presence or
conversation as A.B.'s. I never took my eyes or ears off him the whole
evening. He seems to me to have such a perfect mind & character – & his
lack of infallibility *is* so attractive – besides his wonderful kindness &
courtesy to the smallest & dullest & most insignificant (i.e – self).'

As the notoriously cold-hearted Balfour was then, and for six and a half
years subsequently, the leader of her father's opposing party this was by
any standards a remarkable tribute. It would have been the more so had
she then been able to foresee that Balfour, whom her father liked to regard
as with him the co-captain of the gentlemen in politics, none the less
delivered the decisive blow against him by marching calmly out on to the

field in December 1916 under the leadership of the arch-player Lloyd George. But Asquith, I fear, although by all tests except that of charm the more considerable figure, always admired Balfour more than Balfour reciprocated the compliment.

Towards Lloyd George himself Violet was ambiguous. With her great gift of phrase she was later to contribute two most memorable epithets built around him. In the second Paisley contest, when Asquith was fighting for re-election in a campaign dominated by Bonar Law and Lloyd George, Violet said that the electorate was offered a choice between one man suffering from sleeping sickness (Law) and the other from St Vitus's dance. At the next Paisley election, when Liberal reunion was attempted, Lloyd George and Asquith spoke from the same Clydeside platform and there were many trite remarks made about the lion lying down with the lamb, Violet, from the same platform, said that 'she had never seen Lloyd George looking less voracious or her father less edible'. But in the days when he was her father's more or less loyal chancellor of the exchequer she was more equivocal. At lunch at 11 Downing Street in April 1910, she was basically patronizing although not without shrewdness: 'quite an amusing meal – I sat next to Ll G. who has charm no doubt but no sense of humour & I think an inferior sense of words to Winston's. Mrs Ll G. very homely & pathetic & Megan delightful.' Then seven months later, when Lloyd George had opened his campaign for the just-announced election at Mile End with one of his more demagogic speeches ('an aristocracy is like cheese; the older it gets the higher it becomes') she occupied a train journey by letting herself go on Asquithian prejudice:

[Have] just read & *heaved over* one of Lloyd George's very worst speeches. It *is* hard on Father to be bound to a man with so little instinct of taste or dignity – & poor darling F[ather] hasn't unfortunately that tinge of the governess in his nature – which might help him to deal with this class of outrage. I hope he won't be upset by it. Luckily he has beyond all people I know the wonderful gift of 'looking in steadiness'. . . .

The other future prime minister of erratic genius over whom Asquith presided with non-governessy steadiness was of course Churchill. Violet was widely thought to have been at least fleetingly in love with him. Her diary however provides little supporting evidence for this, although she writes about him with indiscretion as about Lloyd George, albeit with more affection, none the less mingled with criticism. What is distinctly odd is that there is no diary reference to the Churchill encounter to which she herself was to give great prominence in the book she wrote about him in the year of his death (1965). There she describes with vividness the dinner party at which she first met him:

I found myself sitting next to this young man who seemed to me quite different from any other young man I had ever met. For a long time he remained sunk in abstraction. Then he appeared to become suddenly aware of my existence. ... And he burst forth into a eloquent diatribe on the shortness of human life ... and ended up with the words I shall always remember: 'We are all worms. But I do believe that I am a glow-worm'. ... Until the end of dinner I listened to him spellbound. I can remember thinking: *This* is what people mean when they talk of 'seeing stars' – that is what I am doing now. ... I knew only I had 'seen a great light'. I recognised it as the light of genius.

That was a wonderfully descriptive passage, but was it true at the time, or did it require a combination of the golden glow of memory and Churchill's subsequent rise to full fame to burnish the exchange to brilliance? When his engagement to Clementine Hozier was announced two years later Violet received it with brittle calm, although maybe with an undertow of jealousy.

The news of the clinching of Winston's engagement to the Hozier has just reached me from him. I must say I am much gladder for her sake than I am sorry for his. His wife could never be more to him than an ornamental sideboard as I have often said & she is unexacting enough not to mind not being more. Whether he will ultimately mind her being as stupid as an *owl* I don't know – it is a danger no doubt – but for the moment she will have rest at least from making her own clothes & I think he must be a *little* in love. Father think it spells disaster for them both [not one of Asquith's more prescient judgements]. ... I don't know that it does that. He did not *wish* for – though he needs it badly – a critical, reformatory wife who would stop up the lacunas in his taste etc. & hold him back from blunders.

In fairness to Clementine Churchill it must however be added that, less than four years later, Violet was writing, 'I love her so much now – more than W[inston].'

It is of course of the essence of undoctored diaries that they illustrate the instability of human judgement. And Violet's swooped more than most, except in regard to her father, or indeed to her brothers, where there was less worship, but a steady and mostly admiring love. Her romantic attachments are more difficult to see clearly. She had plenty of attendant swains. It would have been surprising if as the fairly striking and socially active only grown-up daughter of a prime minister she had not. But my guess is that she inclined more to epistolary flirtation than to earthy passion (although the two are not incompatible). From 1905 to 1909 (*aet.* eighteen to twenty-two for her) Archie Gordon, a younger son of the 7th Earl of Aberdeen, was probably the favourite. He was a Balliol Wykehamist and his father Liberal viceroy of Ireland, and he was therefore very *echt* from an Asquithian point of view. But he was not decisively ahead of the field.

Then at the end of 1909 there struck the great tragedy of Violet's young life. Gordon was gravely injured in an early motor crash and died in Winchester hospital nearly twenty days later. Violet was at his bedside for the last of them. The drama had the not unnatural effect of concentrating her affections, they entered into a febrile but exultant engagement, and Mr Asquith came and blessed the union. Then Gordon was gone, but remained in some ways even more of a presence in Violet's life than he had been previously. For several years her diary entries all took the form of letters to him. This may sound mawkish, but apart from her unfortunate habit of sometimes addressing him as 'thee' it was neither that nor deadening of her style. The sentimentality lay in the concept and not in the content. She continued to lead her highly active, *mondaine* but politically involved life. She founded a boys' club at Hoxton in Gordon's memory, and she perhaps visited his parents, both at the Vice Regal Lodge in Dublin and at Haddo House in Aberdeenshire, more than she would otherwise have done, but this apart she did not allow her life to be distorted. And she wrote about it all, allowing for her natural high emotional style, with an unforced spontaneity which makes it a constant effort to remember that what is being read is a memorial diary and not normal letters of eager description to a living person.

An obvious difficulty of such a pattern of imaginative 'widowhood' is how you bring it to an end. She kept it up for a good three years, although as she moved through 1913 the diary entries came increasingly to lose their specific direction. Then at the end of that year she found herself in Khartoum with a desperately ill younger brother on her hands. Cys Asquith survived, but the emotional strain may have finally put to rest the tragedy of four years before. Nineteen-fourteen brought other obvious preoccupations. And in late 1915 Violet (at the age of twenty-eight) married Maurice (Bongie) Bonham Carter, her father's principal private secretary, who had been a devoted correspondent with her for the previous eight years. For this event, and indeed for the war years as a whole, we must await the next volume of diaries.

Apart from their compelling general interest, the diaries provide for me, as an old toiler in the Asquithian vineyard, one new shaft of insight and explanation. Asquith, as is now relatively well known, had a great prime-ministerial infatuation and epistolary romance (and maybe more) with a then young woman called Venetia Stanley, later Mrs Edwin Montagu. It ran from 1911 to 1915. These letters, sometimes amounting to as many as four a day, were made available to and first made public use of by me in my 1964 life of Asquith. Although these letters came to me by the agency of Violet's son, who was my publisher as well as my friend, we between us rather fumbled telling her about the cache. There came a time when she had to be shown my manuscript. When I went to see her after she had read it the atmosphere was distinctly fraught. She claimed that she had not hitherto had the slightest idea of any special relationship between her revered father and Miss Stanley. This was on the face of it implausible for I knew that Venetia had been quite close to Violet, and, as her friend, had been in and out of Downing Street during the relevant years. But the terms in which she denied knowledge tilted probability back to her side. Lady Violet (as I then called her) did not say, 'It cannot be true. My father would never have done it.' That would have been a routine protest. What she said was, 'It cannot be true. Venetia was so *plain.*' This gave a ring of spontaneity and therefore of conviction to the denial.

Since then I have often pondered both over what was the truth and over what made Lady Violet's reaction so extreme. Although patched over with propriety our relations were not quite the same for the remaining five years of her life. It was never 'glad, confident morning' again. These diaries and letters answer not the former but the latter question for me. While I did know that Violet and Venetia were companions (as well as exact contemporaries), I did not know that Violet thought of Venetia as her most intimate friend, with whom she exchanged long and frequent letters of apparently complete confidence. The news, fifty years late, that Venetia exchanged even more frequent and more intimate letters, and perhaps other intimacies as well, with her father was therefore a natural and profound shock, for which I did not fully allow at the time.

Compared with today, when the existence of even the most minor and boring scandals is shrieked out from every tabloid, pre-1914 England was full of hidden sexual reefs. But it was also full of skilful and discreet navigators, of which there now seems to be a paucity. Violet Asquith was not nearly cynical enough to be a winking guide to the *beau monde* as was Greville to mid-Victorian times or Channon to the 1930s, but she had a vivid command of prose and emotion which enabled her to illuminate many fine tracts of now remote terrain.

Roy Jenkins
30 July 1995

The drawbacks to keeping a
diary are manifold; if it is
intimate enough to be interesting
to oneself it invariably becomes
a prey to the inquisitive housemaid
if it contains criticisms on
ones near & dear ones one runs
the risk of alienating them for
life – the only alternative is to
keep a record of ones meals
walks & literature & this is
hardly worth the ink & paper
to say nothing of the waste of
time. So though beset by
many dangers trusting to
Mrs Macmichael's lock as

The first page of Violet's diary, 17 October 1904

ONE

Paris

1904–1905

'We can't have three barristers in the family,' said Raymond. 'We should look as ridiculous as a row of lamp-posts.' It was thus decided that Oc Asquith would not follow his elder brothers to the bar, but would pursue instead a career in the City. For this an understanding of French was considered essential, and in October 1904 Oc was sent to Paris to acquire the necessary skills, taking with him, at his own request, his younger sister Violet. He was then twenty-one, and she just seventeen. They were accompanied by Violet's maid Janet, who was herself only nineteen. Apart from the condition that Violet must not go out alone, they were free of all parental restrictions. They did agree to take their main meals daily at the Casaubons' famous pension in the Latin Quarter, and this became their social base during their sojourn in Paris.

Diary – Monday 17 October 1904 – Hôtel Corneille, Paris

The drawbacks to keeping a diary are manifold; if it is intimate enough to be interesting to oneself it invariably becomes a prey to the inquisitive housemaid; if it contains truthful criticisms on one's near & dear ones one runs the risk of alienating them for life – the only alternative is to keep a record of one's meals walks & literature & this is hardly worth the ink & paper to say nothing of the waste of time. So though beset by many dangers trusting to Mr. Macmichael's lock as my sole security I have resolved to enter on the former more repaying though more risky course.[1]

My leavetaking of Cavendish Square was totally devoid of any sentimental regrets. I left behind me housemaids & dust-sheets, with the prospect of Paris & Artie [Oc] with whom Siberia would be Elysium. Beb hustled us off the steps expressing hypocritical regrets at our departure & we rolled off in a heavily laden four wheeler. My heart sank at the sight of the sea which was rough & filled me with awful presentiments as to my condition on arriving at Calais. However I boldly scaled the ladder leading

---

[1] The diary is secured by a sturdy metal lock, fastened to the black leather covers.

to the deck with my petticoats over my head leaving Janet – who like all maids had started the journey assuming that every one on the ship were scheming to steal my dressing bag (I wish them joy of it!) – below. The first 10 minutes were bliss, but a reaction soon set in. Artie began to play the letter game to distract me but my spirits utterly failed me & I staggered below to gnaw Captains Biscuits & pray. I had just resigned myself to the truly horrible fate of the ladies Saloon when the ship stopped (just in time). We lunched at Calais & had an ideal journey from there to Paris. I was struck by the Gare du Nord; except the Hauptbahnhof at Dresden it's the finest station I've seen. We suffered severely from the dearth of porters & staggered down the platform laden with holdalls & portmanteaus.

Oc packed Janet & I into a fiacre after previously awaking the corpulent coachman who was dozing on the box & we drove off to the Hôtel Corneille leaving him to wrestle with the Douaniers. We had an interesting drive through gas-lit streets thronged with bareheaded women, waisted soldiers, leather clad chauffeurs. Everyone looks picturesquely shabby; so different from London where people either shine with offensive respectability or else repel one by unattractive dirt. The Hôtel Corneille being reached we descended & were told that our rooms were 'au cinquième sans compter l'entresol'[1] which was rather a blow. After a long & weary climb we settled down into 3 little attics at the top whose squalor might have depressed me but didn't. Artie soon arrived & we mutually 'praised each other up' (as E. says) for having chosen not the 4th floor of the Ritz which Margot offered us but the 6th of the Corneille. We had quite a nice little meal marred only by the loquaciousness of a waiter who wanted as he himself put it 'to perfection his English on us'. We then went up to bed; one of the many drawbacks of our rooms were their capacity for creaking. The man 3 rooms off turning over in bed invariably woke me – but these & other little contretemps we accepted with the stoicism of a Cornelian hero,[2] & the philosophy born of high economical ideals.

Diary – Tuesday 18 October – Rue St Jacques, Paris

This morning we resolved to leave Hôtel Corneille as the airlessness of our passage was more than Le Cid himself cld. have faced – so leaving Janet to pack, Artie & I set off to visit Mdme Casaubon. We found Monsieur at home – a male frump of the deepest dye who harps on his estomac & is never so happy as when giving graphic descriptions of his last indis-

---

[1] 'on the fifth floor without counting the mezzanine'.

[2] Violet puns on the name of the hotel, alluding to the French dramatist Pierre Corneille (1606–84), who wrote the heroic tale *Le Cid.*

position. Madame soon came having been fetched from the butchers. She is a dear old girl with a heart (& wig) of gold. We arranged to come to her till our flat should be ready & then started off in search of it. No 14 which was shown us by a colloquial concierge had two delightful sets of rooms on the 4th & 5th floor. The 4th was the best from a point of view of the stairs – it was not quite so clean as the 5th but this cld. easily be remedied. 'C'était un membre du tribunal de la Martinique et ils avaient une domestique nègre. Ah Madame n'ayez jamais des domestiques nègres.'[1] I assured her that Janet was white. After a little time M. Casaubon turned up & said: 'Pourquoi appelez vous cette jeune demoiselle Madame' – 'Comment' she said looking at Artie with anguish, 'elle est seulement votre soeur'? & on his assenting 'Dieu quel désappointement! Et moi qui croyait que c'était un voyage de noces!'[2] Artie & I were much amused at being taken for a honeymooning couple.

Lunch [at the *pension*] alarmed me rather; we were surrounded by odd people of different types; a swarthy little Servian, a gentle religious fanatic with a fair curl on his forehead & a wonderful touch (on the piano), a rather good looking bounder, a Mephistophelian professor with tufts of black hair all over his face a cousin of Artie's old tutor Moulinier, a robust Englishwoman of the type one always meets abroad; shady neck, retiring chin with a habit of bellowing after meals in a rich contralto. Of Monsieur Casaubon's two sons one is an overbearing bore with a passion for dogmatizing on subjects he knows nothing about (I heard him telling some innocents at the other end of the table that Englishmen had only begun shaving since Chamberlain set the fashion & hastily disabused them) & the other a henpecked martyr with a barbe a l'Impériale & a shrewish wife. There are also an English couple the Powys's – he rather Tussaudian & she a Pigeon with an appreciative giggle, harmless except for her unfortunate illusion that she has a voice; she massacres those lovely Indian love-lyrics ruthlessly.

The only other lady is Mlle. Henriette a poor little governess whose capacity for happiness, sense of humour & everything that makes life worth living have been dried up by its dulness, dreariness, disappointments. She's rather a pathetic little creature, her worn harassed expression only leaves her when Berthier enters the room, & she watches him bally-ragging with the Servian with adoring eyes.

I sit next to a young man who has a twitch in his nose; he is studying to be a gunner & is in a blue funk at the idea of learning to ride: 'Voyez

---

[1] 'He was a member of the Martinique tribunal and they had a black maid. Ah Madame, I would never recommend negro servants to you.' The use of *nègres* here is derogatory.

[2] 'Why are you calling this young woman Madame' ... 'What, she is only your sister?' ... 'Lord, what a disappointment! And I thought that this was a honeymoon!'

vous Mademoiselle cela doit être si dangereux – le cheval peut faire un faux pas et puis....'[1] I roared with unsympathetic laughter there was something so absurdly funny about his anxiety. I was trying to re-assure him when Mdme. Casaubon who is the incarnation of an almost tactlessly frank type of tact (she has an ear on every conversation round the table keeps them up whenever they show signs of waning & tries to reconcile all differences of opinion by a sweeping & usually ambiguously couched platitude) turned to me & said: 'Ah Mademoiselle il parait que vous montez beaucoup à cheval; ce doit ce pendant être bien difficile de tenir le fusil en galopant après le renard'[2] !!!! Voces populi! ...

This is far & away the most beautiful town I've ever seen. I love the great open places (like Place de la Concorde) surrounded by fine buildings & monuments & flooded by light & air & sun. The long look through the archway near the Louvre up the Champs-Élysées to the Arc de Triomphe, the changing trees, red & brown & orange that grow down to the edge of the Seine, the distant glimpses of Montmartre swathed in mists – are all bits of loveliness one doesn't expect to find in a metropolis.

I came home tired & pleased & found letters from Arnold Ward, Billy Grenfell & the Bishop of London – an odd trio[3]....

Diary – Sunday 23 October – Rue Gay Lussac, Paris

We have had a very wearing week – of which it may be said that it was a severe test for our French our legs & our tempers. All three have come out of it brilliantly. After exasperating difficulties 2 flats having slipped through our fingers we have at last succeeded in getting a pied à terre at 38 Rue Gay Lussac.[4] We have inspected almost every flat in Paris signed dozens of contracts all of which proved invalid at the critical moment, coped with the dishonesty of propriétaires, locataires & sous-locataires,[5] engaged a charwoman with eyes fixed in opposite corners, & hired every necessary of life from a tin foot-bath to a Louis XVI sofa for the modest sum of 12 £

---

[1] 'You see, Miss, this must be so dangerous – the horse can stumble and then ....'

[2] 'Ah Miss, you are said to be fond of horse-riding; it must however be very difficult to hold a gun while galloping after a fox.'

[3] Arnold Ward had been an Oxford contemporary of Violet's eldest brother Raymond, and Billy Grenfell a preparatory-school contemporary of her youngest brother Cys. Arthur Foley Ingram (1858–1946), bishop of London 1901–39, first met Violet in 1901, when she was recovering from suspected polio, and he visited her regularly during her long convalescence.

[4] The unfurnished flat was above a chemist's shop in the Rue Gay Lussac, near the Sorbonne.

[5] 'Owners', 'tenants' and 'people who sub-let'.

– achievements of which we are justly proud.[1] And now at last the turmoil is ended Artie signed the contract at cock crow this morning, our flat is assured, it only remains to get the furniture in & our ménage can begin. . . . I think for sane, sound judgement & levelheadedness Oc surpasses anyone I've ever met. He has the rare faculty of cutting himself & his personal prejudices loose & of looking on any question however near it may be to him, however entangled with his wishes his hopes or his fears – with as much coolness & impartiality as if he had been the man in the moon. Of this faculty I am hopelessly devoid; I see most things 'through a glass-darkly'.

Diary – Tuesday 25 October – Rue Gay Lussac

After a dictation on art with Fairfax – who grows more blatantly insular every day, Cristiche – who scintillates with absurd witticisms having passed his examination & Miss Gretton, Oc & I made one more weary journey to Janiauds, rated them as soundly as our vocabulary would permit for not sending our furniture, blushingly bargained for & shyly selected a few of the necessaries of life they had omitted & finally took a bus home & read with boiling blood the account of the Russian outrage on the North Sea fishermen.[2] The criminal carelessness that makes such a mistake as this possible, combined with the wanton, inhuman indifference to the states of its victims after it was discovered to be a mistake staggers one – & the state of nerves it testifies to must be highly encouraging to the Japanese. The Baltic fleet crew ought to go home & have a rest cure instead of embarking for a great war.

[1] Twelve pounds was a modest sum by Violet's standards, but the same amount would have paid the rent on an average artisan dwelling in London for eight months. At the other extreme, it would not have covered for a single week the costs associated with the London house of a wealthy family (*Cornhill Magazine* (1901), vols 10, 11: series on 'Family Budgets').

[2] On the evening of 21 October 1904 the Russian Baltic fleet was sailing through the North Sea, on its way to war against Japan, when it encountered a flotilla of Hull trawlers, fishing on the Dogger Bank. The Russians incorrectly identified some of the trawlers as Japanese torpedo-boats, and opened fire, killing or wounding nearly a score of British fishermen. The Russians then departed, apparently still in fear of attack, without giving assistance to the stricken trawlers; they did not inform the mainland of what had occurred. There was anger and incredulity in Britain at this 'North Sea outrage'. Sir Edward Grey later recalled: 'It was not credible that the Russians knew they were firing on unarmed peaceful fishing vessels, though it was difficult to believe that they really thought it possible for Japanese torpedo-boats to be in the North Sea, as they said. It was therefore not easy to understand what the Russians did think they were firing at, and why their guns went off at all' (Viscount Grey of Fallodon, *Twenty-Five Years*, i, 54–5).

To our joy we got into our flat this afternoon & we are tasting of the full sweetness of proprietorship to-night sitting in our Louis XVI salon (curtainless it is true & only illuminated by one lamp which smells more than it lights) in front of a log fire – reposing on two Gladstonian busts called chernêts which are more economical & picturesque than grates – & would be perfection if they didn't let the fire go out every time we looked out of the window.

Diary – Tuesday 1 November – Rue Gay Lussac

Tuesday Nov. 1 <u>La Toussaint</u> [All Saints' Day]
The pious Berthier who has been living on omelettes for the last 10 days in anticipation of this fête celebrated his change of diet by a large slice of stringy veal this morning. Fairfax still poses as a vegetarian & comes in bloated after a large beef-steak lunch at the Foyot to toy with lobster salad & haricots verts.

Mlle. Henriette had laid away the little tartan blouse we know so well for a creation of sandy alpaca, & Cristiche was bubbling over with joy at the prospect of hearing 'une très belle cantatrice Americaine jouer dans "Lakmé" à l'Opera Comique'.[1] Le jour des morts as it is called has a wonderfully cheering effect on everyone's spirits. Drunkards reel to & fro between the cabaret & the cimetière.

After lunch we went to the Luxembourg & found it shut. We then made our way to St. Sulpice – the music was just over. In despair we took a bus labelled Auteuil in the hope it would take us to the Bois which I haven't yet seen. After $\frac{3}{4}$ of an hour of awful frowst a mingled smell of cheap scent, soap & soaplessness pervading the bus – we arrived not at the Bois but at Auteuil (as we might have guessed). We resolved to make the best of it though we were rather at a loss what to do – so we strolled down the suburban pavement just outside the fortifications which was crowded with endimanché people who were keeping Le jour des morts by wearing their best clothes. It struck me as ridiculously pathetic & paradoxical – but I suppose that nothing – not even one of those yellow-plush bonnets with pink ospreys can obstruct that strange & subtle converse one holds with one's dead.

Suddenly through a leafless gap in a tree we saw a confused mass of human beings – & it flashed across us that Auteuil had a big race-course &

---

[1] 'a very beautiful American singer playing in [the play called] "Lakmé" at the Opéra Comique'. The opera *Lakmé*, by Delibes, a three-act tragedy, was first produced in Paris in 1883.

there were probably races going on.[1] Our conjectures were right & after paying a franc we went in & mixed with the scum of the earth. There were such types as I had never seen before & probably shan't see again till I next go on a race-course; dirt & degradation moral & physical were incarnate in the surging crowd drinking odd beverages pink & brown & yellow, eating greasy sandwiches wrapped up in La Patrie waving pink papers, 'selling' tips shouting, pushing, hustling, picking pockets – it was as squalid a sight as I've ever seen.

We saw one race very well – the 2nd a military one we missed as we stood at the outer instead of the inner circle. One man had a fall but I don't think he was badly hurt. We luckily found a taxametre fiacre to take us home, any other would have rooked us. After a longish meal at our pension & a still longer toilette Cristiche giving way at last to my repeated entreaties danced a pas-seul. Wrapped in the dining room curtain clicking castagnettes with oblong eyes & a black lace head-dress he looked strangely oriental. I must say his agility & grace are wonderful & the way he stands on his toes quite extraordinary. The faithful Berthier played the valse out of Faust patiently during the bulk of the evening.

Diary – Thursday 3 November – Rue Gay Lussac

We are anxiously awaiting money – having spent our last farthing (extorted from Janet) – in a feverish telegram to Father for 15 £. . . .

A new Turk came to the Pension. Disappointingly occidental looking but with a name which compensates for all physical defects 'Kara-Theodore'. (It doesn't look so well as it sounds.) Artie had his first fencing lesson. I love the salle d'armes with its weapon covered wall & gentle Méringac with his velveteen suit & feline movements. Madame covered with clothes & powder, with her volubility & almost embarrassing civility is a jarring element – & was happily absent.

We walked back through the Luxembourg gardens among the sparrows & the statues & the falling leaves. It was cold & the sun rolled through the frosty air like a large orange. Sitting on a wooden bench munching two gaufres we had bought from the old man who toasts them in the open air we watched the children spinning their wooden tops with untiring energy, the fat nurses with white bonnets & brown eyes jigging tiny infants up & down, the seedy-coated artistes with slouch hats & hungry handsome faces strolling arm in arm along the leaf-strewn paths. We went as far as Notre Dame which shut at our arrival & back home where we spent two cosy hours before sallying forth to our evening meal.

---

[1] The race course at Auteuil is on the edge of the Bois de Boulogne.

M. Louis was intolerable. I can't think why illogical people are always given such loud voices. He cried down everyone who opposed him & his views on the subject of capital punishment. Kara Theodore's really intelligent & convincing arguments where entirely lost on him. Chambry is doing a series of brilliant silhouettes of every member of the pension for my Album. Berthier thought he had a sore-throat to-night came in muffled in an enormous silk handkerchief & played sad dirges till 9 when he went upstairs to wrap himself in his counterpane & work. Artie wishes me to add he has thought great thoughts to-day. Looby!!

Diary – Friday 4 November – Rue Gay Lussac

I sit down to write with my brain benumbed by 8 pages of composition on Le Curé de Cucugnan for Dupuis.[1] We got a telegram this morning from Sassbags asking us to Laversine. I daresay it will be an amusing experience passing 2 nights at a French Chateau in a nest of Rothschilds – but pension life makes one socially lazy & I grudge the grind of worrying about my clothes & thinking of subjects on which to converse with the Bombay Duck. Three nights at Dalquharran during which he took me into dinner have drained my resources.[2] I remember we fell back on midges the last night a theme more original than suggestive. . . .

I had my first fencing lesson with Mérignac – I began quite gently so it didn't tire me. Artie grappled with a rough subordinate. . . .

. . . Margot speaks alarmingly of the probability of war.[3] Out here the chances are thought very small – & I really don't see what we can want more than an International tribunal. Our case is so strong that if the judges are impartial we must be offered compensation – so far as life wantonly taken can ever [be] said to be compensated for.

Diary – Saturday 5 November – Château de Laversine

Having carried our luggage downstairs [and] given our last instructions to Jeanne we embarked in a rickety fiacre & reached the Gare du Nord just in time to catch the 2.40 to Chantilly. After an hour & a half in a first-class carriage of indescribable frowstiness which we shared with a retired jockey & his wife – we reached Chantilly. We were accosted at the entry

---

[1] Alphonse Daudet, *Le Curé de Cucugnan* (1895).

[2] Dalquharran Castle, in Ayrshire, was taken by the Asquiths for their autumn holiday in 1904.

[3] Between Britain and Russia over the 'Dogger Bank incident', above, p. 5.

of the station by a fat little footman who told us to get into a landau in which a plump, chic obviously English Lady was already seated. We got in with that semi-simper of embarrassment common among strangers who feel acquaintance impending. At last the lady leant forward & [said] in a sugary voice: 'Il y a [une] autre dame qui vient'![1] This broke the ice. Great was my astonishment when hearing a frou-frou of silk petticoats I turned round & beheld in the 'autre dame' no other than Widow Powell renowned at Glen for her proverbially 9 boxes which the horses used to go backwards & forwards between Innerleithen & Glen fetching & depositing for the best part of a week after she arrived.[2]

We drove for about 5 miles in the shut landau whose deafening vibrations drowned all efforts at conversation – a kind of terror creeping over me as every mile took us nearer. . . .

The conversation opposite would have born me up if anything could; our vis-à-vis were anxiously questioning each whether they ought to change for tea & if so into what . . . (a solemn oath was taken that neither would put on a tea-gown unless the other did) . . . we reached the house through several long regularly planted avenues of changing beeches. It is a great white square place with an enormous open space in front. 5 lackeys leapt out & backed up the steps before us – quibbling round the doors (of which there were 3) ensued. Artie & I found it monotonous at the 3rd. We were eventually ushered down a long voluptuously carpeted passage into a still more voluptuously furnished room with an atmosphere of unhealthy luxury produced by the hot air apparatus & the orchids. A second or two elapsed & then in walked

1st) Madame Gustave a Semitic matron of the Lady Battersea type.
2nd (abreast) Sassbags & her sister Lucie. S. in the best of looks clothes & health, Lucie tired & éreinté looking with a pronounced kink in her nose
3rd) 'Ma fille' Mdme Claude Stern a raffinée edition of Henriette
4th) lagging behind Gustave – a jolly old boy with an absurd voice & a henpecked look.

We shook hands with all & Sassbags then did the most tactful thing she's ever done in her life – namely despatched Artie & I to the links for the hour which remained before tea. I cannot describe the joy I felt at being spared that hot room & those beastly females for even this short trêve.

We had a chilly round of golf in the twilight which wld. have been divine unharassed by anticipations. The links are quite pretty no obstacles – & a bad lie quite impossible as the grass is cut short & mainly composed of tiny clover & moss. There are some jolly drives across tiny valleys & typical

---

[1] 'There is another lady coming'.
[2] Glen was the Peeblesshire home of Violet's step-grandfather, Sir Charles Tennant.

views of misty woods & red-roofed villages with those long rows of tall poplars one only sees in France. A very good-looking & competent little boy carried Oc's clubs a great relief after the Cruden Bay caddies.[1] We came back very much à contre-coeur – a footman in white gloves came to meet us & ask us to go to tea. We asked to see our bedrooms & were shown a little suite, we each had a bedroom, dressing room, big bath & W. C. (which a woman in black satin frock hired for the purpose tactfully shows one on arrival!) My heart leapt at the sight of the big bath. I changed & we went down to tea. With quaking hearts & knocking knees we entered a still larger hotter & more gorgeous room than before which was thronged with people. Madame Gustave overwhelmed us with kindness & chocolate & we dragged out a more or less miserable existence for an hour & a half till Sybil & three other little French girls with Sarah Bernhardt waists came down & did some plays & dialogues – really very well.[2]

At dinner I sat between 'ma fille' who is very nice & her husband. The men took the ladies out on their arms instead of staying in like they do in England. In the course of the evening I had the pleasure of hearing Widow Powell called 'un monstre' by Lucie in a venomous undertone. I went to bed 10.30 & wrote this. Now 10 hours of oblivion what joy!

I wish I wasn't so bored by what ought to amuse me. I'm afraid the social part of me is either under-developed or not-existent – I rather fear the latter!

Diary – Sunday 6 November – Château de Laversine

Almost immediately after breakfast lunch began for the shooters; there was a large shooting party amongst the others a man called O'Beirne from the Embassy who is an immense relief among all these French Jews.[3] To use Artie's famous phrase 'Like good milk after vile champagne!'

Sassbags & I started off in a little motor brougham which sprinted across ploughed fields regardless of springs or tyres. On the whole I had a delightful morning marred only by the thought that poor Sassbags was bored with me; we have so little in common – it is hard to find

[1] Cruden Bay lies on the Aberdeenshire coast, about eighteen miles north of Aberdeen.

[2] Sarah Bernhardt (1844–1923), famous French actress renowned for her figure, and particularly her slim waist.

[3] Hugh James O'Beirne (1866–1916), secretary at the British embassy in Paris, 1900–6. O'Beirne, a highly successful diplomatist 'of great charm and ability', was included in Lord Kitchener's ill-fated mission to Russia in June 1916. This ended when HMS *Hampshire* sank, with the loss of almost everyone on board, after striking a mine in heavy seas off the Orkneys.

anything to talk about. We walked from one cover to another & sat on comfy stools watching fat fluttering pheasants emerge from the coverts & succumb to the guns. The whole shoot was conducted on a regal scale & the ploughed field across which we started looked like the battle plain of Liao Yang.[1] The guns were numerous – each was followed by a loader in a uniform which rivals that of a Blue Hungarian Bandsman on the Cromer pier[2] – holding in one hand a chained retriever – in the other an unfolding armchair for the attenuated sportsman. 50 beaters in white livery followed & then a mule decked out with yellow pom-pom to carry the game. I couldn't help smiling as I thought of our homely Dalquharran on the moors Wily & Whiskers & the black retriever & the rare wild birds. The sport itself was of a brutal kind at Laversine; there was a beater for each bird & they were shot at about 4 yards range.

Sassbags polished off a hare & 3 pheasants. I was amazed to see how recklessly they fired at blackbirds, jays, woodpeckers & anything they saw; & amused at the whiffs of different scents I got passing each sportsman! We went in about 5 & had a large goûter after which Artie & I & two other men played Bridge until Sybil & the others came down. An awful proposition had been made to play Dumb Crambo after tea which made our blood run cold with horror. Imagine charades as we conceive them – lack of clothing is one of the essentials – acted before such an audience. Sassbags was happily occupied at Bridge & Artie & I deftly & tactfully kept Sybil Betty & the little Leoninos quiet at Happy Families & old maid. They afterwards dragged us up to play hide & seek – but we considered we had got off easily.

At Dinner I sat between the old Baron & a rather nice young Frenchman – one of the few who will consent to talk French to me – the others insist on talking English which is as a rule – I say it in all modesty – worse than my French. After dinner having got becalmed in a conversation with Lucie I betook me to looking at the visitors book. I saw Father's & Margot's name there & dear Tommy's signed 11th Nov. 1902 – just two years ago.[3]

I went to bed happy, though, to-day has been quite nice. To-morrow we

---

[1] Liao Yang, a city in southern Manchuria, was the scene of a fierce ten-day battle in the Russo-Japanese war, August–September 1904. Russian casualties were 15,000, and those of Japan, nominally the victor in this confrontation, 24,000. There is an account in Maurice Baring's *With the Russians in Manchuria* (1905).

[2] Cromer is on the Norfolk coast, about two miles north of Overstrand, home of the Asquiths' friends Lord and Lady Battersea.

[3] The Hon. Thomas Lister (1878–1904), eldest son of 4th Baron Ribblesdale, Margot Asquith's nephew. Lister served with the 10th Hussars, and was killed in action in Somaliland in January 1904, aged twenty-six.

go! to-morrow we can taste the joys of freedom & stringy meat & a vagabond life in the Quartier Latin far from Semitic patronage & hot rooms, constraint & orchids & champagne! Oh Valenciennes! Oh Valenciennes!

Diary – Monday 7 November – Rue Gay Lussac

To-day, oh joy, we went home. After a journey passed in some constraint with the Gustaves we packed into a fiacre & reached Gay Lussac with Jeanne squinting on the doorstep & the Boethos goose-stealer waving us a welcome from the mantelpiece with his sealing-wax stuck wings. We hurried on to lunch which we eat in semi-obscurity as the day was dark & the stained glass windows made it darker.

If I rejoiced yesterday in the anticipation of stringy meat I was not disappointed – for toughness of fibre & grisly strength I'd back my slice of mutton against the world. After lunch Oc & I & Fairfax & Dupuis went to the Sorbonne to have a look at the cours. I was in favour of Experimental Psychology but the weight of public opinion was against me & I was compelled to resign myself to German Literature & Political Economy. We had a fencing lesson with Mérignac, bought some vases carnations & chrysanthemums, had one more heated dialogue down the telephone with Janiaud (whose remissness surpasses anything I've ever heard of – he has not yet sent the tub or the lamp or come to hang the curtains) & went home.

Diary – Tuesday 8 November – Rue Gay Lussac

Nov. 7th 1904. we spent feverishly writing a composition on l'Elixoi du Père Gaucher for Dupuis. We also paid a visit to the lending-library where I got my II vol. of Tolstoi, & Artie Rouge et Noir, which Kara Theodore recommended me to read.[1]

I had a very interesting conversation with him after dinner; he is extraordinarily intelligent & possesses a sound fund of knowledge on every imaginable subject, Free Trade in England, Japanese Art, German Literature, Turkish politics, etc. Roger Low turned up late & Oc escorted him to Rue St. Jacques where he is sleeping.[2] He told us he got a comic

---

[1] Alphonse Daudet, *L'Élixir du Rev. Père Gaucher* (n.d.); Stendhal (Henri Beyle), *Le Rouge et le Noir* (1831).

[2] John Rogers Low (1881–1907), a Balliol friend of Violet's brothers. He joined the Indian Civil Service in 1904, and died of enteric fever at Banda in the United Provinces, March 1907.

wire from Beb on the boat exhorting him to crush Bishops marry a Buddhist & beware of cobras! Very characteristic advice. He also told us Bernard Shaw had written a new play John Bull which I shall be keen to read.[1] Raymond has already been offered several briefs which he was unfortunately unable to take not being called yet – especially disappointing as one was in the Divorce Court where (he says) he longed to make his début!!!

Diary – Wednesday 9 November – Rue Gay Lussac

... We set off for lunch almost immediately after breakfast & spent the afternoon pottering about among the fascinating bookstalls on the Quai Voltaire from which Artie had to drag me by main force to prevent my squandering my entire allowance the cheque book for which I received this morning. We had tea at the Café near St. Sulpice & then after one last furious dialogue with Janiaud down the telephone went to the Odéon book-stalls where we dallied a long time. Roger Low gave me Clio a book of Anatole France full of lovely water-colours.[2] I am afraid he is very depressed at going to India. It must be awful after 5 glorious years at Oxford surrounded by friends to emigrate to an unknown continent where you do not know a soul & to know you are doomed to stay there for the bulk if not the whole of your life. He is clever & facile & ought to do well I think; he should guard against the danger of becoming too epigrammatic; unless one is very brilliant they are apt to be risky & tiring. He possesses a tremendous amount of miscellaneous & usually superficial knowledge which makes him an amusing companion; he has also a keen sense of humour, a great affection for Beb & a culte for Ronsard – all three help to make him attractive – to me at least.[3]

After dinner at Madame's we took him to the Gare de Lyons & while waiting for the train drank coffee in the restaurant, he talking with that forced merriment which betrays depression quicker than silence. I made him the present of a complicated cigar cutter (which was in the basket in the middle of our table together [with] a pig-match box & other, foolish things). Then we looked in vain for a tolerably comfortable place in the Marseilles train. He eventually had to reconcile himself to a corner in a first class carriage – a Marquis occupying the whole of the opposite side.

---

[1] Bernard Shaw's play *John Bull's Other Island* was written and first performed in 1904, though it was not published until 1907.

[2] Anatole France, *Clio* (1900).

[3] Pierre de Ronsard (1524–85), French poet and humanist.

The train went off after that cruel delay after goodbyes have been said during which one has to keep up a little meaningless small talk referring to the journey, return, etc. & other sterile subjects. Oc & I drove home on the top of a bus.

Diary – Saturday 12 November – Rue Gay Lussac

... Cristiche came to tea & took us on to the Boulevard des Italians where we heard the most marvellous reproductions of Melba, Cabré, Caruso – & selections from the Walküre, Carmen, Lucia de Lammermoor, Tannhäuser etc etc. on a gramophone. He is a funny little fellow – <u>such</u> a baby, loving his embroidered gilets & socks & the Opera Comic & phonograph passionately.

After dinner to which a friend of Miss Grettons, a great singer, came I had rather a good talk with Fairfax. I find now that his tremendous facial contortions are partly owing to deafness – not entirely affectation of denseness. He thinks the Russian blunder quite excusable – in which opinion I cannot agree with him. He says he is an adherent of the maxim 'Shoot first! talk after' & confesses to having shot at his own sentry in the dark in the South African war – though he happily missed him. To my joy Kara Theodore came in later; having with difficulty resisted the temptation of blowing his brains out & giving up smoking! (both of which things he has told me he was going to). The first ought to [be] easy now as he is in a Pension with 7 Englishwomen two old & 5 young, <u>all</u> Jingos. Miss Gretton's friend sang very well & Mrs. Powys chirped 'Oh dry those tears' which convulsed Lousteau & made it hard for Oc & I to keep our self-control. Fairfax says he saw Chamberlain was mad in the French papers. I can't believe it though I should think the starting of a big thing like this would be just the kind of thing to make you insane – especially if you have such a bad head for figures as Jo!

Joseph Chamberlain, H. H. Asquith and tariff reform

'Tariff reform' had dominated public debate since May 1903, when the Unionist colonial secretary, Joseph Chamberlain, made a speech in Birmingham urging the abandonment of the existing policy of free trade. He argued that Britain faced, simultaneously, the decay of its trade and the dissolution of its Empire, and that the introduction of a tariff on imports, with preferential treatment for goods from countries within the Empire, would solve both problems. It would protect Britain's home industry, and at the same time strengthen imperial ties. This speech had an explosive effect, shattering the existing consensus on free trade, and splitting the Unionist party. Chamberlain himself resigned from the cabinet in September 1903 in order to campaign freely on the issue. At the same time his initiative unified Liberals. Asquith greeted Chamberlain's Birmingham speech as 'wonderful news', and predicted that his party would sweep the country at the next election. He was proved right, and could claim a large personal share of the credit for the Liberal landslide in January 1906, since it was he who had championed free trade, and emerged the victor, in a prolonged public duel with Chamberlain.

H.H.A. to V.A.   *Tuesday 15 November*
1, Paper Buildings, Temple,
London, E.C.

Dearest Violet

I was very glad to get your letter a day or two ago.[1] You seem to have been tossed on a troubled sea before you found your harbour in the Rue Gay Lussac. Who was G.L?[2] You don't say anything of your lectures & other studies. I gathered from Oc's last letter that the Sorbonne would not be open to you for another fortnight: which is a pity.

We have been leading a rather uneventful life. The family is still in Cav. Sq., & Margot & the small ones do not settle down at Manton until next Monday the 21st.... Beb is now an inmate of Cav. Sq. & comes to law lectures at the Temple. Raymond is to be called to the bar on Thursday, & I hope that before long the 'briefs will come trooping gaily'.

I have a good many speeches to make still between now & Xmas – Cambridge, Southend, Preston, Cardiff &c. I trust that Joe will soon return & provide us with some new mis-statements & fallacies. The old ones are pretty threadbare by now.

[1] Asquith destroyed most of his correspondence, and this letter has not survived. Only about four dozen of Violet's letters to him are extant, the bulk of them written during her childhood. Asquith wrote to Venetia Stanley in October 1914: 'One can recreate the past from letters better than in any other way, and how different the perspective often is, when, after years, one reads them again, from what it was when they were written. They are real milestones. I have destroyed by far the larger part of those I have received during my life, sometimes not without a malicious complacency at the disservice I am doing to any biographer who may be foolish enough hereafter to take me in hand' (M. and E. Brock (eds.), *H. H. Asquith: Letters to Venetia Stanley*, 299).

[2] Joseph-Louis Gay-Lussac (1778–1850), French chemist and physicist.

Margot & I spent Sunday at Hartham with the Connaughts: we had divine weather, just like summer. She went on to Easton Grey & returns to-morrow (Wed) when we go to the State dinner at Windsor in honour of the King & Queen of Portugal. I have just got Cys's mid-term report: which is quite good. Rendall says 'I sometimes wish he were more communicative'.[1] So do I. He is the worst correspondent in the family

Love to you both yr loving Father

Diary – Wednesday 16 November – Rue Gay Lussac

Dictée & Dupuis. The Rothschilds lent us a box for the Opera to-night – the worst in the week cela va sans dire but very kind of them all the same. I asked Lousteau, Cristiche & Chambry as tactfully as I could – I fear nevertheless that this step will make me more enemies than friends as the omissions are necessarily more numerous than the invités....

Artie went to see his Americans in the afternoon & I stayed at home & practised & rested. Chambry arrived with his fresco which is quite brilliant at 4; I think he is a nice little fellow but all these Frenchmen are the same; the moment Oc left the room to hurry the chocolate he began telling me I looked like a Madonna!!!! I told him he meant a banana & hastily changed the subject. He stayed some time & we had a good talk over all the people in the pension. I almost pointedly refrained from mentioning Gretton – but I think that wound has healed if it ever existed.

Poor little Kara Theodore does not appear to be popular. Even the charitable Chambry said 'Il n'est pas commode' when asked for an opinion.[2] I defend him hotly daily; his argumentativeness doesn't irritate me at all as he is always ready to listen to reason & is never illogical. I wish the same could be said of more of them. The fact is his brains & character overawe them slightly; one terrible anecdote is repeated with bated breath of how he knocked Cristiche down among the flowerbeds one day last year! I'd have given anything to have seen it!

Oc & I hurried on to meet Dorlier, Gretton, Mrs Powys & Cristiche at the Bouclé. It is an enormous place under cover like a fair, the kind of thing which appeals strongly to my low mind which a merry-go-round sends into raptures! The sight of the bouclé terrified me & I assured Artie nothing would induce me to go into it. We soon met the whole party including Loustau, Fairfax & Miss Shipley a friend of Miss Grettons. Dorlier

---

[1] Montague John Rendall (1862–1950), second master at Winchester College, 1899–1911, and headmaster 1911–24.

[2] 'He is an awkward customer.'

a spick & span little bounder (reminding me strongly of Jack[1]) a great pension blood who thinks himself socially superior to everyone there advanced to meet us. Oc & I smiled & nodded & said hollo or words to that effect to which he only answered by taking off his hat, bowing & saying: 'Monsieur Asquith voulez-vous me faire l'honneur de me présenter a Mlle votre soeur' which Artie convulsed with internal giggles did. It is a farce; here have I been living in the same house for a week – eating at the same table he has never addressed a single remark to me which we attributed to enmity but which was apparently only stickling. He really is what Cys would call an ape.

We slid gaily down the 'toboggan' as they call a long slippery curling slope down which one glides 6 on a carpet! Fairfax implored me not to go in the bouclé assuring me it made him feel 'beastly sick' but Cristiche, Lousteau & Dorlier surrounded me & insisted so I got reluctantly into the lift & from thence into the little car. Oc, Cristiche & Dorlier went in front, Lousteau & I behind. We held on to a strap & were shut in by an iron bar. After a second of awful suspense – 'Nous Allons à la mort' said Dorlier – & swish down we went. I never, never felt anything like the violence of the movement, it was like as Cristiche said comme si on tombait dans le vide.[2] The speed is 1000 kilometres an hour, with one's body at a hitherto unknown angle face down as if one was about to be dashed face on to the ground. My breath left me entirely, being pressed out of lungs by the extraordinary force with which one met the air. The actual turn is not at all bad but one arrives gasping & the sensation though interesting is not agreeable. Cristiche is very amusing about it as having a passion for it himself he makes a test of courage out of it & doesn't realize at all that [it] is a question not of safety but of physical comfort. The arguments he used to make me go were 'Allons! courage vous êtes une Anglaise' & Fairfax has gone down several points in his estimation for refusing to do it again. After shooting a little & having several more peaceful toboggans we hurried home to dress for the opera....

Diary – Sunday 27 November – Rue Gay Lussac

My diary has been neglected this week in a way which points to great industry but now I come to think of it I can't remember anything worth writing down we've done. It has been icily, bitterly, cold....

[1] Harold John ('Jack') Tennant (1865–1935); the youngest of Sir Charles Tennant's children by his first marriage. Liberal MP for Berwickshire, 1894–1918, and under-secretary of state for war, 1912–16.

[2] 'like falling into empty space'.

I've had 3 fencing lessons Mérignac assures me regularly that I'm 'éton-nant' which keeps me happy. They are a great resource in this weather as they make one tingle with warmth as nothing else would. On Thursday Oc & I spent a divine afternoon at the Louvre & saw 3 large rooms more or less thoroughly. We walked on down the lighted Rue de Rivoli & I bought a beautiful little Nike on the prow of her ship for Beb for 12 francs I couldn't resist the temptation of unpacking it & putting it on my writing table in spite of my firm conviction that it will fall a victim to Jeanne. Oc found a nice little coloured print called La Gigue Anglaise which he got for 10 francs. We went on & had tea with Venetia who told us some postcards of General André having his ears boxed by Syveton were being sold though forbidden by the police.[1] Hearing this Oc & I immediately resolved to get some but our search under the arcades of the Rue de Rivoli would have been quite fruitless if it hadn't been for an old curé who pointed the place out to us with a diabolical smile. 'Là, c'est là'! I was much amused by this old cleric's fostering of vice but Artie told me all the church loathe the Government & André especially for taking away their rights whilst leaving the Freemasons every privilege.

Diary – Sunday 4 December – Rue Gay Lussac

Berthier urged me so fervently to go to St. Sulpice that I made a mighty effort & got up early this morning & went. I see what he means about loving the interior of the church; it is full of light & strength & large simple lines. But the modern frescoes ruin it for me. The music was marvellous; the organ the finest I've ever heard except St. Paul's – & there was one wonderful soprano voice in the choir. The service was a farce – a very magnificent one no doubt but nothing more or less than a mas-querade – & appealing no more to one's moral side than a Drury Lane pantomime transformation scene. Three fat priests in gold brocade pirou-etted on the altar ringing little bells; 6 splendid baritones carried colossal cierges up the aisle; then a little procession advanced bearing in its midst an immense dish of brioches surrounded by candles like a birthday cake & finally a bevy of girls in blue & white (who looked best with their veils down) brought up the rear with an enormous white & gold banner. In

---

[1] On 4 November 1904 Gabriel Syveton, a nationalist deputy, had crossed the floor of the French Chamber and slapped the face of General André (1838–1913), the minister of war. Syveton was outraged at André's alleged use of informants to uncover information prejudicial to the careers of Catholic officers within the army, part of a government campaign to separate church and state.

the dome behind the altar the choir was singing conducted in a most businesslike way by a black monk with a bâton.

I do not wish to be flippant or unsympathetic – God forbid that I should about anyone's religion – but I cannot believe that hundreds & thousands of thinking, reasoning men & women look on at it all & believe. And the sad part about it is that there is no middle course in Roman Catholicism – you either resign yourself & your conscience to the church & submerge your own individuality, reading only what the Index permits, eating what the Calendar commands – or you are excommunicated, shut out, damned & done for.

All the same I'd give anything to be one – it must be so comfortable & restful to have something to protect one from one's own mind.

Diary – Saturday 10 December – Rue Gay Lussac

We have had another busy week of classes & lectures. One especially on Schopenhauer thrilled me. It was extraordinarily lucid lacking all those technical terms which make most treatises on philosophy incomprehensible except to the elect few who are initiated into the mysteries of its vocabulary. I remember Beb quoting a sentence of Hegel 'The quantum is that which despatches itself beyond itself!' . . .

On Friday afternoon we went to hear Bergson at the Collège de France on Free-will.[1] He is more brilliant than convincing – but I confess I was quite carried away by his defence of the libertist theory – of course I know I am strongly biassed by my own opinions. . . . We spent one hour of awful discomfort & interest standing in a stifling crowd at the back of a tiny packed hall to hear him on Spencer this afternoon. I have no natural tendency for science so that evolutionist theory doesn't attract me so much but it was very interesting & I heard every word though tightly jammed between 4 garlic-reeking men. . . .

The weather has been foul all this week – quite depressing. Sloppy streets, gas in the Salle d'armes, & a sopping brolly to hug thro' dim lectures. Wednesday I was quite giddy with fatigue after Dupuis, Dictée, Faguet, Schopenhauer & a composition for Lacour. . . . Thursday night old Loustau took us to King Lear in French. It was really extraordinarily interesting. We first had a little dinner at Durands which was <u>Elysium</u> after Pension fare. Loustau's anecdotes about our fellow-pensioners were very indiscreet & amusing. We then drove off to the Théâtre Antoine where we had excellent places in a tolerable temperature. Shakespeare in French is

---

[1] Henri-Louis Bergson (1859–1941), renowned French philosopher; lecturer at the Collège de France from 1900.

almost as incongruous as Wagner or the Bible. All the dignity, the grand philosophy & harrowing tragedy of Lear was transformed by high art scenery, mediocre acting & cruel hurrying into a fifth-rate blood & thunder melodrama. It was characteristic of the French to lay great stress on the grisly details such as the putting out of Kent's eyes, poisonings, stabbings etc etc. Still it was interesting & I'm glad I saw it though I'm afraid it will mislead Loustau in his estimate of Shakespeare. We came back here & Oc & Loustau drank beer while I nibbled chocolate & biscuits & mixed a lemon squash. We laughed a great deal over nothing & went to bed tired & happy.

Diary – Thursday 15 December – Rue Gay Lussac

We lunched with Sassbags in her palatial house 23 Avenue Marigny teeming with Greuze, Van Dycks & priceless furniture. Conversation flagged at lunch. I always feel tongue tied in that atmosphere of almost oppressive kindness. The old Comte [Baron de Rothschild], Madame Gustave, Madame Leon & Sassbags were there – we escaped as soon as possible, fenced, went to Lacour & ordered a dinner at Durands.... The awful problem of Xmas presents is forcing itself upon me....

Diary – Friday 16 December – Rue Gay Lussac

A long day of shopping & packing up. Newspaper & desolation are beginning to reign here & I am already feeling what Father calls 'journey-proud'. I tried on at Duperier in the afternoon, then we hurried back & heard an extraordinarily interesting Bergson Lecture....[1]

Loustau has read in the paper that Joe has accused Father of 'méthodes de vulgarization' & I have gone up several points in his esteem since. To have one's father even accused of vulgarity in the Matin is a great thing.

Diary – Monday 19 December – 20 Cavendish Square, W.

We are at home. We have a big bath every morning & a clean fork for every course. Coal bills are a thing of the past – petrol & boot blacking take care of themselves. The change is so sudden I can't help feeling as if Paris & Cristiche & Jeanne & the Casaubons had been a dream.

---

[1] Duperier was one of the *Grandes Maisons* of French fashion. Violet 'ached with boredom' during 'trying-on', when clothes were pinned to her for measurement.

Our journey yesterday was <u>ideal</u>. The Rothschilds reserved us a carriage to Calais. True to his word Loustau turned up at the station dressed in black with a fine orange tie. Kara was ill. He kept the conversation going well till the train started – it is usually so hard to do.

We made an excellent little meal in the dining-car & then came back & I read Anatole France's Opinions Sociales & La Princesse Lointaine alternately till we reached Calais.[1]

Our crossing was ideal; perfectly smooth with a most beautiful sky streaked with fire in the west, cold clear slate-colour with a rising moon in the east. It was almost dark by the time we arrived at Dover & they were sending up rockets from the pier. We got a carriage to ourselves & smoked & read all the way home. Artie picked up an unemployed to carry up the boxes who talked intelligently about the Aliens all the way home.[2] Cave however characteristically refused to let him carry up a single box on the ground he might make away with Father's fur-coat (he'd have his work cut out for him) & Artie had to dismiss him with a shilling.[3] When I woke up this morning I lay waiting for Janet to pull up the blind as my room was so dark. Looking round I saw it was not the blind but the fog which was so dense I couldn't see the Square trees. I shall go to Manton to-morrow.

Diary – New Year's Day, 1905 – Manton, Rutland

My days go very peacefully here. I read – Ibsen & D. G. Rossetti to myself, Heine with Fräulein, Sartor Resartus with Cys & the Arabian Nights to Elizabeth.[4]

[1] Anatole France, *Opinions Sociales* (1902); Edmond Rostand, *La Princesse Lointaine* (1895).

[2] In 1904 the Unionist government proposed legislation to restrict immigration into Britain, which had increased dramatically in the last decades of the nineteenth century. The subject gave rise to considerable debate: Liberals strongly opposed the proposals, which became law in a modified form in the 1905 Aliens Immigration Act.

[3] Cave (n.d.), the Asquiths' butler. He was, Violet later recalled, a great character, whose management of the Asquith household was impeccable. In her unpublished memoir she remembered the following dialogue with Margot as an example of one of his 'fearless initiatives': 'Cave: "Lord Spencer called this afternoon, M'm". Margot: "Oh Cave – why didn't you ask him to wait?" Cave: "I did, M'm, but he wouldn't". Margot: "Oh, Cave – <u>why</u> didn't you ask him to dinner?" Cave: "I did, M'm, and he's coming". Cave would never have asked the wrong man to dinner on the wrong night.' Oc's tip was a generous one, roughly the equivalent of an hour and a half's work for a London bricklayer's labourer.

[4] Fräulein, commonly referred to as 'Fräu', and probably Anne Heinsius (later Meyer), the Asquiths' governess. She returned to Germany in September 1914, after the outbreak of war. Heinrich Heine (1797–1856), German poet whose lyrical verse inspired Wagner's *The Flying Dutchman*.

The rest of the time I talk to the boys, drive to meets or play with Puffin who is more divine than words can say & hasn't forgotten me a bit. It is a reaction after Paris & rather a welcome one in a way as my eyes & head were rather tired when I first came back. Christmas went off well father gave me some pearls & the boys books. Fräulein & Philip tied things together & made a Xmas tree very ingeniously: Elizabeth & Puffin came into my bed at an early hour to pull toys & tangerines out of the boys shooting-stockings.

Raymond has been here for a few days but has now gone to Belvoir. Father & I motored over there with him. It is a vast dark place sham mediaeval with all ancient discomforts & modern hideosities. The boys have had one or two days hunting but the frost has been too hard most of the time. We stay on here till the 20th.

Great excitement over young Pearson standing, Finch having been unopposed for years, Margot has carried on a heated correspondence about it with Peggy Finch a perfect ass who had the cheek to write & tell her father was guilty of bad form & had a lower standard than herself.[1] All this sheds rather a halo round Pearson who is otherwise not remarkable, tho' quite nice – beautiful rider & dancer – unfortunately got white eyelashes.

Diary – Saturday 21 January – Rue Gay Lussac

We had the iciest crossing imaginable yesterday & staggered frozen into the Buffet at Calais. The train was crowded with people on their way to the Riviera & we were packed like sardines in our carriage. I was alternately amused & irritated by the manoeuvres of two old Scotch women who eat high chicken & hard-boiled eggs the whole way while cream oozing out of the luncheon basket above dripped drop by drop on their bonnets. The people at the Douane were very kind to us & let us off easily & we were greeted with almost hysterical fervour by Jeanne who received us. We dined at the Foyot as we were rather late for Pension dinner, but to-day we returned to Rue St. Jacques & ran the gauntlet of its inhabitants. They are all very much the same as we left them – only more so. . . .

---

[1] Harold Pearson (1882–1933), son of the Liberal peer Lord Cowdray, contested Rutland at the 1906 general election, but was defeated by the veteran Unionist George Henry Finch (1835–1907). Finch had held the seat since November 1867: when he was first elected neither Disraeli nor Gladstone had yet been prime minister.

Diary – Wednesday 25 January – Rue Gay Lussac

Last night as we were trudging home rather low spiritedly after a rather worse dinner than usual we were suddenly elevated to the 7th heaven of joy by the arrival of a letter from Mrs. Dubs asking us to go to her to Florence in the middle of March for three weeks.[1] I wrote & thanked her as effusively as I could & forwarded to Margot with a pressing appeal. Florence it would be <u>too</u> divine to go out there alone with Artie, Italy has always been the dream of my life, it seems almost too good to come off. I feel guilty at being happy over anything just now; two thousand Russians headed by Gapon a priest have been shot down in the streets while on their way to the Winter Palace to ask for the rights which every human being in a civilized country has enjoyed for the last 200 years.[2] Gapon's letter to the Czar was full of courtesy & moderation; he puts the case clearly before him, begs him to see the people & hear their wrongs & adds that if he doesn't he will 'briser le lien moral qui existe entre lui et son peuple'.[3] As an answer to this the soldiers are sent out to put an end to discontent by death. I cannot think of it without tears. The censors block the telegraph wires at present so no news can go through & we know nothing. . . .

Diary – Tuesday 31 January – Rue Gay Lussac

Artie's friend Berwick sent us two tickets for the North Sea Inquest commission so we chucked Mérignac & Dupuis & went.[4]

It was <u>very</u> interesting. We arrived at the Ministère des Affaires Étrangères an hour too early & walked up & down the Pont Alexandre III for some time pursued by men who wanted to sell us picture post cards & maps. Artie at first discussed political economy with them & when this failed told them to percher themselves on an orgue de

---

[1] The Dubses were family friends from St Andrews, who had a villa at Arcetri, above Florence. Violet was about the same age as their daughter, Alison.

[2] The massacre of 'Bloody Sunday', in which as many as a thousand Russian demonstrators were killed, and several thousand injured, had taken place in St Petersburg the previous Sunday. The vanguard of the protest was a deputation of workers led by a priest, Father Gapon (1870–1906). The killings sparked demonstrations across Europe, and in Russia a nation-wide revolt that marked the beginning of the violent phase of the 1905 Revolution. Violet's passionate reaction was entirely characteristic.

[3] 'to break the moral bond that exists between him and his people'.

[4] Thomas Noel-Hill (1877–1947), 8th Baron Berwick; honorary attaché to the British embassy in Paris, 1903–11. The sittings of the commission were mostly held in public: the first was on Thursday 19 January, and the last on Saturday 25 February.

barbarie.[1] Neither expedient was successful. At last we went back & were ushered into a huge frowsty room full of red-velvet & gold & chandeliers. It was a glorious afternoon but every ray of sun was shut out & the electric light turned on which gave a very dingy effect.

After another half hour of tropical heat made worse by the nauseating mixture of different scents, everyone stood up like one does in church when the choir comes in & Fournier, Beaumont, Maartens, Fry, Taube, Sir F. Bertie, O'Beirne & other minor officials entered & sat down at their different tables.... Klado was called.[2] He wasn't ready. Another long suspension resulted. At last he came in. He is a middle-sized man, in figure like a German waiter with a beastly roll of fat lapping over the back of his collar; his hair is very short, blue black sharply defining his rectangular head.... He gave his evidence in a rather forcedly decisive manner I thought. I was amused at one passage which I see has not been reported 'Après avoir tiré pendant 9 minutes je regardai la flotte des pêcheurs; pas une ame sur les ponts des vaisseaux; c'était comme une flotte des morts'.[3] Not very astonishing after firing for 9 minutes at 300 yards range.

Several other witnesses were called some spoke in Russian & others in French. All said more or less convincedly (none of them very convincingly) that they'd seen torpedoes. Fournier turned to one a young man of about 25 & congratulated him with great gentleness & courtesy on having sacrificed so many of his family in the war to the interests of his country. He seems to me a tactful moderate well meaning man; one ought always to have a French-man in a position like his; they are sometimes too sugary but they keep relations well-oiled.[4] We came out about 5. I wished I'd heard Klado heckled, I believe that takes place to-morrow afternoon.[5]

[1] In trying to get rid of the unwanted vendors, Oc has suggested that they 'get perched on a barrel organ'.

[2] Admiral Fournier was the French presiding commissioner. Francis Leveson Bertie (1844–1919), newly appointed British ambassador to France (1905–18), was the most senior member of the British delegation. Hugh James O'Beirne, the British agent at the commission, presented the British case; Admiral Sir Lewis Beaumont (1847–1922) was the British commissioner; Sir Edward Fry (1827–1918) the British legal assessor, and Baron Taube his Russian counterpart. Captain Nicholas Klado was a key Russian witness: he had been on the bridge of the *Kniaz Suvaroff*, the flagship of the Russian Baltic fleet, when the British trawlers were first sighted, and he had identified at least some of the vessels as torpedo-boats.

[3] 'Having fired for 9 minutes I looked at the fishing fleet; [there was] not a living soul on the decks of the vessels; it was like a fleet of the Dead'.

[4] According to *The Times* correspondent, Fournier's 'soldierly directness' dispelled any notion, which might have been raised by his civilian dress, that the commission would be diplomatically cautious in its deliberations. His manner was misleading, though, for this is exactly what the commission proved to be: see below, p. 26.

[5] From the outset witnesses before the commission were sometimes heckled by members of the public. Captain Klado, who spoke in fluent French, was an obvious target for British observers.

Two bombs were exploded last night after the Tivoli meeting one on the doorstep of Troubetzkoi a harmless old diplomat who has been in Paris for years – the other on the pavement wounding 5 people. I can't see the point chucking them about at random like that. In my mind the only thing which makes a bomb justifiable is a praiseworthy object, a philanthropic object – like that of sweeping a fiend like Plehve – or Trepoff off the face of the earth. I think doing this is a wider & more unselfish philanthropy than Quintin Hogg's he might be accused of interested motives, of laying up for himself treasures in Heaven at compound interest; but Plehve's assassin sacrifices his soul, runs the risk of flaming eternity (!!) for the good of humanity.[1] I think Jesuitical principles are justifiable in this as in many cases. . . .

Diary – Wednesday 1 February – Rue Gay Lussac

At dinner Henriette asked me suddenly & à-propos of nothing if I should be offended if a young man said to me 'Vous avez de très beaux cheveux'. I said I should certainly think it very crude & rather impertinent. Everyone protested & said that en France cela se faisait couramment[2] & Loustau after a desperate struggle with his chronically entangled tongue suddenly burst out with: 'Vous les avez du reste – de très beaux cheveux – maintenant je l'ai dit.'[3] After a short tussle we made peace & talked of the English constitution & other safe & cool subjects until it was time to go home – Henriette veering round & becoming quite friendly –

Diary – Monday 20 March – Rue Gay Lussac

It is disgraceful of me never to have written a word since the beginning of Feb – but it testifies better than anything else to the fullness & interest of our life here. An ideal 6 weeks have elapsed since then. We've worked a good deal. Besides our philosophy lectures we have had political economy at the École de Droit twice a week – a man called Deschamps lectures very

---

[1] General Dmitry Trepov (1855–1906), former minister of police in Moscow, appointed governor-general of St Petersburg in the wake of the disturbances of 22 January. He was unflinching in the suppression of further disorder. Vyacheslav von Plehve (1846–1904) had been Russian minister of the interior, 1902–4; he was succeeded by Prince Sviatopolk-Mirski. The ministry was responsible for the controversial decision to use the army, rather than the police, to control the demonstration. Quintin Hogg (1845–1903), merchant and alderman of London County Council; well known for his Christian philanthropy.

[2] 'in France this was commonly done'.

[3] 'You have besides – very beautiful hair – now I have said it.'

well on Socialism. The more I hear about it the more convinced I feel that Liberté & égalité are two incompatible ideals which cannot co-exist & that to possess the one, one must sacrifice the other. I think people were created unequal – unjust as it may seem – & that nothing will keep them on the same level except restraints which must fetter the individual & hamper all personal initiative. I am working rather slowly & thoroughly through an excellent book by a man called Gide rather stiff but quite lucid. I bought at Smiths the other day a book of Ruskin's called Unto this Last & have read the first three essays. It sounded very fine & quite plausible – but I don't know if it is possible to treat finances so emotionally with any success.[1]

Bergson thrills & engrosses me. He chirps on week by week about la contingence & I listen raptly among all the red-haired students with someone's knees in my shoulders & mine in someone else's. I have made futile efforts to get the Cours 'sténographies' but as he always publishes them a few years later this is impossible. When I heard it I almost asked Oc not to go to Italy – it seems so unsatisfactory to have heard him working up this subject slowly & surely & to miss the grand clinching conclusion that man is free which I am sure his will ultimately arrive at. . . .

We went to the final sitting of the North Sea Commission with Venetia & heard that most illogical of all verdicts read. The only merit of the whole thing is to have given everyone time to cool down. There were a good many mutually buttering speeches Fournier more than usually sugary.[2] Venetia is a good creature sound, sane & healthy.

To-night we leave. If I say much about it & what we both feel I shall become maudlin. It is very rending to see our beloved flat stripped & bare with dismantled walls & empty shelves, string tissue paper & bills on all the tables, Boethos – whose sealing wax wing has nobly stuck to the last – lonely on the mantelpiece.

I feel the last 5 months have been a unique experience in my life – & one which can never be renewed. The perfect freeness & fullness I have

[1] André Gide (1869–1951), French writer and humanist; John Ruskin, *Unto This Last* (1862).

[2] In the lengthy interval that had elapsed before the commission's report was made public there had been considerable speculation, fuelled by reports in the French press, that Russia was exonerated. The verdict, though, was generally regarded as a vindication of the British case, in the words of *The Times*, 'a condemnation of Russia with extenuating circumstances'. The 'illogicality' lay in the commissioners' desire to identify error without attaching blame: they found that the Russian admiral's precautions 'to repel a torpedo attack were justified', but that 'the fire opened ... was not justifiable'. To British opinion it seemed that undue efforts were being made not to alienate Russia, and *The Times* mocked the commission's assertion that the episode had not compromised the '*valeur militaire*' of the Russian admiral, nor the 'humane sentiments' of his squadron (27 February 1905).

specially revelled in – & I cannot feel that coming out or anything else can ever be so divine. I don't know whether I have learnt very much – except what one unconsciously learns through coming into contact with new things & people. I don't think I have really specialized enough in any subject but I have started interest in a good many which I mean to develop if I have time. And now I solemnly promise to myself that I will not when I am out let all my time run away from me – I will arrange one or two hours a day in which to do something fixed & settled. . . .

Everyone is packing – & I am perfectly idle. I never seem much good in the practical dilemmas of life. People always try & settle me somewhere with a book. I get out of a good deal of bother thanks to this happy lack of competency. We lunch at the Foyot today with Lousbags & then Deschamps for the last time. We go by 10.30 train to-night. I shall read Bergson's book on Le Rire till lunch.[1]

Diary – Tuesday 21 March – Genoa

Our goodbyes have been many & harrowing – from Gonnet & the butter-merchant to Madame whom I boldly kissed before <u>four</u> witnesses a feat of which I am justly proud. Our déménagement was so difficult & complicated that pride in our own napoleonic organization rather took the edge off our sorrow & the pain at seeing our dear little diggings swept & garnished was mixed with a good deal of satisfaction at having got everything safely out. We drove away in a fiacre swaying with luggage leaving the Concierge & her dear grimy little husband & Jeanne semi- hysterical waving on the pavement.

Faire enregistrer les baggages lasted a good long time & when we got to the right platform we found dear old Loustau pacing it with a large bunch of really lovely flowers violets & roses & lilac which he gave me.

We walked up & down & talked of the last 5 months made a few plans which we all felt would never come off then hopped into the train which steamed away. I spent the night with a poor little Italian lady quiet & inoffensive who told me with a pathetic little smile that she had 'toujours mal à l'estomac'. It was very hot so I didn't sleep much but lay dozing & fanning myself with M. Casaubon's little fan with my roses beside me on my pillow.

I woke up in radiant sunshine & after a toilette of great difficulty – I wriggled into most of my clothes between my berth & the ceiling – I went out in the passage & sat on a few boxes & looked at the country. We were passing through Savoie – Swiss drop-slip scenery white peaks & grey glacier

---

[1] Henri-Louis Bergson, *Le Rire, Essai sur la signification du comique* (1900).

streams with here & there a clump of houses round a tiny church. By the side of the line I could see the primroses coming up through the snow. At Turin we changed & got to Genoa very tired & sleepy about 6.30. We failed to get rooms at the Savoy Hôtel so went to Hôtel de Londres near by & after washing & an interminable Table d'Hôte among voracious Germans went out for a damp walk in the town. It was wet & dark so we saw very little but I think it looks promising; we eat some preserved apricots & came home to bed.

Diary – Wednesday 22 March – Genoa

This town is really very picturesque, yellow & rose-coloured houses with green shutters palms & pampases in the public places, washing of every colour hung across the streets & far away the brown masts rising from the port.

I was rather sorry we had to 'rush' it so. I like strolling thro' churches calmly not bustling from altar to altar with a garrulous guide. However they are inevitable here one is mobbed by them directly one gets out one's fiacre.... We went to two picture galleries Bianco Rosso & then had to rush & catch our Pisa train.

Diary – Thursday 23 March – Pisa

We got here after a long journey with 5 chattering old French women & one of their husbands. The country dazzled me by its amazing colours. We kept on diving into tunnels (of which there were over 30) & then emerging from them to find ourselves among the orange trees & almond blossoms & olive-covered hills with here & there a big cypress like a sentry against the sky. We got occasional glimpses of a grey sea; the trees grow down to the very edge of it like at Clovelly....

We arrived at Pisa in a steady drizzle & took a fiacre to the Nettuno Hôtel which to my joy is on the Arno embankment. The town looks lovely full of old churches & Palazzos, I wish we had longer here. I haven't caught a glimpse of the tower yet but I believe it's just outside the town. We dined in the Restaurant below which is teeming with Germans like all Italy at this moment I fear – they are even worse than English people travelling; they eat so much & look so hideous – I admire them as a nation from the bottom of my heart but I cannot bring myself to like them individually with a few exceptions.

We went for a short wet walk ... & we then dispatched some postcards to madame, Loustau, Jeanne, Mérignac etc & went to bed. Vagabonds with beautiful baritone voices sang the Marseillaise outside my window till nearly two.

To-day (24th) we saw the Campo Santo the most beautiful burying place in the world & the only cimetière except Clovelly & perhaps Wanborough churchyard which I wouldn't mind being buried in[1]. . . .

. . . We climbed the Tower & had a glorious view over flat table-like plains which Artie calls 'alluvial' & distant purple hills which I believe were either Appucan or Apennine according to Baedeker – it matters little.[2] To me the tower is more curious than beautiful. Its arcades are all the same which is monotonous & it is shaped like a rolling pin & the colour of a meerschaum pipe. (This last characteristic is its one redeeming feature.)

We left for Florence by the 5 train & arrived at about 8 in the station where a surging crowd of pushing people balotted[?] us to & fro until we eventually found Alison [Dubs] a short sturdy creature in a grey coat & skirt. She has not changed at all since the days we rode together at St. Andrews. I am beginning to doubt if she ever will. After a long drive in the dark during which conversation was nobly sustained under difficulties we arrived at Villa Placci.

Diary – Saturday 25 March – Florence

I know no sensation more thrilling than that which one experiences on the 'next morning' in a new house after a dark arrival the night before. This morning's awakening was particularly delightful for the first thing I caught sight of was a magnolia tree outlined against a patch of Reckitts blue sky.[3] I leapt out of bed & put my head out of the window. Bright sunshine & slight wind – just enough to make the leaves of the olive trees in the podere show their silver linings.

The dining room is delightful all red tiles & a dark wood. I sat down to breakfast with Mrs. North our only fellow guest. She struck me as being very kind I will not say well-meaning as it is always slightly disparaging.

We set off almost immediately after breakfast to go down to the town. Dubs talked the whole way – he is an extraordinary conversationalist; his

---

[1] The churchyards in question belong to All Saints, Clovelly, in Devon, and St Bartholomew's, Wanborough, in Surrey. The latter is the churchyard where Margot Asquith's infant children are buried.

[2] Violet was probably looking at the Apuane hills, north of Pisa and to the west of Florence. The famous *Baedeker* guidebooks, named after their German publisher, Karl Baedeker, were a permanent feature of Asquithian excursions abroad.

[3] 'Reckitt's Blue' was the brand name of an agent once commonly used in laundering white linen, and manufactured by Reckitt & Sons Ltd.

little doubtfully-brilliant epigrams hop out so unhesitatingly I cld. almost say 'pat'-ly that one cannot help suspecting them of being old réchauffés. He told me the whole history of Florentine politics & art going down – never omitting a date – I am ashamed to say my attention wandered more than once. After all whose wouldn't with such a distractingly beautiful thing before one as Florence itself lying in the sunshine a mass of red & white houses grey churches & brown palazzos gathered round Brunelleschi's dome & Giotto's Campanile, the one deep dark red like the heart of a great city – the other white & green & rose coloured the most beautiful thing that was ever built[1]. . . .

Diary – Monday 10 April – Florence

I feel a strong inclination to go straight on with my diary from to-day & skip the last two weeks as if they had never existed – though they have been two of the fullest & most interesting in my life. Facts are always dull & stamped forever on one's mind – amusing trivialities are the only repaying things to write down. . . .

Siena is an ideal town, very medieval, a dusky blood-red, suggestive of all kinds of dark deeds & mysterious romances. . . . Our three days there were very arduous – we traipsed about sightseeing from 9.30 to 12.30 & from 15 to 2 till 15 to 5 & usually another half hour after tea. Dubs is indefatigable & very keen which is so inspiring. I love him for his great youthfulness in everything & the almost romantic chivalry which made him carry Anna to the very top of the Torre del Mangea the highest Campanile in Italy (Palazzo Vecchio a mere stump beside it). She is the best but the most prosaic of wives – I long for her to give him a little more chaff & love out of her great devotion.

Diary – Saturday 15 April – Train from Basel to Paris

I am 18 to-day but did not realize it till I saw it on an immense calendar in the Buffet here while drinking some coffee after a dirty but comfy night journey. I really haven't the self control to go on writing tepidly about Siena & Lucca with Venice so close behind me with its dazzling, startling beauty so utterly surpassing & eclipsing everything I had ever seen & leaving me only a few grey & mouse coloured memories of what had come before. Any attempt at description would be profanity. The two days I

---

[1] The dome of Florence cathedral was built by the architect Brunelleschi, 1420–36, and the campanile, or bell tower, a century earlier, to a design by the painter Giotto.

spent there were the happiest in my life – every moment was full of <u>acute</u> joy & the thought of them is like a rainbow in my mind. . . .

Our first morning was radiant. After the necessary preliminary of cashing a cheque at Cooks we engaged a beautiful copper coloured gondolier called Francesco & made our way down the Grand Canal. A kind of filmy haze of heat lay over everything. We just leaned back silently in perfect content & gazed around at all the beauty the wonderful churches & palaces & bridges, the brown masts & the open sea with here & there an orange sail on a green island. I forget what we went to see – there is a kind of dreamy blur over all the details of these two Elysian days. . . .

After lunch we embarked again & 'glid' down narrow by ways & alleys under arcades of drying clothes of different colours. The slums are very attractive so picturesque in their own dirtiness & each with their box of golden brown wallflowers or chirping canaries in the window. We saw the Frari with its Bellini madonna & ordered ourselves lunch for to-morrow at such a nice little tiny inn with wooden tables & chairs & little low rooms full of tortoise-shell cats. San Marco dazzled me. I never saw anything so gorgeously, regally bright, gleaming with jewels, brilliant with mosaics paved & roofed & lined with gold & red & green it is more like a great pagan joying house than a church. . . .

I felt a great longing to see one of those blood orange sunsets behind the masts in the port so we set out at 6 & floated up towards the Lido. The evening was perfect – coming back a great path of burnished gold stretched before us across the water to the Doge's palace. The surface of the sea was opalescent with a thousand rainbow lights like lubricating oil as Artie said – a true simile if not an attractive one.

Unfortunately we were just too early & when the sun had reached its reddest it dropped behind a tower after illuminating it for a few seconds which reminded me of Shelley's description in Julian & Maddalo[1]. . . .

We went home feeling rather emotional. There is something intensely sad about Venice despite the great happiness one must feel in its beauty. I think it is probably this element of sadness which distinguishes it from any other happiness I have ever felt.

We dined gaily & after a walk in the Piazza where I bought <u>shoals</u> of beads we started out down the Grand Canal in our gondola. It was <u>glorious</u>. . . . Great flashes of purple summer lightning gave one momentary glimpses of the town; unfortunately they were followed by thunder & rain & we were forced very much à contre coeur to turn in at 15 to 10 instead of staying out till 11 as we'd hoped to.

Happily the next day – our 2nd & last – was fine & everything was fresh &

---

[1] Violet goes on to repeat two stanzas of Shelley's poem, beginning: 'And on the top an open tower, where hung / A bell which in the radiance swayed & swung'.

clear & watery after the rain. We sallied forth at 9 with the beautiful Francesco, saw San Giorgio Maggiore where unfortunately all the pictures were invisible through the strings being off. We were very irritated at being deprived of them by such a triviality but we saw a magnificent old wood choir & climbed the Campanile from the top of which we got a good view of the town....

... I have never loved a place so much nor been wrenched from it so soon. However Father's telegrams are inexorable & it would be a shame to waste any more of Cys's holidays poor darling. We resigned ourselves & resolved to buy a few photographs before going.... We rowed sadly to the station by the Rialto & up the rather forsaken bit of the Grand Canal then said goodbye to dear Francesco & turned our minds to the sordid cares of luggage registration.

We reached Milan at 11 where thanks to the cooperation of a diabolical porter with a half-witted guard we were placed in a beastly little tiny carriage without any of the comforts of life & which we were turned out of a few stations later. We were very angry – but glad to get into a beautiful 1st class to ourselves with broad comfy seats on which we stretched ourselves & spent as good a night as one ever does in the train.

We breakfasted at Basel & are at present spinning along green level French country with rows of poplars & red-roofed cottages & here & there an old woman in a blue apron working in the fields. Alas! my olive trees & cypress groves, marble churches amongst the almond blossom, orange-covered hills & blood-red skies!

I do hope I shan't resent Dinard too much – I have horrible presentiments of windy links & whooping cough.

Diary – Monday 17 April – Dinard

I smile at re-reading my worst anticipations! Windy links and whooping cough! If that were all!! I little thought – but how could I?

I had imagined Dinard a French village red & white on a cliff, old women in blue aprons & white caps clattering about in their sabots – yellow sands & little mediaeval churches. What was our despair on arriving on a dank, damp grey morning to find a squalid, hideous, hotel-ridden sea-side hole, over-run with 3ʳᵈ rate English & opulent Semites of the worst type. Our hôtel which we had imagined a rural Ritz is a measly hovel furnished in drab & mustard-colour. The links are reached by a steam tram! running once an hour & are governed by a hidebound oligarchy who have ejected Cys after a heated altercation on a green this afternoon. The town is papered with advertisements. The High-Life Casino seems the only attraction?

This after Venice. I need say no more to describe my état-d'âme except that I have a heavy cold which I am struggling to suppress by large doses of quinine which leave me deaf & muzzy....

Diary – Saturday 22 April – Dinard

Raymond & Father have arrived. The 1ˢᵗ evening we all puzzled vainly over a time-table in hopes of finding out some way of escape from this hole. We were disappointed; neither Jersey, Guernsey, Alderney nor Sark can be reached before next Wed., no boat goes to Southampton till Tuesday – in fact there is no exit from Dinard at all except by Paris & this means 12 hours journey.[1]

Raymond has already booked a berth on the Cherbourg boat for Monday night; neither his clothes, his clubs, nor Father's clubs have arrived here so the links our only solace is wrested from us....

Raymond Asquith to V.A. *Tuesday 25 April*
Cherbourg

My dear Violet
you may have Thought when we parted that I should not have time to write to you from Cherbourg. But quite the contrary is the case.

I have plenty of time & lots to say: for I have decided to spend a day here on my way home. The idea was put into my head last night by an accident which at first (I am ashamed to say) caused me some annoyance but which I now recognise to be one of the many ways in which God fulfils Himself – one of the blessings which he sends to His favourites disguised in sombre wrappings that they may shine with a brighter light when the coverings are removed; a sugar plum found by a tired child on Xmas morning in the dark toe of the seemingly depleted stocking; a joyous

---

[1] Raymond wrote to Katharine Horner: '... finally we arrived here at 9 tonight cold and tired and hungry to find a snow-swept watering place with bad overcrowded golf links 3 miles away and squalid rooms with oil stoves and match-box walls in an hotel full of Jews, hunting women, hunted men, and all the congested vulgarity of Leicestershire, Park Lane and Bayswater. Cys has been already turned off the golf links for insulting an aged member of the club, and Violet and Oc (who have come straight from Venice, from lying in Francesco's gondola and eating pink risotto in our smuggler's cabin by the Frari) quite in the abyss of despair. And the most damnable part of all is that the place is a lobster pot: we are in fact cut off from getting out' (John Jolliffe, *Raymond Asquith: Life and Letters*, 126).

and surprising aftermath of His Paschal Bounty which we might well have thought had exhausted Itself in the profusion of our Dinard happiness – so small is our Faith.

It happened in this way. Last night my train was $\frac{3}{4}$ hour late & on driving down to the Quay I found that the boat had just started. For a moment I gave way to one of those outburst[s] of vexation to which the petulant & rebellious clay of which we are partly made is alas! too prone. Then I saw through a glass darkly; but now, face to face. I came to this Hôtel – I was hungry & thirsty, having had no nourishment since some chocolate at 5 & it was now past midnight. No one was up except the Hall Porter. But he was the soul of kindness. He procured me a piece of bread & took me to my room where I washed it down with some excellent water which had been thoughtfully provided in case I should wish to clean my teeth. And indeed nothing could exceed the consideration with which I have been treated throughout. I said my prayers & went to bed: & there it was that I fully realised the startling good fortune to which I had at first been so strangely blind. It was as if scales fell from my eyes: the veil of carnal lusts & trivial appetitions which too often obscures & obstructs our ter-restrial vision was withdrawn as by an Unseen Hand and the wiser work-ings of the mysterious mind of the Universe broke overwhelmingly upon my illuminated gaze.

What, I asked myself, could be more providential than that I should have been directed even against my will to a spot so rich in historical associations, in architectural beauty, in literary & artistic interests, as Cherbourg? Was it not here that Napoleon said 'J'ai résolu de renouveler à Cherbourg les merveilles de L'Égypte'?[1] Was it not here that Pepin the Fat declared that the Trumpets of Burgundy were thicker than his father's loins. Was it not here that Racine & Molière laid the deep foundations of the French Drama? Was it not here that Rabelais drank & Villon sang? and was it not here also that Fulke de Brèanté, most notable of mediaeval swashbucklers, was found in his bed, dead black stinking and intestate?

And if it was not, what of that? Has Calais its six brave men, and shall not Cherbourg have its one? Yes, I cried, Yes : a thousand times Yes. And after all, what heroism is there in spending a day in Cherbourg? Maybe it has been done before; aye, & will be again. And if I were not here tomorrow where <u>should</u> I be? Why, only at Avon[2] – a common English country house in a common English county, in the society of people who are perfectly

---

[1] 'I am determined to re-create at Cherbourg the marvels of Egypt.'

[2] Avon Tyrrell was the Hampshire home of Lord and Lady Manners, close friends of the Asquiths, and also of Sir John and Lady [Frances] Horner. The children of the Horners often stayed at Avon, and it was around this time that Raymond began to court Katharine, the younger daughter.

familiar to me – a trite & limited circle who have nothing to offer either to my mind or to my heart but the catchwords of a côterie and the stale endearments of a semi-domestic intimacy. Am I a man, I cried, or a fly, that I should stick for ever upon the rim of the same old honey-pot? The question had only to be put to be answered – Flieh auf hinauf in weite Lande[1] came the ringing response of the German poet. New faces, new interests, new horizons for me – aye, and a new Argo and a new Perseus too: and who knows if there may not even now be rising a new morning star for him to shoot his fountains against? Away with this fondness of decay, this docile dotage, this inertia of stagnant emotions & contracted sentiment! I call in Cherbourg to redress the balance of the Ringwood. Such was the tenor of my austere & masculine reflections; which were at length terminated by a deep & refreshing sleep from which I arose to begin my new life about 2 o'clock this afternoon.

I had been told overnight that the boat went again to Southampton this evening: but I was now cheered by the information that there was no boat till Wednesday night. After walking thoughtfully in the streets for 10 minutes or so I felt the clinging & retentive charm of Cherbourg enveloping my whole being like a cloud of incense: the powers of my will seemed to be growing numb and my spirit to be anchoring itself in the soil of Normandy. Angel voices sang in my ears to a tune of ravishing beauty –

> 'You may sing of Calypso and Circe
> Of their isles in a faëry sea,
> You may whisper of Olive or Hersey,[2]
> But Dinard & Cherbourg for me'

and other words of a seductiveness so indescribable that I refrain from setting them down.

I saw that my new enthusiasm had already gained a dangerous ascendency, & I determined to fight it down lest I should find myself tied to Cherbourg as fast as I had once been tied to Avon. 'Self-reverence, self-knowledge, self-control' I muttered to myself, & such other fragments of Lord Tennyson's poetry as I could recall.[3]

Thus braced for the effort I approached the master of a small boat which I was told was to convey cabbages this evening to Southampton & persuaded him by the offer of money to take me as a passenger upon his

---

[1] 'Fly up and away to distant lands'.

[2] Olive Macleod, daughter of Sir Reginald Macleod, and Hersey Maltby were friends and contemporaries of Violet.

[3] From Alfred, Lord Tennyson's 'Oenone': '"Self-reverence, self-knowledge, self-control", / These three alone lead life to sovereign power'.

voyage : and at 10 o'clock tonight, once more master of myself & my desires I shall lay my tired body with the burden of its unconquerable soul upon a couch of tender vegetables & there amid the mysterious shadows of their succulent foliage the lemon-coloured stars of an April dawn will distil upon my spirit the blessed freedom of Peace, so sadly lost, so strangely re-won

> 'Annihilating all that's made
> To a green thought in a green shade.'[1]

Raymond

Diary – Thursday 27 April – Hôtel Ritz, Paris

We have left Dinard! Oh the intense relief! The transition has been very sudden between the tapping masons, screeching housemaids, tepid water & swivelling looking-glasses & this palace where all what R. calls our carnal appetitions are sinfully pandered to – where we bask in scented baths & sink ankle deep in mossy carpets. We came here Wed. the day before yesterday – I saw Cys off at the Gare du Nord & found Margot here with slight whooping-cough poor darling.[2] She luckily rarely whoops except at night & when she does we call it a crumb in the throat!

Thursday we spent in & out [of] dressmakers & hat shops. Callot, Muelle, Esther Meyer, Louvre in the morning, Duperier, Suzanne & countless others after lunch. I am beginning to get quite interested in my clothes though I am still convinced that nothing will ever be able to be done to make the slightest difference to my appearance. However we ordered two lovely dresses at Duperier a mauve shot silky one for the day & a black tulle for the evening, – Mdme Muelle is making me my bazaar dress – white brocadey stuff with pale blue velvet ribbons. I also got a nice blue hat with pink roses. M. thinks it lovely its height alarmed me a little at first but as she says it is rather Watteauesque.

Artie & I dined together alone in this sumptuous place. I never saw such luxury & extravagance – it's like a Rothschild house. . . .

Diary – Sunday 7 May – Wampachs Hôtel, Folkestone, Kent

M. & I came here Friday night. We had a rough & icy crossing & were only saved from sea sickness by intense cold & discomfort, waves sweeping

---

[1] From Andrew Marvell, 'The Garden'.

[2] Margot's expert knowledge of French couture was to be put to Violet's advantage in readiness for her 'coming out' ball the following month.

over us continually & a boisterous wind tearing our hats from our heads.
It was not cheering to hear on arriving drenched & depressed that that
damned fool from the Ritz had registered all our luggage wrong & not one
thing had arrived....

Folkestone is one huge suburban boulevard planted with limes, clean &
airy & smelling of sea & summer. It is ruined for me by being so fashionable,
asphalt parades & lifts up & down the cliffs, bicycles & bandstands & bath-
chairs make life easy & hideous; I feel the sea is desecrated by being made
so accessible. One ought to scramble to it over slimy sea-weedy barnacle-
covered rocks instead of gliding down with a little band of dowagers &
invalids on a trottoir roulant.

The population is almost entirely composed of convalescents & holiday-
making clerics; hospital nurses flit about in great quantities. I also notice
a type I know so well – the middle-aged caretaker, an unmarried woman –
about 50 blurred & faded with a tired, kind wornout with sympathy for
other people look.

TWO

Coming Out

1905

At the end of May 1905, shortly after her eighteenth birthday, Violet made her début in 'society', crossing, as she later put it, 'the Rubicon' that flowed between youth and adulthood. With this rite of passage came changes to her appearance, and much else besides: 'every rule and canon of behaviour, which had governed schoolroom life, was now reversed'. She was suddenly released from a 'Trappist seclusion' and thrown, with little preparation, into a 'whirling vortex' of dinners and dances. The season then included between five and eight balls every week, and the great houses – Devonshire, Dorchester, Stafford and Lansdowne – were in their full glory as the principal venues. Public recognition of 'coming out' was bestowed on a débutante when she was formally presented at Court, a potentially nerve-racking rite that Violet accomplished early in June. The carefully regulated world into which she was admitted did not survive the upheaval of the Great War, and Violet experienced both its heyday and its twilight.[1]

Diary – Tuesday 23 May 1905 – 20 Cavendish Square, W.

I went to my first ball last night. I think I enjoyed it, it sounds blasé to say I didn't – at the same time I don't think any very acute joy is to be got out of balls.[2] I was very bewildered & interested; in the intervals of being whirled giddily round by a young man who was new every 5 minutes I

---

[1] Edwardian 'society', Mark Bonham Carter has observed, 'existed', it was 'a serious expression' (Mark Bonham Carter (ed.), *The Autobiography of Margot Asquith*, xiii); and Kenneth Clark recalled a conversation with a friend who knew 'society' from the inside, Bogey Harris: 'I said something to Bogey about [Oscar] Wilde going into society. Bogey replied "Wilde was never in society. He never dined with the Devonshires"' (Kenneth Clark, *Another Part of the Wood*, 180).

[2] Violet's first impression did not last. Cynthia Asquith, who also 'came out' in 1905, enjoyed 'a long, long vista' of dances that summer, later recalling that 'Violet Asquith and her brother or brothers, and myself and my brother or brothers, were "swept out" of every single one' (Cynthia Asquith, *Remember and Be Glad*, 73).

was conscious of a confused mass of seething people, people I had known all my life looking strange & disguised & different. Everyone seemed to be being crushed or pushed or complaining of the heat or making banal conversation.

They too looked bewildered & rather sad. No one seemed to be able to concentrate themselves to say a connected sentence. I have confused recollection of shouting inane things up to Arnold Ward, whose massive features, more like an oriental potentate's than ever, I could see somewhere far above me in their usual condition of passive weight & undisturbed gravity. I wore my Worth dress a very lovely one all white satin & tulle, with lily of the valley in my hair – people said it looked nice & was well done – I only felt the necessity of holding my eyebrows constrainedly up the whole time to prevent it coming down. Grandpapa's necklace made me feel like a dowager & was admired.[1] I think I danced a good deal on the whole but I have no clear recollection of my partners; May introduced me to a measly looking young man who asked me to dance – I refused Mr. Chaplin in anticipation of his appearance, but as he never turned up I danced with A.W. the most intrepid mover I've ever seen – he skips like the hills in the psalms. The 1st man afterwards accused me of perfidy.

2) Mr. Henry Chaplin a young man who humiliated me by shaking my hand up & down like a pump handle.

3) Archie Gordon whom I sat next to at dinner – I find him very attractive & easy to get on with, one can have quite a good effortless talk with him which is such a rest. His knees coil round one valsing rather too much but this is a detail.

4) Jack asked me waggishly to 'take the floor' with him.

5) Ernest Crawley.

6) I began sitting out with Baker but was borne off by Arnold Ward who took me down to supper & talked to me for the best part of $\frac{1}{2}$ hour about the mental development of Neville Lytton & how that germ of genius, the travail of the brain of his great grandfather which had lain so long dormant within him had reawakened in the aesthetic milieu of the Latin Quarter, startled out of its inertia by etc. etc. He is worse than ever.[2]

7) Joan's young man Lindsay[3] who tho' not amusing is easily amused – this is the next best thing, a good many fall between these two stools. He

---

[1] As 'coming out' presents, Sir Charles Tennant gave a diamond necklace to Violet, and one also to Frances Tennant, her step-cousin and his granddaughter.

[2] Arnold was one of the few young men that Violet met in the course of her first season with whom she was already acquainted. Neville Stephen Bulwer-Lytton (b. 1879), younger brother of Victor, 2nd Earl of Lytton; a painter by profession, he exhibited at the Royal Academy.

[3] Joan Gordon Duff, Margot's niece; she later married James Lindsay.

also insisted on taking me down to supper & we talked over different things. He guffaws encouragingly on the slightest provocation.

Oblivion follows this list – I only know I ended up with Phil Kershaw.[1] He is very amusing & made me rock at dinner; I was faintly disillusioned by A.W.'s suggestion that a good many of his jokes might be dished up from Belloc. He told me he went up to a lady called Ada Cavendish whom he had ogled at between the ages of 11 & 17 & said 'You're the only woman I have ever loved' upon which she turned & fled from the house. He is a Satanic looking man his chin hangs like a great jagged stalactite.

I came home with Artie about 2.30. Francie looked pale poor darling she had everything against her heavy cold & leprous spots but I always love her face. Ruby Lindsay looked quite lovely wild fox coloured hair & white face & Clementine Hozier was in yellow a very fine classical head. Marjorie Manners very pretty, Marjorie Eden perfect head spoilt by a frumpy dress, Barbara Jekyll beige coloured from top to toe, eyes hair dress cheeks; Katharine a dream; Barbara Lister very good looking in black velvet & white roses but rather elderly I thought.[2] I came home at 2.30 with Artie & slept till 11 next day.

Diary – Wednesday 31 May – 20 Cavendish Square, W.

I splashed about in a swimming-bath in Bayswater which sounds squalid but wasn't really bad. Misty green water & odd clammy beings & a lady with a strong Cockney accent who towed me up & down on a hook for a quarter of an hour. I think swimming would be a nice cool thing to do in the summer & I must have some exercise now Margot has knocked off riding, fencing & dancing as too hot. Beb & I Barbara Jekyll went to the Meistersinger in the evening – it was wonderfully given van Rooy doing

---

[1] Philip Southwell Kershaw (1877–1924), a Balliol contemporary of Raymond Asquith; barrister and clerk in the Land Registry Office, 1901–10.

[2] Frances Lucy Tennant (1887–1925), Violet's step-cousin, the second daughter of Francis John Tennant; she married, 1912, Guy Charteris (1886–1967), an elder brother of Cynthia. Ruby Lindsay (1884–1951), daughter of Colonel C. H. Lindsay and Emelia *née* Brown; she married, 1909, Ralph Peto. Marjorie Manners (1883–1946), eldest daughter of the 8th Duke of Rutland; she married, 1912, the 6th Marquess of Anglesey. Marjorie Eden (1887–1943), only daughter of Sir William and Lady Eden, and sister of Anthony, prime minister 1955–7; she was at finishing school with Violet in Dresden in 1903; married, 1909, the 6th Earl of Warwick. Barbara Jekyll (1887–1973), daughter of Colonel Sir Herbert and Lady Jekyll; a first cousin of Katharine Horner, and a lifelong friend of Violet; married, 1911, Hon. Francis McLaren (d. 1915). Barbara Lister (1882–1943), eldest child of Lord and Lady Ribblesdale, and Violet's step-cousin; married, 1905, Captain Mathew Henry Wilson.

Hans Sachs & Richter conducting.[1] I saw Cicely & Katharine looking perfectly lovely in a box with Ronald Graham who reminds me of a newborn child so pink & hairless.[2]

Diary – Thursday 1 June – Munstead House, Surrey

... Tuesday I had rather a nice ball at Mrs. Marshall Roberts.[3] Glorious room but a floor like toffee. I danced with John Flower, Sturgis, Prinz Fürstenberg a German Mrs. Chauncey introduced me to who valsed & reversed wonderfully & Beb with whom I really had my best turn.[4] I don't know many people yet & no one is ever introduced – the hopeless stage to get to must be when like Elsie Graham one knows people & they don't dance with you.[5]

Diary – Saturday 3 June – 20 Cavendish Square, W.

I went to the Court last night. Long & arduous preparations took place between 7 & 8.15; the witty Simpson did my hair & Aunt Eva sat by & asked a string of fatuous questions which I answered mechanically for some time & then gave up hopelessly. My train never arrived so I had to borrow Frances'.[6]

When Margot had pulled down Simpson's feathers & Newson [had] pulled off Janet's veil & when they had been satisfactorily reinstated I climbed the stairs once more in some trepidation & received my bouquet of white roses at Mrs. Baynham's hands; my train was then tried on & I was obliged to practise my curtseys to the rocking horse before a large but not critical audience. Margot said they were too jerky & spasmodic &

---

[1] Anton van Rooy (1870–1932), Dutch baritone; made his début at Bayreuth. Hans Richter (1843–1913), Austro-Hungarian conductor who had worked with Wagner.

[2] Ronald Graham (1870–1949), eldest son of Sir Henry and Lady Margaret Graham. At the foreign office, 1903–7; agent and consul-general in Egypt, 1907–9. He was a half-cousin of Cicely and Katharine's mother, Frances Horner.

[3] Mrs Marshall Roberts, *née* Irene Murray.

[4] (Horace) John Flower (1883–1919), a Winchester contemporary of Arthur Asquith; joined the King's Royal Rifles, 1902, transferred to the Queen's Westminsters, and died of wounds sustained in the Great War. Mark Sturgis (1884–1949), assistant private secretary to H. H. Asquith, 1906–8; private secretary, 1908–10.

[5] Alice Katrine ('Elsie') Graham; half-sister of Ronald Graham (see above); she married, in 1911, Captain Harold William Knowling.

[6] Violet was assisted in her preparations for her Court presentation by, among others, her aunt, Mrs Evelyn 'Eva' Wooding, her father's sister.

lowered herself slowly with a melting look. . . . A.W. took me into dinner &
amused me very much. À-propos of my hand-writing he said: 'If I thought
you would not take umbrage at so personal a remark I should like to say
that yr. hand-writing is singularly consistent with your character. If you
will permit me I will venture to apply a particularly descriptive word to
both.' I waited breathlessly. After a time with the same oracular delivery
'Limpid.' – I (gurgling hysterically) '<u>Limpid</u>!!' – He (with perfect gravity)
'Yes I could almost say pellucid – but the word is a little pedantic.' I rocked
with uncontrollable laughter. I was sorry at not being able to say more to
Bluetooth.

The Court itself wasn't half as dreary as I'd expected. There's no doubt
about it the Entrée is the only thing that makes Buckingham Palace
bearable. I patted myself heartily on the back when I saw the rooms &
rooms full of mothers & daughters mauve with fear & fatigue with an
hour or two behind & probably more in front of them in long disconsolate
rows. . . . I felt acute disappointment at having so little to do – after all the
arduous preparations & practisings there is a certain flatness about the 2
summary curtseys & the 100 yards walk. I enjoyed what followed
immensely. M. & I sat down opposite the K. & Q. a little to the right &
watched strings & strings of people making the <u>most</u> comic curtseys – the
heavy chin-scoops & projecting backs & the extreme archness of most of
them made us shake with laughter – we became quite hysterical when a
lady in feathers diamonds & a <u>flowing</u> beard came through. The orders &
uniforms were quite beautiful & delighted me – Benckendorff's was
especially lovely all silver with a cherry-coloured ribbon; poor man what
must he be feeling after this awful smash.[1] He took us into supper – we
eat a little standing up at a buffet & then went home. It was a glorious
sight.

Diary – Thursday 8 June – 20 Cavendish Square, W.

Last night Annie's ball – my most glorious. We had 27 to dinner I sat
between Eddy Cadogan nice but uninspiring & whom Margot accused me
of neglecting & Hugh Godley Sir Arthur's son who delighted me by his
keenly responsive sense of humour; I had never met him before & enjoyed
my talk with him very much.[2] I talked to darling K. after dinner – she may

---

[1] Count de (Alexandre) Benckendorff (1849–1917), Russian ambassador in London from
1903. The 'smash' refers to the 'Dogger Bank incident', above p. 5. His children Natalie (d.
1968) and Constantine (1880–1959) were friends of the young Asquiths.
[2] Hon. Edward Cadogan (1880–1962), a Balliol contemporary of Herbert Asquith and a
barrister; unsuccessful Unionist candidate for King's Lynn, January 1910.

be dumb & monkey-ridden but she is as beautiful as a dream & I love her passionately. The other women were V. Meysey-Thompson nice but conventional & insipid, Hersey – cheerful, Meessee Lyttelton to whom I hardly spoke & Maud Lyttelton[1] whom I do not know & Clementine Hozier very fine & classical looking but leaving me quite cold. The joke of the evening was sending in Hersey with A.W. they took each other absolutely seriously as I foresaw they would.

We went on early to Annie's; Felix Cassel was the first person I saw[2] – I danced the 1st valse with him then 2 strange men I was introduced to Seymour & Richards, then Godley who frightened everyone by shouting on the stairs, then A.W., then Bury, then Sturgis, then Franklin, then Ernest Thesiger then my mind becomes a blank.[3] I was introduced by D-D to a Bohemian diplomatist & by someone else to a German prince but as I got engaged 10 deep at once I missed them all.[4] I went into supper with Hugh Godley & had a long talk with him – he interests me very much & his intensely melancholy expression is a never-failing source of amusement. A.W. harassed us rather; I wrangled rather with him last night, that silly Oxford book is a fatal groove to have got into.[5] Sturgis & Godley were both furious with me for dancing with Ernest – they don't seem to realize that he is a joke – a kind of 3rd sex to be treated as such. I stayed till the bitter end & enjoyed myself wildly. A. Ward irritated me by cutting strips of tulle off my dress & putting them in his pocket & Olive by coming mysteriously up to Beb & saying Bury was a dangerous character & I oughtn't to dance with him – which is the greatest rot. Bury is dreary & a vile dancer but quite incapable of vice – Olive is a Heygate & a gossip. Beb & I & Oc drove home about 4 in a 4-wheeler all the birds chirping.

[1] Maud Mary Lyttelton (1880–1953), eldest daughter of 8th Viscount Cobham; she married, in 1908, Hon. Hugh Archibald Wyndham.

[2] Felix Cassel (1869–1953), barrister; an ardent admirer of Violet, he proposed to her several times during the next two years.

[3] Walter Egerton Keppel, Viscount Bury (1882–1979), eldest son of 8th Earl of Albemarle; ADC to the governor-general of Canada, 1904–5; to the viceroy of India, 1906–7; unsuccessful Unionist candidate, January 1910. Ernest Thesiger (1879–1961), English actor whose career began on the Edwardian stage and continued in film: he appeared in *The Winslow Boy* (1948), directed by Violet's half-brother Anthony Asquith.

[4] Edith 'D-D' Lyttelton (d. 1948), second wife of Alfred Lyttelton, whose first wife was Margot Asquith's beloved sister, Laura (d. 1886).

[5] Arnold had 'stolen' Violet's *Oxford Book of English Verse*, and written a humorous poem in apology.

Diary – Saturday 10 June – Ewhurst, Surrey

I was so tired on Thursday night I hadn't the energy to go to Mrs. Mackie's ball I went to bed at 10 & was vexed & distressed at not being able to go to sleep till past 3. Every hour which struck left me more angry & feverishly keen to sleep as I saw my night ebbing away before my eyes & thought of the Court Ball the next day. I expect I am a little overtired & this country peacefulness will give me back my sleep. I spent Friday morning with Eileen in the National Gallery kept Sturgis to lunch & drove about in a hansom in pouring rain most of the afternoon.[1] After an early dinner with Beb who is going up to have a look at Thurso[2] I rested – then put on my green tulle & silver dress & had a good talk with dear Simpson who was doing my hair – he is a charming man so witty I'd rather talk to him than most people I meet at balls. F & M picked me up – there were masses of carriages – three rows deep – we didn't have to wait long – went into the same enormous room which was unfortunately frightfully overcrowded, worked our way deftly up to the top slipping between fat officials, & finding the thrones still out of sight hopped boldly up on the seat where we stood – our legs well hidden by other people. . . .

The Royal Quadrille was a lovely sight & went off without a hitch.[3] I climbed down from my perch for the 2nd & by a stroke of luck stood just behind the King of Spain heard him speaking German quite beautifully. . . . I enjoyed it very much on the whole & should have still more if I hadn't been so sleepy. I came here this morning having met Eileen & the Duchess & a small dog on Paddington platform.[4] The house is really lovely full of nice things pictures & furniture perfect, comfort & beauty combined. A big bath is the only thing lacking.

The Duchess is a very kind, benign creature, a good deal cleverer than

[1] Lady Eileen Wellesley (d. 1952), only daughter of the 4th Duke of Wellington. She had been in Dresden with Violet in 1903, having been sent out, Violet later recalled, with only one coat and skirt to wear: 'She laughed at her own plight, which filled the rest of us with indignant commiseration. We got together and presented a collective petition to her governess (a dragon with a row of teeth encased in gun-metal) appealing to the Duchess that Eileen might be allowed to buy a second coat and skirt in Dresden, as at present she had to go to bed on rainy days till her clothes dried. This did the trick, and Eileen bought a dashing brown outfit frogged with gold braid and brass buttons. . . .'

[2] Thurso Castle, home of Sir John Sinclair of Ulbster, lay on the Caithness coast, at the extreme north of the British Isles.

[3] Court balls opened with a 'royal quadrille', in which the royals present, including visiting monarchs and consorts, took part. After this the rest of the assembly was allowed to dance, 'though a respectful vacuum was carefully preserved around the more august of the rotating couples by watchful officials, armed with, (what looked like), long white billiard cues'.

[4] Kathleen Wellesley *née* Bulkeley, Duchess of Wellington; she married the future 4th Duke in 1872.

one would think – very appreciative & finely critical of art of any kind – she has made this place what it is. Her relations with Eileen strike me as being distinctly unsatisfactory – she is quite out of touch with her I can see; most tactless tho' very devoted & knows no more about her than the butler. I think Eileen is alternately irritated & amused by her mother; she doesn't love her enough to feel pityingly protective & tender as to a weaker....

Diary – Saturday 17 June – Littlestone-on-Sea, Kent

I came here Wednesday from Ewhurst. The Bishop of Stepney arrived the last night.[1] I thought him clever & interesting & had a very good talk coming down in the train with him. He is broad & big & doesn't niggle over details or technicalities. At the same time I can imagine his being socially ambitious & talking down to people like Eileen whose criticism is disarmed by their hero-worship for him. Beb says he did it to Kissa.[2] Not quite such a fine character as my dear little Bishop [of London] but better brains I should think. He exhorted me to go down to the East-end – there's nothing I should like better if I wasn't afraid of boring the people! I joined Fräu & came on here the same night. This place is shadeless & shingly; flat arid stretches of grass & sand without a tree or a mound or a molehill of any kind. Our house is built at the edge of the shore so that one hears the monotonous lapping swish of the waves all night & on waking sees a sweep of wet green water bounding foam. We have had brilliant sun all the time; I sit out in it & read & write on the beach or in the garden & go for an occasional dusty motor-drive or chilly bathe. The air makes me feel quite bestial: a strong inclination for air food & sleep is my only sensation. Evan, Ld & Ly Elcho & Mr. Balfour are staying in the hôtel & some of them have dined here every night so far.[3] Friday night there was rather an interesting conversation about Bernard Shaw.

Margot said his sense of humour was so destructive that she couldn't regard him in the light of a prophet with a mission; negation never goes

---

[1] Cosmo Gordon Lang (1864–1945), suffragan bishop of Stepney 1901 to January 1909, when he was nominated archbishop of York by Asquith; he held this post 1909–28, and was archbishop of Canterbury, 1928–42.

[2] Clarissa ('Kissa') Bramston, daughter of the Reverend John Trant Bramston (d. 1931), housemaster and founder of the Winchester house which still bears his name, and which Beb, Oc and Bongie all attended during their time at the school.

[3] Evan Charteris (1864–1940), barrister at the parliamentary bar. Evan was the younger brother of Lord (Hugo) Elcho (1857–1937), the future 11th Earl of Wemyss. Elcho married, in 1883, Mary *née* Wyndham (1862–1937). Lord and Lady Elcho were the parents of Cynthia Asquith, and Lady Elcho a special friend of Arthur James Balfour.

very far & the constant ridicule with which he treats his audience & his characters becomes a little tiresome in the end. Just as one begins to take him seriously – for one cannot but expect some undercurrent of seriousness somewhere – the whole thing becomes broad burlesque, & these farcical developments insult one. I must confess that personally I took the one in three & three in one speech of the mad parson <u>absolutely</u> seriously. I thought it was a bathos – but I thought it was an unintentional one. However when M. lunched with him he amazed her by saying 'One in three! Three in one! Seriously! of course I didn't mean it seriously.' – I am sorry as I loved the mad parson & can't bear to see him degraded by his creator. To me there is something wrong & unnatural about this cuckoo-like indifference & lack of tenderness for your own creations. Arthur Balfour & Raymond take him more seriously than M., they say he is a teacher as he has enthusiasm for one thing – socialism. It is a cause he has never laughed at or given away. In the Unsocial Socialist he only attacks the half-hearted propagators – not the cause itself.[1] He will never be really popular with the public as they want to be touched sometimes – not perpetually laughed at. As it is they shake like jellies thro' his plays in pure self-defence. I can never remember feeling such joy in anyone's presence or conversation as A.B.'s. I never took my eyes or ears off him the whole evening. He seems to me to have such a perfect mind & character – & his lack of infallibility <u>is</u> so attractive – besides his wonderful kindness & courtesy to the smallest & dullest & most insignificant (i.e – self). Beb & I motored in the dark after dinner.

Sat. I dined alone at the hôtel with the Elchos & A.B. I went in much joy & some fear; the latter was speedily dissipated. Miscellaneous conversation not to be written down. Arthur Balfour was amused at my telling him about Charles's bomb-agent in Hammersmith.[2] We played Bridge Ld. Elcho & I won 2 rubbers against the other two. I motored home in a fine thunderstorm.

Sunday – I clung feebly to a breakwater in the morning with chattering teeth walked round warm sunny links with May & Beb in the afternoon, reading the Egoist in the grass while they did loops & grappled with the intricacies of bisks.[3] The P.M. & Elchos dined with us we scrambled into dinner anyhow no-one taking anyone else in & had a most amusing meal. A.B. said Winston made a mistake in thinking violent invective the surest way to success; he thought that with his name chances & capacity he ought to have gone further by now; abuse may advertise one as a platform

---

[1] Bernard Shaw, *An Unsocial Socialist* (1887).

[2] Possibly an allusion to Charles Lister's youthful radicalism: he was passionate about social causes, and joined the Labour party while still at Eton (L. E. Jones, *An Edwardian Youth*, 57).

[3] George Meredith, *The Egoist* (1879).

speaker but it won't go down in the House. I couldn't help secretly wondering whether he minded the same things trebly magnified in Jo. We played Bridge, A.B. & I won a rubber against R. & Lady Elcho & he offered us the motor for to-morrow.

Diary – Sunday 25 June – 20 Cavendish Square, W.

... Being Ascot week not much has happened. Tuesday I dined with the Lewis's – sat between A. Ward & Felix Cassel. I had quite an amusing talk with A.W. – poor dear he kept on striking out desperately at the Russian novelists & the paradoxes of Chesterton etc. etc in vain efforts to get the conversation out of the Ethel Clifford groove.[1] Cassel is quite a good fellow but better to dance with than to talk to.

We danced afterwards in what I had always thought would be the ideal conditions for a ball – 40 couples twiddling in a cool empty room. As a matter of fact I realize now that a ball ought to be overcrowded to be a success; one ought to be crushed & squashed & pushed & hot & harried to really enjoy oneself. There was a kind of flatness about everything I thought. I may have exaggerated it in my imagination thro being depressed about Beb[2] & meeting no-one I was particularly fond of & seeing so many jews. I danced with Cassel, Arnold, Franks Librarian of the H. of C. & several unknown Semites.[3] I enjoyed talking to a man called Mason (who wrote Miranda of the Balcony, the Four Feathers, etc.) at supper – I found him quite amusing.[4] Sturgis cheered me up by asking me with pathetic sérieux not to hail him like a hansom when it was his dance – his conventionality is an inexhaustible fund of amusement for me. Drove home with the Jekylls. ...

Yesterday Sat. I had a glorious day of brilliant sunshine, cool, green, friends & new mown hay at Eton. Charles & I & Edward & Oc & John & Mark & Cys watched the cricket – or rather I didn't watch it – all the

---

[1] G. K. Chesterton (1874–1936), important Edwardian writer who made frequent use of paradox. Ethel Clifford was the butt of a standing joke between Violet and Arnold.

[2] Beb had an unspecified, but minor, operation that week.

[3] William Temple Franks (1863–1926), assistant librarian at the House of Commons, 1902–5.

[4] Alfred E. W. Mason (1865–1948), author of *Miranda of the Balcony* (1899) and *The Four Feathers* (1902).

morning.[1] I never feel more at sea anywhere than on a cricket field & no one will explain anything, they seem to think it so obvious or else expect one to have a mysterious intuition into all its intricacies – they nearly crept under the chairs with shame when I said how unfair I thought it that two poor little Wykehamists in black stockings should be pitted against 22 athletic Etonians. It was pointed out to me that they were the Umpires, & that they wore trousers not stockings & I was implored to make my ingenuous comments sotto voce if at all. We lunched all together in a green garden full of nasturtiums at the back of a Pub called [The] Sun. The cloth was laid under two trees & an umbrella & Charles & Oc grappled with pink fish & cold lamb & we all eat cherry tart & strawberries & were ideally happy. Dear Charles & I had a most amusing talk about Free Russia, Gapon, Spence Watson, etc.[2] I love his enthusiasm & violent Radicalism & intense seriousness.

We strolled back to the cricket ground where I met Archie Gordon. He asked me to walk about with him & broke it to me that Elsie & Ly M. Graham were to live in St. Michael St. for Commem.[3] I behaved very wickedly, pretending to know nothing about it & acted a politely but badly veiled shock at the news. I couldn't help it, it was such a temptation but his evident discomfiture & distress made me feel very rude & guilty. We had an amusing talk otherwise, I love his frankness & transparency & joie de vivre which I sympathise with so acutely. We were laughing very weakly & foolishly over something when I was suddenly confronted by Hugh Godley, sombre but pleased looking. He <u>made</u> me sit down with him in some chairs & introduced me cursorily to a few female relations; meanwhile Archie rôdé-d about discontentedly & finally sloped off. I had some pangs – but had too good a talk with H.G. to be able to repent very much. He was peculiarly delightful, really amusing in a morose way; I felt that whole time that he thought I was very crude & young & unformed & startlingly unconventional – but I also felt to my relief that he wasn't

---

[1] Four of these friends died young, three of them in the Great War. Edward William Horner (1888–1917), eldest son of Sir John and Lady Horner, and a Balliol contemporary of Cys Asquith, was killed in action in France in November 1917. John Nevile Manners (1892–1914), elder son of Lord and Lady Manners of Avon Tyrrell, joined the Grenadier Guards as a 2nd lieutenant in 1913, and was killed in action in France, 1 September 1914; he was the first member of Balliol, and the first of Violet's close friends, to be killed. Charles Lister (1887–1915) died of wounds sustained at Gallipoli, 28 August 1915. Edward Horner's younger brother, Mark, died of scarlet fever in March 1908.

[2] Dr Spence Watson was until 1902 the president of the National Liberal Federation; he was succeeded by Augustine Birrell.

[3] For an account of the Oxford 'Commem' balls that June, see below, pp. 49–51. Lady Margaret Graham *née* Compton (1847–1931), daughter of the 4th Marquess of Northampton, was the mother of Elsie; she married, in 1884, Sir Henry Graham.

shocked only rather grimly amused. Archie has told me since that I talked to him for an hour & a half by his watch with some bitterness – however that may be – we all – Bluetooth, Artie, Archie, H. Godley & I had a delicious tea in Edward's rooms which shocked me by their comfort & beauty & then joined by Bongy we motored to Slough where the others took the train & Oc & I & Bluetooth motored on home – I hadn't seen him Bluetooth for such ages – it <u>was</u> fun.

Diary – Monday 26 June – 20 Cavendish Square, W.

I had a hot ball at Lady Wimborne's – not very amusing – I danced with [Lord] Bury & the Morton boys saw no one I knew well or was fond of. The heat was crushing, not one window open in the ballroom. Father & Margot came & fetched me & took me home.

Diary – Friday 30 June – 20 Cavendish Square, W.

I ought to have written about Oxford just after it happened – while I was yet red-hot with happiness but I had no time to, so I suppose I must make a few lukewarm comments now.[1] Not that I am depressed or that anything has happened to damp my joy since – merely that I am reduced to <u>pulp</u> body & mind thanks to dancing two nights running from 9. to 6.

It was <u>glorious</u> – one of the nicest things I have ever done in my life. Hersey & I & Mrs. Maltby went down on Tuesday afternoon in tropical heat; we had just subsided each in a corner of the carriage when the gigantic face of Arnold thrust itself thro the window – we weakly begged him to come in & then I bought a Times to fan myself with & struggled with the Egoist & some of Roger's letters firmly resolved that no conversation should be made. I was drawn into a little discussion with Arnold about women's education. I said I almost preferred people with not much brain to those who having little tried to develop it violently like Sandow muscles & produced abnormal bumps & knobs which stick into other people & cause much discomfort.[2] He argued a bump was better than no brain; I said symmetry reached its highest point in a dot & we meandered on for some time to a constant accompaniment of puzzled giggles from Hersey. Oc was at the station & we drove to St. Michael Street in a cab. I

---

[1] Violet went to a 'Commem' ball at New College on Tuesday 27 June, and to one at Merton College the next evening.

[2] Eugen Sandow, head of the Sandow Curative Institute, promoted a system of exercise treatment as a cure for illness.

remembered so well last time I came giving Roger & Beb tea in the little
downstairs room & lurking behind a door to try to catch a glimpse of
Warty – then the triumph & joy when his profile was revealed to me
silhouetted against a yellow blind! ...

   We had a very odd dinner; Oc & I, Maltbys, Grahams, Arnold, Archie &
Lord Compton.[1] He (Lord C.) I was introduced to for the first time that
night – I think he is particularly nice; I found him a little teeny bit stiff &
conventional at first & even now I don't find perfect confidence in his
sense of humour but it is a good deal shyness & he is [a] very good sort
quite unspoilt, very frank & most unselfish catering for partners for Elsie
for every dance. I don't quite know what to make of her poor dear – she
appears excessively dank & dreary with distressingly little joie de vivre or
capacity for enjoyment of any kind but I've no doubt she is really nice.
We left directly after dinner & drove in flys to New College. The ball room
was a large covered tent already thronged with people. We were handed
little cards (such as one reads of in the Heir of Redclyffe) to write our
partners' names on.[2] Archie Gordon startled me rather by asking me for 8
straight off! I bewilderedly granted them stipulating that they should be
discreetly strewn over the evening. I danced every dance till dawn. It
was too glorious. Enthusiastic partners & cool windy gardens hung with
Japanese lanterns did a lot towards keeping one going. I didn't feel quite
up to Arnold which was rather sad as we usually get on so well together –
we didn't quarrel tonight but I felt things flagged a little. ...

   Archie took me to see a window in the chapel towards sunrise & we had
an interesting talk there untranscribeable – but which I shall never forget.
I have not yet quite reached his motives – I thought they were those of an
unselfish & energetic youth discharging a duty towards his 'party' at first
but his zeal is beginning to make me doubt it. We broke up at 6. Arnold
making a speech at the last supper in which he compared me to Tabitha![3]
We slept 6 hours got up at 12 & went on the river dozed in punts & eat in
hayfields all day had tea in Archie's rooms & came back to St. M. St. for
an hour before dinner. Elsie & Ly Margaret have gone – they insisted
though I beseeched them not to, assuring Elsie that she was the centre
round which all things turned & that she would leave a flatness &

---

[1] William Bingham 'Bim' Compton (1885–1978), son and heir of the 5th Marquess of
Northampton. A Balliol contemporary of Beb and Bongie, he served with the Northamptonshire Yeomanry, 1903–6, and the Royal Horse Guards from 1907; captain and
adjutant, 1913. Bim was a cousin of the younger Grahams – Alan, Elsie and Marjorie.

[2] In her youth Violet had read Charlotte Mary Yonge's *The Heir of Redclyffe* (1853) seven
times, 'from cover to cover – never failing to cry at the end'; there is, though, no specific
reference in it to dance cards.

[3] A biblical allusion, Acts 9:36: 'Now there was at Joppa a certain disciple named Tabitha
... this woman was full of good works and almsdeeds which she did.'

depression behind her. She insisted on going in spite of these enthusiastic tho' untruthful asseverations.

And we danced all another night. I loved it almost more than the first. Bongy was there! dear Bongy, I have a passion for him, & Gibbie & Gugs & lots of nice new people whom I have forgotten & one or two blighters whom I am trying to forget.[1] I got to know Compton much better & danced with him a lot; my pleasure was rather spoilt by Archie's complaints in the early morning; he said he felt unhappy & neglected & harrowed me rather but I did dance with him 7 times so I don't feel really guilty. I had one moment of complete mental collapse towards 5 when introduced by Timmy Jekyll to a man called Trench whom I was told was brilliant & interested in the Celtic revival. I sank down on a basket chair my mind a perfect blank & said after a few minutes silence (I blush for it) 'Have you seen any Bernard Shaw plays'? – He replied 'No – but do you know that Pantaloon is an allegory of the fiscal question'.[2] I said 'No' feebly & conversation ceased. I thought his was a brilliant repartee. My heart bled for poor Timmy Jekyll whom his mother was hurtling from one young lady to another clamouring at the same time for a fresh supply of partners for Barbara 'smart & clean, mind' was one parting injunction I heard! He looked spotty & sad & out of his assiette. I sat out one or two dances with him. We came home at 6 in a ramshackle fly Artie & Archie one on each step & Ld. Compton on the roof & danced down St. M. St. in brilliant sunshine. The next morning the Maltbys hied away by an early train to see the actors & authors cricket match at Lords! So characteristic I thought. Archie came to say goodbye to me with a small gift. Oc & I lunched together then strolled thro a few quads & chapels – then he saw me off in the train. Bless him.

I felt very, very tired & happy when I reached home. I went slick into bed at 7 & tried but failed to sleep till 11 when arrayed in my green & silver dress looking very white & jaded I set off to Grosvenor House with Margot. It is a glorious house lined with Rubens frescoes. The King & Queen were there & every famed & lovely person I have ever heard of. I danced once or twice rather sadly with dotty guardsmen & tepid diplomatists all blasé & then to my joy espied Archie's face pink & joyous sidling thro the crowd. I ran to him & we went out in the garden & talked for a long time & danced once with him & came home. The little Japanese princess Arisgawa who is over here on a visit was there Geoffrey Howard told me she made inquiries about the Christian religion & on being

---

[1] Francis 'Gugs' Weatherby (b. 1885), a Winchester and Oxford contemporary of Oc; with Messrs Weatherby & Sons.

[2] J. M. Barrie's one-act play *Pantaloon* was staged at the Duke of York Theatre, London, in 1905.

explained the mysteries of the Trinity said 'Just like you English! you do everything by committee!'.[1]

Diary – Sunday 2 July – Seal, Kent

... Our dinner party on Friday was amusing. I sat between Belloc & John Poynder.[2] The former thrilled me; talked brilliantly & incessantly of himself & his works, mapped out the ideal life bacon & beer 6 to 8 riding till lunch writing till 5, tea with beautiful ladies till 7. etc. etc. I was so tired & in very bad form but I enjoyed him immensely. He harped on a good deal on his penury saying repeatedly I'd do anything to get 10 pounds. I advised him to go to Cave who pays all my clothes on delivery & cabs on arrival. I had a heated discussion with Sir John Poynder as to whether personal & political relations should be kept separate or not. I said decidedly that they should. To me the whole beauty of public life in England lies in the independence & robustness of private friendship which continues untouched & uninfringed upon thro' party feuds & splits. So far from weakening enthusiasm for any cause it swells it & makes fighting big & broad not personal & niggly. All this is abominably written. I return home to-morrow.

Diary – Monday 3 July – 20 Cavendish Square, W.

I had a hot unsatisfactory tea-party. Hugh Godley & Archie & Compton came & I couldn't talk to any of them & was very disappointed & vexed & so were they all of them except Archie whose cheerful persistence brought him $\frac{1}{4}$ before anyone else & kept him $\frac{1}{4}$ after. Hersey came for about 5 minutes & rambled on incessantly about Eileen & Harry & her ankle. We arranged a play party for Friday.

---

[1] Geoffrey Howard (1877–1935), fifth son of the Earl of Carlisle, a first cousin of Venetia Stanley, and a familiar figure among Violet's circle. Liberal MP for Eskdale, Cumberland, 1906–10, and for Westbury, Wiltshire, 1911–18; parliamentary private secretary to H. H. Asquith, 1910; Liberal whip, 1911–18.

[2] Sir John Dickson-Poynder (1866–1936), 1st Baron Islington, 1910; Unionist MP for Chippenham, Wiltshire, 1892–1906; Chippenham as a Liberal 1906–1910.

Diary – Tuesday 4 July – 20 Cavendish Square, W.

Dined with the Edens – sat between a great hunter called Kennaird who told me he had killed 10,000 wild goats & promised to send me the head of one – & an aide of Baden-Powell's called Greaves or some such name. Kennaird was quite amusing – he married Cora Lady Strafford a lady justly famous for having made a success of her life. En premières noces she married a millionaire who tactfully dropped early from the perch leaving her a daughter & a fortune. She then very rightly resolved to get the thing she lacked – a title – & accordingly married Ld. Strafford. Him also speedily despatched & having now acquired all the good things of life she has married the love of her life Mr. Kennaird with whom & the fortune & daughter of the first & the title of the 2nd she lives happily to this very day....

Diary – Wednesday 5 July – 20 Cavendish Square, W.

A long weary lunch at the D^{ss} of Wellington's lasting from 1.30 to 3.30.... I lay down for half an hour when I got home then dressed & went off to the zoo in a hansom feeling like a somnambulist. Wild horses wouldn't have dragged me to Olive's tea there if it hadn't been that Archie was keen I should go & it is the last time I shall see Hugh Godley before he embarks on circuit. I was much cheered by Mrs. Walters' greeting 'How <u>very</u> unfortunate you have got no chaperon!' in a tone of deep melancholy.[1] I sidled up long rows of chairs & sat by Olive & Mr. Godley at the top; I waded sadly thro' an ice saying inane things from time to time. Archie made a tardy appearance a little later & was caught in the nets at the bottom of the table. Then we broke into little bits & wandered about. Hugh Godley & I perfunctorily visited a few fishes & then settled on a seat & talked. I went home....

---

[1] By the standards of the day Violet was loosely chaperoned, which reflects her stepmother's upbringing. Margot recalled in her *Autobiography* how she and her elder sister Laura had entertained male friends late into the night in their shared bedroom at Glen. Laura was upset to learn that because of this they were 'considered "fast"', but Margot was unconcerned: 'That these midnight meetings should shock anyone appeared fantastic; and as most people in the house agreed with me, they were continued' (Mark Bonham Carter (ed.), *The Autobiography of Margot Asquith*, 28–29). Referring to Edwardian social conventions, Violet later recalled: 'I was ... always allowed to have young men to tea with me unchaperoned, and this, though it won me the envy and respect of my contemporaries, was, by many mothers, considered very fast, not to say sharp practice.'

Diary – Friday 7 July – 20 Cavendish Square, W.

Last night I dined with the Lytteltons – sat between a man called Egerton & Lord Alexander Thynne <u>very</u> good looking like a cross between an ascetic Nero & Pooley my nurse.[1] I liked him. We talked about Oxford & various kinds of lives interests religions etc. After dinner Archie came & talked to me, then we all went off. One girl tumbled out of the fourwheeler & grazed her elbow on the step – mopping with wet handkerchiefs ensued & lasted quite a long time. I danced with Archie & Arnold & sat out with Ld. A. Thynne for a span which Arnold afterwards referred to as the 'Thynne Epoch'. He accuses me of doing what he called 'too much groundwork'! Beb & I drove home late. He said he had enjoyed it more than any other ball he'd ever been to. I was quite happy but not wildly....

Diary – Monday 10 July – 20 Cavendish Square, W.

I don't think I have ever experienced a greater nausea of mankind in general & my friends in particular than I got on waking on Sat. morning. A great longing to go somewhere, anywhere where was wind & a sea & no people swept over me so I told Janet to wire for rooms at the Wampachs Hôtel [Folkestone] & sorted out books & arranged the next two days in my mind.

Everything was neatly settled & I was just going downstairs with a sigh of relief when I met Father who told me kindly but firmly that I couldn't possibly go away alone anywhere & had far better spend 'a nice cool comfortable Sunday in Cav. Square'. My fury at being thwarted in this tenderly hatched plan may be imagined. I tried to work on Margot's unconventional, airloving heart but all in vain. They none of them seemed to realize how stifled & breathless I was feeling. I hopped & stamped & clicked sadly thro' a dancing lesson. Archie came to see me – still distressed. I assured him it was all right & that I had had perfect confidence in him the whole time & had never really been angry & he went away more cheerful. At lunch Margot suggested that Oc & I & Eliza should go to Cookham a place on the river near Taplow for two nights & sleep in the inn. I leapt at this proposal & in spite of father's gloomy predictions of sleeping above the kitchen & coming home hot & midgebitten we wired for rooms, & set off at 5 in the most suffocating heat I have ever felt. Oc insisted on going 3rd as the journey was short – he is <u>as</u> <u>good</u> <u>as</u> <u>gold</u> – I

---

[1] Lord Alexander George Thynne (1873–1918), younger brother of the 5th Marquess of Bath. A major in the Royal Wiltshire Yeomanry, and Unionist MP for Bath from January 1910; killed in action near Béthune, in France, September 1918.

could have wished E. had not been, she was very good dear darling but I should have been so happy alone with Oc.

Father was right! – E. & I's joint bedroom was over the kitchen & stiflingly hot but we were consoled for this by the beauty of the village & the river – a little spoilt by people with parasols & banjos – but lovely in spite of them. We had tea in the garden then drifted along in a punt Elizabeth enthusiastically holding slime dripping weeds over different parts of me. Then she went to bed & Artie & I after a little dinner all to ourselves spent 2 ideal hours under a full yellow moon on the river. It was so long since I'd seen him to talk to properly – Oxford didn't count a bit for either of us. We had a heavenly talk – I rather longed to tell him many things I didn't.

I spent the next day either on the river or reading the Egoist on the bank. There was an awful storm which we escaped by skulking in a summer house covered with crimson ramblers at the bottom of someone else's garden. We went home that night as I couldn't bear my hot room any longer. I felt ever so much better for our little jaunt.

Diary – Tuesday 11 July – 20 Cavendish Square, W.

I had the most glorious ball last night at Stafford House. We swarmed in thousands up the wonderful stairs shook hands with the Duchess looking divinely beautiful at the top, in a gold dress with all her diamonds & little ruby bows.[1] Margot & I then took up a stand near the balustrade & watched to see the King & Queen arrive. It was not certain that they were coming so only half the people were in kneebreeches & Beb not knowing this & having none didn't come which was very sad. I watched the Royal Quadrille standing against the band. I thought every moment the conductor would hit Arnold Ward (who was standing beside me) on the head. I danced with, Archie, Bury, E. Thesiger, Felix Cassel, Lord Compton a sequence which we spent in the garden – then a blur comes.

I think I danced with Arnold & Ld. Compton several times. At about 4 when I began to think of going home I sent Archie & Arnold to look for Raymond who Margot had entrusted me to. Imagine my despair at hearing he had gone home. Archie & Arnold then both begged me separately to let them take me & amused me very much by each advising me disinterestedly not to go with the other. The difficulty was solved by Mrs.

---

[1] Stafford House (now Lancaster House), in the Mall, was the home of the 4th Duke of Sutherland, and the duchess mentioned is his wife, Millicent ('Millie') (1867–1955), eldest daughter of the 5th Earl of Rosslyn. The Sutherlands were numbered among the 'Souls', and she was a famous society beauty.

Horner taking me as far as Buckingham Gate (for appearance's sake) & my then setting sail across London alone in a 4 wheeler. I arrived at Cav. Sq. without a latch key or half a crown. I broke my nails on the square in vain efforts to raise a flint to hurl at the boys' window. Finally I sat down nodding on the doorstep & pressed my thumb upon the bell for about 5 minutes when Park very somnolent & décolleté turned up with salvation in his hands. I hurried up to bed & to sleep & am just off to have tea with Elsie & go on from there to the Hugh Bells' river party.[1]

Diary – Wednesday 12 July – 20 Cavendish Square, W.

The river party was very nice, windy & healthy & cheerful. I made friends with a delightful man called Arthur Stanley, Venetia's brother, he looks like a little cock-robin & raged with me about eschatology, subjective idealism & the pre-Socratics the whole way to Kew & was finally shut up in the cabin. We had dinner at Kew on the bank I sat between Archie & Arthur Stanley.[2] Archie neglected Barbara Jekyll shamefully. She looks very jaded & tired & as if some catastrophe had happened to her & there is something rather tragic about the mindlessness of the convulsive smile which still clings to her. I talked to Archie coming back & begged him to take a little trouble. He said 'how can I? being with you makes me rude to everyone else'. I told him I hoped I should soon cease to have this disastrous effect on him – but that meanwhile he must play up. When I reached home I found a very oddlooking man whose eyes looked as if they were on tentacles standing by the fire in the library. I was told it was Aubrey Herbert.

Diary – Friday 13 July – 20 Cavendish Square, W.

Last night I went to the Leconfields' ball. I enjoyed myself wildly but didn't admire the house at all. The marble carried no conviction (marble rarely does) – & the sitting out rooms reminded me of the Palace Hôtel at Aberdeen. I had supper with Aubrey Herbert who amused me very much, I love his lisp. For the rest I danced with (same old lot) Archie & Compton &

[1] Sir Hugh Bell (1844–1931), 2nd Bt; ironmaster and colliery owner. Contested the City of London as a Liberal in January 1910. He was the father of Gertrude Bell, the traveller and archaeologist.
[2] Arthur Lyulph Stanley (1875–1931), eldest son of 4th Baron Stanley, and elder brother of Venetia. A barrister and Liberal MP, representing Eddisbury, Cheshire, 1906–10.

Alan Graham[1] & sat out a long time with Ld. A. Thynne, & missed Bluetooth alas! & cut Franklin & got a valse with Oc & Beb & others. Oc pleased me by saying I danced better than <u>anyone else</u> – with the heartfelt sincerity of a brother. I came home tired & happy towards 4.

To-day just as [we] were having our dancing lesson Arnold strolled in & watched us for $\frac{1}{2}$ hour with a kind of mournful contentment. The boys then went out to fence in the yard & he sat with me 2 whole hours perfectly happy rambling on about remote subjects, I stopping his stories, laughing at the wrong moments & arguing about what I know nothing about. Seeing I had two 2nd Jungle books he asked me to give him one – which I did – he in return presented me with a large handkerchief with a red border & green horseshoes![2] I thought it quite a promising sign of thriving sense of humour. I am trying hard to foster it within him. We all had tea together in the schoolroom. Arnold said (as a large plate full of cucumber sandwiches, a pot of marmalade & a stodgy yellow cake were placed round the teapot) 'How admirable Violet! this maintaining of the habits of the manor house in the midst of the metropolis'!...

Diary – Sunday 16 July – Kiddington Hall, Kiddington, Oxfordshire

This is without exception the dullest Sat. to Mon. party I've ever been to. I sit & look at my watch on my wrist & pray for the hours to pass. I find one's friends spoil one so – I made disgracefully few efforts to all these dull young men, it is a matter of complete indifference to me whether I find favour in their sight or not. Three weeks ago I should have taken <u>such</u> trouble!...

Friday night which I see I haven't written about was most amusing. Billy & Julian came up for the night & as Mrs. Grenfell couldn't take them to the play owing to a King & Queen dinner they asked for me instead which pleased me <u>so</u>, <u>so</u> much.[3] We had a little dinner at a tiny table in the middle of that vast dining room in St. James's Sq. & we talked over Dalquharran & all the amusing things we had done & meant to do

---

[1] Alan Charles Douglas Graham (b. 1888), only son of Sir Henry and Lady Margaret Graham; cousin of 'Bim' Compton.

[2] Rudyard Kipling's *The Second Jungle Book* was published in 1895, a year after the original *The Jungle Book*.

[3] Julian (1888–1915) and Billy Grenfell (1890–1915), Ettie Desborough's eldest children. They were educated at Eton, and afterwards Balliol, where they were contemporaries of Cys Asquith. Both were killed during the Great War: Julian died of wounds at a hospital in Boulogne, in May 1915, and Billy was killed leading a charge near Hooge, in July, within a mile of where his brother had been wounded.

together.... I went on afterwards with Beb to the Stanley dance which was great fun.

Geoffrey Howard was very uproarious & quite uncontrolled being in his cousin's house & ran about attacking people. I danced with Edward Horner, & Alan Graham, Archie, Arnold with whom I had a fiscal talk the first for a long time – Aubrey Herbert who sat down with me on a doorstep in Mansfield Street & talked to me about the respective mental development of men & women. He said women developed quicker because they were made love to which I absolutely denied as at 13 they are far ahead of boys of the same age. He disregarded my objection & went on to say that when a man proposes he puts himself in the position of the rabbit lying open to dissection by the surgeon – he also said joie de vivre made the hills blue etc. etc. He amuses me very much. One funny incident occurred just as we were going home when Beb & Oc seized by one common impulse rushed at Arnold & slung him up kicking & struggling in their arms & carried him down the street: All the ball-guests assembled on the steps & cheered. Arnold & I & Archie & Beb & Oc walked home together & the last sight I saw was Archie up a lamp-post at the corner of Cav. Sq. & Arnold tie-less at the bottom reproving him. The boys were in such high spirits that Beb snatched the electric light globes off the nursery landing & sent them crashing down the stairs! Silly boy!

Diary – Tuesday 18 July – 20 Cavendish Square, W.

I am not going to Taplow to-day to the river party as last night was tiring & I am keen to be very fresh for our dinner party to-night. Beb & I & Archie set off at 3.30 in the motor yesterday & reached Richmond pier before any one else. The Sunbury Belle was covered with cherries & grapes & bananas & iced coffee & every kind of luxury. After about 5 minutes wait we saw the rest of the party emerging from the Underground in a dismal little cavalcade headed by Waxworks & Olive. Most of the people I had never set eyes on before – but I recognized the familiar & inevitable Edgar Dugdales, Mrs. Walters, Compton & the two Lytteltons.[1]

Compton & Archie sat down one on each side of me which made me rather apprehensive. All my worst fears were realized, they soon began to bicker & wrangle & haggle till at last I said: 'I won't be quarrelled across – you must go away for a bit Archie & pay yr. respect to Mrs. Edgar Dugdale' which he did. I had a good talk to Compton – I was conscious the whole time of Olive's basilisk eye resting upon me! Then Archie returned & I

---

[1] Mrs Edgar Dugdale (d. 1948), *née* Blanche Elizabeth Balfour, A. J. Balfour's niece and the author of a two-volume biography of him. She married, in 1902, Edgar Trevelyan Dugdale.

made him introduce me to Ewen Cameron a friend of Hugh Godley's who is dining with us to-morrow.[1] I somehow expected him I don't know why – to be like an understudy of H.G. & Geoffrey Howard had told me he was very like Archie only stupider. I found him very different to either – easy & cheerful with a hinny like a goat – but I don't think we had what I call a very satisfactory talk as I was conscious once or twice of casting about in my mind for topics. The races were very dull. People sat & shivered on the bank while other people sat & sweated up & down the river & old Wax-works was as blind as a bat & judged consistently wrong. We were in a fever to get back to catch our train at Hampton Court for the Apsley House ball.

Compton had eaten nothing since breakfast & was quite faint with hunger. We had a large meal coming home. I chaffed him about his letter of apology to me for the too personal remarks made in the heat of the moment at Stafford House & said it only came to oil the wheels for the getting of his Apsley House invitation. He denied this indignantly & said he really had felt very contrite & would have written anyway. He said 'I know you think I disapprove of you Miss Violet – how can you? please, please don't – it will ruin our intercourse if you think over what you're going to say'. I said I should certainly count 9 before every utterance after the very harsh rebuke I had received – I could see the whole time he didn't quite know whether to take me seriously or not. He & I & Archie & Beb & Ewen Cameron & his brother went back by the early train & got out at Vauxhall. Beb & I quickly changed & went on with Margot to Apsley House. The house was beautifully lighted & organized 'Mind your head' printed over every window leading into the garden which I thought so thoughtful.

The King & Queen had already arrived & the Royal Quadrille was in full swing. The Waterloo gallery in which we danced was splendid – the pictures of course were not quite at their best but band floor & light perfect. I danced a lot with Archie & Compton & Guy & Ld. Gerald Wellesley Eileen's brother who seemed to me extraordinarily nice & clever.[2] Cynthia looked lovely. The garden was bitterly cold – with policemen skulking behind every evergreen to prevent one killing the King. Eileen was having a high old time & gave me a distant smile whenever I saw her for which I chaffed her afterwards. Archie came home in our fourwheeler & when we stopped at 58 Grosvenor Street to drop him Beb insisted on getting out & taking me in with him meeting all my objections of sleepiness, propriety etc with 'Don't be heygate!' Archie & I nodded over our

---

[1] Sir Ewen Cameron (1841–1908), fellow of the Royal Geographical Society.

[2] Lord Gerald Wellesley (1885–1972), third son of the 4th Duke of Wellington; in the diplomatic service.

soda-water & tried our very best to get Beb home – nipping the political discussions in which he tried to embark in the bud. I was just awake enough to notice a really lovely Titian over their mantelpiece.

Diary – Wednesday 19 July – 20 Cavendish Square, W.

I got a letter from Arnold yesterday morning saying 'May I put in a respectful plea for the apple green to-night' which amused me not a little. However I was quite firm, wore my Worth & wreath of green leaves Eileen made me & flew to the drawingroom to find Aubrey Herbert & Viola already arrived.

This dinner given by Raymond & myself had been thought out weeks ago & much looked forward to. I need hardly say I have had all the grind & all the glory. Writing out the cards was a bit of menial drudgery I resented – & I went thro' awful qualms over the chuckings which were maddening 3 Edens – ill-health – Arthur Stanley – engaged to be married (I forgot to say this was announced on Friday night at the ball). Barbara Lister – indecision. Finally a distracted wire brought Bluetooth to the rescue & after an hour of severe brainwork I settled who was to go in with who & gave the paper to one of the boys – alas! the wrong one.

When almost every one had come I said to Raymond – you tell everyone who to take in. To my despair he answered 'I haven't the foggiest idea'! I wrent my hands! & was just going to announce a general scramble which seemed the only possible dénouement when Beb turned up with the paper – the key to all mysteries in his hands. Lady Elcho our only chaperon who as Father said gave a tinge of faint respectability to the dinner went in with Raymond – Compton took me. Our guests were all so nice I must make a diagram of the tables.[1]

I had a very good talk with Hugh Godley at dinner. He has come up for a short entre acte in the middle of his circuit. I have had one or two amusing letters from him which we discussed a little, not much – I am just trying to think what we did talk about the rest of the time but can't remember.

After dinner I talked to Cincie & Venetia & tore a bit of tulle off the bottom of my skirt & sat out on the stairs with Archie & Guy having it mended. Then I talked to Aubrey Herbert & to my fury he made the same old conversation about the comparative mental development of men & women. I felt quite shy of using the same retorts lest he should recognize

[1] Violet sketched two circles, around which she wrote the names of her guests, a dozen at each table. With the exception of Lady Elcho, the nominal chaperon, they were all from her age-group.

them! I hustled everyone off early at 15 to 11 – & got quickly engaged about 5 deep with people I didn't care for much then I had a bout with Archie, Compton & a sequence with Hugh Godley. I can't remember ever, ever seeing so many people I was fond of at a ball.[1] Every dance I longed to be with 3 different people. Arnold whom I had forgotten to get an invitation for came to the door & sent in a line to Lady Poynder saying 'May I join the merry throng?' He seemed upset & unstrung. I couldn't think why at the time but have since had revelations from Margot which fill me with remorse & distress. The tale of the soda-water party was in all mouths! I was amused at its getting about so quickly. I supped with H.G. & had an interesting talk about friendship. His theory is that one's capacities of loving are limited & that the fewer friends you have the more you are able to love each. I deny this absolutely. I can see no horizon to my powers of loving – & the more friends I have the more I am capable of giving to each – because each new friendship is a kind of education in sympathy & insight & so far from robbing the old ones – deepen & broaden them. He said time by itself forbade one having many friends – one hadn't space for thoughts of them in the shortness & hurry of life. He may be right – I hope he isn't. When he went I danced with Arnold & Guy & Gerald Wellesley & Archie & was discovered by Ewen Cameron & Geoffrey Howard whom I had cut for the 3rd time! They both said it was their dance. I rather like Geoffrey – despite his boisterousness I love his enthusiasm for temperance & I feel he is handicapped in life & sees stupider people getting on better & minds it.

There was a dance in cloaks at the very end which I did half with Wrench & half with Archie & then I hied home with Beb having had a glorious time. I have liked this & Stafford House & Annie's better than any other balls in London I think.

This morning Ld. G. Wellesley came to fetch me & we went to see Clifford's Studio in South Kensington together; he has some lovely Burne Jones's & some very good copies by himself. Archie came to see me at 4. I hustled him off the doorsteps as I thought just in time to avoid Compton but they met on the pavement outside the house! I had a good talk with Compton who had come to say goodbye to me – he played me his version of the Pilgrim's March & spoke to me very earnestly about Archie saying how important it was that he should set seriously to work & begging me to send him out of London. I said I should certainly keep him as long as I wanted him but that he might go on Sat. as I was leaving for Scotland then. He didn't know whether to be irritated or amused. He then told me he was going into the army & asked me whether I advised him to go to India. I begged him to – as you get some soldiering there & at any rate a

---

[1] This was the Dickson-Poynders' ball, at their home at 8 Chesterfield Gardens.

fine sporting life. Hanging about London & Windsor & going to balls is a poor profession for a man. I warned him to come back before he had become white haired & domineering from the hommages of the rajahs & the foul climate. . . .

Diary – Thursday 20 July – 20 Cavendish Square, W.

Guy lunched with me to-day & was very dear & amusing. M. & I tried on at Miller's in the afternoon. . . . We also chose a lovely Iris chintz for Beb & I's room – though if there's a dissolution I suppose we shall all be turned out.[1] Hugh Godley had tea with me & sat with me for an hour. We had a nice talk. The Connaughts are dining here to-night.[2] I must run & rest.

Diary – Saturday 22 July – 20 Cavendish Square, W.

I am alone in the house to-night & unable to get up to Scotland till to-morrow. Our Connaught dinner went off very well. I had to have a lonely quail in father's room as they unexpectedly brought an adc as well as a lady in waiting but I was quite happy reading Chesterton's book Heretics which thrills me & on the whole rather relieved to have escaped a long hot dinner.[3]

I went up directly afterwards & was introduced to the Duchess a kindly substantial creature with a strong German accent who asked me if I had enjoyed my dancing this year – the same old question. Margot always says 'Look up brightly & say "yes"'! but I feel deeper gloom stealing over me every time it's put to me. Mrs. Crackenthorpe a pretty little American turned up her skirts & danced to the Duchess with castanets. . . .

That evening we heard the glorious news of the Government's defeat on the Irish Supply Vote – not a snap division at all – it was carefully organized & engineered. We are all in wild spirits over it & wondering whether A.B. will resign or put off the Dissolution till Oct. The latter would

---

[1] Violet expected that the Liberals would win the election that would follow a dissolution of parliament, and also that her father would become chancellor, meaning a move for the Asquiths to 11 Downing Street.

[2] Arthur William Albert (1850–1942), 1st Duke of Connaught and Strathearn, was the third son of Queen Victoria, and the younger brother of Edward VII. He married, in 1879, Princess Louise Margaret Agnes.

[3] G. K. Chesterton, *Heretics* (1905).

suit us best.[1] Margot is already talking sadly about leaving Cav. Sq. Father is not so sanguine. It had never occurred to me before I spoke to him this afternoon that C.B. might not be so easy to hustle off into the House of Lords with a peerage. It wld. be madness on his part to try & lead the House but he is cursed with a robust self confidence which neither papers nor party splits can shake.

Last night I dined with Cincie Guy & Ego & went again to the Messenger from Mars. I cannot make head or tail of Ego. He appears so utterly devoid of sense of humour or responsiveness of any kind.[2] Then the Marshall Roberts' my last ball. I spent the evening almost entirely talking to Archie. He seemed low & depressed & I had my work cut out for me to steer the conversation off the rocks. I said goodbye to him.

---

[1] Violet's preference for a later election date may have reflected her father's wish for more time in which to influence the composition of the next Liberal cabinet. The famous 'Relugas Compact', which was meant to tackle this question, was made that September.

[2] Hugo 'Ego' Francis Charteris (1884–1916), eldest son of Lord Elcho; honorary attaché in Washington, 1908–9. Re-reading her diary in later years Violet retracted this 'Extraordinary first impression!', noting: 'How dearly I was to love him when I got to know him – far more than any other Charteris – (which is saying a good deal).' He was killed in action in April 1916.

THREE

Courtship

1905–1906

At the end of each season, 'society' migrated from London to the Scottish Highlands, a location that had become fashionable during the reign of Queen Victoria. In August 1905 the Asquiths travelled to Glen of Rothes, in Moray, where they rented a house (of the same name) that would be their base for the next two months. Among their many house-guests were several of the young men that Violet had met in London during the season. They were for the most part the Balliol contemporaries of her brothers. Their presence at Rothes meant for Violet a further broadening of social horizons. But this new-found freedom caused her some difficulty with her brothers, as she explained in a letter to Arnold Ward: '. . . you see up till now my life has hinged almost entirely on the boys. . . . Oc resents the new régime, like Cys.' The 'new régime' was a natural extension of the courtship that had begun in the ballrooms of London. That autumn a number of young hopefuls paid suit to Violet, who gradually became aware of the complexities of adult life.

Diary – Saturday 5 August 1905 – Glen of Rothes, Moray

I came here on Wednesday after a divine week of North Berwick bathing & reading & eating gooseberries under hedges. I got there feeling rather limp & colourless after my hot London but 5 days of sun & sea made me brutally well & drunkenly happy. I feel braced for some great moral or physical effort like juggling with cannonballs or sleeping on the Embankment & giving Bovril to the outcasts in the small hours of the morning! As a matter of fact I find ample scope for my spirits here; a very hardy optimism is necessary to weather a prolonged stay in this place. On my arrival Margot met me on the doorstep saying: 'I wish I was dead! This is the foulest hole we've ever been to yet!' I confess the drawing room did give me rather a shock. It was just like the Wooding's house in Canonbury on a rather larger, uglier scale.[1] Mustard is the scheme of colour of the

---

[1] The Woodings, Violet's aunt and uncle, lived in Canonbury, an undistinguished suburb of north London.

house – with here & there a terra cotta bas relief. Gold clocks under glass domes & gilt chandeliers with festoons of crystal drops litter the mantelpieces. Not one comfy chair, not one useful table, not one patch of colour one can look at without nausea. One sofa – like a Canadian canoe.... No library. The pictures in this room are: Carola, Queen of Saxony, Portrait of a Countess, Her Royal Highness the Princess of Wales (inky photographs); 'Lost & found' a coloured leaf out of a magazine of two children standing in some cotton wool (which is meant for snow), against some grey cardboard (which is meant for rocks) with an unconvincing fox-Terrier in the background – all in blatantly gold frames.

Oh for Dalquharran with its Raeburns & ruins & long green garden full of clematis! & the fishless stream & the beech-trees! It was like lovely Hertfordshire whereas this is like very tame Scotland. Low round brown hills – pretty when you're on them but not from a distance & measly firs encaged round the house. The pond which thanks to wily foreshortening looked like a lake in the prospectus is in reality a small stagnant pool full of mud & weeds. The garden is not 'Homeric' but useful being full of raspberries & peas. There are also lots of midges & black rabbits. The links are not within 10 minutes. They take an hour by train & you have to change at Elgin & usually miss your connection. There is only one post – which arrives & departs simultaneously at 12 & never brings any letters – at least I've had one very nice one from H.G. so I oughtn't to grumble as I've only been here two days.

It has rained most of the time. I've been for long wet climbs on the hills with Oc & read out of doors on the lawn in the fine moments. It is a very odd & sudden change after London where I was hardly alone for 5 minutes my last 6 weeks. I look forward now to a good 2 months to cultiver mon jardin – what father calls 'make my soul'. I have done the Egoist which I thought brilliant. The first 3 pages made me so angry by their obscureness & incomprehensibility that I nearly left off there & then; but I possessed myself with patience & loved the rest[1]....

I have enjoyed my summer acutely, every minute of it. The human side of life is to me so intensely, engrossingly interesting; I feel unless one was possessed with rare creative faculties & could contribute something new to the thought or the art of the world – one ought to measure the success of one's life by the amount of love one had given & taken, by one's capacity for establishing oneself quickly on a personal basis with all with whom one comes in contact, railway porters & dentists & housemaids, by

---

[1] Violet's appreciation of Meredith, whom her father had known when she was young, was not shared by her brother Raymond, who considered him 'a kind of unhealthy mixture between a snob and a contortionist thinly veiling adulation of the upper classes by the disingenuous obscurity of his style' (John Jolliffe, *Raymond Asquith: Life and Letters*, 11⸜).

one's sensitiveness to outer things & quick apprehension of beauty & fineness of character when it is disguised in ugly grey lives; (& so much heroism passes unnoticed thanks to a sordid mise-en-scène). I can see no horizon to my powers of loving (as yet!) & 'coming out' gives scope & freedom & the power of mapping out more or less one's own life. Every new friend is to me a lesson in sympathy & insight – & clothes & my appearance & hot rooms & bores are only very minor troubles & soon swallowed up in joy. I long to enumerate a few of my friends & append a short résumé of their character to each – but I <u>daren't</u>! I have done nothing useful this summer – nothing that cost me a single pang or effort. Not one stodgy book have I struggled with. Languid strummings of the Moskowsky valse & futile efforts to swim have been my only regular occupations. In this sense it has been a failure.

Margot told me I should have to resign myself to it but I don't think I strove against the stream quite energetically enough....

V.A. to Arnold Ward   *Thursday 17 August*
                                           Glen of Rothes, Moray

My dear Arnold – You neglect me almost as badly in absence as at balls – & now, in anticipation (& some fear I hope) of an early meeting you dispatch a perfunctory little St John the Baptist to straighten the way for you! Crude tactics – whose transparency is their only justification. I loved getting your letter; – the 'incident' points to a sad lack of foresight, glibness & guile on Archie's part. I am anxiously awaiting his version of it which I expect will be duly reported to headquarters.

... I am very, very happy – going for long wet walks on the hills with the boys & reading in prickly woods of Christmas trees. It felt so odd at first after London where I was hardly alone for a quarter of an hour my whole 6 weeks – but it was quite time for me to 'cultiver mon jardin' a little – I'll do my best to grow you a little groundsel as a by-product.

yours <u>Violet</u>

Arnold Ward to V.A.   *Monday 21 August*
                                           25 Grosvenor Place, S.W.

Dear Violet
I cannot resist sending on a postscript to my letter of Saturday, tho' not

without some concern (not exactly fear) as to your opinion of it.[1] Although the composition is in excellent taste, & distinguished by an undercurrent of sobriety & restraint, it is nevertheless one of the most ferocious onslaughts in literature. Please regard it as a discretion provoked by the heat of the moment (although that moment is now more than two days old). Let it be excused by the hot blood of its occasion, be its execution never so deliberate & cold. Let it be commended by the flash of its inspiration, however many hours I gave to chiselling & polishing & copying it out.

Yours, with some concern lest Herodias shd ask for my head,

Arnold.

P.S. What rankles is the false charge of neglect. Neglect, after Dickson-Poynder![2] After the bitter blow of that betrayal – the anguish of that desperate resolution – the humiliation of that wait in a cab at the front door – the trepidation & the triumph of that entry – after bowling in Suffolk till five, and darting up & dancing at Poynder till four a.m., and darting back & reappearing on the cricket ground in the heart of East Anglia before eleven the same morning, apparently not having suffered, apparently not, no, but an 'angel, though in pain, Vaunting aloud, but rack'd with deep despair,' – after ringing down the curtain on that vista of arduous and adorable nights with the superb effort of endurance pushed to the point of idiocy, and peacocklike perfidy requited with doglike devotion, – if this is neglect, may I always neglect you thus.

As a matter of cold fact, (icy), who did the neglecting? ... Who hied her to hours of hushful haverings with Hughs? Who acclaimed with abandon the ardent – but this A clause is too enormous to be written out.[3] It would decorate a dozen ball rooms. It would festoon a hundred Tortajadas with flounces. It would paper a thousand Rothes, not with mustard but with coals of fire.

I did not begin this interchange of amenities. This is retaliation. It is red, riotous revenge. It is unfair, untruthful, unjustifiable, unfeeling. It

[1] Arnold alleged that in her letter of 17 August Violet had accused him of '1. neglect 2. fear 3. perfunctoriness 4. crudeness 5. glibness 6. guile'. He responded, characteristically, in verse: 'O rather than that this were true, I'd lose my books, my skirt's tear too; E'en Tolstoy I would lightly prize, and our Great Countryman despise; fits of inanity should seize me, and even Temple Franks should please me; what though in apple-green I dressed, perfidious, limpid, self-possessed.'

[2] Violet had forgotten to secure Arnold an invitation to the Dickson-Poynders' ball on 19 July: above, p. 61.

[3] Arnold alludes to Hugh Godley and to Archie Gordon, his principal rivals for Violet's attention, and affections.

exaggerates all the qualities of its original, but it is not perfunctory. It is not neglect.

V.A. to Arnold Ward   *Tuesday 22 August*
                                           Glen of Rothes, Moray

The post is going in 5 minutes. I have not time to think out – still less to polish or to chisel what I am going to say to you – but I must write <u>at once</u>. I have just emerged from that fiery furnace you call a P.S – <u>scorched</u>. Do you think even alliteration justifies quite so much abuse? I shall take it lying down (as a backboneless Freetrader should) partly because I'm incapable of retaliating in the same vein – partly because I don't feel either angry or witty – partly because I do feel a little guilty. I think on the whole I would rather you were unfair & untruthful & unjustifiable & unfeeling – if perfunctory & neglectful are the only alternatives – but it does hurt rather
                Yours Violet

Diary – Wednesday 30 August – Glen of Rothes, Moray

Father got a wire early this morning to say peace had been declared.[1] (The Daily Chronicle as usual hankering after 'a brief message'.) The terms look to me most disadvantageous to the Japanese. I can't think what induced them to knuckle under so quickly – if they had gone on they could have crumpled up Linevitch & extorted any indemnity they like.[2] It is absurd to attribute it to mere magnanimity – national Quixotism is rarely repaying. The Gladstones & Bluetooth are gone & we are en famille for the moment. I rather like it provided I am not summoned to the parental rubber in the evening. I so infinitely prefer playing Lettergame with the boys.... Now the boys are clamouring for hot baths & Beb is reading a letter from Arnold in which the following passage occurs

           'More subtly raymonded, more violet-wild
           Than Margaret's lone loin lulling of her child'

I think he's mad.

[1] The Treaty of Portsmouth (New Hampshire, USA), signed in September 1905, brought to an end the eighteen-month Russo-Japanese war.
[2] General N. P. Linevitch (1838–1908), commander-in-chief of the Russian forces in Manchuria, 1905.

The rows in India have been thrilling & very useful in providing stuff for conversation for many family meals. Father seems to think the Government are right in trying to modify a system which has so far produced much friction without any great success. The controversy is a good deal complicated by the fact that everyone has lied heavily so-far St. John & Curzon & Kitchener.[1]

Diary – Thursday 7 September – Glen of Rothes, Moray

Margot went down to Barbara's wedding on Sat. Poor darling it is a grind for her such a foul long journey. I refused to budge & the boys & I have got a small house party of our own. Archie & Mervyn Herbert & Sir Timothy Simpson[2] – between them & Puffin & Lunnon I have very little time to myself.[3] Mervyn is a strange looking being – like a pale-eyed Velasquez – less affected than Aubrey I think – I like him better – but perhaps that is because he has not yet begun to talk to me about the comparative mental development of men & women! Sir Timothy I don't feel I know much about yet. I'm afraid he approaches women from quite a different standpoint to men – which is always fatal to good comradeship. I have not yet had a really satisfactory talk with him. . . .

It is very nice seeing Archie again – we go up & sit in the heather & talk for the best part of an hour every night before dinner. He has a charming character – so full of joy & breeze & sunshine. I always feel out of doors with the wind in my face when I'm with him – they are all out shooting to-day – it is wet as usual when we have a grouse drive. Mrs. Grenfell & Monica come this afternoon.[4]

---

[1] The rows in question involved St John Brodrick, secretary of state for India; Lord Curzon, the viceroy; and Lord Kitchener, commander-in-chief of the Indian army. Through a military representative on the viceroy's council, Lord Curzon could effectively veto the military decisions of the commander-in-chief. Lord Kitchener, supported by Brodrick, opposed this system of 'dual control'. Despite an eleventh-hour compromise between Kitchener and Curzon, the latter resigned in August 1905, in an atmosphere of great bitterness, after being ignored in the appointment of the new representative on the viceroy's council.

[2] Mervyn Herbert (1882–1929), youngest son of the 4th Earl of Carnarvon, brother of Aubrey, and a Balliol contemporary of Oc Asquith; attaché in the diplomatic service, 1907. This *may* be Sir James Simpson (1882–1924), Bt, who was at Balliol with Archie Gordon, and to whom Violet was possibly referring by a preferred name, or even a nickname.

[3] Lunnon was Margot's maid.

[4] Monica Margaret Grenfell (b. 1893), Ettie Desborough's third child and elder daughter.

Diary – Wednesday 13 September – Glen of Rothes, Moray

They have just gone – every one of them & yet I feel equal parts of relief & regret. The last week has been very, very delightful in some ways but <u>so</u> trying & difficult in others.

Archie & Arnold both absurdly babyish & exacting & excitable. They can usually look after each other fairly well – their mutual squabblings spare me a good deal – but when they unite against a common enemy they give me a really bad time. I had resolved not to make friends with Simpson from the first – his pretty speeches galled & humiliated me – how could he think I should tolerate them? Besides I realized his rottenness, his lack of backbone & grit, his intense self-consciousness; he poses as a rotter, irresistibly charming in spite of all his faults & waiting to be reclaimed by some good & beautiful woman. His methods are quite melodramatic but absurdly crude – & he showed great lack of common shrewdness & insight to think they would go down with me.

At last nauseated by perpetual compliments & innuendoes of sickly fatuity I turned round in a noisy moment at dinner & said to him : 'Do you suppose I don't realize that you've said this dozens of times before to dozens of different people? Do you suppose you are pleasing me? If so you must think very very poorly of women in general & me in particular. I delight in you when you are talking to the boys but when you're with me I <u>can't</u> stand you'. I said all this & a great deal more – he took it very well humbly & protestingly & has since thanked me. He has a great charm & keen realization of his own defects, unfortunately also a certain smugness & satisfaction in them. So long as drunkenness etc. is considered chic at Oxford I suppose this will continue with many people – Archie shocked me by his revelations – it is merely a question of convention & if people put their backs against it it would be eradicated as completely as heygatism (which I should think was either extinct or deftly concealed – except by the very brave!)

After this little row we got on better – great persistency on his part joined to an untiring patience under many knocks (he has counted 25!) brought me to a state of passive acquiescence – & now thanks to constant thwarting on all sides & abuse which would have thrown a halo round the head of a less attractive creature than Timothy – I regard this poor little friendship for which I have had to pay so dearly with something like triumph. The first bother took place on the moor on Monday morning – Archie kicked down his grouse-butt because I sat with Timothy during the last drive. I tried to pacify him very gently & humbly – but as he went on raging & storming I lost my own temper which had the effect of at once reducing him to penitence & contrition. I told him he had ruined my morning – he begged me to retract – I refused – & didn't see him again before he went away. I felt sorry we'd quarrelled our last hour – especially as he looked so unexpectedly unhappy. A surly retraction over the cold beef pacified him a little – then he went off to Elgin in the motor. Father & I & Margot & Elizabeth & Mr. Haldane went to Tulchan after lunch – an icy drive of great discomfort – one too many in the motor is fatal to everyone's happiness for long distances.

Tuesday – Arnold & I & Gibbie knocked 3 ball round 9 holes – all playing vilely – then lunch at the club-house after which I was going home but Timothy begged me as one last favour to go round with him. I said I would. Arnold was playing a single with Father & was <u>furious</u> with me – & I thought most unreasonable & exacting. When they came in he sat down on the doorstep <u>quite</u> determined to take me for a walk – Tim & I slunk out thro' the billiard room door & sat up on the heather hill for an hour & a half. He is a very, very good actor – but to-night I really think he was at least momentarily sincere. He told me about his great longings & his poor prospects accusing not so much his circumstances as his character. He has all the most attractive vices – fecklessness – & happy-go-luckiness & that capacity for drifting which makes people – usually rotters – such charming companions. He was very unhappy at my incredulousness & when he had convinced me begged me not to repeat anything to Beb or <u>anyone</u> 'because men are always ashamed of the best part of them'. His frankness & generosity & powers of loving are very delightful but I should say he was as unstable as the sands of the sea. He sat next to me at dinner again – brushing Arnold lightly off to where he remained beside Raymond with a face like a thunder-cloud. After dinner lettergame – & then feeling really sorry for Arnold I walked up & down out of doors with him for a good hour mildly chaffing & soothing him. He said he had decided to go away the next day & that he had seen nothing of me. I said if he minded seeing nothing of me so little as not to stay one day longer for the sake of it I felt no remorse at having spent my time with someone who valued it more. I left him quite happy in the end & made him sing a Persian song to Beb & I & Tim in the tent. I lay on Beb's bed & talked over everything with him till about 1.30. He said Arnold couldn't be taken <u>entirely</u> as a joke. I quite agree – I see a tragedy looming ahead & <u>no</u> way of averting it.

Diary – Tuesday 26 September – Glen of Rothes, Moray

A new lot have come & gone. Compton on the 15th, then Hugh Godley, Aubrey Herbert ... & Harry Cust perfectly delightful more witty & clever than anyone I have ever seen.[1] We had a merry little Sat. to Mon. the house cramfull then they some of them dribbled off & we were re-inforced by Arnold on Tuesday & Archie on Wed.

Compton only remained three days – enough to confirm all my previous judgements. He is very courteous diffident & humble, conventional & unimaginative with an uncertain sense of humour & not (I should say) much sensitiveness to beauty in art – nature – literature or other people.... I tried hard to talk to him & be interested in him but with very indifferent success – as soon as anything that touched either of us at all nearly was mentioned he instantly withdrew taking shelter behind some ambiguous platitude which committed him to nothing. I was more surprised than words can say when a few mornings ago I got a really extraordinarily nice letter from him saying he realized how disappointed I must be in him & deploring what he said was almost constitutional with him – absolute incapacity of disclosing his real self or any of his opinions. A kind of shyness semi-cowardice & semi-nerves makes him fear & guard against any betrayal of self & regard any forcible invasions such as I may unwittingly have made with terror. I wrote to him at once apologizing for any intrusions on his inner life & explaining to him that to me so much of the joy & preciousness of life depended on my friendships & relations with others in general that I unconsciously tried to establish myself on a personal basis with all with whom I come into contact. I haven't either patience or self-control enough to hover for long on conventional borderlands where mutually uninteresting opinions are delivered on mutually uninteresting subjects – people might just as well be lumps of blancmange all cast in the same mould. Individuality is the only thing which makes friends worth making & life worth living. It is useless trying to smother it – the very effort at concealment is an involuntary disclosure. I daresay I am obtrusive. Time & rebuffs will cure me. Meanwhile he was to tell me if ever he thought I was leaving the borderland for that dangerous country of vital interests & problems where personality is out in the open & hiding-places are few.

We had a glorious walk on Sunday afternoon 'en masse' thro' the prickly Xmas wood to the brown burn ravine & back by the moor with Hugh Godley. I delight in him – such a fine character, a rare combination of humour & sensibility & powers of sympathy & understanding, a friend for both joy & sorrow. (My descriptions of people I'm really fond of are so

---

[1] Henry ('Harry') Cust (1861–1917), Unionist MP for Bermondsey, Southwark, 1900–6, and editor of the *Pall Mall Gazette*, 1902–6. He was an old friend of Margot Asquith, who recalled after his death: 'With his youth, brains and looks, he might have done anything in life; but he was fatally self-indulgent ... a fastidious critic, and a faithful friend, fearless, reckless and unforgettable' (Mark Bonham Carter (ed.), *The Autobiography of Margot Asquith*, 142).

unsatisfactory they depress & disgust me by their inadequacy on re-reading.) He is as sound as a bell, such a relief after strangely twisted minds like Aubrey's – possessing a kind of contorted cleverness which takes some people in. He (Aubrey) amuses me very much tho' I find him more eccentric than original; his eternal pose wrecks him – he is no more a reality to me than a wax figure at Madame Tussauds.[1] I was amazed to see how little he had read – no Shelley whatever except the Ode to the West Wind & very poor appreciation of that [and] two to me irreconcilable cultes for Tennyson & Swinburne[2]....

Thursday morning – was glorious. Archie & I played against & beat Arnold & Hugh a foursome which has since become historic – 3 up – 1 to play. Lossie was looking beautiful.... Sat. there was a grouse drive. I went up to the butts in spite of my oath. It was foully windy & cold – peat-dust blowing into my eyes the whole time. I sat the first drive with Arnold who was very inquisitive – then Archie – then Hugh when Bongy lent me his coat – the first bearably comfortable $\frac{1}{2}$ hour. After lunch Father & I played a single at Lossie & found the Brodricks here on our return.[3] Sybil looking very pretty & rather bewildered by a large shooters, tea. She is to me like a being whose spring has been broken – snapped inside her by constant tyranny & repression. St. John's family despotism makes my blood boil – & I can't help feeling mildly irritated with Sybil for her submissive acqui-escence in her fate. It is wrong to be a victim – one owes it to oneself to preserve one's own independence of life to a certain degree. I daresay I am talking thro' my hat & I should have been just as quickly cowed myself – tho' I can't see myself settling down unmurmuringly to an overlooked-existence without scope or freedom in books friends thought or action.

I begged her to rebel, defy her father, take the veil, run away with the coachman, anything to assert her own right of being; she only smiled sweetly & hopelessly & said 'If I only knew'. Sunday – I walked in the woods with Arnold for $1\frac{1}{2}$ [hours] & he spoke to me with some feeling about women's education. I inveighed against & he defended the exotic upbringing now nearly extinct.[4] His three objections to the laisser-passer

---

[1] Reading her diary much later in life Violet was shocked at this assessment, and wrote in the margin: 'How wrong all this was! What gross misjudgement.'

[2] Violet was equally amazed to detect a similar lack of reading in Winston Churchill, and it is a reflection on the education system of the day that such gifted men were more familiar with the Classics than with modern literature and languages. See Violet Bonham Carter, *Winston Churchill as I Knew Him*, chapter 1, 'First Encounter'.

[3] (William) St John Brodrick (1856–1942), eldest son of the 8th Viscount Midleton. Unionist MP for Guildford, West Surrey, 1885–1906; secretary of state for India, 1903–5. He had seven children by two marriages; Sybil (d. 1934), mentioned below, was the second of four daughters from his first marriage, to Lady Hilda Charteris. She was a cousin of Cynthia Charteris.

[4] What Violet and Arnold discussed was not 'education' in its conventional sense, but

laisser-faire method I gratefully advocate (having thriven on) are: 1) that the breath of rumour has time to play. This I swept away as not an objection at all – they say – what say they? Let them say. 2) that through preliminary chafferings the great fund of affection needed for the crucial moment of life may be wasted & weakened. This I utterly disagreed with. Much loving cannot possibly exhaust love & a tried, tempered love that has seen & judged & endured must be of a stronger fibre & more worth having than the first gush of hysterical enthusiasm that leaps forth seeking for an object to spend itself upon. 3) that by too free intercourse one is exposed to falling in love (he is an old protectionist to the end).

Here I fell upon him & rent him. Free intercourse between the sexes is the one thing which makes it almost impossible to fall in love (at least so I find). One never falls in love with one's cousins or country neighbours – one might thro' a nunnery-window with one passing in the street below – of whose profile one had had one passing glimpse, whose voice one guessed at. The freedom which admits of strong close intimate friendships with neither wish for nor fear of sentimental intrusions has given my life so much that I tremble to think how stripped & bare it would leave me were it withdrawn or even restricted. When I think of what I have enjoyed in my friendships with the boys' friends! so much more strange to say than I have ever got out of my own. Except darling Moll I don't know that I have ever had a great friend of my own age & sex – I blush to own it, but it is so.[1]

After arguing for about an hour Arnold pretended he'd really agreed with me the whole time & only wished to get me to recognize what a lot of poetry there was at the back of the old ideal. He spoke to me with a good deal of feeling & some aggressiveness. I thank God every day for the inscrutability of his face – it spares me such a lot.

The Sunday walk was wet & comfortless. I went 'there' with Arnold & 'back' which means over the moor with Hugh with whom I had an interesting talk. He told me he had believed firmly in everything till he was 23 – then the whole fabric of faith to which he had clung thro' childhood & even Oxford – collapsed leaving him on the whole happier without it. I said I couldn't help feeling our attitude was perhaps more reverent & certainly more imaginative than that which is generally called

rather the upbringing of young women in society, and in particular their exposure to men. Violet had not experienced the kind of cloistered existence advocated by Arnold, and their own friendship was testimony to this. Their differing views on this subject mirrored their approaches to 'tariff reform', Arnold advocating the benefits of 'protection', and Violet the efficacy of 'free trade'. In their correspondence with one another they made extensive use of tariff reform as a metaphor for courtship.

[1] Molly Manners was a close childhood friend who died of dysentery in India in February 1904.

'religious' with its arbitrary way of disposing of the incomprehensible, its cock-sure certainty in its own infallibility, its creed hard as nails – absolute exclusive too narrow for one poor little doubt to creep in.

At the same time – as I confessed to him then with great frankness & some shame – I believe if some great calamity were to overtake me to-night – or even some very acute physical pain – I believe I should crawl cowardlily back & invoke my own little private God & persuade myself that he existed – to spare me suffering if for no greater end. (Sidgwick said 'Humanity cannot & will not acquiesce in a godless world.'[1])

We got drenched – sat & dripped & dried on the hot pipes in the melon house & then strolled down to tea. Archie behaved so well – with such self-control & sweetness. I went out & sat with him for $\frac{1}{2}$ an hour before dinner....

Diary – Tuesday 24 October – Windlestone, Ferryhill, Co. Durham

Sat. I went to Edinburgh early by train & saw the Watts exhibition which is most beautiful 'Love & Death' I thought far the finest picture there – such a God-sent inspiration, & 'Progress' I thought fine the rider advancing thro' the sunset. After lunch at the Cafe with May Tomlinson I went straight to the Synod Hall & sat down to wait in the little dusty Committee room; a struggling fire & a deal table littered with letters of apology & Liberal rosettes. People came in & were introduced to me & talked about Barkston Ash[2] – & J. M.'s speech & without I could hear the murmur of a vast audience & occasional outbursts of stamping & whistling; nothing excites me so wildly I could feel my heart dancing up & down with a mixture of joy & terror & anxiety & triumph.... I was in despair when I read J. M.'s speech this morning – he did his very worst for Father – it was so spiteful & unnecessary.[3]

---

[1] Henry Sidgwick (1838–1900), Cambridge philosopher who lectured and published widely on ethics. He was a prominent member of the 'Synthetic Society', a philosophical society that aimed at 'facilitating the reconstruction of essential religious beliefs' (*Dictionary of National Biography*).

[2] Barkston Ash was a notable by-election victory for the Liberals in mid-October. The constituency, in the West Riding of Yorkshire, had been Unionist since the 1880s, and it was, observed *The Times* (16 October 1905), 'undoubtedly a striking victory' for the opposition, increasing the difficulties of Balfour's government.

[3] In a speech to his constituents at Forfar, on Friday 20 October 1905, John Morley spoke at length on Home Rule, a potentially divisive issue for Liberals. He had a personal interest in the subject, having been chief secretary for Ireland when the first Home Rule bill was introduced, in 1886. Professing to speak 'entirely on his own individual responsibility', Morley presented Home Rule as a moral obligation for the Liberal party, an historic legacy that no Liberal cabinet could ignore. His speech came the day before Asquith was due to share a

The hall was large filthy, frowsty & overfilled; I sat on the platform between Ld. Reay & Ld. Dalmeny who is ugly but quite nice & intelligent.[1] One dreary letter from St Loe Strachey was read out, a few apologies then Ld. Rosebery said a few words & then Father.[2] His speech was a very fine one; firm, cool & moderate a summing-up of his Fife campaign. He didn't refer to John Morley's speech – not having read it – except most sweetly & generously saying that there might be differences of dialect but he was convinced that when they all met round a table they would soon be smoothed away. Ld. Rosebery then made a very amusing – rather theatrical speech – comparing the Gov. to a thing at an auction – going – going – gone! & with 'gone' he smashed the desk which pleased the audience immensely. I hate seeing him work himself up into a platform passion over things like Chinese labour[3] for which he doesn't care two brass buttons & speaking tremulously of the loss – the temporary loss (the wish being father to the thought) of Lord Spencer whom he cordially hates.[4] Father quoted a fine thing from Bacon – 'In this theatre of Life only Gods & angels should be onlookers'. I wondered if he meant it for Ld. R. who is for ever making dramatic exits from the political arena.

We went to the station & saw Puff & E. then M. & I motored to Dalmeny in the dark & cool – my head ached with heat & noise. It is a large chilly gloomy house full of oak & fine pictures & elderly interesting people....

... I awoke to find the sea, an unsuspected sea, which was really the Forth in front of my window – dotted with islands – hemmed in by dim outlines of green coast with North Berwick Law vague & misty in the

platform with the chief Liberal opponent of Home Rule, Lord Rosebery, and it thus placed Asquith in a difficult position, pressing him to make a statement.

[1] Donald Mackay (1839–1921), 11th Baron Reay, chief of the Clan Mackay; first president of the British Academy, 1901–7. Albert Edward Primrose (1882–1974), Lord Dalmeny, eldest son of the 5th Earl of Rosebery; Liberal MP for Midlothian, 1906–10. Dalmeny was a keen cricketer, who captained Surrey, 1905–7.

[2] John St Loe Strachey (1860–1927), journalist; editor and proprietor of the *Spectator*, 1898–1925: his letter stated that '... as a Unionist free-trader who regarded the cause of free trade as of vital importance, he should have felt it an honour to appear on Mr Asquith's platform' (*The Times*, 23 October 1905).

[3] In 1904 the Unionist government sanctioned the use of indentured Chinese 'coolie' labour in the gold mines of the Transvaal. For economic and racial reasons the liberties of the Chinese were severely restricted, and Liberals condemned their employment as tantamount to slavery.

[4] John Poyntz Spencer (1835–1911), 5th Earl Spencer; Liberal leader in the House of Lords from 1902, and the designated head of any future Liberal government until he effectively retired from politics in October 1905, after falling seriously ill. He had been Rosebery's political adversary, but at Edinburgh the latter paid glowing tribute to 'the singleness, the elevation, the nobleness of character of that high-minded English gentleman'.

distance.[1] After breakfast ... we set out for church, a walk between trees & the sea. We were ferried over the river by a grizzled old Charon & climbed up steps into the village.[2] The kirk is quite pretty & ivy hidden from without, & like all Scotch U. P. churches the inside is delightfully oddly shaped full of nooks & crannies & recesses where one least expects them. To my delight we sang – 'all people that on earth do dwell' & 'Oh God our help in ages past' – almost too much luck for one morning. We heard a magnificent sermon delivered in broad Scotch by the local minister – the finest I've heard for a long time. Besides great gift of expression & rare choice of words I thought he showed extraordinary boldness & courage; handled the drink, church education & other questions, touched on politics & politicians without winking! From time to time I shot a side-glance at our host [Lord Rosebery] who sat at the further end of the pew seat, solid & inscrutable. Everyone seems to tremble before him from Ly Leconfield[3] downwards – I can't understand it. I feel if I stayed here long I should too – there is nothing so infectious as fear. I felt quite funky sitting next to him at dinner Sun. night – I needn't have we got on quite well but he makes one feel that possessing such a mind, all others must seem dull & trite & commonplace mere intellectual pygmies – whereas with Arthur Balfour one feels that his mind is great enough to transfigure everything it comes in contact with & colour the greyest thoughts.

In the afternoon we went over to Hopetoun in Dalmeny's motor an 80 Horse power Napier. I think it is the most beautiful place I've almost ever seen. An Adamsy house (vases etc) built by a man called Bruce in lovely grey stone, square & long with round it sweeps of green & trees stretching to the sea. The Forth Bridge which has sprung up directly in front of it rather dwarfs things; it must have been a dream before that came into being. We spent the afternoon going over stables one horse after another was patted & fed. The only gleam of joy was when a shabby looking ostler whom Dalmeny nearly tipped was discovered to be the Lord Advocate![4] The house is enormous & with lots of fine pictures Van Dyck etc. We motored back. I was so disappointed at not seeing Barnbougle where Ld. R. sleeps & keeps all his treasures. We left the next morning F. & M. motoring to N. B. & I going into Edinburgh by train with Ly. Leconfield. I lunched with Mr. Haldane's brother & his wife at their little house in

---

[1] North Berwick Law is a small mountain (613 ft) near the East Lothian coast.

[2] Violet and the other members of the party were probably taken across the River Almond at its mouth: the church at Cramond is near the ferry, and opposite Dalmeny on the other bank.

[3] Constance Evelyn *née* Primrose (b. 1846), Lady Leconfield, granddaughter of the 4th Earl of Rosebery, and widow of the 2nd Baron Leconfield (d. 1901).

[4] Lord Scott Dickson (1850–1922), lord advocate, 1903–6.

Melville St & then set out for Windlestone which I reached after an icy journey.

This place is very lovely – like an enormous Easton Grey without the river. Built in nice brown stone, pure Italian with Gothic pillars & balustrades à clair & vases & round all a green stretch of park full of elms & beeches. Frosty mornings & cawing rooks & over all a smell of damp ribes & falling leaves. The party have been myself – a muscular young man unselfish & useful called Sutton, a Russian diplomatist from Newcastle Baron Heyking, Mrs Tree – maudlin – Viola whom I now know better & love more, Marjorie beautiful & resenting life in general; Sir William gallant & not chary of bad language. Lady Eden a dream of loveliness arranging everything, patiently worried, & that's all.[1] Everyday we motor into Darlington a town of smuts & squalor & grime & gloom & I dance every half hour from 2 till 10 on the platform of the Café Chantant for the clearing of a Hospital debt & ply people with food tea & coffee & dangerous coloured cakes in the intervals. Fairly tiring. Viola sings. Mr. Gage a genius from the pit accompanies alternately with Mrs. Rayner a lady with quite short woolly hair which she combs in the intervals. Heyking also sings Tosti in a fruity tenor & an insufferable bore called Miss Franklin wheezes out her own compositions to a harp. Mr. Jack Pease announces the performers in phonographic tones.[2] It has been going on so long that I can hardly remember a time in my life when I wasn't in the Drill Hall at Darlington dancing & handling provisions. The 2nd night was my worst.... A kind of hectic energy came over me the next day – perhaps because I felt it was the last – even Mr. Winpenny's comic songs seemed funnier. Viola & I grew quite hysterical when 'for pains in the back take Ja-jah' was repeated for the third time. She (Viola) sang divinely. There were two new performers a 'siffleuse' called Miss Margot Lethbridge who has a middle-aged figure & wears her hair down her back & sham ermine & an ultra-refined lady called Miss Hewitt who sings 'I hiiiiiiid my love' with great feeling & pathos – Viola & I both wired home to be wired for, which we were & left the next morning.

---

[1] Lady (Maud) Tree (1864–1937), actress who played many leading roles on the London stage after her début in 1888. She married, in 1883, Sir Herbert Beerbohm Tree (1853–1917), actor, proprietor and manager of His Majesty's Theatre, London. Viola was one of the Tree's three daughters; she became an actress and a theatre manager. Sir William Eden (1849–1915), 7th Bt; soldier, master of hounds, painter and landowner. He married, in 1886, Sybil *née* Grey; they had four sons and one daughter, Marjorie.

[2] Joseph Albert ('Jack') Pease (1860–1943), Liberal MP for Saffron Walden, Essex, 1901–10, and for Rotherham, Yorkshire, 1910–17; chief Liberal whip, 1908–10.

Hugh Godley to V.A.   *Wednesday 25 October*
11 King's Bench Walk, Temple,
E.C.

My dear Violet
If I had the smallest sense of dignity (which thank God, of whom more later, I have not) or the least consideration for your feelings, I should fulfil my intention of abstaining from writing to you. As however I want continually to hear from you I am compelled to be only amused by the thought of you like a trainer of performing dogs beckoning one correspondent after another from his seat to go through his or her little performance. You see I am quite docile. All the same I don't see why Arnold should 'make comments on me in the margin' of his letter. I never accosted him (I hope I know my place better) & if it comes to be a question of comments in the margin two can play at that game.[1]

I read most of your Father's recent speeches with much interest & attention & admiration. They almost persuade me that it is possible (in spite of what you say) to be 'at once inspiring & accurate' about the fiscal question (always assuming that anything accurate can be inspiring). I heard indirectly about yr party from a letter to my Father from Lady Leconfield. I am amused to hear you say that Dalmeny is nice. You are the first person I ever heard speak a good word for him. I always think that the son of a Prime Minister, whose profession is cricket, & whose recreation gambling, & who is as ugly as that, must have a great future – if only as a study for Bernard Shaw – before him. Does he write to you by the way?

I am a Home Ruler too – I can't make out whether you are interested in home rule or not, but I suppose it is possible that there may be depths in your nature, such as an intelligent interest in politics, which I have even yet not plumbed long as I have known you. In any case I will reserve my lecture on the 'trustworthiness of the trusted' till I am more certain that it will be appropriate & will only say at present that I don't agree with you[2]....

... As regards God, to whom you refer, it is a painful topic but I suppose one can't deal with him (I beg pardon – Him) as the Christian Scientists

[1] In the margin Hugh has written 'Arnold's face too big – called you limpid – stole your book – slices ball into whins etc etc'.

[2] Violet had written to Hugh from Dalmeny three days earlier: 'I am a rank Home-ruler (I know nothing about it but I always think trusting people is enough to make them trustworthy) but of course if it's introduced now we go out again for another 10 years.' Hugh later shifted his position on Home Rule. He owned an estate in County Cavan, Ireland, which was then leased to a relative, and when he stayed there several years later he was strongly impressed by the strength of local feeling against the planned legislation: below, p. 328.

deal with disease, by denying His existence.[1] I think for myself that without in any way accepting the lachrymose-looking old man peering through a bank of cloud with which Raphael has familiarized us, or the malign spirit which hits people when they are down & w[d] have them believe it is all for their good, one must have some term to describe everything, or that part of everything, which is not human. I think 'God' does as well as anything else, though I don't suppose your sermon was about that. But of course you are only begging the question when you say you wish you believed in God. The question is not whether God but what God. 'And man said – come, let us make God in our own image.'

I apologize formally now for this little excursus – I know it's not in the best of taste. . . .

I must go and have lunch. . . . Yrs Hugh. Write!

V.A. to Arnold Ward   *Friday 27 October*
Windlestone, Ferryhill,
Co. Durham

Dear Arnold – Did the Liberal colours of Edinburgh bring light & inspiration to you – you poor lost groper in the mists?[2] Someone came & pinned them on me on the Synod Hall platform on Sat. (Father made such a good speech to an audience less glacial than usual at Edinburgh. I thought he behaved so generously to John Morley who'd done his very worst for him the night before.) As to your retort which I got this morning – now where <u>did</u> you cut it from? The Globe?[3] . . .

Forgive this wretched letter I feel dissolution of the brain impending I am coming home to-morrow for a week before Stocks.
Your <u>very</u> <u>resolute</u> <u>Violet</u>

[1] Christian Scientists followed a religious system, developed by Mary Baker Eddy in America in the 1860s, that taught self-healing through prayer.

[2] Writing from Dalmeny on 21 October, Violet had sent Arnold a small silk rosette with the message 'Be worthy of it'; the rosette is a tricolour of red, yellow and blue.

[3] The *Globe* was a Unionist evening paper: it was in favour of tariff reform, and against Home Rule.

Arnold Ward to V.A.   *Sunday 29 October*
Stocks, Tring, Hertfordshire

Dear Violet, I asked everybody in the Temple, everybody at the Club, I
consulted friends in the city & inquired of the Station-master at Tring. I
looked in history books for the colour of Nelson, & in Ruff's guide to the
Turf for those of Rosebery & his sons. All the halos in heaven could have
thrown no light on the meaning of that gaudy but obscure conundrum,
which the solution shows to have been the mere offspring of factious
exuberance and a delirious desire for Downing Street. I have been reading
Mr. Asquith's speeches with that respectful attention & admiration which
our side never fails to give to the utterances of the leaders of the opposition....

... I must stop, without speaking of Beb, here today, or Archie, at Oxford
last Sunday. Post really is going Arnold.

Diary – Wednesday 1 November – 20 Cavendish Square, W.

Yesterday afternoon Father & I went to the Wild Duck – the only Ibsen I
have ever seen except Hedda Gabler which I heard in Italian & didn't
understand.[1] It was well done except for Werle & his is a very difficult
part. I loved it – I suppose it is almost the maddest of all the Ibsens full of
elaborate & intercrossing metaphors which are hard to follow in all their
intricacies – but which haunt one tho' only half-realized.

I felt at the end like Hedwig who pertinently remarks at the end of one
act: 'This is all very strange'. Lucy came into my room about 12.15 last
night whilst I was sleepily brushing my teeth & said in that excited twitter
which always makes me smile: 'Violet dearest I hope you realized clearly
from the beginning the three things the Wild Duck symbolizes – earthly
wealth – lost illusions – & oh what is the 3rd? don't you know dear child,
don't you know?' the queries becoming more & more feverish & my mind
blanker & blanker.[2] A few days after I went to the Enemy of the People
done by Tree.[3] Father & I had good places sent us – the theatre was packed
with all sorts & conditions of men; many socialist ladies in scarlet dresses &

---

[1] Henrik Ibsen (1828–1906) completed *The Wild Duck* in 1884. It was staged at the Court
Theatre, London, in November 1905, and has remained one of the most popular of his plays.
Hedda Gabler appeared in 1890.

[2] Lucy Katharine Graham Smith *née* Tennant (1860–1942), Margot Asquith's elder sister;
she married T. Graham Smith of Easton Grey, in Wiltshire.

[3] Ibsen's *An Enemy of the People* (1882) was staged at His Majesty's Theatre, London, in
November 1905, by Sir Herbert Beerbohm Tree.

an incongruous medley in the stalls John Burns, the Carl Meyers,[1] Blue-tooth sandwiched between two Grosvenors, Winston Churchill in the Trees' box shocked by Stockmann's bungling tactics with the crowd & Cicely beside him looking beautiful – a box is her element – a large dark frame which seems to get her into focus. Tree didn't act Stockmann very well I didn't think; it is too subtle & complex a play for him – he does rather crude melodrama best.

V.A. to Archie Gordon   *Monday 6 November*
                              On the East Coast Dining Car
                                                Express

Dear Archie. I never said goodbye to you unless you count a perfunctory handshake in a crowded hall – so this is instead a palsied line in the train to be posted over the Border. I know so well what we are all three feeling to-day – feeling that we have left the palm trees & the watersprings behind us & must set our faces bravely forwards for another month's trudge across the desert. Let us do so resolutely – without any repinings or regrets – let us turn our backs on the Stocks oasis, hugging the lumps of happiness we have looted & determined not to think what ensues more flat & arid & dun-coloured than we can help. Our friendship must not make life in general seem pointless or insignificant – it must paint it [in] gorgeous colours & fill it with joy. All of which little sermon is preached more to myself than you who need it less.

Arnold & I travelled up alone together this morning. I cannot tell you how I admire & love him for his <u>wonderful</u> goodness; his loyalty & unselfishness & self-control touched me deeply & made me feel for the <u>first time</u> (I blush to own it) how utterly unworthy of him I am – so infinitely his inferior in all the things that really matter.... I can feel nothing but intense surprise & great humility & anguished gratitude that he should care for me. He ought to marry someone strong & good & clever like himself, someone with 'sterling' qualities – not a poor flimsy being like me. He told me a little about his conversation with his mother & relieved me a good deal by saying she hadn't been at all shocked or disapproving; but he said she was full of anxiety for me as she thought I was so young & ought to be allowed to develop quietly in the next 2 or 3 years instead of having to cope with what he calls 'list-work' which (she says) destroys peace & often endangers happiness. Oh – how bewildering &

---

[1] Carl Meyer (1851–1922), director of the National Bank of Egypt; he married, in 1883, Adele *née* Levis.

complicated Life is & how I long for a little more wisdom to help me through! I always used to think it was so silly of Solomon to ask for such a dull thing – I would have chosen great beauty – or to be a poet – or to understand the birds like St. Francis – but now I'm beginning to understand him.

Write to me to Hutton Castle – Berwick on Tweed – at once & at great length

ever your Violet

Arnold Ward to V.A. *Wednesday 6 December*
25 Grosvenor Place, S.W.

Dear Violet, Is it possible that you & Beb (or Raym) will dine here one of the first three nights of next week at 7.30, with Dorothy & me for a theatre: I propose to try & get the George Trevelyans (whom you have not met) Archie & Olive Macleod.[1] I am told that Tuesday is the best, but either Mon. or Wed. wd also suit. Have you seen Lights Out? (from the German, H. B. Irving).[2] Will you graciously let me know as soon as possible? And will you also excuse this hasty heygate note from one whom the waves of politics seem about to engulf?

I hope Hatfield is being delightful Yrs Arnold.

V.A. to Arnold Ward *Thursday 7 December*
Hatfield House, Hertfordshire

Dear Arnold – Thank you <u>so</u> much – either Mon. or Tue. would suit me. Beb will be at Pixton till Wed – so you must make arrangements with Raymond. Hatfield <u>is</u> being delightful – so delightful that I must stop without writing another word. Why do the waves of politics seem about to engulf you? I should have thought that on the contrary a time of

---

[1] George Macaulay Trevelyan (1876–1962), the distinguished historian, married Arnold's elder sister, Janet Penrose, in 1904. Dorothy was Arnold's other sister.

[2] *Lights Out* was an adaptation, by Henry Havelock, of Franz Adam Beyerlein's play *Zapfenstreich* (1903); it played at the Waldorf Theatre in London in December 1905. The leading role of Lieutenant von Lauffen was taken by Henry Broadribb Irving (1870–1919), actor-manager, and the eldest son of Sir Henry Irving, one of the great actors of the Victorian stage.

peace & quiet was setting in for you & yours. The coals are at rest when the flame flickers out

              Yrs V.

Archie has been wired for & is coming here to-night

Arnold Ward to V.A.   *Friday 8 December*
                                              25 Grosvenor Place, S.W.

Dear Violet, Thank you very much for your letter. It is very good of you to name Monday or Tuesday. We'll fix <u>Tuesday</u> 7.30, & I will get Raymond. Will you very kindly tell Archie to come & to let me know if he can't. I am so glad that Hatfield is being delightful.

My meeting at Cambridge last night was not bad. I repeat that the waves of politics seem about to engulf me. I can't help thinking that you are rather narrow-minded about politics. Opinions, firmly held, are one thing. The spirit in which they are held is another. I don't think I have ever heard you say a word in acknowledgment of the public spirit of a single one of your opponents, tho' I have heard you speak of Balfour's personal charm. It is the same thing as about public schools. I hope you don't mind these remarks.

I had a civil but not cordial note from the owner of the motor which Archie & I bagged the other night. Archie is missing a great deal by not being at Oxford tonight. Arnold –

Arnold Ward to V.A.   *Monday 11 December*
                                              25 Grosvenor Place, S.W.

Dear Violet, I must congratulate you very warmly on Mr. Asquith's appointment to his new office.[1] Looking at the matter from a wider than party point of view, there is of course no doubt that it is far the best thing about the new Government. It would be presumptuous for me to say more – as an Englishman, I hope he'll soon be Prime Minister & stay there as long as your side is in power.

To turn to very little things, the waves of politics <u>have</u> engulfed me. I'm going to stand for North Wilts – (Cricklade Division) against Lord Edmond Fitzmaurice – at least the local executive today recommended my adoption

---

[1] H. H. Asquith became chancellor of the exchequer on 10 December 1905.

to the meeting which will be held in a few days, & I suppose it will be all right.[1]

Looking forward immensely to seeing you tomorrow 7.30 – Oc is coming, & we got tickets for Lights Out.

I hope the 'ordeal' was successfully faced.[2] Arnold.

One of the best things about Downing Street will be the existence of telephonic communications with the Pole.

V.A. to Arnold Ward   *Friday 15 December*
                                                            Manton, Rutland

Dear Arnold – I feel I owe you a Collins for Tuesday night; you were too busy haggling about how Olive should be conveyed home to say goodbye to me or let me thank you outside the theatre. I enjoyed myself so much tho' I'm sorry so much of our time at dinner was frittered away on Joe – unworthy object for anything so precious to be lavished on!

I came here for the night go back again to-day for a dinner – & back here again Sat. to Mon. & then Stanway till Sat.

Downing St. has been weighed & found wanting. Neither 10 nor 11 will hold us with comfort so we shall remain in arctic obscurity at Cav. Sq. I am so glad.... I see a man called Massie is opposing you; is he any good 'from a wider than party point of view' – that point of view of which you deem me incapable.

Well – good luck to your fishing – Yrs. <u>Violet</u>

Arnold Ward to V.A.   *Sunday 17 December*
                                                            Stocks, Tring, Hertfordshire

Dear Violet Thank you very much for your nice letter, I am very sorry for not saying goodbye properly on Tuesday, especially as I shall probably not

[1] Lord Edmond Fitzmaurice (1846–1935), Liberal MP for Cricklade from 1898, was elevated to the peerage in 1906, and Ward, standing as a Liberal Unionist, faced instead John Massie, formerly a professor of theology at Oxford. Massie won with a majority of 1,578, almost double that gained by Fitzmaurice in the 1900 general election.

[2] Arnold refers to a house party at Terling, which brought Violet and 'Bim' Compton together at a time when they were rumoured to be engaged. Violet had no intention of marrying Bim, or indeed anyone, at this time, and felt acute embarrassment at the situation: see below, pp. 91–92.

see you again for some time, as I shall not be in London till the end of January.... This sanctum is a wilderness of pamphlets on Chinese slavery, logic for labourers, points for publicans, & cheap cheers for the church. My opponent, Dr. Massie, is an elderly nonconformist divine, & passive resister – but I know very little about him. Walter Long is going to open my campaign for me on Wed^n, but I am finding great difficulty in securing an all-British motor car.[1] It is splendid to hear that the Pole is to remain fixed: the great landmarks of the globe must not be uprooted, nor must the compasses of enlisted mariners be disarranged by the nomadic freaks of the magnetic Lode.

Now I must stop & look after Artie and the Heygates – why fishing? fishing of men? Free-feeding Wiltshire Hogs? I hope you will enjoy Christmas, yrs Arnold.

Diary – Christmas Eve – 20 Cavendish Square, W.

I have not touched my diary for two months – I <u>cannot</u> write up this time which has been packed with events but I suppose I must face a short résumé.

I went to Stocks for Sunday on the 5th Nov. the party were R. & I & Archie, Mrs. Gaskell, Daphne, Frank Mitchell & Miss Ilbert.[2] I was treated with overwhelming, frightening kindness, loaded with biscuits & shawls & other creature comforts by Miss Ward – the Yak – (who is most unattractive but as good as gold). All this in virtue of my position of one who has found favour in the sight of that Great One whose whims are law – I felt my unworthiness & longed to reassure them as to his fate – to promise them that he should not be allowed to 'throw himself away' on me! Arnold himself was nicer than I've ever known him. I feared he might be a little pompous & overbearing in this atmosphere of cringing deference & adoration – but it suits most people to be liked & he was at his very best. The women of the party frightened me rather by their feline amenities; Mrs. Gaskell gave me 'one' whenever she could & I was amazed & amused by this unprovoked hostility which I was encountering for the first time. Arnold & I & Archie golfed much together & withdrew to Arnold's little room at the top of the house where we had several amusing talks à trois.

---

[1] Walter Hume Long (1854–1924), a leading figure in the Edwardian Unionist party, and a Wiltshire landowner. He entered parliament in 1885 and had represented five constituencies by 1911, when he was a candidate for the party leadership.

[2] Frank Mitchell (1845–1936), secretary to the congested districts board for Ireland, 1898–1910. Miss Ilbert was one of the five daughters of Sir Courtenay Ilbert (1841–1924), barrister and parliamentary draughtsman.

Arnold's attitude to Archie is an enigma to everyone in the house & I confess a little bit to me – tho' I am oh so grateful for it! They are very sweet & chivalrous to each other rigorously observing a code of mutually understood etiquette; sharing honestly & unselfishly offering each other the best chances; after sitting together for some time Archie says with raised eyebrows in a courteous undertone 'Would you like me to go'? Arnold simply goes.

After dinner games were rather gloomy; heavily classical charades – actors – heygates – properties – fire-arms & travelling & rugs. Result failure. The only thing which makes charades amusing is the possibility of coming down in as few & as odd clothes as you like – & the very suggestion of déshabillé in a Ward milieu makes me quail. Overdressing was one's only chance there. The alternative to this was Arnold imitating the German Emperor – really very good – & a Falkenhurst – elaborate duologues got up by two glib & witty people to disguise a proverb such as 'Procrastination is the thief of time' which no one has the ghost of a chance of guessing. I regretted not seeing more of Mrs. Ward – the one of A's family who attracts me most – I hate old Humphry who is waggishly galant & minds losing games.[1] Miss Ilbert gave me one parting shaft. She took me behind a screen where holding my hand tenderly she imparted several very thinly veiled home-truths!

I left by an early train with Arnold – we travelled up together & had a good talk he more simple & natural & sweet than I have ever known him. I cried bitterly going up to Hutton in the train & prayed that this thing might pass from him that I might be spared giving him such pain. Somehow I had never realized before what it would be to him. . . .

I went to Alderley 16th till 20th the party I have enjoyed least of all. People did nothing but butt & knock each other down; & as I wasn't on butting terms with any of them even if I had been fond of it I was rather bored. Life was very strenuous; we danced every night in the big ballroom (built by Paul Phipps) till 12 – ragging ensued for an hour while jaded guests stood first on one leg & then on the other.[2] Then bed. Breakfast at 9. Out with the shooters at 10 & a 3 hours stand up to the ankles in frost & leaves with people whom you didn't want to talk to enough not to mind getting your feet cold. On Sunday we skated on perilously thin ice – Venetia fell in. The family have a very strong dye of their own; everything is specialized about them down to their very bearfighting. Beside several

[1] Thomas Humphry Ward (1845–1926), journalist and author; fellow of Brasenose College, Oxford, 1869–81. Violet prefers here the French adjective, *galant*, to the English.

[2] Paul Phipps (1880–1953), architect; a Balliol contemporary of Beb Asquith, Phipps was reputedly the best dancer in London, and Cynthia Asquith later recalled that no girl was truly 'out' until he had danced with her (Cynthia Asquith, *Remember and Be Glad*, 62).

obscure cousins Bells & Johnston & an ass in the Guards called Barton there was Paul Phipps, who surprised me by his intelligence & sense of humour. I had been reared on the Balliol tradition that he was 'smart' a snob & a fool; but Balliol men are apt to say this of people who are clean & dance well. . . .

The Unionist government resigns: 4 December 1905

During 1905 the position of Balfour's Unionist government became increasingly difficult. A string of by-election defeats made its majority uncomfortably small, while disagreements over tariff reform, which could be traced back to 1903, grew uncomfortably wide. In November the annual Conservative Conference moved strongly in favour of imperial preference, prompting Chamberlain to criticize Balfour for failing to give a lead in that direction. This attack decided the timing of Balfour's resignation, which came on Monday 4 December. In resigning office, however, Balfour did not seek a dissolution of parliament, thus forcing upon his Liberal adversaries the dilemma of whether or not to accept government. It would be demoralizing to party workers, and unimpressive in the eyes of the electorate, not to do so. On the other hand, accepting office meant forming a cabinet, which Balfour expected Campbell-Bannerman, the Liberal leader, would find extremely difficult. Towards the end of November there were signs of a re-emergence of historic Liberal divisions over Irish Home Rule. In a speech at Stirling on 23 November Campbell-Bannerman made a clear statement of his desire to see 'the effective management of Irish affairs in the hands of a representative Irish authority'. Two days later, at Bodmin, the former Liberal premier Lord Rosebery attacked his party leader for hoisting 'once more in its most pro-nounced form the flag of Irish Home Rule'. He declared 'emphati-cally and once for all that I cannot serve under that banner'. Had Rosebery spoken with the backing of his Liberal imperialist allies Asquith, Grey and Haldane, Unionist hopes of Liberal disunity might have been realized. That they were not reflects upon the acumen of Campbell-Bannerman who, unlike Rosebery, had agreed the substance of his speech with Asquith beforehand. Rosebery was seen to be out of touch, 'ploughing his furrow alone'.

     There remained a threat to Liberal unity, though, in the tension that existed between the imperialists and 'Little Englander' radicals in the party. In September 1905 Asquith, Grey and Haldane had met at Relugas (in Moray), and entered into a private agreement subsequently termed the 'Relugas Compact'. Grey was to become foreign secretary in the next Liberal cabinet, Haldane the lord chancellor, and Asquith chancellor of the exchequer. Crucially, Asquith was to lead the House of Commons. The three rising stars believed that the double burden of leading the country and the Commons would prove too great for their ageing leader. 'C-B' was expected to take a seat, and a role of less importance, in the Lords. This was not to Campbell-Bannerman's liking, and exhorted by his wife to stand firm, he refused to be 'kicked upstairs'. He knew that he had the support of the Liberal *Daily News*, and that a very large section of the party, headed by John Morley and Lloyd George, regarded his presence in the Commons as their guarantee that the imperialists would not dominate. He also declined to make Haldane lord chancellor, offering him the war office instead. The Liberals thus overcame a difficult trial in December 1905, and were rewarded with an historic victory at the January 1906 general election. The Unionists were smashed, losing 214 seats, failing to win a single Welsh constituency, and securing only 12 from 72 in Scotland. The new House of Commons consisted of 377 Liberals, 157 Unionists, 83 Irish Nationalists, and 53 Labour. It was the Liberals' largest majority since the days of the Great Reform Act.

[*diary continued*] On Mon. 4th the Government resigned. A crisis had been long expected – so expected that I had begun to look forward to it in the same way as one looks forward to the Resurrection of the Body – something one has been taught to believe in & hope for but in one's heart of hearts knows will never come off. I woke up on Tuesday morning with an odd feeling that something had happened for the moment not knowing what – then it broke on me in a flash 'They're out'!

It was very characteristic to pursue their tortuous policy to the end; to put off doing anything till the 1st week in December & then to resign instead of dissolving so as to put us in the awkward position of either refusing office which wld. have looked like dissension in the ranks owing to Home Rule (thanks to Ld. R.'s tactful Bodmin speech) or else relinquishing the offensive (always an advantage in an Election) by taking office. I'm glad to say they unanimously decided to do the latter; it will not hurt us much as their tactics are too obvious to be very potent. Father spent the whole day closeted with C.-B. (who the King sent for) M. & I went down that night to Hatfield & he followed late by motor. . . .

I had a delightful three days there . . . tho' I couldn't really concentrate myself on anything but the crisis; – the excitement of it kept me awake at night wishing & wondering & praying for a happy dénouement. Father told me, after exacting an oath of secrecy on Puffin's Head!, how things stood; Grey & Haldane had refused to come into the Government at all unless Father led the H. of C. C.B. was against this not from any personal ambition – but because he thought it would look like cowardice & of course – though he didn't plead this – the Daily News section of the party wld. have regarded it as a betrayal, a handing-over of power to the Imperialists. Father couldn't even attempt to influence him in the matter – tho' his advice would have carried more weight than anyone else's. Edward Grey was as rigid & inelastic as it is possible to be & rendered more so by a few surviving illusions about Ld. R[osebery] – Haldane disappointed at Bob Reid getting the Ld. Chancellorship & urging Father to stand out.[1] Father was torn between his duty to his party & his loyalty to E. Grey & Haldane. I'm glad to say I think the former wld. have prevailed in the long-run – but it was a harrowing position to be in & I've never seen him look more unhappy. His sweetness & self-control thro' it all has been marvellous – dancing Sir Roger de Coverley with all the foolish people at the cotillion without a touch of irritability or boredness. I <u>was</u> moved by it.

The next day he & M. left early by motor & to my despair I found all these dark & jealously guarded secrets given to the world at large in the columns of the Times. Who betrayed them we've never found out. I was bombarded at breakfast & tried to be as discreet as I could; I had to acknowledge there was some foundation in the rumours – it would have been fairly futile not to – but I said I hoped nothing was definitely settled as yet – feeling in my heart of hearts it was all over – our party split, half our majority gone & for Father the necessity of forsaking his friends or the party. I was very unhappy – talked hectically to Archie for an hour in the train about trivialities – once vital – he quite satisfied & noticing nothing amiss. I found Herbert G. closeted with Father & sat in the hall on the chilly slab of grey marble by the umbrella stand listening gloomily to the paper-boys proclaiming 'Sir Edward Grey's refusal to enter the Cabinet'.[2] <u>At last</u> they came out. Father said: 'It is all right Grey & Haldane are coming in; Arthur Acland & Spender have done it.'[3] I felt giddy with joy – my whole being knelt in thankfulness. Margot was in tears poor darling – the strain had been very great & when Herbert said 'All is well!' with his dear glowing face she thought it meant C.-B. going to the Lords. But apparently his wife put a stop to this plan arriving nervous & fussy

[1] Robert Threshie Reid (1846–1923), 1st Earl Loreburn, 1911; lord chancellor, 1905–12.

[2] Herbert Gladstone (1854–1930), youngest son of the Liberal premier; MP for Leeds West, 1885–1910, and chief Liberal whip, 1899–1905; home secretary 1905–10. In 1910 Gladstone was appointed the first governor-general of the newly-formed Union of South Africa.

[3] Arthur (Dyke-) Acland (1847–1926), Liberal MP for Rotherham, Yorkshire, 1885–99. Acland made an influential appeal to Sir Edward Grey not to disrupt Liberal unity on the eve of a general election by refusing office. J. A. Spender (1862–1942), journalist, and editor of the Liberal *Westminster Gazette*, 1896–1922; he was the author, with Cyril Asquith, of the two-volume *Life of Lord Oxford and Asquith*.

after a night journey. I rather sympathise with her wishing her husband to have the kudos of leading the H. of C. if she thinks it will bring him kudos – the certain loss of it is the only possible result to my mind.[1]

Beb & I dined with the Grahams where we met the Kenmares & Drummonds again. I sat next to Paul Phipps who talked to me after dinner; he is very easy – almost too easy – rigid impartiality to all subjects is a little discouraging. I spent all Sat. screwing up my courage like the spring of a clockwork toy – as soon as I relaxed my will-hold it all slackened & unwound. Terling was upon me – long dreaded & anticipated. Rumours of my engagement to Bim confronting me as they have on every side & meeting with universal belief & encouragement have worried me a good deal & I couldn't help feeling very apprehensive on the eve of seeing him for the first time since they started – tho' a short correspondence had done a good deal to relieve the pressure which was weighing on us both. Inaccuracy in matters of this kind is criminal – thunder & lightning should come down from Heaven & blast such liars where they stand. If they have empty heads & active tongues why shld. we, innocents, be slain or rather married to feed their flagging conversation?

Rumours of this kind are responsible for the early death of many harmless friendships; happily tho' I like Bim very much his loss will not leave much of a gap in my life! but it might have meant tragedy for both of us. I cowardlily longed for him to refuse Terling & wrote offering to do so myself in the hopes that he would then volunteer to – but he replied that tho' he fully realized what a trial it would be to me & deplored it – yet it was one which he felt ought to be faced. Throughout he has been calmer & braver than I & I can't help smiling rather ashamedly when I remember how often I have taunted him with conventionality! In this dilemma I have been far the most perturbed by conventions & outside opinion. I am a good deal galled & humiliated by the idea most people seem to have that his determination in the matter suffices; that his intentions as disclosed by himself (so run the libels) are conclusive & sufficient to justify any rumour; that marriage is the inevitable result of his being in love – that the only course open to me is grateful acquiescence. The snobbishness of my nearest & dearest friends makes me sick.

[1] This proved to be an extremely poor prophecy, since Campbell-Bannerman greatly enhanced his reputation. His cabinet colleague Lord Crewe remembered: 'Starting as the subject of some prejudice and with only a few ardent followers, he finished with unchallenged authority and in an atmosphere of universal affection' (quoted in James Pope-Hennessy, *Lord Crewe*, 60–1). Of Lady Campbell-Bannerman's role in the events of December 1905, Haldane later observed: '[she] was a woman of much character, and her decision was "no surrender"' (Mark Bonham Carter (ed.), *The Autobiography of Margot Asquith*, 169).

Archie Gordon to V.A.   *Friday 10 November*
                                        Balliol College, Oxford

Dearest Violet

A short line, this, for time rather presses. . . . I don't think you need mind about the Compton floater. It is not as though we were in the season, when rumours become facts in two hours. After one or two contradictions it will disappear, in fact, it has probably done so already. And if you ignore it, I feel perfectly certain it won't make the smallest difference to him. And that will be the best way to give the lie to fools. . . .

This letter already pines for the flames, but contains necessary things, I suppose.

yr
  Archie.

[*diary continued*] I can't imagine any doom more black & hopeless than marrying a 'parti' – spotty & half-witted as they invariably are. Poor hunted beings I pity them! I tendered all my sympathies to Bim & reassured him – begged him to be at rest on my account at least 'You know I wouldn't marry you if you were the last man on a desert island'. He replied that I had never given him any qualms (gallantly) – if such a prospect could awake qualms – on that score.

He behaved well at Terling with great nerve & tact – I shuddered when I saw him advancing towards me across an expectant room after dinner.[1] He sat down & we talked. I felt myself for the first time in my life getting hot & scarlet – on glancing furtively round I seemed to see every eyelid rising from a wink! We danced after dinner 8 couples in an empty room to a pianola. The next day church & after a little judicious hedging Bim having let himself in for golf I went for a walk with Eileen. . . .

. . . Bim & I & Wolmer[2] & Eileen & Father & the Duchess travelled up together B. & I had half an hour's talk in the long damp wait at Chelmsford where we changed. The Cabinet was out. C. B. Prime Minister, E. Grey Foreign Affairs, Haldane War . . . Aberdeen goes as Ld. Lieutenant to Dublin but is out of the Cabinet (very rightly). Father went to take his seals in the afternoon & got lost in the fog coming back. Rosebery held a meeting of the Liberal League at the same time & made an absurdly egotistic speech explaining motives for Bodmin indiscretion full of obscure & uninteresting soul analysis. Father & I went to the crush at Berkeley Sq. the same night it was very empty; our host wearing a masque of unnatural gaiety more

---

[1] Much later Violet inserted a 'so' before the 'well': 'He behaved *so* well at Terling . . .'.

[2] Roundell Cecil Palmer (1887–1971), Viscount Wolmer, eldest son of 2nd Earl of Selborne, and grandson of Lord Salisbury. Unionist MP for the Newton division of Lancashire, 1910–18.

benign than I have ever known him.[1] I talked to Harry Graham & Munro
Ferguson;[2] the fog was so thick when we got out there wasn't a cab to be
had. We had come in Haldane's motor rather a tight fit Father & I & Sir E.
Grey! but they having left earlier we were reduced to groping our way
back by the area railings.

On Monday I left for Stanway where I spent a glorious 5 days. Guy &
Ego & I & Cincie alone the first part of the time joined later by Ly Elcho,
Ly de Vesci & Mary & Smallbones.[3] The house is a dream Elizabethan; grey
stone covered with orange lichen & a porch one drives thro' like a thing
of melting stone in a ghost story. Inside it is icy & comfortless but very
attractive with stone floors & rush carpets, most beautiful windows of
discoloured glass & a stage wind always whistling. I played golf with Ego
in the mornings receiving large odds & at night we either hypnotized
Guy's tutor or went to balls in Broadway Inn given by the Cotswold
spinsters in aid of Poultry Funds. I found them very dangerous, the Lancers
like a football match. Instead of ambling sedately round in a starfish at
the corners in the visiting figure one was swung horizontally in the air. I
felt my heels tinkling among the chandeliers.[4] I never misjudged anyone
more than Ego. He is most delightful & made very good remarks with that
vacant expression never-varying which discouraged me so much at first. I
missed two big speeches Father at the Queen's Hall & C.B. at the Albert
Hall but I was so happy it was almost worth it. . . .

The [Xmas] good cheer was a little exhausting. It began by E. & Puffin
pulling tangerines & tissue paper out of shooting stockings in my bed in
the yellow twilight of a London morning & ended with a Xmas tree round
which we all stood from Father to Oddman & received presents with

---

[1] The 'crush' at Berkeley Square was a Liberal League gathering, and Lord Rosebery, president
of the League, was its host. Rosebery had begun the League in February 1902 as an organ of
Liberal imperialism, and among his vice-presidents were Asquith, Grey and Haldane. He could
not but be disappointed that they had all accepted office under Campbell-Bannerman, when
he was excluded.

[2] Ronald Munro-Ferguson (1860–1934), Liberal MP for Leith Burghs, 1886–1914, and governor-general of Australia, 1914–20.

[3] Mary Vesey (b. 1889), the only child of the 4th Viscount de Vesci. Violet had come to
know her when they were in Dresden together in 1903, and had been struck by her 'fierce,
beautiful eagle face'. She married, in 1910, Aubrey Herbert. Robert Townsend Smallbones
(1884–1976) was a friend of the Charteris family, and particularly of Ego Charteris; he joined
the consular service in 1910.

[4] Writing about her first season, Cynthia Asquith remembered the 'lancers' as 'positively
dangerous', recalling: 'The girls were all lifted right off their feet and swung by their four
partners who with arms interlocked revolved in a ring. Higher and higher we were swirled,
until our legs hurtled through the air on a level with our partners' shoulders. I once saw the
tiara knocked clean off an onlooker's head by the whirring heels of a swung girl. . . .' (Cynthia
Asquith, *Remember and Be Glad*, 74).

conscientious exclamations of surprise, surpassed expectations & ecstatic thanks.
Bongy & Timothy were our only guests. Bongy gave me a jar of acid drops & Timothy something silver. Then Bongy crowed – well – & I played Chopin Preludes badly. The next day the boys (Beb & Oc) & I went to Overstrand to stay with Batterdogs. It <u>was</u> so funny. He treats us all as if we were 6 & 9 provides crackers at every meal, calls Beb 'my chicky' quite tenderly, whilst Connie raves openly about B's dimple, tells Oc he's a '<u>perrfect darhrling</u>' & shouts in high tremulous treble 'Is she not original, Cyril?' after my every banality at meals.... Our host is in <u>splendid</u> form delighted with a laurel plantation on the cliff & with the New Government which for him has the one paramount all-eclipsing virtue of <u>not</u> containing Rosebery. 'A rotten turnip in a rotten furrow – that's what he is my dear'! He dines in pomegranate velvet & a perfumed beard. Connie shrieks amorously every night 'Cyril you have a <u>very</u> good appearance, a very good appearance! Your nose is so straight to-night.' She told me Bernard Shaw had been at Overstrand & said when she offered him tea 'Don't give me tea Ly B. I implore you; it makes me tell lies.' 'Is it not strange that tea shld. make him lie my dear'?

V.A. to Hugh Godley   *Thursday 28 December*
                                      Overstrand, Cromer, Norfolk

My dear Hugh.... Beb & Oc & I are staying here with Ld. Battersea – do you know him? – he's an odd character narrow & violent & personal in politics – intensely generous in private life; very rich & childless & fond of pictures & gardening & devoted to all of us whom he has known since we were born & still treats as if we were 6 & 7. He has only just left off kissing Beb! & provides crackers & Xmas trees for us every day. I am leading a very comfy 'slack' life taking no trouble about anyone else in the house; I have all my old rooms which have evolved from nurseries so it is like being at home without any responsibilities.... Everyone here treats me rather like the Wards only more so; as something very young & weak which must be amused & kept warm & not overtired; it irritates me a good deal especially when stories are told about me in a loud aside before me, or when at meals Ly. B. <u>shouts</u> from one end of the table to the other 'Cyril! Cyril! She's talking about Home Rule! Dear child! How clever she is'!! It makes me laugh too much to make me <u>very</u> angry – but do you think people will go on treating me like this long? So many do it & I <u>can't</u> think why. If only I were old & strong & gloomy! Never mind, I will be soon.... I am going to Manton to-morrow for nearly a week. Then Haddo. Yrs <u>Violet</u>

[*diary continued*] During the day I potter chillily about the garden & farm with Ld. B. & when I get too cold to be able to bear it I go for a walk in the wind on the cliff with Miss Brand or Mrs. Head two nieces staying here. The boys & Bertie Flower golf. The house is warm & dark & scented with low wide yielding sofas & jars full of roseleaves & spikenard & oriental curtains shutting off room from room. We play gambling games like sympathy & antipathy & 30 et quarante after dinner & 'Connie' always loses. I left Friday with a bad cold & went to bed feeling rather ill. I joined the rest of the family at Manton the next day. Puffin was cold-stricken too & Margot rather worried about him. I spent 4 days there ending in a Bribery & Corruption Ball & then went up to London for Haldane's speech on Thurs. 4th. It was <u>brilliant</u> in substance & so well delivered & received. I took Fräu & May Tomlinson; the crowd was so great that our platform tickets availed us nothing. Thanks to a signed paper from Father we got two chairs & heard well. He spoke in the Cannon St. Hôtel which was <u>packed</u>. Not one woman (except perhaps Ly Colebrooke whom I afterwards saw emerging with Algy West) rows & rows of baldheaded frockcoated astute city men.[1] Nothing cheap wld. have gone down here. . . . H. pointed out the mistake of thinking efficiency & extravagance synonymous. They were often directly opposed – as for instance in the case of the Navy where Sir J. Fisher had cut down the estimates & thereby increased the strength & mobility.[2] . . . He was very much cheered & then Schuster the city candidate who looks as if he came straight out of an illustrated Old Testament spoke.[3] I went away before the end & lay down for an hour at home. Then took the 11.30 from Kings Cross to Haddo.

Beb & I plunged out of our night journey into a <u>brilliant</u> day – brilliant enough to assert itself even in the dingy gloom of Aberdeen station. The motor which was to have met us broke down cela va sans dire. We eat poached eggs at the Palace Hôtel & then proceeded to Udny by train whence we drove 9 miles to Haddo.

I had expected mist & turnip-fields – a kind of sea-less Slains & was

[1] Lady Colebrooke, *née* Alexandra Paget, the wife of Sir Edward Colebrooke, Bt. Sir Algernon West (1832–1921), private secretary to Gladstone when prime minister.

[2] Admiral Sir John Arbuthnot Fisher (1841–1920), GCB 1902; 1st Baron Fisher of Kilverstone, 1909; first sea lord, 1904–10 and 1914–15. In order to pay for the construction of Dreadnought battleships, Fisher implemented strict economies in areas of the service that he regarded as non-essential, closing foreign dockyards, and cutting back ships of low strategic value. He reduced the navy estimates by £3,500,000 for the year 1904–5, and by £1,500,000 for the year 1905–6.

[3] (Sir) Felix Schuster (1854–1936), 1st Bt, 1906; Liberal banker, and unsuccessful candidate for the City of London, January 1906.

amazed at the wet greenwoods with moss & lichen & roe-deer. We were waylaid in one of them by Archie who shyly & apologetically ushered us into a shed where dozens of strange young men – all Heygates as we were told – sat eating. I couldn't focus them all in my mind for a long time but they were mostly A.D.C's from Dublin on approval.

Two called Colthurst 7 feet high – just like Fafner & Fasolt.[1] Ld. Anson clean looking but deeply uninteresting.[2] Jasper Ridley Matt's brother the only person on whose sense of humour I felt the <u>least</u> reliance & his sister – rather stodgy but quite nice tho' a Heygate to the core.[3] There were lots of others I can't remember. Lord & Lady Aberdeen drove down later on he fidgety with a high falsetto voice always jumping & twitching & jerking out one anecdote after another, she heavy & heifer-like with an odd hesitating delivery & I should think no sense of humour – or if any not worn on her sleeve. She rather disturbed me by always laughing quite unexpectedly at things I didn't in the least mean to be funny. I was rather frightened of her the whole time tho' I don't think she was really hostile – only compassionate which is worse. To her Life offers two vocations suffering – & ministering thereto. I fall between both these stools – I am neither maimed nor hurt nor do I do anything to help anyone who is – one of the tinsel superfluities of life which lie in the way of so many reforms & to whom its greater issues are a closed book. If I had been lopsided or an orphan – or ever so little forlorn she would have loved me. I afterwards found out from Archie that my poor little starved soul had awakened some interest & concern – nurtured as it had been in that black hole of Calcutta of scepticism & impiety (Cav. Sq) amongst blasphemers & Anti-Christs (R. & Beb) & living the gay empty butterfly life I was what chance had I? Do men gather figs off thistles?

There was no chance of dodging the great truths of existence (selon Ly A) at Haddo. If either Beb or I had flinched at holy water we shld. have had a very bad time for prayers went on intermittently during most of the day. Archie seemed a good deal relieved at Beb & I behaving so orthodoxly & well I believe he expected us to do something 'unusual'. But we didn't. And I only once talked half thro' grace after dinner.

Life was otherwise peaceful & fairly happy tho' meals depressed me a good deal. The atmosphere was heavy with angels' wings. I usually sat

---

[1] Sir George Colthurst (1882–1951), 7th Bt, captain in the South Irish Horse, and Irish landowner; his brother was also an army captain. 'Fafner' and 'Fasolt' are giants in Wagner's *Das Rheingold*.

[2] Lord Thomas Edward Anson (1883–1960), eldest son of the 3rd Earl of Lichfield; ADC to the lord-lieutenant of Ireland.

[3] Jasper Nicholas Ridley (1887–1951), barrister; unsuccessful as a Unionist candidate at both the general elections of 1910.

between both Colthursts who offered me food & spoke rarely & invariably simultaneously. I always eat a tangerine to cheer me up at the end of one of these gloomy hours – peeling it & the smell amused me – & they <u>always</u> commented on it – till at last by dint of constant repetition it became a joke one of the worst groove jokes I've ever been involved in. Beb used to pinch Archie's calves under the table which was very upsetting to both them & me – especially when Ly A. leant forward with the mild query 'What are you giggling about Archie? What's the matter darling child?' After dinner we played Lettergame or clumps except on Sunday when photograph albums & hymns were the only diversions. I dared not look at Beb for fear of losing my composure.

The situation got so on my nerves toward the end of the 3rd day – Archie pressing hotly & no refuge anywhere but half witted ADCs stodgy & disapproving Miss Ridley & Ly A. pitying condemning & yet so deliberately kind – I could bear it no longer & arranged to leave on Wed. when Father reached St. A[ndrews]. which required the more diplomacy [in] that the telegraph office was in the house & consequently the inviolable secrecy of the wire was not to be relied upon.

I had <u>one</u> glorious evening – when there was a tenants & servants ball in the big hall – a vast place hung with antlers & skis. I wore my Worth dress & looked quite nice – (I never look <u>very</u> nice but Miss Ridley looks even less nice & these things are purely relative) I think I looked quite nice. I remember feeling a little nervous before going down lest Ly A. should be shocked, as I rather feel with her frumpiness would be accounted to one as virtue. However she was <u>not</u> shocked – on the contrary pleased – she called Archie out of the room & poured unwary dewdrops into his ears – I was so amused that the first little feeble élan of her heart towards me shld. be provoked by a Worth dress of all things!

I danced with the loader & the keeper & the coachman & the chef & countless gillies & yokels & talked to the Established Minister between each dance[1] – Ld. A. has a special dance played for him called the Canadian Rush which he danced alone 'very neatly' as someone remarked to me. I was <u>very</u> happy – a remark Ly A. made to Archie about me perturbs me a little when I think of it now but I luckily didn't know it at the time. She said (it makes me shy to write) 'Archie she looks like some poor little white butterfly fluttering out to bruise her wings in the world – those wings that should be so carefully shielded & sheltered from its rough contact.' It gave me a nasty shock when this was repeated to me!

I left for St. Andrews on Wed. & joined Father at Rusack's [Hôtel] – we had several meetings a night for about a week with cool dark motordrives

[1] The minister of the Church of Scotland, which was (and remains) the established church in Scotland.

between each & endless official meals with Provosts & Ex-Provosts at odd hours.... F. & I had an awful drive to Perth 30 miles in a hurricane of wind & rain to speak for Wallace.[1] We dried a little in the 'Salutation Hôtel' a haunt of Commercial Travellers littered with spittoons & whisky decanters & other horrors & then went on to the meeting.

Wallace I thought a good speaker of the cheaper kind – wonderful hold on his audience which <u>breathed</u> with him. Father says he won't go down at all in the House. I left on Sat. for Hutton where I spent 4 days listening to Jack's oratory; he is a bad speaker fidgety & repetitive & instead of being light & conversational with his half a dozen yokels he is very rhetorical & laden with periods which don't come off. I found him very hard to listen to – but was quite happy. Hutton is such a healthy place & one can more or less arrange one's own day there. Charlie Tennant was the only other guest; he & I drove miles to meetings in a dog-cart every night – fording the river wheel deep in water never failed to produce mild excitement!

I spent Sun. 19th with Ettie at Taplow.... I had to leave on Sun. night to join Father at Rusack's. We had 6 days heavy electioneering 5 meetings a night – very tiring for Father. Towards the end he got rather hoarse & I fairly blasée of the Fiscal controversy which was our pièce de resistance but the way he <u>never</u> repeated himself & varied his illustrations & expositions incessantly filled me with wonder. It sometimes made my heart ache to hear him speaking like a God to 25 unresponsive bumpkins in corduroy but the audiences were very good & appreciative as a rule. One night we had a bad motor breakdown & had to grope our way for 2 miles along a desolate road in the most deserted part of Fife – the next night we had an accident which might have been very nasty in a borrowed car covered over with glass. We had no headlights & the night was foul & the chauffeur clumsy & we went full tilt into a stone curb wrenching the back wheel completely off. The car lurched heavily onto one side & then luckily for us recovered itself – why we weren't shot thro' the glass & cut into smithereens I can't conceive. As it was we were not scratched only a little shaken. Poor little Ketchen had to wend his way back to Auchtermuchty in the rain for a fly – in which we drove 20 miles only to find our last meeting (Dairsey) at which we were due at 9 still waiting for us at 11.30. I had to put on my hat & mount the platform & Father to explode the countless times exploded fallacies all over again.

---

[1] Robert Wallace (1850–1939), Liberal MP for Perth, 1895–1907.

Hugh Godley to V.A.   *Tuesday 16 January 1906*
11 King's Bench Walk, Temple,
E.C.

My dear Violet

The year is <u>1906</u>. I am not a labour candidate & I don't address letters to you as 'Violet Asquith'.

On any day that you like to name I will come & see you with the greatest joy & delight & thank my stars that the prospect of meeting Archie is sufficient to allure you from Scotland for four days. I hope he has got through a good deal of work this vac. & of <u>course</u> he is going back to Oxford on Thursday & does not intend to take a single day's leave this term. I am amused at the thought of your little three cornered party at St Andrews. What did the Provosts & Ex-provosts think he was? a chauffeur? Your flight from Haddo seems to have been rather futile. I thought you said you were strong.

Yes, beating AJB by 2000 was splendid, but I am beginning to view the enormous access of votes to the Labour candidates with the greatest possible concern.[1] I would far sooner be governed by Mr B. than by John Burns (in spite of your 'tendresse' for him) & I am sure that once the Labour party really feel their power they will exercise it on the class to which I belong, the 'idle rich' (not even rich) & I shall have to go & live in Switzerland. I honestly care very little about Free-Trade, & all the other things like Chinese labour & the Education Act seem to me absolutely unimportant, so I regulate my convictions almost entirely according as any particular measure affects or may affect me personally – & I believe nearly every one does the same unless they are actually in the game – as you are.[2] I should like to compose a cabinet of those people whom I am graciously pleased to approve of personally & to like reading the speeches of. It w^d include A.J.B. & w^d not include Lloyd George. . . .

This is not really a letter only to say I w^d like to come. I will turn up at 5 on Thursday unless I hear from you but if you have a minute you might send a card to say when you will be there. I have the most miserable cold, & may be dead by that time in wh. case I will send my executors. . . . yr H.

[1] In the Liberal landslide of 1906 Balfour lost his Manchester East seat to the Liberal T. G. Horridge, polling 4,423 against Horridge's 6,403, a majority for the latter of 1,980. Balfour was elected the following month at a by-election for the City of London, a safe Unionist seat.

[2] At the turn of the century education in England and Wales was a deeply political issue. Balfour's 1902 Education Act, though a progressive measure, drew fierce opposition from non-conformists, who argued that it gave a state and local government subsidy to Anglican education. They looked expectantly to the next Liberal government to change this and, with tariff reform and Chinese labour, education was a decisive factor in the 1906 general election.

V.A. to Hugh Godley   *Friday 26 January*
                                      Rusack's Marine Hotel,
                                          St Andrews, Fife

My dear Hugh. It is 9.30 & we're just back from our polling-stations. There are 22 strewn over the whole county – we started at 10 this morning & have been to every one of them. How mysterious voting looks – I was thrilled watching one dirty décolleté man in corduroys after another mumbling his name crossing his little paper & dropping it into the inscrutable box. Outside large (sometimes small) cheering crowds who shook me by the hand grinding my knuckles together till I nearly cried from sheer pain. . . .
Sat. one line before I leave. I have been at Cupar all the morning watching the counting of the votes (I was first sworn in with a good deal of solemnity). The result was too much of a certainty to make it really exciting but it was quite amusing. We half expected the majority to be smaller than last time as Gilmour, Father's opponent, is a local man with a good deal of influence & has worked hard for two years as against our one week.[1] After the declaration we all sat in a large committee room & everyone tossed off heavy bumpers of claret whisky & champagne & made speeches. Not wishing to appear unconvivial I eat a large slice of yellow cake full of sultanas which stuck in my throat every time I had to say Thank you very much gentlemen etc. etc. which was fairly often. Now we are going to have one more round of golf & then south by the night-train. . . . Haste yr V.

Arnold Ward to V.A.   *Thursday 1 February*
                                      1 Essex Court, Temple, E.C.

Dear Violet,
    I drove up in my sledge this morning but found that a Polar migration had just taken place. You can't want to hear about the election – I can only tell you with awe stricken admiration of the intense self-control of my opponents, their moderation in the hour of victory, the cautious truthfulness & classic self restraint of their statements about loaves & slaves. After this superb display, who doubts that the next thing to do is to enfranchise the remainder of our ungullible masses, including of course the mothers of babies saved from starvation, & the wives of workingmen

---

[1] Asquith polled 4,723 votes and the Unionist J. Gilmour 3,279, a majority of 1,444; at the 1900 election Asquith's majority had been 1,431 on a considerably smaller turnout.

who have so nobly protested against the introduction into England of the manacled Chinese. Amidst the serene calm of our disputations, there was only one incident which touched a jarring note – & that was the expulsion without trial of free born English women from the meetings of the Prime Minister. Such methods savour of Continental Protection, or worse of the legislation of the late Government[1]....

Please let me know when you will be at home. I hope you enjoyed the campaign in East Fife. What is the Polar programme? Yours Arnold.

V.A. to Archie Gordon   *Wednesday 14 February*
20 Cavendish Square, W.

Dear Archie – Thank you for the letter which was a <u>very</u> long time coming – but so chiselled & polished a production I feel one ought to be kept waiting for; – it makes me feel rather nervous about dispatching <u>my</u> reams of raw material all jagged-edged & angular! ('I liked the guilty conscious clause'!)....

... Arnold came to see me a few days ago. I made the fatal mistake of mentioning politics. I shall never do it again – as his views irritate me to such a pitch that I find it very hard to control myself even to the point of listening civilly to his expounding of them. I know they ought to only amuse one – but I find them depressingly absurd....

... A-propos of next week. I know nothing against Tuesday as yet but do you mind a definite line. I go down to the East-end twice a week & it would be so dreadful if you came just one of these days.

<u>Don't</u> be depressed about schools beloved Archie, <u>grind</u> but keep gay for me

Yr. Violet
Telephone not in yet.

---

[1] Arnold's irony bears witness to his party's crushing defeat at the polls: the Liberals gained an overwhelming majority in the new House of Commons. They had won the important debate over tariff reform, defending the 'big loaf' of free trade against the 'small loaf' of protection, and had also scored off the issue of Chinese 'slave' labour in South Africa. Arnold derived some consolation from the 'arbitrary' ejection of suffragettes from Liberal political meetings, chiding Violet about Liberal claims to be champions of 'freedom', in its widest sense. The election was notable in that it marked the start of the suffragette campaign.

FOUR

Politics and Society

1906–1907

V.A. to Archie Gordon   *Sunday 25 March 1906*
                                             Manton, Rutland

I tried to avoid coming here with all my might – <u>longed</u> to catch cold or fall down stairs – anything to disable me & secure me a peaceful Sun. with Beb & Oc in Cav. Sq. But in vain. Here I am in this small & noisy house now <u>full</u> of Arnold – trains below & snow all round. I went for a long walk along muddy roads with A. this morning. Archie dear – it <u>is</u> sad – he does get on my nerves rather now. I used to quite like being with him when I was in good spirits & had slept well but now I don't know what I mind him talking about most – politics, the 'Lists' (!) – me – other people.

I like him talking about you best – he is really devoted to you & very simple & delightful in his loyalty – I sometimes want to criticise you to see him spring to arms (which he does with more alacrity & grace than anything else). He scolded me a little 'But Violet it shocks me – your aversion to – your rebellion against – anything that approaches discipline – you go thro' this life mentally & morally as unrestrained as a wild Fijian – you have no steadying fetters – no anchor anywhere – wild random pirouettes' etc. etc. etc! He is alone of his kind. . . .

Why do you <u>never</u> write? I'm sure you have a long margin in the evenings at Hoylake after the daily round [and] the common task are over. You neglect me more than <u>anyone</u> Yr V.

Archie Gordon to V.A.   *Monday 23 April*
                                             Balliol College, Oxford

Only a line to meet you at Easton Grey – & to signalize the end (for me) of happy times, & the beginning of the dry season. May it be for you anything but dry! The hope is needless!

Your coming here to-day delightful, & most gratefully to be remembered.[1] I was amused at Oc's rather anxious & very heated countenance where he arrived & found you chaperone-less! What pangs must have been his as he sped hot-foot thro' the town!

Goodbye. Throw a thought occasionally in my direction – & a line? (I am humbler than I was, but not less hungry.) A.

V.A. to Archie Gordon   *Tuesday 1 May*
                                                    20 Cavendish Square, W.

Dearest dear Archie – Thank you for your beloved letter which I got this morning. I thought it such a good one as well as being beloved. I went straight to the House on my return from Terling – straight that's to say after a short & very noisy lunch M. & I & Charty (Ribblesdale) & Jack Tennant (Hutton-hares).[2] Much as I love M.'s family I do prefer them singly – collectively they tire without amusing me. M & I then ensconced ourselves in the ladies gallery; first a futile division lasting 25 minutes then Father's speech which he made in 2 hours – wonderfully short considering the ground he had to cover. For anyone as unversed as I am in the technicalities of finance – to whom 'sinking fund' 'national debt' are words as empty as Sligger & Hancock once were – it was very bewildering.[3] I leapt at a familiar word like coal – stamp – tea – sugar – picture postcard! But it was wonderfully lucid on the whole – he stepped quite unfalteringly

---

[1] Violet and Archie had shared an idyllic Easter at Nuffield Rectory, in Oxfordshire, which her father had taken as a retreat in which to write his first budget. She accompanied Archie back to Oxford, where he faced revision for his final exams that summer, leaving him at the entrance to Balliol 'with mixed exhortations to work like a beaver for schools & think of me & waste not a second & write very often – which then seemed & perhaps in fact were quite mutually compatible'.

[2] Charlotte Monkton *née* Tennant (1858–1911), Lady Ribblesdale, Margot Asquith's elder sister; she married, in 1877, Thomas Lister, 4th Baron Ribblesdale (1854–1925). Their children Barbara, Charles, Laura and Diana were contemporaries and friends of Violet and her brothers. 'Hutton hares' alludes to the political gossip emanating from Hutton Castle, the Berwick home of the 2nd Baron Tweedmouth, Jack Tennant's predecessor as Liberal MP for the constituency of Berwickshire.

[3] Francis Urquhart, 'Sligger' (1868–1934), fellow and tutor of Balliol, 1896–1934. Ezra Hancock (d. 1914), head porter at Balliol, 1891–1914; Hancock is commemorated by a plaque in the Balliol lodge inscribed 'A better friend had no man'.

thro' mazes of figures – theatrically reserving the semi-anticipated surprises like coal tax repealed, 1d off tea etc to the very end![1]

Arthur Balfour made a little formal congratulatory speech with some wld.-be depressing & very platitudinous warnings such as 'But my friend the Ch. of Exch. has a very difficult task before him' – 'I doubt very much if when next year the Ch. of the Exch. stands before the House he will have found economy & efficiency so easy to combine' etc. etc. etc.

But enough of this – (how cruel to have someone else's Father's Budget inflicted on one!). When I got home I fainted which depressed & humiliated me a good deal. It is hard at the very beginning of the season with 3 weeks country behind me & 3 months London before me. I suppose it was the hot – tent atmosphere of the Ladies Gallery but I've been there for 6 or 7 hours during fiscal & other debates & this was only $3\frac{1}{2}$. Alas!

I had a sleeping draught & am all right to-day & went & stood in the Park at a Socialist meeting which Ly Warwick[2] was supposed to be going to address but didn't & heard 2 Socialists duller than Labour members – then came home – tea – etc.

To-morrow is Elsie's ball. I have 7 or 8 in the near future & 3 Operas. God keep me untired. Oh for the strength of an ox! I could make my life so perfect if I had that. Ld. Northampton has written to ask M. to let me go to Ashby – rather an amusing letter saying I shall be very safe as he is considered goodnatured but particular![3]

Why do you press me to go to a Taplow party to which I have not been asked? No – I'm not going to dine with the Stanleys but with the Brodricks but I would have seen you afterwards & oh why aren't you in London? Ld. Battersea (Cyril) & 'Connie' are giving a dinner for a ball & beg me to bring as many young men as possible as they know none. Why aren't you here? I want you badly yr. V.

[1] In his budget speech of 30 April, Asquith outlined the need for economies to reduce public debts arising from the South African war: there were to be immediate reductions in naval expenditure, and a review of the rates of income tax for the following year. There was little to which either side of the House could take exception, and the speech, 'which departed from the hallowed traditions of Budget day in being comparatively brief and compact', was well received (J. A. Spender and C. Asquith, *Life of Lord Oxford and Asquith*, i, 181).

[2] Frances Evelyn Greville (1861–1938), Countess of Warwick; social reformer and member of the Social Democratic Federation, an early British Marxist movement. The park to which Violet refers is Hyde Park.

[3] William George Compton (1851–1913), 5th Marquess of Northampton, the father of Violet's friend 'Bim' Compton. Lord Northampton planned a lavish party at his country seat at Castle Ashby, in Northamptonshire, to celebrate his son's coming of age on 6 August 1906.

V.A. to Archie Gordon   *Saturday 5 May*
                                                      20 Cavendish Square, W.

Dearest Archie – I loved your letter & smiled at your encontre with Bim –
<u>how</u> it would have irritated me. I think not-being-able-to-understand-
things is almost the worst quality anyone can have – I mean anyone one
has to live with – like husband, butler etc. It's so <u>exhausting</u> having always
to explain. Explaining & want of air were the only things wrong at Elsie's
ball on Wed. not enough windows open & too many weak-minded men.
But I enjoyed it <u>very</u> much & stayed late in spite of my resolve to leave
every ball 2.30. I wish I didn't always enjoy myself <u>im</u>moderately – I wish
I could be staidly happy – controllèd-ly – balanced-ly gay....
Train
I am out of London! The minute we left the station & got out into air &
green my spirits went up like a <u>blind</u>. I don't feel as if I should mind living
permanently in the country at all – I daresay I should if it came to the
point, it is a harrowing choice between people & air. If I married someone
poor whom I was very devoted to I should choose air; if a plutocrat I liked
lukewarmly (God forbid!) I should choose people. Which will you do
when you marry Mrs. Marshall Roberts or Miss Coats?[1]
    I think reading G.B-S an <u>excellent</u> plan – I shall be so amused at
discussing them with you later. <u>My</u> favourite as a whole is John Bull which
isn't published tho' I think I like parts of Barbara better than anything.[2]
Doesn't he strike you as very inhuman? Such a corrosive sense of humour
always demolishing – & such cuckoo-like indifference to his own creations!
he <u>always</u> gives them away.
    Mrs. Sidney Webb (wife of goat-bearded bore) said such a clever thing
to me about him.[3] 'B. Shaw is a gambler – he gambles in many ideas but
invests in none.' I think it so true. I'm dining with them on 15th which
ought to be very interesting – elderly & intellectual – I'm so looking
forward to it. I've not sat next to anyone even intelligent for ages – I really
<u>am</u> beginning to talk automatically 'as if I were wound up'.
    E. Horner & I went to the Academy yesterday morning. It was a sorry
show – a few fine Sargents I'd already seen in his studio but nothing else.
I met old Humphry W[ard]. Write to me immediately. I liked hearing from

[1] Mrs Marshall Roberts, a figure in Edwardian society, must represent the 'plutocrat', and
Miss Coats the 'poor' alternative.
[2] Bernard Shaw's *Major Barbara* was first performed in 1905, and published in 1907. The
principal characters are the eponymous Barbara, a major in the Salvation Army; her millionaire
father, the armaments manufacturer Andrew Undershaft; and her fiancé Adolphus Cusins, a
classical scholar. For *John Bull*, see above, p. 13, n. 1.
[3] Mrs Sidney Webb *née* Beatrice Potter (1858–1943), social reformer, and member of the
Royal Commission on the Poor Law, 1905–9. She married, in 1892, Sidney Webb.

you 4 days running. I will try & telephone Tuesday if W.S. goes early enough Yr. V.

Diary – Sunday 3 June – Littlestone-on-Sea, Kent

Writing up is a hopeless task & I shan't attempt it. I spent 2 very full & happy months in London (Feb. & March) a few balls cool & not too tiring – Greek lessons from Frl. B. twice a week – a hospital in Shadwell every Wed. afternoon & visiting invalids in their own houses in a district every Tues.[1] This last I found interesting but <u>so</u> depressing. I had no idea there could be such unequalities in the world – the injustice of life is glaring & my impotence to level or adjust anything fills me with contempt for myself & hatred of my hidebound surroundings & their <u>cast-iron</u> conventionality. One gets so quickly inured too – the first time I went & saw a child of 13 with <u>everything</u> the matter with it – lying in grey sheets in a dark stuffy room I felt I must sell my diamond necklace & never motor again in my life; – but now I go away feeling almost at ease after dropping an azalea & a few books – my conscience needs very little chloroform. I try & persuade myself that it is not pure selfishness but the feeling of how futile anything I could do would be which stops me doing more; these things oughtn't to depend upon the caprice of the philanthropist or the fluctuations of individual charity – they ought to be made firm & fixed & unevadable – there ought to be equality of opportunity at least. But how?

Manton is over & the horses sold.[2] In their stead we have a large red cheap slow uncomfortable motor – bought from a bankrupt freak called Chirgwin the white-eyed Kaffir who used to show himself at music-halls. M. & the children spent Easter at E. Grey – Father & I in a little Rectory called Nuffield on Huntercombe links – the most beautiful inland course I know high up on a table land with misty landscapes stretching on every side confused & blue – <u>not</u> panoramic & distinct which I hate so. Father wrote his Budget all the morning & golfed afternoon & evening – we were

---

[1] Violet continued her study of Greek for many years, and it was a partial fulfilment of her resolution, made in Paris in March 1905, not to let all her time 'run away' after coming out. It was not common for a young woman, even one of Violet's social standing, to learn Greek, and she had been warned against giving publicity to the fact: 'It doesn't matter your knowing French and German, but don't mention to anybody that you have been trying to learn Greek. Men are afraid of "clever girls".' 'Dead languages', she later observed, 'apparently unsexed one!' The subject had special appeal for Violet because of the exceptionally strong tradition of Greek scholarship within her family. In addition practically all of her male friends were conversant with the subject, and by studying it she gained admission to their intellectual freemasonry.

[2] Manton, in Rutland, was Margot's base for hunting.

<u>literally</u> the only people on the links & felt like the mad King of Bavaria who had Tristan and Isolde played for himself alone in the empty Opera house. I loved the peace & beauty of our life there the awakening every morning in <u>brilliant</u> sunshine to the same small & homely party (F. & I & Cys & Archie – sometimes Lawso).[1] I usually played 2 rounds of 12 holes – & we (A. & I & C.) used to lie on a haystack after tea & talk & read. I'm afraid we talked most – Archie worked <u>very</u> little tho' I sometimes limply urged I never concentrated my will & mind on making him. It was <u>too</u> sunny! & we were all so unruffledly happy. We motored into Oxford one day & Archie made me stand in a cranny of the porch whilst he exhibited Sligger to me – that great & almost mythical personage was led past me & turned round like a Traefitt mannequin – profile full-face $\frac{3}{4}$ etc! I laughed a good deal. An introduction to Hancock ensued then a chilly $\frac{1}{4}$ of an hour in A's rooms & a visit to the bookshop.

He left us Friday – I dropped him in Oxford – we motored there alone – with trusty Park in front beside Horwood – down the hills towards Oxford thro' arcades of sprouting green & white – leaving Huntercombe behind on the height – the time there turning as we sped along from present to past. 'I can't bear its becoming a memory – <u>I can't bear it being</u> over – go round by Abingdon – that will be 5 miles more – only 5 miles more <u>please</u>' Archie said. I stiffened my every nerve & we went towards Oxford – which at that moment seemed to him like a grave....

Tuesday 5th June the news of Grandpapa's death reached us.[2] He had been ill for very long – but these things always come as a terrible surprise & he had been apparently gaining ground every day lately.

M. & F. went up to Glen for the funeral which Father said was very beautiful & pathetic in the little Traquair churchyard, Father told us that Grambo who seems to prevent any situation being absolutely tragic <u>insisted</u> (after following the coffin 3 miles out of Innerleithen) on walking all the way back to get his hair cut saying he couldn't trust his own razor on such an occasion.[3] Our plans for the next two months are chaos.

Margot & Father have to cancel <u>everything</u> till the end of July – I for not quite so long. Grandpapa was a remarkable character generous & vital an almost unerring instinct taking the place of judgement – of which he had none so far as people or politics went. In business & pictures he never

---

[1] Frank Lawson (d. 1920), a friend of the Asquiths, and owner of Ewelme Down in Oxford-shire.

[2] Sir Charles Tennant died at Broadoaks, Byfleet, on 4 June 1906, aged eighty-three.

[3] T. Graham Smith, husband of Margot Asquith's elder sister Lucy. Violet remembered him as 'a lovable country squire with a rosy weather-beaten face.... But though he looked the acme of normality, in fact he was far from being normal.... As it was he had a safety valve. He knew all about horses and had always been a beautiful rider and keen follower to hounds.'

made a mistake. He enjoyed life up to the last second & talked sanguinely of golfing next week the day before he died. Father & Margot wrote a little thing in the Times about him – & Storey the agent at Glen a most excellent appreciation in the Scotsman.

Diary – Tuesday 10 July – 20 Cavendish Square, W.

Commem. went off very well – our party were Rosamund – pretty – easy – active – an ejaculation of ecstasy ever on her lips – thrilled by every man, punt, building, luncheon-basket. Mrs. G. languid, patient, fondly following R. with her eyes & still rejoicing sleepily in her happiness at 5 in the morning.[1] Barbara, neat, brisk, accommodating, & very happy in a practical business like way.

They none of them ever suggested anything, but as they fell in with every plan readily this did not matter. We all dined in Oc's rooms & then went on to Univ. where we danced till dawn – spent the next day on the river dined with the Charteris's & went on to Trinity for another 9 hours.

I was dog-tired when I got home on Thurs. (I had stayed one more night with Oc who had many things to settle & arrange). I dined at the House with Geoffrey Howard where everyone was much amused by the Suffragettes' onslaughts on our house. Nice Collins'es from Bim & Archie. Oc & I had a tête-à-tête week-end in Littlestone hôtel. I read Walter Raleigh's book about Wordsworth which I thought beautifully written.[2]

I shan't treat the summer in detail. I went to balls & danced groovily with Archie & Bim & Guy & Ego & Willie Strutt & Gerald Wellesley & Eddy Marsh & Ld. A. Thynne & Ld. F. Blackwood & Alan & Harry & Ronald Graham etc. etc. etc.[3] I met no one new. . . .

---

[1] Rosamund Grosvenor (b. 1888), daughter of Algernon Henry Grosvenor and Catherine Dorothea *née* Simeon.

[2] Sir Walter A. Raleigh, *Wordsworth* (1903).

[3] By 'groovily' Violet means that she danced with the same people as before: to her, 'groove' had the connotation of something that was well-worn or, more negatively, a 'rut'. Lord Frederick ('Freddie') Blackwood (1875–1930), fourth son of the 1st Marquess of Dufferin; captain in the 9th Lancers, and later the Grenadier Guards. Captain Harry (Jocelyn Clive) Graham (1874–1936), author and journalist; private secretary to Lord Rosebery, 1904–6; wrote *Fiscal Ballads* (1905), etc.

V.A. to Hugh Godley   *Sunday 26 August*
                                    Glen of Rothes, Moray

My dear Hugh. It is Sunday & <u>very</u> wet. Wherever one looks one sees sad green things dripping. Bongie & I have read the Oxford Book of English Verse all the morning & then gone for a walk on the sopping sheep path on the side of the hill – then we've all had a vast lunch – then the boys & I have tried to turn the mossy acres above the kitchen garden into links – Oc digging an enormous <u>quite</u> deadly bunker. Then tea – now peace....
   ... I simply daren't <u>think</u> of Oc's going away on the 9th – he feels to me at this moment quite, quite indispensable. Up to now I've taken his companionship as I've taken air or sleep or food or being amused & I <u>can't</u> bring myself to realize that it – a thing I want & have always had – & love – is going to be taken away from me. It is 'away' – because what are a paltry 3 months? to him they will never be anything but an entr'acte – all his real life will be concentrated out there – in that <u>horrible</u> place full of fevers & bores & tombs & jackals.[1] Yr.V.

Hugh Godley to V.A.   *Wednesday 29 August*
                                    The Pleasaunce, Overstrand,
                                    Cromer

My dear Violet
   Your letter just missed me at Minley, & has just reached me here....
   Ld B. is so different from what I imagined him, & he is very kind & playful but spends almost all his time in Norwich having his eyes doctored & has to wear black goggles always. Lady B. trots me about, looking neither to right nor to left except to say from time to time 'That is the water garden – pretty – is it not' & doesn't wait for an answer. There is no one else here. My bed is wonderfully comfortable but there are neither gold cords nor nards in the bath room, which disappoints me. The conversation at meals is on these lines: Ld B. 'Where's my Raymond? I do wish he were here' Lady B. 'Don't you think he's very clevah, Mr Godley?' I. 'Yes very clever Lady Battersea' Ly B. 'Yes. He ought to marry a clevah wife. Violet's so clevah too, don't you think?' I. 'Yes, very clever' Ld B. 'Yes – dear Violet – I wish she were here too' Ly B. 'She ought to marry a very clevah man' & so on all through the family. This morning they have both motored to the ends of the earth (different ends) & left me quite happy....

---

[1] Oc was shortly to depart for Khartoum, and a career in the Sudan Civil Service, which promised three months' leave each year.

Dear Violet I can think of nothing but trite consolations to offer you about Oc. When he was at Oxford you never saw him for more than 3 months in the year, & his heart was more in New College garden than it will ever be in the Sphinx or Krofi and Mofi. What really matters is that there will be nine months consecutively in every year in which he will be absolutely out of your reach. The only possible thing to mitigate that is that if he were a soldier or a sailor or an Indian Civilian he would go away for five years & never come back again if he could help it, & of course that is not really a mitigation. Your brothers are more to you than ever my sisters were to me or than $\frac{1}{4}$ of me ever was to any one of my sisters. . . .

This letter is too long; don't not write for fear you should get another

yrs always
Hugh.

Arthur Asquith to V.A.   *Sunday 7 October*
                                              Khartoum, Sudan

My dear Violet, So far none of my family's handwriting has filtered thro' to Khartoum. I shall wait in hopes for tomorrow's mail before despatching this.

There should be some quarantine in this sort of place to save one from the contagion of mental flatness and lethargy. I have felt its drowsy numbness creeping over me with stealthy stride from day to day; and I can well understand how Anglo Indians and dwellers in hot and distant lands are so hospitable, and how they must welcome the stimulant of every newcomer. The authorities behaved very stupidly in bringing us out here this month. It is absolutely the deadest month of the year as far as work is concerned. All the heads of departments and governors of provinces foregather in Cairo and discuss together with Cromer and Wingate: and while they are away nothing is allowed to happen.[1] For instance I am in an office which is practically a combination of the Home and Foreign Office. Everything of interest passes thro' it, boundary disputes, explorer's reports, and scandals of all sorts. But the head of this office, Major Phipps, left for Cairo three days after we arrived: and the man left in charge is quite a nice little Artillery officer, intolerably longwinded in work as well as in conversation, and as ignorant as I am of what he ought to do: he only came into the office three weeks ago. When Phipps was here there

---

[1] Evelyn Baring (1841–1917), 1st Earl of Cromer; minister plenipotentiary in the diplomatic service, attached to the governments of India and (later) Egypt. Sir Reginald Wingate (1861–1953), governor-general of the Sudan, 1899–1917.

was masses of work, and he sometimes couldn't get away 'till 2. or 2.30. Now that there is absolutely no work, the little chargé d'affaires feels he must show his zeal making up by length of empty hours for what he lacks in work. So we sit and yawn from 9–2.45. every morning.

Now and then the tinkle of a bell disturbs one from some useful task upon which one is trying to concentrate oneself: and the little chargé d'affaires gives one some little mechanical task, pretending that it is a matter of great importance, and dissimulating in the most ingenuous way the fact that he has already done it himself.

Thus profitably do I spend my days.

Three mornings a week we are drilled 7–8. a.m. by Quarter Master Sergeant Fridlington! This is that we may be able if necessary to take the command of police, and may know the native words of command. I have been suffering from want of exercise: but tomorrow I am going to try a pony, and then one will be able to get away from the flatness of the country and desert that surrounds Khartoum. One longs for a hill. Please tell Erchie if you see him that his present to me was a wrist-watch which has been 'a source of considerable comfort' to me. Now I dine.

<u>Monday evening</u>. I received a wonderful budget of letters today – : your sheaf about Waxworks, and the dinner of frocked funnies and kilted dames made me rock with laughter. The inventor of such an original beano at the tail end of the summer holidays is deserving of much praise and admiration. I wonder whether I shewed you the inkpot with the gift of which Beb anticipated Cys? It is most characteristic of its donor – a masterpiece of the silversmith's craft, chiselled and fretted, with graceful taper-holders and pierced caps of silver – a fit wedding-gift for the inhabitant of a Louis XV boudoir, but utterly unsuited to the vagrant life of an Empire-building cadet! But don't tell him this roughly, or he might mistakenly think me ungrateful.

I have just read over what I wrote to you yesterday – and I see that I was in a grumbling mood. This was partly the result of the little chargé d'affaires: a business-like superior of his has since come back from the hospital, and we have shorter hours and more work. A great number of men who have been out here all the summer, cracked up last week with fever and dysentery. The weather was at its worst – thunderstorms, damp oppressive heat and 'huboobs' i.e. sandstorms. There have been two of these since I have been here, one yesterday. First comes a violent wind and a cloud of dust. Then it changes into dozens of little whirlwinds which make the dust eddy and swirl up in a great spiral with a misty top, – like the clouds out of which Jinnees develop in illustrations of the Arabian nights. The 'huboob' generally lasts an hour or two and it is very unpleasant to be out in it.

I have read very little, only Mme Bovary and part of Middlemarch, and

Sudan literature. I think Middlemarch quite excellent.[1] No time for more:
and I expect you have had about enough! Love Yrs Oc.
P.S. For family economy – one penny is postal charge from England–
Sudan. I hope however that this will not discourage my family from
sending me letters at 2½ᵈ.
   Great favour you could do me – send a hard hair-brush: I have had mine
for years and the bristles are all binged in. If you do this, please let there
be no nonsense about the money side of the affair: I am a rich man now:
prospective horseowner! and I shall probably keep bothering you to send
me things: so please keep a little account. This is like a Ldy. Eileen letter,
what? (as my soldier acquaintances here say) Very many thanks for the
excellent photographs

V.A. to Venetia Stanley   *Friday 12 October*
                                              Rusack's Marine Hotel,
                                                   St Andrews, Fife

Dearest Venetia – I would love to come to Alderley on the 11ᵗʰ Dec – what
fun it will be – do – do let's have the Morris dance for hours & hours....
   We left Rothes yesterday alas! alack! The Capable Scot (who is a good
stayer) remained behind on Lossie links whilst Father & I whizzed south-
wards to Dundee – were ferried over in thick fog & dark in a ship which
looked like a phantom, had a meeting in the Liberal Club at Newport – I
rather touzled but still comparatively tidy – then a long chilly motor drive
on here. We have tiresome functions – & damp golf in the intervals. Father
is going to receive a deputation of the matrons of Fife on Sat. afternoon
who are going to beard him on the Suffrage. This ought to be funny. We
go on to Gosford that night....
   I must stop now – write at once & say you are glad I'm coming – to
Gosford Longniddry. Yr. V. P.S. Thank you for asking me.

'Votes for Women': H. H. Asquith's opposition

On Saturday 13 October 1906 supporters of women's suffrage
staged a demonstration outside the Masonic Hall in Ladybank,
where Asquith was due to address the local Liberal association.
Since October of the previous year women suffragists had targeted
Liberal political meetings, and among the demonstrators at Ladybank was a pioneer of suffragette protest, Annie Kenney (1879–

[1] Gustave Flaubert, *Madame Bovary* (1857); George Eliot, *Middlemarch* (1871–2).

1953). As he left the hall Asquith ignored the group gathered outside, but later that evening he met a deputation of local women. They had the backing of the Women's Liberal Association of nearby Newport, and he recognized among their number the wives of some of his constituents. The essence of their argument was that those who paid taxes should also take a part in electing the government. Asquith did not conceal his opposition to their views. He argued that there was no evidence that a majority of women actually wanted the vote. Nor did he believe that in pursuit of it women ought to exchange, as he felt they must, their 'real authority' and 'unique influence' in society. His arguments against votes for women were not shared by the majority of his cabinet colleagues, and his opposition was, as his official biographers have observed, less intellectual than sentimental. Though he respected the intelligence and judgement of women, it offended his sense of 'decorum and chivalry' to think of them engaged in the 'rough and tumble' of a 'masculine business'. This outlook was undoubtedly a strong influence on the thinking of his elder daughter. Violet's own anti-suffragism, however, was reinforced by the increasing militancy of suffragettes after 1905, and by the violence that she saw directed against her father.[1]

V.A. to Hugh Godley   *Saturday 13 October*
Rusack's Marine Hotel,
St Andrews, Fife

I am just this second back from a meeting at Ladybank 15 miles off – we went there & back in the open motor & my hands feel <u>silly</u> with cold. Father is in a hot bath – I shall have mine before going to bed; – meanwhile a little waiter darts in & out of this oddest of all tiny rooms laying our dinner – china menu very elaborate napkins, glasses cut like chandeliers & all the funny things I enjoy because one <u>only</u> has them in an hôtel. . . . I've just had a letter from Oc – he writes pages about camels & Arabs & sand & about 8 lines about himself & me. But they're enough. Bongie's the only other person he talks about at all. . . .
I <u>wish</u> you'd heard Father's interview with the female delegates on the Suffrage. I insisted on being present – it was one of the best moments of

---

[1] *The Times*, 15 October 1906; Spender and Asquith, *Life of Lord Oxford and Asquith*, i, 360. For Violet's anti-suffragism, see below, p. 395. For an account of the suffragette violence directed at Asquith, see Herbert Asquith, *Moments of Memory*, 155–6, 158–9.

my life. The spokeswoman of the party a mild fifty-year old – looking like
a retired housemaid put their case with tremulous fussiness but on the
whole coherently – meanwhile another – Mrs Death by name – hairy-
faced bald headed & glittering with jet – utterly discountenanced Father
by ogling at him sans trêve in the most pointed & purposeful way. (He
thought she was a maniac – I knew her to be an accomplished coquette.)[1]
All the time outburst upon outburst of cheering (high falsetto) reached us
from Billington's hostile meeting encamped at the door of the hall.[2] Father
was honied but very cautious. He dwelt much on his pleasure in having
met them, on their 'admirable persuasiveness' but begged them not to
sacrifice their great intangible influence for a paltry vote.[3]

How much I want to see you – I should think in about another fortnight
I ought to be coming south. Then! – then! think how glorious. But
meanwhile now takes rather a long time going, doesn't it? yr. V.

Diary – Thursday 18 October – Gosford House, East Lothian

I can't write up the Epoch which has elapsed between this & Commem.
an epoch crowded with events & books & thoughts & people. Three big
things have happened (1) Ashby – this is the smallest – being 5 days &
nights of conventional revelry on a gigantic scale[4] (2) The Floater which
K. has begged me to write an account of but I have been so often over its

---

[1] The spokeswoman of the deputation was Mrs James Mill, of Newport. The other woman
named here, Mrs Death, came from Tayport, about twelve miles from Ladybank.

[2] Teresa Billington-Greig (1877–1964), one of the first suffragettes to be imprisoned for 'the
cause' (1906); she had been involved in the demonstration outside the Masonic Hall at
Ladybank earlier that evening.

[3] As the disappointed suffragists left, one of them asked Asquith if there was any hope
for women, to which he replied, 'The women must work out their own salvation.' Their
spokeswoman commented, 'Just as we expected' (*The Times*, 15 October 1906).

[4] The celebration of 'Bim' Compton's coming of age, at Castle Ashby in Northamptonshire,
took place at the end of the 1906 season. Writing to Violet on Saturday 4 August, as he
watched the remnants of the party disperse, Archie Gordon reflected: 'I must say, the whole
thing was an experience I wouldn't have missed for worlds, & as Beb says, it will certainly go
down to posterity as the event of our generation.' Cynthia Asquith, who was among the many
guests, recalled how the women were accommodated in the house and the men outside, in
'lovely tents far more luxurious than most bedrooms, each hung with tapestry and rigged up
with electric light' (Cynthia Asquith, *Remember and Be Glad*, 83).

squalid intricacies I can't face it again[1] (3) Beloved Oc's going to Egypt which is one of the acutest physical wrenches I've ever had.

The anguish of the week of delirious merry-making which preceded his departure I shall never forget & the last few days – we dared not look at one another & when some homely old Cracknell joke was made at lunch I couldn't bear it – I rushed from the room. The cruelty of detail is so unbearable – I felt I had no tears left for the rest of life. His precious companionship has been a necessary of life to me up till now – so essential that I have barely been conscious of it – I took it for granted like air & sound & movement & sunlight & food – & now that it is gone it is like losing a limb or a sense. . . .

We had a kaleidoscopic two months at Rothes – odd & sometimes unlucky combinations of people. I didn't get through much reading except Anna Karenina which I thought magnificent & Ld. R.C.'s life which I pecked at ineffectually & have not finished.[2] I went to Gosford with Father on the 14th a long cold motor drive from St. Andrews where we had spent 3 days of meetings, deputations (suffragettes among others – headed by one Mrs. Death – Father tried to cajole them!). We went round the Firth feeling loth to use the ferry on Sunday – lunched at Alloa where we saw a freemasons' procession, set faces & silver trowels, green quangle-wangles & locked thumbs! I laughed a good deal.

We reached Gosford about tea-time – went in by side door thro' the big marble hall, almost the only quite unwashingstandy marble – it is more like alabaster – translucent. Ettie gave me tea under the Mantegna madonna in a bright Chinese wrap red & green & gold. The permanent party were Evan, Ly Elcho, Margot, Ettie, I, Archie & Cincie. The atmosphere of the house was not really formal except for the rigid punctuality & a certain grimness Ly Wemyss brings with her into every situation;[3] but the first few days (after Rothes too!) I felt like being in plaster of Paris!

However I soon got acclimatized & drifted more patiently about in ante-rooms sprinkled with unemployed in the odd half hours before meals.

The pictures make one quite dumb. I care for the Mantegna & the

---

[1] Ettie Desborough's flirtation with Archie Gordon, who was at Balliol with her eldest son Julian, became embarrassingly public in August 1906, and caused a mild scandal among their friends. Violet's relations with Archie were inevitably clouded, though Ettie gracefully disengaged. She also made clear how highly she valued Violet's friendship, and wrote a year later: 'My own dear, the first item of London stock-taking is a letter of gratitude to you – you have been so untellably darling, & of the new joys of this last year so far far the highest & greatest' (ED to VA, 1 August 1907).

[2] Leo Tolstoy, *Anna Karenina* (1873–7); Winston S. Churchill, *Lord Randolph Churchill* (two volumes, 1905).

[3] Grace Blackburn (d. 1946), second wife of Francis Charteris (1818–1914), 10th Earl of Wemyss.

Boticelli most; for the heaps of dead hares lobsters & gourds pêle-mêle by Snyders & the half dressed families at food by Jordans <u>least</u>. . . . on Wed we all went en bloc like an acrobatic troupe to Whittingehame. Cynthia & I arrived at Dunbar having had 5 different telegrams & were met by Ly Elcho & Miss Alice Balfour who has a roofless mouth & not much brain power. The relations between her & Ly Frances were disappointingly mild & friendly; (I was waiting for asides like 'Venomous old toad') – but I am told our two days of comparative peace was only a momentary lull which is comforting.[1] The atmosphere of the house is <u>quite</u> unparalleled. Miss Alice clinging doggedly to her little official rights – Ly Frances with flamingo hair, dressed in a little blue velvet bolero buttoned up with silver fish, talking crisply & at times very brilliantly I thought. I admire her mind – it's so powerful & clean-cut like a man's – there is no kind of fluffiness about it – a rare absence in women. At the same time I can't help feeling that where there is so little tentativeness there must be great limitations.

Mr. Balfour is the most all-round perfect being I've ever met; the kind of success which would have turned one's head a little if one had been the Almighty. He looks helplessly & resignedly on at the domestic cyclones & occasionally retires with Ettie – Margot or Ly Elcho. Eustace who has had bad D-T for 40 years reels thro' the room from time to time – clinging to a black stick – his only point d'appui – he is bright blue like a gentian & his legs are tortuous & undulating like a fish's tail. Thank God! I didn't have to sit next to him at dinner – the first night I had Evan & Lady Betty[2] who is an <u>angel</u> – a 'battered sunshining peacemaker' & the next one Archie – Miss Balfour who talked to me about Californian bulbs – I was a good deal out of my depth but fared pretty well till I had to refer to Archie 'What <u>is</u> the name of that little yellow flower – you know – yellow & round'? A. suggestively 'Buttercup'? I broke down over this.

It snowed steadily all the time we were there & we were driven to lettergame after lunch varied by a gramophone. We had sunk to Personal Remarks before tea-time. I went out for two long slushy walks – red hot pokers & lupins covered with snow. The discipline made life indoors like an Orphanage routine, no smoking – bed at 11 rubber finished or not. A. broke a handsome leather armchair doing his head over heels trick!

---

[1] Alice Balfour (d. 1936) was A. J. Balfour's younger sister, and Lady Frances Balfour his sister-in-law, the wife of his youngest brother, (Colonel) Eustace Balfour (1854–1911).

[2] Lady Betty Balfour *née* Lytton (d. 1942), married 1887 Gerald Balfour, younger brother of A. J. Balfour.

V.A. to Arnold Ward   *Tuesday 30 October*
20 Cavendish Square, W.

My dear Arnold.

Your last letter was <u>almost</u> faultless; it contained no carps or harps or haverer harryings – & it enshrined one priceless phrase i.e 'Your shy little seaside life' – really one of your very best. I am looking forward to showing it to Anatole this evening. The <u>only</u> blot – the fly in the ointment, the blob in the amber was 'hoping that you are still enjoying your stay in the North'. You <u>must</u> cure yourself of faults like that; they come like a peroration at the end of every letter; tear the evil thing out by the roots. . . .

We all go down to London to-morrow; – at least we <u>were</u> all going down but for the first time parental care has swerved in the direction of the cloister & it has been suggested (not more than an insinuation) that A. should follow by a later train. This petition has been granted, but as I pointed out he & I have done worse things in our time than sit in a corridor carriage full of Vena & Puffin (King of chaperones) & Elizabeth & Frau[1]. . . .

Ly Agnes thinks my 'liveliness' demoralizing; I have also had one blackball for 'frivolity'! <u>of all things</u>! How obtuse people are! Yrs <u>Violet</u>

Hugh Godley to V.A.   *Monday 19 November*
Union Club, Trafalgar Square,
S.W.

My dearest Violet, I have not had one second since I got to London very late, & now it is 10 to 7 & unless I send this off at once it won't reach you before you leave Stanway. Bluetooth A.J.B. & I travelled up peacefully & chillily, & had a greasy lunch in the train together. I suddenly got shy of him, & couldn't speak, he having hitherto been much more shy of me. But I liked him very much.

I have just come from the H. of C. Outside it a suffragette meeting was being held. Three poor little shingly suff[ttes] mounted on the Rich. I statue & unfurled their poor little banner with timorous hands. Immediately about 200 police bore down upon them bore them from their pedestal & bundled them out of sight. I held my manhood very cheap that I didn't go to their assistance, they looked so respectable & chirruped so piteously.

Do write at once & say how Puffin is & how you are. A nice letter – 10

---

[1] Vena was Puffin's nanny.

times nicer than this. I shall perhaps write again tonight at leisure, but may not be able to till tomorrow. I did enjoy my visit to S[tanway]. so much. Did you. I should have enjoyed it less if you had not been there. Good night dear Violet. yr H.

V.A. to Archie Gordon   *Tuesday 20 November*
                                             20 Cavendish Square, W.

I am at home again – the house reeks of disinfectants (my landing) is full of crockery & carbolic-soaked sheets – Elizabeth shunned by the world like a pariah strays about dogged by Fräu, occasionally venting outbursts of accumulated affection on me. Puffin is better thank Heaven! & Margot intensely relieved tho' rather white & overtired....

M. had a long talk with me to-day; Arnold & Olive were touched upon. . ... She made revelations to me about A. which struck me <u>dumb</u> with surprise; she has concealed much from me all thro'; he has apparently <u>begged</u> for permission for lasher (not lately) & been thro' many phases of acute feeling of which I had no inkling. M. says he suffered very much at Rothes this year & spoke to her a little the night of the Drummuir ball. However – all's well that ends well. I <u>mean</u> this to end well. I drove home with his cousin Mrs Wodehouse (owner of Barley Mo) to-night – she said she heard I'd been very <u>witty</u>!! at Stocks this time!!!! ME! WITTY!

Now I'm quite! quite alone – sitting in my night gown with a <u>pink</u> shaded light in front of me – very sleepy.... It is 11.35 – tell me when you next write what you were doing at the same time. One week is over to-night ... one week since we panted thro' musical chairs & sat in silence over our soda-water at home with the chill of separation on us. <u>Write</u> Dream about me often yr. V

Archie Gordon to V.A.   *Saturday 1 December*
                                             Vice Regal Lodge, Dublin

Your letter this morning was so <u>much</u> more un-ill – it gave me quite a start. I received it with genuine gratification, & I really believe now that you are going to get well nice & quick, & that I shan't find you lying limply on a sofa with books & fruit on a small table & somebody saying 'Hush!' outside the door – as I had half-feared....

This is the last Sunday, thanks to Heaven, & I can soon begin to count by the little sand glass. It really <u>has</u> been rather a rotten time, even apart from meaning Absence. How <u>any</u> civilian was ever induced to do a similar job I cannot conceive. The utter futility of it has so impressed itself on me that I find myself launching out into a diatribe to every stranger I sit next at dinner – as they <u>invariably</u> say 'Isn't it great fun being on the Staff?'.[1] I always shock them. It gives one a glimpse of the demoralization which must await anybody in the army, for the life there is apparently very similar. Never mind. I ought to be glad not to have had more of it....

... I want to thank you again, dearest, for your letters. You don't know what they have been. yr A.

Arthur Asquith to V.A. *Tuesday 11 December*
Omdurman, Sudan

The <u>Mahdi's</u> House
Omdurman.
<u>Dec. 11. 1906.</u>

My dear Violet, I came over here from Khartoum yesterday, and am writing this partly on the chance of its reaching you in time for Christmas, and partly because the address looks interesting. This house is next door to the ruins of the Mahdi's tomb:[2] it is one story high, built of mud-bricks; the floor is hard mudcoloured sand, the walls inside sandcoloured mud, and the roof palm-matting. There is a sand compound outside with a few mud-huts dotted about where the Mahdi's wives and retainers used to live: no tree nearer than Khartoum, and no attempt at furniture except the beds, tables and chairs without which one never moves here. This is a great come down from the luxurious bungalow of 'Phippsey Bey' in the way of comfort, but the life here is infinitely preferable. At last one sees something of the natives, and almost all one's work is in the open air.

A poverty stricken Government has taken it into its head to assert its claim to all the land upon which Omdurman has been built: and to charge rent for most of the twenty eight thousand houses of which it consists. So four of the newly joined Deputy Inspectors including your brother have been told off to assess the 28000 houses to see how much rent shall be

---

[1] Before beginning work with the Dresdner Bank in Berlin, in May 1907, Archie served as an aide-de-camp to his father, who was lord-lieutenant of Ireland.

[2] The 'Mahdi', Muhammad Ahmad (1844–85), a self-styled Islamic messiah, who led a successful rebellion against the Anglo-Egyptian rule in the Sudan, culminating in the capture of Khartoum in January 1885. He died in June 1885, and was buried in Omdurman, where he had based his administration.

charged for each. Each of us is President of a Board of which there are two other members – the Sheikh of the Quarter in which we work, and a Notable of that Quarter – remarkable fat men who roll up on colossal donkeys, and try to get their friends' houses assessed low and their enemies' houses high : and dissolve in perspiration as one bustles them from house to house. By house you must understand one story of mud kneaded with the hands into a habitable shape, roofed – usually with matting, and surrounded by a compound inhabited by donkeys goats and camels. The interiors are more primitive than any Bible illustration. I worked from 6.30 a.m–1 o'clock, with an hour for breakfast, and only got thro' about fifty of my seven thousand. After that I tried two women who were fighting over the body of a slavegirl and did not get back to lunch till a quarter to three. So you can see one has lots to do.

The status of women in this country is extraordinarily low: in the hospital in Khartoum where I was taken to see grisly sights before breakfast the other day, the men have cool comfortable wards; the women wretched mud hovels because, the doctor explained, they are not used to being well-treated and would feel so out of their assiette as to be wretched in the clean cool wards. They do all the drudge work of fetching & carrying. I wanted a bath last night; there was no water in the house, so I told my servant to have some fetched. After a few minutes enter three wretched women with enormous pitchers on their heads.

Now I must go and dine. Please write and give me news of Margot. I have had excellent letters from Con and Bluetooth. By the time you get this I shall know my fate – whether I am to be kept in Khartoum or sent out into the provinces. Love to Eliz & all. Yrs Oc.

The enclosed beads are probably valueless. I bought them for a very small sum from an old villain at Luxor in one of the temples. He swore they came from one of the tombs of the Kings; at any rate they are quite a jolly colour, don't you think.

V.A. to Archie Gordon   *Saturday 22 December*
                                              20 Cavendish Square, W.

6 p.m. <u>In Train to Minley</u>
Your wires have come one after the other each mowing down a hope. I am now on my way to Minley & I shall not be able to see you before you go. It is <u>unbearably</u> harsh & unreasonable of Everything – why <u>couldn't</u> you come to-day – <u>one</u> day sooner wouldn't have mattered surely....

I had a wearing day yesterday – presents – invalids at home – brown paper & string & bores on the telephone. And in the evening Bongie & Cynthia & Mary Vesey all fell together at 4 (which sounds a safe hour!) & when I bundled them all away by 5.30 Felix came & had the worst lasher of his or my life. I've never experienced anything more rending – the agony of having a knife put in one's hand & made to stab because one would otherwise torture. I hope there was some finality about this last scene – but I cannot say I will never see him again as in spite of all it's the only thing he enjoys. [Sir] Timothy [Simpson] is another harrowing problem – he is terribly ill & telephones to me daily in despair in a breathless halting voice – he has aphasia. What can I do but promise I will see him again – he may be dying for all I know. I have sent you a dull little temporary present forgive it – oh why can't I see you again.

Goodbye beloved A. write to me yr. V.

V.A. to Venetia Stanley   *Saturday 29 December*
                                                20 Cavendish Square, W.

Darling Venetia – I loved getting your letter. I know you will realize what we are all going through just now. I was wired for on Monday morning & arrived in an anguish of fear to find M. very ill. The baby was born at 3 that afternoon (Xmas Eve) very tiny & fragile from coming so much too soon but so vital & well-developed that the Drs. were very hopeful about it especially when it got over the critical hours so wonderfully. It was a boy which I had longed for – such a darling – neat little nut-head about the size of Puffin's 2 fists. We went to bed quite happily – leaving the nurse triumphantly sanguine & it died at 6 the next morning – just flickered out from weakness & unreadiness for the world.

Margot had not one fear for it after the first few hours & of course we did not like to worry her with possibilities. Her anguish when she asked for it in the morning will haunt me always. She never saw it alive – they carried it in afterwards & it lay in her arms. I've never felt such help-lessness – such blind misery & agonizing ignorance. Her courage all through has been marvellous. Poor, poor darling how inexplicably cruel it seems that all her hopes & pain & looking forward should end in death. It has been an extraordinary experience – I feel as if a hundred years had passed over me & all my own affairs which till now have been paramount in my life seem so dim & small & jarring & unimportant.

It is the first time I have been near anything real. Father & I motored yesterday to Wanborough thro' the country all white & silent with snow & buried it in the little churchyard there. I am glad this is over & M. has no more leave takings before her. She is going on <u>so</u> well thank Heaven. I am absurdly busy as I am a lot with her & children, servants & automatic letters gobble my time up. Forgive this one being all about us – I can think of nothing else. Was your Xmas nice? I had a tree for the Chils but it seemed such an irony hanging up shiny green & red balls with death in all of our hearts – Goodbye dearest

         Yr V.

V.A. to M.B.C.   *Monday 7 January 1907*
                                                          20 Cavendish Square, W.

Dear Bongie – I write you a short line in the train partly to show you how firm & free from palsy my hand is … & partly to thank you really seriously & gratefully for being such an <u>angel</u>. … I never believed in Death before. And you were so – <u>so</u> good & really helped me so much. I'm afraid it must have been at the cost of much time & fun. But I did love it – & I shall always wonder at the imagination which could inspire such understanding sympathy.

         Yrs. <u>Violet</u>

M.B.C. to V.A.   *Tuesday 8 January*
                                                          Shaw Hill, Melksham

Dear Violet.

I have not earned nearly such a nice letter as you have sent me, but if what has given me a great deal of pleasure, has also brought you something in the way of help in a hard time, I can only thank providence for giving me the opportunity, and trust that you will not later find me out. …

I hope you will have [a] peaceful & pleasant time at Mells … yrs Bongie.

Archie Gordon to V.A.   *Thursday 31 January*
                                                          The Castle, Dublin

Two drawing rooms & much tinselly pomp, feathers, trains processions & all the rest of it have reduced me to a terrible dankness, & a state quite unworthy of one writing to you. Which reminds me that I am looking with a good deal of anxiety to another letter from you. You will remember V. dearest, won't you, that the veriest Puffin makes the whole difference to my day? You don't know what a light it sheds.

I scarcely dare contemplate the effect of 6 weeks of this on one's mind & morals. Imagine giving a dance in London every night of the season to people you didn't know & hadn't asked, & having to treat them as tho' they were your nearest & dearest – & you have it....

With the 230 women I told you of I had some amusement last night. I seated them carefully, but at the first opportunity they rose en masse & made for the door. I stood in the middle like Otto Twigg at the Hippodrome, & shouted that those who stood up should be the last to leave the room.[1] In two seconds every chair was being competed for, just like musical chairs. In the 'presence' chamber itself there were also joke scenes. One woman lost her head, & scuttled rapidly past my P. & M. without noticing them. Before leaving, however, she felt herself bound to relieve herself of her curtsey to somebody, & perceiving a lackey, she turned her back on my M. & made a hurried obeisance to him....

All these items, which loom quite large here, will illustrate for themselves the tenor of the life. They will also bore you.

I do get such pangs at being away, & <u>needlessly</u> away from you, but am staving off the invidious things that will try & come.

> 'By absence this good means I gain
> That I can catch her
> When none can watch her
> In some close corner of my brain'[2]

My V. darling Goodnight. <u>Write</u> Yr A

M.B.C. to V.A.   *Saturday 2 February*
                                      5 Hyde Park Square, W.

Dear Violet.

You told me to write you an amusing or at any rate an interesting letter, I have little to write that is likely to be the one or the other but I shall send this partly because 'Countess etc' and partly because if your

---

[1] The London Hippodrome, in Cranbourn Street, off Leicester Square, opened in 1900 as a circus, with a large water tank in the centre of the stage for 'aquatic spectacles'.

[2] Archie quotes here the first four lines of the last stanza of John Donne's 'Present in Absence'. The missing two lines, which conclude the poem, read: 'There I embrace and kiss her; / And so I both enjoy and miss her'.

brain is at any time tired of being educated you may send an answer.[1]

I had a tête à tête dinner with Beb last night at Cav Sq, we talked more than we usually do when we are alone together sometimes, on topics very well worn but still interesting, though we discussed them quite without bias or at any rate with a friendly one.

One subject is male, the other female. I have practically no acquaintance with the latter. You may have I guess? I also heard a piece of scandal under a strict injunction of secrecy. . . .

. . . you must be glad to have a free day to yourself and not to be bound within the strait limits of a time table Yours

MBC.

V.A. to M.B.C.   *Monday 4 February*
                                                      Easton Grey, Malmesbury,
                                                      Wiltshire

My dear Bongie – <u>How</u> nice you are to write to me. I loved getting your letter – wire the piece of scandal <u>immediately</u> – unless – as is just possible – it emanated from me originally. Did it? Was it about Edward Horner? You & Beb seem to have had a thoroughly gossipy dinner – I should have put a stop to it very quickly if I'd been there; – as you know I rarely talk about people – my staple topics are discreet & helpful: gardening, the Opera, cycling, poetry. (Poor little Ettie – I hope you weren't unkind about her – she goes Dublin to-day.)

I am leading a very strange life; my only companions are my uncle – plum-coloured & quite mad, a blind clergyman & a bullfinch. Aunt Lucy is in London with a specialist but returns alas to-night to plumb my ignorance of bulbs, battles etc for the 100th time. I can't tell you what the <u>delight</u> of waking up to silence & sunshine was – the first morning; the clean air, the elms & the rooks & the river & the stretches of frosty field – oh it <u>was</u> so glorious. If only Aunt Lucy wldn't arrange every meal with a different neighbour – each drearier than the last. It is trying when I particularly want to be alone & drift & read. I wish you were here – we could be quite happy – you are possible to drift with.

Are you having a nice time with Mush Face? Please go on taking care of & reporting on Beb's health & Hugh's frame of mind. I'm so glad the healthy principle expressed in Countess etc still has some hold on you –

---

[1] It was a private joke between Bongie and Violet that she was a 'Countess' and he her 'attendant'.

I'm coming back on the 8ᵗʰ lest its grip shld. slacken – for no other reason –
Yrs <u>Violet</u>

Isn't it awful Grambo has gone to sleep in this room & I'm afraid of getting up lest he should awake with a start & do something to me

Hugh Godley to V.A.   *Wednesday 6 February*
                                                Office of the Parliamentary
                                                Counsel

Dearest Violet

I haven't heard from you since yesterday, but you have been very good about writing & I don't complain!

That dirty swine Lloyd George has given my job (it really ought in justice to have been mine, all my predecessors had it) to a blasted needy Welshman of his own.[1] It is £300 a year straight out of my pocket which I am sordid enough to mind. Damn him. Even a Tory president wouldn't have done that. I don't believe anyone else would. . . .

I have recommended Cuthbert Headlam[2] for the post of secy to Sir F. Schuster! I believe it to be as good a road to wealth as a needy man is likely to have. But I don't think it wᵈ have been a good thing for Bongie to take. It wᵈ be like becoming a butler.

I shall see you tomorrow. Are you glad? I am <u>so</u> glad. You will dance with me so often won't you. Don't disappoint me by not. Even if you think it good for me. Don't teach me a lesson! Yr H.

Diary – Saturday 16 February – 20 Cavendish Square, W.

Stanway is over. It was amusing & exhausting as ever. I arrived to find Ego, Guy, Edward, Smallbones & Beo Campbell. Eddy Marsh, Letty & Venetia followed quickly – a party tiring in a way but also <u>so</u> full of peace & freedom for me.[3] I felt for the first time the relief of utter untrammelledness – the possibility of talking to whoever you like for as long as you want. How infinitely refreshing people who don't care for one very much are. How smooth & kind.

Broadway Ball happened the first night. We drove there in a large bus –

[1] Lloyd George was then president of the board of trade.

[2] Cuthbert Headlam (1876–1964), barrister; clerk in the House of Lords, 1897–1924.

[3] Lady Violet ('Letty') Manners, middle daughter of the 8th Duke of Rutland; she married, in 1911, 'Ego' Charteris.

our skulls vibrating on the windowpanes – & mental gibbets going on à tue-tête.[1]

I was wired for to go home the next day & found a dinner party of the drearier members of the cabinet waiting for me. Lord Crewe took me in – I give him 20 for Impossibility.[2] Besides looking as if he'd been made at Harvey & Nichols he never utters except to say 'Really' & 'Isn't it?'[3] I tried him on every subject – Ireland – sense of humour – the Papacy – sleeping out of doors – mangos – wearing jewels in one's teeth – or teeth in one's jewels – & had a more dismal failure than I can ever remember.

Afterwards we talked in clumps which is always deeply unsatisfactory. Mine was Dolly, Mr. Horner who can't hear – Herbert who can't think & Mr. Birrell whom I loved.[4] He told some excellent stories about Lord Portsmouth & discussed the varieties of religious baptism.[5]

The Grahams' ball happened the next day – I dined with the Jekylls & went in with Bim which was very démodé – I felt as if I were wearing crinoline.[6] Ewen was on the other side rippling with laughter & delightfully unfastidious. I danced till 3.30 with him & Hugh & Bongie & Bim & Harry Graham & other phantoms & then came tiredly home & travelled wearily back to Stanway the next day....

M.B.C. to V.A.   *Friday 22 March*
                                            5 Hyde Park Square, W.

Dear Violet.

It is twenty minutes to four a.m. but as I am going off tomorrow morning to play golf at Cassiobury with Archie I shall write you a short line now, as there will be no time then. I have carried out your directions fairly, as in addition to playing golf tomorrow with A, I dined with Hugh last night and saw him again tonight at the Poynder's. I think he is comforted about your health. I spent a very sleepy day at Cartmell's and in the evening

---

[1] 'at the top of one's voice'.

[2] Much later in life Violet qualified this judgement, writing in the margin of her diary, 'How wrong I was!'.

[3] Harvey Nichols was, and remains, a well-known department store in central London.

[4] Dorothy 'Dolly' Gladstone, *née* Paget, married Herbert Gladstone, 1901.

[5] Newton Wallop (1856–1917), 6th Earl of Portsmouth; parliamentary under-secretary for war, 1905–8.

[6] A crinoline was a hooped petticoat, used in Victorian dresses, and it, like the French *démodé*, suggests something old-fashioned, which is perhaps how it struck Violet to be paired with Bim more than a year after it was rumoured that they were engaged. The Grahams lived at 4 Cadogan Gardens, S.W.3.

dined with your two brothers Charlie Meade, Archie, Edward Horner & Eddy Marsh.[1] I don't associate them together as a bachelor dinner party but it was quite fun. Then except Beb & Charlie who went to bed, we went to the Poynders' and saw Rosina Filippi acting Jane Austen rather well and afterwards danced a little.[2] I danced with Viola Tree, Cynthia Charteris, Rosamund Grosvenor & Etty, and quite enjoyed it encouraged by your philosophy.

The last Lancers had a somewhat startling conclusion, as Edward Horner was discovered 'flying' Lady Poynder by himself and for no obvious reason & he continued to do so, until her tiara fell off. The band stopped in mute amazement and Hugh & I laughed. Edward when he recovered his equilibrium looked somewhat foolish. It will make a good 'par' for Eddy Marsh's next contribution to the D.M.

Thank you for your letter. I do not deserve one quarter of it, & feel guilty in consequence. I am supposed to have a German lesson at 9. tomorrow that is in five hours about exactly.

Goodbye yrs Bongie.

V.A. to Hugh Godley
Monday 22 April
Clarence House, Littlestone-on-Sea,
Kent

I hadn't one second to write from Taplow – charades, bumblepuppy, golf, walks, waterfights, hockey & pencil games in whatever threatened to become an interval. Even Ettie was quite worn out on Monday morning – she told A. she could never remember feeling so tired before. It was a good deal like other Taplow parties in its organization & unceasingness. I was quite amused & liked Winston (whom I'd never properly spoken to before) very much. He's got the uncertain sense of humour of the last generation – which (for me) invests conversation with a new excitement.

He was brilliant at charades – our troupe was He – A – Charlie Meade – Julian – I – Miss Chaplin (heavy cousin of the Dss of Sutherland) Ivo, Monica, Guy Benson etc.[3] We did Drag – A glorious Hell scene (in which I found myself really sticking pins into people's eyelids!) – Rizzio's murder – Alpine accident – & the Gorgon's head – I wish you'd seen my Gorgon's

---

[1] Charles Francis Meade (b. 1881), mountaineer and author. A first cousin of Billy and Julian Grenfell, and a Balliol contemporary and good friend of Bongie.

[2] Rosina Filippi (1866–1930), singer and actress on the London stage.

[3] Ivo George Grenfell (1898–1926), the youngest son of Ettie Desborough. Guy Holford Benson (1888–1975), a Balliol contemporary of Cys Asquith; a banker.

hair! & Julian approaching as Perseus with his shield. Beb & I went there & back in Charlie Meade's motor which he calls Runnymede – isn't it a good name? ... Goodbye – write to me every second – I am thinking of you V

Hugh Godley to V.A.   *Wednesday 24 April*
                                 Office of the Parliamentary
                                                    Counsel

Thank you so much for your letter, which was brought to me in bed this morning....

I took the Ireland Bill home with me to read last night (of course a <u>very</u> confidential doc^n) & left it in the underground![1] I was paralysed with fear, & went at cock crow to the Lost prop. office, where, thank God, I found it. Thring would certainly have killed me if he had found out.[2] It was partly your fault; because if I had been reading it instead of thinking about you I shouldn't have left it there at all....

Now I must go to the House of Commons to a committee on Lights on Vehicles. Send me a line sometime. Yr H.

Diary – Tuesday 21 May – Ewelme Down, Oxfordshire

Father & I are spending Whitsuntide in Frank Lawson's new house – one of Walter Cave's best efforts in sand coloured stone on the top of a juniper hill – stone terraces with pansies in the rifts – tulips shooting up fierily all over the grass – <u>vistas</u> of country rolling in lovely curves towards Oxford & there mixing with the blurredness of the hills ('What are those blue remembered hills?' they always make me think of).[3] There is to me great-great beauty about this place. The blossom is out making everything lovely – Father & I motored down thro' alleys of pink & white & green.

---

[1] The Irish Devolution bill, introduced in the Commons by Augustine Birrell in May 1907, gave powers of local government in Ireland to an executive body of elected and nominated officials. It fell considerably short of the demands of the Irish at Westminster for a parliament in Ireland. In June 1907 the government reluctantly accepted that without Irish support it could not proceed with the bill.

[2] Arthur Thring (1860–1932), first parliamentary counsel, 1903–17.

[3] Walter Cave (d. 1939), architect, vice-president of the Royal Institute of British Architects. Cave designed two of the houses in which Asquith stayed, Ewelme Down in Oxfordshire, and the Wharf in Sutton Courtenay, Berkshire. The quotation is from A. E. Housman's *A Shropshire Lad* (verse XL), which Violet later associated closely with Ewelme, and with memories of Archie Gordon.

We are absurdly comfortable in the way of bathsalts etc but our house-mates are <u>too</u> ghastly – squalidly vulgar – I didn't know such people existed & they lie about marringly like orange peel by the sea. One of the women – Mrs Tufton – calls her golf ball 'Arabella' & often remarks when luck goes her way at games 'Well that's a cert. for yrs. truly'. Father & I alternately rock & shudder. I have never made less effort & put out fewer feelers. I feel momentarily tired out by the double strain of the last week – Margot's complete nervous breakdown & A's rather long drawn out preliminaries to departure were a trying combination of evils, though in a way antidotes to one another. He (A) was wonderfully brave & good – but he felt going away acutely – not only because it is a really physical wrench for anyone who has invested so recklessly in any single idea as he has but also because of the torturing uncertainty one cannot help feeling with a fluctuater like me – (with whom being on the spot is everything).

I have only realized properly in the last two months what an exceptional being he is – & how easy it would be to underrate him in what H. calls 'one of my lightning judgements.' – pink – normal – plausible – pleasantly athletic – with aggressively high-spirits & great assertiveness. This is how I should have sized him up I feel – for the 'charm' which is vaunted by every woman from Hallahan to Ettie has never acted at all potently with me. What I love about him is this great cleanness & soundness of his whole being – the strength & simplicity of his emotions & the courage with which he feels – never holding back for fear of ultimate pain. I think his singleness of heart very rare – & it gives him untold power. He also has undefeated hopefulness & the greatest capacity for joy I have ever seen, unparalleled aplomb redeemed by a strong foundation of real humility; faith in the unseen – reverence for the mysteries of life as well as for its conventional institutions – such as God & our parents. He ought to go far & pray God I may not hamper or injure him; – his recuperativeness gives me hope even if I do my worst! ...

Diary – Monday 17 June – Easton Grey, Malmesbury, Wiltshire

Penrhôs is over – & the beginning of the Season. How unlike a season it has felt – ceaseless rain, bananas instead of strawberries, winter com-binations & <u>every</u> friend stricken down by some mortal disease. Con at Avon with bad heart, Charty at Westgate – lungs, Margot in a state of utter breakdown here sleeping badly losing weight, constant deadly sickness & no progress of any kind in spite of a fortnight's peace & air. I am very unhappy about her & utterly at a loss as to what to do. I wish I could stay with her continuously but this is alas out of the question as Father is alone at home & there are a thousand things to be done.

I had a full week before coming here – Annie's ball on Tuesday for which I had a dinner of 24. . . . Dorothy Beresford whom I imported from E. Grey in a fit of hope was coiffed by deft Simpson & looked <u>too</u> lovely[1] – I thrust young man after young man upon her & had my work cut out for me mapping out her & my own complicated courses between 11 & 4. She only stood out one dance – so I was on the whole proud – & I triumph to achieve! – danced with 3 utter strangers. . . . Altogether my conviction that new means worse is strengthened. But it is a gloomy belief. Ettie spoke to me seriously about grooviness – my 'impenetrables chevaux de frise'[2] – she says I am too engrossed – have not loose interest left to expend etc – but I feel as if I had <u>masses</u> only no recipients – for the only people I ever come in contact with are my intimate & beloved friends & unnegotiable fishfaces. She won't believe this & thinks me criminally passive. 'There are tracts before you to ravage darling – crowds I wish to see in the dust at yr. feet'. But I am a believer in accident where friendship is concerned – the plodding system doesn't appeal to me & I don't feel at all like setting out with a sword. She is very wonderful & one of the cardinal points of my life; her unflagging – tireless radiance & all-embracing sympathy. But I sometimes wonder if the <u>pain</u> of life has ever touched her. I don't think so.[3]

The Court Ball happened Wed – I had a new, hardy, banal, white & silver Marte dress – very clean & glittery – the King looked a perfect portent in a kilt – (of all garbs to choose for his peculiar figure!) but considering <u>how</u> grotesque he looked comported himself with tolerable dignity. I stood & gasped through the Royal Quadrille – wedged between Father & Soveral[4] – afterwards talked to Venetia & Cynthia & danced with Ld. Granard.[5] Then supper off one of those poisonous buffet erections in the plate room with Father, Pamela Lytton & Winston – & home to bed.[6] Father was very chilly

---

[1] Dorothy Beresford (d. 1978).

[2] 'impenetrable barbed wire'.

[3] It would have been remarkable if the 'pain of life' had not touched Ettie, who was an orphan at the age of two, lost her only brother when she was eight, and her favourite grandmother when she was thirteen. Perhaps as a response to these tragedies, Ettie developed a strong personal ethic of 'playing up' to the game of life, and Nicholas Mosley has written of her 'stubborn gospel of joy' in his biography of her son, Julian (Nicholas Mosley, *Julian Grenfell*, 181).

[4] The Marquis de Soveral (1862–1922), Portuguese ambassador in London, and a popular figure in society: 'No social function of any importance takes place without his presence, and he is in all probability one of the most intimate friends of the King and Queen' (*Daily Mirror*, 16 November 1909).

[5] Bernard Arthur Forbes (1874–1948), 8th Earl of Granard; lord-in-waiting to King Edward VII, 1905–7.

[6] Pamela Lytton *née* Plowden (1874–1971), a lifelong friend of Winston Churchill. She married, 1902, Victor, 2nd Earl of Lytton.

in his kneebreeches & white silk stockings & looked rather like the Frog Footman. He said he was intriguing to be made an elder Brother of Trinity House a naval distinction which means you need never wear anything but trousers all yr. life. The <u>last</u> thing I should want – I can't think why he doesn't welcome <u>any</u> variety. I took Dorothy to the House Thurs. found Runciman & Winston in Father's room.[1] He (F) took us all over it & we then went up & heard Arthur Balfour make rather an ingenious speech on the Small Holdings (Lulu Harcourt's bill) characteristically catching on to the most trivial points first – such as degeneration in the physique of the nation.[2]

I dined with Ottoline (<u>dog</u> tired) sat between Max Beerbohm & Noel Buxton – normally a bore but we abused the Aberdeens together which is fun with anybody.[3] Max Beerbohm tried to discuss religion which was perhaps a mistake. After dinner Adkins – a middle aged Liberal on a sofa. Joe discussed – & A.J.B. I felt much too overtired & excited to go to bed on getting home so Beb & I went to Glen-Coats' ball an <u>awful</u> gathering. I danced with Jimmy Tomkinson – Eddy Marsh & Felix – 4th lasher to my despair.[4]

Arthur Asquith to V.A.   *Thursday 20 June*
                              Omdurman, Sudan

My dear Violet, Many thanks for your last letter, finished at Huntercombe. I expect you will be tired of London by the time this reaches you.
    I am curious about this marriage. When is it to be? What has Bertie

[1] Walter Runciman (1870–1949), Liberal MP for Dewsbury, 1902–18; parliamentary secretary to the local government board, 1905–7; financial secretary to the treasury, 1907–8; president of the board of education, 1908–11; of agriculture, 1911–14.

[2] Lewis ('Lulu') Harcourt (1863–1922), only surviving son of Sir William Harcourt, Liberal leader, 1896–8; Liberal MP for Rossendale, Lancashire North East, 1904–17; a determined opponent of women's suffrage.

[3] Lady Ottoline Morrell *née* Cavendish-Bentinck (1873–1938), a friend of H. H. Asquith, and an important figure in Edwardian literary and artistic circles; she married, 1902, Philip Morrell, Liberal MP for South Oxford, 1906–10, and for Burnley, 1910–18. Max Beerbohm (1872–1956), author and cartoonist, drama critic of the *Saturday Review*, 1898–1910. Noel Edward Noel-Buxton (1869–1948), Liberal MP for Whitby, 1905–6; for North Norfolk, 1910–18.

[4] Archie Gordon wrote to Violet from Berlin, on the same day that she wrote this entry: 'The Felix lasher disturbs me a little – I cannot understand what sort of end each of such scenes can have which admits of their repetition. Poor man – I am sure he suffers fearfully, but it <u>must</u> be made worse for him to have lashers, & it <u>must</u> give you pain.'

done with my money? If there are any titbits in the journals, you might send me them, and I will return them: so far I have only seen the one about K. being <u>quite</u> cultivated.[1]

I am disappointed at having as yet heard no tattle connecting your name with that of a titled landowner. Time flies, and the comfortable country seat no nearer. I ask for no precipitancy – nothing but a mental glance at the battered toilers of your family.

I am glad the cloth reached you: it did not look to me as if it could be schooled to play a useful rôle in the feminine wardrobe. I should like you to tell me honestly whether it has really any practical utility, so that I may know whether to ship off more bales of it. I am sending you a shoe: if you could contrive to catch the Bridegroom a clout with it, you would earn my gratitude. Who is to be Best Man?[2]

This month came in with wearisome sandstorms, but the last ten days have been delightful, clean days, fine sunsets and cool winds. My present prospect is Omdurman till the end of October at least – rather monotonous but not uninteresting.

Last week I spent a night with Bongy's brother, the Lord Chancellor of the Sudan.[3] He has the best house and the best cook in Khartoum. We shot about twenty brace of sandgrouse the next morning. Tomorrow being Friday, I am going to shoot betimes, so must go to bed. Here are some photographs. Goodbye, your loving Oc.

P.S. Friday. This morning a letter came from Bertie for which please thank him. I am contemplating the purchase of a <u>third</u> pony – for polo. Altogether with loans from friends on leave I hope to have the use of 5, which should lighten the burden of the dogdays.

V.A. to Hugh Godley   *Wednesday 3 July*
                                20 Cavendish Square, W.

Just back from my H. of C. dinner between John Burns & [Edwin] Montagu. John Burns in <u>wonderful</u> form – defined Father & I & Montagu's & his own political opinions.

[1] Oc refers to Raymond's marriage to Katharine Horner, which took place in London in June 1907. His playful irony draws attention to the fact that Katharine was exceptionally cultivated.
[2] The best man at Raymond's wedding was his Balliol contemporary Auberon 'Bron' Herbert, 8th Baron Lucas.
[3] Edgar Bonham Carter was the judicial adviser to the governor-general of the Sudan.

Himself – a High Old Tory
Father – Radical with the veneer of a Whig
Me – a despot in the making
Montagu – An anarchist with tory tendencies.

I was sorry you didn't come last night – but it was a very jostling ball –
teeming with people I knew. I stayed till 3.30....
Goodnight & bless you Yr V.
I shall see you at Stafford House. Go early.

V.A. to Archie Gordon   *Thursday 4 July*
Train to Penrhos

WRETCHED Letter
    I am taking a morning off (in bed) – the week so far has been exhaustingly
amusing. Mond. Venetia's dinner & ball at which I stayed till 4 – the next
day Eton match – memorable scene of First Embarkations....
    I was in despair yesterday morning at hearing Venetia had got pleurisy &
will probably be in bed for a fortnight – sat with her in the afternoon....
Dinner at the House between John Burns & Montagu. Burns in brilliant
form. He said: 'You must never wait for money to make a marriage or a
career. I married at 23 on nothing – I'd been out of work for 6 months &
after the wedding I had to take the ring off my wife's finger & pawn it to
pay for my honeymoon – which was tea at Hampton Court. It (marriage)
is the greatest – divinest – happiness in life'. I was startled but not convinced....
    I'm just off to lunch with Aubrey – Stafford House to-night. Bless you
dearest dear A yr V – always

V.A. to Venetia Stanley   *Saturday 27 July*
20 Cavendish Square, W.

Goodbye darling – I wish you weren't gone. When I see you again it will
be in air & peace & joy – how glorious to think of. I feel momentarily in
utter collapse of spirit from balls & tears & lashers but Wed. is coming &
the end of all tension. Write to me very often & don't stop loving me
        Yr V.

Archie Gordon to V.A.   *Sunday 28 July*
                              Berlin W., Friedrich Wilhelm Str.
                                               4.

My V. – Somebody gave me a Daily Graphic to-day, with pictures of R. & K. & all the bridesmaids, so I know it came off, & that Mrs Horner received her guests at 11 Downing St., kindly lent for the occasion.[1] Also that the bride groom gave the bridesmaids crystalline brooches.

It does feel so odd to reflect that a thing which would be a vital & all-important thing if one were there, (& which is) should become by the accident of absence a blurred photograph & a few lines of print, as far as it strikes the outward scene. It is the first wedding in which you have felt a <u>real</u> personal concern, I suppose, since Margot's.[2] My own experience of the first important one was that I forgot the trashiness & the cheap sentiment & was very profoundly affected, but I believe that the occasion is one when the <u>least</u> glimpse of the obviously ridiculous side of every wedding would break down the other atmosphere in a minute. The music makes a good difference, as well as the voice of the man doing the service. . . .

I am on very short rations just now my dearest. 11 days with only one letter! I really hardly dared hope you would have time all this last busy week. I shall be so happy when I hear. Bless you ever, dear one yr A

Diary – [August] – Highfield, Muir of Ord, Ross

I shan't say a word about the end of the season – it tires me to <u>think</u> of it. My last week I had 5 balls running & Raymond's wedding – an almost unbearable combination of grind & wrench. The atmosphere of fuss & bustle in our house was exhausting to a degree – wreaths & veils & hymns & food – they <u>insulted</u> my private feeling of finality & loss. When it was all over I lay down with mauve cheeks & bleary eyes there was still the ball to face – I minded it acutely at first but enamelled on emergency spirits for the first 2 or 3 hours & began to feel quite happy after dancing an 8-some reel with Waxworks. It lasted till 4.30! . . .

---

[1] The Asquiths had elected not to move into the chancellor's official residence at 11 Downing Street because it was too small. It was taken instead by Herbert Gladstone, home secretary, who had no London house (Roy Jenkins, *Asquith*, 161).

[2] Violet had been a bridesmaid at the wedding of her father and Margot in May 1894.

Raymond Asquith to V.A.   *Tuesday 13 August*
Avon Tyrrell, Christchurch,
Hampshire

Dearest Violet

I was very glad to get your letter. Highfield sounds far from perfect, and I am glad to see in today's papers that the grouse prospects are quite unusually bad. It is clever of me to miss Scotland in a year when there is nothing to shoot & nowhere to live.

We have had rather a rainy time on the whole but with a fair percentage of beautiful days. . . . Runnymede is a great resource – enormously powerful, very comfortable, and driven in a most lyrical manner by a reckless but extremely skilful chauffeur who by great good luck has fallen in love with Katharine's maid; so everyone is satisfied. We live a very pleasant but rather lazy life, reading & writing & rather limply learning Italian in the mornings & motoring or walking or both in the afternoons. If you want my impressions of being married they are that it is incomparably more agreeable than being single.

At the beginning of last week an insufferably pompous little man turned up to sculpt a coat of arms in the chapel & insisted on dining with us & talking till midnight about Montaigne, Luini, Pericles & many other things, about which he had opinions but little information. Luckily on the following day (Tuesday) we drove off to Mells where we stayed, in the big house, till Saturday. It was a pleasant visit, except for one awful day when the vassals assembled to the number of nearly 1000 in the Park. Rustic sports took place, Mark played music-hall songs upon the gramophone, rockets went up, and friendly relations were maintained between the classes till a late hour of the night. In a flabby tent where we dined with masses of farmers I struck a deep note in response to a toast of our health. Miss Padford, a woman of 83, expired shortly afterwards from sheer emotion. She ought never to have risked it.

Shaw-Stewart was there – Hugh tells me that Ettie has abandoned herself to him without reserve – to Stewart, I mean.[1] I have written to Archie to come back & defend his title. We stay here till next Monday, sleep that night at Buck-Gate, start Tuesday morning for Porto Fino & hope to arrive there Wednesday night.

---

[1] Patrick Shaw-Stewart (1888–1917), a Balliol contemporary of Cys Asquith and, like him, an outstanding scholar, winning the Eldon Law scholarship, and an All Souls fellowship by examination, in 1910. He was a director with Baring Brothers bank, a position that Ettie Desborough helped secure for him. They enjoyed a close friendship, but probably not an affair in the modern sense (see Nicholas Mosley, *Julian Grenfell*, 173–4). He was killed in action in France at the end of 1917.

Give our love to Margot. I hope she is improving. Write again.
      Yr Raymond

Arthur Asquith to V.A.   *Sunday 25 August*
                                              Omdurman, Sudan

My dear Violet, Very many thanks for your first letter from the Muir of
Ord, and the Graphic and Mirror illustrations. The Graphic group amused
me most. Either the camera has acted like those shortening looking glasses
at Earl's Court, or all the young women have put on a good deal of
condition since last I saw them.[1] It must have been a trying ordeal for R.
and K. But I expect a large London wedding has the advantage over a
country one of sinking the sorrow of leaving friends in the joy of being
rid of busy buzzing swarms of acquaintances.
    It is nearly a month since we have had any railway communication
with Egypt. Many miles of railway have been washed away by the floods.
Letters have been taking twenty days and more to dribble through by
steamer from England. Meanwhile the temperature has been ideal: but
September and October are bad months. . . .
    August 29th I got out of Omdurman last night to some hills – or rather
heaps of black rock – about ten miles away. I missed a gazelle, and a fox
(Asiatic!), and saw a hyena. Today has been the most sweltering close day
I can remember – not a breath of air and a hanging mist of sand. When I
got back home I found a pile of letters – a delightful one from Margot for
which please thank her very much: and several from the Clovelly party
largely about one another which was interesting. Love to Margot Father
and all. Yrs Oc.

V.A. to Hugh Godley   *Tuesday 17 September*
                                           Highfield, Muir of Ord, Ross

There has not been one instant's lull for me since Monday – days at Tain,
teas at the loch, Archie, Bongie, Venetia, Lizard, Arnold, Cys. We had a
ball on Friday night with reels Triumphs & Petronellas & Flowers of
Edinburgh, it lasted till 4 & I was as wildly happy as I always am on such

---

[1] Earl's Court, the exhibition centre in central London, was also the site of a permanent
funfair.

occasions & was whirled round by keepers & odd-men. I wish you'd seen Father. He was much more active than ever before & galloped up & down the room in the Lancers with one arm round Park's neck & the other round Nye's. And the beautiful lady from the Dingwell level-crossing came. I have been too criminally spoilt by Archie & Venetia – who think of <u>nothing</u> but what I want all day long – it is humbling to be so loved & overrated – it ought to make one very good. And Bongie brings realization before one has time to wish.[1] Yesterday was the most wonderful day of my life – I started at 15 to 8 in the Darracq motored to Tomich (where Ld. Tweedmouth lives) & he & I & Archie then rode 10 miles (through country which made me dumb with beauty) across the hills-thousand-coloured.[2] We got off our ponies when it became too wild & walked a very rough 5 miles on – I covered in an invisible cape & a kind of Tarnhelm on my hair because I should otherwise have been prohibitively garish.[3] And then at last at about 2 we reached our destination a most wonderful pass in the hills. The stags were 'moved' we saw them galloping towards us – literally over a thousand! I can't convey the wonder of it to you – we got back to Tweedmouth's house about 7 & motored home 40 miles after dinner getting here 11.30.

To-day is a very sad one – Archie & Cys go – they are both wretched & I too. I shall see A. again before Berlin. He (A.) has been an angel of goodness & his joy is really infectious – it has done M. a world of good. She is having another terrible breakdown to-day & won't let anyone except Father & I go near her – so my heart is full – but as is usual on such occasions I have to amuse Eddy Marsh who has just arrived....

... forgive this letter – I am in the middle of a very bad Maelstrom & hardly being given time to feel Yr. V.

---

[1] Violet had written to Bongie on 3 August: 'Your friendship is the greatest thing gained in this last year of turmoil & disaster – & you have been a most dear & sparing friend.'

[2] Edward Marjoribanks (1849–1909), 2nd Baron Tweedmouth; chief Liberal whip in Gladstone's last administration, and first lord of the admiralty under Campbell-Bannerman, 1905–8. Asquith made him lord president of the council, a post that he held for just six months; he was replaced by Viscount Wolverhampton. The Darracq 'Flying Fifteen' was an early production automobile, manufactured by the Frenchman Alexandre Darracq (1855–1931), who expanded his business using British capital, and built an assembly plant for his cars in south London. The more expensive models sold for around £400, and had top speeds approaching 45 m.p.h.

[3] In Wagner's *Der Ring des Nibelungen*, a tarnhelm is a magic helmet which allows the wearer to become invisible, or change appearance.

V.A. to Venetia Stanley   *Tuesday 15 October*
                                    Archerfield House, Dirleton,
                                                East Lothian

Darling – I have been meaning to write every single day to thank [you] for your beloved last letter but winding-up Highfield was a long drawn out operation. The last week there we were all alone – Father, M., Beb & I except for Hugh & May Tomlinson (who get about $1\frac{1}{2}$ for buoyancy between them).... It seems odd to think that my two variegated months there are over for good. I should have been <u>perfectly</u> happy if it hadn't been for M.'s health – she is not really better yet.

Father & I & Margot got here for dinner to find the <u>Dubs's</u> about whom you've often heard A. & I speak – (she is one [of] my best imitations) & an unknown, middle-aged rather piano golfer called Mansfield (a brother of Ld. Sandhurst's[1]). I am behaving like a timid unassuming young woman – anxious to please but a little unsure of her ground – saying safe things tentatively in a low voice. Dolly has not yet asked me how many people are in love with me but I can feel it coming – I am playing a single with her this morning....

What news have you of A.? Have you written goodly? & bracingly Goodbye <u>really</u> Yr V.

V.A. to M.B.C.   *Sunday 1 December*
                                    Archerfield House, Dirleton,
                                                East Lothian

Dear Bongie – Thank you for your last two letters. I write in bed – (which is oddly enough the only place in my day for letters) after an uneventful evening spent with Elwes, May, Fräu & Miss Lemon – who has been here from Sat. to Mon. (I had my lesson from her yesterday but didn't like to ask her to read with me to-day – though I <u>longed</u> to – because poor little thing she works so hard – <u>8</u> lessons a day – however I employed her to carry round my clubs in the afternoon!)[2]

The only incidents of to-day have been 1) Margot's departure to Whittingehame for two nights (I follow to-morrow) 2) An access of faintness on the part of May – <u>nothing</u> like one of my operatic tumbles – only 5 minutes on a sofa with a green smelling bottle – 3) the appearance of Miss Lemon for dinner (who is 3 feet high & has a face like a Nibelung) in a

---

[1] William Mansfield (1855–1921), 2nd Baron Sandhurst; under-secretary for war, 1892–5.
[2] Miss Lemon taught Violet Greek, and became a lifelong friend.

highly classical mustard satin drapery hanging straight from the chin &
traversed at intervals by the key pattern in gold. . . . Park & Nye were ironly
controlled – but I think moved. . . .

I come back from Whittingehame Tues. morning – have 2 more Greek
lessons – & then Bongie think how exciting!! London Thurs – Winchester
Fri. – Minley Sat.! It is a head-turning prospect – after my even turnip's
life here. But I have loved the peace & air & regularity & if only things
had always been smooth with M. I shld. have a very green vista to look
back down.

My reconciliation holds good & I am determined it shall but I think it
is praps just as well I am going as she is beginning to think my Greek
lessons bad for me – first on the ground that they overtax my brain (!!!!!)
then because I might so easily break a tyre going in to Edinburgh & be
stranded on the road. Also that my philosophy class is dangerously
stuffy – & that I tire myself by going for walks! So you see there is a good
deal of scope for controversy though none has luckily arisen as yet.

Keep Monday evening free for me – I want to take a play party to the
Sins of Society.[1] Goodbye very dear Bongie
       yr V.

---

[1] *Sins of Society*, by 'Cecil Raleigh' and Henry Hamilton, played at the Drury Lane Theatre
in London, September to December 1907.

FIVE

Downing Street

1908–1909

V.A. to Edwin Montagu   *Tuesday 4 February 1908*
                                   Palace Hôtel, Montana,
                                   Switzerland

Dear Mr. Montagu.

This is a line from my lonely ice-fields to remind that you promised to let me know if anything the least amusing happened – (or exciting – or interesting – or approaching the tiniest tea-cup crisis). Please be a man of your word – I feel so exiled & out of range & the papers say nothing – & anyway there are only last springs here with pictures of the Russo-Japanese war.

This country is very theatrical – the mountains are stupendously big – really verging on the improbable – & the sky Reckitts blue & the snow clean & deep & the Xmas trees innumerable.

I have done nothing violent yet except toboggan a little – which thrilled me – it's so frightening & so harmless, one has all the anguished expectancy without any bump at the end. I'm afraid I shall come back a snow-bore

Yrs Violet Asquith

H.H.A. to V.A.   *Wednesday 5 February*
                           House of Commons

My dearest Violet

I was glad to get your letter last night, & also to see yours & Eliza's to Margot. I am afraid your first impressions of Montana were not altogether alluring. I am surprised that there shd. be such a crowd of the vulgarer class of English encamped there now, when the holidays are or ought to be over. Margot, however, declares that it is just the same at St. Moritz where she got her best lessons in skating & other forms of 'winter sport' from bounders & 'trailers' of our own race. I hope you will soon have a sitting room to yourselves, and the company of Venetia. I haven't heard whether she is starting to-day.

As regards your private enclosure, I am living a most virtuous life (perhaps in the absence of temptation) & all the hours of the day & night (except from 12.30 to 10 am) are spent at the Treasury, or at or in the neighbourhood of the House. So far nothing very critical has occurred, but there are all sorts of possibilities in the immediate future.

I was interrupted by Victor Lytton who came to see me.[1] He is strong for Celerina, where he & Pamela were for a month, but he will write to you himself on the subject.

Margot is beginning to complain of her back & inside, and I am afraid she misses the exercise, golf & c which she had at Archerfield. It is a pity, I think, that she came to London, but it is difficult to see where else just now she could be. I must stop now & go into the House – Always your loving Father

Raymond Asquith to V.A.   *Friday 7 February*
                                              20 Cavendish Square, W.

Really, Violet, patch or no patch, you ought not to have taken my Liddell & Scott;[2] not only was it bound in light blue morocco but I have had it for 15 years; so for God's sake tell me what you have done with it, as my position without it is exceedingly difficult & painful. As to my Ibsens – they turn up one by one in various corners of your room; & I have no serious complaint to make about them. But I do implore you to bring back safely the 3 vols of Arthur Machen which you have taken.

If you had any conscience it would take more than the company of Eliza to keep your spirits up. But you have none: and it is with difficulty that I sign myself

       your loving brother Raymond

---

[1] Victor Alexander Bulwer-Lytton (1876–1947), 2nd Earl of Lytton; married, 1902, Pamela *née* Chichele-Plowden. Appointed chairman of the Royal Commission on International Exhibitions, 1909.

[2] H. G. Liddell and R. Scott's standard Greek dictionary was reprinted many times after its first publication by Oxford University Press in 1843. The 'patch' to which Raymond refers is the area of infection on Violet's lungs that was the reason for her stay in Montana.

V.A. to M.B.C.   *Sunday 16 February*
Palace Hôtel, Montana,
Switzerland

Dear Bongie – I have had 3 wonderfully good letters from you – (all prompt
up-producers) bringing news of everyone I wanted to hear about. The post
is <u>paramountly</u> important here – where I have not much human contact
(divine vegetable intimacy with Venice & Fräu excepted)....

... As I longed for some fixture in the day with no hygienic object I put
up an advertisement anonymously in the hôtel hall saying would anyone
give 3 hours very, very elementary Greek teaching a week. There were
immediately 2 answers – one from the hôtel zany – a confirmed dip-
somaniac (which was disregarded) & the other from an unknown quantity
called Law.[1] It was very exciting when this <u>pitch</u>dark horse presented itself
at the given hour at the door of our sitting room.

It turned out to be a quite nice young man – fairly well-informed but
having never taught before consequently explaining a little irrelevantly at
times – I mean irrelevantly for someone at my stage. But I feel it will just
prevent poor <u>darling</u> Lemon's last tottering erections from crumbling.
What I <u>know</u> I ought to do is to grind over my grammar but it is so difficult
picking up threads after this lapse. The threads of the Contracted Verbs
for instance!

I am sorry you are depressed about your Law – but I feel convinced that
nothing can go very far wrong so long as you realize – as you do – to an
almost morbid extent – the importance of annexing large tracts daily &
irrevocably. I'm sure you can do anything you like – you have a <u>very</u>
exceptional amount of will – and concentration is only a question of
turning it on at the right moment. I know that the aridity & greyness of
what you have to do is probably quite outside the reach of my imagination – but <u>dear</u> Bongie – think of Easter when your desert shall blossom
like the rose – when we can sit on Littlestone shingle in the sun – or go
for long green walks among windmills & larks & eat cherry-jam in
orchards & dance by the sea under the moon! <u>Then</u>! – the long grey
regiments will vanish like ghosts before the delight of that then....

Bless you – I wish you <u>so</u> much happiness
Yrs Violet
Please try & see Hugh.

I have had particularly funny letters from Elwes, Montagu, Sturgis, &
Beb & Waxworks. Patrick & Ettie have both written to me 2 or 3 times &

---

[1] Henry Duncan Law (n.d.), joined the India Civil Service after the 1905 examination, and
was assistant magistrate in Bengal; educated at Edinburgh University and Trinity College,
Cambridge.

K & Father & Raymond & Cys & Olive & Lilian Tennant so I have been well treated on the whole.

H.H.A. to V.A. *Monday 17 February*
20 Cavendish Square, W.

My dearest Violet
It is midnight & I have just returned from the House & was delighted to find your letter. I suppose a gain of $\frac{3}{4}$ of a lb. is good, & it is well that your temperature is on the down grade. I am sure if you persist & are patient all will go well. I was amused at your adventure in the way of Greek lessons. Tell me how the exuberant Law goes on. What are his credentials. Oxford or Cambridge or whence?

I am still leading a virtuous life & leading the House also; our poor old CB, after a bad heart attack, having succumbed for the time being to influenza which is ravaging the town.... We had the old Bencks here last night & the Lyttons & Evan. Also Arnold Ward & McKenna – whom Margot thinks you have ceased to appreciate. Aggie Jekyll, however, has fixed her steeliest hooks into him, with Mrs Spender lending a hand, and he seems to be for the time completely Jekyllised. I suppose it may be a phase; Aggie is a past mistress in these psychological & educational experiments.

I am glad you are pursuing your episcopal investigations. I went to St Paul's yesterday afternoon & heard Stepney, who surprised me & still more his congregation (I shd. think) by declaring himself & his Church on the side of the Socialists....

... Oc comes home at the end of April for 3 months. Margot is on the whole wonderfully well – rather shocked that Cheyne has shaved his beard, just when old [?] has begun to grow one. But the Doctors are past finding out: as some one said of the Treaty of Utrecht 'My Lord Harley, Peace is like the peace of God – it passeth all understanding'. Always your loving (& harried) Father

V.A. to Archie Gordon *Friday 28 February*
Palace Hôtel, Montana,
Switzerland

Thank you for all the letters I have had since I wrote last – Buxton plays a very important part here & you are reckoned upon as a three-times a week certainty. My only real time for writing is during one of my rests (the after-lunch one I'm allowed to in) & struggling with a pencil, on one's back, in thick gloves & very often snow whirling round makes it rather slow work....

I have been so thrilled by politics – & hardly able to keep still when C-B was so ill – I believe I kept him alive by sheer prayer – I couldn't have borne anything so crucial as his demise to happen with me away. Father has done & is doing magnificently I'm sure he's improved his position a great deal – & disposing of what he has on his hands now is a tour de force in its realest sense. Besides all C-B's work & his own, he leads the House, does the Licensing Bill, prepares the Budget, bears a great deal of the Education Bill brunt (& Hugh says does most of McKenna's work too). He writes me divine long letters – never mentioning the strain. Isn't his strength of mind & body iron & wonderful? He turns all other men into women. I long to be there – but people are angels about writing me everything – & H. sends me the Daily Mail from Paris! – so I get news only one day late instead of two; I don't expect you have time to read the papers.

Now I must stop this endless letter – write often to yr V.

V.A. to Edwin Montagu   *Thursday 9 March*
                                            Palace Hôtel, Montana,
                                                  Switzerland

Dear Mr. Montagu – Your letter was a great joy & excitement – & I felt like the triumphant decipherer of the Rosetta stone when after 2 or 3 hours hard labour I succeeded in making out every single word of it. But thank you really for writing – I have been hardly able to sit still in my ice-fields through this thrilling time & you told me everything I most wanted to know.

... I delight in the boldness of the Licensing Bill. I suppose it will lose us myriads of by-elections on grounds of spoliation – but I suppose a little temporary despoiling of the despoilers is necessary & inevitable in the process of annulling long arrears of injustice?? I am deeply ignorant of this – & also of how much temperance depends on the number of public-houses, I should have thought the inner citadel of the drunkard was the thing to attack first – but no doubt this would need some storming![1] I agree with what you say about McKenna – but I feel myself to be a bad judge of him (though I like him) because I think his table-talk & links-badinage do his brains an injustice – he is a different man when he talks shop. Father deals with him professionally & probably sees him at his best – but however 'competent', 'able', & 'efficient' he may be I can't imagine him anything but rather banal-ly sound. (Please be silent about all this – not that it cld. be of any interest to anyone!)

Will he be Ch. of the Exch. do you think under a new régime? I heard John Morley wanted it when the last Gov. was formed – but I can't see him at the Treasury can you? You don't know the <u>tent</u> anxiety I've been through over C-B's health – the thought he might die when I was away kept me awake at night ! & I'm sure I kept him alive by <u>sheer</u> prayer. Poor old boy. Aren't you happy now at F's relations with the King? How does he stand with the rank & file – & do Eddy & Jack Tennant continue to vote against the Government every night?[2] I still want to know <u>such</u> a lot of things – please be very kind & write me a line of answer when Austen Chamberlain is speaking or in some other free moment.[3] Tell me how angry the Cabinet are with Tweedmouth – he seems to have behaved like a school-girl, I blame him much more than the Times whose profession it is to make mischief.[4] No room for anything about me – I am better – out

---

[1] Successive Edwardian governments attempted to tackle the social problem of drunkenness by controlling the licensing of public houses. The April 1908 Licensing bill went much further than the 1904 Act, and if carried into law would have forced a substantial reduction in the number of licences then in operation. The drink trade was a powerful lobby within the Unionist party, and it was inevitable that the measure would face tough opposition in parliament. The ferocity of this resistance, though, was unexpected. Not even the intervention of the King in support of the bill could dissuade the Unionist peers from rejecting it on 28 November, by 272 to 96.

[2] Edward Priaulx Tennant (1859–1920), 1st Baron Glenconner, 1911; Sir Charles Tennant's eldest surviving son, five years older than Margot. He was Liberal MP for Salisbury, 1906–10.

[3] (Joseph) Austen Chamberlain (1863–1937), a leading figure in the Unionist party, and a candidate for the leadership in 1911; MP for East Worcestershire, 1892–1914. He was the son of Joseph Chamberlain, and the half-brother of Neville, prime minister 1937–40.

[4] In February 1908, against a background of public anxiety in Britain concerning German naval building, the Kaiser wrote to Lord Tweedmouth to proclaim the defensive purposes of the German navy. Tweedmouth was given authority to acknowledge this letter, but not formally to reply to it. It was agreed that his acknowledgement would contain details of the coming year's navy estimates, which had not yet been presented to parliament. Tweedmouth subsequently, and indiscreetly, allowed the existence of the Kaiser's letter to be known in political circles. In March *The Times* supported demands for the correspondence to be made public, in the 'national interest'. Only the co-operation of the opposition leaders saved the government from an inquiry. One of Asquith's first acts on becoming premier was to remove Tweedmouth from the admiralty. See Peter Rowland, *The Last Liberal Governments, 1905–1910*, 194–5.

all day in snow & ice & <u>pray</u> <u>God</u> coming home in 3 weeks yrs Violet
Asquith

V.A. to Ettie Desborough   *Saturday 21 March*
                                                  Palace Hôtel, Montana,
                                                          Switzerland

My Beloved – What a joy yr. 3 last <u>glorious</u> letters have been – I don't
know which of the 2 fragments of life I could best have <u>borne</u> to have
missed – Hugh in the twopenny tube or M. in the shop.

It speaks badly for my brightness in the family circle doesn't it that the
name of a (well-known) skin-disease (alas running hither & thither on too
many faces) should be reckoned as one of my 'good things'![1] I am rather
nervous though that my mention of McKenna's spots, spats, speckles &
tricot tights shld. have reached her (Heaven knows through <u>what</u> channel).
I expect she will write & warn me against 'the trivial aspect of things' & say
'believe me – you <u>can't</u> do better than marry a man with a sunny nature
(swing Puffin for <u>hours</u>) who's <u>bound</u> to be in <u>every</u> Cabinet'. I daresay one
can't – I wld. sooner marry someone for a career than a country-house, but
one wld. have to take a long farewell of most of one's expectations from life
before one cld. resign oneself to McKenna for either – or any consideration.
As a matter of fact – he is <u>very</u> <u>nice</u> & has a good head – banal to the verge of
soundness – I mean vice versa. I think rather commonplace people do best
in politics don't you – (by do best I mean 'arriver' most) look at this Cabinet
Sydney Buxton, Herbert Gladstone, Ld. Crewe, <u>Ld. Elgin</u>, <u>C-B</u>!![2] Winston the
only in-the-least <u>unusual</u> one.

I have written P. Jekyll a guarded letter but cldn't resist asking her if she
felt like Isolde.[3] Most marriages seem to me to present the awful alternative
of cramping one: either emotionally (by marrying a well-to-do Funny who
gives one practical scope) or intellectually – by living with a nice pauper
(whom one likes) among the dankest of the dank. It sounds rather a crude

---

[1] Ettie had written to Violet in March, saying that Margot had asked her what she thought
of Pamela Jekyll's engagement to Reginald McKenna, and on her replying 'Well, I wish he
hadn't got eczema' had remarked 'Oh, you get that from <u>Violet</u>, how often I hear of you
repeating Violet's good things!'

[2] Sydney Charles Buxton (1853–1934), president of the board of trade, 1910–14; Liberal MP
for Poplar 1886–1914. Victor Alexander Bruce (1849–1917), 9th Earl of Elgin and Kincardine;
secretary of state for the colonies, 1905 to April 1908.

[3] Violet offers ironic comparison between Pamela, who in her eyes has made a 'career
marriage', and the heroine in Wagner's opera *Tristan und Isolde*, who is possessed by passionate
love.

sheep & goat division – but don't you think detrimentals <u>as a whole</u> more satisfying than drumbores? in fact in almost every instance[1]....

Alas – no Taplow possible for me – I shall be back 1st May at earliest. Do let me have one later. The thought of our first dentist makes me see stars! My Darling – I <u>am</u> tired of being away from you

         Yr V.

H.H.A. to V.A.   *Sunday 22 March*
                                          20 Cavendish Square, W.

My dearest Violet.

I have just time for a line & only a line about your plans. Though I need not say I should be delighted to see you at the earliest possible moment, yet the climate & general condition here are so bad at present – quite at their worst – that there would be a real risk of throwing away all the good you have got at Montana if you were to come back now.

Moreover you would have very soon to make tracks again in order to meet Oc, who will I hope arrive at Venice just about Easter time.[2] Probably as the snow & ice are breaking up you shouldn't lose much time in leaving your present quarters....

The situation here is full of strain & suspense which tries some people more than it does me. Charles II apologised for being such an unconscionable time in dying. No one wants poor CB to die, tho' I fear his case is really hopeless, but it is time that the inevitable was recognised. As it is, the whole political world is given up to every kind of idle & mischievous gossip. The brewers & their hangers on are up in arms over the Licensing Bill, which will cost us a few by-elections, but we shall carry it through, & this kind of fighting does the party good. Margot on the whole keeps well, tho' of course she agitates herself from time to time over the future.

Always your loving Father

[1] Victorian and Edwardian mothers, considering their daughters' possible suitors, were said to classify the latter as either 'eligibles' – rich and well-connected, or 'detrimentals' – lacking such advantages, and perhaps showing other defects too. 'Drumbores' is Violet's dismissive term for the nondescripts ('bores') that she would expect to meet at any large social gathering ('drum').

[2] Oc made a diversion through Italy on his way home to England on leave from the Sudan in 1908, and Beb and Violet met him in Venice, as planned, towards the end of April; Violet wrote to Venetia Stanley on the 23rd: 'He is <u>very</u> thin & I think not looking well but over the moon with joy & exactly like himself. I don't think I've ever been so excited by anything as at the thought of seeing him....'

Hugh Godley to V.A.   *Monday 23 March*
                                                  Office of the Parliamentary
                                                                    Counsel

My darling, I have your perfectly glorious letter this morning. I had forgotten that it was the turn for its being addressed here. But I must tell you
that I think your writing a mocking letter to Pamela Jekyll is <u>inexcusable</u>,
just because at the outset of her career she had done her duty like a <u>woman</u>, &
made a <u>most advantageous</u> engagement, instead of wasting her time by ring
fencing herself with unsubstantial trifles (like me), you are pleased to scoff.
You have no reverence Violet, that's what it is about you. And in order to
show you that I am not alone in my opinion I send you this extract from a
letter of Etty's. Seriously, I hear of the fixed event now for the first time, & I
think that it is eminently satisfactory, & likely to prove absolutely successful.
They neither of them could expect perfection, & I think their respective
short comings balance very nicely. I would sooner marry McKenna than me.
(At least I think it w^d be far wiser) And I tell you what – if you go on making
<u>cattish</u> remarks to & about P.J. I think it very likely that when the time comes
for her to be giving one of her smart evening parties at the B^d of Education –
or by then it may be at the Treasury – poor little Violet will be left out in the
cold, with nothing to do but go & kiss herself in her bath. At best you will
only be asked like this

> *The Prime Minister and Mrs Asquith*
> Miss Asquith
>
> The Chancellor of the Exchequer and Mrs McKenna
>
> At Home
>
>   R S V P
> *11 Downing Street SW*   *Music 10.30*

Your Elysian, but not serious, suggestion that I should come straight out
now with an untidy bag simply makes my mouth water. It is of course
impossible. Bongie told me he had no idea of going abroad, & unless there
is anything he w^d like to do more I hope he will go somewhere with me,
esp^{ly} if the James' come too. . . .
    You will make what arrangements you like with Archie. If he goes out

now for a fortnight, it will drive me quite mad of course, the thought of it makes me want to dash my head against a wall, but I am aware that that is not a consideration which ought to, or would, influence you. . . .

Let me know your address at once please, & your plans, so that I may know. I am so happy that you are better that I daresay I shan't mind so much about anything else. I had great faith in your complete recovery. May I say this now, without touching that nerve.

The sooner you leave this letter & all my letters in a snow drift the better. . . . Goodbye dearest. Yr H.

Venetia Stanley to V.A. *Saturday 4 April*
18 Mansfield Street, W.1

My darling I got a most glorious batch of Bellagio letters this morning. . . . One from Archie in a wild state of joy and then your most admirable & slightly unexpected one. Poor dear Hugh I am really sorry for him it must be bitter for him to think of Archie with everything he can possibly want having a divine dentist (circumstantial) while poor Hugh has to work at boiling Willie in rain and slush. I haven't yet seen him, perhaps he feels too strongly that I as one of A's little band will be triumphing over Archie's successful 'touching up'. . . .

Eddie and Bongie are coming to lunch so I shall wait and finish this till after in case they say anything good. . . . I have just heard of C.B.'s resignation. How <u>thrilled</u> I am.[1] Oh darling it is exciting and at the same time <u>the</u> most cruel thing that you shouldn't be here. I hear your father goes to Biarritz on Wed to see the King. It does seem wrong that he should have to go all that way to see him when he (the K) has nothing to do and is only having fun.[2] . . . I have just come in from the most <u>divine</u> dinner at

---

[1] Sir Henry Campbell-Bannerman resigned on Friday 3 April, after a long illness. It had been publicly known for some time that H. H. Asquith was his undisputed successor.

[2] The King was holidaying at his favoured resort of Biarritz when he received news of Campbell-Bannerman's resignation. He wrote to Asquith the following day, 4 April, inviting him to form a ministry, and making clear that he did not intend to return to England to oversee this: 'The King now calls on the Chancellor of the Exchequer to form a government, and will be glad to see him here at any time that he can conveniently come in order to hear from him what proposals he has to make' (J. A. Spender and C. Asquith, *Life of Lord Oxford and Asquith*, i, 196). Before leaving for Biarritz he had given Asquith an intimation of this arrangement, and to Asquith it presented no difficulty. In other quarters, though, the King's wishes met with less accommodation: a French hotel room, it was argued, was not the proper place for a British monarch to appoint a new prime minister. The case was most forcefully stated in a *Times* leader, discovered afterwards to have been written by Colonel Repington, by

Cav. Only Margot, Beb and your father. During the whole of dinner and after messages kept on coming from every imaginable paper to ask him what he was going to do about the Licensing Bill to-day and when he meant to start for Biarritz. Mr Park looked far far more as tho' he had just been made Prime Minister and as tho' he had all the secret codes at his fingers end.

After dinner we played bridge and then talked. Margot complained of the heart of stone of all the Asquiths which manifests itself by 'Henry always bangs the door when he goes out'. She was navigating away. O.S. was very anxious to know whether Stephanie was susceptible or not! I have never known your father in such good spirits. He was as happy as a hind, tho' of course rather tired at the thought of having to pack off to Paris by a night train, getting there at 6 a.m. Margot tho' seemed rather ill. She went away during dinner and again at bridge and looked generally rather ill. I am sorry for her she does really have a bad time.

This is a boring letter, worse than any of Archie, but it has been so terribly interrupted. I haven't told you one single thing which you want to know. Give my love to Fräu and Archie and tell them I am going to write to both of them soon. Are you still taking care. You must otherwise I shall feel it is my duty to come out to you at once.
Write Your V

V.A. to Venetia Stanley   *Tuesday 7 April*
                                              Bellagio, Italy

My Darling – First – what an angel you are to send me the 3 books of all others I most long for in the world. . . . Your letters have been wonderful – easily first as news-givers – & very well couched! You will know what a wretched day I had yesterday; Fräu came in with a telegram before I'd opened my eyes – unsigned 'I salute the Prime Minister's daughter'. Montagu sent it I think. I really nearly cried with dépit & rage – how cld. C-B be so inconsiderate – after holding out all this time too – Oh how I mind. I gave Archie & Fräu a dog's-day – they were soothing & patient but not really sympathetic. I sent O.S a furious wire to Biarritz, & M. a short one asking for all the newspapers. You would do me such a giant-service if you cld. en passant ring the bell & ask Park or Margot if they have all

no means an unbiassed commentator where the King was concerned. Asquith's absence meant a rearrangement of Commons business, and a week 'unnecessarily lost at a critical period of the session' (F. Ponsonby, *Recollections of Three Reigns*, 253).

gone – <u>all</u>. I want Monday's – & I shld. like the Times or some daily for the next week or so tell Park – till the House rises. . . .
Forgive this staccato rag Yr V.

H.H.A. to V.A.　　　　　　　　　　　　　　　　*Wednesday 8 April*
Hotel du Palais, Biarritz

Dearest Violet
I was delighted to get the flowers which arrived here fresh & intact this (Wed) evening about tea time.[1]
The only thing that makes me sad is that you should have been away in these trying & exciting times. You & I have been through so many adventures together.
I arrived here lateish (as Viola would say) last night, & at 10 this morning I put on my frock coat & went to the King, who was similarly attired. I resigned my office of Ch^r of Ex^r, & he then said 'I appoint you Pr. Min^r & 1st Lord of the Treasury', and thereupon on bended knee I kissed his hand. 1½ minutes sufficed for the ceremony.
I then breakfasted with him tête à tête on fish eggs & coffee & talked for an hour, unfolding my scheme of reconstruction. He was most amiable, & made no objection to anything.
The weather here is vile beyond description, but in the aft. I walked half round the golf-links with Irene Murray – that was, now Mrs Marshall Roberts – and watched a three ball match. Then I dined with the King at the Cassels, & in the morning I start for London, where I hope to be on Friday aft.[2] Nothing cd. be nicer than the King's way of taking things. Ever your loving Father
Love to Libby.

[1] Violet had sent her father a telegram, as well as flowers, from Bellagio, and this he received in Biarritz on 7 April: 'How dare you become prime minister when I'm away great love constant thought Violet.'
[2] Sir Ernest Joseph Cassel (1852–1921), financier and philanthropist, friend and financial adviser to King Edward VII; he married, 1878, Annette *née* Maxwell.

H.H.A. to V.A.   *Monday 13 April*
                                                  20 Cavendish Square, W.

My darling Violet
    This is to tell you that I love you & wish everything that is bright &
good & great for you, now that you are 21.
    It is so sad that you should not be here in these critical times. I miss you
much. But it would have been madness for you to come back into these
black icy days & possibly lose all that you have gained. So we must try to
be content.
    I opened your letter from Brescia to-night to Margot, & shall not show
it to her. I feel all that you say, but M. could not wisely have done
otherwise.
    I wrote to you from Biarritz & I hope you got my letter, wh. was
addressed to Bellagio. I got back here on Friday evening, after 1500 miles
of travelling, & since then I have been forming, or re-forming, the Cabinet.
It is a gruesome task, but I think the result is not bad. In another week
you will have Oc & Cys with you, & very soon thank God! you will be
here again. I am as you know always & everywhere
                    your loving & devoted Father

Venetia Stanley to V.A.   *Tuesday 14 April*
                                                     Penrhôs, Holyhead

My darling I had rather a funny dinner last night at Cav. quite unlike any
I have ever had there before. It was chiefly for bridge and consisted of Sir
George and Lady Murray (I rather like her, she was very nice about you) 2
dummies called Hamilton, 'John Revelstoke' (Beb was very angry with
him as he, Lord Revelstoke, went in with Natalie Benck and hardly said
one word to her.[1] Beb said 'No man whatever his amatory distinction has
any right to behave like that') Olive, Mr White and the Ivor Guests[2]. . . .

---

[1] Sir George Herbert Murray (1849–1936), GCB 1908; permanent secretary to the treasury,
1903–11; he married, in 1879, Helen *née* Mulholland. John Baring (1863–1929), 2nd Baron
Revelstoke; a director of the Bank of England and a partner in the Baring Brothers bank.
Revelstoke was a long-time admirer of Ettie Desborough, and had courted the beautiful Nancy
Shaw (Lady Astor).
[2] Harry White (1830–1927), secretary to the American legation, London, was married to
Daisy *née* Stuyvesant Rutherford, and together they were popular figures in society, entertaining on a large scale. Ivor Churchill Guest (1873–1939), Unionist MP for Plymouth, 1900–6.
Like his cousin Winston Churchill, Guest broke with the Unionist party over tariff reform,
and fought the 1906 general election as a Liberal, representing Cardiff District, 1906–10;
paymaster-general, 1910–12. He married, in 1902, Hon. Alice *née* Grosvenor.

Did I tell you that Pamela said to me that what she was waiting and longing for was for someone to write and say she was the only person he wanted to marry. She wasn't pleased with Beb's letter as it was mostly about golf and not about her. Won't she be happy at being at the Admiralty in Uncle Edward's place.[1] I think it is rather fun for her. As I went through Cavendish Square this morning I found the door of 20 thick and black with cameras and reporters. They were waiting for O.S. to come out, encouraged by a motor which was standing at the door. I am dining with Beb this evening, I don't know who he has got besides Felix, I think Natalie.

I am trying to finish this in the train but Bongie's brilliant conversation makes it rather hard. We had a joke dinner with Beb – Natalie, Mother, I, Felix, Jimmy Tomkinson and Beb ... Felix was in extremely good form. I sat next him at dinner and at the play (it wasn't very well chosen for him as it was the Merchant of Venice but he didn't seem to mind and applauded all the abuse of the Jews most loudly,) and he didn't mention the streets of London or the Architecture of the Theatre....

Goodbye very dearest Your V.

V.A. to M.B.C.   *Wednesday 15 April*
Hôtel Villa Regina, Lido-Venezia,
Venice

My very good & dear Bongie –

How wonderful you have been about writing – your letters are the greatest joy always & to-day a telegram came to remind me I am 21. I feel such a sudden & overpowering consciousness of majority & all it implies – age & dignity & legal responsibility & balance & presence – & other inheritances of middle-age....

I can't tell you what the torture was of sitting still near that damned lake at Bellagio – with what I'd dreamt about & prayed for all my life happening at home. I cried over every paper for days & wired at last begging M. to let me come home as I felt quite ill with wanting to. But she wouldn't – she is sometimes unimaginative & conventional or she wld. have realized that no journey cld. have tired me so much as staying still. However it's over now – I wish I'd wired to Father but I didn't like to worry him. I got 2 divine wires & a letter from Biarritz from him – which was angelic of him wasn't it? He said the one thing that made him sad

---

[1] Archie's uncle was Edward Marjoribanks, 2nd Baron Tweedmouth, first lord of the admiralty, 1905–8.

was that we hadn't been through this together – like every other adventure of his life since I've been born....
		Goodbye, bless you, write here Yr V.

V.A. to Edwin Montagu		*Thursday 16 April*
		Hôtel Villa Regina, Lido-Venezia,
		Venice

Dear Mr. Montagu
	I feel sure it was you who wired me the News anonymously – wasn't it? Thank you so much – I was grateful to know though miserable to hear it. I had so hoped & prayed that C-B would hold out till I came back. I have cried over every newspaper this week.
	But the worst is over & now comes this blessed Easter dulness & by 1ˢᵗ May I think I shall really & truly be home with a thrilling summer before me. Father has been an angel & written & wired nearly every day – but I long to hear about him & everything from someone else – do write. What do people think of Masterman's appointment?[1] I suppose it is considered a sop to the extrême gauche – & how on earth did Father get rid of Ld. Elgin! I don't like the thought of McKenna on the quarterdeck of a Dreadnought do you? Is Bron very happy?[2] What a shout of joy must have gone up over Ld. Portsmouth's weeding.[3] That was 'popular' surely. Please write to me about it all – I know you are the only person in the world who is half as glad as me
		Yrs Violet Asquith
I am on an island with green sea all round & Venice 10 minutes off. Beb Oc & Cys come to-morrow. Tell Wheat how sorry I am that our paths are

[1] Charles Frederick Masterman (1874–1927) was appointed parliamentary secretary to the local government board on 12 April 1908. He was Liberal MP for West Ham North, 1906–11; for South West Bethnal Green, 1911–14. Masterman entered the cabinet as chancellor of the duchy of Lancaster, 1914.

[2] Auberon Thomas Herbert, 'Bron' (1876–1916), 8th Baron Lucas; under-secretary of state at the war office, 1908–11, and the colonial office, 1911, and parliamentary secretary at the board of agriculture, 1911–14. He was a first cousin of Aubrey Herbert.

[3] Lord Portsmouth had served as parliamentary under-secretary for war under Campbell-Bannerman, and wrote to Asquith in April 1908 asking for cabinet rank in the new administration. Not only was he disappointed in this, he was dropped from the government altogether. Asquith had tutored him as a boy and, as Lord Jenkins has observed, had enjoyed 'exceptional opportunities' for gauging his abilities. Portsmouth's protests against the decision were to no avail, though they did result in his successor at the war office, H. T. Baker, being blackballed at Brooks's (Roy Jenkins, *Asquith*, 183).

diverging now I feel very jealous of the Lloyd Georges being at the Treasury.

Archie Gordon to V.A.   *Sunday 19 April*
Vice Regal Lodge, Dublin

My V. I have finished my first Vice-Regal day – a day so far removed from last Sunday at Brescia that I think the other must have happened in a former existence.[1] No surprises awaited me – the party was just 3 A.D.C's (Anson remains at his post) Gracie, & the manager of my Father's Canadian Ranch – (a golden man of 45, who married last year after grinding all his life, was bird, & then lost his wife when their baby was born. He is going back again now to the old game, & his face makes one twist w. pity). The A.D.C's all dank & snuffy, an up w. Gracie, who is meek & mellow. Bad & dull church all the morning, & a very unusual escape, performed by stealth, to the golf-links in the afternoon, attended by Grace. A little talk w. my M. who is simply beloved, very pleased about Italy, very solicitous about you, & generally super-mellow – only – the Tweeders affair![2]

I confess I blushed for O.S., for he made it rather extra harsh for poor old T. It seems that during all the rumour time T. had no notion of the truth, & that his first intimation of the change was long after Biarritz, on the very day before the list came out, when he got a note announcing the blow, without further explanation or comment. He then had an interview, in wh. O.S. said every sort of nice thing, agreed with all his plans etc. but said he must have the 1st Ld. in the Commons.

The poor man is naturally feeling it terribly, not only because he loved his ships & his guns, but because in the eyes of the world it is the finishing at a blow of a long career of hard work for the party – & of course all the foolish papers fly to that absurd Kaiser's letter.[3] And he doesn't even get the pretext of becoming leader in the Lords.

But I am glad to say that he is as loyal as loyal, tho' quite stricken, & I feel rather proud of him. He hasn't made one complaint. Elgin, too, apparently, was sacked at a day's notice – a rude awakening for these old

---

[1] In an effort to cheer Violet's stay in Bellagio, her father and Margot agreed to allow Archie to pay an extended visit. He arrived early in April, and spent more than a week there, returning to England via Brescia.

[2] Archie refers to the recently announced ministerial changes in which his uncle, Lord Tweedmouth, was moved, against his will, from first lord of the admiralty to lord president of the council. Grace Ridley was a first cousin of Archie's, the sister of Jasper.

[3] For the 'Kaiser's letter', see above, p. 137, n. 2.

chaps who fancied themselves the stays of the Liberal party![1]

Best & funniest of all, I hear Portsmouth <u>wrote</u> to O.S. saying the time had now come when he thought he ought to go into the <u>Cabinet</u>!!! & got an answer saying that there wd. be no place for him! You will probably have heard all this from Beb when you get my letter....

My Italy is rising higher in the firmament every hour as it recedes....

I shall stop writing. Bless you my belovedest. A

T. had invited a party & planned a cruise on the Admiralty yacht, wh. was to have begun <u>this week</u>!!

Arthur Godley to V.A.   *Friday 24 April*
                                   29 Sloane Gardens, S.W.

My dear Violet: it was a great pleasure to receive your post-card from Venice, with that delightful procession upon it, and to know that you had served your time or got your ticket of leave....

To turn to less important topics, I am very glad that your Father has become Prime Minister, & I wish him health and strength & all the other 101 qualities which he will require; luckily he has them, whether I wish it or not. I know too much about it to talk about it in a light-hearted manner, but I end as I began by saying that I am very glad.

It grieved me very much to think of him & Margot being in the thick of this terrible business at Easton Grey; but their presence must have been everything to poor Mrs Graham Smith. I hope Margot is none the worse for it.[2]

You must be prepared to be snap-shotted on arriving, & disembarking from the boat at Dover. I can see you in my mind's eye, in the Daily Mirror, with one foot well uplifted, as people always are when snap-shotted, on the gang-way between the steamer & the pier. There will be a heading – 'Prime Minister's Daughter's Home-coming – Miss Asquith disembarks at Dover'.

Well, I shall write no more. Ever yours very sincerely Arthur Godley

---

[1] Lord Elgin, secretary at the colonial office, was surprised to be dismissed from his post and, like Lord Tweedmouth, protested against the decision, refusing to accept the marquisate that was offered in consolation. He was replaced by Lord Crewe.

[2] Margot Asquith wrote in her diary, 15 April 1908: 'Henry ... told me Graham Smith had fallen with a lamp ... & been terribly burned.'

V.A. to Eddie Marsh   *Tuesday 5 May*
20 Cavendish Square, W.

My dear Eddie.

Your going to Dundee directly I get back from Venice, though it affronts me a little, gives me an opportunity of answering yr. letter to Bellagio. It <u>was</u> a good one – unnervingly good for an answerer – but I am emboldened to write this one by the thought that you certainly won't have time to read it. Are you having a thrilling time? & are <u>you going to win</u>? A 2nd defeat would be beyond bearing – what is a Prohibitionist? Do maul him.[1] We are in the throes of moving – leaving <u>beloved</u> Cavendish Sq. for Downing St. which is an 'interesting' house of the most accepted type – pitch-dark – with highly official wholly uninfluenceable furniture – (different Prime Ministers having lived & died in every chair) & not a bathroom or a bookshelf anywhere (how <u>can</u> they have neither washed nor read?) When we have had these put in the glamour of the Great Shades will begin to assert itself – but so far it is dim.

One nice thing is a garden full of daffodils (& a detective) which you must come to tea in every day. You must have all yr. meals with us now you'll be so near – yr chief has asked me to tea with you & him in the Board of Trade which will be fun if it happens won't it?

Do write to me about Dundee & <u>oh do</u> win
      Yrs Violet A.

Eddie Marsh to V.A.   *Thursday 7 May*
Dundee, Angus

My dear Violet

If I let a decent interval elapse before answering your letter, I should never do it, as I hope we shall now meet quite soon – so I take up my pen at past midnight, after 5 meetings and supper.

You say my letter was unnerving to an answerer, but yours is simply shattering. Your description of Downing St is sure of a place in any worthy

---

[1] Winston Churchill was required to stand for re-election in his constituency after being made president of the board of trade, and was defeated by the Unionist W. Joynson-Hicks, who turned a 1,241-vote deficit at the previous poll into a majority of 429 in April 1908. The next month he was given a second chance, at Dundee, a relatively safe Liberal seat. Here he comfortably defeated three other candidates, re-entering parliament as the youngest cabinet minister of the day. Edwin Scrymgeour (1866–1947), the prohibitionist who came bottom of the poll in May 1908, went on to win the seat from Churchill in the 1922 election.

anthology of Edwardian letters. Your invitation to meals there is most welcome – I feel like Neville, when he was living in Paris on a bob a week – & wrote home to his mother that a lady to whom she had given a letter had been very kind, & asked him to come whenever he liked. 'I think', he said 'that I might lunch there every Tuesday and Friday'. I hope you will be a better hostess than you were the other day, according to the Daily Mail, when you gave Eliza all the work & confined yourself to looking graceful in a picturesque robe of blue Shantung, with necklace of coral. Do tell me next time I see you in Shantung, whenever my friends' clothes are described in the press, they are always made of Shantung, & it's so tiresome not to know what it is.[1]

This is rather a horrid place, & the hotel is very economically managed. There are only two armchairs, which have to be moved about from room to room. If you ask for coals, a man comes in with a large lump in each hand, which he puts on the fire, & as pokers are not allowed these last the whole day. I am writing under difficulties, as the ink is peculiarly rich & viscous, and clings to the pen; also my candlesticks have been taken away because Ly Wimborne wanted them, but the waiter said never mind, I'll give you a plate – so I am writing by the light of one candle, insecurely fixed on a saucer by melting the end.

Yes, we are going to win all right (I think). Tell your Father his budget has had a succès fou. A Prohibitionist is one who wishes to prohibit strong drink. Conrad thought they wished to abolish Slavery, but that is an Abolitionist, & quite another pair of shoes[2]....

I hope you are dining with Venetia on Wednesday.

  yours Eddie M

V.A. to Venetia Stanley   *Saturday 9 May*
           20 Cavendish Square, W.

My Darling.

Only one line to say the joy & help you have been to me in these 2 strangest of strange weeks. Living has felt like dreaming – & a thick veil has seemed to hang between me & what have always been the realest &

---

[1] Shantung is a soft undressed Chinese silk; formerly undyed, from 1907 it could be produced in any colour.

[2] Conrad George Russell (1878–1947), a Balliol contemporary and close friend of Raymond Asquith; private secretary to the secretary of state for colonies until 1907; with Medwin & Löwy, stock exchange jobbers, from 1911.

clearest things – (I mean things like my relations with people I know as well as my carpet).

I don't know what has happened – perhaps everything will soon resume its normal course & tea will be spread among the vines as regularly as ever – perhaps it is the beginning of a lasting revolution & instead of beginning to dream I am beginning to live!!! I wonder.

You have been my one firm footing all through

Bless you – I worry about yr hand.

V.

M.B.C. to V.A.   *Sunday 31 May*
5 Hyde Park Square, W.

Dear Violet

It was rather delightful to go into the country yesterday & play cricket in the sunshine. Oc was playing too & with much more success than me.

I hurried back last night just in time to go to Miss Smyth's concert at the Queen's Hall with Cynthia's party.[1] People seemed to think the music was good. I could not say more than that one might like it after hearing it again. . . .

I wish I were in the country with you, one is missing so much in London & I really have not been out of it for a long time or Sunday which is admirable for my pocket but not for much else. I hope you are resting. Downing St seems a tiring place I think. Violet dear, I think you show a good deal of wisdom & self restraint in not going to many things. I think it is worth while not tiring yourself out if you can. It is rather [a] bore that you should spend yourself on Partingtons & Guests to which I do not go but that is the burden of being Prime Minister's daughter, which has its merits except sometimes for your friends, who don't see you. Bless you

Yours Bongie

V.A. to Hugh Godley   *Wednesday 22 July*
en route for London

I write in the train on my way back from Dover with a very heavy heart.

---

[1] Ethel Mary Smyth (1858–1944), composer, author and suffragette; Bongie went to see a concert performance of her most famous work, the opera *Wreckers*.

We talked the whole way there as practically as we could then I went onto the boat with him [Oc] (& nearly got left there) then 3 minutes of tearing goodbye watching the narrow strip of water between me & him inexorably widen.

I don't know anything which gives one such a feeling of complete & final severance as seeing a boat go off. I cried a little but not much & hardly at all at the time. Then I had lunch (which Father told me to) at the Lord Warden Hôtel, all alone with my cold beef it felt so funny – then I sat on the beach & was wretched & now I'm coming home – still fairly wretched. You don't know what an angel he was & how brave; I know he hated going back to 9 months in a suburban desert – I mean a deserted suburb or whatever you would call Omdurman. And I feel in a way I've had so little of him & he's wasted such a lot of his leave in London talking to the dull & left-out. If only he might have stayed for August on the rocks....

... Write V.

Venetia Stanley to V.A.   *Wednesday 5 August*
                                  Alderley Park, Chelford, Cheshire

My darling as I write this you will just about be arriving in Aberdeen. I do pray that you aren't too tired and that you haven't fainted. I have followed you very continuously in your journey and imagined exactly what you and your father looked like. If it had been a year ago you would have had 'Confessions of Belief' as a show piece, in little purpley, as it is you probably withdrew an official report (concealing a Hardy) from that extremely pompous bit of plunder you have now. Even your bag you see marks that change in you which makes it impossible for you any longer to appreciate Bongie & Arnold. Good simple souls....

I want you to read Far From The Madding Crowd and see what a plum Bongie gets in that. 'Gabriel Oak' I need hardly say, you will see at once when you have started it. I am just going to embark on the Heart of Midlothian & the life of Charlotte Brontë which I expect will keep me some time.[1] Please write Yrs V

[1] Thomas Hardy, *Far from the Madding Crowd* (1874); Sir Walter Scott, *Heart of Midlothian* (1818); [prob.] E. Gaskell, *The Life of Charlotte Brontë* (1857).

V.A. to Venetia Stanley   *Friday 7 August*
                                              Slains Castle, Aberdeenshire

My Beloved – I got yr. letter with joy this morning & smiled at your
forecast of the journey – which was fairly accurately realized. Father & I
sat among rugs & bags (the <u>divinely</u> official new dispatch box figuring
largely) from 10 in the morning till 11.30 at night when we motored out
here 30 miles through a sea-mist arriving about 1. I felt the wonderful
freed feeling that August always brings & the unspeakable joy of being on
the threshold of my 2 <u>halcyon</u> months when the porters' accents began
to change in the turnipy lowlands short of Edinburgh. This place is exactly
as we left it except for 2 new bathrooms & the Gainsborough being a little
paler.
    ... I've devoured Far From The Madding Crowd which I think very very
fine – such a wonderful atmosphere of hay isn't there – & <u>Troy</u> what a
marvellously drawn character. (What most people think A is like I'm
afraid!) Of course I thought of Bongie <u>at once</u> with Oak – what an up with
him it does give one – & Boldwood oddly enough <u>in his dealings with
Bathsheba</u> is the image of H.!!! – much more than any of them really –
because A. is not as vulgar as Troy or as vicious – or as charming & B is
only like Oak in his inarticulateness & ill-fortune, not in his strength. But
H. has Boldwood's outward dignity & reserve – & every inch of his real
madness. (Burn this sheet.) Life's Little Ironies are good too aren't they?
but almost unbearable – I'm having a tremendous Hardy wave & am just
going to begin Tess. For my solid I've got Purcell's Life of Manning (as yet
untouched) & the Inferno with Carlyle's translation opposite – you know
it. I didn't want to read it a bit as I shall have Lemon here with Greek by
Monday but the old Haverer coerced me[1]....
    Oh if only Bluetooth wasn't coming to-morrow! & the entire Tennant
family the next day – I shld. be completely happy. Come to us whenever
you want darling. I do pray you're better V.

V.A. to Venetia Stanley   *Friday 14 August*
                                            Slains Castle, Aberdeenshire

My Darling – I loved your letter – but you haven't written <u>half</u> often
enough. I have a slight fluid-ish ridge with you about it which will however
soon crystallize into IRON if not levelled by a little brisk Buxton-work.

---

[1] Thomas Hardy, *Tess of the d'Urbervilles* (1891); *Life's Little Ironies* (1894).

Life here is gloriously strenuous & healthy. I do 3 hours Greek a day with Lemon who is installed & golf with Father on far the longest & most tempestuous links in Scotland – & sit with Cys on the very edge of slimy barnacley rocks hauling up shimmering 'sathe' out of green deeps.

... The news of the clinching of Winston's engagement to the Hozier has just reached me from him, I must say I am much gladder for her sake than I am sorry for his. His wife could never be more to him than an ornamental sideboard as I have often said & she is unexacting enough not to mind not being more. Whether he will ultimately mind her being as stupid as an owl I don't know – it is a danger no doubt – but for the moment she will have rest at least from making her own clothes & I think he must be a little in love. Father thinks it spells disaster for them both (unberufen).[1] I don't know that it does that. He did not wish for – though he needs it badly – a critical, reformatory wife who would stop up the lacunas in his taste etc. & hold him back from blunders. But as in Arnold's case no one who saw these things would have the nervous system to cure them. I have wired begging them both to come here (as he was going to) on the 17th – won't it be amusing if they do? Father is a little chilly about it – & W. generally, & Margot has an odd theory that Clementine is mad! which she clings to with tenacity in spite of my assurances that she is sane to the point of dreariness. Meiklejohn is impending too – otherwise a fairly clear bit. The entire Frank Tennant family have just gone.

If you want to know what you're in for look at the vast pictures of Slains in Monday's Daily Chronicle & the Sphere & many other papers headed 'The Premier's Eyrie'!![2] I long for you dearest – mind you're not a second later than the 9th yr. V

Venetia Stanley to V.A.   *Sunday 16 August*
                              Alderley Park, Chelford, Cheshire

My darling Aren't you thrilled about Winston. How I wonder whether Clementine will become as much of a Cabinet bore as Pamela, I don't expect she will as she is too humble. Poor Pamela I'm afraid will be awfully bored at no longer being the only young liberal matron. I had a very

---

[1] In this sense the German *unberufen* is the equivalent of 'touch wood' (to ward off ill luck).

[2] Perched on a high cliff above the sea, Slains Castle looks very much like an 'eyrie'. The *Sphere* of 15 August carried a large picture, noting that it stands 'on the wildest part of the Aberdeenshire coast', and the *Daily Chronicle* of 8 August displayed a similar photograph, with the caption 'The Premier's Refuge from the Suffragists', with the wry comment: 'Even militant suffragists will find access to the castle somewhat difficult.'

ecstatic letter from Clemmy saying all the suitable things. I wonder how stupid Winston thinks her. I have just got up to see Beb out of the house, he has been here since Friday, very nice but I'm afraid rather bored, tho' he was in excellent form. It is a shame that he should have to go on working, without the solace of the cool retreat at Stanway.[1]

I've just found your letter, it made me leap with joy to see it. Isn't Eddie a gossip I suppose Katharine had told him, as it can't have been Cynthia. He does rejoice in something of the kind. I have not yet seen any pictures of Slains, but there was an excellent account of your father's day in the Daily Mail saying he enjoyed a good game of tennis every morning in the beautiful Castle grounds. I expect you saw it. Also what do you think of Clementine's accomplishments as set forth in the Manchester Guardian – six languages, a good musician, a brilliant conversationalist. Surely that influences Margot's opinion a little. Father has a theory that her mother is mad, but I've never heard any doubt cast as to her sanity. I think he must be a good deal in love with her to face such a mother in law....

... In three weeks I shall almost be at Slains. I count the days.... Your Venetia

Arnold Ward to V.A.   *Sunday 30 August*
                          Alderley Park, Chelford, Cheshire

Dear Violet

Your very kind & interesting letter was received with gratitude and very much appreciated. It must be delightful to be back at Slains, redolent of Early Violantine vivacities, black silk ballets, and brown Beb fishing in a brown pond.

It must be delightful to look back over the interval between the two Slains. And to consider how some types of vessel, once formidable assailants, are now obsolete hulks: others, once experimental toys, now successfully perfected monsters of the air & deep. But I can't help feeling anxious as to the prudence of allowing the Omnipotent [HHA] to reside at Slains, as it is such an exposed place in the event of a sudden German raid.

Thank you very much for most kind invitation to revisit scene of highly valued recollections. I should very much like to be allowed to do so, and

---

[1] Beb was then well advanced in his courtship of Cynthia, whose parents put a bar on him visiting the Charteris home at Stanway, in Gloucestershire. It is not clear why this obstacle was placed in Beb's path, but by the autumn he had found ways around it (see below, p. 166). He and Cynthia were married in July 1910.

could come on 11th or on any subsequent day during September which was convenient to Polar plans. . . .

Apologies humbly tendered for lack of attendance at Downing Street, due to circumstances entirely beyond Arnoldian control. Naming of time of pilgrimage humbly requested. Arnold.

'Premier's daughter missing . . . House party's thrilling search'

During the Asquiths' 1908 autumn holiday at Slains Castle, in Aberdeenshire, Violet was at the centre of a bizarre episode that briefly made headlines in the national press.[1] Just before dinner on Saturday 19 September she told her maid that she was going out on to the cliff-tops, in search of a book that she had left there earlier in the day. When she failed to return for dinner the assembled house party grew alarmed. Darkness had by then fallen, and the guests began a search, assisted by the coastguard and the local police. Three hours later Violet was found lying unconscious on the cliff-tops at nearby Cruden. She was carried back to the castle, and attended by a local doctor. Thereafter her recovery was fairly swift, and there were no lasting effects from the accident, the circumstances of which remain unclear. Violet later claimed in a letter to Arnold Ward that she had slipped as she was climbing down the cliff to retrieve her book: 'I slid scraping & scratching with my knees & palms – then a jutting ledge underneath knocked me outward like a ball & I fell down about 7ft onto the back of my head. Why my skull wasn't smashed into smithereens I can't think.' But the press reports gave no indication of a fall. They mentioned only a 'faint', surmising that 'the darkness and eeriness of the lonely cliffs had acted on her nerves'. The episode is perhaps revealing of an attention-seeking side of Violet's character, and it increased the tension in her relationship with Margot, who recalled in her diary:

'I was considered very unsympathetic because I didn't think this unfortunate foolish and <u>most</u> dangerous episode should be made too much of – constant talk of all that was said & that happened; charts of her temp. copied out & distributed, newspaper cuttings, letters & telegrams all of course dwelling on the affair put into her

---

[1] The *Daily Graphic* and the *Daily Chronicle* of Tuesday 22 September each carried a similar story, based on an extensive report that appeared in the local *Aberdeen Free Press*. The headlines stressed the potential dangers to which Violet had been exposed: 'Miss Asquith's adventure', 'Search party's long quest', 'Dangerous plight', 'Found unconscious on heights at Cruden', etc.

hands at all hours could not be good for any one of V's temperament – I wanted her just to thank the fishermen & poor people who had found her & to say nothing more about it: poor Violet! Nothing was further from her ideas & she felt hurt I cd. see by my attitude'.[1]

Hugh Godley to V.A.   *Tuesday 22 September*
29 Sloane Gardens, S.W.

My very dearest, I have just got back here, & have not had an answer to my telegram yet, but I at once rang up Viola & found out from her that you were really recovering, & all about it. I can't imagine what you must all have gone through. The notice in the Dublin paper simply said that much excitement had been caused at Cruden Bay by a rumour that Miss Violet Asquith had fallen over the cliffs, then after a good deal more came at last your Father's telegram to say that at least you were alive. I can't describe to you what I felt; I have never known anything like it; & being on a ship in the middle of the sea gave one a curiously helpless feeling – though of course even on shore one could only have sent useless telegrams.

I got a much more reassuring paper at Euston; but as I drove through London the streets were covered with immense affiches

'PREMIER'S DAUGHTER MISSING
MISS ASQUITH'S ADVENTURE
HOUSE PARTY'S THRILLING SEARCH'
&c &c.
The Daily Graphic has a large portrait.

Bless you my dearest, & Thank God that nothing worse has happened. I will write from North Coast. I am only here for a minute or two. H.

V.A. to Venetia Stanley   *Friday 16 October*
Archerfield House, Dirleton,
East Lothian

My very Dearest – <u>Don't</u> be angry with me – this is nearly my first letter since I saw you last – & the only others were to Ld. Curzon & Mr.

[1] Diary of Margot Asquith, 1907–9, p. 125; Bonham Carter MSS.

Cracknell & a line to keep H. out of the Thames[1] – & I've got 28 letters of inquiry from <u>blighters</u> to answer directly I've done this – besides K, & Frances & Ettie & up-till-now unfed Bongie, & poor little Oc in the burning sand & divine Cyril & the Old Haverer & Sir John Williams & Aubrey & Arnold & Bluetooth & Felix & Foxie & all the Secretaries & superidi [*sic*] Bongies & odd-men in Downing St & Father himself. <u>Oh</u> when shall I ever ever get them done? ...

Thursday back here in the evening to find that Beb (who had apparently lain low at Hyndford all that week) had been dentisting with Cynthia since early morning & that they'd had all their meals alone!! Wasn't it like them – How pathetically futile parental precautions are. . . .

Write at once darling to Yr V. Burn this letter because of vulgar allusions to various navigations.

V.A. to Edwin Montagu   *Monday 19 October*
                                        Archerfield House, Dirleton,
                                                    East Lothian

Dear Mr. Montagu.

Thank you so much for writing about my accident. I wasn't given your letter while I had a respectable temperature of 106 – & now I'm ashamed to say I'm drearily normal again in every way so it seems very flat to answer it. I escaped death narrowly in about 5 different ways – such as drowning, smashing into smithereens, brain fever, 'exposure' (!) etc etc – but now I feel as far away from it as ever.

How did your holidays go off & what a coward you were not to come to Slains. Which of the bugbears kept you away – probable death, certain loneliness, or the Balliol Mind???

You must be pretty busy now I expect – tell me if anything exciting happens won't you. <u>What</u> <u>do</u> <u>you</u> <u>think</u> <u>of</u> <u>McKinnon</u> <u>Wood's</u> <u>appointment</u>[2]

I am coming on the 12th Nov.

                              Yrs Violet Asquith

---

[1] George Curzon (1859–1925), viceroy and governor-general of India, 1899–1905, and an Irish representative peer from 1908. He was a 'Soul', and a friend of Margot Asquith from the days before her marriage.

[2] Thomas McKinnon Wood (1855–1927), Liberal MP for St Rollox, Glasgow; appointed under-secretary of state at the foreign office, October 1908.

Edwin Montagu to V.A. *Saturday 24 October*
59 Bridge Street, Cambridge

Dear Violet

If I don't write to you by means of the type-writer I never shall, and so I think that you will have to excuse my resorting to this weapon.

You <u>do</u> seem to have had a bad time; but you must not talk of brain-fever because I have been brought up to believe that there is no such thing, and I had far rather think that you were contemplating death from exposure, which always sounds to me so audacious and courageous, than from anything so unsightly as drowning or smithereening.

My holidays were a transcendant success, for I satiated a sponge-like blood-lust and killed, killed, killed! . . .

Am I to take up your challenge about Slains? I wanted to come because the name attracted me; I wanted to come because staying with you is always delightful at the time and only frightening to contemplate, and afterwards most of my complaints emanate from the fact that they afford a convenient basis for some of my pet theories. But for he or is it him who plays no golf, climbs no rocks, never exposes his over-rated body to any physical danger, plays only one game (which I think you think is rather low) and, yes, comes from Cambridge, Slains was more frightening than your normal seats.[1] Besides, the light which beats around you now is so appalling fierce – and when you take a house by the sea and instead of a mere dinghy at your landing-stage you have the 'Enchantress' it is no place for humble folk like me.[2] Besides, there was the effort of really deciding which shoot I should give up to fix a date, and when the date was fixed for me the notice was too short. . . .

Yes, I am pretty busy because I am most fearful keen on the Licensing Bill, which I think the best thing we are doing. But I rather suspect that a large part of our party will not be sorry if it is chucked out. They want money from the poor trade next year. It is a poor game from some points of view because when the Bill is in the House I am not allowed to speak and quite rightly. Samuel, of whom in this connexion I am extraordinarily jealous, does all the talking.[3] He is getting a very great man now, and yet I am afraid loses none of his goodness.

[1] The only game that there is record of Montagu playing, and being good at, is cricket (see Naomi B. Levine, *Politics, Religion and Love*, 30).

[2] The *Enchantress* was the admiralty yacht, at the disposal of the first lord (then Reginald McKenna) for official entertainment, and used by him to make inspections of naval bases.

[3] Herbert Louis Samuel (1870–1963), Liberal MP for Cleveland, North Riding, 1902–18; parliamentary under-secretary at the home department, 1905–9; chancellor of the duchy of Lancaster, 1909–10; postmaster-general 1910–14.

What do I think of McKinnon Wood's appointment? Extraordinarily safe. I am convinced that no international imbroglio will ever be the result of him. Thank God, he is not a journalist. The House is amused at its safety and the way it has caused the avoidance of Trevelyan in that office.[1] I wish you had been in the House last Wednesday. Our Man surpassed everything that I have ever heard in the House.[2] And silenced all of those who differed from him. Two things have resulted which make me want to shake the party of progress. The Labour Party thoroughly satisfied with what he said are compelled by the methods that they have chosen to prove their raison d'être and are pretending not to be satisfied, and many of the knock-kneed poltroons who form our party, after trembling for a fortnight that the Whig element which they are so fond of talking about in the Cabinet would prevent us going far enough, now turn round and say that once again we are 'on the knee' to Socialism. Let me assure you that it was an awkward parliamentary situation, as awkward as I have seen. Various conflicting private and public forces intra- and extra-governmental were battling for an excuse and an opportunity. He got over the lot! – and on we go to the next bad place.

How long are you coming for on the 12th? I suppose the usual thing will happen. You will immure yourself somewhere in the fastnesses of Downing Street for a month or two. I shall know of your presence by an occasional hat, and very possibly I shall charge against you one day in the passage to find that you are about to leave London. But if you are ever inclined for a new form of boredom ring the bell and tell your messenger, secretary, maid, or what-not, to lure me from the company of the muttering Meiklejohn.

   Yrs Edwin Montagu

Churchill, Lloyd George and foreign policy: 1908–1909

In late October 1908 Violet was prevented from speaking on the same public platform as Winston Churchill, by a telegram from her father. Only weeks before she had been involved in a cliff-top

---

[1] Charles Philips Trevelyan (1870–1958), Liberal MP for Elland, Yorkshire, 1899–1918; parliamentary secretary at the board of education from April 1908. Trevelyan was known for his strong views on foreign policy; he was often critical of his own leadership, and resigned in August 1914 in protest against British intervention in the European war.

[2] In parliament on Wednesday 21 October, Asquith made a detailed statement on the government's immediate plans to deal with the exceptionally high levels of unemployment, greater than at any time since 1886. The government proposed to increase the loans made available to local authorities for public works, and also to accelerate the building programmes of government departments. His plans won the qualified approval of *The Times*, as having struck the right balance between philanthropic intent and sound finance.

accident at Slains, but his 'prohibition' was not because of special
concern for her health (the 'hygienic' grounds that Violet mentions
in her letter to Venetia Stanley, below). The prohibition stemmed
instead from Asquith's dissatisfaction with Churchill's unau-
thorized interventions into foreign policy. In alliance with Lloyd
George, Churchill was then vigorously opposing increases in the
naval estimates, to make money available for social reform. In
order to justify reductions in those estimates, at a time when
Britain was involved in a naval building race with Germany, it was
necessary to minimize the danger of conflict between the two
countries. To this end Churchill scouted the notion of a war with
Germany in a speech at Swansea on 17 August 1908. The speech
was well received in Germany, and Lloyd George, then in Hamburg,
telegraphed a message of congratulation.[1] Their joint efforts at
reaching an Anglo-German accord differed markedly in content
and style from those being made at the same time by the King.
After a meeting with the Kaiser on 11 August, the King wrote to
Sir Charles Hardinge, at the foreign office, complaining at the
behaviour of his chancellor and his president of the board of trade:
'I cannot conceive how the Prime Minister allows them ever to
make speeches on Foreign Affairs, concerning which they know
nothing'.[2] While Asquith disapproved of his ministers' conduct,
he was obliged to recognize the support that they enjoyed among
radical, anti-militarist Liberals. The dangers of war with Germany
were soon underlined, however, by the international crisis that
followed the Austro-Hungarian annexation of Bosnia and Herze-
govina, on 7 October 1908. On 6 November Asquith informed
Balfour that 'the internal conditions of Germany were so unsatisfactory that they might be driven to the wildest adventures'. An
attack on France through Belgium 'might prove irresistible', in
which case Britain could be drawn into a European war in defence
of Belgian neutrality.[3] The crisis of 1908, which subsided without
conflict, eerily foreshadows the events of 1914: by then Churchill
was a determined advocate of naval spending. In the winter of
1908, however, he was an 'economist', and with Lloyd George
exerted great pressure on Asquith to reduce the naval budget. In
February 1909 Asquith complained: '[they] go about darkly hinting

[1] See Randolph Churchill, *Winston S. Churchill: Young Statesman, 1901–1914*, 282, 511–14.

[2] Philip Magnus, *King Edward the Seventh*, 411.

[3] A. J. Balfour to Lord Lansdowne, 6 November 1908; quoted in Kenneth Young, *Arthur James Balfour*, 271.

at resignation (which is bluff) ... but there are moments when I
am disposed summarily to cashier them both'.[1]

V.A. to Venetia Stanley   *Tuesday 27 October*
                                      Archerfield House, Dirleton,
                                                    East Lothian

My Dearest – I <u>have</u> loved both your letters & now thank Heaven the
Albatross is <u>off</u>! & I can resume my normal clockwork Buxton. Life here is
very renewing & I can feel my springs getting back into wonderful condition – they have been a little less resilient than usual since the rock-
affair & no wonder – but now I am gathering steam & impetus daily &
emitting very little. Archerfield is an ideal cocoon.... I am slowly picking
up Greek threads & go into Lemon twice a week. I nearly spoke for Winston
at a meeting in the Oddfellows (!) Hall but was stopped by a wire from
O.S. I was sorry as I had thought of one or two things I quite wanted to
say!! but the prohibition was not on hygienic but political grounds which
reconciled me a good deal to it. I gather there is a slight recrudescence of
the summer Winston-down – don't <u>breath</u>-this.
     What do you think of <u>Raymond</u> having a daughter? isn't it funny &
thrilling? I wired to K. (who wanted a boy) 'never mind its being a girl she
will be like Helen' (meaning 'of Troy') & now I hear R. wants to call her
Helen – which was our Mother's name[2] ....
     ... When M. has gone back here again I shall see Douglas Powell &
get my Montana doom definitely sealed or lifted.[3] I am cheered by the

---

[1] See Randolph Churchill, *Winston S. Churchill: Young Statesman, 1901–1914*, 517.

[2] Writing to congratulate Violet, Archie Gordon recounted how he had been told the news
by her father: 'I came in, saw O.S. who said "Well, have you heard of the event in our
family?" – very weightily, I blanched, then simpered, & asked the truth, with the usual
appendage – "Is it a boy". "No, <u>not</u> a boy", said O.S. with such fearful solemnity. Now I had
an awful fear of <u>twins</u> for a second, then relief ... We tried to imagine the relationship of R. &
a <u>daughter</u> – almost the most incongruous in the realm of hypotheses' (22 October 1908).
Bongie observed: 'Raymond accepts his daughter as if she were a Varsity scholarship. I do not
mean that he is not pleased, as he obviously is, but I do not think that he would dream of
mentioning it to anyone as a possible piece of news of interest' (28 October 1908). After
Asquith was made an earl, in 1925, both Helen and her younger sister Perdita were granted
the courtesy title of 'Lady', as if their father, Raymond, had lived to inherit his father's
earldom: he had been killed on the Somme in September 1916.

[3] Violet feared being sent to Montana for health reasons, as had happened the previous
spring; cold air and altitude were considered beneficial to chest complaints, from which she
was suffering. There was of course a constant fear of tuberculosis.

thought that if I do go <u>divine</u> Cyril will be removed from Winchester & go with me. But E. Fräu Puffin & M. too! Write again at once please darling Yr V.

V.A. to Venetia Stanley
Friday 20 November
10 Downing Street, Whitehall,
S.W.

My Beloved. It was a joy to see your writing & to hear the horrid wound will soon be allowed to close. . . . I have had the usual dentist press of the first few days – Hughley is wonderfully balanced & happy, consequent <u>giant</u> up – A. quite speechless with glumse (worse than this May) & extremely importunate – using the 'last-day-before-I-go-to-America-where-I-shall-probably-be-till-after-Easter' plea very freely. Bongie is equable & rather bald, Charlie Meade bearded & mild, Eddie as yet unseen, the Lizard exceptionally civil. I lunched with Clemmie & Winston on Tuesday & drove him to the House in a taximetre afterwards during which time he confided to me that Clemmie had more in her than met the eye <u>Padlock</u> I thought I got out rather well from a point of view of combined truth & emollient as I cloyingly reiterated: 'But so much meets the eye'. Archie has as you've probably heard been made Dunn's <u>partner</u> (which means an income of 2 to 3 thousand a year <u>at once</u> – awkward for me) & he brought the great man to lunch to-day.[1] I was on the whole relieved. He does look too young to be <u>very</u> wicked & though not very like a gentleman he is not <u>very</u> unlike one. . . .

I have got into D-D Lyttelton's clutches & go to an <u>embroidery</u> class! once a week at her house! isn't that a funny thing for me to do? & I write letters for Miss Violet Markham for $1\frac{1}{2}$ hours a day about this personal service thing for the Unemployed.[2] So altogether I feel I've taken a turn for the better. . . . Father & I have got Sat to Mon parties at Ewelme which

---

[1] Even at the lower end of the suggested scale, Archie's starting salary was remarkably high, and was more than enough for him to marry on: his prospective father-in-law's ministerial salary was £5,000.

[2] The Personal Service Association was a philanthropic body established in London in 1908, in response to the high level of unemployment. It co-ordinated and directed the work of volunteers who wished to establish 'personal relations with their less fortunate fellow-citizens'. Edith 'D.D.' Lyttelton was its chairwoman, and its honorary secretary was Violet Markham (1872–1959), daughter of a wealthy Derbyshire colliery owner. Markham had a notable career as a public administrator, educationalist and Liberal activist.

has been lent us by the Israelite (Lawso) but I cld. come any Mon to Sat after this next week.

Bless you my <u>Dearest</u> I think of you unceasingly yr V.

Archie Gordon to V.A.   *Friday 11 December*
                              R.M.S. Lusitania, en route for New York

My V. This curious blank interval of no-man's land has not been a very great success. I had hoped for novel sensations, experiences & acquaintances. Instead, something closely resembling a hyper-dull hotel with the doors & windows shut.

I came on that morning at Queenstown with a real thrill, having been quite affected by the pink sky & the steel sea, & the monster ship in waiting – as well as by the emotion of some Irish emigrants who were thoroughly conscious of being engaged in the most momentous act of their lives. They behaved just like people at a wedding. – Before lunch I had discovered that nine tenths of the passengers were Jew commercial travellers, & before dinner we were struggling in a gale, & everybody was sick.

The first three days were all the same. I was one of the very few who were unaffected by the pitch & toss, but I was thoroughly depressed by the vibration & general discomfort & lack of exercise. Dunn was trying to pretend he wasn't ill, & was in a terrible temper, & Mrs D. (who came after all) had neuralgia.

I exchanged a few remarks w. John Revelstoke daily, & didn't find him very attractive – also, when I introduced Dunn to him & they talked, J.R. took the opportunity of saying to D. (à propos of me) that <u>he</u> had tried to train up many young Englishmen in <u>his</u> office, but they were never any good, & he didn't suppose Dunn wd. do any better! I bore him malice for this.

All round an atmosphere of snappiness. Dunn frequently down my throat. The last two days have been much better. The sea calmed, the sun came out, & people hitherto undreamt of came out like rabbits.

Among them Melba, in great spirits & full of arch Archerfield harkings.[1] I played Bridge with her & her retinue.

---

[1] Dame Nellie Melba (1861–1931), Australian-born opera singer, who became famous in England in the 1880s and 1890s, appearing many times at Covent Garden. With Archie and Violet, she had been at a house party at Archerfield early in November. In a letter to Bongie, Violet wrote of her: '[she] is an extraordinary creature. Very colonial & colossally built (of course) but with the manners of a wispy minx. She looks less like Grandmamma Melland in real life than when singing Traviata' (VA to MBC, 5 November 1908).

Now we are near New York. When we are once landed I shall realize rather more sharply what has hit me a good many times on this dreary ship – distance & still more <u>inaccessibility</u> of <u>you</u>. It will be no good my writing to you about it – it is to be a condition of existence for some time – a commonplace. It gives me an odd sensation which I am sure Nelson would have if you took him off his pillar & put him to walk down in Whitehall.

I won't weary you w. plaints. – you will have been w. Venetia, – sadly, I fear, for the most part. I shall hope, faintly, to hear about it from you....

Bless you – dear one. I am there with you when you want me – (& when you <u>don't</u>, I am afraid?) Yr A

Archie Gordon to V.A.   *Saturday 19 December*
The Plaza, New York

My V. Owing to the tempestuous weather no English mail has got here yet since I arrived, so I am without news of you, & feel horribly out of date & isolated.

It would be easy here to forget that such a thing as England had ever existed. The papers contain not a <u>word</u> of news from outside America – for all I know there has been a General Election & the King is dead....

– Things have been going much better. Dunn mellow, & a number of interesting men & women met. Not conspicuously among this last some cousins of Arnold's, who have been very kind to me, & who are strangely Stocks-ish in general type. They dislike & deprecate Arnold a good deal. They gave a dance, which I went to – where all the men were the same age & had the same faces, & looked ridiculously <u>un</u>-ballroom-y, & where the women promised <u>half</u>-dances. A plan wh. might commend itself to you.

I am going up to stay with the Greys about Christmas day. & shall <u>sail</u> very soon after N.Y. – Dunn having found he will have to stay some time & not wishing to keep me uselessly here, which is good. I hope I shall get a schedule of yr. movements in January, so as to get an early view of you. I feel Taplow toils closing, & I also feel you getting out of them.

I pray you are being happy, most dear one. Bless you. yr A

V.A. to Venetia Stanley   *Tuesday 26 January 1909*
Grand Hôtel Victoria,
St Beatenberg, Switzerland

My Beloved – You don't know how wonderful it was to find my little foul room here (furnished with oil-cloth & hot water pipes) full of yr. divine carnations & violets & roses – thank you ten thousand times my dearest – you are the most magical friend anyone ever had. Also a sumptuous box of brown luxury from Barbellion! You do spoil me – & I do love it so – & you! – Travelling out here alone with Cys was like an adventure in the Arabian nights, so thrilling – & fancy we didn't miss one train or lose one object (except 8 books left in the Foyot – loose! which I hope will be sent on) & in spite of giving a franc to everyone we met we've arrived with far more money than we started with.

I was very ahuri at Victoria & could not calm myself sufficiently to distinguish anyone from anyone else – & lost Bluetooth & disregarded Hughley & flung rugs & bags at Meiklejohn & yelled to Philip – 'write to me constantly won't you' – to which he replied 'Yes Miss' with splendid impassivity quite untinged by surprise. Bongie came to Dover & was funny on the white cliffs till they melted out of sight with him. We had a smoothish ice-cold crossing – & then ¼ of an hour's anguish in that Hell of Douane mangled & mauled by everyone in the world's luggage – final production of the F.O. Sesame & installation in the crowded Paris train where I found myself beside Lord Vernon! with whom I had a long & good talk about Turkey & Aubrey – whose position out there he gave a very good account of.[1] At Paris was Archie with a Swift & Reliable. We visited Mdme Casaubon & then went on to the Foyot where Arnold was grappling with the menu. The waiter suggested chevreuil.
Arnold – (perplexed – adenoidally) : Est-ce que cela demeure dans la forêt – ou est ce que cela demeure dans la ferme?
Waiter – Dans la forêt Monsieur
Arnold – (still nasal & hesitant) Est-ce que cela est bon pour les dames ? (glancing solicitously at me)
On the waiter affirming that it was we had chevreuil![2]
Afterwards we all went to the station together & established ourselves in our salon-lits – (which are infinitely nicer than those stuffy berths). Arnold was much disconcerted on finding a swarthy stranger was going to spend the night with us & in spite of my assurances as to the futility of

---

[1] George Venables-Vernon (1888–1915), 8th Baron Vernon; honorary attaché in Constantinople, 1908; at the British legation at Munich, 1909.

[2] In response to the waiter's suggestion of venison (*chevreuil*), Arnold asks: 'Does it live in the forest – or does it live on the farm?. . . Is it suitable for ladies?'

the enterprise insisted on abordée-ing the guard & summarily ordered his removal. I overheard the guard protesting : 'Mais le train est plein m'sieur tout est complet. C'est impossible' – & Arnold with his most magnificent gesture 'Impossible? On peut franchir les Alpes n'est ce pas?'[1] – but needless to say the stranger remained to A. & A's disgust. Archie said to me 'You won't take off much – will you?' rather nervously! which made me rock! I lay down in my red dressing gown & Cys & I talked a lot & slept a little & breakfasted off honey at Bern in the cleanest coldest sunniest air you can imagine. Then on to Interlaken & 2 hours drive up the mountain – rather like Montana only lower which means less snow (it is <u>dreadfully</u> scarce & patchy) but there is oddly enough a finer view because the valley is narrower & all the giants on the other side Jungfrau, Mönch, Eiger, Schneckhorn etc. are nearer to one than 'Ruskin's favourite mountain' used to be there.[2] There are more trees & rocks & things to see & places to go to than at M. but I foresee the ski-ing will be worse even when it does snow....

My Dearest & Best every moment's acutest joy I have with Cys sends a shoot of anguished realization through me for you.[3] I feel I <u>couldn't</u> bear it – your courage fills me with wonder & reverence. I think of you & love you in the depths of my heart always – all ways Yr V.

Oh!!! the post has just brought the dream of my life a blue shawl – but Darling you <u>must</u> <u>not</u> give it me you <u>mustn't</u>. I will wear it for you till you can with the greatest gratefulness. I do <u>love</u> it. It's my favourite thing.

The 1909 'People's Budget'

When the new session of parliament began in February 1909, Liberal morale was at a low ebb. During three years in office the party had seen its majority in the Commons repeatedly overridden by an unelected Unionist majority in the Lords. Only a funda-mental change in either the composition or the powers of the upper chamber could correct this, and nothing of the sort was outlined in the legislative programme for the coming session. The government, though, was about to take the offensive, through its budget for the coming year. Lloyd George needed to raise nearly £16 million in new revenue, with which to fund old-age pensions and the construction of Dreadnought battleships. In meeting this deficit he planned to take advantage of the convention that money

---

[1] 'But the train is full, monsieur, every seat has been taken. It is impossible' ... 'Impossible? The Alps can be crossed, can't they?'

[2] John Ruskin (1819–1900) spent time painting at Chamonix, from where he would have seen Mont Blanc.

[3] Venetia's brother, Hon. Edward Stanley, had died of illness in Africa late in 1908.

bills were the sole concern of the House of Commons. He would force upon the peers a 'People's Budget', one that redistributed the burden of taxation on to the wealthy and landed classes. To this end he introduced a super-tax on incomes above £3,000 a year, and increased the death duty payable on inherited estates. The budget also included four new land taxes, which met with violent opposition from landowners. These would raise a modest £500,000 only, but their implementation would necessitate a complete valuation of all land, and prepare the way for Liberal land reform. Prior to his budget speech, on 29 April, Lloyd George was told that no chancellor had ever before enacted such heavy taxation in peacetime. In the Commons he made this his battle-cry, declaring, 'This is a war budget! It is a Budget for waging implacable warfare against poverty.' The peers regarded it as an act of war directed against them, and on 30 November 1909 they rejected the bill. The conflict then took on another form. What had begun nominally as a battle over finance became overtly a battle over democracy.

Edwin Montagu to V.A.   *Saturday 13 February*
59 Bridge Street, Cambridge

Dear Miss Asquith,

I thank you most sincerely for your letter. I only wish that you would write oftener....

I can imagine you kicking about in a whirl of snow and cold, and sun and frost-bite, and public-school boys' sports, and Dr Lunn, and skis and châlets and pine trees, and glaciers and avalanches, and diaries, and I do not think that I will write you much more. But thinking of what I have written I am rather afraid that I have not set a bait for a reply, so I am going to unload my mind.

Things are not well in London. The Constituencies are in excellent heart, ready and eager to be led, but dismayed for want of a lead. The fireworks of last Session are to be succeeded by soaked squibs this Session. People are complaining of your father's silence, and it almost looks as if your father did not know what to do. Politicians are getting weak-kneed, constituents are getting more and more enthusiastic. As my confidence in your father grows my lack of confidence in his colleagues grows too. I hope to goodness history won't say that they proved too strong for him. And as for Winston – you can if you like discount everything I say because of my ungovernable prejudice against him; but I deny altogether that

Birmingham was abnormal;[1] it was the true Winston – cowardly at the last pinch, vague and hasty, with no thought or depth; and what you call the normal, is the restraint of the actor. You ask that he may be controlled by his wife. I do not know her, but I should not have thought that she would have set herself, or would be able, to control anybody, and that she worships unreasoningly, that she has married not to improve, but to adorate. And as for Marsh – why should he interfere with the amusement he gets from the antics of his chief? Winston hates his present office – longs for other men's shoes, and – oh well – enough said! I daren't go on!

Meanwhile, Haldane makes at least 75 thousand speeches a week and nobody reads or listens to them. The Cabinet sits every day and its deliberations are published in the newspapers, and all the time we poor Members keep our Constituents in feverish expectation of the great day that is to come when – ! And the newspapers publish growls at the Government, vide The Daily News, The British Weekly, The Nation and even The Westminster Gazette.[2]

You don't know how well we get on here in Cambridgeshire. If only I felt certain that better political instinct would rule in Town. Yrs ever Edwin S. Montagu.

V.A. to Edwin Montagu

Saturday 13 March
Montana

Dear Mr. Montagu.

You must have thought me very ungrateful not to have answered your last excellent letter before now – but I have been afraid of warding off all others for life by the nature of my reply. This place doesn't furnish good straw to make letters out of – & rather than write you an Alpine one (full

---

[1] On Wednesday 13 January 1909, Churchill addressed the Birmingham Liberal Club, as its president, and dwelt at length upon the Unionist peers' obstruction of Liberal legislation. He invited the peers to reject the budget, too, thereby perpetrating a 'constitutional outrage' that he was certain would lead to their downfall: 'I should be quite content to see the battle joined as speedily as possible upon the plain simple use of aristocratic rule against representative government' (*The Times*, 14 January 1909). Whatever else it was, Churchill's speech was prescient, anticipating both the nature of the political battle ahead in 1909–11, and its outcome.

[2] All of the papers mentioned were Liberal, but the *Westminster Gazette*, an evening paper edited by J. A. Spender, was the most loyal to Asquith's government. Successive Liberal whips had been involved in its financial affairs, and when it was in danger of collapse, 1908–9, Asquith allowed his name to be used to attract investors. See Stephen Koss, *The Rise and Fall of the Political Press in Britain*, 541.

of 'skis & Glaciers & Dr. Lunn & diaries & avalanches') I will confine myself to monosyllabic thanks. But <u>very</u> grateful ones. You really have been an angel in keeping me au courant of things. I hope all is smoother now than when you wrote. I really don't know what programme of campaign against the Lords the constituencies were expecting. I thought it was understood that all punitive measures were going to be contained in the 'predatory' Budget to come. À-propos of Budgets how <u>abominable</u> of Lloyd George – (at least I suppose it was him) to give away the Navy Estimates dissensions to the Daily Chronicle. Father is very much handicapped in coping with squalid little situations like that by his generosity & big-ness of heart – & aloofness from all suspicion. But I <u>do</u> think it's inexcusable to trade on this absence of 'governessiness'. Ponsonby too behaved pretty badly – but it gave Father a good opportunity of stating his position which I thought he did very satisfactorily.[1] I wish I'd seen yr. weekly letters to him during this period! Has he been 'discouraging, irrelevant, & off-the-point' lately? That was what you were scolding him for just before I went away.

I shall be home on Tuesday about tea-time – in <u>transports</u> of joy & relief. Don't accuse me of imparting this news 'as if it were likely to be of importance to you' as you once before did! I hope you will see me for more than 4 minutes between now & Easter. Yrs.

Violet Asquith

I don't agree with you about Winston – as you know.

Edwin Montagu to V.A.   *Tuesday 13 April*
10 Downing Street, Whitehall,
S.W.

My dear Miss Asquith
    I wonder whether you have found a minute to investigate my purpose during the time I was making inordinate 'draughts' upon your patience yesterday.

---

[1] In the debate on the address from the throne, 22 February 1909, the Liberal MP Arthur Augustus Ponsonby (1871–1946) attacked the government for not committing itself to reform of the House of Lords in the coming session. He proposed an amendment to the King's speech to rectify this. Ponsonby's loyalties lay with the past and not the present Liberal leadership: he succeeded Campbell-Bannerman as member for Stirling Burghs, 1908–18, and his motion amounted to a vote of censure on the government. Asquith made a confident response, explaining that the government had decided not to make reform of the House of Lords its priority, even though it accepted its overriding importance, because to do so would entail an election, and the premature end of the government and its other legislative plans.

Smitten with keen pangs of fear that I may be acting without absolute candour in my [Lloyd] Georgian excursions, I denied the sympathy if I could get it of a keen observer who has always shown me surprising toleration of my vagaries.

I do not regard the existence of camps and cabals – they are to be recognised neither by the head of the Gov. or by his myrmidons – but only by his colleagues. And so I work with those that want me – for him and him only. But lest you may hear in the language of those that think in terms of conspiracy of my meanderings in Wales I felt uneasy lest there might at least appear to be good ground for the assertion that I was deceiving everybody in turn.

I know I have the reputation for ambition inordinate and ludicrous. The death of that ambition – and how it is dying faster and faster with the growth of loneliness and solitude and old age I alone know – makes no difference but it barbs the shafts of those who are acquainted with it.

And so I talked, on and on, to you. I am ashamed of it rather now for after all, what does it matter. But if you will forget it all and the sordid thoughts of those about whom I prattled, I shall have one more reason for gratitude

My very best regards to the [?] Olive Macleod

Yrs Edwin S. Montagu

V.A. to Edwin Montagu   *Friday 23 April*
Sealand, Littlestone-on-Sea, Kent

Dear Mr. Montagu.

Do send me a line about Father's Glasgow speech, it read very well – I wish I had heard it like you did.[1]

Thank you for your letter – I have never dreamt of any lack of candour on your side either in your relations with Father (!) or in your relations with Ll.G. All I meant was that the slightest misconstruction of yr. motives in Georgian quarters (by them not by us of course) wld. be too heavy a price to pay for any advantages reaped – (such as indiscretions elicited, influence gained etc). I think Ll.G. should realize the definiteness of yr. position, see it in black & white, not in mauve & grey. He probably does not believe in loyalty anywhere – not knowing what it means himself. I hear (this is between ourselves) that he was furious with Thring for sending

---

[1] Asquith addressed a large Liberal gathering at the St Andrew's Hall, Glasgow, on 19 April 1909. In his speech he attempted to reconcile the government's decision to spend more on naval building with its continued commitment to social reform.

<u>Father</u> a copy of the Finance Bill!! Don't repeat this – it really is too grotesque to believe.

I'm afraid Welsh Disestablishment won't make us more popular – but I suppose it was a pledge & had to be gone through with.[1]

We've had such divinely peaceful days here – sunny, windy, flatness & larks singing & lambs bounding & windmills twirling all day long. I am coming up for the Budget – 29th isn't it?

        yrs. Violet Asquith

Edwin Montagu to V.A.   *Tuesday 27 April*
                                      10 Downing Street, Whitehall,
                                                          S.W.

Dear Miss Asquith

To my shame I have not answered your letter and now you are here....

I quite see what you mean about [Lloyd] George. I've given up. Partly because I see what you think about it although you don't say it – it's dishonesty you see in it. And I don't think I can make you see it properly....

Where did you hear the story of the bill which Thring did <u>not</u> send but was accused of sending to the P.M.

I long for the twirling rabbits and the skipping windmills. Of course you are dining with me on Thursday.

        Yrs Ed S. Montagu

Hugh Godley to V.A.   *Wednesday 12 May*
                                    Office of the Parliamentary
                                      Counsel, Whitehall, S.W.

My dearest Violet

I have torn up a long letter which I was writing you about the Budget. It seemed so ludicrous & grotesque solemnly to sit down & pen my views on economical & social questions. We will talk more about it, or we won't.

---

[1] The government's proposals for ending the special privileges of the Anglican church in Wales were delayed by the conflict with the House of Lords, which followed the peers' rejection of the 1909 budget; a bill for Welsh disestablishment was not introduced until April 1912. As Violet indicates, the measure was not likely to win many votes. It was, though, integral to Liberal objectives, as defined in the 1891 Newcastle Programme. Asquith had himself introduced the Welsh Disestablishment bill of 1895.

I think 'undeveloped land' is the only thing I really object to & that probably because it will I think completely remove any value at present attaching to the only valuable property belonging to my poor brother in law, who can hardly be accused of being a rich man. Your Father told me at L[ittlestone]. that he thought the tax was 'very hard to defend', so as it raises practically nothing perhaps they will drop it.[1] Anyhow it is of small consequence what happens to one man or another.

I know I am bad tempered but I am very humble about my views on any subject, & the fact that I feel strongly on any subject usually makes me doubt my rectitude; you are on the other hand angelic tempered but <u>colossally arrogant</u> about your views to the point of despising & rejecting people who differ from them. Aren't you? Say you are.

It is a great pity that we have such atrocious rows. I don't have rows with other people either, & yet I don't believe we were made to have rows with one another, & I think that we survive them is the most wonderful proof of the vitality of the sympathies between us. I admit to much of the blame; but not quite all. It is partly a helpless struggle for independence, as you pointed out to me not long ago, & it shows how <u>very much more you like me than any one else</u> that I did not perish in the attempt....

Thou shall arise & have mercy upon me; for it is time that thou have mercy upon me, yea, the time has come – Please H.

Arthur Asquith to V.A.   *Sunday 18 July*
                                     P. & O. S.S. Arabia

Dearest Violet, It was sad leaving you just when I thought I might have been of some use to you. I ought to have invited your confidence before: but I was blind: the possibility of your regarding Hugh in a new light had not occurred to me. Please don't be put off if I seem to lay down the law in what I am going to say: my intention is only to give you my personal opinions and impressions for what they are worth.

I understood from you that you thought of him as a possible husband because he had been in love with you for four years; and because he was the best companion you knew; and because you had not yet met anyone who stirred you to any deeper feeling than this. You were sorry for him: you despaired of meeting anyone you might fall in love with yourself: and you could not bear the idea of not only losing the monopoly of his companionship but of losing it altogether.

[1] For the political significance of the land taxes, see above, pp. 175–6.

You would marry him, if you married him, with the best part of yourself consoling itself for unrealised ideals with the knowledge that at least you were sacrificing yourself in a good cause, in pity of him – as a man, despairing of finding work by patient waiting, might give his last sovereign, against his principles, to a beggar, and salve his conscience with the thought that at any rate it was his last: – while the creature of habit in you that hates jars and discomforts would sigh with relief at the substitution of massage for the knife.

I can only explain to myself your ever having come to think of him as a possible husband as being the result of persistence sympathy and charm on his side and of your overfatigue, and perhaps loneliness in the sphere of emotions, and the restfulness of companionship with one who understands you and in whose affections you know that you come absolutely first.

If it were not for overfatigue and Hugh's and Archie's constant badgerings I am convinced that nothing could have brought you to contemplate as possible what you recognize would be only a second-best sort of marriage when you are only twenty two. If you were thirty, and still love had not come into your life, it would be different.

But surely you have the same sort of ideals of marriage as me. In it surely you would like to find a background of quiet and simplicity against which the real values of things would shine clear: and in a husband surely you would like to find a rock to build your house on: someone who would never allow the line of least resistance in important things: a man of broad humanity, not glib but understanding; one in whose courage and character and sense of honour and of proportion you could have implicit reliance; one who could guide your energies into right channels and help you to see all things clearly and in proportion, if in the glare and turmoil you lost your bearings or your vision became blurred. I can imagine that the man I have described so imperfectly might be superficially unromantic compared to Hugh: and – don't be offended at this – that unless you were thrown with him constantly or in trying circumstances, you might be inclined – at your present age – to sum him up and dismiss him in two or three epithets, bearing possibly on superficial characteristics – not because you are incapable of appreciating qualities of the sort I have described, but because I think your, as everyone else's, <u>every day</u> criterion for judging people must result from your every day atmosphere: and your every day atmosphere is social not domestic: and in <u>practice</u>, in a social atmosphere, Liberty scarves are bound to have it over homespun, and Wit over Worth.

My point is that you could not think of Hugh as a possible husband, at your present age, if you were to bring him before the bar of the higher criterion by which you appreciate as fully as anyone the quality of character that Father has and Hugh has not. But this higher criterion is apt to fall into disuse with all of us – unless the regular practice of religion, or self-denials and unselfish drudgeries or sorrows are there to keep it unrusted.

All this reads very priggishly: I expect you are sick of the school-master and family moralist in me: but it is difficult to talk naturally about things one so rarely talks about.

I only feel very strongly that your nature is capable of becoming richer, deeper and broader: married to Hugh you could not reach your highest: he has a perfect appreciation of the vistas you see from those windows which are habitually open: but with you the blinds are down over other windows opening on vistas he knows nothing of, and can know nothing of either because he has not got these other windows, or because from permanent neglect his blinds are down, and will not go up.

Also I feel that it would be very wrong for you to be impatient and to despair so soon: give your ideals longer credit, and suspect your every day criterion. I feel that at present you are inclined to specialize in gold and diamonds when you go mining: there are so many other minerals more worth getting for domestic life.

Then, think of Hugh, Father and Beb put through every sort of test: don't you feel by instinct that Father's and Beb's metal would always ring true: but that possibly in Hugh's there might be a flaw? I do, though I know nothing to justify me in feeling so. Don't think I'm unsympathetic towards Hugh: I have every reason to feel for him. For Heaven's sake tell him you cannot care for him in the way he cares for you: and that if he cannot go on being just a great friend, he had better avoid you. I would not give interfering advice of this sort, if I did not feel sure I was right: I feel all the surer because I know Father agrees with me.[1]

I did not mention all this to Margot in Paris – beyond saying, when we were talking about you, that I hoped you would not think of marrying Archie or Hugh, particularly Hugh. I would <u>much</u> sooner see you marry Meiklejohn, or Archie than Hugh.

I am having a peaceful voyage on a large uncrowded boat in perfect weather. This letter reads shockingly: remember it is meant well.

Your loving Oc.

---

[1] Asquith had written to his daughter on 4 June 1909 beseeching her 'Don't do, or think of doing, this thing, until you & I have talked it over <u>many</u> times. It would break my heart if you didn't make the best of your life.' Hugh was aware of the opposition, not only of Violet's father, but also of other members of her family, and he wrote to her on 1 July: 'You can let your Father come between us if you must, but you owe no duties to anyone else, & I do think you owe it to <u>me</u> – if I may say so – not to let them say such things to you.'

Hugh Godley to V.A. *Tuesday 10 August*
29 Sloane Gardens, S.W.

My darling & most beloved,
    The darkness is closing in upon me, so I write quickly, & shall send to you by a messenger, the few <u>business</u> matters which still remain to be said. It is mostly a recapitulation.
    We part tomorrow. We are parting to find out how much we mind being without one another. The moment either of us finds that we don't mind, or only minds a little, or wavers one inch from its present determination, it is under a solemn pledge immediately to write & tell the other....
    On February the 11th we will meet at 5 at Overtons.[1] We shall then have to decide (not immediately, but soon) whether we really belong to one another, or whether we are to part for good & finally. Remember all this, & think of it often....
    ... You have been never anything but noble & brave & generous, & if I never see you after tomorrow, you will still have been the best & the most wonderful element that entered into my life, & a treasure beyond price for all time.
    My conviction is that tomorrow is not the end. Goodnight my own loved one. I am glad our last day was a happy day. The spectres are rising thick round me now. Ah how cruel it is. Violet. Goodnight.

V.A. to Hugh Godley *Thursday 19 August*
Lympne Castle, Lympne, Kent

Beloved Hugh –
    First I must tell you that my temp. is down to-day for the first moment since I've been here & I feel a different <u>creature</u> in consequence – you mustn't worry or <u>think</u> about me so far as health's concerned now as I shall get better in no time & be able to sleep & everything once I'm cooler, which I am to-day.
    Margot showed me a letter from you yesterday which I wanted to say one or two things about. I don't think it is quite accurately describing my attitude to say I have arrived at the 'absolute conviction' (which is I think the way you put it) that I ought to marry you. If I had done that Hugh – should I have asked Father's advice & been to a certain extent, certainly so far as action was concerned influenced by it? I might have asked his

---

[1] A famous fish restaurant in Victoria, London.

permission as a formality, but my going to him on this occasion had nothing to do with his relationship to me as my Father – I went to him as the person whose judgement & opinion I most valued. And it is in that capacity that he influences me now (filial piety is neither here nor there).

I don't want you to think of him as a sort of ogre who makes me wretched & ill & spoils my life – I am ill & unhappy thro' my own irresponsibility & sanguineness about life & taking everything glorious which came tumbling to me like golden apples out of the sky as a very wonderful but at the same time natural largesse of Fortune's.... Now I see that Life knows no such word as largesse – only strict commercial transactions – tears for laughter, the blackness of the pit for every moment on the rainbow, the loneliness of desolation for that most sensitive & tender intimacy – all these are paid with mathematical precision.

And I do not grumble & wld. willingly spend 4 years as unhappy as I am now (tho' perhaps not quite as ill as I felt last week!) to keep the actuality & the memory of my 4 years with you. But this is a deviation. What I want you to understand is that Father influences me from <u>within</u> not from <u>without</u> – it is his opinion which deters me, not his keys –

If I said to Father that I was going to marry you to-morrow that I had made up my mind & that nothing would prevent me – of course he wldnt. try to after a time. The reason I don't do this is that, as <u>I</u> know you know, my feeling for you held the possibility but not the <u>inevitability</u> of marriage. I felt I couldn't bear losing you – not that I <u>must</u> marry you. Now when I cry for hours on end I know that I am sad at being parted from you for the moment & terrified of being parted from you for ever, lonely without you, longing to see you & hear you speak – but not wretched because I can't marry you. Do you see what I mean? I'm sure you knew all the time because we talked it over so often but in yr. letter to Margot you seem to have got the 2 ideas – torture at parting – & willingness to marry rather mixed & she in consequence thinks I must have misled you or given you some definite promise which of course I haven't.

Oh dearest it is so difficult to write you this sort of letter seeming to try & minimize everything I feel, but they worry me & say you are under a misapprehension & you know honest is the one thing I've always tried to be – to the verge of crudity – & it's only clumsiness if I've failed.

Now I'm crying again so I must try & finish quickly. Another thing Margot says is that if I've left myself or you any hope, which of course I have, Feb. is <u>much</u> too long to wait in uncertainty. She says I shall be ill <u>with</u> uncertainty all the time & anyway it's <u>cruel</u> to you. And I rather agree about the last.[1] ... What I want to do is to see whether I am being self-

---

[1] In spite of her awareness of the need to make a decision, in Hugh's best interests, Violet

indulgent & shrinking from parting with my joy & pleasure in you – or whether you are a <u>necessary</u> of my life without which I can't live. Of course if I felt sure of the last there wld. be no question of argument & advice & time-limits – that's what I should call a 'conclusion'. The feeling I have got is so much more tentative & inchoate, so much more 'it might be' than 'it must be'....

Will you write & say what you feel about <u>time</u> & also if you had misunderstood anything – so that I can reassure Margot. Yr V.

V.A. to Venetia Stanley   *Friday 15 October*
Stanway, Winchcombe,
Gloucestershire

My Darling – I must thank you for my Sunday which I enjoyed <u>acutely</u>; I've never known heterogenii blend more happily.

No doubt the common denunciation of Vesey Holt & Marjorie Graham proved wonderfully cementing![1] It is a thing to remember for the future.

Barbara took me on to lunch at the Admiralty with her, Pamsky & Eczy who <u>revolted</u> me by his cock-a-whoop, vulgar & utterly senseless conversation more than I shall ever be able to convey to you. Remind me to tell you about it sometime – it is too long to write, I had a hot encounter with him during which I'm afraid Pamsky suffered a good deal (not thro' my coups but thro' his blunders). His only feeling about Lloyd George's speech[2] (from which I was suffering acutely at the time) was exultation that he had made a faux-pas, his only reason for wishing the Budget to go through was that Ll.G. would be a hero if it didn't. It made me perfectly

was unable to do so. It was not until the summer of 1913 that she appears finally to have ruled out the possibility of marrying him. Hugh's unhappy predicament furnished Edwin Montagu with a salutary precedent in his own protracted courtship of Venetia Stanley, to whom he wrote in April 1915: 'Remember I have your promise that I shall not be "Hugh-ed". I rely on that and can wait for ever' (M. and E. Brock, *H. H. Asquith: Letters to Venetia Stanley*, 530 and n. 2).

[1] Marjorie Winifred Graham (d. 1937), daughter of Sir Henry and Lady Margaret Graham.

[2] In a speech at Newcastle on 9 October 1909, Lloyd George defended the land valuation proposals in his budget, warning the Unionist peers against rejection: 'They are forcing a revolution, and they will get it. The Lords may decree a revolution, but the people will direct it.' Questions would be raised, he said, that the Lords little dreamt of, fundamental questions of government and property ownership. It was revolutionary rhetoric, delivered in spite of an entreaty from Asquith, who had written two days earlier asking Lloyd George not to do anything that might compromise an attempt by the King to mediate with the Unionist leaders. See Bentley Brinkerhoff Gilbert, *David Lloyd George: A Political Life*, 384–96.

sick to hear him admit such things – his soul is worthy of the dark cottage bald battered, eczema-ridden & decayed in which it is lodged![1]

Father & I had a glorious tête à tête dinner & <u>long</u> talk about <u>everything</u> ranging over Budget, Balmoral, Cabinet, & (of course) Raymond's hair as a child! I could see he thought Ld. Lansdowne wld not be able to hold the Peers – but don't quote this. He also indiscreetly admitted to me that he thought Eliza looked 'beastly'!!

I went with him to Orpen the next morning – the picture is improving a lot though still on the ashy & cadaverous side. It will be incomparably better than the Solomon.[2] Then to Buckingham Palace & then after lunch with A. & Montagu we went to E[aston]. Grey, deserting a play party whose component parts were Micky, Bongie, Archie & Beb. Life at E.Grey peaceful except when a detective (of which there were 11) leapt out of the shadow of a shrub at one's throat. I was twice held up coming back in the dark from the Rectory. Father motored me over here Thurs. morning – we found an ideal party consisting of Melcho – Ego & Cynthia – & the usual Squidge contingent. Ld. Elcho arrived in the evening in a state of utter collapse owing to a financial contre-temps – (I believe some more than usually murky proceeding on the part of his discredited firm which seemed to necessitate resignation). He sat all through dinner with a fixed & glassy eye – a telegram quivering on his knee his family unsympathetic but depressed at the thought of the bailiffs. I was driven towards cheese to ask if he had any god-children! so low had my resources run. He left at 6 the next morning & returned last night with his serenity completely restored – in fact every symptom of having sealed a dishonourable peace.

Life here is perfect – I walk with Cynthia for hours – & play golf in the garden & stump cricket in the barn with Ego whom I really love. The atmosphere is very congenial to me! & Cynthia always helps me wonderfully towards calm & concentration. We sleep together, with Ld. Elcho behind that tissue paper wall! Love to you Dearest yr. V.

---

[1] In her comments on McKenna Violet consciously echoed Edmund Waller's 'Old Age': 'The soul's dark cottage, battered and decayed, / Lets in new light through chinks that Time has made.'

[2] The portrait of Asquith by Sir William Orpen (1878–1931) was completed that year, and exhibited at the Royal Academy. The study by Solomon Joseph Solomon (1860–1927) was also completed in 1909.

Archie Gordon to V.A.   *Thursday 18 November*
10 Downing Street, Whitehall,
S.W.

My Darling – You will be surprised to see this paper. It is due to my having dined here with Beb & a very nondescript party.... The place is sadly shorn & despoiled of its glory without your vivifying presence. I sometimes think how it would be if in some time to come I were to see this room as I once saw it before, full of Baffy's & Rayleighs – after it had been the centre of the world for so long.[1] The speech I have as the pocket-list. I love it, V. dearest, & am thrilled with pride in you over it, & over the thought of your coming to your own in every sphere that you approach. May I be? Your triumphs are so infinitely dear & precious to me.[2] Did you see the Daily Mirror? – (in which I note Heap!)

I have just spoken to Edgar – (who says he dined here last night – & apparently felt himself badly cheated by your absence). He told me to tell you once more that you had behaved very badly. I play with him & Evan Saturday morning.

Get very rested at E.G. darling. You will be made tired by the H. of L. debates again.

I will Buxton again to-morrow. Bless you ever & always yr A

Hugh Godley to V.A.   *Sunday 21 November*
Stanway, Winchcombe

My dearest one
I want to write to you to say what I have been making up my mind to say for some time back.

---

[1] Archie alludes to the period of the preceding Unionist government, when the relatives of A. J. Balfour were to be found at 10 Downing Street: 'Baffy' was his niece, Blanche, who became Mrs Edgar Dugdale; the 'Rayleighs' were his elder sister, Evelyn, and her husband, John William Strutt, 3rd Baron Rayleigh.

[2] On Tuesday 16 November Violet gave a speech while opening a sale to raise funds for the Hammersmith Liberal and Radical Association. In it she reflected on the achievements of the party during four years in power, and amid loud applause urged party workers to redouble their efforts in the cause of Liberalism: 'We have a cause worth fighting for. We are like Crusaders outside the Holy City.' There were reports on the speech in the national press the following day. In an atmosphere of intensified political conflict, Violet's own political involvement increased. Bongie wrote to her on 17 November, 'Don't overdo your political spadework & leave London a wreck,' adding, 'I thought you were pleased with your speech, it was a very good one....'

It is really clear to me now that you will never marry me. I think you are not in love with me & never will be. I am not even necessary to you. If I were to marry you under these circumstances the result could not be anything but disastrous. I believe, & shall believe till I die, that if circumstances had been a little different, we should have married, & I don't think we could have been anything but happy. Six months ago I thought it was certain to happen; I didn't see how else the position could resolve itself; I still have great difficulty in imagining you for one moment married to anyone else.

I cannot tell you what it costs me to write these few formal sentences, but I have said, without comment, what I believe to be right. Some time during the present week I will come & see you about it.

If you agree with me, & that is the conclusion we come to, I don't think I could bear to see you very much just at present. I don't think we could either of us bear it. . . .

The only other thing I will say now is that in spite of everything you have made me happier, & been better for me, than anything else that has ever come near me, & that never as long as I live shall I think of you as anything but good & great & wonderful, or with anything but love & gratitude & blessing

    My darling Violet

    Always yr

    H.

SIX

Archie Gordon

1909–1910

On the last Sunday in November, 1909, Archie Gordon was fatally injured in a motor car accident just outside Winchester. He was driving his brand-new Daimler 'Silent Knight' towards Chippenham when he collided with a Renault landaulette at a badly sighted crossroad. The Renault, carrying a driver and three passengers, cut across Archie's path from the left and, though he tried, he could not quite swerve behind it. The other car crashed into an earthen bank, hurling one of its occupants more than twenty feet, while Archie's car overturned, trapping him underneath. He sustained severe injuries to his abdomen, and was taken by horse-drawn carriage to the Royal County Hospital in Winchester, bravely enduring an agonizingly slow journey on a hastily improvised stretcher. Characteristically his first concern was for his chauffeur, who had been riding as a passenger in his car. In fact Archie was the only person who was seriously hurt. Violet was staying in Oxfordshire at the time of the accident, and travelled to Winchester the following Saturday. She was not allowed to see Archie until the early hours of Wednesday 15 December, when it was clear that he was losing his battle for life.

Diary – late December 1909 – Archerfield House, Dirleton, East Lothian

I am going to try & write down as simply & as accurately as I can everything that I remember of the greatest day of my life.

At 10 [pm] I drove up to the Hospital with Venetia & Fräu – left them below on the 'Visitors' bench in the iodoform-y hall & ran upstairs to Lady Aberdeen. The wind was <u>howling</u>. We talked a little about houses – plans etc – & in about 10 minutes the Drs. came out of A.'s room.[1] They were silent at first & I thought the usual measured & judicial evolution of the bulletin was in process & tried not to interrupt. Presently I tugged

---

[1] Archie's room in the Royal Hampshire County Hospital was later named 'The Gordon Room' in his memory. Violet had a china vase placed in it, which was filled with violets.

Godwin's coat & said: '<u>Do</u> let it be "progress" – I'm so tired of the day before yesterday's improvement being maintained'.[1] He looked at us compassionately & then away – then with difficulty he told us that heart-failure had set in & that the outlook was very grave. I asked if there was any hope & saw at once in his eyes that there was none. I think Lady Aberdeen still had a flicker.

She sent off some telegrams – & I asked Fräu & Venetia to let Father & Beb know & bring me my jade beads from the Inn.

Godwin promised I should see him before he became unconscious – & said he might live till the morning. From 11 to 4 I watched our precious sands running out – then they came to tell me I might go in to him.

He had asked for me during the day & Godwin told him I was passing thro' Winchester & would come now. He didn't seem to think it strange – he said: 'You'll get her here for me all right Dr. won't you? – I don't <u>look</u> bad do I? Give me a little brandy before she comes in to buck me up – & put a good high cushion on the chair so that I can <u>see</u> her properly.' When they said: 'you may go in now' I felt the greatest joy I have ever known. I could not see beyond it.

I had put on my hat & coat & veil in as tidy & 'travelling' a way as I could – & my jade beads round my neck. Godwin took me in.

The first thing I was conscious of was dim light & an all-pervasive smell of Eau-de-Cologne – then I saw <u>Archie</u> – propped up in bed by pillows on every side – his face changed & transfigured beyond recognition – his breathing coming & going in short, sharp gasps – his arms held out to me.

'<u>Dearest</u> – you've come – <u>how</u> good of you. Now I know what Tristan felt'![2]

'Only for us it's the beginning – not the end. Shall I for a great treat kiss you?'

'Ah' – he lay back breathlessly & I kissed him. Then I sat down beside him & held his hands while he asked me 10 000 questions – how I had come – why they had let me – wasn't it too late for me etc. etc. When I had satisfied him that it was quite a normal proceeding I said I had something to tell him – only he mustn't allow it to excite or tire him. Then I told him in the words Heaven sent me for such a moment that I loved him – that everything I had to give was his. It would be sacrilege to write of what followed – an ecstasy too holy for expression either then or now....

[1] Of the three principal doctors who attended Archie, Violet placed the greatest trust in the surgeon who first operated on him, Herbert Godwin, who was on the staff at the Royal Hampshire Hospital.

[2] In Wagner's opera *Tristan und Isolde*, the mortally wounded hero dies in the arms of his beloved, after bidding her come to his bedside. Violet and Archie shared a passion for Wagner, and especially the *Ring* cycle.

I called Godwin & said 'Dr. Archie wishes me to tell you we're going to be married' – A. 'Yes tho' perhaps at first sight I don't look it Dr. I am at this moment in the most enviable position of any man alive. And she's cured me Dr. I could walk now – I can't feel the beastly pelvis or the rib – no pain – no breathlessness – I'm treading on air'. When he had gone – with infinite emotion: 'Beloved how great & glorious you are! You come here & see me torn to bits, smashed up & full of tubes, you take me from the depths & raise me to the heights – your heights'.

I told him how proud I was of his heroism – & how like a knight he had covered my name with glory by his prowess – & he glowed with all his old joy at a comparison from his favourite Age of chivalry & lists & Graals & armour. 'Proud of me dearest? proud like you are of Winston's speeches – & Maurice's books'?

I tried to tell him what waste paper they all seemed now compared with this – 'They're all nothing – Cys is nothing'! He lay back & shut his eyes & gave a little high moan of delight.

I told him how all the things I used to expect of life & think I prized had dwindled & disappeared – how now platform oratory, verbal memory, 'interest' (one of his worst bogys!) & all my other nominal essentials were so many melted mists – all I cared about all I longed for was just to be his wife. This seemed to me [the] greatest thing that could happen to any woman. – 'Do you still feel up to having 7 sons Dearest?' V. 'Quite up to it.' – A. 'Oh how wonderful they'll be – your children – my children –' then smiling – '& glorious, unapproachable You – my chattel before the world! Why has it all come to me?'

They brought in some tea which I poured out for him (I had been giving him water & brandy & ice & meat-juice & oxygen at intervals all this time). . . .

Godwin came in & gave him heroin a derivative of morphia which he loved – he said: 'Dr. fancy being engaged' – & then went off wonderfully quickly into a sort of drugged sleep with his eyes half-open but his mind apparently at rest. He murmured things about the motor 'I can't get in the clutch' & then turning to me (he had been holding my hands tightly the whole time) 'Do you know what my motor is there for? To attend to your wants' (with great emphasis). He had said this to me several times at Littlestone at Eastertime when I used to sometimes tease him by refusing to use his motor.

When he woke up he asked them to leave us alone again & made me put my head on the pillow again by his. We were talking very happily when a spasm of pain crossed his face – & when I asked him what was the matter he said 'That poor man' – 'What poor man darling?' – 'You know who I mean – Hugh.' I was deeply moved by this. . . .

The Dr. came in while I was still quite close to him – & he was amazed at my not starting away: 'Darling – you have changed! you used to hardly speak to me when there was anyone there – & now' – – – I said to Godwin 'Archie thinks I'm an abandoned woman not to be shyer of you – he's quite ashamed of me' – & A. just turned & looked at the Dr. with an expression I shall never forget of such radiant pride – mixed with a sort of 'just-listen-to-her' look! He said to me a little later on: 'You don't seem to think me half as <u>wrong</u> to-day as you usually do'. I said: 'No Dearest – I think you right – & perfect' – 'How strange that a motor coming down on the top of me should make <u>you</u> – relentlessly logical you – think <u>me</u> right' – V. 'Yes – I suppose it's what people would call feminine. <u>How</u> I always used to mind your calling me feminine! And I still don't think I am'. . . .

He had another little sleep & then Haddo came in ostensibly to congratulate him. 'Well done Archie – this is splendid – this is better than the Eighty Club.'[1] – 'Yes won't she give me a lift there – I shall get on the Committee if she writes my speeches! Bless you Doddie' – 'Bless you Archie'.

Dudley came in & talked for a bit which he loved[2] – & then I tentatively mentioned Beb – '<u>Oh</u> yes – what fun – let's have him up. Is he pleased about it' – & as Beb reached the door – 'Here comes the burlesque element'.

'Well Beb – this <u>is</u> fun isn't it – this is splendid – but I can't have you for my best man Beb as I would under any other circumstances' 'Why not Archie?' – 'Well you see Violet will be given away by her Father – & the best man's business is to prod the bridegroom into action. That would look very bad Beb wouldn't it – towards your own sister'. . . .

Venetia came up which made him very happy: 'What did the people at Mansfield Street say to <u>this</u>? – then to me 'Venetia will have to nearly live with us won't she' – then 'Kiss me Venetia'. She went away & he seemed very tired & said: 'It's odd – not one visitor before now & to-day about 14 – if congratulations come in at this rate I shall [have] to put a notice in the Morning Post saying the number is so great it can't be coped with individually'. . . .

He seemed a little uncomfortable once or twice when I mentioned Bongie: 'This does make one so sorry for all the poor fellows in the world who aren't going to marry you.' V. 'Not half so many want to as you seem to think. It isn't everyone's idea of fun' A. 'Oh <u>don't</u> they just! I know what it feels like.'

He was beginning to grow much weaker & I had to be constantly giving

[1] George Gordon (1879–1965), Lord Haddo; eldest son of Lord and Lady Aberdeen. Contested East Berkshire as a Liberal, 1906; London county councillor for Peckham, 1910–25. The Eighty Club was a Liberal dining club and political society, which took its name from Gladstone's historic election victory in 1880.
[2] Hon. Dudley Gordon, second son of Lord and Lady Aberdeen.

him brandy, oxygen, & ice. He was looking forward to seeing Father & grew worried & impatient at his delay: 'Will he be here soon?' . . . At 3 Father came – he almost broke down altogether on seeing A. but recovered himself splendidly when I reminded him he must congratulate us. He said 'I've always wished it Archie – I've always wished it' with tears in his eyes & voice; A. looked a little puzzled – but then suddenly seemed to understand his emotion: 'I know you're giving me the most precious thing you've got Mr. Asquith' – 'It's my very best – the best thing I've got to give' – A. 'I will try & make her happy' – They talked on about it a little & then A. said in his 'City' voice 'So now we've put all this on a thoroughly business footing Mr. Asquith – it's settled up.' Then 'Will you kiss me?' – & when Father had done so 'Will you bless me?'

As he went out of the room A. said to me 'Divine man!' then turning to the nurse 'There goes the finest man alive!' – 'Much talked about just at present Mr. Gordon' A. 'Not only just at present – always & everywhere.'[1] . . .

A message came from his Father which Dudley brought in : 'You answer it darling in your <u>excellent</u> way'. I held the oxygen tube for nearly 2 hours during which he only spoke to ask me for ice – water etc or to have his forehead bathed or lips moistened. . . .

His breathing became terribly distressed at one moment as if the tubes were getting blocked & a dreadful choking fit came on – the worst thing that happened. His Mother & I were with him & a nurse & we tried in vain to adjust the pillows in such a way as to help him to spit – his agony & helplessness were dreadful to watch – he clutched me with terror & shouted – 'I'm dead – I'm done' – & I had to try & look into his eyes with confidence & serenity & promise him that it was all right – that he'd only to make another effort & it would come away – & he would be all right. . . . at last thank God it came & the terror left his eyes & he sank back exhaustedly saying '3 days' strength gone'. He seemed a good deal upset & tired – & I looked from him to the clock & longed for Lord Aberdeen.

At last he came. . . . A. had revived a good deal & said as he bent over him: 'Father say <u>lovely</u> things to Violet.' – & he kissed us both. Then Ettie came. She said 'Darling – this is what I've always longed for – to see you two together' – & he turned round & gazed at me again with that radiant look of joy & pride. It was the last time I saw it. . . .

Another lapse of consciousness & then he drew me towards him & whispered 'May we be married in bed darling – now – at once' – 'In bed beloved – why? we can easily wait' – 'I don't know why – but I want to be

---

[1] With Margot, Asquith had journeyed through the night to be with Violet during Archie's last hours, arriving at Winchester at two o'clock on the morning of Thursday the 16th. He remained there for the whole of that day, missing a cabinet meeting in London at which he had been due to preside.

Violet Asquith, aged 19

Violet, in childhood, with her father

Learning German, and acquiring a taste of Wagner: a group of young English-women being finished in Dresden, in the winter of 1903. From left to right: Mary Vesey, Cynthia Asquith, Violet, Eileen Wellesley, Fraülein Schneider, [possibly] Lady de Vesci.

Family scene at Glen, Peeblesshire, Easter 1904 (left to right): Elizabeth Asquith, H. H. Asquith, Olive Macleod (standing), Margot Asquith (sitting), Katherine Horner, Violet, Cyril ('Cys') Asquith (sitting, front), Arthur ('Oc') Asquith (sitting, middle), H.T. Baker (standing), Edward Horner, Raymond Asquith. Katherine is looking up at Raymond: they were married three years later, and their courtship began around the time that this photograph was taken.

Hugh Godley (second from the left, standing) at the New College Commemoration Ball in Oxford, 1899; aged 22. To the right of Hugh is his sister, Kitty, and seated at the front are his other sisters Eveline (left) and Helen (middle).

Cyril ('Cys') Asquith, when at Oxford.

Hon. Archie Gordon at Oxford, 1905; aged 21.

'5 days and nights of conventional revelry on a gigantic scale': some members of the birthday party at Castle Ashby, seat of the 5th Marquess of Northampton, August 1906. 'Bim' Compton, heir to the marquisate, whose coming of age was the cause of celebration, is seated at the front, third from the right.

Standing (left to right): Cynthia Charteris; Herbert Asquith ('Beb'); Violet; Archie Gordan; Venetia Stanley; Lord Loch; Amherst Webber; Hon. Evie Loch; Hon. Rupert Keppel; Lord Elcho; Hersey Butler; Hon. Arthur Brodrick; Nellie Kerr; — Ponsonby; Rosamond Grosvenor; Constantine Benckendorff; Hon. Gerald Wellesley; Marjory Graham; Phil Williams; Hilda Lyttelton.

Seated on chairs: Lady Loch; Hon. Nan Lyttelton; Sally Carpenter; Melville Balfour; Hersey Maltby; Hon. Alec Cadogan; Clementine Hozier; Lady Margaret Graham; 5th Marquess of Northampton; Mrs Kerr; Elsie Graham; Hon. Hermione Fellowes; Horatia Seymour; Ronald Graham; Claire Stopford; Harry Graham.

Sitting on the ground: Hon. Guy Charteris; Ewen Cameron; Lord Henry Seymour; Hon. Douglas Kinnaird; Sir Lionel Earle; Earl Compton ('Bim'); Lord Bury; Hon. Jack Mitford.

Violet with her elder brother Herbert ('Beb') and their spaniel 'Sambo', 1908.

Violet, Venetia Stanley and Katharine Asquith at Archerfield, East Lothian, in the autumn of 1910.

The Archie Gordon Club at its summer camp at Littlestone-on-Sea, Kent, July—August 1911; Maurice Bonham Carter ('Bongie') is standing at the back.

'Dukes on my yacht are as plentiful as blackberries — if you don't know a man you're safe to call him your Grace.' Violet on board Sir Thomas Lipton's yacht *Shamrock*, August 1912.

The crew of HMS *Enchantress* with the First Lord of the Admiralty and his guests, May 1913. In the front row, from left to right, are: Violet, Winston Churchill, Clementine Churchill, H. H. Asquith, Margot Asquith, —?, [probably] Mrs Cornwallis-West,—?.

The *Enchantress* in the Mediterranean, June 1912.

Violet and her father in Tunis, June 1912, during their cruise on board the *Enchantress*

Violet with her friend Sir Rufus Isaacs, attorney-general, at a cricket match, July 1912; allegations against Liberal ministers, including Isaacs, over dealings in Marconi shares were then gathering momentum.

H. H. Asquith addressing the East Fife Liberals at Ladybank, 1913. Sharing the platform are Maurice Bonham Carter ('Bongie') (on the left), Violet, and Clementine Churchill's sister Nellie Hozier ('The Bud') (on the right).

Violet at Hopeman, Moray, in August 1913; aged 26.

married <u>now</u> – I feel such a strange impatience.' This was the last thing he said to me before he became finally unconscious.

Cys & Margot arrived – & I went out for a moment & had something to drink – then Godwin fetched me. I hurried back to his bedside – he was looking round him with searching eyes & groping hands – he said 'has she gone?' – then 'Violet!' & taking my hand drew my arm round him with great strength & force – clutching it tightly with one of his & holding me to him with the other. He stiffened himself with what looked like some effort & murmured '<u>I</u> <u>won't</u>'.

He never recovered consciousness again. . . .

The death of Archie Gordon

Archie died of heart failure at twenty minutes to seven on the morning of Thursday 16 December. A memorial service for him was held in the Temple Church in London the following Monday, and he was buried in the private cemetery at his home, Haddo House, on Thursday 23rd. A large congregation of friends and family weathered a heavy snowfall to be present, and they were joined by a deputation of the Aberdeens' tenants and estate employees. The pall-bearers included three members of the government – H. H. Asquith, Lord Aberdeen and Lord Pentland, as well as two ex-ministers – Archie's uncle, Lord Tweedmouth, and Lord Balfour of Burleigh, the former Unionist Scottish secretary. Archie's brothers, George and Dudley, and his cousin Jasper Ridley, completed the group. Despite the recent bad weather, the day itself was fine, and the carriage bearing Archie made its way from the private chapel to the cemetery in bright sunlight. Violet followed walking between Lord and Lady Aberdeen. Her parting gesture was to cast a wreath of violets into the grave, bearing the inscription 'To my beloved'.

Winston Churchill to V.A.   *Thursday 16 December*
                                        10 Downing Street, Whitehall,
                                                          S.W.

My dear Violet,

Accept my profound sympathy with you in your sorrow. I know how useless words are. This is a most cruel event. All that can be said is that we are all in the grip of the same chance. Poor poor fellow –

Yours vy sincerely,
Winston S. Churchill.

Dudley Gordon to V.A.   *Thursday 16 December*
                                             Winchester, Hampshire

Dearest Violet

Our hearts were too full for us to say all we felt to each other this morning: but may I be allowed just to thank you for giving dear Archie such a gloriously happy ending to his life. I feel proud of the fact that you are his, and I can't put it higher when I say I feel you are indeed worthy of him. It was your wonderful courage and love which made his end so contented and peaceful, and all my life I shall remember how wonderful you were, and be made a better man for the memory.

Archie told me more of his feelings for you than he did to anyone else, and I can appreciate all you have meant to him.

God bless you, your affect. Dudley.

Hugh Godley to V.A.   *Friday 17 December*
                                             Minley Lodge, Farnborough,
                                             Hampshire

My dearest Violet, In writing to you yesterday I said nothing about what I had seen in the Evening's papers because, although it was what I had expected to hear, I thought it just possible that it might only be conjecture.[1]

Now this morning I have letters from Venetia & Bongie. The former says that 'her .... thoughts & sympathies have been with you since'.

Now you must believe that what I have to say I say absolutely from my heart & with no idea of saying what you would like me to say, & also that I am under no impression but that you acted from an absolutely sincere conviction, having found out then what you would have found out in the long run whatever happened.

That you did right goes without saying, but I want you to know – although it is of no importance – that you did what I should have wished you to do. I very nearly wrote & said this a week ago, but I refrained partly because I thought it would have been impertinent & partly – mainly – because I knew that no thought of me would stand in your way or, if it did for a moment, that I could trust you to know my wishes.

I think he was a better man than I am; I think he loved you more than

---

[1] Hugh refers to the news of Violet's engagement to Archie, which appeared in the national press on 17 December. The *Daily Telegraph* reported an 'official statement' to the effect that: 'An engagement of marriage was entered into between the Hon. Archie Gordon and Miss Violet Asquith shortly before Mr. Gordon's death.'

I do, more unselfishly; I think he would have made you happier than I should have. And if I, dear Violet, in pursuing my selfish ends, have stood between you & the realization of your best self, you must try, in the course of years, to forgive me; for although one learns too late what one should have done, I did honestly believe I was doing right....

... I only ask & long & pray that you may have strength; if you have I know you can only use it in doing what is right. I will not write more dear. You must dismiss me totally from your mind unless I can be of use to you Yr H.

'A Suffragette' to V.A. *Sunday 19 December*
Dublin

Dear Miss Asquith

Although I am a stranger to you, my heart goes out to you in the deepest sympathy.

No one could feel more for you in your overwhelming sorrow than I do – for I have loved & lost through Death. Here in Ireland everyone feels keenly for you, as they do for the family of your Beloved one. He was very popular & much esteemed here, & to know that you possessed his love & were to have borne his good name must ever be a consolation to you, although a sad memory.

God bless & help you to be brave.

Yours in sympathy

A Suffragette member of the Women's Freedom League.

I do not give you my name for private reasons of my own, but you & I have many mutual friends.

I read in the Papers that your Father (I always hiss his name!) is a devoted Father. Yet he is the sole cause of so much trouble & suffering & imprisonment, loss & giving up of so much money, comforts & c etc of hundreds of brave noble women & young girls of good birth & education who are fighting & will continue to fight for their rights in this 'so called' free country England. Can you not in your sorrow feel for them & get him to see how unjust he is on the subject. It has become a more serious & desperate matter than he cares to see. It is quality not quantity of women who must be judged.

It is when Death approaches & takes from us our beloved ones that our hearts should be softened towards others. I find consolation now in being a suffragette & would give up my Life for the cause.

Raymond Asquith to V.A.   *Friday 24 December*
                                              49 Bedford Square, W.C.

Dearest Violet
    Father gave me a very moving account of the last days at Winchester. I
was very fond of Archie and I am glad to think that as long as he was
conscious he was completely happy; and that you also were happy – in
'this little moment mercifully given'.
    At any rate no future event can ever blunt the edge or taint the flavour
of what you then enjoyed. It is preserved in memory as in amber, beyond
the reach of questioning and the battery of facts; and you will be spared
the effort, so often & so vainly made, to reinstate an unique emotion &
recapture an evaporated essence. To this extent it seems to be true that
the half may be better than the whole. However this letter is not intended
to add to the unbearable weight of consolation which from many and
diverse quarters you must already have received, but only to tell you that
I also in my degree shall miss Archie very much.
    He had humour and brains – much better brains in my opinion than
almost anyone gave him credit for – and that delightful unprofessional
vitality which is based on blood & lungs instead of on nerves and drink.
    It is a terrible pity.
                                              your loving Raymond.

V.A. to M.B.C.   *Thursday 10 February 1910*
                                              Valescure, France

Dearest Bongie – I expect Venetia will have given you most of our 'fleshly'
news – how we had the longest foulest journey imaginable round by every
capital of Europe & found Father installed in a vast hideous comfy villa
belonging to the Rendels – surrounded by about 90 acres of fabulously
expensive baobabs.[1] I felt about as lively as a <u>mummy</u> on arrival – & still
feel hopelessly impulseless & inert.
    Monday Father settled us up here in a little puffin house among the
pinewoods. It is quite lonely & nice & there is much less motor traffic &
confetti than down below at Cannes. The climate is quite incredible – but
somehow I feel too tired & sad to face these radiant mornings. The colours
are so mercilessly joyful – scarlet rocks jutting into the sea – oranges
blazing in a cloudless sky – & such a bursting crowding, tropical overflow

[1] Stuart Rendel (1834–1913), 1st Baron Rendel, 1894; an ex-Liberal MP, Rendel was a wealthy
industrialist, with villas in Italy and the south of France.

of <u>life</u> pushing up all round one. It makes me feel such a <u>corpse</u> – it doesn't heal. But <u>what</u> does? . . .

Goodbye Bongie dear bless you

Yr V.

Isn't it awful I simply <u>can't</u> read.

Hugh Godley to V.A.   *Friday 11 February*
29 Sloane Gardens, S.W.

My most beloved, A lavish post has brought me two letters from you & a post card with edelweiss in it. How wonderful your first letter was! No one but you could have written such words.

. . . all I have to say to you is, by way of selfish appeal, that if you cannot find anything worth living for in what is left to you, if it turns out that your most precious all important life, your life which, arithmetically reckoned, is only beginning, which has only just emerged from childhood, is something manqué, something which has aimed at a million, & missed a unit, then it will just break my heart, as it will break the hearts of <u>all</u> those whose destinies are inextricably involved with yours. All of them, Beb's, Cys's, Hugh's, your Father's, all those of whom you speak, it rests with you whether the future state you foresee for them is possible or not. You must do your duty by them (– by us). As a matter of plain duty you must survive, & with us find out millions of things that you do not know. If you do not, you are a selfish woman. Yes, a bad self-indulgent woman. A woman who will lie down & give up the ghost at the first knock down blow that you get.

Courage is what I expect from you my dearest. I think you have abundant stores of it, but you have still got to prove to me. . . .

. . . Yr H.

The first general election of 1910: 15th–22nd January

The general election of January 1910 was brought about by the House of Lords' rejection of the Liberals' 1909 budget, on 30 November. On 2 December a resolution was passed in the Commons condemning the action of the peers as unconstitutional, and the next day parliament was prorogued in readiness for a general election in the New Year. The immediate issue was the budget, but the wider question was the constitutional power of the upper chamber. Asquith, Churchill and Lloyd George all publicly declared, early in December, that they would not again hold office in circumstances where the peers could overrule the people. The Liberal leaders were aware, though, of the impasse that loomed. Any bill to limit the power of the House of Lords was likely to be vetoed by that chamber. The only certain solution was a mass creation of Liberal peers, to guarantee the government a majority. This lay within the power of the crown, but such a dilution of the nobility was unlikely to be welcomed by Edward VII, even on the recommendation of his prime minister. The King had still to be approached about this sensitive matter when Asquith opened his campaign at the Albert Hall, on 10 December. His speech was widely interpreted as an indication that he already held the King's assent to the creation of peers. When parliament met, on 21 February 1910, he was obliged to make a frank admission that he did not. It marked a low point in his long premiership. Liberals felt that they had lost the initiative, and there were 'cries of disappointment from even loyal members of the Party.'[1] Asquith's position was made more difficult because the Liberals were now dependent for a majority in the Commons upon the eighty-two Irish Nationalist members. In addition to objections to clauses in the budget, they feared that once it was passed, with their aid, the Liberals would abandon the constitutional battle with the peers. Unless this was successfully prosecuted, Home Rule would not pass. In return for Irish support for the budget, John Redmond, the Irish leader, therefore sought a guarantee that in the coming session the peers' power of veto would be tackled. Asquith could not guarantee success but, in effect, he promised to try. The budget was finally given the royal assent on 29 April, exactly a year after it had been first introduced in the Commons. In the same month Asquith outlined the government's proposals for ending the veto power of the House of Lords, beginning the next stage in the battle.

Roderick Meiklejohn to V.A.   *Thursday 17 February*
10 Downing Street, Whitehall,
S.W.

Dear Miss Asquith

It was very good of you to write & I was very glad to hear from you altho' I quite understood your silence and feel that every time you write

---

[1] J. A. Spender and C. Asquith, *Life of Lord Oxford and Asquith*, i, 273.

about Archie it must renew the sense of your loss and that of all of us who knew him....

Here things are in a very exciting state & many expect the Government will be out in a week or two tho' who is to take their place it is difficult to see. Personally I believe the Irish & Labour revolt will collapse as the futility of their action in turning the Government out must be plain even to them. John Burns had a mot which may amuse you 'Tell Redmond to go to 'Ell & he'll come to 'eel'.

I suppose the Prime Minister has told you that he is making Montagu Under Secretary at the India Office. The Government appointments so far have been well received except that some people rather demur at Pease being put in the Cabinet & many think that the senile Wolverhampton should be made to retire.[1] Your father, however, is kind hearted to a fault & so probably has let the old man stay on as the only harm he does is to keep other people out....

I will write again if I have any news. I do hope you are feeling better in health. Please remember me to Miss Stanley if she is still with you.

Yours Roderick Meiklejohn

H.H.A. to V.A.   ***Sunday 27 February***
Easton Grey, Malmesbury,
Wiltshire

My dearest Violet – I was very glad to get your letter. I hope the weather has gone back to normal: your country needs the sun. You will have heard by this time that Olive Macleod proposes to come out to you & probably Frances Horner a little later. I think it is important that you should prolong your stay – not necessarily at Valescure – as much as you can: and [Dr] Lawrence is very strongly of that opinion, for the sake of your heart & your general health. March is the worst time of the year in England, and this year, in addition to climate, there will be all the worries and anxieties of the political situation. There has never been anything quite like it; one party is as badly off as another, and it looks as though we might find ourselves in an impasse from which there is no visible outlet. I have come down here in the motor to get a few hours' peace: only Lucy & Ribblesdale are here; unfortunately I have to go back to London this afternoon.

We went to the first Court on Friday night: Clemmy Churchill was the

[1] Jack Pease had entered the cabinet on 14 February, as chancellor of the duchy of Lancaster. Henry Hartley Flower (1830–1911), 1st Viscount Wolverhampton, was lord president of the council from October 1908 to June 1910; he was succeeded by Earl Beauchamp.

success of the evening in the way of looks. London is seething with gossip, and a most undesirable place to live & move in just now.... My dearest love – Your Father

Edwin Montagu to V.A.   *Monday 7 March*
                                                   India Office, Whitehall

Dear Violet
    (I am going to begin as a regular practice to address you as I think of you and hence without permission this opening) I <u>am</u> glad to have received your letter.
    I take it as a sign that you have used your 'rest' to take stock and that you want and feel that you can use your friends. That is the great thing – that you can use them....
    Let me offer you my share to take on paper or in talk as often as you like. I have learnt to live by friendships because – Well whenever you ask it you shall have my story to make my claim good....
    Your father is behaving with courage which masquerades as cowardice, and is the victim of cabinet carelessness in the past.
    The Albert Hall was a colossal mistake. Our party is divided into those that think it retrievable and those that don't. I believe your father is ready to sacrifice himself. I wish he would look on contingent possibilities more and lead rather than focus.
    Goodbye, dear Violet, his [Archie's] courage remains with you and you have a regiment of friends eager to do service. Tell me when to come to you and what to talk about, to sit still and I am ready now and always to help. yrs Edwin S Montagu.
    This lacks coherence and reserve. But it's spontaneous.

V.A. to Edwin Montagu   *Monday 11 April*
                                        10 Downing Street, Whitehall,
                                                              S.W.

Dear Mr. Montagu.
    You wrote me such an ideal letter – & I have begun you several long answers on different days – & then torn them up. It is so difficult to say what <u>I</u> feel – because no words come within <u>range</u> of it – what I <u>say</u> must

sound either stilted or hysterical – but there is no need of words to send to a friend who can understand like you.

You do help me so much – your <u>trust</u> in me gives me back confidence – Thank you from my heart

Violet

Diary – Monday 18 April – 10 Downing Street, Whitehall, S.W.

... <u>Night</u>

A bad half hour before lunch – then the weary daily task of trying to sponge my eyelids into respectability (they are now permanently scarlet!) then lunch next door with the Lloyd Georges – quite an amusing meal – I sat next to Ll G. who has charm no doubt but no sense of humour & I think an inferior sense of words to Winston's. Mrs LlG. very homely & pathetic & Megan delightful.[1]

Afternoon spent in the Ladies Gallery – O'Brien made a violent denunciatory speech accusing Lloyd George of every sort of breach of faith & honour – Ll.G. followed – very clever & sinuous but I thought not convincing – then Redmond.[2]

I dined alone with Margot & had rather a <u>nice</u> talk with her afterwards. I found a little Anthology from Raymond waiting for me – 'Words & Days' – which I had always wanted – it was sweet of him wasn't it?

Diary – Thursday 21 April – Vice Regal Lodge, Dublin

My own Darling[3] – After a long journey & <u>mill</u>-pond crossing I got here yesterday. It <u>was</u> exciting & driving up through the strange sad streets – everything different in a way one could not define from any place one had seen before – & past the sentries into the courtyard. How I felt at every stage – from landing onwards – 'he will meet me here' – & longed for the joy in your eyes.

Up the stairs & through $\frac{1}{4}$ of a mile of passages & rooms into a long

[1] Megan Lloyd George (1902–66), the fourth child of David and Margaret Lloyd George, was the same age as Violet's half-brother Anthony.

[2] William O'Brien (1852–1928), journalist and author, and Irish Nationalist MP for Cork City, 1900–18; O'Brien accused Lloyd George of deception over the whisky duties in the 1909 budget, during a debate on the allocation of parliamentary time for the final stages of the bill.

[3] From late December 1909 until June 1913 Violet's diary entries took the form of letters addressed to Archie, generally beginning 'Beloved', or 'My Darling', and ending 'Your Own', or simply 'Yours'.

narrow drawing room where people were having tea. An embarrassed scone or two & then they left to practise a strange dance for St. Patrick's ball that night – & then a sudden fanfare of trumpets & several outriders – & in drove your Mother & Father in a wonderful carriage on high springs covered with postillions & wigs & crowns & every sort of grandeur....

I struggled through the complexities of the country dance with a man called General May – then a short feverish rest – then I dressed – stuck 3 feathers into my hair – (alas! – I've got <u>such</u> a bad feather-face!) & dinner happened – with a lot of Viceregal ritual – the King's health etc.

I sat between Anson (who is fundamentally offensive – but spared me a good deal – I believe thro' contempt for my sense of humour) & Chichester – nice.

After it & an interminable succeeding wait – my <u>Presentation</u> happened. You would have laughed Dearest – at hearing my name bellowed by the last of a long row of ADCs & seeing me curtsey to yr. Mother & Father – The Procession was then formed – trains pages, God Save The King & all – rather like Tannhäuser – & we entered St Patrick's Hall – which looked very big & brilliant – quite full of glittering uniforms & swords & medals & hideous women covered with feathers of every colour. First the Country Dance happened – then I talked to General May a little & Sir Anthony Weldon & then went & sat on a seat between Lady Jekyll & Lady Lyttelton.[1]

All our own tunes happened & there was that sort of gala atmosphere of clash & glitter & movement & sound that both our hearts have always leapt to – & I thought of that wonderful feeling we used to have in crowds of <u>absolute</u> alone-ness – in the middle of everybody – I just clenched my teeth & sat still.

Your Father & Mother sat on a dais – & he sent for me to go & talk to him there. He was divinely imaginative & sweet – he has your genius for emotion Darling – minus yr. splendid ballast & focus & control. We danced together then – he had not done so the whole year till then – but I was so moved by it & by his seeing that we were both suffering enough to be able to – with one another – I sat on for hours – yr. Mother came down to my bedroom & undid me.

Through all the pain I was so <u>proud</u> Beloved to belong to you – – Yr own.

[1] Sir Anthony Weldon (1863–1917), 6th Bt; Irish baronet, and chamberlain to the lord-lieutenant of Ireland, 1908–17.

Diary – Sunday 24 April – Vice Regal Lodge, Dublin

I hadn't one second to write all yesterday. Déménagement from the Castle happened & your Mother was <u>ill</u> – which made me very unwilling to go but she was afraid of infection etc. & made me. Aggie, Barbara, Katharine Lyttelton & I made a strange expedition to tea with Horace Plunkett a rather earnest bore who lives in a house like some hybrid cross between a Lutyens & the Danish Pavilion at Overstrand.[1] We were taken over every room – onto the roof where a high gale was blowing – by him & an American called Pinchot – (Roosevelt's right-hand man – Ly Lyttelton described him as) who disserted on the American 'conservation policy' which means that they haven't got trees enough to last them 10 years in fires.[2] We had an uncomfortable à 6 at tea – & the only gleam in the whole expedition was the appearance of Russell – who is A.E. the poet & painter – & looks <u>exactly</u> as he ought – hairy visionary – & <u>very</u> amusing.[3]

We had a peaceful dinner. I sat next Sir Neville who is a most beloved creature & bumbles away about battles & Wellington.[4] He read aloud to us to-night – battle descriptions by Napier getting so keen & moved himself as to become quite incomprehensible.[5]

We had military church this morning with a <u>band</u> – & everyone in uniform. Rather a good sermon on immortality preached by Canon Tristram (!) – & the King of Love my Shepherd is – I love its simple touching little tune.[6]

Afterwards all the band mustered & played in the big hall – hung with deadly weapons of every age & riddled banners – & all the old pensioners

---

[1] Katharine Sarah Lyttelton *née* Stuart-Wortley; she married, in 1883, General Sir Neville Lyttelton (below). Sir Horace Plunkett (1854–1932), commissioner for the congested districts board, Ireland, 1891–1918.

[2] Gifford Pinchot (1865–1946), professor of forestry at Yale, 1903–36, and director of the United States Forestry Service, 1898–1910. Roosevelt's administration placed heavy emphasis on the conservation and development of natural resources, and Pinchot was central to this policy: 'Tall, lean, and hardy, with a flourishing handlebar moustache and intense eyes, Pinchot was a man of action … and he quickly became a close companion and adviser in Roosevelt's select circle' (*Dictionary of American Biography*).

[3] George William 'Æ' Russell (1867–1935), Irish poet, painter, economist and journalist.

[4] General Sir Neville Lyttelton (1845–1931), brother of the 8th Viscount Cobham, veteran of many campaigns, including the River War (Sudan) and the Boer War (South Africa).

[5] Sir Neville probably read from General Sir William Francis Napier (1785–1860), whose *History of the War in the Peninsula and the South of France* was widely reproduced after its original publication, in six volumes, 1828–60.

[6] The Reverend John Tristram (d. 1926), canon of St Patrick's, Dublin, 1908–22. Tristram was a leader-writer for the *Irish Times*, and played a prominent role in resisting the second Home Rule bill, 1893.

eat their lunch – thick chunks of meat & bread – & little barelegged boys came in to hear the music.

Professor Mahaffy sat next to me at lunch – he looks very bloated & gave way to terrible excesses in the way of food – disappointing in the finest Greek scholar alive.[1] He said several good things to me but most of them were quotations from what he'd said to other people. As for instance to Lord Spencer: 'Ireland is a place where the impossible is always happening & the inevitable never comes off'....

Diary – Friday 6 May – Vice Regal Lodge, Dublin

Night – While your Mother & I were talking on my bed to-night there was a knock at the door – & a secretary told us the King had died at midnight. There had been an alarming bulletin in the morning papers – that his condition caused anxiety – & I (with my Winchester experience of bulletins) felt it was hopeless at once.

The news got worse & worse during the day – they were evidently letting the public down gently. And now it is all over.

The King dead – <u>dead</u> – the same thing people call you – I can't realize it. He was to me only a splendidly characteristic figurehead – full of personality. A function property – I think of last year's Court Ball – & you & I valtzing round & round before him on the daïs – who could have dreamt then that <u>you</u> & <u>he</u> were destined to the same strange adventure within a few months....

V.A. to M.B.C.   *Friday 6 May*
                                            Vice Regal Lodge, Dublin

Dearest Bongie.

I feel that I have behaved rather badly about writing – but I have led a very variegated life since arriving here. First 3 days of great pomp at the Castle – trumpets & postillions & sentries outside the bathroom & a band at breakfast – then a peaceful week at Abbey Leix – a <u>most</u> beautiful place – with Cynthia Ego & Mary – then back here – where the Viceregal ritual is somewhat modified.[2]

[1] John Pentland Mahaffy (1839–1919), first professor of ancient history at Trinity College Dublin, 1869, and provost of the college, 1914–19.

[2] Mary Charteris (b. 1895), younger sister of Cynthia, and the sixth child of Lord and Lady Elcho.

It is a delicious house in the middle of the Phoenix Park – with an enormous garden gleaming with early greenness; – wall-flowers – yews – sentry boxes – miles of glass – avenues of kennelled cats & dogs – a shelter which revolves with the wind – & a <u>wonderful</u> view of distant hills which changes every day. We usually have busy afternoons of cattle shows, Industry centenaries – tubercular congresses etc – but in the morning & evening I'm very free to write or stick or drift about.[1] I've got a sitting room in which all my properties are installed, I should sit in the garden but it's so arctically cold. I'm going to ride a little mildly – as I feel sure it would be very good for my sleep & food. I feel such dreadful <u>permanent</u> physical lethargy – & walking is too dull unless one has got someone who makes one forget one is doing it. It suddenly occurs to me that Venetia will have told you all my news. She was a transformed <u>being</u> here! very painstaking, feminine, bright & avenante – her gruff baritone changed to a siren soprano – shooting glittering glances hither & thither – wearing a new 'fish' every night & spending tête à tête days at the zoo with the A.D.C's! A Viceregal Court is certainly her assiette – & bogus-captains her element (All the ADCs here are called Captain though civilians – they are mostly bounders of the deepest dye – & one – Ld. Anson a cad). It is sad to think how much time she has wasted in the wrong place!!...

It is very extraordinary how strong & how utterly indefinable the atmosphere of Ireland is. It is as different from England as Cairo – & yet there is not one <u>concrete</u> symptom of difference one can put one's finger on (such as pyramids – black men – oases etc) except perhaps these ridiculous little outside cars.

I drove with Barbara on one – in a vain attempt to balance Aggie on the other side – I am very bad at them – scramble up – cling to an iron hook & then take a flying leap onto the pavement when dismounting. Write please & give me all yr. news <u>Love</u> from yr V.

Diary – Sunday 8 May – Vice Regal Lodge, Dublin

It is the evening – your Mother & I & the Lord Chief Justice had tea together & Birrell has just come....

The Service for the King happened in the Chapel Royal this morning. Everything draped in crepe & purple ribbons & the 2 funeral marches Beethoven & Saul – well played – 'Oh God our help in ages past' sung to the <u>wrong tune</u> – which I found it hard to bear.

I <u>didn't</u> tell you that I went yesterday to Russell's studio.... It is one of a long row of rather Tooting-like houses – semi-detached with strips of

---

[1] Sticking pictures into scrapbooks was a common Edwardian pastime.

garden at the back. Russell opened the door to us looking shaggier than ever – & we looked at his pictures which are very uneven some really inspired – others just irrelevant splashes of colour – all highly individual. He has absolutely no draughtsmanship – & draws only what he sees <u>inside</u> his head – not what he observes without – so if ever the vision is cloudy or blurred – which it is in the nature of visions to be, the picture suffers – especially in detail.

He showed me one – very promising sea-shore with airy children playing on it – 'But what am I to do? I forget what their legs looked like – & I can't draw anything like a leg now' – 'Shall I get a girl with nice long legs to come in & stand to you George' – (said his wife a kind of practical adoring inferior) – 'No – no – models upset me – I can only draw from within – I must wait till it comes back – that's all'.

I had an excellent talk with him – & he delighted me by saying when I reminded him of the stiffness & constraint at Horace Plunkett's – 'But <u>conversation</u> is only possible between two people' – voicing my own much persecuted opinion. He went on to talk of vision & achievement – he thinks there is no void between these two which cannot be bridged – granting one has sufficient faith in oneself – 'As one's aspiration – so is one's inspiration'. And when I mentioned Alfred Austin – whose goal was poetry – 'Well he has achieved it according to his lights – he has reached his conception of poetry'.[1]

I couldn't abandon my opinion that those of greater enlightenment must realize without being able to span it the gulf that separates them from their desire – but he was full of glorious optimism about this – & only said 'Not if you have faith in yourself – not if you have confidence'.

He spoke rather amusingly of Roosevelt (à-propos of Pinchot) – 'the only man who has made the commonplace – intense. And can't you hear him coming now – can't you hear his great feet splashing up the Nile'.[2]

He talked very well & amusingly – (I wish I could remember more he said) & with delicious unself-consciousness & amusement in what he was saying himself – & no misgiving as to how it was going to be received by his listener.

I bought a picture – with rather a lovely landscape & a boy's figure blowing a horn on a rock – full of rhythm. All his positions & movements are. We discussed how children always have this quality – & those in

---

[1] Alfred Austin (1835–1913), poet laureate from 1896 until his death in June 1913. His verse was much derided, and as poet laureate he was overshadowed by Rudyard Kipling, who had been considered for the laureateship, but had indicated his disinclination to accept.

[2] Theodore Roosevelt (1858–1919), twenty-sixth president of the United States, 1901–9; after leaving office Roosevelt undertook a ten-month hunting expedition through central and northern Africa, and afterwards made a grand tour of Europe.

contact with the earth & sea – but how quickly & entirely top-hatted men & life in towns destroy it....

Diary – Monday 9 May – Vice Regal Lodge, Dublin

Beloved – This morning I rode! It was wonderful.... All the Park gleaming with green loveliness – & the blackthorn out. We had a little mild jumping – over a ditch coming home. Then a rest – lunch – & off creaking with stiffness to the Proclamation.

The Castle yard was lined with troops the cavalry keeping back the crowd – & some infantry drawn up in front of the entrance – who went through a wonderful series of complex salutes when their Excellencies drove up.

We were all ushered after some delay into the Privy Council room where Generals & Judges & other great men sat round a long table in medals & wigs. Some reading was done – very well – by yr Father who wore the order of the Thistle – & after a good deal of signing we went out onto the balcony where we heard the Ulster King at Arms (mounted on a charger & dressed like a character in Alice in Wonderland) proclaim George V. He did it very well & looked magnificent – & there was a good deal of cheering as he clattered out of the Castle Yard – to repeat the ceremony all over Dublin....

Your Father & Mother drove away with pomp & postillions – & I followed with Johnson in a motor. Seeing Anson & Williams in your uniform was strange Darling. I thought of our last Court Ball together – & how you were bullied by all the Royal hags – & fledglings wanting to dance with you – & we finally had to fly from the room. Then back to the Speyers'[1] – do you remember – where we had the most wonderful dance together I can ever remember almost – such extraordinary swing & rhythm & unity of élan – & the feeling that so much more than our bodies was moving together....

[1] Sir Edgar Speyer (1862–1932), 1st Bt, 1906. German-educated financier; partner in family firms based in London, Frankfurt and New York. A generous supporter of the Liberal party. He married, 1902, Leonara *née* von Stosch, a professional violinist, and they held concerts at their homes in Grosvenor Street, London, and at Overstrand, Norfolk.

Venetia Stanley to V.A.   *Tuesday 10 May*
                                          18 Mansfield Street, W.

My darling somehow I haven't written to you at all during all this week, but as you haven't either it makes it all right. Everything has been so horrible tho', since the King died, deep gloom, not real but enforced and a permanent feeling of Sunday everywhere. I certainly shouldn't come back to London an instant sooner than you need for the funeral. I am thankful to be leaving Thursday and don't ever want to come back. I wish I was still in Dublin. How was the riding, you went out yesterday didn't you? By the way I owe you 10/ for the horse I rode, so will you pay it and I will give it back to you.

I lunched at Downing St on Saturday, Margot, Eliza, Beb, Fräu, Mikky (he puts up such a funny face when he asks how you are and always alludes to you as 'her' or 'she' only) Lulu Harcourt, Zelle Zelle and a man called Sir Vincent Corbett.[1] M. was in tip top form, as you can imagine she absolutely revels in the excitement of the sudden death of a King. She did all her imitations of both the K. and Queen several times. . . . On Sunday I went to the afternoon service at St. Paul's. Very splendid. A Brahms anthem Behold All Flesh Is As The Grass and at the end The Dead March in Saul with drums wonderfully concealed and placed in the dome, and straight after it God Save the King. Marvellous but it was a kind of stage effect which makes one cry but doesn't really move one, or it didn't me. I couldn't help thinking all the while of the last time I heard the March and with what different feelings[2]. . . .

Everyone says G. V is a knurd. I never heard it before had you.[3]

Write Venetia

---

[1] Captain Sir Vincent Corbett (1861–1936), financial adviser to the Egyptian government, 1904–7, and minister resident to Venezuela, 1907–10.

[2] The 'Dead March' from Handel's oratorio *Saul* was played at Archie Gordon's funeral at Haddo, Thursday 23 December 1909, at which both Violet and Venetia were present.

[3] Rumours that the Prince of Wales was a drunk (i.e. 'knurd') persisted after his accession as George V in May 1910. In September the Austrian ambassador, Mensdorff, wrote in his dispatch to Vienna: 'His Majesty hears all sorts of remarks about his alleged alcoholism made by crowds in the streets. At pious meetings in the East End of London, prayers are said for Queen Mary and the royal children, begging the protection of Heaven on their unhappy drunkard home. The Archbishop of Canterbury and the clergy . . . are now trying to fight this risible legend of the drinker King, but it will take a long time to eradicate' (Kenneth Rose, *King George V*, 81–2).

Diary – Thursday 19 May – 10 Downing Street, Whitehall, S.W.

... Father & I have just come back from Westminster Hall. It was a most extraordinary & impressive sight. Hundreds & hundreds of people – men & women & boys & girls & little babies streaming silently like a great sea down the steps & filing past the coffin. It lay in the middle of the hall guarded by 6 motionless Lifeguardsmen with bowed heads – a splendidly impassive Ghurka & some Beef-eaters. On it some flags & the regalia. Above the wonderful vaulting of the roof. From time to time the guard was changed – glittering against the stone in slowly moving lines. Father & I & Ld Carrington & Lulu & John Burns stayed on & watched the Foreign Legations arrive & walk past – blazing in every variety of medal & uniform.[1] Then a wonderful thing happened – the Queen arrived quite unexpectedly with the King of Denmark & the Emperor of Russia, shook hands with all the Foreign officers – & knelt down on each side of the coffin. She did everything with extraordinary dignity & pathos & grace – I was much touched.

Father & I drove home through the crowds....

V.A. to Edwin Montagu   *Monday 6 June*
10 Downing Street, Whitehall,
S.W.

I write to ask whether you would care to give some small sum to Archie's memorial from his friends? Lots of different schemes were suggested to me. Evan Charteris wanted to have a window in Balliol chapel – but I felt very strongly that if Archie was to be commemorated it must be in life & if possible in happiness – not in stained glass or stone.

The present idea is to form a fund the interest on which is to be devoted to starting in life a number of boys – whose conditions are otherwise too hopelessly destitute to give them a fair chance at the outset.

These boys should be recruited from one district (Stepney) through schools & care Committees (who would be likely to have the most accurate knowledge of their circumstances). They would form a Club called after Archie – meeting regularly for purposes of pure enjoyment (no insidious undercurrent of improvement!) This would have to be carefully organized by people like Bongie & me – once a play, once a meal, once a Magic

---

[1] Charles Robert Wynn-Carrington (1843–1928), 1st Earl Carrington, 1895, and 1st Marquess of Lincolnshire, 1912; president of the board of agriculture, 1905–11, and lord privy seal, 1911–12.

Lantern, once the zoo etc. & at the age of 14 or 15 having graduated in fun – they would be apprenticed & placed – & new boys would step into the vacancies.

The old ones would not be disbanded but our financial obligations towards them would be discharged. By this I mean the disbursing of the premium for Apprenticeship – which costs from 15 to 25 £.

I'm told we should need an income of 80 £ a year to start with 10 boys. These would mean a capital of 2000 £ – or which is far more likely to come to us a smaller capital – & a supplementary income through yearly subscriptions.

Will you give an infinitesimal yearly subscription for life! – or a slightly larger donation? I ask from sentimental as well as mercenary motives.

This is a purely business letter. I should like to see & talk to you about many other things. I am away with poor Olive – you will have seen by the papers what has befallen her.[1] She had only seen him 3 times but she had woven a good deal round him – I'm in D. St for lunch on Wed. do come I return here Thurs. I loved yr. letter from the yacht. Yrs V.A

Diary – Monday 11 July – 10 Downing Street, Whitehall, S.W.

... A very wonderful meeting of the Salvation Army – I gave away 300 certificates to cadets – it was strange looking into face after face as they passed me – & I had an odd feeling that you must be coming soon – that our eyes were just going to meet.

I spoke more or less spontaneously the audience was keen & vibrant & the atmosphere very electric. Mrs Lloyd George rambled a little about porridge & cancer & hygiene generally – there were hymns sung in very rough touching voices to a band of drums & cymbals & brass – & prayers.

I was much moved – & had a flicker of the feeling of the shortness of life & how fully one should live it....

Diary – Tuesday 12 July – 10 Downing Street, Whitehall, S.W.

A morning of letters & a tiny walk with Bongie in St. James's Park among the pelicans. We thought how you would have envied his Secretaryship & being able to nip in at odd moments for freakish lightning dentists at irregular hours. Then a rest – I am feeling very exhausted just now – & on to the House where I listened with real interest & curiosity to the Suffrage

---

[1] Olive Macleod's fiancé, Lieutenant Boyd Alexander, had been killed while on an expedition in Africa.

debate.[1] Such strange & unexpected facets of people revealed – one realized for the first time how dreary it had been to hear them steadily contradicting each other across the floor of the House. Winston spoke <u>very</u> well – & Father <u>marvellously</u> – so sanely & temperately & with such <u>breadth</u> & size in his treatment of the subject. Then AJB – very supple & clever & frivolous & quite academic.

I had to hurry off to a dinner the McKennae were giving at Greenwich – & arrived (mercifully) to find it nearly over.

We looked at stars through a telescope afterwards.... It was a very wonderful view from the observatory – London all wrapped in smoke & mist & the glorious buildings – & the river covered with lights. We went back by boat & I was just in time to hear the Division figures. A good deal bigger majority for the Bill than they thought there would be (110) but it was shelved all right which showed the voting to have been fairly theoretical.

And now bless you my Dearest & Best – I have given you all my ant-heap news. Send me your love – & the peace & courage it should bring Your very <u>own</u>

Diary – Tuesday 2 August – The Manor House, Mells, Somerset

Here – after lunch with Jasper & a long train journey in a packed carriage. A walk in the wet but <u>brilliant</u> with flowers garden – with Maurice – puddles standing in the little tiled paths. We spoke of Edward's 3rd over which there is apparently a great sickness – <u>poor</u> Frances very upset.[2] I am so sad for her I know she invests those rather concrete hall-marks of success with deep significance – & feels them to be symbols. I suppose one would mind for anyone one really cared for. I should have for you – I shouldn't have been content with my own private recognition of you however certain – I should have wanted the world to know too....

---

[1] The Commons debated the Female Suffrage bill proposed by the Labour member D. J. Shackleton. It was, remarked *The Times*, an 'interesting and non-party' occasion: F. E. Smith and Lord Hugh Cecil, firm Unionist allies on the central issues of the day, found themselves entering different sides of the division lobby.

[2] Oxford 'honours' degrees were then divided into four classes, and great kudos attached (then as now) to the gaining of a 'first', the highest. This would undoubtedly have been Frances Horner's wish for her son.

V.A. to Venetia Stanley   ***Thursday 4 August***
                              The Manor House, Mells, Somerset

My Darling – One line of thanks & blessing for my three delicious days of rest with you. I did love them – & having a real span of return to uninterrupted vegetable intimacy – & glorious tracts of night-talk.

It is nice being here – the best atmosphere I know – Frances, Katharine, Sir John & I. Edward left this morning & Maurice last night. I was sad to part with him – & don't feel a bit happy about him poor darling. He is so helpless & hopelessly unequipped to manage the rather sordid financial side of life – & bound to be bullied by publishers & agents – I rather wish I had offered him Father's Secretaryship – it would have just kept him & North St going & given him time to write in between whiles. I'm sure he ought to have some regular occupation & be pinned down to a stool for a few hours a day. It would make him write better if he wasn't free to do it whenever he wanted....

Goodbye Darling bless you. I am so glad this summer is over – it has been the most tiring & difficult bit of life I've ever lived through
        Yr own
I will see you <u>Friday</u> in Munich—

Diary – Friday 12 August – Munich

My own Darling – How different to the usual 12th – with lunch out of doors on the heather – & paper bags popping & scones being thrown about – & cherries being caught in people's mouths & ginger beer bottles going off....

The journey was very long & exhausting.... Cys hasn't come yet. I hope he hasn't bungled but think it more than probable that he has....

... I feel rather a sadness at being alone in this big hot far away town – but Scotland without you would hurt much more. I hope Ober A[mmergau]. is going to be a really wonderful experience & the Operas too. Those sort of detaching impersonal sensations are rather reprieves – though of course music we both always <u>immediately</u> applied didn't we....

Cys has come! When the very very last bus – of many buses – drew up empty my heart <u>did</u> sink – but a few minutes later up he drove in a fly <u>with</u> his luggage – in his brown Skipworth coat! I thought it must be a mirage at first – I had looked for him in so many flies – but no – there he was darling beloved – looking so well & when we got upstairs he put both his arms round me & hugged me again & again 'Visey I am glad to see you – I've never been so glad to see you in my life. I've been so lonely these last two days' – <u>Poor</u> Darling – he'd had all my desolation only much worse – & had even been dog-alone for the night at an hôtel in Geneva (I would have gone there to meet him if I'd known) & had had not one penny of money to get himself food in the journey – so he was starving with nothing but a schinken brötchen behind him since 6 in the morning. I ordered him fried eggs & cold ham & beer – & he eat them downstairs with joy – & we've now been having a glorious talk before bed. He sleeps in the next room with a door through – I do love him.

Bless you my Dearest & Best – I feel a shade less unhappy <u>Yr own</u>

Diary – Tuesday 23 August – Train to Garmisch, Bavaria

Beloved – All this week in Munich – while my thoughts have been hardly ever away from you I haven't written one word – mostly because Cys has talked so late in my room every night – often till nearly 2 – when I have been dropping with sleep.

We have had rather an amusing life. Restaurant meals – & <u>glorious</u> Operas & a little lazy sight-seeing in the mornings. Once we went to the Ausstellung – a sort of Earls Court at night – & I went on a switchback. Somehow 'fun' without you seems to hurt the most of all. Once we had dinner in a Biergarden – Lowenbräu Keller – & Cys & Bongie consumed enormous Bocks with pewter lids – & a band played & afterwards they were photographed looking 'lusty' – (Fräu has been with us & in her best German form. I imagine rather like what she was with you at Berlin). Once we went to a lake called Starnberger See for the day & lay in hayfields in the shade with crickets whirring all around.

I have <u>loved</u> the music – though at times it was torture listening to it alone – especially the first act of Walküre & <u>Tristan</u> last night.[1] In spite of the perfect arrangements the theatre a little lacks size – it isn't vast enough to detach oneself in.

I tried to think of you listening to it all in Berlin – & perhaps wanting me – about a millionth as much as I longed for you now....

Diary – Friday 2 September – 10 Downing Street, Whitehall, S.W.

Dearest – I got here yesterday morning – very tired – after a smooth night's crossing. We drove through the well-known streets with autumn strangeness upon them – foreigners reading Baedekers under Westminster Abbey – workmen pickaxing up most of the pavements. An odd man in the hall....

---

[1] *Die Walküre* is the second opera in the tetralogy that comprises Wagner's *Ring* cycle.

V.A. to M.B.C.   *Tuesday 13 September*
                             Archerfield House, Dirleton, East
                                                      Lothian

I loved getting your two letters. Bless you for all your grind over my
affaires – I am grateful <u>always</u>. You don't think I ever forget to be – do you?
I am sometimes so afraid of its seeming to you that I am taking things for
granted – & indeed dearest Bongie I never, <u>never</u> do....
    ... I think you were right about Nan [Tennant]. Poor dear – she will
never get her deserts from life. I think women's lot is almost the <u>most</u>
arbitrary & capricious feature of this slipshod scheme – nothing seems to
come to them because they're worth it. The greatest things come quite
unearned – often unrecognized – because of some irresponsible chance –
gold-dust quality without which the <u>realest</u>, & finest natures seem to be
sacrificed to a dusty lot.
    There was a general Exodus here to-day – Lizard – Nan – Ernley (who
was overtaken by bad earache) – 2 Pauls & Bluey come to-morrow. Simon
is being sapless – but with a fascinating face – <u>Love</u> – go on writing V.

The Archie Gordon Club

Violet's living memorial to Archie Gordon was a boys' club bearing
his name which she founded in Hoxton, a deprived area of East
London, in the autumn of 1910. She raised over £1,000 from
among fifty of Archie's friends, with which to finance the club; it
had rooms in an Anglican institute called the Maurice Hostel.
Violet's mainstay in the enterprise was Bongie, who had for several
years been involved in running the Balliol College Boys' Club in
Hammersmith. Archie's Club had at any one time around a dozen
members, between the ages of eleven and fourteen, specifically
chosen because of their disadvantaged backgrounds. The emphasis
of Club activities was on educational entertainment, and in spite
of Violet's playful avowal to the contrary, there was an 'improving'
aspect to the proceedings. She wanted the boys to have 'pure fun',
but she also wanted them to have prospects, and this meant self-
improvement. They were encouraged to attend night-school, to
read and to debate. She enthused at the thought of their enjoying
translations of the Classics, and perhaps unconsciously modelled
them on her brothers. When the boys reached working age efforts
were made to find them apprenticeships: to this end Violet and
Bongie enlisted the help of their wealthier friends. The philanthropic aspects of the Club, though, were overshadowed by the
recreational: there were annual summer camps, sightseeing trips

and a weekly 'Club night'. Running the Club helped Violet over-come the loss of Archie, and it also brought out how much she enjoyed this sort of social activity. Bongie wrote to her in July 1911, when she was with the Club at camp in Littlestone: 'I am afraid of you getting rather tired out, especially if rounders becomes popular. How you ran.'

Diary – Friday 7 October – 10 Downing Street, Whitehall, S.W.

My own Darling – Such a thrilling day – I embarked in a taxi with Cys after lunch & we plunged through deepest darkest London to Wenlock Road School. I was led up flight upon flight of stone steps by a little boy called Price – to Mr. Ramsden's room at the top of the house. He was looking more alert & less weary than the first time I met him – & I had a distinct up. We proceeded (he & I & Cyril – with blazing hatless hair & grey flannel trousers!) to go through every class in the school – till we culminated in the top one whence the nucleus was selected.

It was extraordinarily interesting – & very funny! You would have smiled if you had seen the poor little oddities called up one by one 'Now Miss Asquith – this is a very good nice-spoken little boy – you speak to him & see' – or 'This boy Miss Asquith is a little hero – step up Yeats – he saved his little friend's life in the canal'. All this without an attempt at sotto voce. The boys themselves I thought very delightful – & most touching – I had a succès (in humour) with one of the younger classes when being not too rigorously chaperoned by the master & made them all roar with laughter – I don't quite know how!

It was very exciting reaching the ultimate class & setting eyes on the boys that might be mine – like the Israelites seeing the Land of Promise. Fourteen possibilities were sent up to me – I liked them in varying degrees – but all a good deal. I tried rather vainly to vary my formulae in interrogation & to veil the indelicate probing into family circumstances etc. which fell to my lot – but it all resulted in a rather crude Aubrey I'm afraid. However all their strange little names & addresses are written down – & how I am longing to begin.

You can't think how pathetic it all was – the brave drudgery & cheerfulness of the poor little undermasters – grinding away their lives in these dismal class-rooms – the pale plants trying hard to grow in pots on the window ledge – one or two small fishes caught in the canal & kept in a small tank of opaque water in which floated one slimy strand of weed. The wild spirits of the boys in the midst of all the squalor was very wonderful – they were all let out into the stone playground at 3.30 for 10 minutes – you never saw such riotous joy. We looked in on the Club Room on our way back – the mystic fabric is springing – though by no means noiselessly. Hammers & saws & planks & paintpots & men in aprons as busy as bees. It gave me an intoxicating sensation to go in & know I had put it all in motion & that it was <u>Yours</u> – I saw dear little Hyde[1] – who alas! says it would be <u>quite</u> impracticable & impossible to have 2 green bay trees in tubs outside the door – as they would be torn down & turned into firewood before you could say knife! Otherwise he didn't discourage anything (though Bongie said he was a little governessy about the cocoa to him!) Cys & I & B – went to the Follies for the first time since we were there together <u>Dearest</u> – that perfect – disreputable party of you & I & Bongie & Venetia & Cynthia & Beb. <u>How</u> you loved 'I've eat a maggot'. You took me home yourself do you remember?

V.A. to Venetia Stanley   *Monday 10 October*
                                               Vice Regal Lodge, Dublin

My Darling. Alas the 26th is impossible I'm afraid – as Father's Aberdeen Rectorial Address is on the 24th – & I shall be at Archerfield for a few days after that – till about the 1st when I come South to start the Club. . . .

I got here by the late train on Saturday – & found the Pirries[2] – & that decayed old aunt of A's Ly Harriet Lindsay with her moth-eaten husband – & a rather dwindled & changed staff. . . .

Yesterday was Sunday so I didn't attempt games with them. We went to Castle Knock church in the morning – & I did Davidson & the kennels & gardens in the afternoon. Birrell came to tea. I am always terrified of what he is going to say next when he is with them – & torn in half between a desire to protect them from him & a passionate appreciation of his jokes.

Ly A – What did you think of Miss MacNeill Mr. Birrell? the Secretary of this new Pasteurized Dépôt? a very very able – – –

Birrell – The ugliest woman I ever saw – the very ugliest.

Ly A – (smiling rather bewilderedly) But <u>most</u> efficient.

B – Oh that face!

   etc. etc.

Just in from a long & gossipy drive with Lady Lyttelton. Between her & the Birrells I shall find a good deal of civilized companionship.

---

[1] The Reverend Robert Robertson Hyde, chaplain of the Maurice Hostel, Diocese of London, from 1907.

[2] William James Pirrie (1847–1924), 1st Baron Pirrie, 1906; married, in 1879, Margaret *née* Carlisle. He was the chairman of Harland and Wolff, Belfast shipbuilders and engineers, and an ex-lord mayor of Belfast.

I'm going to play golf at Dollymount to-morrow & am intriguing to get the first footman Alec (who won a cup at Braemar) to go with instead of Captain Hunter.

I am going to Peggy's on the 18th. This letter is almost Olivian in length & matter. Prompt Buxton – wide in outline & rich in detail expected from you.

Love – V

The Women's Health Assoc. is going to sit from 11 to 8 on Friday

Venetia Stanley to V.A.   *Wednesday 12 October*
Alderley Park, Chelford, Cheshire

My darling glorious Buxton received with great joy in spite of the unpleasant news contained in it, that you could not come here. I resent you being in Cheshire and not here, perhaps I shall see you for an instant when you are at Crewe. . . .

As for my Buxton your suggestion that it should be wide in scope is rather hard to follow, but I will give you some rich detail as to Mrs Humphry [Ward]'s visit. I had warned Margaret before she came that the first thing she would do on seeing me would be to ask how you were, it used to be Margot.[1]

She hadn't been in the house 5 minutes before she said: 'Have you been to Archerfield lately. How is Violet. Arnie has just been there. He is so happy with all there'. And then afterwards she said 'Does Arnie talk politics much at Archerfield. I am always afraid he may be so overbearing, he is so intolerant if people disagree with him'. I think it's rather pathetic the way the poor old thing imagines that Arnie is treated as an oracle in other houses besides his own, she doesn't in the least realize that you 'make a butt of him'.

She asked me (whether she was thinking of Arnie or not I don't know) if I thought you could ever bring yourself to marry a conservative. She was very affectionate and purred at me the whole time. She also read part of her new book aloud, I believe it was terribly boring.[2] Since she left Mother, Margaret, Arthur and I have been alone. . . .

. . . Your V

---

[1] Henrietta Margaret Goodenough *née* Stanley (1874–1956), Venetia's eldest sister.
[2] Mrs Humphry Ward's *Canadian Born* had been published that April.

Diary – Sunday 16 October – Vice Regal Lodge, Dublin

... We had tea at the Chief Secretary's Lodge – where to my amazement I found Lady Lewis & Katie – beside the Master of Elibank, 2 Illingworths & a host of unknown fishfaces. Mr. Birrell & the Master walked back with me in a fine drizzle – he in his very best form.

The Master wants me to try & make Edgar stand for Colchester. I wish he would – I gather it needs more money than grind.[1]

V.A. to M.B.C.   *Saturday 22 October*
Train to Archerfield House,
East Lothian

... I left Dublin not till Thursday – because I was anxious to see the Olympic launched, scenting a 'sensation' in the distance – & being strongly urged to by the Pirries & Ld & Ly A.[2]

We left Dublin at crow of cock on Thursday – about 7.15 in a special train – he, she, I & 2 A.D.C's glittering & clattering with swords & medals & buttons & martial glory – had an amusing train breakfast – Kedgeree out of thermos pots etc – & reached Belfast about 10.30 – drove through the town with Mayor, Mayoress & mounted escort to the docks – WHERE The biggest ship you can imagine – far & away the biggest in the world – was standing – under a gigantic archway of scaffolding & ironwork – & supported by a forest of props which a thousand men were hammering away as hard as ever they could. You can't think what a jolly noise it made – the thousands of hammerstrokes & the crashing down of the timber. Finally – just upon 11 – she was only held by a sort of iron clutch – a rocket went up – a man pressed a tiny tap which released her – & she glided wonderfully down & took the sea with a lovely dip. If only you could imagine the stupendous size – you would have some idea what it felt like. It's quite the most extraordinary sight I've ever seen. A. would have loved it.

We got back to Dublin by tea-time & at 7 I started for Crewe – had a very rough crossing without a blot on my scutcheon – & ended the day at Crewe station hôtel at 4 in the morning – feeling fairly tired. ...

---

[1] Sir Edgar Vincent was persuaded to stand, and Violet helped in his campaign: below, pp. 230–1.

[2] The *Olympic* was a White Star liner, built by Harland and Wolff of Belfast, the sole builders to the line. At 46,000 tons, she was a very large liner, only marginally smaller than her sister ship the *Titanic*, which was launched in May 1911, displacing 46,328 tons.

... I enclose good news from Hyde – <u>Love</u> & blessing from V.

Diary – Wednesday 2 November – 10 Downing Street, Whitehall, S.W.

My Darling – The Club's first evening is just over – & I feel happier than I have done since you left me. You can't <u>imagine</u> how wonderful it was – the <u>glittering</u> blue & white paint & cherry coloured curtains – & Halma & Ludo & draughts boards & ping & pong & rifle range – & <u>brilliantly</u> happy – <u>darling</u> little boys. They <u>did</u> have fun – I felt as I saw their faces that you would have said 'Do this in remembrance of me – '

They had cocoa at the end & buns & bread & butter – & then Bongie & I knelt down & rather shyly said the Lord's Prayer with them.

I have a wonderful sense of attainment to-night – though of course I am really only at the beginning. Few schemes could have such a gloriously <u>tangible</u> fruition as this one. Wish me luck Beloved

Yr own

Diary – Thursday 3 November – 10 Downing Street, Whitehall, S.W.

Rather a typical London day (of the better sort) just over.

Personal Service Committee in the morning as usual very frowsty & technical – I said not one word – there were only about two to be said about anything & it was only a question of time before everyone said them several times over.

The kind of lunch I <u>love</u> – Father & I & Nash[1] & Sir G. Murray & Jack Pease (only blot) then a Liberal crush of Mrs. Henry – a dentist with Charlie – very piano but charming as ever – & just contemplating another Himalayan journey – then Bongie – rest & dinner between Winston & Birrell. <u>Wonderful</u> talk à trois – here raised as to whether aeroplanists, engineers, explorers, etc were impelled by a desire for the truth – good of humanity etc. or by quite small & personal motives – Birrell mentioning the latter – Winston was very Blakeish & inspired – 'No – no – it's because every man is half an angel' – & on Birrell's laughing – 'I know I'm an angel'.

Birrell spoke of mathematics as the loftiest scheme where the greatest universality was reached – where men 'thought the thought of God'. Not

---

[1] Vaughan Nash (1861–1932), H. H. Asquith's private secretary, 1908–12, inherited from Sir Henry Campbell-Bannerman; he had previously been on the editorial staff of the *Daily Chronicle*.

my idea of them. He said it was the nearest akin to music which I didn't know before.

After dinner we had a good pie talk. Birrell was a little hard on Edward Grey whom he said saw & dramatized himself in every situation of life. He said his speaking was beneath contempt – & when I argued with him about this maintaining it had a certain Doric dignity & impressiveness – he said it had the style of all times – & ages – the style of a stone inscription on a wall – adding 'Clay has no style' – but obviously preferring clay.

V.A. to Venetia Stanley   *Thursday 10 November*
                                        10 Downing Street, Whitehall,
                                        S.W.

My Darling.

The <u>most</u> glorious flowers have arrived & are going to be taken down to the Club to-night. Thank you a thousand times – they <u>will</u> make a difference.

I believe Bongie has told you about our First Night. It really went off with great éclat – the room looked lovely – glittering with new paint & cherry-coloured curtains – & St Georges & the dragon etc – & the boys were divinely responsive & 'malleable' & 'elastic'. They couldn't quite make out what Bongie's raison d'être was – & one of them said to me 'What's he here for? To conjure?' which I thought rather a good idea.

Another asked me whether Halma was called after the battle of Halma – & I was so rattled as to say it was! I foresee the crux will be not to make them have <u>fun</u> – <u>that</u> they have on the very slightest provocation – but to make them have fun in ways which afford a certain amount of imaginative scope. Not always draughts & race game & ping pong etc – I am going to try reading aloud this evening – & devoutly hope I shan't be lynched. My favourite boy's name is Joseph Judd! I am very intimate with him.

... I'm in bed to-day with a cold after the Guildhall dinner & am making a <u>tremendous</u> fuss about it – pouring orgies of grouse down the telephone by my bed.

Aubrey lunched yesterday in his very best form – telling Father how the Wolf Hound bespattered the ceiling with blood whenever he shook his head etc. I thoroughly enjoyed him but he must be strange as daily fare....

It will be fun when you come up darling – mind you let me know & we will arrange aeons of dentist. Egypt still very vague. I shall be at Pixton with you –

        Yr lovingest V

Diary – Thursday 10 November – 10 Downing Street, Whitehall, S.W.

My Darling – Just back from the second Club night – it <u>was</u> just as gloriously successful as the first – & made better by a closer intimacy with the members – 'poor little fellows' – they <u>really</u> <u>do</u> come under this comprehensive heading. They contrive to be marvellously happy on wonderfully little. Each one has a skeleton in his family cupboard which has to be carefully avoided – I blunder heavily on to them now & then 'Jenkins – you can take these flowers home to your Mother'. 'She's been in a lunatic asylum for seven years Miss'. I tried reading aloud to them Rikki Tikky Tavi – I'm not sure they liked it much – but I daresay as Bongie says it's good for them.[1] It's so difficult to get anything in the least corresponding with their ordinary every day experience – & of course in a way one would like to extend it. Father & I went this afternoon to see the lovely new Venus at the British Museum. It was <u>most</u> amusing as the two rival critics collared him – & expounded their opposite theories – he maintaining a splendidly judicial poise between them. . . . Mary & Aubrey were there – she looking very married & lovely – in blue velvet clothes & waved hair – he very much the same as usual – carrying her off to the zoo to buy a wolf.

Father & I had the Guildhall dinner together last night – I thought of last year. It is so strange watching the old landmarks coming round again – like meeting ghosts in a new life. There was a good deal of Alice in Wonderland about it. Sheriffs & Aldermen, & Halberdiers & Toast-masters – but it was <u>dreadfully</u> long & I was sitting between Beauchamp (much improved) & Herbert Samuel the most smug & sapless type of Jew. Father spoke very impressively & well – leaving out of course any reference to the Conference – & confining himself to Trade Returns & Anglo-Persian intervention etc – which was rather a disappointment I'm afraid to the audience – they were as frigid as ever.[2]

---

[1] 'Rikki-Tikki-Tavi', one of Rudyard Kipling's most famous stories, belongs to the first *Jungle Book* (1894).

[2] It was a convention that at the annual lord mayor's banquet at the Guildhall the prime minister, who was the principal speaker, would avoid topics of partisan controversy. Asquith therefore made only passing reference to the government's plans to tackle the veto power of the House of Lords, despite the fact that the failure of an important cross-party conference on the subject had been made public that day. Instead he dwelt on foreign policy, in particular the possibility of British intervention in southern Persia in order to protect the freedom of trade.

Diary – Friday 11 November – 10 Downing Street, Whitehall, S.W.

Just back from a Liberal Social Council party at Palmer's Green – a distant suburb. Lady Haddo had asked me to go – & I did it for your sake than Liberalism's I'm afraid.[1] It was an icy evening – I had luckily pinched Bluey's motor in which I was fairly snug – till I arrived at a large gaslit hall at the corner of a dark row of villas – entered to find Liberals already streaming in shook hands for $\frac{1}{2}$ an hour or so – mounted a jerry built platform – listened to speeches by Ewen, Ginsburg the chairman & Haddo (who was surprisingly good) & then mixed with the throng & talked to nice poor eager people sitting among table loads of buns. A woman sang Annie Laurie at the end – it always moves me rather – it has slightly Scotch harmonies don't you think? Then Haddo & I & Lady Southwark[2] trained back & crept through raw & draughty Kings X into a taxi – & so home – he dropping me.

One ought always to do things like to-night's when asked. For the smallest of grind they give an extraordinary amount of pleasure – far more in proportion than grind usually produces....

Diary – Saturday 12 November – 10 Downing Street, Whitehall, S.W.

My very own Darling – My day began with a disappointment – but ended in a certain amount of compensation. I had written to Ramsden asking him to let my boys know I would take them to the zoo – & my heart leapt when it turned out fine – only to fall heavily when a note arrived saying they didn't go to school at all on Saturdays – so he had been unable to let them know anything.[3] I was miserable – I had been thinking of it all night – it was my cherished darling plan – & also you know how I abhor 'thwarting'.

First I wouldn't accept it – & wanted to start straight off for Hoxton & honk them out of their homes – but Ramsden & Bongie overrode me by pointing out what bad luck it would be on the ones who were out – so I

---

[1] The Liberal Social Council brought together leading Liberal women: its proceedings had a social as well as a political emphasis, with luncheons and dinners. In 1912 the executive included Lady Allendale, Lady Swaythling, Mrs Harcourt and Elizabeth Haldane. Lady Haddo (d. 1937) *née* Mary Florence; married Lord Haddo in 1906.

[2] Selina Mary Causton *née* Chambers, wife of the newly created Liberal peer Baron Southwark, paymaster-general, 1905–10.

[3] Violet's assumption that the Club boys would go to school on a Saturday was based on the fact that this is what her brothers, and all of their friends, did. They, however, were educated at public schools, where Saturday classes were the norm: at state schools such as the Wenlock Road School, Saturday school did not exist.

sadly sat down to lunch among the débris of my hopes with a very flat afternoon stretching before. Rather an amusing talk with the Master of Elibank who is keen to have an election at once – as I am too. The 'indignation of the people' cools before you can say knife – they will soon be blasé of the Conference break-up – just as they were of the Budget's Rejection by the time the election began. This time last year that was just happening – my Darling we were going through that & every other thrill closely together. How well I remember turning rather furtively round in the House of Lords to see the points telling on your beloved 'gold-fish-bowl' face. And you asked to have Father's speech read when you were at yr. very worst – Dearest – closest to me in everything – – – Though I have lost so much I yet do feel that there is more of me there than there was last year.

After lunch a new scheme began to germ in my head – St. Paul's evening service with them to-morrow. So I was just about to slink off to Hoxton when Bongie & Micky caught me & insisted on coming. We changed into tram after tram & finally reached Britannic St. Bastendorff's house was empty & very deserted looking – dirty children crowding into the doorway. We went on to the Carmichaels' in Shepherdess Walk – much more respectable though rather grim – & here I found Alick – who promised to tell 4 of the boys for me – himself. Then we wandered in through the strangest byways to some of the other boys' houses – called at above 5 & came home. R. & K dined – we are a perfect à trois. Bless you my Sweetest & Best Yr own

Diary – Sunday 13 November – 10 Downing Street, Whitehall, S.W.

... A wonderful evening crowned my day. We took the boys to St. Paul's! It was well worth it – Bongie & I fetched them from the Club – they were all outside the door bless them – & off we went down the wet City Road pavement & across the muddy streets 'as merry as grigs' – me trying to shelter as many as I could under Bongie's umbrella – & steer the ones with colds out of the way of the puddles. We plunged down into the tube & up again after one or two changes – emerging quite near St. Paul's. The boys were a good deal impressed by it I think. I must say it did look very splendid rising out of the rather Whistlerian fumes of a wet night. They all took off their caps & walked very reverently in & I settled them in 2 long rows – sitting between the 2 smallest Wood & Blackmore – with whom I tried to follow in your Prayerbook. The lights & the gold glittering in the dim vastness looked very lovely – & I watched their faces like a lynx & wondered what they were thinking. We brought them home &

gave them cocoa here – & then Bongie & I & Micky dined late & talked. Oh my Darling this is being such a joy to me. It is your last gift to me – Yr own.

SEVEN

A General Election and a Journey
1910–1911

Diary – Monday 14 November 1910 – 10 Downing Street, Whitehall, S.W.

Dearest – An immediate general election seems almost certain now & all to-day the house has been thronged by people of every most varying kind – Loulou – Ld. Esher – Winston – Spender – Ld. Knollys – in quick succession after tea – I saw Hugh.[1]

Cynthia came – Dinner of too well-known ones – Edgar, Helen – Evan Manners, Ettie – Frances etc etc. I sat next George Grey a brother of Sir Edward's – & Sir John Horner.[2]

What facts to send you Beloved. Sometimes it seems so absurd that I should write to you of such things – but the absurdity & incongruousness of not telling you everything would be so much greater. You are nearer than anything in the world or out of it – I feel you – as I used to feel God – Yr Own

Diary – Wednesday 16 November – 10 Downing Street, Whitehall, S.W.

Most dearly loved – Just back from the Club where my life seems to centre more & more. Slightly jarred on by Winston & Clemmie (who came down & sat with me while I had my supper) – talking about 'good works' – 'Good works' – my God how little they know. How dare they touch on my sacredest joy & call it 'good works'.

It is a little odd to me (quite apart from this & you & all it means to me)

---

[1] Reginald Brett (1852–1930), 2nd Viscount Esher; deputy governor of Windsor Castle, 1901–28. Francis Knollys (1837–1924), 1st Viscount Knollys, 1911; private secretary to King Edward VII, 1870–1910, and joint private secretary (with Lord Stamfordham) to King George V, 1910–13.

[2] George Grey (1866–1911), younger brother of Sir Edward Grey.

to feel <u>so</u> little curiosity or interest or responsibility about other people's lives as most people I know do. I can never remember not feeling it – not being haunted by the thought of the poor – & longing to do something – I suppose it is just a kink in one's temperament – perhaps a purely intellectual one. With me it is absolutely detached from any <u>moral</u> instinct. I am about as self-centred & as self-indulgent as it is possible for a human being to be – yet I am haunted & obsessed by the thought of the squalor & greyness & sunlessness of some lives – & by the arbitrariness with which our fates are dealt round.

I feel a slight failing of courage to-night – I pray the morning may bring me back my strength – which is yours as is all else I live on – Yr very <u>own</u>

Diary – Tuesday 22 November – Train to London

Darling – Going back in the train – having just read & <u>heaved over</u> one of Lloyd George's very worst speeches.[1] It <u>is</u> hard on Father to be bound to a man with so little instinct of taste or dignity – & poor darling F. hasn't unfortunately that tinge of the governess in his nature – which might help him to deal with this class of outrage. I hope he won't be upset by it. Luckily he has beyond all people I know the wonderful gift of 'looking in steadiness'. . . .

Hugh Godley to V.A.   *Wednesday 23 November*
                                             29 Sloane Gardens, S.W.

My dearest Violet, I mind very much where you are, & what you do. On the whole I am glad that you are not in London at present, because if you were you would be stoned by the suffragettes. Also you would be lost in the fog. Last night Miss Lilah Locke, & Miss Ethel Nettleship & Miss Olive Strutt & I played in a quartet together after dinner, & when we had finished

---

[1] The previous evening Lloyd George had addressed a packed hall on the Mile End Road, in East London, to mark the opening of the Liberal election campaign in Tower Hamlets, a strongly working-class area. Eighteen months previously, at nearby Limehouse, he had delivered one of the most memorable speeches of the era, during the public debate on his 1909 budget. He had then ridiculed the landowning classes, and in November 1910 he returned to the attack, suggesting that an aristocracy was like a cheese, 'the older it is the higher it becomes'. According to *The Times*, some of those on the platform winced at the tone of his remarks, but the same paper acknowledged that his oratory was 'greatly to the liking of the "East-Enders"'.

there were no cabs to be got, so first of all I had to walk with Miss Lilah Locke & Miss Olive Strutt to Chelsea Embankment, feeling my way along the area railings, & then I had to go by the tube to Baker Street with Miss Ethel Nettleship, carrying her violoncello.

You ought to have devoted yourself more seriously to the arts from the first, & not concerned yourself with politics, & other matters which you are not really capable of grappling with. I think you have a very true instinct, although deficient knowledge, in artistic matters, but in politics you always have sided & always will side with sentiment against sense. It is the woman's way....

Dearest Violet are you tired? I would so love to see you happy. I would so much sooner you were happy than I was. That is quite true. Yr H.

The second general election of 1910: 2nd–20th December

The December 1910 general election was necessary in order that the government could proceed with its plans to limit the powers of the House of Lords. Its proposals were enshrined in the Parliament bill, which was introduced in the Commons in April 1910. The bill stipulated that any future budget, or 'money bill', would come into law one month after being approved by the House of Commons, whether or not it was sanctioned by the Lords. The Lords' veto over other legislation was effectively limited to the duration of three successive parliamentary sessions, or a period of two years, whichever was longer. And the maximum duration of a parliament was reduced from seven years to five. These terms were certain to be rejected by the Lords, but the death of King Edward VII, in May, delayed the inevitable conflict. The new King, George V, proposed a truce, and somewhat reluctantly the leaders of both main parties agreed to seek compromise through a Constitutional Conference. This broke down after twenty-one sittings, and its failure was made public early in November. Soon afterwards Asquith decided to recommend a dissolution of parliament, in order to put the veto bill to the electorate. Before he did this he sought from the King, and gained, an assurance on the creation of peers: if the government secured a majority in the new parliament the crown would, if necessary, exercise its prerogative to ensure the passage of the Parliament bill through the House of Lords. Parliament was dissolved on 28 November, by which time the election campaign had already begun. Asquith delivered his first address on Friday 25th, at the City Hall in Hull. The audience included the delegates of the National Liberal Federation, whose annual meeting had concluded in the city earlier that day. Asquith gave a commanding performance, setting the tone for an election that he dominated. He identified the 'veto bill' as 'the first and the greatest task' faced by the government, without which the Liberal programme of plural voting, Welsh church disestablishment, and Irish Home Rule could not proceed. The Unionists were, by contrast, on the defensive, unable to decide on the place that tariff reform should occupy in their campaign, and forced to accept the need for some measure of constitutional reform. At the Albert Hall on 29 November, Balfour ingeniously conflated these issues, promising a referendum on food taxes: there were cries of 'that wins the election' from the audience. In fact he was more at the mercy of events than in control of them. After the election there was virtually no change in the position of the parties, but the Liberal government now had the popular mandate necessary for tackling the peers.

Diary – Friday 25 November – Kingston-upon-Hull, Yorkshire

Darling – A splendid meeting just over – packed north country men clever & keen & lightning quick – taking every point before Father had made it almost – electric atmosphere – & thank Heaven well-ventilated hall with good 'acoustics'. I am so afraid of Father's voice giving way – it is not quite so hardy as it used to be & there will be a great strain on it in the next few weeks. We went on to an Overflow meeting (which I always do think a great cruelty). Ure was holding it at bay – the atmosphere was like a furnace – Sir J. Barran was behind me on the platform & I saw Bluey in the background with his little shiny beetlehead glistening – & his eyes quite out of sight – so well put in – & Lord Brassey booming away like an old foghorn 'Sit down sit down' whenever a Suffragette was thrown out.[1] This only happened about three times to our great surprise & relief. We came home & had a small supper party here....

Diary – Tuesday 29 November – Colchester, Essex

I came down here this afternoon to help Edgar. He met me at the station in a large orange rosette & wonderful spirits & we drove round all his

[1] Alexander Ure (1853–1928), 1st Baron Strathclyde, 1914; Liberal MP for Linlithgowshire, 1895–1913; solicitor-general for Scotland, 1905–9; lord advocate, 1909–13. Sir John Barran (1872–1952), 2nd Bt, Liberal MP for Hawick Burghs, 1909–18; parliamentary secretary to H. H. Asquith, 1909–16. Thomas Brassey (1836–1918), 1st Baron Brassey, 1886; Liberal MP for Devonport, Devon, 1865; for Hastings, Sussex, 1868–85.

Committee rooms & Liberal Clubs. He was splendid with the people & greeted by loud boos & cheers wherever he appeared. Winston came later & they had a splendid packed meeting in a biggish hall – W. spoke marvellously – I'd never heard him on a platform before. He was tremendously cheered. Sedgar's delivery is alas rather dreary & clerical – the last thing one wld. expect from him! & he spoke rather above his audience – I shld. think he wld. be better in the House. We drove back thro' crowded streets. Poor W. got pelted with rotten fish![1]

It is a strange way of spending my Holy Week – my spirit is miles away – this was the day I got a wire saying I might see you – & was so happy – Beloved – I am yr very own

M.B.C. to V.A.   ***Wednesday 30 November***
                                        5 Hyde Park Square, W.

Most dear. It really [was] wonderful to have half an hour of you alone tonight. . . . Rest these days if you can because I think you may find the tour with your father tiring enough.

I suppose it is impossible for you really when you are in London & everyone is about. I have been talking to my sister about your Egypt trip, she says that you must have these things (& I suppose Morrison too)

pith hat   ⎫ A & Navy
green lined umbrella   ⎬ Stores
veil such is worn to keep off
glare in snow i.e of gauze & green
blue or smoke colour.
Boracic powder to make wash for eyes important if eyes are sore.
motor veil useful for dust.
remedy for mosquito bites may be needed
Remember travelling in train is very dusty & nights on the river may be very cold.
I think you ought to take a camera.

This is an unfair letter isn't it because it is filled up with these directions. But it is half past one so I shall stop it. Bless you. B.

---

[1] The *Daily Chronicle* of 30 November 1910 described how Churchill was 'Pelted by rowdy Tories' as he travelled between election meetings in the constituency. The windows of the local Liberal committee room were smashed, and the Young Liberals' van partly wrecked. The election was won by the Unionist, L. Worthington-Evans, with 3,489 votes, to Vincent's 2,874.

Diary – Friday 2 December – 10 Downing Street, Whitehall, S.W.

One line of goodnight love – It's very late & we start for Newcastle at crow of cock to-morrow. I'm a little depressed about the Election now – as I feel this last acrobatic feat of AJB's will go seriously against us. The Referendum has a fictitious veneer of the democratic about it which I'm afraid may take in the average greenhorn elector who doesn't see the almost insuperable technical difficulties.

Also the abandonment of Tariff Reform will rope in the Free Traders – & it doesn't seem to have upset the Confederates so far.[1] Altogether they have dropped everything we could have attacked & except for complete absence of any programme – are much in the same boat.

The Master of Elibank & Lloyd George lunched – & were very amusing – I did 'last things' hectically all the afternoon – as except for 2 or 3 days this will be the last time I shall be here before Egypt....

Diary – Saturday 3 December – Bywell Hall, Stocksfield-on-Tyne, Northumberland

Darling – Bongie & I & Father & M travelled up here together – how you would have loved being him! We read columns of oratory – Lloyd George really rather good[2] – & eat a messy lunch – drove straight to the meeting which was a very fine one in the self same theatre as I came to 7 years ago – just before I went to Dresden. It is odd to think I was as old as 16 as long as 7 years ago – & practically grown up as long as 5 years ago. As a matter-of-fact I think I've been really grown-up for just a year – I was a child before with a little mis-leading precocity but none of the instincts of the developed being – except a few stray maternal ones for Cys! When I think of all the time I wasted with you Dearest.

Father spoke very well but his voice sounded a little tired to me. He afterwards went on to an overflow & Bongie I. E. Fräu, Ld. Allendale, Ld. Nunburnholme & 2 Noah's Ark Beaumont girls meandered back to Bywell

---

[1] The 'Confederates' were a loosely organized group of Unionist MPs who were strongly in favour of tariff reform, and equally determined to drive out of the party the few remaining advocates of free trade. From 1907 onwards they put forward rival candidates in the constituencies of free trade Unionists. In 1910 they proved more tenacious in their advocacy of tariff reform than Violet realized.

[2] *The Times* of 3 December carried a report on a speech given by Lloyd George at Ipswich the previous night: the government, he said, 'were not destroying the House of Lords, they were simply chaining it as they would chain up a vicious dog, for the Lords had bitten every Liberal bill'.

by slow train.[1] I rested & after dinner we waited tently for Election results &
I licked little coloured squares onto my election map Marjorie gave me –
Bonar Law is beaten thank Heaven – but we are 3 down on the evening[2]. . . .

Diary – Tuesday 6 December – Archerfield House, Dirleton, East Lothian

Dearest – We tumbled out of the train at Burnley yesterday into the midst
of a Suffragette mêlée – & were driven off by Ottoline – looking very rich &
strange – to a lodging house where we eat sandwiches – then on to the
meeting – a vast packed skating rink with over 8000 men sitting &
standing.[3] The platform was above like a Punch & Judy one – & one felt a
sort of burning steam ascending all round. I trembled for Father's voice –
but it held out splendidly though his face was streaming with the effort – &
he said he couldn't have gone on another 5 minutes.

We proceeded to 3 other meetings an overflow in Burnley – reached at
great peril through a seething, under-policed but friendly crowd & then 2
of Bluetooth's at Accrington & Osstlethwaite.[4]

He (Bluey) amused us by appearing in quite a new rôle as the mellow
demagogue – not the least academic or a shade above his audience – tub-
thumping away talking of throwing their badges in the gutter etc! I was
vastly amused – I was glad to get Father away & back to Gawthorpe for
some food. He had made 4 speeches on a very meagre luncheon basket
provided by the Allendales. . . . Afterwards we sat up waiting for returns –
I giddy with fatigue. We ended all square on the evening & 3 down on
the whole thing – but we have since recouped ourselves & are at present
one up – after 3 days tough fighting.

---

[1] Asquith addressed two large meetings in Newcastle; there was an audience of 8,000 at the
'overflow' at the St George's Drill Hall. Wentworth Beaumont (1860–1923), 2nd Baron Allendale, and 1st Viscount, 1911; Liberal MP for Hexham, Northumberland, 1895–1907. Beaumont
married, in 1889, Alexandrina *née* Vane-Tempest; they had three daughters and two sons, and
lived at Bywell Hall.

[2] Andrew Bonar Law (1858–1923), Canadian-born Unionist MP for Blackfriars, Glasgow,
1900–6; for Dulwich, Camberwell, 1906–10. A vacancy was soon created for him at Bootle,
Lancashire South West, where he was elected on 27 March by a comfortable majority. He
became Unionist leader in the Commons in 1911, following the resignation of Balfour.

[3] Ottoline Morrell's husband, Philip, had lost his seat at South Oxford in January, and stood
at Burnley in December, where he secured a narrow 173-vote victory over the incumbent
Unionist. The construction of many roller-skating rinks across the country, in the years
preceding the 1910 general elections, provided new and larger venues for political meetings.

[4] H. T. Baker held Accrington, Lancashire, at the December 1910 election, but with a reduced
majority from January (2,513 to 1,668).

Father & I & Bongie came on here – (It is being a halcyon time for B.) & motored out our lovely coast-drive in the dusk. We are actually dog-alone in the house (with M. Fräu & children) <u>such</u> a change & relief. I have not minded being here so little since last year. Bless & keep you for me – my most beloved – & intimately possessed – I feel you very near. Don't let it be too long – Yr own.

Diary – Thursday 8 December – Kilmaron, East Fife

My Darling – Father addressed a little out-door meeting to the night shift to-day at Guard Bridge – during their luncheon hour – troubled only by one Suffragette.[1] We had a huge 'Fife' lunch on return – masses of courses – champagne – no minor necessaries such as potatoes! – & lasting on until far into the afternoon. I then dragged Bongie out for a rather lovely walk along wet roads in twilight deepening to darkness as we returned, & got blown about & rained upon & felt much better. B. said à propos of some trifling assertion of will on my part that I was the most undisciplined person he had ever come across. It was like an echo of you – beloved disciplinarian – how governessy you used to be about it & how terribly arbitrarily & successfully you set about to remedy it – I told B. the only effectual discipline I could imagine was being in love.

Just back from 4 wonderful little meetings – St Monans – fishermen standing jammed like dates in a schoolhouse – Largo where some heckling took place – Leven – & <u>Kennoway</u> – the scene of our boomerang speech <u>Dearest</u> do you remember? & the meal at Carberry where my beads broke & all the Provosts & Ex Provosts crawled about under the sofas & chairs after them. All this life is such an echo after that – –

Father spoke marvellously at all meetings – his fertility of word thought & arguments & the way he shakes the Kaleidoscope of the same case into a different combination every time is <u>amazing</u>. His voice held out well & I think he was happy – Ketchen very chirpy & alert – Bongie on the water – Goodnight – love of my life – Yours

Diary – Friday 9 December – Kilmaron, East Fife

Most Dearly Loved – I am just back after a twelve hour day round the Polling-Stations. We started before 7 – got back about 9 for dinner. Every conceivable motor-disaster alas! took place. First the Napier – brilliant with tenderly wound red & yellow ribbons – broke a vital part of its axle –

---

[1] The workers in question were employed at the Guard Bridge paper works.

then a series of more or less gusty hirelings – a long lunch at Carberry (the scene of our meal) Provost Balfour more gaga than ever – & on – crawling in the Siddeley with a cracked cylinder – till we were relieved by a Kircaldy hireling which broke down in the most desolate waste near Crail – where we had to wait in wind & rain till the police took pity on us & returned with theirs.

Then followed a nightmare drive through wind & rain – mud spluttering, hat rearing – heap against my face my only shield & comfort! It was a real joy to go into the Dr's house at Crail & warm & dry – & eat scones with a few beloved old local funnies in front of the fire. The keenness of the people for principles whose action they must only very remotely & rarely feel the effects of – & their love for father whom they very rarely see is extraordinarily touching.

Dundee looked quite wonderful on the way back. I was given 3 bouquets one by Miss Ketchen – one bunch of green roses by Dr Horsley & some violets by the Ladies Liberal Club at Newport. We found Margot & Eliza on return.

It is extraordinary how little the battery of concrete fact can avail against my citadel of peace – where we are alone. My thoughts hardly left you to-day – Yr own

Diary – Saturday 10 December – Archerfield House, Dirleton, East Lothian

Darling – Father's poll was declared this morning – we sat [and] watched the counting of the votes – & I thought of last year – & my feeling of dazed misery & deadness – & how I was now going through all the mechanical movements of life – like so many exercises it is true – but in a way that quite looked like living.

Father's majority was reduced by two hundred & poor little Ketchen cried with misery![1] We adjourned to the Tontine for the usual ceremony of wine & cake & endless speeches. I had to comfort poor old Ex-provost White who was also in tears & made the only really good speech – saying it's not all right – the majority shouldn't be reduced – the weather oughtn't to matter to anyone – we should have worked harder – at which the Executive looked rather blue. However Father smoothed away the creases by a mellow speech & we dispersed – I thought we should never get away from Kilmaron. There's no doubt (as M. said) grocers shouldn't be in

---

[1] At the December 1910 general election Asquith polled 5,149 and A. Sprot, Unionist, 3,350, a majority of 1,799. At the January 1910 election Asquith's majority, against the same opponent, and with a similar turnout, had been 2,059.

castles. No <u>real</u> comfort such as writing paper – hot water or a candle – & these endless champagne orgies in the middle of the day.[1]

We left at last at about 7 – & got back here to find May Tomlinson – poor dear – more sucked & wrung than ever. Dearest – that she should live – & you should die – I must stop – will my life soon be over? I am very tired of it – Yr own.

V.A. to Venetia Stanley   *Sunday 11 December*
                                        Archerfield House, Dirleton,
                                                    East Lothian

Darling – I was so sad to miss you on Tuesday – I thought you were following & only realized when we reached the other platform that you had stayed behind. We went on to Fife the same day – (F & I – Margot stayed at Archerfield) & had 2 or 3 days of 4 or 5 meetings a night – declaration of poll yesterday, & to-night I go down to London. It would be <u>glorious</u> to see you on Wednesday if you are in London – but you mustn't on any account come on purpose as I shall be ridden with Xmas tree cares – clothes, looking out books etc. & a very tiresome companion – & should feel guilty the whole time of having dragged you there.

Write me a line in any case. It is strange to think how far I am going in how few days – & how small a sense of uprootal I have. Isn't the Election going oddly – all square in losses & gains after a week's hard fighting – I suppose in a way it isn't odd – as it is more or less of an endorsement of last year's – except for the production of our bogy Home Rule – & the burying of theirs – Tariff Reform – both of which ought to go a little against us.

I do <u>hope</u> yr. brother does well.[2] Has he had a message – & does it bear the stamp of Me, Nash, Bongie, or Meiklejohn?

Love to you Darling – & let me know yr. plans V.

There is no one here but May Tomlinson & Bongie – an empty house <u>is</u> a luxury.

The Master of Elibank & Haldane are frowsing in thick luncheon fug over shandigaff dregs next door – 3.15!

---

[1] Kilmaron Castle, near Cupar, Fifeshire, was owned by Sir James Low, created a baronet in 1908; he was a Liberal activist, and the managing director of Lindsay and Low Ltd of Dundee.

[2] Arthur Stanley lost Eddisbury, Cheshire, which he had represented since 1906, in January 1910. He could not regain it in the December election, though he reduced the deficit from 688 votes to 289.

M.B.C. to V.A. *Monday 12 December*
5 Hyde Park Square, W.

Dearest. I am comforted by the thought that your Egyptian journey is panning out well. I think you will find the Red Sea way much less tiring as well as being quicker & everyone has so far shown a laudable desire to look after you well.[1] I hope to be able to slink down to Dover with you. You have got busy days before you, I am not sorry but I do not want you to go away quite tired out.

Your Father & I had a rather amusing time at Bury St E[dmunds].[2] We arrived in a shower of harmless missiles & left in a seething booming badly managed crowd. The only hurt was to the motor whose window was smashed. We were treated much better in the way of our train meal than we were by any of our millionaire friends.

Bless you B.

Diary – Saturday 17 December – S.S. Delhi, en route for Port Said

I didn't write on our two holy-days.[3] There seemed no need – I felt our hearts so close. It seems incredible that a year has gone – such a cold dark struggling age – I couldn't have lived through it without you.

No one else could have left such a legacy of hope & courage behind.

Thursday morning I started – Margot, W.W., Micky saw me off & Bongie took me as far as Dover. His poor faithful dog-eyes looked sad as the water widened between us – & the ship slipped out to sea. He has been so indispensable bless him & I feel really quite happy about leaving the Club with him – (though I am divided between longing for it to go on on oiled wheels without me – & longing for it not to get on too well without me!) We had a calmish crossing – then followed the mêlée in the douane me being binged by everyone else's hold-alls! then a long vibrating night on the upper shelf of a sleeping compartment – & up in a very dark dawn as we neared Marseilles. It is a hideous place like a manufacturing town in the north of England – but boarding the boat in a rather eerie morning twilight amongst streams of half-castes in coal-stained coloured clothes carrying heavy bags Nibelung-like – was rather strange & picturesque. We

---

[1] The Red Sea way to Khartoum involved travelling by train to Ismalia, and then by boat along the Red Sea to Port Sudan – a journey taking roughly two and a half days. From Port Sudan it was a further twenty-four hours by train to Khartoum. Violet left London on Thursday 15 December and arrived in Omdurman on Christmas Day, after eleven days of travel.

[2] Bongie had been appointed H. H. Asquith's private secretary several months earlier.

[3] Violet refers to 15 and 16 December 1909: see above, pp. 190–5.

didn't start till about 12 – & I was sitting solitarily on the top-deck reading A Room With A View[1] – when I was abordéed by a particularly delightful man whose face I had noticed in the train. He turned out to be an Indian Judge – & plunged in medias res with extraordinary promptitude but without offensiveness. He thinks the world is a soul-factory & that the more we suffer the luckier we are because the nearer the attainment of the object for which we are created.

I asked if he was quite sure suffering did improve one – & he said yes – if one was strong enough which I suppose is true. The glorious natures emerge like tempered steel from a furnace – the less finer metals just melt & lose by it – I felt a little nervous about myself. . . .

Lunch between his wife & another Anglo-Indian – between whom & me not much passed – brownish-black servants – a cross between Portuguese & niggers waiting on us – & then an afternoon lying up on the deck tucked up in rugs – reading & trying to write a little but overcome with sleepiness. I had a glorious big bath before dinner turned on for me by a mulatto who kept his little black hand in it till the last moment – & felt almost afraid was going to wait there till I got in. . . .

Diary – Sunday 18 December – S.S. Delhi, en route for Port Said

Beloved – I didn't write to thee all yesterday – the days are interrupted tho' in a way so empty – & at night I don't like to keep my poor old fellow cabin-inhabitant awake by scribbling. I've never had such a sense of space before – & time & room for all things – even thought.

There is no crowd or hurry anywhere – one has the whole sky & the whole sea to look at – & all day long to look at them in. I lie & gaze on wide horizons with delight. The lights are very lovely. The sea is the colour of the blade of a knife & curves like a charger's neck on each side of us as we cut through it. . . .

I feel very rested in mind & body. Being alone was a very good plan. I have made one more friend – an engineer going on to Khartoum – he has the charm of great simplicity & a certain gentle virility about him – & carries coats & rugs about with activity & solicitude. We had rather a good talk about books at tea – I, Crouch & another Anglo-Indian who proved to be very well-read & with the zest of the self-taught.[2] We touched on Shelley, Keats, Bernard Shaw, <u>Spender,</u> St <u>Loe</u> Strachey! I was a little controversial & I wondered if you would have thought me overbearing &

[1] E. M. Forster, *A Room With a View* (1908).
[2] Probably Henry Newton Crouch, a judicial commissioner in the Indian Civil Service.

dogmatic like the time with Sir G. Murray under the Cedar-Tree[1]....

Night. At this point I was abordéed by the engineer – & then church happened in the dining-room. A union Jack on the altar – a layman officiating (as all the clergy are travelling 2nd class!) & very tentative & wavering hymns. It was rather a touching little service all the same – I thought you would have liked me to go....

In the evening a long walk with Crouch & a very glorious orange & green west – & then <u>just</u> as I was settling to long-deferred Raleigh the engineer who had been badly nobbled by Mrs. C. (who instead of being a homely housewife as I had imagined has all the arch avenance of the Anglo-Indian) & no reading was done before bath-time. I must fight hard to-morrow or my last day will be gobbled up – I feel a little sad & lazy about my uprootal now – having eingelebt myself so cosily. Darling how glorious it would have been together. <u>Excellent</u> talk with Jones at dinner – he spent ages speculating how much of my 'unusualness' was intrinsic & how much acquired by 'infiltration'!...

Diary – Monday 19 December – S.S. Delhi, en route for Port Said

My Darling – This morning I woke up early – & knelt up in bed with your cloak round me & gazed out of my port-hole – the sun was rising – & Crete lying like a cloud on the horizon – the sky pale yellow deepening every moment to orange.

Suddenly everything turned into gold the waves, the clouds, the snow on Crete – & the next thing I saw was the sun lying in the sea – blazing. It was wonderful – & I was sad to have to lie down & shut my eyes again when my cabin-mate began struggling with her wig.

I am lying on deck now after about $\frac{1}{2}$ a mile's walk with the engineer – the sun is much hotter – the wind much colder & the sea much bluer to-day – Crete is passing out of sight. I must write a few letters. The fishface on this boat would amuse you – there are <u>shoals</u> of them defiling before me now – I think I have struck rather lucky veins of ore on the whole. Night.

A lovely sunny day is over – I read a little – a very little of my Johnson – & embroidered & wrote 3 letters & talked to Crouch for hours – Montagu (as I hear the engineer is called – <u>how</u> different from the picture the name

---

[1] Violet was friendly with Sir George Murray, whose office in the treasury looked on to the garden at 10 Downing Street: 'Having my tea in the garden on hot summer afternoons, I would throw a pebble up at the window in the Treasury ... and down he would sometimes come to share some strawberries and a gossip with me.'

calls up) was faintly skimped. I like him – his simplicity surpasses anything I have ever come across.

Jones gets better & fonder of me every night at dinner I am glad to say. I am beginning to find out how his land lies – the territory is circumscribed but good.

Wheat is his great subject! To-night his eyes blazed as he discussed it – & he gave a description of a cholera camp worthy of Kipling. Last night talks with Crouch – who said it had been an inspiration to meet me (dewdrop) – Montagu who after a long silence said tentatively – 'Do you mind if I ask what yr. Xtian name is' – 'Violet' – 'Oh.' 'What did you think it was?' – 'I thought it might be Angela'! – Uneasy stirrings from bedfellow, blessing & loving you Your own

Diary – Wednesday 21 December – Train to Ismalia, Egypt

Darling. It was extraordinary arriving at Port Said yesterday – I think it is the strangest – wickedest – most frightening place I can imagine.

Unlit sandy streets – where dust whirls & women & children huddle in heaps – men, with pigs, of every colour & nationality howling strange tongues at each other – diseased dogs lapping out of filthy puddles – desolate mud-stretches – horrible hovels – everywhere an atmosphere of filth brawl & squalor. We drove along the sea-front to see the sun go down & I nearly cried at the desolation the forsakenness of it all – like a place that God has forgotten. I nearly 'found it in my heart to pray for it'! ... I should have been really frightened & miserable if it hadn't been for darling Crouch who came to tea with his wife – & gave me dinner later.

I had a wonderful talk with him sitting in the Lounge – a horrible leather place full of smoke with a band – I told him a little about You – & I think he understood. The only thing he said was: I think you are a very lucky woman. We went out after dinner & looked at some of the shops & bazaars. . . . We were both sad to say goodbye to each other – we had come so near & shall probably never meet again – a passing in the night.

I went to bed behind a very stuffy mosquito veil – & listened to the noises of Port Said till far into the night – shrieks – screams – cats – children – quarrels – laughter – baths – I felt a little lonely & afraid.

I woke up not very rested – sent off 17 postcards to the [club] boys very business-likely – paid bills – eat lunch – & now I am in the dustiest train in the world – looking out on stretch upon stretch of sand – with an occasional patch of palm trees – pampas or grass – the blades grown in rows like flowers. I managed the change at Ismalia well – I am very governessy with the Egyptians! – You would laugh. Oh my sweet love how I long for you.

Khedival Boat – night.

Blessed Darling – The boat was successfully boarded. It is small but not dirty – & I pray not cockroachy – I was accosted by a Miss Hanbury who is going out with a party to stay with Currie – but have not had much truck with her yet.[1] I sat next the Captain at dinner & eat slices of huge rose-coloured water-melon.

Diary – Friday 23 December – Khedival boat, on the Red Sea

My Dearest – We have had another boiling day – much, much hotter than yesterday.... The boat below is decidedly smellier & the butter & other foodstuffs in a baddish decline. I went down into the stokehole – & it really haunted me. How can men live there & by what strange act of volition does one decide to become a stoker. It seems to be just like deciding to spend one's life in Hell.

Their poor grimy shiny faces among the oily clashing wheels – in an atmosphere I could hardly stand up in – I felt sad & a little ashamed of my luck – & complete absence of physical endurance....

Diary – Christmas Eve – Train between Port Sudan & Khartoum

My Darling – I got up earlyish this morning after a very breathless night & went up on deck – land was just in sight – & before long we steamed into the harbour of Port Sudan. It is an upstart town only begun about 5 years ago – mainly built of white coral & standing on the edge of the bluest – most crystalline sea you can imagine. Since beloved Tresco I have never seen such clear depths – & such a colour.[2] It was like distilled aquamarines. In the midst of all the beauty & strangeness – standing boldly out against a wild range of hills the most shameless Occidental machinery – steam-cranes etc. such as one might find in Belfast or Oban.

A friend of Oc's with a delightful face called Winter met me – & also an envoyé of Frank Balfour's one Echlin – & together they helped me through all luggage complications.[3] The Douane was thronged with little pitchblack

---

[1] James Currie (1868–1937), principal of Gordon College, Khartoum, and director of education in the Sudan, 1900–14; Currie married, in 1913, Hilda *née* Hanbury, possibly the 'Miss Hanbury' mentioned.

[2] Tresco is one of the Scilly Isles, England.

[3] Lt.-Col. Francis Balfour (1884–1965), joined the public works department of the Sudan government in 1906, and transferred to the political service in 1912; he was a nephew of A. J. Balfour.

nakedish Nibelungs – of apparently rickety build – but of enormous actual strength – heaving vast cases of sugar canes onto their mesquin little backs seemingly without any effort. After an hour or so's luggage fussing – we were taken off in a launch & sailed about a little looking at the sights. Everything in a sort of early February state of growth – streets marked out in the sand – the beginning of a Hospital, a church – the Governor's House where we went to lunch. Even the few hundred yards walk there from the launch was almost impossibly hot. But it was glorious getting into the shade sitting on a cool verandah of shiny stone spread with rugs – & drinking Lime-Juice – do you remember my old favourite chilly drink? We had what seemed after our Khedival Boat fare a very sumptuous meal – waited on by blacks in turbans & lovely clothes. Flies covering everything before one eats it is the only down I have about oriental life so far. Then overwhelming of the Governor with thanks (best done by me!) re-embarkation in launch – boarding of train – & here I am speeding through miles & miles of sand sprinkled with sad grey grass-tufts with an occasional bush, tree or telegraph post – & before us the mountains a glorious range – not high but full of outline & movement & shadow – & the very smallest hummock which at home wld. have an unostentatious mound shape here look like tiny Sinais. The blue sea line is still visible on the other side – but we shall soon leave it. We have just passed a herd of gazelle – Darling what a lot of the world there was left for you & I to see together – I do need you badly to share it with me – Oh – a flock of wild goats has just gone past. . . .

It is odd to think I shall have reached my destination by to-morrow – after 10 days' travel – I am wonderfully proud of arriving as a practical achievement. In these strange days I think of Haddo – the snow on the ground – the heavy sky streaked with yellow. . . .

Diary – Boxing Day – Omdurman

Mess-Room of the 14th
   Sudanese Battalion.
      Omdurman.

Beloved – Isn't my address good? You would be amazed if you could see where I am.

We got to Khartoum about lunch-time yesterday – it was fun finding Oc waiting for me there after my 10 Wanderjahre – as these 10 days now seem. He immediately took over all the cares of my existence – & I immediately shed responsibleness & capability & all my newly acquired assets like a garment – & sat helplessly in a fly in a shade while he fussed over the luggage which was ultimately drawn away on a lorry by two marvellous-dignified looking camels! After a few perfunctory introductions, offers of help etc to the Hanburys – who were unmet by Currie – we drove off in a <u>tiny</u> fly – one of 4 in Khartoum! – down to the river where we boarded a launch & were ferried over to Omdurman. We landed on a sandy bank – where a few natives were loading little timber-skiffs … & just above us – up a little steep path stood our house – this house which Artie has specially prepared for me. It consists of a straight row of rooms with a verandah opening on a little 'garden' – all beautifully cleanly & whitely & newly painted with bright green doors & shutters.

By the gate & separated from the rest is my part of it – a large cool white bedroom – with a shiny stone tiled floor on which lovely carpets are strewn – a <u>very</u> odd – <u>very</u> broad bed – made of strung rushes – a little white table – a looking glass – & next door a large bathroom stone bath – where my clothes – boxes etc. are kept – & where lizards dart about quite freely & vast spiders hang on threads from the ceiling.

It is all wonderfully light & clean & bare & cool & strange. We had lunch served by Achmed Artie's servant & then I rested & had a brown bath in Nile water in my stone bath – then tea on the verandah where a small mad monkey is tethered. We went out for a lovely drive at sundown – among extraordinary little mudhouses which cover the ground for miles around – & saw the Mahdi's old house & encampments – & the Nile stretching away – & many strange figures with melancholy oriental outlines in the distance. One man saying his prayers – kneeling towards the setting sun & kissing the dust – quite frankly in the open street – many women bearing pitchers on their heads – some children – tiny round-headed black Puffins – carried in a shawl. There was a very beautiful & sudden twilight – then the red glow in the west died & dark set in. We dined out of doors & talked a little then I went to bed – I was too excited to sleep very well. Now Oc & I have breakfasted after his early ride & work (I shall go with him to-morrow). . . .

Diary – Tuesday 27 December – Omdurman

Dearest. I missed writing goodnight to thee yesterday – as I had left this book in our living room & hadn't the heart to send Morrison back for it – over the nobbly sandy path in the darkness. I lay awake a long time feeling a faint <u>nervousness</u> for the first time since I was quite little. I had a sense of isolation & things creaked & rattled – & I wondered if I heard stealthy movements outside or not – & what I should do if a fierce, pitch-black face were suddenly thrust through the window. I felt sure of one thing, that I <u>couldn't</u> scream.

I got up early this morning about 6.30 & rode with Oc on his morning tasks. It was very amusing – we went round among the labyrinths of mud huts which I call 'the village' – & which Oc calls Omdurman – & says is the great & ancient capital of the Soudan – (but I can't imagine a capital which is only 2 ft. high). A Sheik accompanies us on a donkey with a sheaf of hieroglyphics in his hand which he shows Oc – one by one – as we reach the houses they apply to. Here the plaintiffs come out & petition to Oc in querulous tones & Oc either (usually) refuses what they ask or refers them to someone else – (the Survey Commission or something) I saw hardly any boons granted. The requests were usually for things like a yard & a half more land or to be allowed to put a wall round a well. Oc looks very judicial in a khaki coat – & a sun-helmet & speaks in low authoritative tones. His verdict is accepted as final.

The maze of huts looks very bewildering – some of the people were making them like mud pies. Goats & donkeys & little black Puffins huddle together in the shade. One old γραυς [old woman] looked very odd – almost quite naked except for a blue wrap which flapped about in the wind revealing the blackest sparest most crinkled up little body I've ever seen.

The sand is a little hard for cantering on – & the dust prevents anything out of doors being <u>delicious</u> or <u>perfect</u>.

We went up to see the polo in the afternoon yesterday – it was rather a lovely sight – beautiful ponies turning & twisting & caracoling in clouds of sun-irradiated sand.

The afterglow is the most wonderful colour here – the mudhuts suddenly burn <u>rose</u>-gold. It is a calmer colour than fire – & a redder one than sunlight.

We had a few people to tea Mrs. More – the wife of Oc's chief an Australian – & a Mrs Charlton.... It was odd dispensing tea on our little stone loggia with the monkey catching biscuit on the wall. How strange it would be – & <u>how</u> frightening – if one could see isolated scenes of one's life in advance – like lantern-slides – without knowing – where they were – or when – what led up to them or what followed. How impossible it would have been to believe that you would be in none of these....

Diary – Friday 30 December – Omdurman

Beloved – I had a wonderful ride with Oc this morning along the banks of the Blue Nile – a fresh breeze blowing – & wonderful smells rising from the bean flowers at our feet. We cantered slowly along the sand past little mud settlements of labourers till we got to a place where sand-grouse are supposed to fly over to water in the river. We sat down in the shade of a little mudwall. A little half naked black loaded Oc's guns & sure enough in about 5 minutes – over came a little golden covey – Artie fired – & a lovely little bird fell at our feet.

I felt a little sad as I thought of the possible widower flying sadly on to his drink – 7 more were shot in an incredibly short time. The boy who ought to have been watching gazed rivetedly at me as if I'd been a strange fauna – & finally asked what stone Unexpected Joy was made of. He admired it very much. We rode home in <u>frightful</u> heat – & I lazed the rest of the morning after a cold bath of brown Nile water in my stone tank.

I read with <u>great pleasure</u> W.'s account of the Battle of Omdurman – <u>so</u> well & vividly told – & one of the few battle descriptions I've ever understood. Also the preface to Gordon's diary which I'm now going to attack[1].

Diary – Monday 2 January 1911 – Omdurman

... I slipped fairly unconsciously into the New Year – coming back from dinner at the Palace – which was rather a formal affair. I sat next to a quite nice good looking soldier called Kinahan – & after dinner an ADC sat down at a Pianola – & gloomy little couples were formed & began to gyrate spiritlessly. I was introduced to a man called Kitchener – nephew of K of K. whom I began by disliking intensely & longing to escape from – & then suddenly came to quite close grips with & <u>loved</u>.[2] He is a sailor & there is a good deal of naval manner & humour to be got over at first – but he has tremendous vitality (a quality I feel real sentiment about now) directness simplicity & reality – & is very amusing in a foolish way. He cross-examined me about going to the Bachelors' ball & when I persisted in refusing said 'why!' – 'I have given up balls' – & on his laughing – 'there is a special reason'. He looked bewildered – 'Perhaps you don't know – about me. How I got as far as this I don't know'. He said very gravely 'Yes – I do'. We talked a little & he showed real heart – though the inexperience of a child.

We returned at 11 to find everyone gone Artie hunting desperately & poor Lady Wingate having fallen back on fortune telling as a last resource. The Palace is rather a good building high & white – built on Gordon's old foundations with large cool empty stone spaces & palms growing, fountains falling etc. The Sirdar who is [a] dear little fellow with divine manners showed me the spot where Gordon fell. In spite of fighting hard against

[1] Chapter 15 of Churchill's *The River War. An historical account of the reconquest of the Soudan* (1899) describes the battle of Omdurman, 1898, the decisive engagement in the successful Anglo-Egyptian campaign to retake the Sudan, which had been lost to the Mahdists in 1885. The eight-month siege of Khartoum, which clinched the Mahdist victory, is recorded in the diary of the town's defender, General (Charles George) Gordon (1833–85). Gordon was killed in dramatic circumstances on the final day of the siege, but his diary was recovered, and published in 1885 as *The Journals of ... Gordon at Khartoum*, edited by A. E. Hake.

[2] Henry Franklin Chevallier Kitchener (1878–1928), the only son of Lord Kitchener's elder brother; lieutenant in the Royal Navy, 1899, and commander, 1911.

it I feel the stirring of a nascent maudlin Gordon culte of the most approved type. Just as I was going I saw Kitchener – & was introduced to him. He looks <u>most</u> impressive & just as he should – a grim iron conqueror – 8 ft high bright red coat square jaw – inaccessible martial eye. Casting about for a conversational opening fatuity I hit upon the most apposite thing I could have said – by praising the s-shaped staircase – which he made & is <u>much</u> prouder of than the Battle of Omdurman. He unbent considerably at this & I could have made good headway! but was hustled off into the launch by Artie & Kinahan....

Yesterday was the Mohammedan New Year's day – I was woken early by drums beating – & strange Oriental rhythmic chants & songs. There was an electric feeling of festivity in the air. I drove out early with Mrs. Meldon (Mrs. More's sister – a kindly little Australian with an extraordinary accent) in a small dog-cart – the streets were thronged with excited groups twanging odd instruments, chanting & dancing. Hired ululaters had been carefully beaten up & placed along the line of the procession. We waited for a good long time in the shade of the Sukh – then the lu-lu's began to rise – & get nearer – & a splendid detachment of camel police in long scarlet boots rode past followed by Kitchener on a white horse looking very grim & victorious – the Sirdar on his left – Major Wilson on his right – then ADCs – & Oc & Ma[jor]. More – Oc's horse hinnying wildly – Kitchener looked splendid crossing the big open square outside the Khalifa's House. The Review of the schoolboys was very funny – the poor little fellows were told to give 3 cheers – & gave 3 little hard – short – punctual – saccadé shouts Hurrah – Hurrah – Hurrah.

I watered the Hanbury's on lime juice & soda – & then Artie & I hurried off to Khartoum where we lunched with a woman called Mrs. Charlton. I sat next rather a nice man Gibbs by name a fine polo player who afterwards rode in several of the races.

The race-course is a vast sandy expanse – with a pavilion built by the finish on which one can sit in the shade & listen to a black band playing & watch these lovely Arab ponies gallop past – I spent a very happy afternoon – talking to Kitchener, Sayer (an Attaché known as the 'Palace Pet' – of very polished profile & manners) & Bonham Carter whose charm for me remains great.[1]

Kitchener was sad at leaving – he asked me more about you – & I was able to tell him a little of the more or less fleshly facts of the case. I think he understood a good deal considering how little he knows. I wonder if I shall ever see him again. We got back late & rather tiredly....

---

[1] Violet had first met Bongie's elder brother Edgar (see biographical note in appendix) the previous day: see below, VA to MBC, 2 January 1911.

V.A. to M.B.C. *Monday 2 January*
Omdurman

I was so happy to get your letter enclosing Barker's excellent one[1] – which I have immediately answered – it is very good & unmercenary of me to go on writing to you because I shall probably not reap any more answers. My present plan is to take a P. & O. either on the 30^(th) or the 6^(th) – probably the 6^(th) from Port-Said – leave here about the 19^(th) & stop at Assouan Luxor & Cairo on the way. My only possible companions so far are the Hanburys (Currie's friends) who consist of 3 tough leathery old does (Miss H. her aunt & faded Swiss friend) & one youngish stag Cecil Hanbury a friend of Aubrey's – plump, civil, & nice, quite uninspiring. He is <u>very</u> anxious I should go with them as he is tired of grinding over the hold-alls of his elderly flock & longs for something rather dewier. Miss H. on the other hand, who regards me with some suspicion I believe as being altogether too bright for my position – socially overbearing, & a distraction to her hitherto concentrated brother, would I think welcome me with less open arms. (All this synopsis of her sentiments is purely speculative on my part.) Anyway I needn't make up my mind yet awhile.

I am being very happy & amused. On Sunday Artie & I rode 8 miles across the desert to Kerreri – where the battle of Omdurman was fought. We started about 7 – the sun already blazing in an implacably blue sky. The party was Currie – Miss Hanbury – a woman called Hicks Beach, Artie, I & a man I didn't know – but who just [as] I had started off cantered alongside of me on a wonderful snow-white Arab barb & said – may I introduce myself to you? I am Bonham Carter. I then turned round & saw the <u>most</u> exquisite Carter with whom I had a heavenly ride the whole way there. I simply love him – he is divinely reserved & aloof & unsusceptible & contained – the sort of person who rather challenges one – & he has got the beautiful & rather ceremonious manners of a misogynist....

... We then embarked in Currie's luxurious launch & went back by the Nile eating the most complicated & delicious breakfast on the way. Your brother has asked me to go down the Nile in it with him & Currie for a night or two shooting on the way. This wld. mean postponing our desert expedition till next week but I think I shall go.

I have made very intimate friends in an incredibly short time with Kitchener's nephew – whom I met dining at the Palace on Saturday night – & who has hardly left us since – until to-day when he was summoned to return to his ship which he very sadly did. He was beginning to exhibit slightly navigatory tendencies so it was perhaps a good thing. I liked him <u>very</u> much – once naval manners & humour were got over –

---

[1] Henry Barker, one of the boys in the Archie Gordon Club.

splendid vitality & youth & mustard keenness – & really amusing in a rather foolish way....

The heat is still Sir Giles – I drink <u>gallons</u> of lime juice & soda & cannot screw myself up to read or write or even embroider. I shall feel drained after this letter. I'm up at 6 every morning isn't it <u>wonderful</u>?

If you write to me to Cairo let it be to Hôtel d'Ingleterre – & if to Luxor where I shall probably spend a few days from 24th to 31st or so c/o Cook.

Goodbye bless you – Yr V.

Tell me about the Club. Shall I communicate with yr. Cairo brother if I go there alone?[1]

Diary – Wednesday 4 January – Omdurman

My own Darling – Just in from polo followed by tea with Mrs More.

The days seem to get hotter & hotter – to-day & yesterday it has been 102 in the shade. I lay on my bed all the afternoon with nothing on but my dressing gown & felt as utterly exhausted & done as if I'd been running in a race.

I went over to Khartoum in the morning about 7 – to breakfast with Mr. Currie [and] go over the Gordon College – a thing which I felt had to be done someday.[2]

I found Mr. Bonham Carter waiting to meet me on a donkey – I got on to another exquisite white one & we jogged up together to his house. We breakfasted à trois. They are a strange contrast – B.C. like polished ivory – sensitive, dignified, silent, restrained – Currie with a face like a cheese moon – spluttering, garrulous, assertive – but disarming by his go & spunk '& snap' & ginger. I was given the only rose in the garden – B.C. looked surpriseder than words can say when I held it up to his face to smell!

Currie drove me to the Gordon College had a short & excellent talk on slavery with me in his little room – & then handed me over to one Udal – a clean – blue-eyed – good – strong – young – wonderful mannered Englishman who proceeded to take me for a most exhaustive 3 hours tour round the whole place[3] – Primary Schools – Secondary Schools – Museum – Engin-

---

[1] Frederick George Bonham Carter (1877–1968), a chartered accountant, based in Cairo on business.

[2] The Gordon Memorial College was the chief educational centre of the Sudan, a large building accommodating a museum, research laboratories, and facilities for several hundred scholars. It had been built in memory of General Gordon, with funds raised by his avenger, Lord Kitchener, and it was the latter who opened the building, in October 1902.

[3] N. R. Udal (1883–1964), an exact contemporary of Oc Asquith; they followed similar paths, through Winchester and New College, Oxford, before joining the Sudan Civil Service in 1906. Udal was later warden of Gordon College, 1927–30.

eering – Carpentering – Townplanning – Bacteriological Dept. Football ground – nothing was skimped or missed – every individual scarab handled & commented on. Finally my interest & strength having held out fairly well – I overwhelmed him with thanks & steamed home on the launch. The camel-ride yesterday was a great success – the mount by far the most terrifying & uncomfortable part. I timidly placed a foot on a great long bulbous stalk of a neck – & climbed into a roomy square saddle lined with a bright blue lambswool fleece – in front my legs hung round a small post too short to get any real purchase on – then three violent convulsions took place as the animal rose – almost dislocating every bone in my body – & we started off first in a swaying see-saw – sea-sick walk then in a very much more comfortable intermediate motion – finally in a jerky jog-trot which played cap & ball with poor little ballastless me very successfully. The intermediate motion is the one to cling to & retain if possible – one has no sort of seat or grasp on the animal's mouth or body – & is a little comforted by the thought that every other camel rider must feel just as helpless as one does oneself. I enjoyed the giddy height & Old Testament feeling & vast Oriental shadow stretched beside me. Oc said I looked very funny – & I felt rather odd & incongruous I must confess – You would have been amused to see me.

I laughed as I thought of young Kitchener's description – 'these blooming swans – you pull them to port & they go to starboard'. We came home with the stars out.

Now I am sitting in our little stone floored room at home with 2 Oriental merchants squatting on the floor displaying rather inferior Liberty goods for exorbitant prices – I am being firm & practical & confining myself to one puce-silk handkerchief for the black boy.

It is a shade cooler to-day I think. We start off in Currie's launch with him & B.C. about 4 – Bless & keep you near me Darlingest & Best – I can feel you helping me to live.

Diary – Friday 6 January – Omdurman

... It was a nice peaceful expedition on Currie's little launch – steaming about 4 hours down the Nile – oilsmooth & flashing back the sunset. I saw a little more of C. & less of B.C. than I should have liked. He (B.C.) is more inaccessible & more <u>limited</u> I think than I thought – but his charming expression which holds so much more than anything he says – & his complete absence of shop window goods or any sort of ease or savoir-faire or modus vivendi with women still rivet me a good deal. Currie is keen & <u>alive</u> & kind & gross – & sometimes says a clever thing – but he is much less fine metal. The thing that amuses me about B.C. is that he has

obviously never been on speaking terms with a woman in his life.
We got up at 6 – I struggled into my <u>own</u> clothes – & bundled up my
own hair! & all 4 started off down the river bank in search of sandgrouse.
It was beautifully cool – & the strips of beans & grass & other growing
things edging the water looked very brilliantly green & fresh. They drew
places – I settled on a campstool by Currie – a few flocks came over
impossibly high – a few guns were hopelessly discharged – one bird was
shot – & the sanguinary expedition returned with fairly unstained hands
to breakfast – which we eat drifting slowly back up stream. Talk – reading &
sleep went on till we reached Omdurman. Oc & I had late lunch a short
rest & a glorious canter in the desert – Now lonely dinner & bed.

Diary – Sunday 8 January – Omdurman

Dearest – There was a garden party at the Palace yesterday – I went over
with Oc & Boyce & a handful of missionaries in the launch – Oc & Boyce
dressed in a Galahad-like uniform of white linen with gold collars & cuffs.
It was a very fine 'spectacle' – & I felt really excited advancing down an
avenue of pitch-black soldiers holding pennons of red & green – into the
garden which blazed with colour – uniforms (& faces) of every shade –
among palm trees & other brilliant tropical flowers – a gorgeous tent like
a Sultan's in a novel flapping in the wind – swords clattering – medals
glinting – a band playing. It gave me the best sort of theatrical thrill – you
<u>would</u> have thought it such fun. Bonham Carter advanced towards me
dressed like Portia in the Merchant of Venice & we watched together the
dignified progress round of Lady Wingate the Sirdar & the Ex-Sirdar –
Wingate looking very gentle & fluffy beside Kitchener's iron jaw & well-
padded chest.[1] Oc & I then strolled about & talked to – Boyle – Currie –
Winch & a few people Oc introduced me to.
I suffered a little from garden party nerves about detachment from
people – it is so difficult to do inoffensively & so impossible not to do at
all. All the men were most wonderfully disguised – the women very
insufficiently so! Either freaks or frumps – not one pretty one except the
sickly Miss Jeffreys.
The variety of clothes really very extraordinary. There were Civil Servants
in white, Egyptian & Sudanese officers, English officers – English officials
in <u>frock-coats</u> & <u>tabouches</u>! & <u>wonderful</u> Mohammedan sheiks in robes of
every colour – Oc introduced me to one called Bowl of Blood – who shook
hands with his elbow. We got home & gave a little dinner to Currie,

---

[1] Sir Reginald Wingate (1861–1953) succeeded Lord Kitchener as sirdar and governor-
general of the Sudan in 1899; he married, in 1888, Catherine *née* Rundle.

Bonham Carter, Winter, a man called Howell – a Wykehamist & as such – hallowed.[1] We eat our turkey who had been battening in solitude in the Khalifa's house. B.C. was in excellent form – & said two very surprising & rather Bongiesque things – one) how much he enjoyed being called by his big toe every morning! 2) that he had had a seal made in imitation of the Shoe-bird in the Palace gardens – that Lady Wingate had taken it from him regarding it as a sort of lèse-majesté – that he had had many others made – but none alas! in the least resembling it – adding pathetically 'it had always been my dream to have a seal with a Shoe-bird on it'!

I wonder if you would like him & think him funny. I somehow think you might not – you were often a little unappreciative of my 'funnies' – especially when you thought you saw signs of an exaggerated culte on my part.

Oc & I are spending a lazy afternoon in the verandah – Oc reading me extracts from a very stale Daily Chronicle – which slightly derail the current of what I am writing: The monkey is dozing in the sun under his brown rug – down by the river the boats are being loaded – prisoners are toiling up & down the garden in the heat with buckets of water followed by a redoubtable black sergeant with a gun. We have had a long & strenuous day already. We got up at 5.30 by starlight rode down & caught the half-past six ferry – mounted the ponies on the other side & cantered on to the most wonderful review of the Troops – which took place on a sandy plain beyond the race-course. We met Kitchener – the Sirdar & their escort on the way & followed them.

At first I could see no army they were so much the same colour as the sand – then I realized a very long thin line of Khaki-clad men – Oc & I & Udal & Bonham Carter dismounted & went into a little roped-in space – & the whole Sudanese army defiled in 3 different ways past Kitchener – sitting like a granite statue on a white horse. Men of every colour – mounted on mules – mounted on horses – mounted on camels – each led by a white officer with a drawn sword – the native bands playing an odd mixture of national Sudanese & national English music. The best moment was the cavalry & artillery gallop-past. One saw their spears glittering in the distance – the pace gathering & growing – & past they swept in a cloud of sand the heavy guns rattling behind. I could have shouted with excitement – I didn't know such love of life was left in me as I have felt to-day. It is the first feeling of living again in that way I have had at all....

---

[1] Alan Berkeley Howell (b. 1884), roughly contemporaneous with Oc Asquith at Winchester and at New College, Oxford; joined the Sudan Civil Service, 1908.

Diary – Sunday 15 January – Omdurman

Beloved – Just back from our desert expedition! – I can't tell you what the glories & delights of these few days have been. Days in the open on camels & ponies & nights under the moon & stars – early starts in the thrilling freshness & dusk of 5 – hot thirsty arrivals at the wells at 10 – long drinks – & rests in sparse shade – & on again at sunset. Nothing could have persuaded me I could ever have loved anything so much again. I longed for you every minute to share it all with me.

We started off on Thursday at about 4 – me in my long red-camel boots with yellow soles! – Bonham Carter, Oc & Currie. I felt quite at home on my camel – the great strength of one for long distances is that one can vary one's position so constantly & need never get cramped. It soon got cool & B.C. & I had happy talk. He has great charm for me quite independent of anything he <u>says</u> – & when he does say something good or amusing I find myself surprised as at a sort of par-dessus le marché.[1] We reached the camp about dinner time – the Hamla had already arrived & made a strange little island of confusion of kneeling camels, half hoisted tents, camp-bedsteads – bustling men in the empty waste of calm all round. It grew darker – & soon fires were lit & the servants crouched round them – & we heard the clink of pots & pans. I put on my orange dressing-gown – & we had an elaborate dinner on a table – with napkins candles etc – which seemed very incongruous! then B.C. & I went on a little journey of exploration round the camp.

The camels looked very like Exodus – kneeling in the moonlight – & the huddled sleeping men. We found the horses tied up & gave them some almonds – at least B.C. did – he wouldn't let me – he has the most exaggerated & inexperienced conception of the frailty of women & always thinks I'm going to tumble down a well or be kicked or bitten by a horse or do something foolish or unlikely. The air was full of the constant loud whirr of crickets & another sound half like a bird half like a frog – which we pursued a little way hoping to identify – but it seemed to recede as we advanced.

I slept in the white light of a full-round moon – waking several times in the night from sheer excitement & towards morning from the cold which was intense – to my great surprise I had to pull up my fur-coat. We started off again about 6.30 – on ponies as it was still quite cool. My little treasure went divinely – Currie & Oc jogged on in front C. looking strangely

---

[1] The French phrase 'par-dessus le marché' – meaning 'into the bargain' or 'on top of all that' – would normally be used to indicate that someone has exaggerated, and carries a negative connotation, but Violet has interpreted it freely to mean 'as an added bonus'.

out of harmony with his surroundings. B.C. rode that beautiful & very mettlesome Arab he had going to Kerreri.

We passed not much that was growing or living till we reached the wells about 9 – very hot & thirsty – they are in rather a wonderful place though quite unlike my conception of an oasis – no palms or gurgle of water or crystal rills. Enormous tufts of stiff yellow grass growing up beyond one's waist a few lowish trees in strange wind-swept shapes – & the wells themselves deep brown holes round which goats & donkeys & sheep & men & women & children were crowding – pulling it up in what seemed to me absurdly small quantities in leather-skins. I stood & watched them for ages – their black bodies bending & tugging at the ropes – & the poor goats nosing each other out of the way to get at the very brown & muddy water.

Then we went back to where a very Omar Khayam-ish table was laid under a bough – like a Tischlein-deck-dich in the fairytale – & we had longed-for breakfast – & then I bathed in a canvas bath in my little green tent & changed into a white cotton dress & sat in the comfiest chair in the blackest shade I could find feeling very cool & clean & sleepy. We lazed away the afternoon among the long yellow grass – drinking limejuice & listening to wonderful little bluebirds singing on the trees – the low cooing of doves sounding strangely like woods at home. Towards evening we rode out to some near hills – & climbed up to the top of them & saw a new stretch of desert beyond – & the sun going gloriously down. The hills were like gigantic cairns of wonderfully coloured very brittle rock – more like lava than stone. It was quite dark when we got back – though they were only a few yards ahead we were only just guided by the white tail of Mr. Currie's horse in the moonlight.

After dinner Oc & I rode a little of the way back with B. C. & it was then I think I got my maximum desert thrill. Camels ought always to be ridden by moonlight – I don't know why but it is a combination – which produces a complete sense of the fitness of things – the silver light – the silence – the infinite expanse – the rhythmic unvarying motion – when at its best – more like waves than an animal moving under one – – – The shadows played strange tricks – with the scrub by the wayside & turned the distant figures of the two outriding camel-policemen into fantastic portents – – – I was sad to turn back.

We rode back into our sleeping camp & slept. I woke just before dawn – there was an odd maize coloured light over everything. Currie Oc & I rode out – & saw a flock of gazelle – lovely furtive creatures – greyish white – almost the same colour as the sand & grass. We spent a lazy day – reading & talking – I practised shooting at glass bottles with a revolver. The Hamla was rolled up all the afternoon & the baggage camels set off at a slow jog. Towards evening we set out again – the sun had set, there was an interval of darkness – then the round pale-gold moon lighted us on our way again. On & on – with never a landmark to mark an advance it was like a ride in a dream. Far ahead we could see Currie's helplessly swaying & wobbling figure – pent round with pillows – but I took care not to go near him or get within range of his fluent tittle-tattle – I longed for Cys.

I was really feeling a little tired when we reached our camp – & was glad to lie down flat on my Farona on the sand & rest. There was not much cover to be taken & a clean coldish wind was sweeping over the sand. We dined hungrily – & then went to bed – my last night in the desert – in that spacious moonlit infinity. If we could have seen it <u>once</u> together.

We rode in next morning – & now I am sadly between 4 walls again.

I think Bonham Carter was right when he said that what one loves is partly the <u>sameness</u> of the desert which transfigures every incident into a thing of marvellous beauty – & also partly the size & the simplicity of the effects – in light & line. There is no niggling detail – only vast, splendid sweeps of colour & outline. It is certainly an experience quite by itself & which one somehow feels nothing else could quite give. . . .

Alick Carmichael to V.A.   *Tuesday 18 January*
Shepherdess Walk, Hoxton,
London

Dear Miss Asquith

I was pleased to receive and read your very interesting letter.

We are getting on all right at the Club and Mr Carter makes the cocoa very nice but I would like to see you at home again among us. I am glad to know you are enjoying your holiday and having hot weather. We are having a spell of London fogs at present which you know are not very pleasant.

I hope when you go on the shooting expedition on the Nile that you do not make a <u>nice tasty bit</u> for some large crocidile.

I would like, very much to see some of the sights to be seen in foreign lands which I have no doubt would appear very grand and strange to us British boys. My jersey fits me (to a tee) I have felt the benefit of it this winter and to whose kindness it is due.

The boys are getting on all right at gymnasium and our Bob thinks that some of us will be all right for the display.

You ask me if I have chosen my profession yet I will leave the matter over till you come home. If I don't get into Mess. Brown Bros. my father would like me to learn wireless telegraphy. I will have to improve myself at night school.

Hoping you have a safe journey home feeling much the better for your holiday. I remain one of your Boys

Alick Carmichael

H.H.A. to V.A. *Monday 23 January*
10 Downing Street, Whitehall,
S.W.

My dearest Violet – I hope this will catch you at Cairo before you are once more involved in the responsibilities & risks of solitary travel.

We came back from Archerfield 10 days ago after a Xmas of quite wonderful sunshine & calm. Last Wed. Margot with Eliz. & Puff & Fräu left for Mürren, and the final parting between Puff & Vena took place.

The great sensation before they left was the West slander case, wh. resulted in a gross miscarriage of justice – poor old Algy being required to pay £1250 damages to his daughter in law, for exclusion from Court & loss of hospitality. Margot gave her evidence very well, & did not give the old boy away. She was content with one epigram – that 'extravagance is a passport to Society' – wh. was economical on her part. Of course there will be an appeal, but it was a badly conducted affair, & the judge (that little ape Darling) behaved far from well.[1]

The same day they left your grandfather Melland died, & I went down to Altrincham to Auntie Joe's on Friday night to attend the funeral. It turned out to be a cremation: the first at which I have ever been present. Rigby's brother Elkanah Armitage, who is a Professor at one of the Dissenting colleges & a very cultivated man, conducted the service & gave quite an admirable address. He had a difficult task – to explain why the old gentleman, who became more & more of a sceptic the longer he lived, was being buried (or burned) with Christian rites. He got through it with

---

[1] In a much publicized court case in January 1911, heard before Mr Justice Darling, Mrs Horace West alleged that her father-in-law, Sir Algernon West, had publicly attributed the failure of her marriage, to his son, to her hopeless extravagance. She further alleged that Sir Algernon and his friends, among whom Margot Asquith was one, gave the same account to Lord Spencer, the lord chamberlain, and that as a result she was excluded from all court functions. It was in this context that Margot was asked by counsel for the defence, 'Have you ever heard of a lady being excluded from society because of her extravagance?' At the court of appeal, on 22 May 1911, the original judgement in favour of Mrs West was overturned for lack of evidence, the lord chamberlain having refused, on grounds of public interest, to divulge the substance of any conversation regarding Mrs West.

great skill & taste. The actual ceremony – the coffin gliding imperceptibly under a canopy of curtains, & being committed to the 'purifying fire' (which you don't see) – struck me as, on the whole, less repellent than the ordinary grave burial. I made the acquaintance of a number of sisters in law, two of whom have attractions – Mrs Norman, who makes £400 or £500 a year out of teaching singing, & Mrs Charles, who is a youngish Australian.

I am just off to Windsor for a couple of nights. I am quite alone here, as Cys has gone back to Oxford. Let me know as soon as you can the exact date of your return. I am glad you have seen so many new things Yr most loving Father

Diary – Monday 23 January – Train to the Nile

My Darling – Such an <u>extraordinary</u> thing has happened to me since I wrote last – I feel more utterly bewildered & perplexed & désorienté than ever before in life – I will try & tell it measuredly & in its context –

Oc & I rode there early – on a perfect morning – got off at Surgham & gave the ponies a sand bath – till the others came up – a large party of Colonels & their wives on camels. Then back by the launch. B.C. & I riding on in front. The next afternoon he & I & Currie & Oc had arranged to go a ride to the hills – but poor little Artie was requisitioned to take part in Fantasia nimra wahid – for the Fifes – & couldn't go. He & I & More sat waiting on the verandah for the arrival of the Royal party – the shore strewn with carefully beaten up lu-lu-ers & camel police – in scarlet waistcoats – when rather to our surprise B.C. stepped through the little gap in the verandah alone. He didn't account for Currie's absence very coherently – & after watching More & Oc make their bow & ride off in clouds of sand & dust we started off together into the desert riding towards the hills.

Bonham Carter seemed distinctly different in some subtle way – he seemed far from his aloof contained self I had first met riding to Kerreri – in fact for so very shy a man I thought him singularly outspoken. He turned to me suddenly looking very full at me & said in the rather intense hard <u>loud</u> voice Bongie uses when embarrassed : 'I have enjoyed your visit immensely – – I wish it could go on' – I replied rather lightly – 'Oh have you – how nice of you – You have made such a difference to it – you have been so wonderfully kind & hospitable'. There was a pause & then he said in rather a too moved voice – 'You have been – most charming to me – I wish I thought it could go on – I'm afraid it won't – it can't – there has been too much limelight – camels & the desert & the moon' – 'You don't suppose I'm influenced by that kind of condition in my friendships do you – I assure you I'm not a sentimentalist at all.'

Then feeling an instinctive desire to give the talk a ruck into safer country – 'By the way you sent me a most insulting message to-day about finding a younger companion to amuse me? What did you mean? do you know I'm 23.'

'Twenty-three are you? & do you know how old I am?' – 'No but I know you're not a day older than me in anything that counts. You see I've got the experience of someone of 100 – I've had all my life compressed & concentrated into these last few years'. We talked of other things then he suddenly & quite irrelevantly asked me how old Bongie was – on my telling him 30 – was silent. Then suddenly in the middle of another subject 'I'm ten years older than Maurice'. It seemed a great relief to him to get this over & without any apparent shock to me! We dismounted for a few minutes at the foot of the hills, great masses of volcanic looking stones & we sat on the grass – talked a little & then rode towards home – dark came on very soon & we were busy picking our way – among stones & tufts & found ourselves among the houses in Omdurman before we knew where we were. We approached the house by the shore – he said 'It is very sad that this is my last ride with you' – 'Perhaps we'll have one in Richmond Park on your leave' – 'Perhaps – (with immense feeling & inarticulateness) thank you most tremendously for this one'. Then as I held out my hands for him to help me jump off my horse – he quite firmly & simply & most unexpectedly lifted me off.

Winch Currie & Haddow soon arrived & we dined – B.C. was in marvellous spirits – (which a little bit clashes with my idea of him – that of a grave & sombre man). He & Haddow went away afterwards – & Currie & Winch stayed the night – & I spent my very last night under the verandah with the Kelb & beloved Oc in his little white nightcap – I feel so ashamed of having ever ever got out of touch with Oc – now that Thank Heaven I have got quite closely back again. We had a last desert ride in the afternoon – I mounted on Nibbler (by Mrs More) whom I had some difficulty stopping – then goodbye to the Mores & some amusement over the Reuter – goodbye & tips to the stud – Hussain – the Slave of the Prophet – the Joy of his Master – the Osta – & into the launch & over the dark water round Tutti Island for the last time.

Bonham Carter was at the landing stage somewhat to my surprise – with an enormous retinue of carts & carriages into which my luggage was slowly transferred. Meanwhile he suggested that I should drive on with him in the little buggy drawn by the white horse – I got in & we rolled off into the darkness I talking lightly & commonplacely about nothing – suddenly he said 'Miss Asquith – I've got a request to make to you. In Oriental legends & stories there is nearly always a moment when supplicants come before a Queen with requests & say "Oh Queen – will thou grant me whatsoever I shall ask" – & sometimes she – the Queen – (speaking very slowly) grants them their request – & then regrets her promise because it is too big a thing to have asked – so now that I come before you. I do not ask you to say yes – I ask you to say either no – or that you will consider my request. What I ask is this – will you marry me ?' I couldn't have been more surprised if he had shot me where I sat. My breath literally left me – then I said 'You can't mean it seriously – you don't know me' – 'Perhaps three weeks is not a very long time – & yet I feel as if I know you very very well – I am not in the habit of proposing to people I have only known a fortnight – or indeed at all – This is the first time I have ever asked anyone to marry me.'

'But – –'

'It is perhaps wrong of me & of course I should not have done it so soon – only – you are going already – & I thought in London I might perhaps only be able to see you once or twice – & I fancied here sometimes – perhaps I made a mistake – that you might possibly care for me more than as a friend'.

I was abasourdi – & have never felt more hopelessly unable to cope with any situation – I felt I ought to say no-no-no – this is impossible – quite impossible but somehow my lips refused to frame the words. I said all the silly conventional things about its being an honour & my being proud – & my being surprised – but the nearest to a negation I could get was would he give me a little time. I had a strange feeling of inability to brush it aside altogether – a feeling which haunts me still – that this may be a thing I don't want – may be a thing which wld. make me & many others unhappy – & yet it is important & not to be put by. I can't dismiss it from my mind or life.

He went on to tell me how I was the most wonderful person he had ever met using pathetically & ridiculously inadequate words like 'charming' – 'No one in the whole course of my life has ever been so charming to me'.

I pulled myself together & tried to tell him a little about you & I – that there was not much left of me to give – that I belonged to you. He said 'I think there is a great deal still left of you – I think you have had great experiences – but there are still great experiences for you to have'. I told him I felt bruised & sore still – that I had thought that side of life over for me for good – that some springs never quite mended – that I was a derelict. He didn't say much but seemed quite undeterred. We reached the house & found Currie & Oc had gone out to hunt for us – I felt in unaccountably foolish & frivolous spirits – & tried in vain to speak solemnly & seriously & as became the situation to B. C. sitting on a basket chair beside me – in the dining room.

Finally Currie & Oc came having been very frightened & thought we were dead. Currie in rather an ominous voice drank my return to Khartoum & B.C. drank long & deep. I shivered – & looked around at the room & actually found myself helplessly wondering whether I should ever live there.

B.C. & I again mounted the buggy to go to the station. This time I was terrified of what was going to happen. I felt an awful nervous smile breaking over my face which happily the darkness hid. I took him to task saying how rash he was – how little he knew of me.... He smiled & said he thought he knew all he wanted to about me.

Then – 'But it isn't fair I'm asking you to give up altogether too much. There you are the centre of everything & having always had everything you wanted all your life – & I have very little to offer you out here.'

He ended by assuring me that he wasn't urging me to give any definite answer unless I felt sure it would be no – & reminding me that he wasn't a young man & was a very cautious one. Think it over as long as you want unless it be no – & don't let it be no – (this was the only solitary note of supplication in his whole proposal) & please believe & remember I'm in earnest about this. This as we got out & parted – joining Currie Oc & crowds of others at the station. I just had time to tell Oc briefly what had happened – in one sentence – as Currie dogged us rather. He seemed not surprised – then goodbyes & the train moved off leaving a very odd situation both with them & me.

I now have ample leisure to revolve mine in my mind rolling through miles of desert – distant Gebels – mirages – the stations marked by numbers. I had breakfast with the <u>engineer</u>! – who by a strange fluke was in this same train.[1]

Dearest – how grim you would be about it – & how all my fault you would think it

Diary – Tuesday 24 January – 'Government Steamboat On the Nile'

My beloved Darling – We got on board this boat last night after a very sleepy & dusty day – & I was glad to be neatly tucked up in a little tight clean berth – with no sand or vibration & the luggage unmissing round me. A man brought me a telegram onto the boat – it said 'Be sure that I am quite certain of myself & do not wish a reply until I come to England shall write to you Cairo – Bonham Carter.'

If it were not for the little orange envelope crackling by my side I should feel the whole thing was a dream & that I should soon wake up at home

[1] Montagu, whom Violet met on the SS *Delhi* on her voyage out: above, pp. 238–9.

with all the people I have known all my life standing round me & telling me there is no one else in the world – I feel such an odd mixture of sensations about it. At times a vague thrill at the thought of such a strange new life – far away from anyone I have ever seen or known & in the possession of an absolute stranger. At others panic & terror at the thought – & the cosy feeling of relief one has waking from a bad dream in the night-nursery of Thank God it's not true – thank God they are still all there at home Father & Bongie & Fräu & my sitting-room & the Club. Oh Thank Heaven – thank heaven – I am still free.[1]

Oddly enough too the last feeling that ever comes in is any feeling of fear or even touching on what is yours. It seems so remote & different – almost as if it were happening to a different person.

Your part is inviolate & inviolable.

This is more the choice of a life – the choice of a state – I think I long for you above all people to discuss it with.

We are steaming down the Nile past vast stone cairns rocks piled into hills – clumps of motionless palms. It is extraordinary how like their art their nature is – or I suppose I ought to put it the other way round. All these hills are the shapes of vague Pyramids & sphinxes. . . .

Diary – Wednesday 25 January – Assouan, Egypt

My sweet Darling – We got to Shallaal early this morning & passed Philae – a lovely temple on an island near some Roman ruins – but hadn't alas time to go in – as luggage fussing had to be done instead.

I was immensely helped by an enormous Welshman called Whittingham who had been on the boat with us coming – with first-class sense of humour & goodish brains – a Liberal – he bought me a splendid sword sheathed in rhinoceros hide with a tiger skin handle & two daggers stuck in. . . . He also bargained for many beads for me – strung on gazelle hide. A man called Captain Stony was delightful too – a little piano & sapped by heat – but so kind & amusable. He told me his regiment was his only home which made me sorry for him – a regiment would be such a beastly home wouldn't it?

You would be amused to find I am getting quite accustomed to military men & good at them! At Assouan I had to say goodbye to them all & get out. I was sorry as I had got to like them – even silly little Charlton. I got into a launch & crossed the water to this hôtel – a gigantic place in a

---

[1] On 23 December, as she travelled down the Red Sea towards Port Sudan, Violet had written to Venetia Stanley: 'Everything is very unusual & different – & I feel what I wanted to – a sensation of rather mythical life.'

rather lovely garden – covered with marvellous purple flowers – with the river just below. I read a few old Times's – & fell rather on my feet as I came across Margot's <u>evidence</u> in the West case! highly characteristic – & also saw that Ld. Swaythling is dead – which means a 'deep note' letter to Edwin. It may facilitate his matrimonial prospects – with the graminivorous wife....[1]

We rode back through a bazaar hung with scarves & beads – I showed praiseworthy restraint meaning to buy some black opals to-morrow. I think I shall get daggers & shoes for the rest of the Club – I wish boys wore beads. I haven't <u>yet</u> written to B.C. which haunts me like a ghost – I can't think what to say. I know I ought to say definitely <u>no</u> & that he must put it out of his head once & for all – but in a way this wouldn't be fair as it is still well in mine....

V.A. to M.B.C.
 Wednesday 25 January
 Savoy Hotel, Assouan

Dearest Bongie – This will be <u>one</u> of the very last letters you will get from me – I may possibly write <u>one</u> more from Luxor to put the 'comble' to one of the most brilliant records of fidelity & style ever sustained over a <u>very</u> long period in a <u>very</u> hot climate. Are you proud of having elicited it? I spent a <u>very</u> sad last few days with Oc – last nights in the open – last sunrise rides – & left Khartoum Sunday night – having been there exactly 4 weeks.

My journey has so far been conducted in a <u>masterly</u> way – transferences of luggage from ship to train & from train to ship (both registered & unregistered) being accomplished without loss – tickets unscathed.[2] Circular notes & Letter of Identification unmissing etc.

I think what makes me such a <u>marvellous</u> traveller is not so much the capacity for helping myself as that of getting other people to help me. I met several <u>angels</u> on the steamer who ground like niggers over my hold-

[1] Samuel Montagu (1832–1911), 1st Baron Swaythling, 1907; head of the bank Samuel Montagu and Co., London, and Liberal MP for Whitechapel, Tower Hamlets, 1885–1900. The 'graminivorous wife' may have been Lady Dorothy Howard, third daughter of the 9th Earl of Carlisle (see Naomi B. Levine, *Politics, Religion and Love*, 178).

[2] Violet's return journey to Port Said took her, by boat and by train, along the Nile valley to Cairo, which she reached on Thursday 2 February, having spent four days at Luxor visiting the ancient sites there. She spent another four days sightseeing in Cairo, and left Port Said on Monday 6 February. Her ship, the SS *Caledonia*, arrived in Marseilles the following Friday, and she reached Downing Street on Sunday the 12th, three weeks after leaving Khartoum.

alls etc. & bargained for beads for me at all the stopping places – & one (called Whittingham) gave me the most wonderful sword sheathed in rhinoceros hide with a tiger skin handle. I have alas left them all now & am sitting with great dignity & self-possession at a little table all to myself in the midst of a buzzing Table d'Hôte room. . . .

Bless & keep you – the best friend anyone has ever had – I should be happier if you did less for me. I wear yr. Heap every night. I didn't get a letter from you my last Friday – perhaps it is at Luxor Goodbye Yr V.

Diary – Wednesday 1 February – Train to Cairo

My Darling – My last day at Luxor is over. . . .

I wonder what the Cairo étape will be like. I feel a good deal of curiosity & some excitement over the thought of finding B.C.'s letter there – I <u>so</u> wonder what sort of a love-letter he will write. Rather a bad one – beginning 'Dear Miss Asquith' I guess – I shall laugh very much if he ends 'Believe me – yours sincerely E. Bonham Carter' – but I somehow feel as if he easily might! Lady Haddo has just written me a line about the cemetery at Haddo – which is very sweet of her. How strangely hallowed the things which were even on the <u>fringe</u> of your life (like her!) seem to me now. The man has come to make up my bed – Goodnight to thee most dearly loved Yr own

Diary – Thursday 2nd – Monday 6th February – British Agency, Cairo

My Darling – I didn't sleep much in the train but was fairly comfy nevertheless – & pulled out at the other end by a Kavass & the station master – instead of wildly beckoning to an unresponsive hôtel porter – & driven off through grey damp streets to the Agency. My first impressions of Cairo were very bad – it has all the oriental squalor & dirt & every European hideosity in the way of advertisement etc. The Agency itself stands in a nice garden with the Nile at the end – I was received by a sister of Gorst's with feverish hospitality – she was very kind & stayed on talking about my bath & my breakfast whilst I longed to throw myself upon a pile of unopened letters.[1] Such a treasure hoard – 1 from Father one from

---

[1] (Sir) John Gorst (1861–1911), GCMG 1911; under-secretary of state at the foreign office, 1904–7; succeeded Lord Cromer as British agent and consul-general in Egypt, 1907. He married, in 1903, Evelyn *née* Rudd; they had one daughter. Violet stayed with the Gorsts at the British Agency in Cairo, and found them '<u>delightful</u> people to live with – so simple & easy & natural. One of the best atmospheres I have been in – from a pt. of view of comfort & glide'.

Cys two from Bongie 2 from B.C. one from little Stony with some kodaks –
B.C's were <u>much</u> better than I expected – so simple & real – though
containing one or two ingenuously hackneyed touches of the very new
hand which would have made an old stager like you smile! His treatment
of you & me is wonderfully reverent & considerate – & I think you would
approve his navigatory attitude – which is the very reverse of the H-
school – what you used to call Hot & gusty – do you remember?

I rested a little & then went down & found Lady Gorst – who is very
kind & rather vacantly pretty – with not much 'mentality' – but simple &
nice with no sort of official nonsense about her. We walked round the
garden & were civil to each other – then in to lunch to which various local
people came. I sat next Gorst who is a very shrewd intelligent little fellow –
also simple & natural & easy to get on with – not listening quite enough
to what one says – but amusing & at times amusable....
(continued in train to Port-Said – Mon 6th)
... Saturday – I spent the morning at the zoo which is the best – the least
smelly & saddening I have ever been in. Nearly all the animals out of
doors – <u>marvellous</u> birds of every colour – gazelle & ibex with twisted
horns – a baby elephant – a rhinoceros playing with a goat on apparently
equal terms....

I went to Salome at night – tried to remember every word of your letter
from Berlin to me about it.[1] As much as I could remember I agreed with
absolutely. It is extraordinary how closely the music follows the action &
reproduces the emotional atmosphere. It is never <u>irrelevant</u> for a moment.

The Harem ladies sit in boxes with a sort of screen in front of them –
through which they but nobody else can see – I believe that's the sort of
way you would have treated me – you were very Turkish at heart in spite
of all your proud boasts to the contrary....

Now I am in the Port Said train having said all my Collinses & goodbyes
to the Gorsts – & seen two last mosques – Sultan Hassan & the blue one –
with Storrs who is really very amusing & incredibly Custian.[2] I think I
must toss off one line to Artie & perhaps one to B.C. to post at Port Said –
I will write again on the ship – Blessings.

---

[1] *Salome* (1905), an opera by Richard Strauss, based on the text of Oscar Wilde's play of the
same name.

[2] Ronald Henry Storrs (1881–1955), officer in the ministry of finance of the Egyptian
government, 1904, later Oriental secretary to the British Agency, Cairo. Storrs was the nephew
of Harry Cust, of whom the *Dictionary of National Biography* records: 'He was, before all things,
a talker, born and trained.'

Diary – Tuesday 7 February – S.S. Caledonia, en route for Marseilles

Beloved – Sitting on deck in a high gale – with a tossing blue sea shooting jets of foam & spray over the side – the ship bounding along. I have been very kindly & cosily tucked up by an angel of a deck-steward who I foresee is going to perform Montagu's functions on this journey – & had a short talk with Duncannon who is <u>much</u> the nicest 'parti' – so clever & civil & apparently unselfconscious about his prospects[1] . . . .

Diary – Friday 10 February – S.S. Caledonia, en route for Marseilles

. . . I have written to B.C. & shall post at Marseilles. He is taking up more of my thoughts than anything has done since your death – I feel in a way that I oughtn't to quite brush it aside as unfeasible because it is off the beaten track – & yet I know I should never have the courage to do it – unless he is a <u>wonderful</u> person – & more compelling than I think him.

I am curious to see what Bongie will say about it – poor little B – He has done more for me than anyone in the world – this year. . . .

Now that I am getting near home a great impatience is sweeping me – to arrive to find all the things I love – Father – Cys within reach – Bongie – the Club. It shows me that I still do love a good many things a good deal – which I have forgotten sometimes in my great love & longing for one.

Diary – Saturday 11 February – P. & O. Express train from Marseilles

Beloved – Once again in this – <u>the</u> shakiest – rattlingest train in all the world. I spent what seemed an aeon at Marseilles between the arrival of the ship & my re-embarkation in the train. Posting my two letters – to Lady Gorst & B.C. – sending Bongie a wire & registering my luggage took only the twinkling of an eye – & I then found myself with hours on my hands & nothing to do but sit on a draughty abandoned deck covered with coal-dust. . . .

I went for a <u>very</u> beautiful drive round the Corniche with Morrison in a rickety Flayosc. A <u>Marvellous</u> coastline jutting ruggedly into a cold – glittering blue sea. The villas & grey olive trees & Riviera vegetation reminded me of Valescure & last year – & a sort of pang of longing to be back there again – in that time of anguish shot through me. Why – how can any thought of tenderness linger round the memory of that nightmare.

---

[1] Vere Brabazon Ponsonby (1880–1956), Viscount Duncannon, and the future 9th Earl of Bessborough; a barrister, and Unionist MP for Cheltenham, 1910, and for Dover, 1913–20.

I suppose it is the feeling of the advancing days leading one further from the East – of new grist pouring into one's life – new claims – new demands – one cannot turn away from....

Diary – Sunday 12 February – 10 Downing Street, Whitehall, S.W.

A night in the train over – tossed mercilessly about in my narrow bed – I never <u>knew</u> a train like this one – one always feels on the verge of derailment.

It is so strange seeing a bright winter sun – the country white with frost – the hand ploughed fields & still icebound pools. A nice homecoming feeling. It is 11 – at 1 I shall get to Calais & at 3 I shall be at Dover & find Bongie – bless him – I got a letter from him at Marseilles – saying – '& then what glory will there be –'. I think of the homecomings from Switzerland & finding you & him & Venetia at the station – Oh Beloved how much there was to come back for then....

EIGHT

Liberal Activist

1911–1912

In March 1911, not long after her return from the Sudan, Violet addressed a Liberal meeting in Camberwell, London. It was not the first occasion on which she had spoken in public, but it marked the beginning of a more active participation in Liberal politics, after the long period of mourning brought about by Archie Gordon's death. In October she inaugurated a Women's Liberal Association at Fife, and in December she spoke on the National Insurance Act to the association's Hammersmith branch, of which she was then president. She even made political speeches on what were not obviously political occasions: opening a Methodist social institute in Kingsway, London, in December 1911, she spoke in advocacy of the state's responsibility for social reform. She displayed on these occasions early signs of her skill as a public speaker, and the deep conviction in Liberalism that she retained throughout her life.

Diary – Wednesday 22 February 1911 – 10 Downing Street, Whitehall, S.W.

My Darling – A very crowded day – beginning with a botany lesson with Reginald Farrer! who sat with me for about 2 hours volubly demonstrating the peculiarities of a large yellow tulip.[1] Then lunch with Venetia where H Paul[2] was – then the House – a good speech by F.E. ending with a fine Burke quotation about fortitude & wisdom & the Almighty which came strangely from him!

I fled off to the Club with Bongie & Dudley – had a delicious welcome & watched a rehearsal of a game of living draughts! – which was really rather pretty – much less absurd than it sounds – & then <u>just</u> got back in time to hear Winston wind up the debate which he did very well. The majority

---

[1] Reginald John Farrer (1880–1920), botanist who travelled extensively in the Far East, India and North America before the Great War. A Balliol contemporary of Raymond Asquith, he contested Ashford, Kent, as a Liberal in 1911.

[2] Herbert Woodfield Paul (1853–1935), author and politician, Liberal MP for Northampton, 1906–10; second civil service commissioner, 1909–18.

was 124 – wonderfully good. It was such fun seeing Father trip down the floor of the House & put the Bill on the table.[1]

Love to thee my own Beloved.

The Club is such a joy & pride – Yr own

Diary – Friday 24 February – 10 Downing Street, Whitehall, S.W.

My darling – I have been at Harlesden this evening at a Liberal Social Council – shaking hands with hundreds. Lady Haddo – Haddo – Ly Roxburgh present & Dudley who motored down with me – & made an excellent speech – coming after an awful one by Sub Rosa – the last word of vulgarity – setting every nerve on edge & making one really almost ashamed of being a Liberal.

Dudley spoke divinely – so sweetly of yr. Mother – saying 'I am not one of those who is ashamed of extolling their parents' – so like you I thought....

Diary – Tuesday 28 February – 10 Downing Street, Whitehall, S.W.

My Darling – I am home again with much to tell you.

First of all to finish off Oxford. I had a wonderful Sunday – conversation for <u>3 hours</u> between breakfast & lunch with the Professor in his book-room about nothing & everything – the best sort of talk.[2] Then we drove into Oxford & Bongie gave lunch in Cys's rooms to a large & motley horde....

After lunch we adjourned into a room which used to be <u>Yours</u>. After a little pie-fun – the Professor Bongie Mrs R. & I drove off in a taxi to call on the poet Bridges who lives in a divine little house up on a hill.[3] We first wandered chillily round a garden & I found him a little farouche & inaccessible – but I afterwards closed with him in a glorious talk after tea –

---

[1] In the House of Commons on 22 February, Asquith moved the introduction of the Parliament bill, to reform the powers of the House of Lords. Churchill was considered especially effective in concluding the government case. The success of the motion could be taken for granted, but the margin of 124 votes gave the government an important moral victory, as it was just two votes short of its full majority.

[2] (Sir) Walter Alexander Raleigh, 'The Professor', at Hinksey, a couple of miles south-south-west of central Oxford.

[3] Robert Seymour Bridges (1844–1930), poet laureate, 1913–30. Bridges, who had been at Corpus Christi College, Oxford, settled at Chilswell House on Boar's Hill, overlooking the city.

good relevage of my favourite kind – books etc. He loathes Tolstoy! & thinks Charlotte Brontë a pure governess but appreciates Emily which is the main thing. He is very beautiful!

Diary – Tuesday 4 April – 10 Downing Street, Whitehall, S.W.

Dearest – I have had rather a tired day. Short bout of H of C. in the afternoon – Veto Bill in Committee stage – AJB, Linky, F.E., Winston, Banbury & others speaking.[1] Tea with Nash & Bongie – the sort of moment you would have loved. Then home & at 7. I saw your Mother – & we had a glorious talk. Just seeing her is so wonderful – there were rather a lot of concrete hares to be chased off the block first – our best talks are the midnight ones – but still I did love it – through all even the most circumstantial 'women workers union' talks I have that undersense of strength & unflinching-ness in meeting life with all her power & all her courage unmaimed by any anguish.

I dined with Frances [Tennant] & sat next Sargent – who is most delightful.[2] He has a delicious trick of becoming absolutely nonplussed by want of words in the midst of a sentence & finishing it off by gestures – of the oddest & most eloquent kind. I had a very good talk with him & also enjoyed little Speyer on my other side who is a strong Liberal & a darling & infinitely superior to her, whom he aptly described as having 50 per cent too much of everything!...[3]

Diary – Saturday 8 April – Munstead House, Surrey

My own Darling – Fräu slept with me the last two nights owing to congestion at home & so baulked Buxton. Since I last wrote Oc has returned – looking better I think than usual. It seemed so much more like the reestablishment of our old relations this time. There's no doubt Egypt made a great difference....

... yesterday we had a vast plutocratic Liberal dinner at Lord St Davids'

[1] Lord Hugh Richard Cecil, 'Linky' (1869–1956), fifth son of the 3rd Marquess of Salisbury, and a first cousin of A. J. Balfour. Unionist MP for Greenwich, 1895–1906; for Oxford University, 1910–37. Sir Frederick Banbury (1850–1936), Bt, Unionist MP for the City of London, 1906–24.
[2] John Singer Sargent (1856–1925), American-born painter famous for his Edwardian portraiture.
[3] Sir Edgar and Lady Speyer, see above, p. 209, n. 1.

(a new peer).[1] Claridges – the whole Cabinet – embarras de food – band etc – (caviare oysters <u>&</u> plovers eggs!) & afterwards the whole Liberal party jammed like figs in a box together –

It was a reprieve to motor down here this afternoon – a <u>divine</u> party – Cys I, Oc Puff & father in the Napier – & nest in this delicious comfy house – Alick had come down earlier with Morrison – he has cheeks like apples & glistening eyes. I am so happy about him – I have settled him in a tiny (but luckily icy room) over the stables & shall try & get him a little work in the garden[2]. . . .

M.B.C. to V.A.   ***Wednesday 26 April***
                                         5 Hyde Park Square, W.

Dearest. A short letter tonight as it is late. I took Dudley down to the Club. I am not very much in favour of his taking England as his home is so poor & it is necessary for an office boy to look smart & I do not think it usually answers very well to make a boy live up to so much higher a standard than his home.[3] I think too that he will be better suited to manual work as he is a strong boy. . . .

. . . Dudley was very nice & laughed at all the jokes in Punch. He had the pleasure of reading the famous Agincourt speech at the Club. K has sent the two pictures & I have taken them down to the Club. Hyde wants to know if you will give away some prizes for him on Sat May 6th 8.p.m. I said I thought you were engaged for the weekend. He wants me to get some one else in that case. I cannot think whom I shall induce to do it.

Bless you. B.

---

[1] John Wynford Philipps (1860–1938), 1st Baron St Davids, 1908; Liberal MP for Pembrokeshire, 1898–1908.

[2] Alexander Carmichael, a member of the Archie Gordon Club, was suffering from a chest complaint which Violet and Bongie feared was tuberculosis. They arranged for him to be seen by a doctor at the Brompton Hospital in London, and it was not until late in the year that he was finally pronounced healthy, after being hospitalized for a short period in September. The same month his mother lost one of her five other children to the disease. Once 'Alick' was healthy, Violet and Bongie tried to find him employment as a gardener; he had left school the previous February, aged fourteen.

[3] Henry England, one of the original members of the Archie Gordon Club.

Diary – Saturday 29 April – Vice Regal Lodge, Dublin

Beloved – Two glorious days of sun & rain – riding in the morning in the
Phoenix Park which is at its very dampest & greenest & loveliest –
blossom & gorse coming out here & there – with <u>delightful</u> Forbes who
has real charm for me[1] – on a comfortable but uninspiring horse procured
for me by Keddy – frowstyish functions with yr. M. in the afternoon –
gladly endured as they are with her. A particularly bad one at the Alexandra
College this afternoon when a woman read a paper on lodging-houses
with Zola-esque detail about lice – vice – stench etc. Your M. dozed in the
Chair. At one point it became so lurid that the Reporters dropped their
pencils & wrote no more – but sat in scarlet silence....

Diary – Friday 5 May – 10 Downing Street, Whitehall, S.W.

Darling – Just back from dinner next 'Sir J Simon' – to whom I am at
present supposed to be engaged – a rear-Admiral on the other side.

Talk afterwards with Mrs. Lloyd George who is a little darling – & has
all her wits about her. Back across the Horseguards on foot with her & LG.

I chose 5 new boys this morning with whom I am fairly pleased – Rowe,
Johnston, Ashley, Sinfield, & little Gunter – saw England's Mother who
seemed quite agreeable to his being apprenticed....

I sat to Barnie – in Artillery Mansions towards tea-time.[2] I have an
amusing letter from Forbes – he says 'since you left I have felt just like
Stephen – very very lonesome –' I like him. Manchester to-morrow –
Bless & keep you – Yr V.

The Parliament Act, 1911

The final stages of the Parliament bill took place during a heatwave
in the summer of 1911. In May the Unionist leader in the Lords,
Lord Lansdowne, made a belated attempt to pre-empt the government by unveiling his own plan for reform. The peers would retain
their veto power, but they would no longer have an automatic
right to sit in the upper chamber, which was to be made smaller.

[1] Violet first met Forbes the previous week, and described him in her diary as a 'very nice
new shy ADC' to Lord Aberdeen. Three days later she was writing of his 'immense charm'.
[2] Possibly Emily Barnard, a portrait and figure painter who exhibited at the Royal Academy.
A watercolour portrait of Violet by 'Barnard' is in the possession of the Hon. Raymond Bonham
Carter, Violet's younger son.

Members would be nominated equally by the Crown, nobility, and the Commons. The bill sank without trace after a second reading, and thereafter Lansdowne bowed to the inevitable. By late July both he and Balfour were advising non-resistance. Their words, however, went unheeded by a determined group of Unionist 'diehards', and Balfour lamented in a letter to Lady Elcho:

'Fragments of the Unionist party seem to have gone temporarily crazy, to the detriment of the party as a whole. As usual the leading lunatics are my own kith and kin; but they have many distinguished allies, and I see at present no signs of returning sanity.'[1]

Balfour's 'kith and kin' included his cousins Lord Hugh ('Linky') Cecil and Lord Robert Cecil, and their brother-in-law the Earl of Selborne, all of whom gathered beneath the banner of resistance raised by the eighty-seven-year-old Earl of Halsbury. On 26 July a banquet in Halsbury's honour was held at the aptly named Hôtel Cecil in the Strand. The organizers were Austen Chamberlain, F. E. Smith, Edward Carson, and George Wyndham, senior Unionists to be counted among the 'distinguished allies'. At the banquet Chamberlain gave voice to the widespread scepticism among diehards about the government's readiness and authority to 'swamp' the House of Lords with new creations, and so effectively guarantee the bill against all odds. He called Asquith's position one of 'fraudulent bluff'.[2] Asquith, however, had the King's guarantee on the creation of as many peers as would prove necessary, and he had drawn up a list of 249 names that he was considering: they included Thomas Hardy, J. M. Barrie and Bertrand Russell.[3] The issue was not put to the test. On 10 August the bill was carried in the Lords by 131 votes to 114; in all thirty-seven Unionists voted with eighty-one Liberals, and thirteen bishops, to make up the majority. The government had won the day, and it was a great personal triumph for Asquith. But for the more pragmatic Unionists there was the consolation that there had been no creation of peers. The party retained its huge majority in the upper chamber, and even with the lesser instrument of the suspensory veto allowed by the Parliament Act, this was to prove significant in the fight against Home Rule.

[1] Arthur James Balfour to Lady Elcho, 30 July 1911: Jane Ridley and Clayre Percy (eds.), *The Letters of Arthur Balfour and Lady Elcho 1885–1917*, 268.

[2] See Roy Jenkins, *Mr Balfour's Poodle*, 163.

[3] The list appears as an appendix in J. A. Spender and Cyril Asquith, *Life of Lord Oxford and Asquith*, i, 329–31.

Diary – Wednesday 10 May – 10 Downing Street, Whitehall, S.W.

Beloved – The Court last night with Father – I had a white dress with pearls & a white & gold train.

I fetched father from E. Grey's & we stood about in the little entrée pen at the bottom of the big room – Father discussing with the Lord Chancellor [Loreburn] & the Archbishop – with huge lawnsleeves – who was to be allowed to crown the Queen – the Archbishop of C. maintaining it was his right & not the Archbishop of York's.[1] We went up the passage & across the room without much waiting – directly after the Corps Diplomatique – the Archbishop & the Lord Chancellor – & immediately followed by the Speaker[2].... The Queen is much less plain than I thought – quite a tidy dreary face – with regular Royal hair in exact imitation of the old one – without any of her beauty or grace. The king looked rather amusingly bored towards the end – two hours of frumps & freaks having defiled past him.

I sat between Mrs. Lulu & Mrs Birrell in one of those pews & watched.... We got back late & tired.

We had rather a wonderful day in Manchester on Saturday – father spoke really marvellously well. Ld. Lansdowne unfolded his scheme of Peer Reform on Monday which was received in icy silence – I wish I'd heard the debate. I think things are going well for us.

Barnie's picture exhibition started yesterday. You would love her first one of me I think. Olive is back – though I haven't seen her – placards are covered with 'Lady explorer's return'.[3] What a fleshly letter Darling – More to-night.

Diary – Sunday 21 May – 10 Downing Street, Whitehall, S.W.

Winston & I talked at the Court Ball. He said rather a good thing about men not daring to combine pomp with power. They must always be

[1] Randall Davidson (1848–1930), archbishop of Canterbury, 1903–28. Davidson was succeeded at Canterbury by the archbishop of York mentioned here, Cosmo Gordon Lang.

[2] James William Lowther (1855–1949), Unionist MP for Penrith, Cumberland, 1886–1918, and speaker of the House of Commons, 1905–21.

[3] The *Daily Graphic* of 11 April 1912 announced the return of Olive Macleod from Africa and the news of her engagement to Charles Lindsay Temple, chief secretary of Northern Nigeria: 'The announcement recalls the wonderful pilgrimage Miss Macleod made eighteen months ago to the grave of her fiancé, the late Lieutenant Boyd Alexander, who was murdered while on an expedition. She travelled 4,000 miles in the heart of Africa, passing through territory never before traversed by a white woman.'

separate – then they were harmless – otherwise fatal – Metternich looked to me dying which made me sad.[1]

We spoke to Princess Louise – the King – Queen – old Christian – Connaughts etc. Not the Kaiser or Kaiserin which I should have loved. He has a magnificent head & forehead I think. The little Princess looks vital & rather attractive – tho' quite plain.

Goodnight – bless thee Yr own

Diary – Tuesday 23 May – 10 Downing Street, Whitehall, S.W.

My own Darling – I came up this morning & the garden party happened – one & a half thousand fishfaces in our garden – I nearly fled with terror when I saw Bongie's brother coming towards me & hid behind serried ranks of Barrans & Bothas.[2] But he grimly waited till I emerged & then – we met. I said all the usual conventional garden party things. What a phantasmagoria it was etc. & then fled – leaving him with Puffin. Forbes appeared presently – an extra complication. Altogether my life is pretty full just now.[3]

I dined in bed – but got up afterwards to see them – Bongie – Micky – Venetia – Bonham Carter – with whom & Léonie[4] I had the oddest possible à trois – Léonie at her very most shymaking – & he bewildered & dazed by her. His best remark was 'I can quite understand Royalties not caring for Americans'.[5] Oh Darling I am a little puzzled by the situation – I must stop – voice better Yr own

Forbes came to say goodbye at 15 to 10 – en route for Euston – I'm afraid incipient lasher is declaring itself.

---

[1] Count Paul von Wolff-Metternich (1853–1934), German ambassador; thought to be too favourable towards Britain, he was recalled to Berlin in May 1912, and replaced by Baron Marschall.

[2] The garden party was held by the prime minister, at 10 Downing Street, for the delegates of the Women's National Liberal Federation. This was probably the first occasion on which Violet had seen Edgar Bonham Carter since returning from the Sudan: he had taken early leave that year in order to pursue his courtship of her. The 'Barrans & Bothas' to whom Violet refers were Sir John Barrans and the Rt. Hon. Louis Botha (1863–1919), who were representative of two obvious types of guest – British Liberals and overseas dignitaries, respectively. Botha, the first prime minister of the Union of South Africa, was in Britain to attend the Imperial Conference, the first meeting of which was held on the morning of the garden party.

[3] Violet feared proposals, or 'lashers', from both Edgar Bonham Carter and Forbes.

[4] Léonie Leslie *née* Jerome (1859–1943), the sister of Lady Randolph Churchill; she married, in 1884, Colonel John Leslie.

[5] Edgar's comment is surprising, given that Léonie was American.

Diary – Monday 24 July – 10 Downing Street, Whitehall, S.W.

Just back from Fife – A most extraordinary scene in the House to-night –
Father denied a hearing. . . .

Diary – Friday 28 July – 10 Downing Street, Whitehall, S.W.

Beloved – A stifling airless week political feeling running high & strong.
Tremendous indignation is felt over the scene on Monday – I must say I
felt shocked & shattered beyond words by it. Linky sat there snow white &
gibbering execrations – like a baboon, epileptic & suffragette rolled into
one. He has the excuse of insanity – not so F.E. who is a mere political
adventurer – with no loyalty or convictions. He has joined the Halsbury
Cave of last ditchers who had a large dinner at the Hôtel Cecil on Wed.
night.

Father has shown a magnificent ballast dignity & temper throughout.
Edward Grey's speech on Monday was most simple & touching.[1]

We had the garden party yesterday 800 people in great heat a good talk
with Winston & Jack Gordon & Bogey Harris at the end of it.[2]

Liberal dinner of 40 to-night – sat between a Scotch member Collins &
Spender.[3] Camp with Club to-morrow – yr very own

[1] On 24 July Asquith was due to deliver a speech to the Commons outlining the government's position on the amended Parliament bill. When he rose to speak an organized uproar
began on the opposition benches, from which cries of 'Traitor' were heard: the ringleaders
were Lord Hugh 'Linky' Cecil and 'F.E.' Smith. Unable to make himself heard Asquith sat
down, after thirty minutes. The next speakers, A. J. Balfour and Sir Edward Grey, were both
heard in silence. Grey had been urged to speak by Margot Asquith, who had witnessed her
husband's plight from the Ladies' Gallery, and had sent down a note to Grey: 'They will listen
to you, so for God's sake defend him from the cats and the cads!' The text of Asquith's
important speech was published in the national press the following day. The disturbance gave
Unionist MPs an opportunity to express their anger at the government, and also their
dissatisfaction with their own leadership, over its management of the opposition to the
Parliament bill. See Roy Jenkins, *Mr Balfour's Poodle*, 158–60.

[2] Bogey Harris (d. 1950) was 'one of those figures that appear in memoires of all ages and
mystify historians. Why was this man, who did nothing, and said nothing, the friend of all
the great, with an entrée into every salon? . . . a short answer is that in a society composed of
bursting egos anyone who is recessive without being dull is always welcome': Kenneth Clark,
Another Part of the Wood, 179–80. He was educated at Eton, and lost much of his inheritance
playing baccarat with the Prince of Wales's set in the 1890s.

[3] Godfrey Pattison Collins (1875–1936), Liberal MP for Greenock, 1910–36, and parliamentary private secretary at the war office.

Diary – Sunday 30 July – Littlestone-on-Sea, Kent

My Darling – In camp with the Club! Bongie took down most of them on Sat. morning – having like an angel spent the previous night here & got up at 5 – & gone back to London to fetch them. After a <u>singing lesson</u> with a woman called Mrs. W. Archer (wife of the Ibsen translator[1]) my 2nd – I went home & had a somnambulist <u>dog</u> tired lunch then fetched Roberts, Bailly & Martin from the Club & drove to Charing Cross where I met the most influential of the Carters.

After $\frac{1}{2}$ an hour's wait on <u>stifling</u> Cannon St. platform we fought for places in an overcrowded train – I popped Martin & Roberts in with Morrison & took Bailly with me, B.C. in front – what was my despair to find we were in a non-stopping train going straight to Folkestone! It was very difficult to bear – but we all behaved with grit & composure. Luckily it was an express so we taxied out & reached the camp rather before the others. It is really a very good place quite near that coastguard station by the 9th hole. The sea & shingle close by – & grass (dreadfully brown & desiccated) for them to play cricket on.

Four rather groggy looking tents went up – & there was quite a jolly building near by where we all had tea. They were all in a state of <u>wild</u> excitement – & didn't close one eye all night in consequence thereby keeping poor Bongie & all the staff awake. We have spent an arduous day playing cricket & rounders – & walking along burning roads & shingle in the sun. I had the pride & pleasure of <u>washing up</u> for everyone after tea! which I did with morbid thoroughness.

We had a little service in the evening – well conducted by Bongie – Hymns played by me on a rather good piano. Now B. & I & B.C. have dined here together & Cyril has <u>not</u> arrived – as he said he would – & I am very sleepy – but less <u>tired</u> than I was this morning – & loving you very nearly & dearly. Your own.

Diary – Monday 31 July – Littlestone-on-Sea, Kent

Beloved – A strenuous day. Blazing skies again under which the boys played cricket with extraordinary grit for <u>hours</u> during the morning – B.C managed them with genius. Cyril turned up in a landau for lunch – he <u>had</u> arrived last night after all – & stayed at the hôtel. He lunched with us & then went off on my bicycle to Dymchurch to telephone to Lympne – & has not returned or sent a word of any kind – which is very sloppy & inconsiderate of him. I suppose with such <u>marvellous</u> points as

---

[1] The 'Ibsen translator' was William Archer (1856–1924), drama critic and playwright.

Cyril has there must be largish cavities in places where the surplus has been scooped from. Certainly over plans & arrangements he is most trying. We went for a very hot & arduous walk to New Romney in the afternoon – & showed the boys the church. They drank quantities of very highly coloured & gassy drinks such as 'cherry cider' & 'raspberry champagne' in a little shop there – & then we walked back & had a little restful time on the beach till dinner. B.C came back & dined with me & had a happy dentist afterwards – I showed him my commonplace book.

I got a very disagreeable anonymous letter about Father – too absurd to really matter but pretending he is in danger – which I can't believe – Bless & keep you Beloved.

I walked back alone in a strange light this evening & felt very strongly that you were beside me – my Strength. Yr own.

Diary – Tuesday 1 August – Littlestone-on-Sea, Kent

Beloved. That saint Artie came to-day which helped me out a lot. We had great heat – bathed twice – played a good deal of cricket etc. No set walk in the afternoon which was a comfort. I read aloud The Man With The Twisted Lip on the beach.[1]

Bongie turned up late to-night. Wonderful stormy sky – B.C releved lasher again which he had refrained from doing with marvellous chivalry – whilst we were alone. I feel perplexed about him – I really love him when we are alone together but when one other is there it seems impossible – Goodnight Beloved

Yr own

Diary – Wednesday 2 August – Littlestone-on-Sea, Kent

Dearest. The Club played the local cricket eleven & were badly beaten poor little things – by 79 runs. They weren't playing their best & got very tired towards the end of it. But it was very exciting & I can truthfully say the only cricket match of my life that has riveted my attention & emotions for a whole afternoon.

We afterwards all repaired to Mrs. Savage's – (the seller of gassy drinks & highly coloured sweets) & had tea in her garden – a nice little sunny plot behind her very stuffy little house – both elevens putting down an

[1] 'The Man with the Twisted Lip' is one of the stories in Sir Arthur Conan Doyle's Sherlock Holmes series.

incredible number of cakes & buns. I bicycled back to camp – Ronald Glover, Ashley, Baily & Pocock running beside me.

Oc is divine with the boys. Cold supper here with him Bongie & B.C. My love to you most Beloved. Yr own.

Diary – Friday 11 August – 10 Downing Street, Whitehall, S.W.

My Darling – One of the most thrilling evenings of my life. I was in the H. of Lords from 4 onwards – & heard Rosebery, Milner, Camperdown, Halsbury, John Morley, Ld. Curzon, Selborne. Everyone was most uncertain about the division & little Benn told me in the Lobby 2 minutes before we should be defeated.[1]

It was strange standing in the short passage jammed up against Wolmers & Salisburys waiting.[2] First the news came that the Die Hards numbered 111 – & that we were beaten. It did indeed look like it. I didn't see how we were to do better – & went through all the emotions of defeat till 3 minutes later a man rushed thro' with the news the Government had won – by 17 as we afterwards found 114 diehards – & 131 Gov. The 12 Bishops voted for us & several Lansdownites whom Knollys had got hold of.[3] (Camperdown had made a speech in favour of voting for the Gov. & Victor Lytton did so too.) It will be amusing to read the Division lists to-morrow. We walked back & talked a little at home Montagu & I & Micky.

Mild uproar & cheering in the streets – Bless you Beloved Your own

[1] Earl Camperdown and Lord Curzon were Unionist peers who supported the Parliament bill; Lord Milner a Die-hard opponent. William Wedgwood Benn (1877–1960) was Liberal member for St George's, Tower Hamlets, 1906–18; junior lord of the treasury and Liberal whip, 1910–15.

[2] Viscount Wolmer, a Unionist MP, and the 4th Marquess of Salisbury, were die-hard relatives, the former being a grandson, and the latter a son, of the 3rd Marquess of Salisbury.

[3] On learning of the government's victory the King wrote in his diary: 'So the Halsburyites were thank God beaten! It is indeed a great relief to me – I am spared any further humiliation by a creation of peers.' His private secretaries Lord Knollys and Lord Stamfordham had, he noted, 'worked hard for this result' (Roy Jenkins, *Mr Balfour's Poodle*, 184). Violet was also intensely relieved, and wrote to Venetia Stanley on 17 August: 'I do feel a load off my heart – a creation would have stripped victory of all romance for me – & I am so glad for Father & the King who really has behaved well. Knollys is after F. the hero of the situation.'

M.B.C. to V.A.   *Friday 11 August*
                                                   5 Hyde Park Square, W.

Dearest one. Your father has won his great game. I do not suppose that
again in his life will he have such a single handed triumph again, and he
will be the last person to mind sharing the merits of his future victories.
But there is no one to dispute with him for the merit of this.
I wish only that you would be in the House to see his reception on
Monday.
   Bless you
      B.

Hugh Godley to V.A.   *Monday 14 August*
                                               Office of the Parliamentary
                                                                Counsel

Dear child I only told Venetia about the watch. I thought she knew all
your tenderest secrets. . . .
   The Lords debate must have been the most thrilling thing imaginable.
Even K[ilbracken]. was quite excited, but of course his vote only meant
that to the question 'Do you want the Bill with 400 peers or without 400
peers?' he replied 'without them'. He said that whatever had been his
intention when he went down to the House he w^d have been induced to
vote as he did by the speeches of the ditchers, especially of Ld Selborne.[1]
Their attitude seems to me one of the most inexplicable of modern times.
Ld Salisbury & Ld Hugh were both at Panshanger, & they both quite
seriously asserted that, after all that Morley & Crewe said, they were quite
convinced that the Gov^t did not really mean to make peers, or at most to
make 50, if the Bill had been defeated.[2]
   Of course I don't like the Bill; it will enable you to carry Home Rule &
lots of other things to which, apart altogether from the question of their
merits, there is every reason to believe the country is hostile, but I needn't
tell you that I have no kind of sympathy with the hysterical cries of
'treachery' & so forth. Your father has just done very skilfully & successfully
exactly what he said he w^d do, & exactly what everyone must have foreseen
that he w^d do, & the opp^n have not only been conquered, but completely

---

[1] William Waldegrave Palmer (1859–1942), 2nd Earl of Selbourne. Governor of the Transvaal
and High Commissioner of South Africa, 1905–10.
[2] Panshanger, in Hertfordshire, was the home of Ettie Desborough's aunt, Katie Cowper.
For the assumption of some Unionists that the government was bluffing in its threat to create
new peers, see above, p. 271.

outwitted. You have all the honours of war. But you have the hell of a time coming....

Goodbye my dear, & I hope you will enjoy your time with your sweet brother. I love you very much in spite of everything & am on the whole of the opinion that your merits outweigh your defects. Which is paying a very high compliment. Bless you. You wrote me a very nice letter. Nicer than I deserve Yours always Hugh.

Diary – Thursday 17 August – Eib See, Garmisch, Bavaria

Dearest – I spent two or three last feverish days in London – saw H. Paul, Jack Gordon – Bogey Harris – <u>Winston</u> – Storrs – & left London Sat. night with Cys. To our despair we reached Flushing at 4 in the morning & had to sit erect in one of those absurd little slices of railway carriage from then till <u>10.15</u> the same night. The filth & heat & jolt were indescribable but we showed great grit.... We slept like logs – & awoke to a cool grey day – with damp pavements – scoured the streets – found neither beads nor ribbons – lunched at the Künstlerhaus – & then dressed for the Opera which we reached with genius in a tram – I can't tell you what a wonderful sensation the Overture gave me – (Meistersinger) partly probably not having heard any music for so long – & partly being with Cys with whom I know every note was telling. Absolute darkness & absolute silence – about two minutes tent expectation – then that wonderful triumphant opening – I had what Cys calls the 'enthroned sense' more than almost ever before.

We met Bernard Shaw in the entr'actes & had some rather amusing talk with him – Caesar & Cleopatra is being acted in Munich & being a great success. I think we must go on Sunday. He was delightfully gentle & natural.

We came on to this place early on Tuesday. It is just as lovely as we had remembered it. A simple little brown inn on the edge of this wonderful <u>black</u> lake....

We have our meals in a long verandah at little tables – surrounded by Tyrolese in delicious clothes – coachmen, country people, lower middle class holiday-making Germans. No English or gentlemen which is nice.

M.B.C. to V.A.   *Thursday 17 August*
                                   10 Downing Street, Whitehall,
                                                       S.W.

Dearest one. The labour troubles here have taken a somewhat serious turn. The difficulty lies not with the dock people, except in Liverpool, but with the Railway Unions, who have decided to call a general strike. Your father intervened today & saw a deputation of the Union leaders at the Board of Trade & gave them the Government terms viz a Royal Commission to investigate the working of the Conciliation Board which would report within a few weeks' time, but if the men struck meanwhile steps would be taken to ensure the working of the railways.

He received them this morning & this afternoon but the Unions have nevertheless decided to adhere to their decision to strike, probably because they feel that the men would not follow them in any other course. Their main grievances seem to be that the companies will not recognise the Trades Unions i.e will not receive the Union officials as representing the men in their employment & that the companies have worked the Conciliation Boards in the letter & not the spirit of the agreement that set them up. The opinion seems to be that the Unions will not be able to get the majority of the men out as their members only number about a quarter of the whole number of railway employees, but the troops are to be ready in case of trouble.

Your father goes to Easton Grey tonight & comes up again tomorrow. I shall not leave London for Munich tomorrow night, as I intended. I do not suppose that my presence here is necessary for the peace of the industrial world, but I think that it would be rather absurd to leave at this moment. Also two Bishops are dead. Will you please write to say how you are & that I am right to stay?

It is time that I heard from you isn't it?

Munich would be nicer now than London & Cyril's company than Leith Ross'.[1]

          Bless & keep you. B.

V.A. to M.B.C.   *Sunday 20 August*
                                   Grand Hotel Leinfelder, Munich

We sent you a telegram yesterday asking you to come out last night or to-

---

[1] Frederick Leith-Ross (1887–1968), private secretary to H. H. Asquith, 1911–13.

day – as I saw by the papers Father was at Easton Grey & I imagine there is not much you can do about the strike.

This morning it looks rather bad by what I can make out from the German papers – & I feel very anxious and worried – I mind it dreadfully for him & if it is going on & getting worse I think I can't stay away. If you think things look bad will you send me a wire to-morrow? & if not will you come out as soon as possible – Cys is very anxious to have a Bock companion.... Yr V. Please don't forget to <u>wire</u> as soon as possible.

M.B.C. to V.A.   *Monday 21 August*
                                              10 Downing Street, Whitehall,
                                                                   S.W.

Very dear one. Your telegram was stupidly never sent on to me from my house so that I only got it at half past one on Saturday night. I had been down here waiting for the finish of the strike negotiations. The settlement has been a triumph for L.G who really ran the whole thing. He induced the managers to meet the men and both sides to accept the Government's proposals. Your father motored up from Easton Grey on Saturday evening. I do not know if you will have read in the papers that his motor knocked over a girl on a bicycle near Newbury....

Here we are feeling how lucky it is that no peers had to be created. We should have had to be doing that business all through the strike, which has temporarily blotted out everything else
        Yr B.

H.H.A. to V.A.   *Thursday 24 August*
                                              10 Downing Street, Whitehall,
                                                                   S.W.

Dearest Violet – best thanks for your two letters. We have been going through a trying time here – what with the Strikes & Morocco & our own trouble over the motor accident.[1]

---

[1] A national seamen's strike in June had been followed in August by strikes involving dockers, London transport workers ('carmen') and railwaymen. The four unions representing

Hayward was driving & was I think quite free from any blame. I was reading inside the car & saw nothing of what happened, but the girl seems to have dashed down a cross road at right angles to the motor & losing her head went bang into it. She was very badly wounded in the face & head & has not yet recovered consciousness, but there is now a faint hope that she may live. I was driving up in response to an urgent message from Winston & Haldane, who were getting rather nervous. The accident kept me an extra 2 hours on the way.

It is difficult to account for the epidemic of unrest which is still not altogether quieted. I suspect the heat had something to do with it. You would see that Ll. George gave Keir Hardie a most tremendous trouncing for his lies[1]....

We go to Archerfield a week this Sat (Sept 2nd). I suppose we shall pick you & C up on the way. My voice is better tho' still a bit husky. Always yr loving Father

Diary – Tuesday 5 September – Archerfield House, Dirleton, East Lothian

Dearest & Best – We reached London very sleepy & hungry early on Friday morning – I with the fateful beginnings of a cold. I slept a little in the morning – bought things hectically all the afternoon – Storrs came to tea to ask for a Bishopric for his father! then rather an amusing dinner Louis Mallet, Reggie, Bencks, Bogey Harris, Bongie, Micky, Cys.[2]

Agadir discussed afterwards by Reggie Louis & Benck – Reggie vehemently maintaining that if we had originally sent a gunboat nominally to 'co-operate' with the Panther this diplomatic situation would

the latter mounted the most serious challenge, and in spite of Asquith's mediation the country experienced, 17–19 August, its first general rail strike. Lloyd George was brought in by Asquith to negotiate, and a settlement was quickly reached. Running parallel to these domestic troubles was the 'Agadir incident': on 1 July the German government informed the foreign office that it had dispatched a gunboat, the *Panther*, to the Moroccan port of Agadir. Ostensibly sent to protect German nationals, the gunboat was used to pressurize the French into accommodating German territorial ambitions in Africa, as a compensation for French gains in Morocco. The crisis was resolved in the Morocco Accord of 11 October, by which France ceded to Germany territory in the French Congo. The affair threatened to bring Germany and Britain to war, and it had important implications for British foreign policy: see below, p. 284.

[1] James Keir Hardie (1856–1915), Labour MP for Merthyr Tydfil, 1900–15.

[2] Sir Louis du Pan Mallet (1864–1936), private secretary to Sir Edward Grey, 1905–7; assistant under-secretary of state for foreign affairs, 1907–13.

never have arisen – as it would have saved Germany the humiliation of withdrawal. I parted with beloved Morrison the next day – it is a dreadful wrench losing her – she has been with me through all my most glorious days – & knew & loved You – Coates her successor (how interested you would have been in her!) is probably a more efficient maid ... Scotch (she comes from Brechin) & a good dressmaker.

Augustine Birrell to V.A.   *Thursday 7 September*
                                       Balmoral Castle, Aberdeenshire

My dear Violet,
    I had already suggested myself to your Father – the 'caged Bird' pants for release. Precisely how I am to negotiate the hour of my release in time to reach you ere the shades of the Sabbath descend I do not yet know but it must be negotiated.
    The Braemar Galkerry (a thing I have for 61 blameless years studiously avoided) is celebrated this afternoon. I fear it will be a 'melancholy spree'.
    It is graceless of me to grumble – for all is kindness. The K. has an excellent library taste. We have had much talk about favourite Authors. He hates R. Kipling – finding him coarse – incongruously he loves Capt Marryat – but for pure library joy give him Harrison Ainsworth. Hall Caine he detests. I am afraid he never really cared for Miss Yonge & even the Queen spoke coldly of the Heir of Redclyffe.[1]
    I will communicate my movements by telegraph
                                        Forever always AB
P.S. I don't think I can reach you until Monday.

V.A. to Venetia Stanley   *Monday 25 September*
                                       Archerfield House, Dirleton,
                                                East Lothian

My Darling – I am miserable about your plight – & feel terribly 'done' by Fate at not having you here. . . .

---

[1] Frederick Marryat (1792–1848), William Harrison Ainsworth (1805–82) and (Thomas Henry) Hall Caine (1853–1931) were popular and prolific nineteenth-century novelists. Much of their writing had an historical or adventure theme. For Violet's appreciation of *The Heir of Redclyffe* see above, p. 50, n. 2.

I wish I could think of any book or possible alleviation to send you. I should be upon you myself like a shot out of a gun (whatever your inclination) if it were not that I am tied here by every limb. I hear Ishbel is at Cromer & shall try to go up to Haddo for a day or two while she is there but I'm afraid it can't be till much later. My Ireland plans are very fluid.

I think I shall probably have to leave the country soon to get out of the clutches of Miss Markham who summons me every day more urgently to take chairs at meetings & serve on sub-committees of the P.S.A. I have got to make two speeches in Fife during October – one on women – can't you give me any suggestions? This is a fleshly letter – darling – forgive it. I will write again. Come soon I need you Yr V.

Churchill at the Admiralty : 'He is determined to make a success of it ...'

In the cabinet reshuffle of 23 October 1911, Winston Churchill and Reginald McKenna changed places, the former becoming first lord of the admiralty, and the latter home secretary. Churchill had been offered his new post by Asquith on 27 September, following a round of golf at Archerfield. McKenna was considered to have outlived his usefulness at the admiralty, and Churchill set about being the new broom, energetically embarking on a programme of fleet reorganization and, in due course, rebuilding. His conversion to the admiralty cause, from his earlier hostility, was undoubtedly influenced by the 'Agadir incident', in July 1911.[1] Germany's apparent determination to settle its grievances with France over Morocco without regard to British interests threatened an outbreak of war between the two countries. A measure of the seriousness of the crisis is the bellicose speech made by Lloyd George at the Mansion House, on 21 July. The chancellor had been a consistent opponent of arms expenditure, and equally an advocate of good relations with Germany, but he there declared, to an audience of City men, that Britain must assert itself in the 'Cabinet of Nations'. Peace at the cost of prestige, he argued, 'would be a humiliation intolerable for a great country like ours to endure'. A month later both he and Churchill were present at a special meeting of the Committee of Imperial Defence, convened to discuss Britain's preparedness for war. From this point onwards Churchill became increasingly

---

[1] For Churchill's opposition to increases in the naval estimates, 1908–9, see above, pp. 168–70.

absorbed in naval matters, and the possibility of conflict with Germany. Three years earlier, in August 1908, he had ridiculed the prospect, declaring that there was nothing to fight over 'but tropical plantations and small coaling places scattered here and there about the world'.[1] It was a remarkable transformation, the explanation for which does not lie solely in the changing picture of foreign affairs. The general elections of 1910 had decimated the Liberal majority of 1906, and the principal casualties were the radical naval 'economists', whose numbers fell from above one hundred to below forty.[2] The power base from which Lloyd George and Churchill had attacked in 1908 and 1909 had disappeared, and both men were pragmatic enough to shift their bearings.

Diary – Sunday 1 October – Archerfield House, Dirleton, East Lothian

I went out for a walk with Winston after tea – & he told me Father had offered him the Admiralty – & to put McKenna at the Home Office. He is over the moon about it (as it has long been his Mecca in the Cabinet) – & tremendously fired by the scope & possibilities of the office. 'Look at the people I've had to deal with so far – Judges & convicts – this is a big thing' etc. etc. He is determined to make a success of it & will put every inch of himself into it. . . .

Diary – Monday 2 October – Archerfield House, Dirleton, East Lothian

Beloved – To-morrow is your birthday – I am so thankful to be spending it with Dudley. I have just written a long letter to Father about the removal of yr. F. & M. from Ireland. How I pray it can be stopped. Anyhow I have stretched every sinew.[3]

[1] See Peter Rowland, *The Last Liberal Governments, 1911–1914*, 106–27; Randolph Churchill, *Winston S. Churchill: Young Statesman, 1901–1914*, 511–14.
[2] Rhodri Williams, *Defending the Empire: The Conservative Party and British Defence Policy 1899–1915*, 176.
[3] Violet's intervention on Lord Aberdeen's behalf may have been effective, as he remained lord-lieutenant until 1915. In the autumn of 1914 Asquith decided finally to replace him, and was in receipt of '7 quarto pages' of pleading from Lord Aberdeen. Asquith wrote to Venetia Stanley: 'Violet also had an even more poignant appeal from Lady A: "how can your Father wreak such havoc upon Archie's parents?" &c (Don't ever say I told you a word of this) . . .' (M. and E. Brock (eds), *H. H. Asquith: Letters to Venetia Stanley*, 271).

R. Farrer came this evening – & R & K – Father went to Balmoral. I played a round with Winston & had wonderful talks about the re-shuffle in the Cabinet & Tripoli – I feel very strongly we should take the Turks' side. The Italians' action seems to me a sheer act of brigandage[1] – Goodnight bless you – Yr own

Reginald gave me the flash of the Kingfisher in epigrams[2]

Diary – Wednesday 18 October – Archerfield House, Dirleton, East Lothian

Dearest – Just back from a meeting at the Synod Hall. Sympne spoke very logically & well – but of course he is like an asbestos fire – little blue & green flame playing that never <u>warms</u> one. It was a chillyish meeting as always in Edinburgh. We motored back Eliza & I & Bongie. The leaves are changing <u>most</u> wonderfully in the woods. I took Willie to the Point this morning & Simon this afternoon – & we came back through a blaze of different <u>marvellous</u> colours – orange – & red & yellow. I made Simon roll in the leaves. Love to you my Beloved – Your own.

Barnie has just left me after a wonderful talk. She says I am too clever to ever be happy – I am not too clever – but I rather agree with her that I probably shan't ever be – A letter from Cys.

V.A. to Venetia Stanley   *Friday 20 October*
Archerfield House, Dirleton,
East Lothian

Oct. 20th 1911   <u>Write</u>
My Darling – I'm afraid Bongie must have caused you some inconvenience this week but I can testify to it that it really hasn't been his fault this time. Complications have been in process which seemed likely to end every day – but which have dawdled on till now – & are not yet over. Long

---

[1] 'Tripoli' refers both to the town and also to the extensive territory to the south, known as Tripolitania, all of which was then Ottoman territory. Italy invaded on 5 October 1911, at a time when the other European powers were still absorbed with the Franco-German confrontation at Agadir.

[2] Violet later recalled: 'Margot thought it was her & that the Golden Snipe was me. She cried indignantly "I won't have the beastly snipe"'; for epigrams, a word-game, see the glossary.

cypher telegrams pour in & without Bongie to translate them O.S would be boiled.

As you may gather a reshuffle is impending but for <u>God's sake</u> keep a <u>morbid</u> padlock about this till everything is out – as the way is by no means clear or smooth yet. I will tell you all about it afterwards. . . .

Beautiful Cyril has gone back to Oxford which is a sorrow – I went to Fife last Sat. to inaugurate a Women's Liberal Association – & spoke for nearly <u>25</u> minutes – of which I am very proud. Several people cried – I notice that is the effect my speaking has! of reducing people to a state of abject maudlin <u>Dickens</u> emotion. . . .

Father goes South Monday I think I shall wait & go Monday week – unless poor little Barker who is rather bad gets worse – I'm afraid he is fatally ill (heart). <u>Love</u> V.

Arthur Asquith to V.A.   *Sunday 22 October*
                                         Buenos Aires

My dear Violet, I have not heard from you yet; – in fact I have only had one letter – Margot's – from my family since I have been here. I am not sure whether I have written to anyone since my trip to the Andes. I was the guest of the local Manager of the Buenos Aires and Pacific (Lord St. David's) Railway: so I travelled 'en prince' in a special train with a party of about twenty – Sir Reginald Tower, (the British Minister) and railway managers and their wives.[1] The railway climbs more than ten thousand feet to a tunnel, lately made, which leads to Chile. It was snowing and we turned back, about a mile short of the tunnel: and spent a night at a little hotel 10,000 ft. up. Here my sponge froze in my bedroom; and my nose bled; and the next morning, which was divinely clean and sunny, I bathed in the hot springs. These are full of minerals and bubbles. It is like bathing in hot champagne; one's body is covered with small tickling bubbles.

The Andes are very stark and grand: and as innocent of any sort of vegetation as are the Argentines of culture or of 'souls'. Much of the rock is red, pink and violet; and I can well believe that Andine sunsets are a marvel. The rock, above snow-level, is too sheer for there to be much snow. Below snow-level, the bases of the mountains are like rubbish heaps of sand and boulders.

From the Andes we came down to Mendoza, the capital of a S. American Lombardy: a flat smiling country of vines, and orchards with weeping

---

[1] Sir Reginald Tower (1860–1939), envoy extraordinary and minister plenipotentiary in Mexico, 1906–10, and in the Argentine Republic, 1910–19.

willows and files of poplars growing along the borders of the irrigation channels. The houses of the country districts are very like the house you lived in at Omdurman, flat, one-storied and built of mud brick – with verandahs. In Mendoza the houses are more luxuriously built: but they are all of one storey for fear of earthquakes. These are of very frequent occurrence: there was a slight one two days before we got there. I left the train at Mendoza, and joined a pleasant old Norwegian, called Don Pedro Christophersen. He took me with him to see an estate, of about 120,000 acres, which a Company he formed with my people Franklin & Herrera, have exploited by making great irrigation works.

Don Pedro Ch. was in a shipping firm, won a lottery worth one million dollars, married one of the richest women in this country, and now owns with his wife 800,000 acres of land in this country and 35 leagues of forest in Paraguay. He was a very good companion....

Ten years ago Don Pedro bought this estate for less than 1s 6d an acre: no-one will sell it now for less than £15 an acre: and I fully believe it will be worth £35 an acre within five years. And these values are based solely on the amount of grapes, fruit etc. that it actually produces year by year: with nothing to fear from droughts. The increased value has been brought about by the railways going there, and about 15s per acre having been spent on irrigation. Investments in agricultural land here seem to me to be perfectly sound and incredibly lucrative. I only wish I had capital to invest in it....

Everything is very big and new and up-to-date and efficient. I go to Rosario, a big port, tomorrow: and to Concepcion, in Uruguay, at the end of the week, to see a 'saladero' or establishment for 'jerking' beef which my people, F.H.Ltd., think of turning into a Company.

I watched an international football match Uruguay v. Argentina today. A crowd of 20,000 people, tremendous enthusiasm and very good football. Love to all. Yours Oc.

Diary – Thursday 2 November – 10 Downing Street, Whitehall, S.W.

Beloved – Just back rather tired after an L.S.C party at Wembley with Haddo & Ly H. I spoke a little – about 500 people – deliciously responsive & keen – back here in Montagu's Rolls Royce (which was invaluable as there's a taxi strike to-day!) & 'approached' Burge in a letter beginning Dear Bishop to speak at the P.S. Annual Meeting.[1] I went to the Committee this

[1] Hubert Murray Burge (1862–1925), the headmaster of Winchester College, 1901–11, had been appointed bishop of Southwark the previous May; he held this post until 1919.

morning. . . . I have so much to tell thee of the last week – but it must wait. Goodnight my <u>Darling</u> Yr own.

'That damned split vote': electoral rivalry between Liberal and Labour, 1911–1914

In the years 1911–14 the Liberal party lost a total of fifteen by-elections to the Unionist party, and in half a dozen cases the defeat could be attributed to the influence of the new force in British politics, the Labour party.[1] The constituencies in question had returned Liberals at every election since 1906, and in four of them there had never been a Labour candidate. Labour's intervention gave voters an anti-Unionist alternative. Paradoxically, it also made a Unionist victory more likely, by splitting the 'progressive' vote. At Oldham on 13 November 1911, the Hon. Arthur Stanley, Venetia's brother, polled 10,623 votes, and W. C. Robinson, Labour, 7,448. Their combined total was far in excess of the 12,225 needed by the Unionist, E. R. Denniss, to win the seat. At Oldham there were strong arguments for Labour being given a clear run against the Unionists. The same could not be said of the South Lanark by-election, on 12 December 1913, where the Labour total was less than half the Liberal, and the seat was won by the Unionists with a narrow majority of 251. It was a graphic illustration of the effect of what Violet called 'that damned split vote'. By June 1914 Lloyd George was publicly talking of the need for an electoral accommodation with Labour.[2]

M.B.C. to V.A.   *Tuesday 14 November*
                                      5 Hyde Park Square, W.

Very dear one. I started writing you a letter last night after coming home from the Opera, but it was not up to the mark & was incinerated.

. . . When I went to Alderley I found Venetia pretty depressed, due I found to the fact that this was the time that her brother died. . . . I saw her tonight after dinner and she was in good spirits though she minded very

[1] They were at: Oldham (November 1911); Crewe (July 1912); Midlothian (September 1912); South Lanarkshire (December 1913); South West Bethnal Green, Leith (February 1914). For C. F. G. Masterman's defeat at Bethnal Green, see below, p. 413 and n. 1.
[2] At South Lanark the result was: William Watson (U) 4,257; G. Morton (L) 4,006; G. Gibb (Lab) 1,674. See: Chris Cook, *A Short History of the Liberal Party*, 58; P. F. Clarke, *Lancashire and the New Liberalism*, 316–17; Peter Rowland, *The Last Liberal Governments, 1911–1914*, 341.

much about Arthur's defeat at Oldham. It is a very amazing thing in this case, because as far as one could judge there was little enough reason for them to vote for the Labour man. His programme was almost identical with Arthur's....

... Don't weave too much pile on the web of Forbes' life but think of the huckaback of mine at D St now & then

Bless you B.

V.A. to Venetia Stanley   *Sunday 19 November*
                                                   Vice Regal Lodge, Dublin

My Darling – I am so <u>miserable</u> over your election. I fear it will be a great blow to you – & it was cruel luck the Labour man splitting the majority like that. What birdlime had he in his programme to get so many people to vote for him?

Did you expect to get in at the last? or were there any rumours? I <u>am</u> sad for your brother – he has worked so hard – it is discouraging. It will be the last straw if Aubrey gets in![1] ...

I lunched with Lady Lyttelton to-day – she was full of good talk & divine discontent. Shall I find you in London when I get back on Wednesday? ... Love Yr V

Venetia Stanley to V.A.   *Tuesday 21 November*
                                                   Alderley Park, Chelford, Cheshire

My darling thank you so much for your letter. We were all quite miserable; as you know at the beginning they all felt rather nervous as to the result, but as the week went on we seemed to be gaining more and more ground and when they got in their canvass, which as a rule is implicitly to be trusted it showed a clear 1000 majority. So on Monday we went off to hear the result in raging spirits, only to see a foul Jew returned with 12,000 votes, when there were 18,000 Liberal votes all wasted.

Arthur and the Labour man had practically the same programme, till the last few days when the Labour candidate became far more socialistic. They count that the Liberals lost 6 votes to the Tory one instead of 5 to 2 as was estimated. I must say it must be rather fun for a candidate to have

---

[1] Aubrey Herbert was successful, by a narrow margin of 148 votes, at the South Somerset by-election the following Tuesday, 21 November, having failed in his attempts to win the seat at the two general elections of 1910.

electors like Conservatives who seem to stick to their official candidate whatever his views and whatever other attractions are dangled in front of their eyes. As you say if Aubrey gets in it will be the limit, but I gather they are anxious. I had all last week in London, Club one night with the introduction of Chess, very bewildering for them at first, it is a difficult game to explain, their faces were a pathetic sight as one intricacy after another was unfolded. I played one real game with Alec and was nearly beaten, 2 chapters of Treasure Island were read. By the way I felt a little anxious about Alec as he was so very husky and hoarse, has he seen the doctor yet? I daresay I am only like Margot tho' with her 'Doomed, doomed'. . . .

Ireland sounds fun I wish I had been there with you, we must have one together some time.

Love V̲

Diary – Saturday 2 December – 10 Downing Street, Whitehall, S.W.

Beloved – I had a meeting at Hammersmith yesterday – & spoke really rather well! & with more ease than ever before on the Insurance Bill. A woman called Miss Garland made a strong Woman Suffrage speech – which I was angry with – it is very wrong & confusing for people to press home a freelance propaganda like that on an official platform.

Just back from dining with R. & K. Conrad was there – I went to see John Glover at the Highgate Infirmary this afternoon [and] spoke to him of you.[1] Rode with Clemmie in the Wellington Barracks riding school this morning. Blessed one goodnight – Yr own

V.A. to Venetia Stanley   *Thursday 7 December*
10 Downing Street, Whitehall,
S.W.

Darling – I think Friday would be the best day for hunting especially as the meet's near. I am so thrilled by the thought.

Do get me a reliable horse with a soft & responsive mouth – malleable & elastic if possible – as it is my maiden-hunt – & I do not wish it to be my swan – or even my ewe one. An apparent lotus-eater – with some biffo in the bush would be the ideal thing. No doubt if you forward this letter to Tinsely he will produce the very article.

---

[1] John Glover was one of the original members of the Archie Gordon Club.

One other practical suggestion – will they hire me a comfy saddle or shall I try & borrow or hire & bring one with me? as I imagine your ones might be a little big for me. Wesley House went off very well – but is cruelly reported – the whole point & sting carefully drawn from every remark. <u>Pamela</u> <u>came</u> – wasn't it odious of her – but she has written me a delightful letter since. Lady Robson, Ly Lawson-Walton, Mrs George Lewis, Mrs. Carr Gomm & Mrs. Crawshay Williams were also there a terrible phalanx of 'known women' – I'm thinking of going to Winchester over Sunday.

Goodbye my Darling bless you – Yr V

<u>Hunting</u>! the thought thrills me to the marrow – Can I rely on you for my stock – & its adjustment?

Diary – Thursday 21 December – Kilmaron, East Fife

Beloved – I am here – just back from a meeting at Newburgh. Every spare minute of the last days has been spent on my speech. It went off quite well – though I think the audience would have preferred less argument & more vague generalizations – Sir James Low – Sir James Scott & Bailly Lamont 'supported me'.[1]

I feel very tired now – & glad it is all over. I will write properly in the train to-morrow. My goodnight love – most deeply loved – Your own

Diary – Saturday 6 January 1912 – Mürren, Switzerland

Darling – I had a hectic day in London – no one in the house but Leith Ross & Miss Way – the two least desirable of our staff – dust sheets in every room – few & chilly cutlets on a tiny table in the very middle of the vast dining room.[2] I rested in the morning – in the afternoon had a tooth quite spontaneously stopped by Dawes – which he told me would have given me <u>anguish</u> in Palermo – a few more shoppings – Club cards etc – & then

---

[1] Sir James Scott (1838–1925), 1st Bt, 1911; engineer, and twice provost of Tayport in Fife. Newburgh is around fifteen miles due west of St Andrews.

[2] Miss Way was H. H. Asquith's personal secretary.

dinner with Olive, WW & Micky & a longish play called Bella Donna in which Mrs Pat. acted.[1]

Cys & I started the next morning – he very white & hollow-eyed after a night journey – roughish crossing – & then safe installation in the train where we remained in a coma with the lights out till after Paris – I felt too tired to read Queed.[2] We got to Interlaken next morning – which we found terribly damp & 'mild' – the grass sticking up blackly through the snow like an unshaved cheek. Snow dripping slowly off the train-roof.

Lunn's face was the first thing which greeted us at Lauterbrunnen – outlined against a thawing bank.[3] Hugh was there too – tall & gaunt in a little khaki mantle. We spent 1½ hours floater in the funicular – as it turned out the Grand Hotel H. had got us rooms at was not Lunn's. Hard lubricant & emollient work done by me. Mürren is perched on the edge of a rock like an eyrie – I don't see how one is to move without going over – but I daresay we shall find vistas of possibilities behind. We spent the afternoon looking for ski boots etc. & I skated round the rink once or twice feeling very wobbly with windmill arms....

Diary – Monday 15 January – Rome

Beloved – I left Mürren yesterday morning – feeling rather weak & wobbly – with a thick yellow mist & the remains of tonsillitis hanging about me. Divine Cyril put me & Coates & innumerable Handgepäck into the funicular & we crept down into the valley – making very slow & jerky cogwheel progress. At Lauterbrunnen a change – into the Interlaken train – snail-slow & exuding hot-air at every pore – in spite of all my privy tampering with the levers – then out again into a slimy platform – I was at Interlaken – no snow – no hills – only mists & mud....

... The railway over the Brünig pass would really have been lovely I

---

[1] Mrs Patrick Campbell, *née* Beatrice Stella Tanner (1865–1940), legendary figure of the English stage, for whom Shaw wrote the part of Eliza Doolittle in *Pygmalion* (1914). Violet remembered meeting her in Dresden in 1903, where her daughter, Stella Patrick, also an actress, was at boarding-school: 'I shall never forget her entry, swathed in furs – scarves – stoles – furbelows – with an odious monkey-griffon called Pinky Panky Pooh on her arm. I was swept off my feet by her fascination, her vitality, her impulsive spontaneity and unexpectedness, her inspired "amusing-ness". Looking back, I suppose that she was then old, but to me she still seemed beautiful and irresistible.'

[2] Henry Sydnor Harrison, *Queed* (1911).

[3] Henry Simpson Lunn (1859–1939), founder of the Lunn travel agency (1909) and a pioneer in developing Alpine sports holidays. He did much to popularize the resort of Mürren. Lunn was a supporter of Asquith, and contested Boston as a Liberal in January 1910. His son, Henry, a year younger than Violet, was a ski pioneer in his own right.

think on a clear day – the height scaled seemed terrific from what one could guess of it & at one moment the clouds did melt a little & one saw the table flat valleys deep down – miles below one & the summits of mountains up above – almost in the sky.... I felt very tired after my two days in bed & didn't read – just dozed & gazed & longed to arrive. At Lucerne I found Venetia who poor darling had been there 24 hours – & was almost dead with boredom. We dined together – rested – reléved – & started by the 11.52 night train to Milan....

Coates – poor dear – was jammed like a fig between five or six swarthy skinned & villainous looking fumatori two doors off. At 11.30 Venetia & I had lunch & saw the whole of the neighbouring table-occupants pouring cascades of spaghetti of all lengths – soaked in tomato sauce down their throats. No hectic tucking in – just slow measured suction – till each most lingering end had been imbibed. It was a horrible sight but held a strange fascination.

I couldn't beat myself into a state of sufficiently hallowed anticipation of Rome – & yet I was disappointed when we drew into a station just like any other – a station which might have been Munich – or Brussels – or Berlin – Arc Lights & porters – & guichets – & hurry & crowd. The only unique feature of the arrival was that just as we got outside the station we were greeted by a loud chorus from a large crowd of porters – each one braying the name of his own particular hotel. We drove off to the one Edwin had selected for us – the Grand – a very luxurious Ritz – & after divine baths & dinner – I am now in bed & very sleepy.

Blessings to you my beloved – I can't remember where you stayed here Yr V.

Diary – Tuesday 16 January – Train to Naples; Sicily

Dearest – I woke about 9 – & went to my window – a large clump of ilexes was growing outside en plein street – & on a shelving roofledge pots of flowers & cactuses stood in a little green procession. A fountain played below in a courtyard – & I thought of Brescia – Venetia & I bathed & dressed – I wondering vaguely which of the 7 collines de Rome we were at present upon? & hoping somehow it was the Quirinal. We took a taxi in front of the hôtel which opened on a large bogus-Parisian square of vast white modern buildings, then drove through a strange medley of old & new to her uncle Monsignor Stanley's flat overlooking the Tiber – which is just as I'd imagined it – yellow & rather sluggish. He was an odd old boy with a large pontifical ring & a red skull-cap – conveying no more idea of sanctity or faith to one than any other Stanley.[1] He had lived in these same rooms for 40 years with a white cockatoo & a man & his wife called Victorina. The wife was just dead.

He took us to St. Peter's – I admired the colonnade & the fountains which lead up to it but not its façade or dome.... I admire St. Paul's infinitely more. St Peter's has no dimness – no drowning vastness or uplift – or mystery. One most beautiful & touching thing we saw – the Pieta of Michael Angelo – I felt tears in my heart as I looked at her – holding his beloved – beautiful broken body – the thing she loved most – the despair & the control of that gesture with her open hand. We saw people kissing St. Peter's toe – poor people touchingly as savages to a dreaded idol – but when the highly cultivated & sceptical old Monsignor went & did so – noisily & effusively & over & over again I was almost ill.

The Forum is pure ruins – overgrown with lovely grasses – & with two fine Arches one at either end – & the Colosseum looks just exactly like itself – it couldn't be anything else. We drove hastily back – wolfed lunch – haggled over tips & bills & embarked in the Naples train where I struggled through terrible joltings & distractions to send out postcards to the Club. The Campagna was wonderful – wild brown country where blue mists floated – then it got greener & hillier – towns on every summit like little citadels – goats cropping by the railway – olives – orange trees.

We passed Capua in the dark alas! – & thirsting terribly by a strange irony – & arrived at Naples in pitch-blackness. Crowds of porters of all sizes & ages erupted into the carriage – but were summarily ejected by the Cook's men – who then led us on board a biggish boat. Another larger one was sailing for Tripoli that night – & little groups of very operatic looking soldiers talked & drank in knots on the quay. I felt a slight theatrical serrement de coeur as I looked at them & wondered which were doomed. After the strangest table d'hôte opposite a row of prize fishfaces – we sat about for $\frac{1}{2}$ hour & went to bed – & this morning when I went out on deck we were nearing a golden shore bathed in sunlight – where lemons & oranges grew in glittering groves – with beyond a magically beautiful range of hills. We glided into a noisy amusing crowded port – brownskinned men jostling each other on the jetty – & amongst them brown too, but differently brown, Montagu stood – a little pinched & drawn after an early rise – with beside him Danostrio (whom I call & who is in fact La Nôtre) our courier – who has supplanted Bongie, Nash, Micky, Leith Ross ... & the Master of Elibank in Father's confidence & affections. We drove through Palermo a funny crowded, coloured town of complex smells to our hôtel the Villa Igiea which is right outside & on the sea –

---

[1] Algernon Charles Stanley (1843–1928), fourth son of the 2nd Baron Stanley. A bishop in the Roman Catholic church, he was consecrated in Rome in 1903.

which laps up quite audibly & visibly day & night a few yards off a marble
terrace broad & cool onto which our 4 bedrooms open in this order:
Father – sittingroom – Montagu – Violet – Venetia. Below is the garden –
full of lemon trees & purple bougainvillaea & rare-brilliant heavy – tropical
Sir Giles flowers. Sunshine pours out of the sky all day like honey – – –
I found Father looking very well & bird-happy. He is a born sight seer –
thinks every 'sight' the best of its kind in existence ('You won't see a better'
is never off his lips) & thirstily laps up the most arid information Baedeker
has to offer. I am galvanized into stamina by his keenness – from being as
you know Darling one of the limpest tourists on record. . . .

Diary – Sunday 21 January – Girgente, Sicily

Dearest – We left divine Palermo this morning – our blue bay – & Monte
Pellegrino – & the Conca d'Oro – & our marble balcony covered with
purple bougainvillaea. We had an early start – the sky was just like mother
of pearl with a golden rift at the horizon – which streaked the sea with
sudden brightness.

We all rumbled off to the station in a regular hôtel bus with vibrating
panes – rather like the one you nearly broke at Alderley (out of jealousy
for Bluey!). Montagu's is *such* a funny face to travel with. The Consul &
the Prefet were at the station to see us off – & 3 Sicilian detectives – looking
like Government cutthroats – accompanied us on our way – besides
George, Coates & La Nôtre – who make an amusing group. George absolutely phlegmatic & unchanged – behaving the whole time as if he were
in the basement at D. St.[1] Coates with her usual genteel & exquisitely
foolish simper – La Nôtre harrying & hustling them both like a gadfly.
There was no incident in the journey – except the combustion of a Noeara
[?] bottle which deluged the carriage. I read the Devil & the Deep Sea by
Rhoda Broughton – not very good (Le Visage Émerveillé I finished last
night in bed).[2] At 12.30 we began lunch – slabs of meat wrapped up in
tissue paper – at 1.30 we arrived – & were packed into a most rickety –
disintegrating landau – drawn by two skeletons in ill-fitting mangy skins
'the finest equipage in Girgente' – as La Nôtre with fine satire proclaimed
from the box. . . .

I wish I cld. give you a little idea of the beauty of this place. The
luminous brown-gold of the ruins – & the flowers – wild-garlic & ground

---

[1] George Wicks (1886–1977), Asquith's valet; at the outbreak of war in 1914 Wicks volunteered for the army, and Asquith arranged his commission, which was signed by Kitchener.

[2] Rhoda Broughton, *The Devil and the Deep Sea* (1910); Anna Noailles, *Le Visage Émerveillé*
(1904).

ivy & marigolds – honied candytuft growing up amongst them. We saw such a wonderful little Greek garden too – with pillars standing in a fairy ring amongst the orange trees & lavender. There is <u>tremendous</u> atmosphere about the place – I felt it peopled with happenings. Right above one sees the town like a large oyster-shell – & the yellow quarries in the side of the hill where the stone for the temples came from. We played hiding in the garden & jumping out after dark. Montagu is the best person in the world to play it with. He is <u>so</u> frightened – & <u>so</u> frightening –

M.B.C. to V.A.   *Monday 22 January*
10 Downing Street, Whitehall,
S.W.

My dearest one, I sent you a very scrappy letter on Friday, as I arranged with Hugh to go down to Sandwich for Sat & Sunday & I was in a hurry to get away....

... Little paragraphs are now appearing in the papers of your movements. I daresay soon I shall hear from you to tell me how successful Sicily is proving. Your Father thought of getting back on the 1ˢᵗ but I daresay that he will stay on a few days later. I suppose he does not worry about the Suffrage question. It is being fought up & down in all the Liberal papers, the Westminster [Gazette] & Daily Chronicle both push a referendum & the Tory Press all look forward to [a] real Cabinet split over it. There is an article by Massingham in the Nation [on] E.G. which you will like to see so I shall send it by the next messenger[1] .... Goodnight my most blessed. B.

Diary – Tuesday 23 January – Syracuse, Sicily

My Beloved – We arrived yesterday evening at this most wonderful & unique place....

To-day we had a strenuous but remunerative bout of sightseeing. You would laugh if you saw us rumbling off in our grotesque landau – Father – Venice – Montagu & I every tooth in our heads rattling – over the most mountainous & flinty roads – the old D. St fur rug spread over our 4 knees – 3 Baedekers in our hands – La Nôtre on the box occasionally

---

[1] Henry William Massingham (1860–1924), journalist; under Massingham's editorship, 1907–23, the *Nation* became an influential weekly journal, the voice of independent Liberalism.

calling our attention to some simple wayside object – 'Mr Asquith – excuse if I bring to your notice the prickly pear' – etc. A church is reached – built on the foundations of an old temple – I struggle up the stylobate in a hobble skirt – the Kodak is produced & found to be leaking & letting in light – all the photographs we have taken so far are no good – Disappointment – Hopes pinned on a chemist in Taormina – La Nôtre proceeds – We go down to the Crypt – then on through some catacombs – Montagu pales at the skulls – shivers at the cold – Venetia & I rally him – we re-emerge covered with cobwebs & drippings into the warm sunlight of the friars garden – full of the smell of Cherry Pie – the friar gives me a little bunch. We re-embark & drive on. We saw an Altar of Dionysus also an amphitheatre – & a Greek theatre where La Nôtre gave us a long dissertation on the Greek drama.

Then the marvellous Latomia del Paradiso – a vast gouffre with caves hewn in the cliff one in the shape of an ear – called the Ear of Dionysus – with an uncanny echo. We also saw which <u>haunted</u> me – a tiny boy of 9 turning a wheel for 12 hours a day at 50 centimes. It made me feel very unhappy & helpless & as if I ought to have taken him back to the Club. All little boys seem to belong to me somehow – through it – & you. . . .

M.B.C. to V.A.   *Wednesday 24 January*
                                              10 Downing Street, Whitehall,
                                                                    S.W.

My very dear one. It was a wonderful thing to get a gloriously fat letter from you last night. Being here without you & hearing nothing was becoming wearisome & to get news of your contentment with Sicily was a great alleviation. I wish now that you were to stay longer, you are the only people in Europe who seem to be in the sun, whether they be in England Switzerland or the Riviera. . . .

There is a good deal of fuss going on about Winston's meeting in Belfast, and questionings as to whether it should be held or not. The Master typically had a conference today consisting of Devlin & 3 Ulstermen & told me that he thinks he has a way out.[1]

[1] Churchill had been invited by the Ulster Liberal Association to deliver a speech in the Ulster Hall, Belfast, on 8 February. The plan met with fierce opposition there, and a riot was threatened. The choice of venue was considered to be particularly provocative, since it was there that Churchill's father, Lord Randolph Churchill, had in February 1886 uttered the words that became a Unionist battle cry, 'Ulster will fight; Ulster will be right.' The meeting was eventually transferred to a large marquee at the Celtic Road football ground, in the Catholic Falls area of the city. Churchill, accompanied by his wife Clementine, still had to

If it could be held without trouble in another hall that would be best otherwise I should abandon the meeting. A real riot would bring us nothing but harm & I do not think that any criticism could be made against Winston if he abandoned the meeting. I sent you the Nation by the messenger yesterday. You will be interested in Massingham's article on E.G. which I have not yet read. I am going through your letters, which at present are few & dull. I have refused for you an invitation to open a Baptist Bazaar in some suburb in March. . . .

Remember that I am hungry for news & do not write to a lot of unnecessary other people so as to knock out my letters. Bless you. B.

Diary – Wednesday 24 January – Syracuse, Sicily

Darling – Such an absurd expedition – in a small painted boat down the Anapo river – followed by a cargo of detectives in another boat – the river about a foot broad – thick walls of papyrus shutting out all other sights – not a fish or a bird or a flower or a breath of air.

After about an hour's hard rowing we reached the Azure springs – a deep clear blue pool where tadpoles darted – disembarked & picnicked in a ploughed field – presenting a view which wld. have done East Lothian credit. Then back. It was a unique expedition of its kind – Father looked very odd in the bows – gliding down a sluggish canal between hedges of papyrus for several hours! We went on to the town where the Consul & the local Salinas took us over the Museum – a dismal collection of urns & coins – with one rather nice torso of a Venus. At one moment Father became subconscious & to our despair began going all over one floor again – till I saved him & us.

Venetia & I & Montagu rambled about the town a little – it is very odd & attractive full of narrow little alleys with the sea at the end of them – & exciting wickedish looking people. The sea redeems what would otherwise be pretty bad filth & squalor. Home – tea – wrote to Hugh – dinner bridge & now bed. Goodnight my sweet Darling – my Share of the World – Your own.

run the gauntlet of Unionists lining the route from the Grand Central Hotel. Joseph Devlin (1872–1934), a leading constitutionalist Irish nationalist; Irish Parliamentary Party MP for Kilkenny North, 1902–6, and for West Belfast, 1906–18.

V.A. to M.B.C.   *Friday 26 January*
                                         Hôtel San Domenico, Taormina,
                                                              Sicily

We came on here from Syracuse on Thursday – it is as beautiful as a dream – perched on high cliffs above a sea like chrysoprase – with Etna in the distance sloping down to the shore in a gentle violet curve. . . .

Your wires have just come about the Belfast meeting. I am boiling with indignation at Londonderry's condescending permit – & very sorry Winston has moved an inch.[1] If we are to have a row I should have thought we cldn't have had one which would have put us more in the right & them more in the wrong. How characteristic E. Grey's speech is – I haven't yet read the Nation article – but am glad to have it & will do so. I shall come straight home with Father I think as the Tennants won't be there in time to go to them. I don't believe I could bear Montagu as a companion for very long in spite of his good points – tremendous efforts to make everything easy for one – cleverness, keenness etc. His physique – & physical habits get so terribly on my nerves – I hate to be reminded of the body – his & one's own – so much. But he has been very nice – really wonderfully good & painstaking. I have read a certain amount [of] a rather clever novel by Miss Sedgwick called Tante – also some Theocritus translations Hugh has sent me.[2] I am suffering terribly from mosquito bites – be prepared to see me covered with spots – Love & much daily & hourly missing from yr V.

Diary – Monday 29 January – Taormina, Sicily

Dearest – We are just back from a really wonderful day out. We left about 10 – got into the train at Giardini & arrived about lunchtime at Catania. The Marchese Capizzi – (San Giuliano's son[3]) a plump little shiny yellow Italian – very voluble & unhealthy looking with a moustache like eye-lashes – met us at the station & motored us up through a biggish squalidish

---

[1] Charles Stewart Vane-Tempest-Stewart (1852–1915), 6th Marquess of Londonderry. A die-hard Unionist peer and, through his presidency of the Ulster Unionist Council, a leading figure in the resistance to Home Rule. Londonderry's 'condescending permit' was conveyed in a letter to Churchill, 26 January, which appeared in *The Times* next day: 'In the interests of peace and order of the city of Belfast I note with satisfaction that you have abandoned the idea of holding the meeting in the Ulster Hall in that city . . . So far as the [Ulster Unionist] Council is concerned, its main objection in the interests of law and order is removed if you determine to hold your meeting outside the districts which passionately resent your action.'

[2] Anne Douglas Sedgwick, *Tante* (1911).

[3] The Marquis di San Giuliano, Italian foreign minister from 1911.

town to his house – a little coloured villa standing on a height – among eucalyptus trees with a marvellous view over the sea. The house was quite hideous inside – (entirely paved with very ugly bathroom tiles) – & contained his wife – who looked like a wan little Spanish maid – very small & pianissimo with 3 little black eyed children called Enrichetta – Nini & Agatina – an English governess who seemed rather at the helm of things – & who made great headway with Father – & a Professor who understood not one word of any language & nearly screamed when I tried him in three running at lunch – the longest & most wonderful meal I think I have ever had – served by a butler of 80. One rich & strange dish after another defiled before us – spaghetti – crayfish – turkey – asparagus pouding de l'Etna – & finally an ambrosial food – made of sheep's milk & eaten with Hyblaean honey extracted solely from orange blossoms – called Ricotto – which seemed to me to hold the essence of Theocritus.[1]

It was far the most poetical food I have ever eaten – & most lovely to look at. We started off after lunch in Capizzi's motor & went for a very extraordinary drive round the base of Etna.

I have never seen anything so strange & wild & desolate as the country – black tracts of land, the earth heaving like an unquiet sea in great bubbles of lava, nothing growing but moss – & tufts which looked like broom – & little brown blasted oak-trees. The desolation was indescribable. Higher up we came to a place where the lava was still smoking – though it had been there two years. It had rolled down to within a yard of a cottage (engulfing thousands) which we saw standing there secure & intact – Capizzi said it rolled very slowly – a yard every 5 minutes & looked just as it did now – in the daytime – but at night it was luminous – & glowed & burned.

We went down the mountain again getting glorious views of the sea at every turn. I was faintly reminded by the look down to the flat bays of Syracuse – but there the thing which strikes one first is the whiteness of the country – the gleaming stone of the walls & houses – here everything was black – burnt & charred looking. . . .

I am amused that the axe has at last fallen on Pentland – Father has offered him Madras – I'm afraid Marjorie will be very unhappy – & that the whole thing will have been a complete surprise & shock. And Madras won't be very nice for the children – New Zealand wld. have suited them better. I am anxious about how much your M. will mind. These things make me very uncomfortable & unhappy.[2] Bless you darlingest & best – Make me like you – strong & pure in heart Yr own

---

[1] The town of Hybla in Sicily was renowned for its honey, produced on neighbouring hills.

[2] John Sinclair (1860–1925), 1st Baron Pentland, 1909; secretary of state for Scotland, 1905–12, and governor of Madras, 1912–19. He married, in 1904, Lady Marjorie Gordon, only daughter of Lord and Lady Aberdeen.

Diary – Tuesday 30 January – Messina, Sicily

On the vibrating upper shelf of a train bed Dearest – & hardly able to write.

It was difficult to leave Taormina on this radiant day of sunshine.

I do think it is the <u>bluest</u> place I have ever been to – such wonderful expanses of sky & sea – & the sea seems to have an <u>intrinsic</u> dye of its own which is not a mere reflection like at home. One feels it wld. keep its brilliancy under the most leaden sky.

We walked up to the Teatro Greco in the morning & lay about there on warm grass in the sun.... We had rather a lovely journey in the steelblue evening along the edge of the bay – & got to Messina by the light of a rather wan moon. Then followed the most extraordinary & moving experience. We drove – in two flies – Father & V – Montagu & I through the ruins of the town houses lying in heaps – inchoate masses of stone – brick earth & mortar – with here & there some touching little patch of wall-paper – or a staircase to show that man once lived there.[1] The pavement heaving in great waves – destruction & desolation on an unimaginable scale – it is not to be described even to you.

The man on our box – who had a strange wild hectic look & talked feverishly in almost incomprehensible American told us that he had lost his <u>whole</u> family – Father Mother wife sisters & children – in it – He himself had been dug out by Russians; he said pathetically 'I had to pay 600 francs to a lawyer – & he give me an order for 200 francs to get out my family. Then I go with the order & get them out – after 24 days. First I find my baby – then my Mother then my wife'.

The <u>horror</u> that comes over me when I think of yr. accident gripped me again then – as I looked round & saw where <u>80 000</u> had been killed. Those who were not crushed to death were burnt – or drowned by the sea which rose & overflowed its bounds.

And the thing which struck me was that the existence of an <u>agency</u> which makes such <u>horror</u> possible should not blight our whole lives – from the root.

Where such an element exists what chance have we – how can such horror be merely incidental. What was all this but your accident – in collective form? Darling this is all so badly put but you understand.

It seems to me that we are all in the midst of a battle really – but most people think it is a cotillion & those who know it isn't pretend it is....

---

[1] Messina and nearby Reggio were destroyed by an earthquake on 28 December 1908. The official estimate of loss of life was 77,283. Russian, American, French and British seamen gave assistance to the survivors.

Diary – Wednesday 31 January – Train to Pisa

Train – My Darling – I woke up at Naples this morning – but only obtained a very blurred topsy turvy impression of Vesuvius by hanging my head upside down out of my Wagon-Lit. I dressed with difficulty – in the small space left over by Coates & the kit-bag – washed an incredible amount of myself – & then read Dolben in Father's compartment – he priming himself with Baedeker.[1] The Campagna looked quite different from a fortnight ago – much more snow on the hills – & less blue vaporousness. We saw the dome of St. Peter's miles away – found Rennell Rodd at the station at Rome – just lacked courage to go far enough to get a Tauchnitz.[2]

Who do you think we found in the luncheon-car? Mendl![3] We have not yet abordéed him. He was eating with a strange rather meretricious looking woman – I thought of the supper after the Opera – when you said 'I did not accuse you Sir of being an aboriginal' – & when he thought you must be everyone's cousin – because they all treated you with such freedom. . . .

---

[1] Digby Mackworth Dolben (1848–67), poet and Anglican Benedictine monk, who drowned shortly before going up to Oxford.

[2] James Rennell Rodd (1858–1941), British ambassador to the Court of Italy, 1908–19. Violet, her father and Venetia feared missing their train in an effort to buy a 'Tauchnitz' – a volume in the series of works of British and American authors produced by the Leipzig publishing house of Christian von Tauchnitz, which could be bought only on the Continent. Edwin Montagu parted company with his friends before they travelled to Pisa.

[3] Sigismund Mendl (1866–1945), Liberal MP for Plymouth, 1898–1900, and chairman of the National Discount Company.

NINE

The Enchantress

1912

In the summer of 1912 Winston Churchill, then first lord of the admiralty, included Violet and her father among a party of friends chosen to accompany him on a Mediterranean cruise, on board the admiralty yacht Enchantress. *For the first lord it was a case of mixing business with pleasure, as the ostensible purpose of the voyage was to inspect the naval establishments at Malta and Gibraltar. The Mediterranean was then the focus of international attention, following the Franco-German confrontation over Morocco the previous year, and there was speculation in the press that the* Enchantress *had a diplomatic mission. On board were the architects of British naval policy, and contact was made with the French fleet, at Tunis. Domestic political pressures, too, impinged upon this cruise, in the form of telegrams from London keeping the prime minister informed about the progress of the transport workers' strike. Asquith resisted calls for his early return to Downing Street, and made the most of what Violet later remembered as an 'interlude of delight' in troubled times.*

Diary – Thursday 1 February 1912 – 10 Downing Street, Whitehall, S.W.

My Darling I am back – after another night & another day's filth & rumble – but rather peaceful fun all the same – reading & eating & being with Father & Venetia. At Paris she & I drove across – & I bought myself the most divine green Crepe de chine dressing gown at the Galeries Lafayette. I finished the Way of all Flesh between Paris & Boulogne – & embarked – a little languidly – on Mill's Liberty which showed some grit after 56 hours travelling.[1]

A calm moonlit crossing – Father abordéed by a Suffragette. At Charing Cross Bongie & Nash met us – & a horrible mêlée with Suffragettes ensued – I had the pleasure of giving one an ugly wrist-twist!

[1] Samuel Butler, *The Way of All Flesh* (1903); John Stuart Mill, *Liberty* (1859).

Home – & food – Bongie was so happy to see me – too happy. Glorious letters – a sad one from yr. M. about P.[1]

Diary – Monday 5 February – 10 Downing Street, Whitehall, S.W.

Darling – Cys is 22 to-day – he comes after you in my heart.

I went with Father – shivering in uniform & a thinnish military coat to receive the King at the station. Icy red-carpeted platform – everyone looking very pinched & rednosed – in hastily improvised mourning for the Duke of Fife.[2]

They arrived – after a longish wait – not changed by one jot or one tittle, not a tinge of new Oriental shimmer or sheen about them. The Queen in the same hat & same smile – the King very kind – asking after everyone's limbs.

Haldane delighted with Ll G.'s reply to Bonar Law – which absolutely crunched him.[3] He goes off to Berlin next week in a philosophic capacity but with diplomatic intentions.[4]

The Granville Barkers came to lunch & were most amusing about the Censorship.[5] I drove with Cynthia in the afternoon – went to a bad palmist – saw Letty & Ego baby.

Hugh to tea – & an interesting talk with Nash about his successor. He is pro Bongie. Just in from Maud Cunard's – I sat next Soveral & had a wonderful talk with him about European diplomacy. I can see that he thinks E. Grey lacking in imagination – & in that Quixotic element which

---

[1] This refers to the removal of Lord Pentland from the Scottish office; see above, p. 301.

[2] The King had just returned from a state visit to India in the winter of 1911–12. His brother-in-law, the Duke of Fife, had died in Egypt on 29 January.

[3] On Saturday 3 February Lloyd George addressed the City Liberal Club, responding to Bonar Law's criticisms of the government's fiscal policy. At the Albert Hall, on 26 January, Law had attacked the record of Asquith's government as 'an example of destructive violence of which there is no parallel since the Long Parliament' (Robert Blake, *The Unknown Prime Minister*, 94–95).

[4] In February 1912 Haldane was dispatched to Berlin on an informal mission to discuss Anglo-German relations, in particular naval building. His known interest in Hegel was used as a cover for the visit, which was ostensibly for academic purposes, but its true nature became general knowledge, and his presence in Berlin caused fluctuations in the stock market there (R. B. Haldane, *An Autobiography*, 244).

[5] Harley Granville-Barker (1877–1946), actor, director, dramatist and critic, renowned for his staging of new plays, as well as for innovatory productions of the classics. He married in 1906 Lillah McCarthy (1875–1960), a leading actress famous for her roles in Shakespeare and Shaw. Censorship of the Edwardian theatre operated through the office of the lord chamberlain, and in 1907 Granville-Barker's own play *Waste* was refused a licence, on the ground that it featured an abortion.

has always distinguished our diplomacy & preserved the integrity of little States....

Diary – Thursday 8 February – 10 Downing Street, Whitehall, S.W.

Beloved – I've just won 50s at the Granards! – at auction bridge.

Dullish dinner – I sat between McKenna & Sir F. Ponsonby – a delightful man.[1]

McKenna <u>ranted</u> about Winston – to <u>me</u> of all people. He must be mad – I had tea with Ruby Peto in a grubby little overcrowded house full of lovely things. Yesterday my first Club – '& Fanny's first play' with Bogey R K & Father in the afternoon. I <u>was</u> happy to be back at the Club – all the boys delicious & well. Tuesday night I dined with Beb & Cynthia – Charlie was there.

The days are going quickly – it is <u>heavenly</u> being alone with Father here – I sadly watch my sands running out – Love & blessing – V

Diary – Wednesday 14 February – 10 Downing Street, Whitehall, S.W.

<u>St. Valentine's Day</u>
Dearest & Best – I have had a very rushed day – Hugh on the telephone & the cook before I was up – then up to Hampstead Heath with Mrs Granville Barker – without any breakfast. She talked vaguely & intensely about things like the Fabian Society – & Socialism – Shaw's genius – Wells's moeurs – her own career – which arose out of the purest accident – her acting [in] an amateur performance of Macbeth at the Queen's Hall to get a tombstone for Mrs Siddons.[2]

We sat on a bench in gentle spring sunshine with our backs to the round pond – overlooking that lovely Constable distance that has such glamour for me. Then home – & a hurried change into deep & low black – feathers etc – $\frac{3}{4}$ of an hour's chilly attente at the H. of Lords – amongst the shivering glittering peeresses – & peers in their red gowns & fur tippets.[3]

[1] Sir Frederick Ponsonby (1867–1935), KCVO 1910; equerry and assistant private secretary to George V, 1910–12, having been assistant private secretary to Edward VII and Queen Victoria.

[2] Sarah Siddons (1755–1851), famous English actress, painted by Reynolds and Gainsborough.

[3] Violet describes the state opening of parliament, 14 February, which traditionally begins with a speech from the throne to both Houses of parliament, delivered in the House of Lords.

Then came the Procession – Rouge dragon pursuivants – amongst them shrivelled old Lindsay – the Cap of Maintenance & the Sword of State – & Ld. Crewe bearing the crown on a little tray in front of him like a seller of penny toys. A delicious Alice in Wonderland-like cortège.

It seemed hours waiting for the Commons to be fetched – church coughings & throat clearings going on everywhere – Ettie standing with open eyes looking incredibly loyal and demure. Then came the speech. It is an absurd position for the poor King – the Peers loathing almost every one of its provisos & thinking them thoroughly disreputable but yet being compelled to accept them from the mouthpiece of authority.[1]

A good speech moving the address made by that fat bestman of Francis McLaren's Sir H. Verney – seconded by young Gladstone rather prim & pompous – but very nervous & morbidly diffident.[2] Then Bonar Law made a not bad & very violent attack on every item of our programme vulnerable & invulnerable. Disestablishment, Home Rule, Absence of preamble, Haldane's Mission. Father crunched him & wrung from him an unguarded & quite spontaneous pledge to repeal the Insurance Bill![3]

Club – Blessed one – Yours

M.B.C. to V.A.   *Thursday 29 February*
                          5 Hyde Park Square, W.

My very dear one. Another day over and one goes comfortably to bed with extraordinary want of real perception of the fact that a million men are

[1] Violet's close friend Ettie Desborough was a lady-in-waiting to the Queen. The address outlined the government's plans for Welsh church disestablishment, Home Rule, and electoral reform, all measures that were deeply resented by Unionists.

[2] Hon. Francis McLaren (1886–1917), Liberal MP for Spalding, Lincolnshire, from 1910, and parliamentary private secretary to Lewis Harcourt. Sir Harry Verney (1881–1974), 4th Bt; Liberal MP for North Buckinghamshire, 1910–18, and parliamentary private secretary to Augustine Birrell, 1911–14. William Gladstone (1885–1915), grandson of the Liberal premier and Liberal MP for Kilmarnock Burghs, 1911–15. Both McLaren and Gladstone were killed in action during the Great War.

[3] Asquith had quickly seized upon a remark made in the Commons by Bonar Law, to the effect that the National Insurance Act would never be operative. He asked Bonar Law if a Unionist government would revoke it, and when Bonar Law nodded in assent the Liberal benches erupted, MPs realizing at once the magnitude of the error. The principle enshrined in the Act could not be extinguished without fierce opposition from Labour and the trade unions. Bonar Law was obliged to try to make good the damage done by sending letters to the press, explaining that what he had meant was that the Unionist party would replace the Liberal legislation with something better (Peter Rowland, *The Last Liberal Governments, 1911–1914*, 146).

on strike and that a fortnight more may see us in God knows what state.[1] When one has been present at a conference of the men it is impossible to believe that such a collection of commonplace respectable insignificant respectful beings can have the power to upset the whole scheme of our daily life. The point they make is that they will not submit the schedule of minimum rates to the arbitration of any body that can have the power to cut them down. The figures they say have been cut down to the lowest point. The answer that your father gives them fails to convince, that in many cases they may before an impartial tribunal get a higher figure, because the corollary is that in some cases they will get a lower one. Unless they will split as the owners have split we have reached the end.

I am glad that I had a little of the play with the boys, I did enjoy it as you know well. Bless you golden one. B

V.A. to M.B.C.   *Friday 5 April (Good Friday)*
                               Le Touquet, Pas de Calais

I got your beloved letter yesterday & this morning a wire from Margot saying Father is much better – so I feel happier. Strength as <u>unbending</u> as his is very frightening – one feels it will never give until it is broken – I have felt this about Father for years – that if ever his health were to give way it wld. be quite suddenly & quite irrevocably. That's why I was frozen with terror about him on Wed. when for the first time in his life he admitted to feeling ill. I hope very much that you haven't <u>mentioned</u> to Venetia even that he was overtired or that we were anxious about him. But I am sure you will not have.[2]

We had a very amusing & most eventful journey on Wed. When we reached Folkestone we found there was barely <u>standing</u> room on the ship – though we were the first section of our train. Raymond absolutely failed to get us any kind of chair or seat I need hardly tell you! & Hugh arrived

---

[1] In mid-January 1912 the Miners' Federation of Great Britain voted for strike action in support of district minimum wage rates: on 1 March 850,000 miners ceased work, making more than a milion workers in dependent industries idle. On 15 March Asquith announced a bill to facilitate the minimum wage rates demanded, and the miners were back at work by mid-April.

[2] Asquith enjoyed robust good health throughout his life, but in the spring of 1912 he was physically and mentally at a low ebb, and was diagnosed as briefly suffering from high-blood pressure. Ironically he later attributed his recovery, from something approaching 'despair', to his love for Venetia, which began around this time, and about which Violet was then unaware (see M. and E. Brock (eds), *H. H. Asquith: Letters to Venetia Stanley*, pp. 1–8, and Lord Jenkins's Introduction to this volume).

very late & did no better. Warty however proved a far more effectual knight than our effete Christian escort – wheedled two beautiful chairs out of parsons for us & remained in conversation with me during the greater part of the voyage to H.'s annoyance 'That's the sort of thing that ha'ppens Raymond – if one leaves one's women for a moment some <u>Jew</u> slips in' etc.... When we reached Boulogne there was one of the 'ugliest rushes' for shore I have ever seen. What would happen in a fire or wreck I can't <u>conceive</u>. The whole boatload stampeded like Gadarene swine – does were mauled & trampled underfoot in the most ruthless way. Warty again came to the fore & piloted K. through the mêlée – they looked a very strange couple surging over the gangway together – topping the crest of a wave of sea-sick stragglers.

Terrible difficulties over the luggage ensued – Hugh being very good & showing more grit & efficiency than anyone else. He stayed behind finally to see about it & K & I & R. went on by the connection – to Le Touquet. We found ourselves in the Annexe – a little pavilion made of pitch-pine roofed over with corrugated iron – an odd little rabbit warren suite of rooms <u>all</u> leading out of one another & mostly impossible to reach except by going through everyone else's. It was very difficult to arrange with any decency.... R. complains bitterly of the discomforts especially of the cotton sheets which excoriate his skin but K & I are fairly comfy & Hugh thoroughly enjoys the interdependence of rooms & slackness of 'moeurs' involved. The place is rather jolly out of doors – a delicious, <u>very</u> ingenious not too long & fierce links among lowish pinewoods, a theatre of sandhills all round – the sea within reach but out of sight. The grass is very parched & brown & arid as if a very hot summer were just over – no lush green lies – & very few leaves on the trees – only embryo cat-kins covered with yellow down.

We have been playing bad golf in a perfect hurricane all day long – under grey skies. I feel giddy & muzzy with wind but rather healthy & well.... I'm going to risk sending this to Penrhôs tho' I feel it's rash. Bless & keep you dearest & goodest in the world Yr V.

Meet me on Wed. I will wire you –

M.B.C. to V.A.   *Tuesday 9 April*
10 Downing Street, Whitehall,
S.W.

Thank you for your beloved letter which I got this morning. I sent you a half sheet by the early post which will be certain to reach you & this which I am writing in a sleeper on my way down to London will probably find you still at Le Touquet on Wednesday morning. I have not spoken to anyone outside Downing St of your Father being unwell but I have said to Venetia & other people that he is tired & that I should be glad for him to have a short holiday after the introduction of the H.R. Bill. If as I hope very much this should happen I think that it is better not to be at pains to conceal that fact, after all if there is no mystery about it, it will not seem strange to anyone that he should go off as Sir E Grey is also doing for a fortnight. Margot writes that he has spoken of going away for a bit & the Master as I think I told has made a plan to enable him to get away so I hope it will now be settled without difficulty. I hope that you will feel more happy about him then.

I have had a happy time at Penrhos chiefly walking & sitting in the heather with Venetia and an occasional clump walk.

Tuesday

I am finishing this in the Turkish Bath where I have just met the Master. He tells me that he has suggested a plan by which your Father could get away until May 7th from tomorrow week. This would mean practically three weeks rest for him. We shall know tomorrow no doubt what he will do as he will have the opportunity of discussing matters with his colleagues and the Master, but I am in great hopes that he will take at any rate a fortnight.... My blessing beloved B.

M.B.C. to V.A.   ***Wednesday 10 April***
                                      5 Hyde Park Square, W.

Beloved. I hope that you went straight to sleep without interruption when I left you tonight. Tomorrow will be a wonderfully exciting day for us all;[1] & we shall be glad for it to be over and done with and for your Father to be able to look forward to a quiet haven of days. I wonder what the Irish members are feeling now. They have worked well for this day & I hope that they will get their reward.

Before I forget, if as seems possible you postpone your visit to Strachan, accept Olive's invitation to Vinters on the 28th.

Bless & keep you B.

---

[1] The third Home Rule bill was introduced by Asquith the following day, 11 April 1912.

V.A. to Katharine Asquith   *Saturday 13 April*
                                   Ewelme Down, Oxfordshire

My Darling – <u>How</u> I love your most lovely present which has just arrived –
thank you a hundred thousand times dearest. I have just read the ones
you mention & think them marvellously good. Father loves the Sicilian
one.

Thursday afternoon was wonderful. Father spoke about two hours – I
thought magnificently though he was very tired. He left the sentimental
brief almost untouched – the centuries of blood, tears, oppression, deci-
mation, inextinguishable spark of nationality etc. etc.! – & presented the
case on the intellectual side. This was very characteristic & much more
effective than a réchauffé of Gladstone would have been. He will have
plenty of opportunities for lyrical outbursts later in this session & next <u>&</u>
the one after I'm afraid!

The speech was punctuated all through by the worst type of private
school interruption from Carson & Bonar Law.[1] B.L. really <u>incredible</u> –
excelling even himself in rudeness & complete absence of point. Carson
followed – not very good but pathetically sincere in his delusions – then
Redmond who made his usual speech but better I thought than he had ever
made it before – ending with a rather good quotation from a prayer[2]....

I believe Father is writing to R. by this post about a Norfolk seat which
the Whips want him to contest. He will tell you all details. Though I am
passionately impatient for him to stand I'm not sure that this sounds quite
the best sort of seat for him. It is rather a scattered county constituency
so far as I can gather & might mean addressing <u>hundreds</u> of handfuls of
yokels in schoolrooms which wld. bore him to extinction. Also though it
is considered as safe as a church – I don't feel anything's safe now with
[National] Insurance – & it wld. be a bore if it went wrong. However of
course <u>this</u> is a very inky hypothesis & ought to be left out of account.

Do let me know what R. feels himself about it. Darling – I am so sad not
to be living with you any longer. Our week together was pure delight – &
my hours with you the best part of it. It was an inspired idea of yours bless
you for it – Yr V – My love to Frances

---

[1] Sir Edward Henry Carson (1854–1935), Kt, 1900; a leading Unionist politician, MP for
Dublin University, 1892–1918, and the central figure in Ulster resistance to the third Home
Rule bill.

[2] John Edward Redmond (1856–1918), MP for Waterford City from 1891 until his death;
chairman of the reunited Irish Parliamentary Party from 1900.

M.B.C. to V.A.   *Friday 19 April*
                                                     5 Hyde Park Square, W.

My very dear one. I am writing this in the train on my way to Alderley. We are rattling along in a way to which I am not accustomed since the coal strike so that I have to write a large childlike hand to obtain any possibility of readableness. When I got to London I went straight off to St. Paul's to the Memorial Service for the Titanic.[1] The choir was boyless, and I missed the unspeakable thrill of their voices which moves me at moments more than almost any sound. But St. Chrysostom's Liturgy sung by the men was beautiful and the roll of the drums through the Dome in the Dead March made an appeal almost physical in its effect.[2] Actually so to some people as several women were led out fainting, and one man opposite me dropped to the ground before the first roll was done. He poor man turned out to be Carlisle the designer of the ship.[3] His burden may well be heavy.

I sent off your letter to Hugh. I think that you must allow fully for the overstatement of his case due to his desire to be frank. Nor do I agree with you in thinking as you said to me on our walk yesterday that it is unnatural that he should wish himself to appear to you without illusion. I don't think that anyone would care to feel that the feelings for him of the woman he wishes to marry are resting on something like a false view of him, or at any rate anyone in the position that H finds himself. I am not surprised that he should desire the relation to be founded on an understanding less precarious than that.

Send me a short line to No 10 will you if you have a moment to write. Bless you B

V.A. to M.B.C.   *Monday 22 April*
                                                     Ewelme Down, Oxfordshire

I got your little line about the Memorial Service this morning. How tragic it all is – I think the whole thing has come home to one more intimately than any other great collective calamity.

[1] The White Star liner *Titanic* sank in the early morning of 15 April 1912, on her maiden voyage, after hitting an iceberg ninety-five miles south of the Grand Banks of Newfoundland; 1,635 lives were lost, 732 saved.

[2] *St Chrysostom's Liturgy* is The Orthodox liturgy, from which an excerpt would have been sung.

[3] Alexander Montgomery Carlisle (1854–1926), formerly general manager of Harland and Wolff shipbuilders. He was questioned at the Titanic Inquiry over the number of lifeboats provided on the vessel, a decision for which he had been partly responsible: the shortage of lifeboats was found to have contributed to the death toll in the disaster.

The man <u>Guggenheim</u>! who changed into his dress clothes to die is one of the most funny & pathetic touches.[1] The cruelty of the separations is almost unbearable – 19 widows under 23 – & one honeymooning couple of 18 & 19 – torn from each other & the one drowned & the other saved. I should have been inclined to send them off in Happy Families – the Pottses in one boat & the Gritses in another – as it is half are dead & the others unhappy for life.[2]

How disgusting this American censure of Ismay is.[3] Poor man I suppose he was wrong to leave the ship – but he has outraged the most unwritten of unwritten laws & no one has a right to arraign him for it before a conventional tribunal. Also he is probably going through hell enough to atone for anything he has done.

It is so <u>heavenly</u> here I wish I hadn't got to come back to-morrow – except that you & I will enjoy having what H. calls our 'weekly lark in Hoxton' – & I <u>won't</u> curse you this time & spoil your evening my poor little thing....

... Expecting Venetia minutely – Bless you – my very dear Yr V.

Diary – Thursday 23 May – The Enchantress, in the Mediterranean

... We all left London on Tuesday morning – Father, Winston, Clemmie, I, Goonie, the Bud, Admiral Beatty, Eddie & Masterton Smith.[4] The station scene was very good – Bongie came & Micky & Montagu & Venetia & Margot & Mrs West & Lady Blanche Hozier[5] – (very blatant & triumphant) & we all rumbled off in a Pullman car full of papers & letters & flowers – till Dover. Calm crossing of bright sun & wind – I read Imaginary

---

[1] Mr B. Guggenheim was a first-class passenger on the *Titanic* who did not survive the disaster.

[2] The 'Pottses' and 'Gritses' were family names in the popular card game Happy Families.

[3] Joseph Bruce Ismay (1862–1937), shipowner, was the eldest son of the founder of the White Star Line, owners of the *Titanic*. He took a first-class passage on the maiden voyage, but not in any official capacity. He survived the disaster, and was subsequently questioned by the American Senate Committee of Inquiry into the circumstances of his escape.

[4] Nellie Hozier, 'The Bud' (1888–1957), younger sister of Clementine Churchill. Rear-Admiral Sir David Beatty (1871–1936), naval secretary to the first lord of the admiralty, 1912. James Masterton-Smith (1878–1938), private secretary to the first lord of the admiralty, 1908–17. Lady Gwendeline Churchill (1885–1941), 'Goonie', Winston's sister-in-law.

[5] The *Enchantress* party left Victoria station on the morning of the 21st: among those gathering to see them off were, Mrs Cornwallis-West (1851–1921), formerly Lady Jennie Randolph Churchill, the mother of Winston, and Lady Blanche Hozier, the mother of Clementine.

Speeches[1] with Winston – (a very good one by Lord Rosebery) – & at Calais we had a meal & then changed into the well-known Train de Luxe.

... We found the Enchantress lying slimy-decked in the harbour – a very beautiful one – & our luggage having all made its appearance we steamed happily off under brightening skies. To-day has been fine. ...

Venetia Stanley to V.A.   *Thursday 23 May*
                                                          Train to Penrhôs

Darling I have been so damnably rushed since you left (and also Bongie very tiresomely kept on telling me I should have lots of time to catch you at Naples) that I now find that I must send this to Malta. ...

In the evening B and I went to the Club. ...

No parents came. Bongie read prayers and I Jekyll and Hyde, we got on quite well, tho' Joe went fast asleep. We came back to Mansfield St and dressed and went to a ball given by Aubrey's sister. It was quite fun. I talked to Duff, Jonah, Bongie and Aubrey and stayed quite late.[2] Aubrey was in very good form and started off by saying, hitting the palm of his hand with a knife, glaring and ruffling his hair. 'Venetia do you notice now with what swagger all the women walk. It's the beginning of the sex war, which is certainly coming. I've noticed a distinct difference in women's behaviour during the last year. It will be terrible. All struggles between two ideals always are. Such as sobriety and drunkenness, manhood and womanhood. I dread it Venetia' and so on in his wildest mood. All the other people round us at supper were intensely surprised.

I went to the Titanic this morning but it was deadly dull, inaudible wireless operators.[3]

The only funny thing was that Margot sent down a note both to Mr Solicitor and Mr Attorney saying 'For God's sake speak up and make the damned witnesses speak up too. We can't hear a word'. It had no effect and I came away early. ...

... I long to hear all your news and how the Bud is getting on. It was a shock to me her going. Did you see La Nôtre. Tell me everything. And don't bother to read this terribly long letter.

Much love to all. V.

---

[1] John Squire, *Imaginary Speeches, and other parodies in prose and verse* (1912).

[2] Alfred Duff Cooper (1890–1954), educated at Eton and New College, Oxford. Lawrence Evelyn Jones, 'Jonah' (1885–1969), a Balliol friend of Violet's brothers, and a member of her inner circle of friends. Called to the bar, 1909; with Helbert, Wagg & Co. Ltd., 1914.

[3] The official British inquiry into the sinking of the *Titanic* began in London in May 1912.

M.B.C. to V.A.   *Friday 24 May*
                                  5 Hyde Park Square, W.

Beloved. It seems a terribly long time ago since I saw you away from
Victoria, and since then my days have passed in a vain attempt to get
away to Penrhos. First I hoped to go with Venetia on Thursday but then
Knollys & the Honours kept me till Friday & then the question of the
strike arose.[1] It is the Transport Workers' Federation which has again called
a strike, but at present it is only certain classes of dock labourers who are
affected, & that only in London. It remains to be seen whether the carters
will come out or the dock men in other places. Of course if this happened
things would be pretty serious in London at least. But as this morning
there was no Cabinet Minister in London & Knollys informed me that the
King was getting anxious at the prospect of the P.M's absence for so long,
for me for the moment things were somewhat serious.

However McKenna luckily came to London & I got hold of Elibank. The
opinion of the authorities, that is Askwith[2] & McK, is that the strike will
go on for some time but M thinks that he can keep London fed without
much difficulty or danger to the peace. Askwith is more gloomy. Elibank
has a really high opinion of McK's value & abilities, not merely for an
occasion such as this, where his good opinion is not surprising, as I think
you will agree that McK. came very well out of the coal strike, but what is
to me unexpected he rates his abilities as a Parliamentarian very high. I
hope your father will not have been worried by my telegrams, though
I have no doubt that Masterton Smith & Eddy will have cursed me
heartily....

... Bless you my golden one B.

V.A. to Venetia Stanley   *Sunday 26 May*
                                  The **Enchantress,** *bound for*
                                  Syracuse

Going past Capri.

Such an odd blur of days has gone past since I left you – I have been
strangely unaware of time & am amazed to find to-day is Sunday. Our

---

[1] One of Bongie's duties was to help draw up the list of honours traditionally awarded on
the monarch's birthday; the official celebration of George V's birthday was 14 June, when the
list was due to appear in the press.

[2] Sir George Ranken Askwith (1861–1942), KCB 1911; arbitrator and chief industrial commissioner, 1911–19.

journey was tiring but rather amusing. The does were rigidly segregated during the London to Dover lap – & were brought 4 glasses of <u>port</u>!! & some sandwiches just before arriving there (which they sipped with apparent shrinking but actual enjoyment) then a delicious sunny breezy crossing. . . .

By the time we got back to the train poor Clemmie was in tears of nerves & exhaustion (<u>padlock</u>) she is not at all strong yet & excitement keeps her going much too much.

Typical French night journey with collisions every few minutes – & a grey dawn on rather dirty & demoralized people the next morning. Clemmie stayed in bed. I made friends with the delightful bluebearded Prince[1] (who had joined us at Paris) & listened to Winston describing Napoleon's exact progress through the Alps as we crept through them. Clemmie when I went in to see her asked me rather weakly: 'Violet – is Winston talking or reading aloud?' which is a very good demonstration of his conversational technique. . . .

So far as the personnel is concerned everyone has been at their most typical. Clemmie spending almost her entire time at Naples in hat & glove shops – being very nice – vital – frolicsome – soignée & kind – Goonie 'drimmy' & vague but full of aromatic charm – Nellie the especial prey of Father & his questions which <u>rain</u> in a steady shower – (We have had the Italian German & French flags & many other old favourites already to-day) – she is very disarming & has an amusing little face – but is thoroughly light metal don't you think? always borrowing, thanking, apologising, fagging, telling one of her country house floaters with attractive frankness.

Eddie – most characteristic, longing not to miss anything & by an evil fate always being left behind. Mr. Masterton Smith <u>delightful</u> – much the best person to have a consecutive talk with & a very good Auction player – Admiral Beatty – nice but impossible to talk to – says 'Curiosity, curiosity – ah Miss Inquisitive' if one asks him the name of an island or the date of a church – Prince Louis <u>delightful</u> very easy – but difficult to have a very good talk to – Winston is passionately absorbed in naval arrangements – his enthusiasms become obsessions – a delightful trait in the abstract but which might a little spoil one's balance as a companion. I think O.S. chafes a little under the continuous shop.

We had a <u>wonderful</u> day at Pompei – it is a magical place. I must tell you about it when I get back. We left Naples this morning & have just passed Capri – swathed in mists in the lapis-lazuli sea. We reach <u>Paestum</u> about 2 – celebrate divine service in the evening – Father reading the lessons – then on to Syracuse. Think of us there. We are due at Malta <u>Wed.</u>

---

[1] Prince Louis Alexander of Battenberg (1854–1921), admiral of the fleet, and second sea lord; promoted to first sea lord by Churchill later that year: '[he] looked the beau-ideal of the British naval officer' (*Dictionary of National Biography*).

Bless you Darling – Goodbye – I am being <u>divinely</u> happy. Give Bongie some of my journey news – I shan't bother to write it all to him yr V.

Diary – Monday 27 May – The **Enchantress,** *bound for Malta*

Dearest – We reached Naples on Friday morning & anchored in the harbour. There was no blaze of sun or colour. Vesuvius was hidden in cloud & it looked strangely like a Scotch shipping town in many ways. We went on shore in the pinnace – straight to the Museum where we saw the most wonderful treasures – Greek statues – a Bacchic procession relief – & an Orpheus & Eurydice relief – marvellous bronzes. No one cared about them much of our party except Father, Goonie & Eddie. The others went back to the yacht for lunch – & Eddie, Goonie, Nellie & I had an odd little spaghetti meal in an eating house called La Starita. In the afternoon a long expedition with Lord Fisher to a most hideous modern Pompeian villa belonging to some people called Pierce. Fisher spent most of our Neapolitan time with us – discussing naval plans with Winston – dancing with us before breakfast & retailing a stock of chestnuts anecdotes riddles & puns which even Puffin would have blenched at.[1]

Saturday we had a most wonderful day at Pompei – in real warmth – It moved me strangely the long lovely silent streets – the little courts & houses of the dead – where grass & flowers grow. One ought to go alone (not as we did with a large crowd of Vice Consuls, Naval Attachés & photographers) & hear one's own steps echo.

The beauty and intactness of everything is incredible. The wall decorations are exactly like the Saloon at Archerfield. We had a vast lunch & motored back through crowded filthy streets where dust swirled – oranges & lemons & nespolis were being sold – children swarming, cows & donkeys & horses yoked together pulling carts in every conceivable direction.

We sailed yesterday morning early – landed at Paestum & had the most heavenly expedition to the temples – driving in couples in toothrattling little gigs & dogcarts & landaus through fields of wild marigold & vetch & love in a mist & giant crimson cornflower & poppies & oats – to where they stood by the sea – the water glinting silverly through the colonnades. They are built like the Girgente ones in gold brown sandstone – double rows of perfect Doric pillars & capitals.... W. was characteristically unaffected by their <u>knockdown</u> symmetry & beauty – & devoted himself to catching the little green backed lizards which darted in & out of the

[1] Until 1910 Fisher had been first sea lord, and he continued to be an influential voice on naval matters. Churchill was to reappoint him in 1914, after the outbreak of European war.

crannies & crevices of the stone with extraordinary agility & elusiveness. He pressed Beatty & Masterton into the service to make a drive muttering to himself – 'We must be more scientific about this – we must be more scientific' – I love his eternal childhood. He & I drove back together & I spoke to him about H. We got out & picked armfulls of wildflowers – how happy you would have been dearest – I need you in sunshine among flowers.

About 3.30 on Monday we sailed into Syracuse harbour. It lay there just as we had left it in February – the white town jutting into the green bay with Plemmyrion sickle shaped beyond – & above the misty upland of Epipolae. Etna was clouded & invisible. We packed into the pinnace & drove round some of our old sights Dionysus ear – the Latomias dell Paradiso (where the little boy still turns the wheel) – & walked in the lemon tree garden in the middle & picked nespolis off the trees & eat them – then towards sunset we strolled up to the Greek theatre – & sat there on the worn stone seats – watched the sea changing colour under the sky – first red – then pale cool green – then steely blue the moment before dark. Eddie said 'Oh suitably surmounted with a hat' in piping scrannel notes from the stage. W. took several photographs – then we all went back & dined & played auction with some of the crew – Philpotts, James & Smyth Osborne the three lieutenants.

Rather an amusing thing happened after dinner. Just before going to bed Eddie & I & Masterton Smith & Goonie began valsing in a mild burst of joie de vivre on the deck – I heard a sudden jerk & bump & turning round saw Goonie & M.S. who a moment before had been revolving quite safely lying prone tightly locked in each other's arms like Paolo & Francesca on the companion ladder with their heads through it overhanging the sea![1] They were pulled back & saved with no loss or hurt beyond a graze on Goonie's elbow & the loss of her diamond comb.

Diary – Thursday 30 May to Saturday 1 June – *The* Enchantress, Malta

On Wed. morning in the early stages of dressing I was roused into activity by an order from the First Lord to come on deck immediately & see the approach to Malta harbour. I wasn't dressed enough but I gazed out of my porthole & saw us sailing up to an island which looked like one vast

[1] The story of Paolo and Francesca, thirteenth-century lovers who were put to death for their illicit union, is recounted in the fifth canto of Dante's *Inferno*, and became a popular theme in nineteenth-century art, the subject of a poem by Leigh Hunt and a tone poem by Tchaikovsky.

fortress of grey & yellow rock – a great heap of battlemented stone built between sky & sea.

We drifted into the most wonderful harbour I have ever seen – strongholds & fastnesses piled up on every side – & men of war – rigging up their flags & saluting by bugle calls from every deck. I dressed & ran up on deck – different grandees were beginning to arrive in pinnaces – all the Admirals in one – followed by their flag-lieutenants, Ian Hamilton with a military contingent – & finally Kitchener looking quite splendid (treble life size) but alas dressed as a civilian in a Homburg hat.[1]

We sat & talked rather uncomfortably to these great men & their suites till lunch – when we all went off dressed as well as we could to a gigantic official lunch with Admiral Poe – (whose wife is a dear old girl & used to be Evelyn de Vesci's near neighbour at Abbey Leix).[2] I sat between an Admiral & a Captain – called Ryan – who groused terribly at the removal of the Fleet. I glibly produced all the arguments I had picked up en route – such as – much better none than too few etc.[3]

We returned to the yacht after lunch & a good deal of dawdling & conversation – picked our way through streets where dozens slept en plein pavement (the Maltese are an odd-looking mixture of Italians & Arabs) – then a long rest & out again to dine at the Palace.

This was a vast & very intimidating function. On arrival we found all the guests (thousands of them) arranged in a large circle – as they are at a Connaught dinner at home. We shook hands & went in. . . .

After the King's health – band etc. we danced – with myriads of young men all looking exactly alike but fortunately all dressed differently in glittering uniforms. . . .

Next morning Thursday – we were given 10 minutes to leave the ship by Captain Ruck-Keene – (a most gloomy & pessimistic character) as the mystic rites of coaling were impending.[4] We went into the town – saw a big cathedral called St. John's paved with the different coats of arms of the Knights of Malta. We then drove exhaustedly off to San Antonio – the Ian Hamiltons' house – in flies like 4 poster beds – with a little flannelette

[1] General Sir Ian Hamilton (1853–1947), general officer commanding-in-chief in the Mediterranean, and inspector-general of overseas forces, 1910–15.

[2] Admiral Sir Edmund Poe (1849–1921), first and principal ADC to the King, 1912–14. He married, in 1877, Frances *née* Sheil, and they lived at Black Hill, in Abbeyleix, where Violet spent a week during her visit to Ireland in April–May 1910.

[3] As part of Churchill's reorganization of the navy its strength, from 1912, was concentrated in the home waters of the Atlantic and the North Sea, and reduced in the Mediterranean. This strategy assumed a degree of co-operation with France, which had concentrated its fleet in the Mediterranean, and in 1912 an extremely ambiguous arrangement was reached between the two powers over the logic of the disposition of the fleets.

[4] Captain William Ruck Keene (1867–1935); captain in the Royal Navy, 1906.

valance round the top called carozza. San Antonio is the most wonderful steamy tropical garden full of bougainvillaea flowering pomegranates & strange blossoming trees of every colour. We sat round a little fountain where stone dolphins spouted & spat & I read Francis Thompson till lunch.

Lady Hamilton is a faded graceful woman – much too elaborate & complicated – for the amount of 'coming off' she achieves.[1] She ought to be either much simpler or else much more of a success. She moves with terribly deliberate & sustained grace. A rather faded lavender sister called Mrs Montcreiff lives with them & is a hell of a bore. I thought Sir Ian much less attractive & more un-first rate than ever before but he is easy to talk to & nice if you can make him forget for a moment that you are a woman.

We drove back tea-ed & rested & returned there for dinner – I sat between His Excellency the Governor – Sir Leslie Rundle – commonly called Sir Leisurely Trundle[2] – & a quite nice man called Hobbs. We danced afterwards & sat in the heavenly garden smelling wonderfully of tobacco plant & other strange heavy fragrances – Japanese lanterns hung in trees – fountains played – it was as good as anything I have seen in its way. I danced with a young man called Colvin – who was quite extraordinarily good – back to the yacht by about 1.

The next morning Friday was thrilling. We were sent on board the cruiser Cornwallis Captain Ryan's ship – for battle practice. Father, Lord Kitchener, Winston, Prince Louis & Admiral Beatty came on board after a little tour in the Destroyer Kennet & we all started off in this large iron grey monster into the open sea in pursuit of the Suffolk which was towing the target. Five minutes before the firing began we were told to put cottonwool in our ears – the Suffolk was 4 miles off. The minutes were counted 3 – 2 – 1 – then it began – I held my hands over my ears. It was less like a sound than a most thrilling shock to the whole of one – every inch of one's body was shaken vibrating by it from the soles of one's feet upwards – then again – & again – & again – till every thought was driven out of one's head. Great bursts of flame flashing out of the side of the ship & then far away where the shell struck a fountain rose from the sea higher than St. Paul's. Great clouds of yellow & black smoke covered one – I felt for the first time what war would be & how difficult it wld be to think in the middle of a battle.

After it was all over we went down & washed our faces – then torpedo

---

[1] Lady Hamilton *née* Muir (d. 1941).

[2] General Sir Leslie Rundle (1856–1934), governor and commander-in-chief Malta, 1909–15; the nickname may be derived from the delays associated with his command during the Boer War.

practice with submarines began. It is almost impossible to see the periscope which looks about the size of an umbrella handle in the waves – but the water is a lighter green just above them & an aeroplane cld. easily mark one out in the Mediterranean I shld think. Only one reached us....

Saturday morning early – a review of soldiers & Marines at the Masa, a large arid strip of ground where polo golf & all other manly pastimes happen. There was a delightful march past – but I thought of Khartoum – & of the camels & horses & mules galloping past Kitchener – this was comparatively flat & ordinary – though the bluejackets were delightful – & the little Midshipmen with drawn daggers. We lunched at San Antonio ... then home to a gigantic reception of 120 dog-strange Maltese on board the Yacht. They all look like halfcastes or octaroons. The flag lieutenants came to dinner – about 28 all together & we danced afterwards to the Russells band. It was very amusing & exciting – far too few women but we had Sir Roger which was a great success & started things well. The men were all quite delightful – unblasé, amusing, simple, active & wonderfully courteous & keen.

I had a good talk with one Fitzgerald rather a nice A.D.C of K[itchener].'s & asked & heard about Cairo & the Sudan. It is extraordinary what glamour & sentiment I feel about it all & how I long to go back. We sailed at 11 – as the last pinnace laden with guests disappeared.

M.B.C. to V.A.   *Monday 30 May*
                                   5 Hyde Park Square, W.

Beloved. Thank you for a postcard which reached me yesterday from Naples. You sent it to Penrhos, where I wish I had been, but I could only stay there for Sunday & Bank Holiday. I did not like to be away while possible demands might recur for your Father's return. As you know another request for this was put forward yesterday this time not from the King, but from all his colleagues who were in London which meant really L-G, McKenna, Elibank & Isaacs.[1] Their point is & I think it is sound that at the moment the chance of a settlement seems small as the employers including the Port of London Authority refuse to meet the men. This makes it very unlikely that the strike will end in the next few days in which case the P.M.'s absence from the House of Commons is likely to be

[1] Sir Rufus Isaacs (1860–1935), 1st Baron Reading, 1914; Liberal MP for Reading, 1904–13; attorney-general, October 1910 to October 1913; lord chief justice of England, 1913–21. Bongie uses the phrase 'colleagues' loosely here, as neither Elibank nor Isaacs were then members of the cabinet.

the subject of awkward comment in the House or to put it at the lowest his presence would strengthen the Govt's position very materially. I personally shall be very glad if he is back when Parliament meets. Of course it may happen that the strike will fizzle out in the next day or two, but that it is impossible to foresee & today the probabilities are certainly against it. This being so and since every strike of this magnitude bears the seeds of a crisis in the House, I hope he will decide to come home.

I don't quite know why I write this to you, you can only get this letter at Gibraltar, when the decision will have been made & you will have forgotten the whole thing; if indeed you ever gave it a serious thought as I quite believe the suggestion that your father should shorten his holiday may seem ludicrous at Malta, though here I have [done] nothing but think of it for the last week.

I have just had your Father's telegram telling me to wire reasons for his return to Bizerta & I must forthwith attend to that....

    B.

Diary – Sunday 2 and Monday 3 June – The Enchantress, *Bizerta*

After a most calm & heavenly journey over oily blue seas – past lovely jagged islands & capes we sailed into Bizerta harbour about 4. The coast is disappointingly un-African – as Goonie said 'not unlike the environs of Bournemouth' – on a rather parched day. No sand or palms or blacks or camels or lions or tigers – a brown sweep of hills – with an occasional chalk-quarry. The harbour itself is magnificent – though nothing like Malta of course. Seventeen guns were fired as we steamed in & the Suffolk replied & ran up the French flag. Shortly afterwards the French grandees began to arrive on board – & most ludicrous rites of reception were gone through. Winston had somehow scraped up out of the depths of the ships 10 marines – none of whom as their sergeant confessed had presented arms for 10 years. These were dressed up in scarlet uniforms & placed in a row at the head of the companion ladder – & made to bugle a salute & present arms when the man we conjectured to be the Commander in Chief set foot on board.

He unfortunately turned out to be the Mayor. However nothing loath they went through with it all again. The Enchantress was soon flooded with French of all ages & sizes & callings all hyper-civil, a little non-plussed by their complete inability to make themselves understood to the men of our party.

Admiral – Vous avez fait une bonne traversée.
Winston – Yes, yes very fine fortifications.
Admiral – Vous n'avez pas souffert du mal de mer.
Winston (rather loud) – We want to see your docks.
Admiral – A la bonne heure – enchantés de vous voir.
Winston louder still – How many torpedoes have you got.[1]

We embarked in a sort of Destroyer & went 10 miles across the great salt lake which forms the inner harbour. Champagne was served on board & everyone drank each other's health with low bows – altogether – the amount of bowing that went on was quite <u>extraordinary</u>. Then we got into several motors – terribly tightly packed & drove round their ship-repairing works & home round the lake by land – Goonie & I & Nellie & Eddie & Masterton Smith & a man called le Commandant Joie in a very gorgeous & garish uniform of the Spahi – bright blue trousers like my Milanese clock & a red coat. Vast official dinner on board – I sat between the General & another military man – then the crew of the Suffolk came on board & we wandered about on deck & talked till lateish.

Next morning at 10 we started (all except poor darling Clemmie who had to stay behind because of health & Winston who stayed with her) for Tunis in several contingents – Eddie & I & Mr. M. S. were in one – Nellie Prince Louis & the Spahi in another – Father, Goonie, the General & the Resident in a 3rd – Mr. Berkeley the English Consul in a 4th.

The beauty of the way on this dazzling day was indescribable – we went by marvellous blue lakes with green shallows & purple fringes – jagged mountain-ranges – passing on the road strange crabbed brown old Testament figures jogging on donkeys – & hobbled camels feeding. It got terribly hot after we had been going about an hour – & I was glad to arrive at the suburbs of Tunis & plunge into the icy cool of a Museum where we saw some lovely Greek bronzes & statues that had lain perdu in a ship at the bottom of the sea for thousands of years. We went next to an hôtel called Belvedère whose garden was full of unknown flowering trees of every colour – oleanders bougainvillaea – & what looked like a sort of mixture between acacia & wistaria. A gigantic meal followed with an ice between every course – I between the Resident & Mr Berkeley – then we were photographed & started off into Tunis. It is a snow white town under a very blue sky with a wall all round – just as I had imagined it. We went straight to the native parts & walked down the Souks which are not unlike the Cairo & Omdurman ones. Cool brown shade – with dazzling flecks of sunshine dancing on the drowsy brown figures asleep on their counters

[1] 'You had a pleasant journey?' ... 'You didn't suffer from seasickness?' ... 'That's fine – pleased to meet you.'

or squatting before their doors. The same kind of merchandise is offered too – pungent jasmine scent & little painted glass bottles – cheap scarfs & coloured handkerchiefs carpets & brass & ugly modern coloured dressing gowns. They have an extraordinary fascination for me in spite of their badness & tawdriness. We went on in motors to the site of Carthage – on the edge of a fabulously blue sea. There is nothing of it left now – then to a gigantic teaparty at the Residente's – I caught a small tortoise in the garden which I longed to take home – but humanely let go – & then regretted it.

Everyone was in their best clothes high collars & hats trimmed with ostrich feathers & I felt a very incongruous note as I blundered in tortoise in hand.

Then came almost the most wonderful thing in the whole day. We arrived at a large open-field where about 4000 troops were drawn up – Infantry & Cavalry – Zouaves – Chasseurs d'Afrique – native troops & the Bey's bodyguard. These marched past – the cavalry going most beautifully past at the gallop. They then retreated to a little distance – a signal was given & the whole cohort of men mounted on the most wonderful Arabs came straight at us full gallop with drawn swords – flashing in the sun – shouting at the top of their voices. It was the most exciting & moving thing I've ever seen. The old General said to me 'Vous n'avez qu' à lever votre éventail Mademoiselle et ils s'arrêteront'[1] – but I didn't – & they charged full tilt at us to what seemed to be within a yard or two of me – I shan't ever forget it – We got back very late & sailed that night. Father to the joy of all of us made up his mind not to go home in spite of the Master's rather alarmist telegrams about the transport workers' strike – so the Suffolk was sent back to Malta.

All yesterday was heavenly – oily calm & sunshine again. I wrote [and] read on deck most of the day – finished Multitude & Solitude & began a book called the Coward.[2] Mr. James has just called me to see some porpoises playing round the ship – there have been flying fish & dolphins too. Winston is in the stokehole – isn't it sporting of him? We reach Gibraltar at midnight to-night. . . .

Diary – Friday 7 June – The Enchantress, *rounding Cape St. Vincent*

Dearest – The Lord Chancellor has resigned – great impending Cabinet re-organizations – I hope Montagu may get something good in the shuffle though I rather doubt it. Personally I am anti Seely as a successor to

[1] 'Just raise your fan, mademoiselle, and they will stop'
[2] John Masefield, *Multitude and Solitude* (1900); Robert Benson, *The Coward* (1912).

Haldane – as I don't feel he will be a very invigorating dash of new flavour into the Cabinet pudding.[1] But Samuel is not a very good figurehead for the Army either. We were turned out of the ship early yesterday morning as coaling was impending & I had my first look at the Rock. It is not quite so stupendously big & rugged & overhanging as I imagined. I had a faint pang of disappointment. We found a landau & an A.D.C. & drove up to the Convent – where that poor brute Inverclyde received us with a good deal of practical kindness. I loved her Scotch accent & the knowledge that she knew you. She showed us innumerable photographs & then settled us in the garden. We drove round the rock in a motor to see their summer cottage – & I got a slight realization of the island fortress we were on. Sheer cliff down into the sea – no ladders allowed & all gates locked at sundown –

Edwin Montagu to V.A.   *Tuesday 11 June*
                                        India Office, Whitehall

Dear Violet

I address you as one concerned with cabinet making.

The Morning Post today suggests John Burns for war office. Would this do? Safe in hands of military advisors, easily kept in order, very popular with the army, quite harmless.

That clears the way for Samuel to L.G.B. and Hobhouse to P.M.G and Seely to Duchy.

Fearing the pseudomilitary orator at the War Office and being brave enough to ignore Winston's ire, I <u>rather</u> like this.[2]

Yrs gratefully ESM.

[1] R. B. Haldane succeeded Earl Loreburn as lord chancellor, 10 June 1912, and was himself succeeded at the war office by Colonel J. E. B. Seely (1868–1947). Seely served in the Boer War with the Imperial Yeomanry, and was elected Unionist MP for the Isle of Wight, *in absentia*, 1900. He crossed the floor over tariff reform and was re-elected unopposed, in 1904; Liberal MP for Abercromby, Liverpool, 1906–10. Under-secretary of state for war, 1911–12, and secretary of state, 1912–14. As Violet suspected, Montagu was passed over in this reshuffle.

[2] The *Morning Post* unwaveringly advanced the views of the Unionist opposition, and Asquith was extremely unlikely to take its lead on cabinet appointments. John Burns remained at the local government board. Montagu's plans involving Samuel and Hobhouse were later realized: in February 1914 they both made the moves outlined in this letter. Charles Hobhouse (1862–1941), Liberal MP for East Bristol, 1900–18, held a number of cabinet posts during the period, and was chancellor of the duchy of Lancaster, 1911–14.

V.A. to Winston Churchill   *Wednesday 12 June*
                                       10 Downing Street, Whitehall,
                                                           S.W.

My Dear Winston.
    I send one line to thank you for my heavenly three weeks – I have never loved anything so much & the memory of it will be a possession for life. I am so very distressed to hear about Clemmie – & pray things may not turn out as long & wearisome as they sound. I am coming to see her to-morrow – would you tell her I might be rather later than I said – perhaps towards 6 as the Board of Trade garden party happens that afternoon. I have just been listening to McKenna's vindication of himself – very good & courageous I thought. He seemed to have an unanswerable case, so this Vote of Censure is probably the best thing that cld. have happened. Austen's data was very sloppy.[1] I feel <u>terribly</u> land-sick & long to be back with you all – lizard-catching at Paestum – or eating at Malta or gliding on that oily Bay.
    Goodbye – & thank you again a <u>million</u> times
                                       Yrs Violet

V.A. to Venetia Stanley   *Thursday 22 August*
                                       The Wharf, Sutton Courtenay,
                                                      Berkshire

My Darling – Thank you so much for your glorious letter. I have been meaning to write to you every <u>single</u> day but every second that passed made the letter a fuller & a longer one & I have recoiled before the enormity of the task. When one lives like you & I do recording what every single person 'said then' – correspondence – if it is to be adequate – should not be lightly undertaken.
    I spent 4 extraordinary days with Lipton in an atmosphere completely

---

[1] Reginald McKenna, then home secretary, faced a motion of censure in the Commons on 12 June. Austen Chamberlain argued that by refusing police protection to a group of strike-breaking dock labourers, the previous week, the home secretary had failed in his duty to protect the freedom of labour. McKenna, though, was able to point out that the government had been so effective in protecting labour that the port authorities had a surplus (*The Times*, 13 June). It was a foregone conclusion that Chamberlain's motion would be defeated, but it strengthened government morale that McKenna made such an effective defence.

differing from any I had ever breathed before.[1] Yacht-owners – aeroplanists & the nobility of Spain – represented by two people called the Duke & Duchess of Santona (she is the Duke of Alba's sister).

The D[ss] of Westminster had just left – Lipton introduced me by saying 'Dukes on my yacht are as plentiful as blackberries – if you don't know a man you're safe to call him your Grace'.

I began by heaving under his ingenuous vulgarity but ended by liking him for his kindness & real humour. He assesses Kings & Queens at about their right value au fond – but talks much too much about them. On the first night of my arrival I had far the most thrilling experience of my life – I went up with Grahame-White on a gigantic biplane & was in the air for nearly $\frac{1}{2}$ an hour![2] I can't tell you what a <u>marvellous</u> sensation it is – I only live to do it again – & feel I must marry an air-man – Do you think H. would learn?

I have made great friends with Grahame-White – who has a keen, spare, alert bird-like charm. Father who would never – <u>never</u> have let me go up – is now rather proud of my having done it & regards it as an indirect feather in his cap – though to me he says it was a very Goneril-like action[3]....

I go to Dallas on 20th. This is a dreary letter of purest news – please write to me darling – to D. St to be forwarded & tell me all your plans yr V

Hugh Godley to V.A.   *Wednesday 28 August*
                                  Killegar, Killeshandra, Ireland

My dearest one

I wonder if you are in Venice; I suppose anything less like being in Venice than being here has seldom if ever been imagined. It has been raining very heavily & quite unintermittently for about 12 hours, & I, in my winter plumage, am sitting almost <u>in</u> a large fire of turf, & am even so not at all too hot.

But I have liked being here, with my mother & my cousin Anna. I have never thought the place so nice. We have had warm soft days till

---

[1] Sir Thomas Lipton (1850–1931), 1st Bt, 1902; the owner of tea and rubber estates in Ceylon, and a keen yachtsman and motorist. Unmarried, he listed membership of twenty-two clubs in *Who's Who*, including the Royal Automobile Club and the Royal Yacht Squadron, Cowes. The names of his yachts, *Shamrock, Shamrock V* and SY *Erin*, reflected his Irish origins.

[2] Claude Grahame-White (1879–1959), aviator and aeronautical engineer, owner of one of the first petrol-driven cars in Britain, and the first Englishman granted a certificate of proficiency in aviation.

[3] Goneril is the heartless eldest daughter in Shakespeare's *King Lear*.

yesterday & wonderfully lovely things like loosestrife & meadowsweet & bulrushes grow all along the river & in the bogs, & the smell of wet earth & turf smoke is very pacifying.

All the people I have talked to, of whatever station, from the Archbishop of Armagh down to the boy who weeds the garden, are passionately anti home-rule. They <u>really</u> think that if it passes there will be a serious rising in Ulster & that all the Protestants in a little outpost like this will be set upon & murdered. Anna is seriously in dread for her life. It is very difficult till one gets among them to realize that all these deep feelings are not merely invented by politicians for party purposes.

The only thing which consoles the people here is that they none of them seem to think it has the smallest chance of passing. . . .

God knows when this will reach you my dear one, but I hope it will find you in a happy nest. You are a poor wandering little saint aren't you. Write to Ardgowan Greenock if you write to me before Tuesday 3rd; to Evistones after that. Always yr loving H.

Lord Murray to V.A.   *Thursday 5 September*
Hôtel du Rhin, Paris

Dear Miss Asquith – Your letter reached me in my wanderings across country from Biarritz to Avignon, whither I had gone for a change after the odious fortnight I spent previous to the rising of Parliament.[1] I have carried it about with me without answering – these are matters on which one feels so deeply that words will not come either to speech or letter. Your words touched me to the quick – only Mrs Asquith and yourself really know my feelings towards your Father, and that you and she should both have written and spoken to me as you have done, overwhelms me. I find myself constantly essaying to banish the recurring thought – ought I to have resigned my post, which he gave me in every confidence, as a personal trust, in the execution of which I know I earned his approval? – ought I not to have let the future look after itself, so long as the Prime Minister wanted me? – and when I think thus – I am unhappy.[2]

I like to think that you know that I looked after his interests <u>first</u>: – and

[1] Prior to the rising of parliament, rumours had begun to circulate of the Master of Elibank's involvement in improper share dealings in the Marconi Company (see below, p. 381), and this is the likely explanation of his 'odious fortnight'.

[2] Murray had accepted an offer from the Liberal peer Lord Cowdray of a business partnership, in a company with interests in Mexico. He resigned from the government on 7 August, with a peerage, becoming Lord Murray of Elibank.

as you say in directions of which he knew not the existence: he is too quick minded to take note of the 'small things' – & yet these count as much, perhaps even more, in the fortunes of Statesmen and Governments as in the humdrum lives of obscure people.

I was always watching.

I am returning home: if you will allow me to find my way into N° 10 in the same unconventional manner as in the old days, I shall not feel so cut adrift from scenes & memories where I had real happiness – for with me so much of my work is personal. I shall watch Raymond's career with warm interest and hopes – and I like to carry with my retirement the thought that his was the last candidature that I arranged.

I am sending you something for the 'little room downstairs' – as a reminder of three vy strenuous years and of one who was vy devoted to all that concerned the interests of his Chief and his family: – and to quote a Welsh proverb beloved by L.G – 'May the dawn always shine on you' is the heartfelt wish of one who will sign himself as You always knew him. <u>Alick Murray.</u>

V.A. to M.B.C.   ***Thursday 5 September***
Train to Munich

We left Venice early this morning & have been rolling for 6 hours through the most wonderful country.... I am <u>miserable</u> to have gone. The last 4 or 5 days the joy in the place itself became so acute that nothing – no people in the world could have spoilt it. The smell of the lagoons – the <u>fruit</u>-market – the wonderful lights at sunset & after – the indescribable beauty of every hole & corner & cranny & crevice in the place became an almost physical luxury. I have <u>never</u> enjoyed 'sights' – & especially pictures <u>half</u> as much in my life – I think I really have sharpened & deepened my aesthetic appreciation a good deal. My last two days were occupied by a very embryonic but still real plait with Vincent Astor who arrived on Monday at the Grand Hôtel & had some meals with us.[1] He is a very odd but <u>I</u> think nice & touching creature – 6ft. 4. with an extraordinary accent – shy – farouche – uneducated – glum & boorish looking – but I think solitary – at sea & fundamentally sound. He sat very silently all the first night at dinner while Beecham etc talked infinitely drearily & flippantly about everything people are supposed to hold in reverence & affection – & minded <u>terribly</u> a tirade against America by an American

[1] (William) Vincent Astor (1891–1959), future head of the Astor family in the United States; educated at Harvard, 1911–12.

called Cluse. When Beecham began to talk about Christ I stopped him quite heygately. Afterwards Vincent asked me to go out with him & I thought him very nice – & rather pathetic. Everyone else wrote him down as dull & loutish from the first second – but I think he is only shy & lonely & undeveloped. One thing I thought very nice of him was that he asked me to arrange for him to see Zelle-Zelle (who used to be his governess) on the one day he spends in England before sailing. I hope he will endow her handsomely – it makes one's brain reel to think how rich he is – $1\frac{1}{2}$ millions a year – which Cys says works out at over 3000 a day – & not a single thing to do with it in the world.[1] No house – no tastes – no ideas. I asked him if he wasn't haunted by the responsibility of having such gigantic levers in his hands – & by the fear that he might not have imagination enough to work them properly. He said rather doubtfully that he was – but I don't believe he'd ever given it a thought – Cys & I are installed by ourselves for a 14 hours journey 8 – 9.40. I have read a book on Venetian painters & one on Woman Suffrage from cover to cover....

I wonder if the most influential of the Carters will meet me at the station – I have had several very pressing & insistent letters from him. He is a man of tremendous determination – & I think wants to achieve this object more than anyone else (except A.) ever has.

People are beginning to get in with knapsacks & little Eib-See hats & Alpenstocks – & the country is getting more Garmisch-like every second – gigantic limerock hills – & stony riverbeds in the valley below. Oh Bongie it gives me such a sehnsucht for a week here with you & C. instead of chilly Dornoch with the McKennae....

... I don't know where to send this – Yr V Have you written me a letter to Munich – I hope so.

V.A. to M.B.C.   *Saturday 21 September*
                                               Train to Aberdeen

I have had 3 days in London with Father, Margot, Oc & Cys – Tante coming to every meal – Lord Crewe, Lord Morley & Sir Edward Grey alternating at most.[2] On Wed. night Oc & I went down to the Club – it

---

[1] A salary of £1,500,000 a year is the equivalent of more than £4,100 a day: either Cys calculated, or Violet remembered, wrongly.

[2] 'Tante' was a nickname given to Edwin Montagu by Violet and Venetia, because of his resemblance to the moody central character in Anne Douglas Sedgwick's novel *Tante* (1911), which Violet read in January 1912, when holidaying with Montagu in Sicily (above p. 330).

fell rather luckily my being there as it was just the psychological nick of time to Svengali them into going to Night school which begins again this week. I coaxed & threatened & bribed & terrorized – & how I hope they will be good & go. Ted Judd had no idea what he wanted to learn – & I was so at sea as to be just about to send him to some classes on 'citizenship'! when I luckily remembered chemistry was what he ought to know about. Dyer was the most tiresome – & I had finally to say to him that unless he attended at least one Class a week he couldn't come to the Club – I think we might make this a rule. Jo was vanquished by an unfair feminine appeal. Roberts is now working prosperously for Oc at 7/6 a week – we gave him 6d to go & get his hair really expensively cut – he looks otherwise enormously improved already. John Glover I am <u>disgusted</u> with – will you believe that a casual enquiry by me elicited from him the fact that he had left Thrupp & Mabberleys without giving a <u>day's</u> notice – simply because his trousers got covered with oil there & he hadn't got another pair!!!

I was incensed as I dragged this from him – & for a moment could have pierced his languid poached-egg eyes with red hot needles – his flaccidness is beyond belief. I sent him to apologise the next morning to Thrupp & M.'s – I think it wouldn't be a bad thing to leave him without help as to work for some little time. He says he is learning his father's business – of making attaché cases which sounds a rather patchy & precarious employment. I have left yr. little black book in your writing table drawer for you.

Vincent was in London yesterday on his way to America – & he & Artie & Cys saw me off at King's Cross at 11.30 after going to a play together – he is an odd creature – I do like him – he now says he is coming back in the Spring so you will see him then.

<u>Station-hôtel – Aberdeen station.</u>

I haven't been here for two years & it is flooded with strange memories for me – of Slains & after. It is extraordinary how accurately every phase & aspect of Scotland brings back A's atmosphere to me – I feel it oughtn't to exist without him.

I want to write about our talk at Penrhôs – before you went away – only these things can hardly be put into spoken words let alone written ones.

It is impossible for you to quite understand what one feels – the difference between the two sides of the same feeling is so great. What I called the longing for 'infallibility' is a little what Brunhilde meant when she said – if I <u>must</u> surrender to someone – then let it be a hero – not only that – let it be a Wälsung – & if possible Siegfried.[1] For a moment one

---

[1] It was characteristic of Violet to use Siegfried, the hero of Wagner's *Ring* cycle, in this context: her feelings for Archie Gordon had been couched in similar terms. Her love of Wagner's operas, which was shared by many of her friends, was cultivated when at finishing-school in Dresden in 1903. For the group of young Englishwomen there, the opera was the

disappears altogether oneself – everything becomes transferred – vicarious – invested in the other person – one has vicarious amour-propre – & if they in any way failed to come up to scratch – it would be very difficult to bear. You would not have the <u>right</u> to assess yourself low-ly or treat any fallings-short with equanimity or resignation if I loved you[1]. . . .

Diary – Saturday 21 September – Haddo House, Aberdeenshire

My Beloved – I came up from London on Friday night. Coates brought me in some tea in the morning & there I was in real Scotch (Aberdeen scotch) country – harvest just beginning in the fields – & the September sunshine clothing everything with gold. . . .

At Udny the motor – & Weir on the box & a letter in blue pencil from your Father recommending me to sit on the box (bless him) for more air & less draught & indicating Mr. Kidd my fellow passenger a 'helpful' man – the organist I afterwards discovered. We buzzed in at the Haddo lodge & up through these glorious woods – the leaves not yet changing much – the heather still out & the 40,000 rabbits scampering in every direction. I drew up in front of beloved Haddo to find them all typically assembled in front of the house being photographed! in one of those family groups we know so well – Dudley & Haddo in kilts – & your Father too – your Mother, Marjorie, Miss Younger, & two Upward & Onward women Mrs Forbes & Mrs Innes.[2]

I joined the group & we afterwards adjourned to a Viceregal lunch about 2.15. Your Mother & I walked down to the cemetery afterwards – in calm sunlight & sat there silently together for a little. The beech tree in front of the house on that side is so yellow one doesn't know when the sun is on it & when not. The fountain is playing & your Father constantly gives directions to higher or lower it a few inches.

At 5 we all assembled in the Big Hall (neatly dressed – I in my pink pannier) & a teaparty of about 200 of the old people on the estate took place. Macdonald MacKinnon – the house carpenter, the forester – the man who winds the clocks – they were all there – I handed buns & biscuits for some time – & then the entertainment began – consisting of songs interlarded with short speeches by your father culminating in Dudley's

'greatest treat', and they made three visits a week: 'We all became passionate Wagnerites and knew every "motif" in the Ring.'

[1] The conclusion to this letter is missing.

[2] The Upward and Onward Association, officially the Haddo House Association, was an educational and recreational project founded by Lord and Lady Aberdeen, for the benefit of their estate workers. It later spread throughout the Empire.

rendering of 'Fairshon' which he did quite beautifully & without the slightest selfconsciousness – whooping in a way which would have roused Belfast – Lord Pentland arrived about 8.30 & farewell speeches were made – I felt an awful ridge of guilt & floater[1] – Dinner – between your Father & Dudley – then back to the hall & glorious dancing – a quadrille with Keddy – an 8-some with Dudley – & a 4-some with delightful Mr Smith whom I do love. Auld Lang Syne happened about 12 then bed.

Diary – Sunday 22 September – Haddo House, Aberdeenshire

... A glorious service in the chapel in the evening – held by Mr Holden – Dr. Brabner preached a most touching sermon. I have never seen the chapel full before – people were sitting on chairs all the way up the aisle – & crowding outside the door. I sat between Haddo & Miss Younger in a rather tightly packed pew. The singing seemed to come out of everyone's hearts.... After dinner I had a talk with Marjorie who was perfectly splendid in courage & generosity but how bitterly I minded Father having hurt them all so – & how difficult it was to know what to say – how to explain what looked like an act of bare capricious injustice & ingratitude. And your Mother was so sad too when she came in to see me in bed – I longed to be able to have done something – anything to avert it.

Diary – Monday 23 September – Dallas Lodge, Forres

Dudley & I spent the most glorious morning at Gight.[2] He motored me there himself in the new Daimler with Weir inside – out of the little lodge covered with scarlet runners & along by the side of the Ythan....

We talked of the de Veres & your upbringing & then blundered oddly onto a brother of Cécile's who had married an actress who used to be taken out regularly to tea by Willie Desborough![3]

Aren't men mysterious & extraordinary – what would Ettie think? Dudley said à propos of moeurs that you had the purest mind (he didn't

---

[1] Lord Pentland's departure for Madras was indirectly the cause of Violet's embarrassment; see above, p. 301.

[2] Gight Castle is on the River Ythan, about four miles north-west of Haddo.

[3] Cécile Elizabeth Gordon *née* Drummond, who married Dudley Gordon in 1907. William Henry Grenfell (1855–1945), 1st Baron Desborough, 1905; the husband of Ettie Desborough. Former Liberal MP, who represented South Buckinghamshire as a Unionist, 1900–5. Renowned for his exploits as a sportsman, he played cricket for Harrow, rowed for Oxford, climbed the Matterhorn, and swam the pool at the bottom of Niagara Falls.

put it like that) of any man he had ever met – he said 'I try & not laugh at the wrong things but it's sometimes an effort – but Archie never <u>wanted</u> to'.

We drove back – were put down at the Gates & walked through Craigie Wood – & back past the lake & the cemetery. My violets are gone – I must write to MacKinnon about it. After lunch & goodbyes Dudley & I started off & travelled together as far as a place called Kennethmont – wasn't it sweet of him to come so far out of his way.

I got here the same night in easy time for dinner.

Diary – Thursday 3 October – Cloan, Perthshire

My own Darling – Your birthday – & I dedicate this year of my life to you – the only gift that can reach you from me Beloved. God make it worthy.

I left Beaufort at 7.30 this morning – after two wonderfully peaceful & healthy days – I have <u>never</u> felt such air – it made me feel better than months of Penrhôs – & even Dallas could. Laura lives like a lovely plant in this bleak but delightful spot – Simon is full of a restless activity of mind & body which I love.[1] He is most attractive I think – as he has <u>real</u> vitality & initiative & great susceptibility to ideas – which tends perhaps to make him unconcentrated but heightens his interest as a companion. He has his iron in every fire – Army reform – cotton growing in the Sudan – afforestation – peat-schemes – besides immense feudal activities – & militant Die-hardism – I liked him awfully....

Who should I see getting into the next carriage to mine but dear old Currie – I hailed him into mine & we spent a pleasant 3 hours of political gossip rumbling through the lovely country between Inverness & Perth. How I needed you to see it – the heather not quite over yet & the trees just beginning to change – past Moy Kingussie Killiecrankie etc.[2]

The motor met me at Perth & I got to dear little Cloan – perching in its homely site above Auchterarder on the low hill-side just in time for lunch. Elizabeth, General Haldane – whom she calls Aylmer – Haldane & I are the party.[3] I had a long walk with beloved old H. all the afternoon & we

---

[1] Simon Lovat (1871–1933), 14th Baron Lovat; raised and commanded the Lovat Scouts in the Boer War, and originated cotton-planting in the Sudan. A Unionist, he married in 1910 Laura *née* Lister, daughter of the Liberal peer Lord Ribblesdale; Laura was Margot Asquith's niece.

[2] Towns that would be passed on the train travelling from Inverness to Perth.

[3] Elizabeth Sanderson Haldane (1862–1937), social reformer, consulted by the 1909 Royal Commission on the Poor Law. She published a three-volume translation of Hegel's *History of Philosophy*. General J. Aylmer Haldane (1862–1950), distinguished soldier who served in the South African war, and was a military attaché with the Japanese army in the Russo-Japanese war, 1904–5.

ran over every conceivable topic – Politics – Land – the Liberal League –
Insurance (which he is strongly in favour of) Carson – Father & his
young days – the Sydney Webbs' courtship – the Under Secretaries – this
generation compared to the last etc. All this very wheezily while panting
up a steep hill through an undergrowth of bracken & tumbledown trees.
I don't think he looks <u>very</u> well. After tea Gen. Haldane & Pat (Willie's
son) & I went up & fished in a little artificial loch they have made by
damming a stream. We all got into a boat – I made one inexperienced
experimental cast with the rod & immediately hooked a fish! became
quite hysterical with joy tried to heave it into the boat – saw it for one
intoxicating moment glitteringly suspended in the air & – lost it! All the
most scientific & prolonged casting couldn't get us another. The sun set
<u>in</u> the loch divinely – the water became a sheet of orange – & the hills a
wonderfully intense violet. Then the sky grew cold & slate blue & the
moors brown & we walked back to the motor waiting on the road – &
home. Dinner is just over. . . . afterwards Haldane's huge St Bernard, Kaiser,
was brought in onto the hearthrug. I saw dear old Mrs. Haldane in bed –
she is 88 & still marvellously beautiful. I'm afraid she will probably never
get about again. Do the dying go to you? It seems so strange to think of
them in the same breath – I don't know where I think of you as being –
In the <u>sun</u> I think Your own.

Diary – Friday 4 October – Cloan, Perthshire

Beloved – I stayed on here to-day & had another morning's fishing at the
loch with Pat & the General – caught two sardines – sat with beloved old
Mrs Haldane for about half an hour. She spoke to me of my mother – saying
that Father had given a photograph of her to Haldane's old factotum – who
had said. There was never anyone looked like that but her & the Virgin
Mary – I felt strange tears coming at the thought of her nearness to
death – & her great tenderness to earth. She spoke of Haldane's engagement – & his misery – very temperately & forgivingly of Valentine.[1] She
has a big oil picture of him hanging opposite her bed by Fiddes Watt.[2]
After lunch Haldane & I walked for an hour & a half – along the glen &

---

[1] Haldane was briefly engaged in 1890 to Valentine Munro-Ferguson (d. 1897); when she
broke off the engagement, suddenly and irrevocably, he was plunged into a deep despair (see
R. B. Haldane, *An Autobiography* (1929), 117–18).

[2] George Fiddes Watt (1873–1960), Scots portrait painter, whose subjects included many
leading Edwardians, including Haldane, Asquith and Balfour.

up the hill where a glorious wind was blowing. We spoke of Emily Brontë & he recited all her best poems word perfectly from end to end – in a thrilled voice – then I got him onto philosophy & he was most interesting. He told me he had read Hegel's Logic 19 times – & that it was to him what the Bible was to his mother – deeply comforting. The idea of life as the vehicle of eternity is a satisfying one to him. He is so impersonal – he doesn't understand my passionate desire for the integrity & survival of small imperfect individual entities – narrow intense passions. He is the only man I have ever met who seems really at home in the Infinite.

Tea – & a Collins to Lovat written – also a letter of thanks to Tree for engaging Waxworks' chauffeur's sister as a programme seller in his theatre!

Miss Spair – The Auchterarder belle came to dinner dressed up to the nines – also Willie Haldane & his wife.

I go to-morrow – goodnight my dearest & best Yr own

Diary – Saturday 5 October – Kilmaron, East Fife

Dearest & Best – I left Cloan this morning after a most touching last conversation with old Mrs. Haldane.

She said to me – I've always loved you so – it's been 'Love in a Mist' – wasn't it a delicious thing to say. I felt very much moved – & did I'm ashamed to say cry a little – her beautiful old sunken eyes seemed to sink down into the very depths of me & stir everything that was realest. I motored here – in a very slow motor – easily passed by every collie dog – & several flocks of sheep. We came through typical East Fife country – long stretches of stubble & green fields – lowly rising ground with little woods – cold little grey villages – built of sandstone – I got to Kilmaron well before lunch – found Father looking not very well I thought....

After the usual endless champagne lunch to which dear old Sir James Scott came we went off to Ladybank – where we found the delegates assembled in the Masonic Hall. About 200 – & many well known old faces amongst them & on the platform....

Father spoke very well – quite firmly about Ulster I'm thankful to say – & also about land – the long awaited pronouncement – at last – I feel infinitely relieved & am eagerly awaiting the press comments on Monday.[1]

---

[1] At Ladybank on Saturday 5 October, Asquith addressed the annual meeting of his constituency Liberal Association. He made clear the government's determination to enact Home Rule, in the form that it was introduced to the Commons in April 1912: the underlying message was that there would be no special treatment for Ulster. His statement on land reform, however, lacked the same clarity. He denied that there was cabinet division on the issue, but he was unable to convince *The Times*, at least, that there was a meaningful consensus: everyone

Dear old Scott was given a rosebowl of his own design afterwards – to celebrate his golden wedding with Mrs Scott – a little tiny mouse of a woman sitting just behind me.[1] Home – & now dinner is over & a long & rather weary talk afterwards with Lady Low & Lady Lang – the men never came out – & now bed – in this icy room where everything rattles & the blinds are light. Old Sir James is perfectly <u>excellent</u> company & just pulls one thro' meals otherwise the clock does tick off the minutes slower at Kilmaron than anywhere else in the world. All the same I get a kind of washy sentimental pleasure even from its worst aspects – Goodnight my beloved one – I am all Yours

V.A. to Venetia Stanley *Tuesday 15 October*
10 Downing Street, Whitehall,
S.W.

My Darling – Thank you a thousand times for your most generous subscription it is sweet of you darling to give so much & I feel guilty at taking it. You will give less unhesitatingly if ever it's more convenient to you won't you?[2]

As a matter of fact we are profoundly grateful for every halfpenny this year as the camp cost a good deal – & I long for the piano which seems to recede further & further into the distance – & this is the greatest news of all – I attacked Hyde boldly about giving up his dining room to us & he has yielded!! & I am itching to get it all cleanly distempered white & some lovely curtains & a tablecloth put in....

I am in bed to-day with a cold which turned into a chill & which has this saving grace that it may prevent me from going up to Newcastle to-morrow to open a bazaar. By the way did Dorothy Howard tell you how the United Kingdom Alliance imbroglio ended?[3] I ended by writing her a <u>very</u> civil letter offering to go – but stating my Temperance views in a few temperate sentences – which evidently so much alarmed her that she

was agreed on the need to put agricultural land to better use, but the fundamental questions of finance and ownership had been left unanswered.

[1] Sir James Scott married, in 1862, Jeannie *née* Brough.

[2] Venetia was a generous supporter of the Archie Gordon Club, as well as being an active participant, and she gave, annually, ten pounds to Club funds.

[3] Lady Dorothy Howard (1881–1968) was the daughter of Venetia Stanley's aunt, Lady Rosalind Frances Howard (1845–1921), a prominent temperance reformer. The Alliance, formed 'for the Suppression of Traffic in all Intoxicating Liquors', enjoyed its heyday in the late nineteenth century, and by 1912 its influence, even among Liberals, was waning.

wrote back imploring me not to come – as I might put the Alliance in a very false position! My brush with Temperance has left me a confirmed disciple of the Grape.

I am just back from a crowded male Sunday at the Wharf. The nucleus of our party consisted only of Beb – Bongie – Artie & I – but Hughley arrived next morning from Yatterdon where he had been staying with his aunts (of whom he has <u>expectations</u>) & a little later Polos & 'Mun' (another of Cyril's little compères) came over from Oxford to lunch tea & dinner – & by teatime Cyril & Gillespie turned up – so the house teemed & bubbled with baritone voices & smoke & the knock of pipes on the wall & the scrape of nails on the floor – & the clink of whiskies & sodas on the 'grog-tray' & the fall of cards on the table – Hughley was rather 'moody' at being fleeced at auction – & gave vent at dinner to the extraordinary assertion that F.E was a cleverer man than Winston – thereby drawing a hornet's nest about his ears. Life here is running its usual course – the usual lunches are beginning – John Burns, Phillips (American), Bluey, Pamela McKenna & Dudley to-day – & to-morrow Haldane, Lloyd George, Lacy & the two Grahame-Whites.[1] The debate on Thursday was quite fun – Father made one of his very best 'succinct' speeches – with the unanswerable point – why give you time to improve & amend a bill you confessedly wish to destroy....[2]

... I am thinking seriously of taking Italian lessons – do you advise me to? I think it might amuse Father if I did. He poor darling has been suffering from a Job like affliction on the shoulder – <u>Love</u> – & write at once – Yr V

M.B.C. to V.A.   *Monday 21 October*
                                         5 Hyde Park Square, W.

Beloved. I have [not] done much more today than see you across the table at lunch. Did you have a good talk with L-G? You must tell me about it. Your father and Birrell were in very good fettle, in fact it was really one of

[1] Claude Grahame-White married, in 1912, Dorothy *née* Taylor, of New York.

[2] On Thursday 10 October Asquith moved a closure resolution, to set the timetable of the remaining stages of the Home Rule bill. His aim was to prevent the opposition from obstructing the bill with a series of amendments which, he argued, were meant not to improve the bill, but to exhaust the parliamentary time available to it. It was a controversial step, which *The Times* strongly disapproved of, calling his speech 'the pleading of a clever lawyer', and contrasting his 'rhetorical treatment of the subject' to Bonar Law's 'grave reasoning' (11 October).

the best Downing St lunches I have had. I think that LG ought to come very often and always when your Tory friends are there, it is good for them & very entertaining for quiet watchers....

Thank you for arranging with Zellie about my French lessons, we might arrange to walk round St James's Park in opposite directions you with Signor Rossi & I with Z.... My love B.

M.B.C. to V.A.   *Monday 11 November [i]*
10 Downing Street, Whitehall,
S.W.

You will want to know about the defeat of the Government in the House this afternoon.

It was a very clever piece of work by the Tory wirepullers which brought on a division at 4.15 with the result that the govt were beaten by 22 as you will have read in the papers. It is of course regarded as indeed it was, as a snap division & I need hardly say that the Govt have not contemplated resigning. But it is an awkward thing to get over & certainly means the loss of some days' business.[1] B.

M.B.C. to V.A.   *Monday 11 November [ii]*
10 Downing Street, Whitehall,
S.W.

I will tell you a little more about our little breeze this afternoon. I was sitting quietly in my room when the division bell rang. It was not much later than half past four which meant that the question that was being divided upon had not required much discussion. The first inkling of danger was the arrival of Bobby Harcourt to ask that the P.M. should vote as we were rather short of men.[2] He went in & voted & came straight back as if nothing unusual were in the air. But Birrell soon followed in expectation that it would be a very close thing, so I went

---

[1] This defeat, on a financial resolution of the Home Rule bill, was a serious blow to the government's prestige, an indication, according to *The Times*, of the 'moral weakness' of its Irish legislation. It did not, however, necessitate resignation, as it was not in a real sense a vote of confidence: Balfour had made clear the distinction when his government was similarly defeated in 1905, and it would have been difficult for the Unionists to deny the precedent.

[2] Robert Harcourt (1878–1962), Liberal MP for Montrose Burghs, 1908–18.

out to the lobby & heard storms of cheers from the House & knew that
it meant a defeat.

Hobhouse & Verney came hurrying out with the figures & then your
father went back & moved the adjournment of the debate. It was really
very clever of the Tories. They had lulled our men into security all these
weeks by not bringing up their forces & then they sent out a 3 line
whip for 4.15 this afternoon, put up Banbury to move a palpably absurd
amendment on which really nothing of moment could be said & got a
division quickly taken.

Where our mistake was made, & why it was made it is hard to
discover, was in not getting our side to talk until our numbers were
safe. Illingworth's figures of members in the House gave him a majority
of about forty & those of our side to be over 200 & this he apparently
thought was safe but of course the Tories came pouring in at the last
moment. I am very sorry for him poor devil as of course he must bear
the brunt of the blame & it must be hard to bear at the outset of his
career as Chief Whip.[1] You will see the statement of our case which has
been issued to the Press.

Your father of course takes it lightly & is as merry as a grig tonight but
Birrell though still merry enough thinks it more serious. Of course it is
not a case of resignation & no one in the House supposes it so whatever
the Tory papers may say. I heard Walter Long himself say as I passed
through the lobby 'Oh they will recommit & go on with the Bill in three
or four days'. Balfour's Government was beaten certainly twice in the
course of his last Parliament, & no one can consider this as anything but
a defeat on the snappiest of snap divisions.

The amendment today practically negatived a resolution which was
passed on Thursday by a majority of 121. But when all this is said it is a
defeat & a defeat on a very important point of the bill & this cannot be
good for the Government. For technical reasons it is not easy to reverse
it.... The result is that at least it is a great nuisance & will cause a certain
loss of time, which can hardly be spared. It means that the Home Rule Bill
cannot possibly be through before Xmas.

Eleven of the Irish were away & most of the Labour men, also Grey,
Pease & Runciman.

Your father got L.G., Harcourt, Grey, Isaacs & Illingworth to dine with

[1] Percy Holden Illingworth (1869–1915), Liberal MP for Shipley, Yorkshire, 1906–15. A
barrister by training, Illingworth became chief Liberal whip in August 1912, having previously
been a parliamentary private secretary to Augustine Birrell. He recovered from this early
setback. Asquith wrote, on hearing of his death in January 1915, 'He is a great loss to me ...
he had great Yorkshire shrewdness, & was as straight and loyal as any man living' (M. and E.
Brock, *H. H. Asquith: Letters to Venetia Stanley*, 358).

him tonight & had apparently a very amusing dinner. I came in afterwards with Oc & found him playing bridge. He seemed very well in spirits & body I thought.

Bless you always
B.

V.A. to M.B.C.   *Tuesday 12 November*
                                           Vice Regal Lodge, Dublin

Bongie – I have made bold to tell Kerridge to commence work at once on receiving this (VERY moderate) estimate – without consulting my [Club] Treasurer – Was it naughty of me?

I have written to that saint Muntzer to say I will be content with the present foul brown linoleum on the floor – but will let him know about curtains when I come back – as I don't like the bricky colour of enclosed. It would swear with the subtle cherry glow of the rest.

Won't it be glorious – think of the rosy effulgence & the dove-grey walls – like the silver lining of a pigeon's wing? And Judd & Pocock & Martin all reading Francis Thompson & Richard Middleton & Homer & Plato & Heine round the table? & their minds flashing like opal-swords out of their Muntzer scabbard?

I was glad to get your letters full of details – but I cannot yet understand why they didn't talk it out till re-inforcements came up – Illingworth has as you say had an inglorious début. I fear I have missed a thrill by going – & the dinner on Monday must have been most amusing – but it can't be helped. Tell me won't you if there's anything I ought to come back for. Poor little Gertrude Dunn is so unhappy. I do hope I'm a little good to her – Dunn seems to treat her in a most inhuman manner. I mean to speak to him when I get back. Write – this is my 2nd letter Yr V.

M.B.C. to V.A.   *Wednesday 13 November*
                                           5 Hyde Park Square, W.

I think that Margot has already written to you something about today's proceedings. I dictated a message through the telephone which I hope reached you. I could hear you speaking perfectly. You know that Rufus was howled down at 7.30 & the House adjourned for an hour & that on resumption he again could not speak & the House was again adjourned.[1] There is no doubt that it was an organised scheme, the front Opposition Bench led the hunt chiefly Law, Long & Wyndham.[2] AJB left the House at 7.30 & never came back. If you look at Bonar Law's speech you will foresee that he threatened this manoeuvre in the closing sentences. It is supposed that they will do the same thing tomorrow & will not allow questions even, & presumably continue, until they force an election. It has occurred to me that they might instead absent themselves from the House, which would be more difficult to deal with tactically. You will be raging at not being present during this, though for watchers there has not really been much to see.

Five minutes noise & then an adjournment is the sum. I was not in the House on either occasion. I will telegraph tomorrow afternoon what happens, as it will be quickly clear what their line is to be.[3] I wish I could have spoken to you on the telephone.

I need hardly say that I did not go to the Club. Oc & Venetia were there.
B.

[1] In an effort to recover from the defeat in the Commons on Monday the 10th, Asquith proposed a resolution to rescind Sir Frederick Banbury's amendment. The effect of this would be that the Home Rule bill would continue as if nothing had happened, other than the loss of a few days of parliamentary time. To Unionists this was a cynical use of the government's majority, used retrospectively to override the earlier judgement of the House. Because they were powerless in any vote where the government's full majority would be deployed, the Unionists resorted to methods of obstruction, and were successful in forcing the day's proceedings to be adjourned.

[2] George Wyndham (1863–1913), Unionist MP for Dover from 1889; former private secretary to A. J. Balfour and a cabinet minister 1902.

[3] There was a surprisingly good-natured end to this impasse. On Thursday the 14th the Unionist MP Ronald McNeill (1861–1934) rose and made 'a very frank and full apology' for having thrown a book at Winston Churchill during the previous day's stormy proceedings. This created 'an atmosphere of forgiveness' in which a repetition of the uproar would have been difficult, and the speaker took advantage of it to propose a three-day adjournment. When the Commons reconvened on Monday the 18th, Asquith proposed a solution to the problem that was 'more in accordance with the feeling and custom of the House': the offending amendment was not expunged from the record, but was instead superseded by another amendment. That the government had to use a closure motion to pass this, on Tuesday the 19th, is a sign that hostilities had by no means ceased (M.B.C. to V.A., 14 November 1912, Bonham Carter MSS).

V.A. to Hugh Godley   *Saturday 16 November*
Vice Regal Lodge, Dublin

Beloved ὑ[1] – Every hour & instant here has been filled or I would have written – I have thought of you & meant to do so all the time – I have been agonized as you will know at being away through all this – & am starting back to-morrow (Sunday) night so I shall see you almost as soon as you get this.

I can't bear to think that you are being glad over a thing I have minded so terribly but of course you are – & that is one of the cast iron facts that come between us just when we least expect them. Of course if one analyses the circumstances they have no significance whatever – simply a moment of sloppiness on Illingworth's part – during which a nonsensical amendment was moved at a time in which they were in a majority in the House – but the name it is called 'Gov. defeat on Home Rule Bill' has an ugly sound to the uninitiated – & I can't can't forgive Illingworth & the Whips for having let it happen or the Speaker for his extraordinary unfairness – in seeming publicly to slightly disapprove of Father's rescinding motion – when he had seen & unconditionally approved of it when privately consulted by Father.

T. W. Russell who was here tells me that the Irish Whip O'Brien & that big Labour man Ward (with the grey hat) each severally & separately warned Illingworth that we were going to be beaten.[2]

Nothing would have been easier than for our men to talk it out till reinforcements came up – but Illingworth only replied we had a majority of 40 in the House & were perfectly all right. I blame him bitterly – anyone can be caught napping but no one has an excuse for disregarding such warnings. Poor man I expect he has suffered terribly. All this is between us two – please don't repeat.

I am just in from a ride (my first) in Phoenix Park – I went this morning to such a divine exhibition of Russell ['Æ'] pictures – Hugh you would have adored them & only 5£ each but all already sold – Wonderful bogpools – & visionary Mothers & babies on the fringe of the foam – & wild dream dances by children by the sea – & on Thursday night I went to the Irish

---

[1] Violet sometimes addressed Hugh (and also referred to him in diaries) by a Greek character that English speakers would pronounce in exactly the same way as they would his name. The Greek letter upsilon (υ), with the 'rough breathing' sign ̔, indicating an *h* before the word, produces the combination ὑ, pronounced 'hyū'. This play with Greek reflects her interest in the subject, which both Hugh and his father encouraged.

[2] Sir Thomas Wallace Russell (1841–1920), Bt, Liberal MP for North Tyrone, 1911–18. Patrick O'Brien (1853–1917), Irish Parliamentary party MP for Kilkenny City, 1895–1917, and a party whip. John Ward (1866–1934), Labour MP for Stoke-on-Trent, 1906–18 (Independent Labour from December 1910).

plays – & it was yourself I was wanting to see them alongside of me – & me all alone in the stalls with the ADCs & no *v̇* at all. They <u>were</u> wonderful – almost more than ever before I thought in their atmosphere & with their own understanding audience. Pot of Broth was given ... & The Rising of the Moon by Lady Gregory.[1] – – – –

It is after dinner now as I was carried off to a Hospital by Ly Aberdeen – & I come back to find my poor little letter has missed the post. We have had a dinnerparty – the Macdonnells & others & your friend Maurice Headlam – who sent his love to you.[2]

Social entertainments here are very heavy – impregnated with duty & almost impossible to leaven.

Lady Aberdeen's life really <u>stupefies</u> one with wonder & admiration – one thankless (but infinitely fruitful) task undertaken after another out of sheer love of <u>humanity</u>. She has really saved life on a large scale in Ireland I think. She makes me feel so criminally idle & frothy & superfluous – instead of the heavy moralist I am with you! Have you missed me a little in London this week? I minded leaving you at Alderley as I had the feeling of in-tuneness which precedes a delicious time together. Come in on Monday bless you – Yr V.

V.A. to Edwin Montagu   *Wednesday 27 November*
                                10 Downing Street, Whitehall,
                                                    S.W.

Dear Tante – I was <u>thrilled</u> at receiving your long & lavish telegram yesterday[3] – & this isn't the letter it asked for only a little St. John the Baptist to say it's coming. I suppose you think it's abominable of me not to have written – but you know you haven't sent me <u>one</u> word about the orange skies you're under – & the blazing rajahs on white elephants – & pouncing panthers – & scarlet creepers – & heavy smells & apes – I will write you a long <u>long</u> letter next week – the last 2 days have been impossible. I am taking Italian lessons – & have a Russian procession to equip for a Fancy dress ball next Wed – & am starting a library for the Club – & 4 new Women's Lib. Associations in Fife – & my life feels like an obstacle race against time. The Snap division was <u>heart</u>breaking – but we

---

[1] W. B. Yeats, *The Pot of Broth* (1904); Augusta, Lady Gregory, *The Rising of the Moon* (1910).

[2] Maurice Francis Headlam (1873–1956), deputy paymaster for Ireland, 1912–20. Headlam was private secretary to the chancellor of the exchequer, 1903–5. His brother Geoffrey ('Tuppy') had been a close friend of Hugh's at Oxford.

[3] In the winter of 1912–13 Edwin Montagu, then parliamentary under-secretary at the India Office, made an official visit to the subcontinent.

had a glorious meeting at Nottingham on Friday I have seldom heard Father better – Lansbury's defeat a joy too.[1] I miss you <u>really</u> nearly every day – Bless you yrs Violet

'Votes for Women': the 1912 Franchise and Registration bill

In June 1912 the government introduced its Franchise and Registration bill, the object of which was to extend the vote to all adult males in Great Britain. The old property-based franchise would be swept away, increasing the electorate by around 2,000,000 to 7,500,000. The bill, framed at a time of intense activity on the part of the supporters of women's suffrage, both militant and non-militant, applied only to men. Asquith, though, pledged that the government would accept any amendment in favour of women's suffrage which had the support of the House. He also promised a free vote on this. Four amendments were tabled for consideration at the committee stage of the bill, in January 1913. The most radical proposed straightforward adult suffrage: the vote to everyone over the age of twenty-one. Around 10,500,000 women would be enfranchised, putting them in a majority in the electorate. The most conservative, the 'conciliation' amendment, proposed to enfranchise propertied women who already qualified as local government electors, around 1,000,000. This was the least palatable to Liberals. On 24 January, however, the speaker signalled his ruling that if any of the amendments were adopted the character of the bill would be so altered as to require it to be withdrawn. In the light of this the cabinet decided not to proceed with the bill in any form. Contrary to the belief of some suffragettes, Asquith was genuinely surprised by the speaker's decision, which seemed to contradict precedents set in 1867 and 1884. That he was also greatly relieved by the ruling gives an indication of how close parliament was to enacting some form of women's suffrage by 1913.[2]

[1] George Lansbury (1859–1940), Labour MP for Bow and Bromley, Tower Hamlets, 1910–12. Lansbury took the courageous step of resigning his seat in order to recontest it solely on the issue of votes for women. In the by-election of 26 November 1912 he stood as an Independent Labour candidate, and was defeated in a straight fight by the Unionist Reginald Blair (4,042 against 3,291).

[2] See HHA to Venetia Stanley, 27 January 1913: 'The Speaker's coup d'état has bowled over the Women for this Session: a great relief – but I dare say the militants will now take again to the war-path' (M. and E. Brock (eds), *H. H. Asquith: Letters to Venetia Stanley*, 27).

V.A. to Edwin Montagu   *Sunday 15 December*
10 Downing Street, Whitehall,
S.W.

Dear Tante – At last I'm going to write you a real letter. Nothing but being
in bed with what's called a 'bronchial chill' (my 3rd this winter) could
possibly have cleared me space to – for I am living in a perfect obstacle
race against time in view of my impending departure to <u>America</u> next
Thursday! Did you know I was going? Lady Aberdeen passionately wanted
me to & as you know I am in favour of experiments – so long as they are
not very long ones – so I decided to go. It is the last place in the world I
have <u>ever</u> had the faintest desire to see – but as the Professor says to me –
'the danger is that you'll <u>like</u> it'. We are going to stay with the Bryces in
Washington[1] – also at New York for a time – & I suppose we shall be back
in time for the Franchise Bill at the end of January.

I must confess to you that I am feeling some considerable anxiety about
<u>it</u> – (the F. Bill) – it looks to me as if one or other of those beastly women's
amendments was bound to be carried – unless Lulu can organize some
new form of outrage between now & then. The amendments are being
put in this order 1) Philip Snowden's – Adult Suffrage 2) Norwegian –
which is what Ll.G. believes in 3) Conciliation Bill.[2] The first two are pretty
safe to be defeated I should think as the Tories are bound to oppose them
(unless they don't! – so as to put us in a hole) – the 3rd Conciliation –
though the worst for us of the whole lot, our keen suffrage men might
vote for rather than get nothing – & trusting to an extending amendment
in the future. Quite apart from resignations (which I gather from Father
aren't contemplated) lots of our Anti-Suffragists will vote against the
Reform Bill if women are included – & tho' Father is sanguine I shouldn't
be a bit surprised if Lulu <u>did</u> resign on it – & then who's to succeed him? –
with the united Tory & anti suffrage Liberal vote against him, who could
get in? This is all very diffuse – but it is so difficult to compress everything
I've got to say to you into a respectable compass. The Session has been
quietish – except for the breeze over the snap-division. . . . Poor Illingworth

---

[1] James Bryce (1838–1922), Liberal MP for Tower Hamlets, 1880–5; for South Aberdeen,
1885–1907. An eminent jurist and diplomat, British ambassador in Washington, 1907–13.
Bryce married, in 1889, Elizabeth *née* Ashton.

[2] In fact the adult suffrage amendment was proposed by Arthur Henderson, like Snowden
a Labour member. The 'Norwegian' suffrage that Violet refers to was the amendment proposed
by the Liberal member W. H. Dickinson; it would have enfranchised women who were
householders, or the wives of householders. Women in Norway were enfranchised in advance
of most other countries, and could also stand for parliament: the first woman was elected to
the Storthing in 1911, eight years ahead of Lady Astor, the first woman to sit in the House of
Commons.

was diddled – & he & every other Whip are changed, reborn men since. Illingworth himself looks as if he'd undergone some terrific religious upheaval – he has a transfigured – Catherine of Siena[1] – recipient of the stigmata, look – Geoffrey too has become wonderfully 'softened & changed' – he is less like the <u>brass</u> part of an orchestra & more like what's called the 'woodwind' – I have begun to make friends with him for the first time in my life. I was in Ireland during all the howling & book-throwing – which was just as well as it might have brought a whole new tribe of 'Arnolds' into being.[2]

I got back in time to hear Father re-establish the whole thing – the only loss being 14 precious days of Parliamentary time.... Except for this we have had calm – Home Rule Bill in Committee & Mr. Solicitor winning daily praise from the Times – rather at the expense of Mr. Attorney.[3] Welsh Dis. oozing very slowly & stickily through – (Eczie is a bad lubricator for a really unpopular measure – whatever his other virtues).[4] I am told young Gladstone made a really <u>very</u> good speech against it yesterday – but can't believe it of him! poor adenoid-ridden young man.

Father's Guildhall speech was one of the best things that has happened – it has added <u>cubits</u> to his European reputation – & was probably one of the most far-reaching in effect of all his utterances. Both Conferences impending here are wonderful tributes to our Foreign policy[5] – & the Gov.'s prestige – I can't help always loving it when a little respectable international κυδος comes our traitor way! The Canadian Dreadnoughts are rather one in the eye for the Ex Canadian Scotchman aren't they?[6]

[1] Catherine of Siena (1347–80), canonized by the Roman Catholic church; she had a reputation for severe asceticism.

[2] Violet refers to the stormy proceedings in the Commons on Wednesday 13 November (see above, pp. 341–2): by 'Arnolds' she means the unacceptable face of the Unionist party, an indication that her friendship with Arnold Ward had cooled considerably in the partisan atmosphere of the times.

[3] The solicitor-general was Sir John Simon, and the attorney-general Sir Rufus Isaacs; in October 1913 the former succeeded the latter as attorney-general.

[4] As home secretary, Reginald McKenna ('Eczie') had the responsibility of introducing the government's bill for disestablishment of the Welsh church before a hostile House of Commons, in which opposition could be expected from among the government's own supporters, as well as from the Unionists.

[5] In December 1912 London was the setting for two international conferences, one a peace conference to settle the first Balkan War (the London Conference), and the other a meeting of the ambassadors of Germany, Austria, Italy, France, Russia and Britain (the Conference of Ambassadors).

[6] In response to a request from the British government in 1912, the Canadian premier Robert Borden agreed that Canada would meet the cost of three Dreadnought battleships, to be used by the Royal Navy in the Mediterranean. His Naval Aid bill was introduced to the Canadian parliament in December 1912, but met with resistance from the Liberal opposition,

We had a <u>marvellous</u> meeting at Nottingham. Father in his very best form – caracoling & curvetting & tossing his tail like a fresh hunter – in the opening passages of what the Daily Chronicle calls 'badinage'. We stayed with Sir Jesse Boot! who <u>kept</u> us like tame rabbits behind wire-netting for fear of Suffragettes – wire-netting all over the motor, all outside our bedroom windows & even over the <u>bath</u>! so they evidently expected them to get to close quarters.[1]

I wonder if you have been very worried by all this silly Eye Witness agitation going on about the silver.[2] I do hope you haven't though I have longed for you to be here, now & then, to put a little of the personal indignation which <u>shrivels</u> such accusations, into your answers at question time – & wipe out Gwynne & his rabble who are only out for self advertisement & party capital.[3]

I <u>seriously</u> think you should sue the Eye Witness (or New Witness as it's now called) on your return. For one thing I should like to see it smashed – for another I do believe there is a section of the public – not perhaps a very important but a very large one – in whose eyes no one is ever cleared of anything except by a libel-action – look at the King who is now considered a sober monogamist – instead of a bigamical Knurd![4] – I am only voicing my own view when I say this – I have heard

which argued that Canada should control, and even build, its own navy. This undermined the assumptions of the British Unionist leader Bonar Law, the 'Ex Canadian Scotchman', about imperial unity. The Canadian parliament finally rejected Borden's plan on 30 May 1913.

[1] Sir Jesse Boot (1850–1931), businessman and philanthropist, founder of the world's largest retail chemists, based in Nottingham. He was a member of the National Liberal Club.

[2] In 1912 the *Eye Witness*, a newspaper founded by Hilaire Belloc and Cecil Chesterton the previous year (it later changed its name to *New Witness*), attacked prominent Liberals, and members of the Anglo-Jewish community, for their alleged dishonesty in financial dealings involving the government. As well as giving publicity to the 'Marconi affair' (see below, pp. 381–2), the journal made disclosures concerning the purchase of £5 million of silver bullion on behalf of the India Office by the foreign exchange bankers Samuel Montagu & Co. The bank, which had links to the government, had made its purchases secretly between March and September in order to avoid the operation of speculators in the market. These circumstances gave rise to allegations of impropriety. Edwin Montagu, then a junior minister at the India Office, was the cousin of Sir Stuart Samuel, a Liberal MP and a partner in the bank in question. As such he was an obvious target for the anti-semitic invective of the *Eye Witness*. Though Samuel's conduct was later subjected to the scrutiny of a parliamentary select committee, the charges against Montagu were quickly dismissed. J. M. Keynes's view was that those involved in the 'little Marconi' affair had acted with patriotic intent, but that their conduct was open to misinterpretation (see Colin Holmes, *Anti-Semitism in British Society, 1876–1939*, 77–8).

[3] Rupert Sackville Gwynne (1873–1924), Unionist MP for the Southern Division of Sussex, 1910–24.

[4] In February 1911 E. F. Mylius was convicted of a criminal libel against the King, whom he had accused of bigamy in an article published in the republican paper *Liberator*. Mylius alleged

no one else <u>suggest</u> it as a necessary or an advisable course. I think one's instinct is to disregard these things as too low for any notice – I know Father & Simon were both opposed to Rufus taking action in the summer – but I think personally he would have done better to have done so – & silenced things, however absurd – once & for all[1]. . . .

Raymond has been up to Derby – & made an earnest platform speech containing passages like 'I am a <u>passionate</u> supporter of the Government's draining policy of 1861' he was cheered to the echo – unanimously adopted & came back with a real platform-glow on him.

How I wish we were going to start off to Sicily in 3 weeks – & that you were at this moment taking the necessary preliminary step of finding out from the Automobile Association what the roads are like in Morocco! The Sydney Buxtons are going there instead.[2] Do you think we might manage it or something like it in this barbarously early Easter? Do let's try.

I have seen darling White twice. Once he came to the Wharf for a Sunday (just before the Snap Division) & once he took me out shopping bless him. He had 'heard from you that morning' both times. How <u>vilely</u> you have behaved in never writing to me – & how wonderful it is of me to send you this dreary & meticulous record of current events. Goodbye I hope you are having a <u>blazing</u>, <u>gorgeous</u>, <u>resplendent</u>, <u>dazzling</u> time of pomp, & wilds & sun & scent & colour

yrs Violet

---

that the King had disowned his first wife, the daughter of a British admiral, when he became heir to the throne, following the death of his elder brother in 1892. Such stories had circulated since 1893, and Sir Rufus Isaacs, the attorney-general in 1911, was hesitant about prosecuting Mylius, fearing that the court case would give the rumours greater currency. The King, however, was determined to proceed, and in the event won widespread public sympathy from the trial. Mylius was convicted and sentenced to twelve months' imprisonment: see Kenneth Rose, *King George V*, 82–7. For the separate allegation that the King was a 'knurd' see above, p. 210, n. 3.

[1] Violet refers to the allegations, which appeared in the *Eye Witness* and elsewhere, that Isaacs was involved in financial misdealing arising from the government's contract with the British Marconi Company.

[2] Sydney Buxton married, in 1896, Mildred *née* Smith.

TEN

The United States and Canada
1912–1913

In mid-December 1912 the New York Times *heralded the arrival in the United States, later that month, of 'Miss Violet Asquith, the daughter of the Premier . . . chaperoned by Lady Aberdeen'. The official purpose of their trip was to visit the British ambassador in Washington, James Bryce. Lady Aberdeen, though, was also engaged in raising funds with which to fight tuberculosis in Ireland, a cause that Violet supported. Their movements in America, and later Canada, were closely followed by the press. Lady Aberdeen, keen to take every opportunity to promote her philanthropic work, welcomed this attention. Violet, though, did not. She 'absolutely refused' to answer the questions put to her by the* Washington Post, *and on one occasion coquettishly declined to pose for a picture, giving its correspondent a single quote, 'snap me if you can'. This behaviour did little to diminish the newspaper's interest in her, and may even have given it the 'angle' that it was seeking: Violet was credited with 'the characteristic modesty usually attributed to the English girl'. It was a wildly inaccurate depiction.*

V.A. to M.B.C.   **Saturday 28 December 1912**
                                        S.S. Celtic, bound for New York

It's just a week & a day since I left you – but I feel as if I were well on in another life – as if you & Father & D. St. & Micky & Hyde & Ramsden were what one remembers of a dream when one wakes up in the morning – & the only solid realities – the only <u>existing</u> things were this ship & Lady Aberdeen & Mr. Norton. Mr. Norton I know better than I have ever known anyone before – I talk to him on an average 8 hours a-day & we have covered every field of human discussion – books, people, politics, religion, objects in life – ethical quandaries – with autobiographical shafts of light (which take some time) to explain our present position & attitude of mind on all these questions. The days have flowed in a wonderfully smooth, even succession – it has been roughish most of the way – & once or twice very rough indeed – but the action of the ship is too gigantic – its lurches & dips & pitches & rolls [are] on too big a scale to upset my ant-equilibrium – I have been a little sad at your not sending me a telegram of <u>any kind</u> either to Liverpool – Queenstown or on Xmas Day – but otherwise it has been far more tolerable & (almost pleasant) than I could ever have imagined it being cut off from <u>all</u> news of any kind – except such as is supplied by the Ocean Times a ridiculous publication which is brought to one's bedroom every morning – containing the photograph of an actress & the court-circular of last July. The attempted assassination of Hardinge is the best gobbet it has produced yet.[1]

Shall I tell you the plot of my day? I have breakfast in bed – after what seems to me for the first time in my life a sufficient night. For breakfast I eat grape-fruit – then I get up & have a heavenly hot salt sticky bath, dress & go on deck where I take a walk with Mr. Norton – of 6 miles or so! There are masses of decks – but I like the top one best where one has nothing but sky overhead – & a fine Dauber aperçu of the Atlantic[2] – I shan't say anything about the sea – because it is such a bore – but it has been very wonderful on this journey – leaping all round one like a moun-tain-range gone mad – sinking below one to infinite depths – & then rising like a glistening wall of steel to break with a crash against the side of the ship – throwing fountains of foam up into the wind. We have had a moon most of the time at nights – & the stars have been marvellously large & bright – but very little sun & cold – wet – 'dirty' weather most of the time. At 1 lunch happens – in a large stuffyish saloon – & then I talk to Lady Aberdeen a little in our sitting room which she rarely leaves. She sleeps a good deal – reads books on playgrounds – & Medical Officers Bluebooks – & sends out hundreds of Xmas letters etc. to people in Canada & every sort of outlandish spot. Then I come up on deck again & am tightly furled like a caterpillar in a cocoon of rugs – furcoats etc – in a long chair with Dizzy's Life (just finished).[3] Mr. Norton reads Nietzsche beside me in another chair – & at 4 when we're both beginning to feel a little chilly & stiff a ministering steward comes round with two hot tea-cups in which little discs of lemon float – & we crunch biscuits comfortingly in the dark.

At 4.30 I go down & have an official tea with Ly A. (who doesn't dream of my first one – I have a thrilling sense of duplicity & double-life-leading

[1] Charles Hardinge (1858–1944), appointed viceroy of India, and raised to the peerage, 1910. Seriously wounded in a bomb attack during the state entry to Delhi, 1912.

[2] The central character in John Masefield's narrative poem 'Dauber' is an artist, who goes to sea in order to realize his ambition of painting it well: 'It's not been done, the sea, not yet been done, / From the inside, by one who really knows.' His artistic efforts and his seamanship are ridiculed, and he is given the nickname 'dauber' by his shipmates.

[3] Probably W. F. Monypenny's *The Life of Benjamin Disraeli*, the second volume of which appeared in 1912.

as I embark on my second) & at 6 or so I re-appear & we walk again lashed
by an icy wind (which has several times thrown me <u>down</u> & bruised me
rather!) then bath, dress, dinner at 7 – accompanied by deafening band –
after which long talk with Lady A. & short talk with N. upstairs in the
library – then bed.

On Xmas morning the stewards sang carols at 3 & I couldn't sleep
properly all night I was so thrilled with excitement in anticipation of your
present. To my amazement & delight I heard a stocking crackling at the
foot of my bed! – never was anything less expected & hailed with more
delight! Ly A. had done one for me & I undid it with feverish haste &
excitement....

A gale has just got up again – about the 5ᵗʰ really bad one since we
started – we are already two days late (due now on Sunday – instead of to-
day) & the whole ship is rocking & creaking – every port-hole shut –
people staggering knurdly about & waves dashing up against the windows
in a way you would have thought irresistible. One came into our sitting
room yesterday & nearly flooded us out.

I've spent all this morning going over the ship with the Captain. The
third-class passengers are marvellously well & humanely housed & fed –
such an odd rabble of Poles & Finns in astrakhan caps – & Yiddish women
with babies in shawls & handkerchiefs over their heads.[1] We then went to
the engineroom & I walked down a steep iron staircase – the heat getting
more impossible to bear every moment – huge brutal implacable machines
roaring & grinding & crashing round me on every side – down to the very
bottom the chief engineer yelling in my ear – then to the stoke-holes –
where fierce, resentful-looking slaves, décolleté, black with coal-dust, hurl
shovelfuls of fuel into hungry glaring mouths – whose burning breath
makes one's head swim. The atmosphere was miraculously cool considering – quite a different thing to the <u>hell</u> I went down into on the Red Sea.
I am going up into the crows' nest to-morrow if only it's fine – up a pitch-
dark shaft not much bigger than the trunk of a tree with a ladder inside.

How I hope I shall find a letter from you <u>directly</u> I get there – you <u>are</u>
naughty to have neglected me so about telegrams. When you get this you
will be back at work in a rather deserted Downing St – M. & the children
at Mürren – I shall have to Aubrey some of my very sparse news to Father
whom I shall now write to so don't anticipate me – by telling him any.[2] I

[1] A transatlantic passage at this time would have cost around six pounds for third class, or
'steerage'; from nine pounds for second class; and upwards of fifteen pounds for first class.
This at a time when a 'working-man in receipt of good weekly wages' in London earned
around thirty shillings. See: *Cornhill Magazine*, 1901; Walter B. Paton, *Canada Handbook*
(HMSO, 1912).

[2] On receipt of Violet's letter of 2 January, in which there was considerably more news,
Asquith wrote to Margot: 'I had a gigantic letter from Violet describing her New York

can't help rather longing to be just going to arrive on some blazing tropical shore – & find your brother with a milk-white camel & a bird of paradise waiting to meet me. It is stiflingly airless with all the portholes shut – I am gasping like a goldfish.

Bless you – goodbye – Yr V.

I will add a word when we get into New York harbour – before posting.

Sat. night
We are within sight of the first light ship – which means 190 miles off America only! I'm told to post this by sea-post is quicker than in New York – so no more – Goodnight – I feel very far away. So long for the Club boys' addresses but alas haven't got them – V.

V.A. to H.H.A.   ***Thursday 2 January 1913***
                                                       Train to Washington

Jan.2nd 1913   America
My Darling Father – I simply don't know where to begin to give you any idea of this extraordinary place – stupendous size, lightning speed, deafening noise, miraculous mechanical ingenuity, no creative imagination, no sense of the absurd, no touch, no 'pile', no bloom, marvellous vitality energy & horse-power, feverish competitiveness, a grotesque standard of values, above all an extraordinary atmosphere of hope – which (however illusory) seems to communicate itself on landing to everyone, down to the most pinched & threadbare & unpotential-looking Pole, Finn & Yidd who disembarks from the Steerage & stands cooped in the Immigration pen – waiting to be passed by the authorities. There is a busy, fussy 'Excelsior' spirit everywhere[1] – but there is no idealism about the ascent, no mystery about its end – it is the spirit of the man embarking in a lift with the perfectly defined intention of reaching the 9th floor – not of the mountaineer setting forth to scale shrouded heights.

We arrived on a glittering morning of sun & frost – it was misty but one cld. just see the land covered with snow & the tops of the sky-scrapers shooting up into heaven. From the moment the pilot-boat arrived (with Drs. etc. on board for quarantine) my life became perfect hell – for a crowd of the most howling cads – the 'interviewers' of various newspapers assailed me & molested me without ceasing till we arrived – discharging batteries

experiences: very graphic & even brilliant: she had 2 long talks with Roosevelt, & fell to some degree under his charm, without losing sense of his limitations' (14 January 1913, Bonham Carter MSS).

[1] Violet alludes to Henry Longfellow's poem *Excelsior*, published in 1841, which figuratively depicts a man's ascent through life: he struggles upwards to the constant repetition of the idealistic motto 'Excelsior', which is heard echoing in the air even after his death, when he has reached the summit of his ambition.

of cameras & Kodaks – & asking fatuous questions about my political opinions etc. & effectually stymying the statue of Liberty (which I missed!) Realizing that by absolute silence I could inflict the deadliest wound of all upon them – I swallowed down (with difficulty) some pungent periods of invective & remained quite dumb – a really fine performance under the circumstances.

Lady A. however to my amazement received them with the utmost benevolence & suavity – 'chatted' to them for several minutes – was docilely photographed whenever asked etc.

However in spite of my reticence the papers are full of the most flowery headings – (one of them 'Serpent's Tongue Furore' wld. please Nash!) & descriptions of how during a terrible storm at sea I went down & alleviated those in the Steerage & the Stoke Hole with fruit! – how I am a passionate Suffragist restrained from action by your domestic tyranny & bigoted opposition etc. etc. etc. I have never imagined anything at all like New York – the houses rise on each side of one like huge cliffs – honeycombed with windows – the streets seem like cracks between them – & one crawls along like an insect in the depths of the crack with such a narrow strip of sky so far above – that one feels at any moment the walls might meet – & crush one to death. The poor live in vast tenements with iron stairs outside in case of fire – they look such grim, heartless impersonal houses – I would rather starve in any streets than New York.

The rich quarters are quite different & rather splendid in a way. Fifth Avenue – the Grand Canal of N.Y. is a marvellous place – miles of palaces some of them rather beautiful – great blocks of marble & stone – with glorious cornices jutting into the clearest – cleanest – most radiant air you ever breathed. They are the symbols of a hard crude commercial success – drifting to smug opulence – & are very accurately suggestive of their inmates & owners.

Our hosts the Phippses (Mrs. Freddy Guest's parents) have by far the best, aesthetically, in 5th Avenue – I think.[1] All white marble within & without, with priceless tapestries & some fine pictures. He belongs to the small bug-like Carnegie type of millionaire to look at – & is evidently on the verge of premature gaga-dom. The first night when he was showing me the house I asked him who the picture over the mantelpiece was by. He rang the bell & said to the butler: 'Davidson – go & ask MacKenzie' (a Scotch stenographer) 'who that picture's by' – After an interval the butler re-appeared: 'MacKenzie says it's a Lawrence, Sir' – 'Oh' (trustfully to me)

---

[1] Henry Phipps (1839–1930), manufacturer and philanthropist. Phipps had a particular interest in the prevention and treatment of tuberculosis. He married, in 1872, Anne *née* Shaffer. Their daughter Amy married, in 1905, Captain Frederick ('Freddie') Guest (1875–1937), Churchill's private secretary, and treasurer of the royal household, 1912–15.

'it's a Lawrence' – Isn't it amazing? I expressed a wish to see the papers – & find out what had happened during my 10 days at sea – but he insisted that MacKenzie should read them aloud to me instead – choosing out the grain & discarding the chaff – 'it is so tiring to read the papers to oneself' – so I reclined effetely in a chair while MacKenzie, whom I cldn't resist winking at, was ordered to read 'anything which was likely to interest me personally which had happened in the last 10 days'. Most of the headings where things like this 'Bridal pair in Ice-box' 'Baby eats Gripe Tablets' 'Thief returns sick fowl' 'Woman with mended spinal cord spends joyful New Year's Day' 'Guggenheim explains 5th marriage' – not a <u>word</u> about anything political or international. I spent a hectic 4 days rushing over gigantic buildings – teeming with human beings – sitting through longish lunches & dinners – getting in & out of taxis, telephone-rooms & lifts.

My most amusing expedition was with dear old Mr. Choate[1] who took me down to Wall Street where I saw the Stock Exchange – in full swing an extraordinary babel of voices – & hurrying men whose incomes were every moment in the balance – then the Bankers Trust C° a marvellous marble office where Pierpont Morgan works.[2] Business <u>is</u> the religion of most Americans – & they enshrine it as we should our Gods or our Kings – their churches are very ordinary & mediocre – but their offices are <u>inspired</u> really tenderly conceived & lavishly executed.

This one was like a Roman Emperor's bath. We buzzed up to the very top (39 storeys) in a lightning lift – & had the most extraordinary view from the top over the roofs & steeples of New York – all the smoke is snow-white – (as they are obliged to burn a kind of hard fuel –) & it curls up in cotton-wool corkscrews & diffuses no haze – & we saw the whole town like a child's game of bricks & far below in the crevices the buses crawling like small beetles.

Mr. Choate also took me to a very wonderful Insurance C° – the 2nd highest building in the world! an insured person dies every 50 seconds (I must get rid of some of these statistics on you – they are rained on me all day long). I saw 2000 women employees having their lunch who all rose & cheered – which was very disconcerting. They are given a ball-room where they dance for an hour in the middle of the day – not I am assured from humane motives – but in order to make them more efficient workers – & a better business investment.

I sat next to Roosevelt at two meals yesterday – a very interesting men's lunch – given by the editors of a kind of Spectator called the 'Outlook' – & dinner at a man called Collier's. I must confess that having started with

---

[1] Joseph Hodges Choate (1832–1917), distinguished Republican lawyer and diplomat.

[2] John Pierpont Morgan (1837–1913), banker who was the leading force in American finance in his day; he died in March 1913.

every orthodox prejudice against him [Roosevelt] – I was completely disarmed & feel a real affection for him now. He has got 'l'élan vital' in a greater degree than any man I have ever met – & though there is nothing rare or recondite about his mind – & his opinions are mostly underlined truisms I can't help liking his continuous bubble & splutter & flow – & real spontaneousness & sincerity. He is like a <u>hot</u> water spring. I had most amusing conversation with him – in spite of his assertiveness he listens to what is said, understands & answers it – a very rare quality among lions. About electioneering he said : 'one's desire to win should not be measured by the difference which separates one's opinions from those of one's opponents – or by the superiority of the arguments of either side?' – which I'm sure was a cri de coeur! He <u>adores</u> E. Grey – loathes Winston & Kitchener. About Winston he said : 'I hate it when a man obliges <u>me</u> to behave like a swine – to prevent <u>him</u> from behaving like one. I had to <u>ask</u> him to go & say goodbye to his hostess – & to take his cigar out of his mouth when he did so'.[1]

We talked about beauty – & everyone cited an example – Dss of Sutherland etc.... Roosevelt became dumb for the first time & refused to cite an instance though he admitted he had one in mind. After dinner he whispered 'I was thinking of Mrs. Roosevelt in her wedding-dress'. Wasn't it pathetic – especially as I hear she's a fright. We talked about the Panama Canal – he professed to be in favour of arbitration – which surprised me. He said 'That was a rotten treaty – I made it so I ought to know' – & 'it's a bore to have to keep a foolish promise'![2] All this was surprisingly ingenuous – I tried to elicit a manifesto of his new Progressive party – & asked how he intended to adjust things between the dynamiters & the millionaires – the disparities of circumstance here are a perfect caricature. He spoke of Income Taxes, Death Duties, Minimum Wage Boards, the Tool-user becoming the Tool-owner – quite an orthodox Liberal election address which Illingworth might pass any day.[3] He is almost as impatient of conversational rivalry as John Burns – tilts his chair & clears his throat

[1] Remembering in later life Roosevelt's antipathy for Churchill, Violet reflected, 'they were too alike'.

[2] In December 1912 Britain made protests to the American government over its policy of allowing its nationals free use of the Panama Canal, when tolls were exacted on the vessels of other countries. The Hay-Pauncefote Treaty of 1901, between Britain and the United States, ensured that the canal would be open to 'all nations': the question arose whether its other terms were inclusive or exclusive of America. A British proposal that the matter be put to international arbitration was opposed in the American senate.

[3] Having lost the contest for the Republican nomination in 1912, Roosevelt founded the Progressive Party to support an independent campaign to become president, adopting a set of radical proposals for social reform that were similar to measures enacted by the Liberal government in Britain, 1906–11.

noisily the whole time. His own delivery is not unlike a blend between Currie & Edmund Gwenn.[1]

I had lunch with Ava Astor one day – she had a lot of dull, saltless, désoeuvré, overfed, overdressed overexcited people – I suspect the 400 of being a drearyish lot.[2] Mrs. Benjamin Guinness gave a pseudo-Bohemian party on New Year's night where I met Harry Wilson to my intense surprise – & Ethel Barrymore! grown quite fat & unrecognizable – not a trace of beauty left.[3]

Barnie & I spent a morning together in the Elevated Railway – commonly known as 'the El' – it is far the best way of seeing New York – buzzing along in mid-air – at the height of the 3rd floor. I also had tea with Borden – sandwiched in between my two Roosevelt meals – & was able to thank him for the Dreadnoughts![4] He sent you all kinds of messages.

I write to you from the train – on my way to Washington. Never believe what anyone tells you about the goodness of American trains – they are asphyxiatingly hot – double windows not a chink open – & full of hot air (which poisons existence here – just as iced water redeems it). Every stop & start feels like a collision in violence & jerkiness & shoots one from one's seat – one is all herded together in Pullmans & has no privacy or comfort. The Pennsylvania Station on the other hand which we started from – is one of the [most] beautiful things I've ever seen. Built on the model of the baths of Caracalla. I hope someone is sending me news – I gather the Drs. have crumpled up & the peace negotiations are going well[5] – & Bonar Law seems to have given us another tremendous lift by saying Ulster wld

---

[1] Edmund Gwenn (1877–1959), English actor who played leading roles in Shaw, Galsworthy, Ibsen, Granville-Barker, etc.

[2] Ava Astor, first wife of John Jacob Astor, financier, who had died in 1912. The '400' [also 'Four Hundred'] is a term given to the social élite of an American city or locality, and notably to New York's exclusive set.

[3] Bridget Guinness *née* Frances (d. 1931), married Benjamin Seymour Guinness, a prominent American businessman, in 1902. Mathew Richard Henry ('Harry') Wilson (1875–1958), succeeded to his father's baronetcy in 1914; the husband of Violet's step-cousin, Barbara *née* Lister. Ethel Barrymore (1879–1959), American-born actress who enjoyed considerable success on the London stage.

[4] Sir Robert Borden (1854–1937), prime minister of Canada, 1911–20, and leader of the Canadian Conservative party, 1901–20. For his support for a British request that Canada provide three Dreadnoughts as a contribution to imperial defence, see above, p. 347, n. 6.

[5] Medical treatment under the 1911 National Insurance Act was due to begin on 15 January 1913. Throughout 1912 the government faced resistance from the British Medical Association, over the remuneration to be paid to doctors for treating patients under the scheme. This resistance effectively ended in the New Year, when it was clear that most doctors favoured the plan. The 'peace negotiations' refers to the London Conference that convened in December 1912, to resolve the first Balkan War between the Balkan League and Turkey, October–December 1912.

prefer to be governed by a foreign country than submit to Home Rule!![1] If it were anyone else one must think it was a misprint – but he's quite equal to it. Also saying that if affirmed by another General Election he would not counsel active resistance – narrows down the whole question to the issue at the last Election. And Carson asking for separate treatment instead of the dropping of the whole iniquitous bill is a step to the good.[2]

Love to you Dearest & Best.

I wonder if you'll ever have time to read this endless letter – there is so much to tell you – you must read a page a day till I get back.

> Your
>
> V.

Roosevelt pretends his bullet is still in him. He said 'I got more bullets than ballots this time' – & roared with pleasure at this little verbal play of his own.[3]

Diary – Thursday 2 January – Washington

My Darling – We left New York yesterday embarking from the glorious Pennsylvania Station – I could say my prayers there it's so beautiful. I rather pique myself on having likened it at first sight to a Roman Emperor's bath! I now hear it was modelled on the Baths of Caracalla! I think it is twice as impressive as St. Peter's at Rome. The train was a terrible disappointment to me – one is herded all together in a large frowsty pen of a Pullman with one's Handgepäck on the top of one & underneath one – & an atmosphere of hot air which made one giddy. Every time the train starts or stops a shock at least as violent as an ordinary collision occurs.

---

[1] Ulster's loyalty to the union between Britain and Ireland, the very basis of Unionist opposition to Home Rule, seemed to be compromised by Bonar Law's admission. It was not, however, the first occasion on which a prominent Unionist had made such a statement: in January 1911 Captain James Craig spoke of a feeling in Ulster that rule by the Kaiser would be preferable to rule by the Irish nationalists. Bonar Law's remark was, however, astonishing in that it came from the official leader of the Unionist party (see M. and E. Brock (eds), *H. H. Asquith: Letters to Venetia Stanley*, 36–8; also chapter 18 of A. T. Q. Stewart, *The Ulster Crisis*, 'The Kaiser's Ulster Friends').

[2] On 1 January 1913 Sir Edward Carson formally moved in the House of Commons that Ulster be excluded from the terms of the government's Home Rule bill. Prior to this the Unionists had opposed Home Rule outright. Carson's amendment, which was soundly rejected, could be construed as a battle won by the government. Such optimism was, however, misplaced: by abandoning the rest of Ireland to Home Rule, the Unionists had effected a tactical withdrawal to a shorter, and much stronger, line of defence around Ulster.

[3] Roosevelt had been shot by a fanatic while campaigning in Milwaukee in October 1912. He recovered sufficiently to continue with the campaign.

I tried hard to write to Father – & your Father – & we had lunch – & at last after many jerks & jars & stops & restarts we got into Washington station.

I immediately felt the most wonderful atmosphere of peace & serenity invading & enveloping my jarred & tingling New York nerves – a little grey town rather like Cheltenham – or Bath lay before me – I could see the tops of the houses – I could hear myself speak – the quiet streets went out all round me like the rays of the sun – & opposite was the Capitol – a lovely stone dome not unlike the Pantheon – with pillars all round. We drove up to the Embassy feeling faint premonitory shyness – & in at the porch. How like an Embassy it looked – very like the Russian one at home with a big central stair dividing off halfway up into two bifurcations. Mrs Bryce was waiting for us – brisk, benevolent, business like – dressed in Sunday coloured grey charmeuse – Kissing me firmly – & sitting us down to a rather tepid & inadequate tea. After a time Mr. Bryce came in – a dear old boy – very gentle & easy to talk to – I went on expecting him (I don't know why) to behave like Lord Sheffield & being relieved that he didn't[1] – I was surprised to find he hadn't seen the text of the H.R. or Insurance Bills – & when I spoke to him of Kiderlen Waechter's death said: was he considered friendly to us or not?[2] We were taken to our bedrooms – & a small dinner party took place that night.

I sat next to a peppery old boy called Adams – & a rather nice attaché Kerr – Muriel White was there with Scherr Thoss – looking most well & prosperous – really happy – & most like herself.[3]

Diary – Friday 3 January – Washington

A gusty morning, hurricanes of wind – trees blown up & some rain – I went to a most amusing & terrifying function – a luncheon party given in my honour by the Attorney General & his wife.[4] I came in to a

[1] Lyulph Stanley (1839–1925), 4th Baron Stanley of Alderley and 4th Baron Sheffield, the father of Venetia Stanley. Bongie wrote to Violet in May 1912 surprised that Raymond had got on so well with 'Old S', 'who one would think would bore him almost to silence'.

[2] The third Home Rule bill was introduced in April 1912, and while it is surprising that Bryce had not read this, it is even more remarkable that he had not seen the National Insurance bill, which was enacted in December 1911. Alfred von Kiderlen-Wächter (1852–1912), the German foreign secretary, had died in Stuttgart on 30 December. He had been responsible for a forward foreign policy that was aimed at breaking Britain's *Entente* with France.

[3] Muriel White was the daughter of the 'Souls' Harry and Daisy White; she married a German landowner, Count Scherr-Thoss.

[4] George Woodward Wickersham (1858–1936), lawyer; attorney-general under President Taft; he married, 1883, Mildred *née* Wendell.

drawing room in which all the electric lights were <u>blazing</u> in spite of bright daylight – to find 16 absolute strangers whom I was bewilderedly introduced to – including Lord Eustace Percy far the most romantic Early Victorian looking young man I've ever seen.[1] We sat down to a <u>very</u> long meal – I had the Attorney General a <u>delightful</u> man on my left & a Mexican with a brown velvet voice & eyes on my right. We eat dozens of complicated courses & afterwards I had rather nice easy talk with them – they all seemed amazingly glad to see me & nice – all talked to me the whole time at once – all rose when I did & sat down when I did as if I had been a Connaught – & none went away till I did at 3.5 – back to the Embassy where shortly after 4 a huge tea-party & crush began. I have never experienced anything like it – one was fallen upon by group after group of affectionate Harpies yelling a chorus of what a pleasure & honour it was to see one – how long had one come for, how long was one staying – what sort of a crossing did I have – what did I think of New York – what did I think of Washington – & just as I had painfully surmounted all these preliminary fences & there seemed an opening for some real interchange – a new group fell upon one & one had to go through it all over again – I was so giddy with new faces & voices towards the end of the time that if I'd been introduced to Father or seen my own reflection in the glass I shouldn't have recognized either.

At last at 6 they all went – & I had a short rest before dinner & the White House at 7.30. I wore my new pale yellow dress & my diamond necklace in my hair – & sat between the Naval Attaché & a Mr. MacVeagh who is something in the Cabinet.[2] He took me on afterwards in his brougham to the White House. It was quite dark when we drove up but to my delight I saw by the carriage lamps as we waited in the queue that it <u>is</u> snowily, spotlessly white – not a mere phrase or façon de parler – & enclosed in a nice quiet yew hedgy garden.

We disembarked & went in finding the rest of our party waiting in the hall – were spirited up by a lift & introduced into a crowded room full of Ambassadors, swords, spurs, uniforms & orders which corresponds to the Entrée at home – I was introduced to several – a nice big Dutchman called Lowdon, a delightful & most witty little Frenchman Jusserand, the Russian with his cherry coloured ribbon like Benckendorff

---

[1] Eustace Sutherland Percy (1887–1958), seventh son of the 7th Duke of Northumberland. In the diplomatic service from 1909; attached to the British embassy in Washington, 1910–14.

[2] Isaac Wayne MacVeagh (1833–1917), lawyer, diplomat and political reformer. He had close connections with President Taft, but Violet was mistaken in thinking him a member of the cabinet.

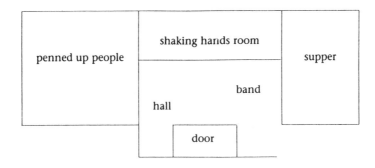

at home – Jusserand went first then Mr. & Mrs Bryce, Lady Aberdeen & myself – & shook hands with Mr & Mrs Taft & then with about 6 Princess Christians holding bouquets – the wives of the Cabinet ministers. They all stood in a row just inside the door – Taft is a distinctly unmagnetic personality – big & rather fat with a pince nez & white hair – no aura of greatness or distinction.[1] Mrs Taft also what is called 'stout' – brown haired & eyed & slightly florid-faced suffering I am told from 'aphasia'.

We all stood in a dense crush behind them – with 6 people a second being introduced to one – & being torn away from each in turn just as one began to like them – I talked to Stimson the war-minister & Judge Holmes[2] – & Harry White & Ld Eustace & another Justice & dozens of others – the band was playing deafeningly outside & my larynx wasn't up to it – also all Americans <u>always</u> talk at the top of their voices & all at once, just out of high spirits – Ld Eustace & I & a young American Rhodes scholar who used to know Cys struggled through to the supper room & eat a little & then got home by about 11.15. The White House is a jolly place – a little small for present conditions but simple & dignified.

---

[1] William Howard Taft (1857–1930), twenty-seventh president of the United States, 1909–13. Taft was then in the last weeks of his presidency, having lost the 1912 contest to the Democrat Woodrow Wilson. (The president-elect did not move into the White House until after his inauguration, then at the beginning of March.) Taft married, in 1886, Helen *née* Herron. His lack of aura may have been due to the fact that at the official presidential New Year's Day levée, two days before, he had shaken hands with 7,052 guests (*Washington Post*, 2 January 1913).

[2] Frederic Jesup Stimson (1855–1943), lawyer, diplomat, author and Democrat politician; Violet was wrong in thinking him the minister of war. Oliver Wendell Holmes (1841–1935), jurist; he served with the Massachusetts Volunteers during the Civil War, and was wounded three times, retiring with the rank of lieutenant-colonel. He made many visits to England, and there formed a friendship with James Bryce.

Diary – Saturday 4 January – Washington

John Barrett – director general of the Pan-American Union – that bald noisy friend of Lady Henry's called for us on a radiant morning & took us over his building[1] – a rather ingenious combination of the classical & Mexican – (with a lovely Patio in the hall) & then he & I went up to the very top of the Washington monument – a rather jolly simple obelisk-shaped column of immense height. We got a most glorious view all down the Potomac river – & over the town. Its resemblance to Cheltenham ceases directly one gets into the public building part of the town. The Treasury is a very fine building near the White House – & Pennsylvania Avenue is one of the most beautiful streets I have ever seen with the Capitol standing at the curve....

Thrilling dinner next to Mr. Senator Root – I cast a few flies over him to which he didn't rise very readily then turned to Harry White with whom I had a high old gossip – & returned.[2] We then had a really interesting talk. Root was a great friend of Roosevelt's but split with him over his propaganda that a popular vote should overrule the decision of the supreme court. We also spoke of Chesterton Shaw & Wells – of whom he is a great admirer especially of Tono Bungay & Marriage.[3] He says the Labrador bit is quite accurate. I had a most wonderful after-dinner time first with Judge Holmes who is fascinating – & so young & goodlooking I cannot believe he is 70 – then with him & Senator Bacon who joined us.[4] They had a most excellent North & South talk – both having been in action in the Civil War in opposing armies – Bacon was at Bull Run – & Bull's Bluff & graphically described how they had routed the north on every occasion – I finally asked ingenuously : 'Then how was it Mr. Senator you didn't win in the end?' – 'How? why because we were so exhausted with licking the Yankees'.

I thought this a very good reason & probably a true one! very much what the Bulgarians may be feeling now.[5] Holmes was wounded 3 times &

---

[1] John Barrett (1866–1938), diplomat, publicist and head of the Pan American Union, an institute dedicated to fostering good relations among the republics of the Americas.

[2] Elihu Root (1845–1937), Republican senator for New York. Root presided over the Republican convention of 1912, which resulted in Taft, and not Roosevelt, being adopted as the presidential candidate. He had once been a political ally of both men, but this resulted in a lasting break with Roosevelt.

[3] H. G. Wells, *Tono Bungay* (1909); *Marriage* (1912).

[4] Augustus Octavius Bacon (1839–1914), Georgia senator who served as an adjutant in the 9th Georgia Regiment during the Civil War.

[5] Between October and December 1912 the Balkan League, comprising Bulgaria, Serbia, Greece and Montenegro, successfully waged war against Turkey, conquering virtually all of the Ottoman possessions in Europe. The Bulgarian army led the drive south to Constantinople,

exposed for two days on the battlefield on one occasion – the present Attorney-General was a kind of powder-monkey under him. I asked him if the negroes are happy now – Bacon gave a gloomy account & Holmes said 'Well you can't expect a man who's just been given moral responsibility to be gay'. We were joined by Jusserand & Lodge & had the greatest fun – I must say Senators & Judges are my two favourite genuses of American citizen.[1]

Diary – Sunday 5 January – Washington

Church with Mrs. Bryce in the morning, an Episcopalian service this time very different to the farce we attended on our arrival in New York. Though my mind revolts from Church doctrines – the efficacy of christening, apostolic succession, etc. etc. so that in conviction I suppose I am much nearer Presbyterianism – I do confess to infinitely preferring the church service – with all the lovely formulae I know. We walked home & proceeded out to lunch with the Henry Whites. They had an enormous party & I enjoyed myself immensely – I met Mr. Underwood who is one of the many people of whom one is told that they were nearly elected President[2] – he is as a matter of fact the leader of the Democrats in the H. of Representatives & the only person I have so far met who undertook to tell me & asserted he knew the exact difference between the Democrats & the Progressives. However he didn't have time to of course! Lincoln's son was there – an unremarkable looking man with a short beard – & a man called Willert who is Times correspondent & was at Balliol – he is married to a sister of the wicked Baronet's – Flo Simpson whom we used to hear about.[3] I sat next to Pinchot – the same old Pinchot I was so reluctantly driven over to visit at Sir Horace Plunkett's. I liked him infinitely better – in fact very much this time. He is extremely good looking in a rather knight-like Gerald Balfourian way[4] – & a real idealist I think – with every orthodox Liberal tenet firmly ingrained – a passionate Rooseveltian. On my other

but it was the threat of Russian intervention, and not exhaustion, that prevented them from taking the city.

[1] Henry Cabot Lodge (1850–1924), Republican senator for Massachusetts; he had specialist knowledge of international relations.

[2] Oscar Wilder Underwood (1862–1929), Alabama senator, and leader of the Democrats in the Senate, 1911–15; beaten by Woodrow Wilson for the Democrat nomination in 1912.

[3] Arthur Willert (b. 1882), joined *The Times* on leaving Balliol, 1905, and was correspondent in Washington, 1910; married, 1908, Florence, sister of Sir James Walter Simpson.

[4] Violet first met Gifford Pinchot in Ireland in April 1910: see above, p. 205. Gerald William Balfour (1853–1945), Unionist politician, was the younger brother of A. J. Balfour.

side was Butler Ames a most re-actionary Republican with the amount of brains & dialectical skill usually allotted to people of this way of thinking.[1]

We had a very good à trois each putting their side of the case – Pinchot scoring hands down. (It has given me a slight shock to learn since that he is supposed to have suborned his former chief Ballinger's private secretary in order to expose him – for what I suppose he imagined was the public weal.[2] The method doesn't seem to me to be justified by any end.) I think I have more or less mastered the political position now – but it is a very complicated one – & I'm afraid rather at the mercy of expediency....

V.A. to H.H.A.   *Monday 6 January*
                               British Embassy, Washington

My Darling Father.

I am having a strange & wonderful time here – & am being treated like a mixture between an Envoy Plenipotentiary & a Music-Hall star of the first water – so that I reap a combination of the advantages that were accorded to Haldane on his Mission to Berlin – & those which are enjoyed by Miss Gaby Deslys on a tour in the provinces.[3]

I have really never known what it was to inspire interest or affection before – nor indeed guessed what the words 'love' or 'kindness' meant – & I look forward with a shudder to the chilly obscurity which will close round me again on my return home! ...

Seriously it is being very funny here & very amusing. The atmosphere of the place is an intense relief after New York – a little grey dignified

[1] Butler Ames (1871–1954), Republican congressman from Massachusetts, 1903–13.

[2] Pinchot accused Richard Achilles Ballinger (1858–1922), secretary of the interior, 1909–11, of abetting the fraudulent claims to Alaskan coal lands of a Guggenheim–J. P. Morgan syndicate. President Taft upheld his secretary, and Pinchot was forced to resign from the Forestry Department, but this conflict between big business and conservation split Taft's administration, and contributed to deteriorating relations between the president and his predecessor, Roosevelt.

[3] Gaby Deslys (1884–1920), a star of the Georgian music-hall. Asquith wrote to Margot of Violet's 'most vivid' description of her stay in Washington: 'She has had the time of her life, and been treated with the same mixture of curiosity and rather snobbish deference & real hospitality which the Americans always exhibit to foreign notorieties. Her descriptions are quite first rate' (17 January 1913; Bonham Carter MSS).

town – like Cheltenham or Bath – where one can see the tops of the houses – & hear oneself speak – inhabited by the politicians, the Judges, Senators, diplomats & Congressmen instead of the vapid plutocrats & crass leery business-men of New York.

Mrs. Bryce is a brisk benevolent woman permanently dressed in grey satin & discharging her functions <u>very</u> efficiently & with intense official gusto. He is a <u>darling</u> – & for a man so chock-full of information conveys it to one in a wonderfully palatable form. One is constantly arrested by the thought 'how differently Lord Sheffield would tell me this' – there is all the difference in their methods of procedure that exists between those of a nurse first stimulating & then satisfying the appetite of a rather apathetic baby – & a gaoler pumping food down the nostrils of an unwilling Suffragette. Social amenities of a sort were almost unintermittent – & began with a large luncheon-party given in my honour by the Attorney-General – to which I went quite alone without Lady Aberdeen or the Bryces. Though it was broad daylight on a sparkling day every electric light & gas-jet was blazing – & I was very much embarrassed & disconcerted to notice that everyone got up & sat down when I did – & that no one could go away before I did!! as if I'd been some stuffy Colonial Governor's wife. However they were all perfectly delightful to me & so uncannily amusable & appreciative that I began to think I must be someone else.

I got home about 4 – to find myself in the midst of a dense afternoon drum at the Embassy. Here I felt like a lonely specimen of some unfamiliar fauna, cast adrift in a jungleful of apes – friendly, welcoming but <u>intensely</u> curious. They rushed round me in dozens shook me by the hand – plucked at my clothes – examined & scrutinized me till I felt like apologizing for my disappointing normality – shot volleys of questions at me – always at least 6 people at a time – (people here always <u>all</u> talk to one at once & <u>all</u> at the tops of their voices) – 'Miss Asquith – <u>proud</u> to meet you – I'm Mrs. Cornelius J. Dimmock – & this is my daughter – my son is the owner of the biggest automatic potato-peeling plants in all America – it's way down Texas way' etc – 'have you been in our country before? & <u>what</u> do you think of it?' etc etc. etc – always the same routine of questions & just as one had got through them & was about to establish the conversation on a more satisfactory basis one was snatched away into another vortex & had to begin all over again. Intercourse is very noisy – & very staccato here – people don't want any interchange of thought or even of words – they just like rubbing up against one another in a crowded room & making a noise....

I had a full day yesterday – beginning with a visit to the Supreme Court which sits in the Old Senate Chamber. I saw the Bench come in in State & hear a few cases – & then went on to the Senate where a sleepy inattentive handful of Senators dozed & droned – then on to the House of Representatives. You have <u>never</u> <u>seen</u> such a place – it's like a vast – disorderly class-room – everyone sits at a desk facing the Speaker's Chair, indescribable babel & confusion prevails – from time to time the Speaker – a hoarse, futile man with a wooden hammer gives a yell like a muffin-man to which no one pays the slightest attention. Several members seemed to me to be on their feet at once – they were not making the slightest effort to be heard by the rest of the House but were yelling with their hands before their mouths at individual reporters or occupants of the gallery – which is open & runs all round. The Speaker seemed to be mumbling something the whole time – but whatever it was it was wholly disregarded – as were the terrific blows he dealt to his desk with his hammer. I was told that he broke several hammers at each sitting – I've <u>never</u> seen such a place!!

We had lunch at rather a wonderful place called the Congressional Library – & afterwards Mr. Bryce & I went out for a 5 mile walk in a lovely gorge just out of Washington called the Rock Creek Park. We had most easy, fluid & delightful talk about books & people & politics at home. He is pathetically out of touch & I <u>think</u> (not from anything he said) feels faintly neglected poor little thing. He had had no copy of either the H.R or Insurance Bill sent him – had the very foggiest ideas of their provisions, asked if Kiderlen-Waechter's death was considered a blow to English interests, had heard nothing about the Anti-Semitic agitation, didn't know Hobhouse was in the Cabinet, or that you had been howled down in the House on the Parliament Bill, or anything about the Cabinet position on the Suffrage – or the amendments to the Reform Bill.[1] He is terribly anxious about the Suffrage position now I have luridly depicted it to him! – I saw a certain amount of Muriel White – who was there with Scherr-Thoss & two babies! – & also of Cys's little friend Davies who is out there for the Times – poor little exotic scholar – I found him 'in tears amid the alien corn' amongst these raw, underdone Philistines.[2] I entertained the entire crew of the Natal at tea at the Embassy – the Captain is very anxious I should go back with them – as a fit substitute for Whitelaw Reid's coffin I suppose![3] We go to Philadelphia to-morrow then <u>possibly</u> to Canada for 3

[1] These were all major contemporary political events: the *Eye Witness* agitation against prominent Jews over the Marconi affair was launched in 1912; Charles Hobhouse entered the cabinet as chancellor of the duchy of Lancaster in October 1911; Asquith had been denied a hearing in the Commons on 24 July 1911; the three feminist amendments to the government's franchise bill were to be considered in January 1913.

[2] The quotation is from Keats's 'Ode to a Nightingale'.

[3] Hon. Whitelaw Reid (1837–1912), proprietor and editor of the *New York Tribune*, and American ambassador to Britain from 1905. Reid died in London on 15 December 1912, and his body was carried home to America on board the HMS *Natal*.

days. Love to you beloved father – all my fun here comes from being your belonging – & lovingest possession V.

Diary – Wednesday 8 January – Philadelphia

My last day in Washington was a terrible rush – beginning with a visit to a coloured school – I had nice talks with dear little chocolate faced boys & longed for them to be in the Club – then on to the Capitol. . . .

We came on here the next day at 8.30 – arrived in a thick white mist & pouring rain. Dr. MacKenzie met us at the railway station & there was the usual discharge of cameras & general importunities of reporters to cope with. We drove up to the MacKenzies' house which lay in the kind of Courtfield Road district[1] – found a large luncheon party waiting – I sat between the Mayor a thick German with a guttural voice & a man called Mallory with whom I had a particularly good talk about Wells & every sort of English writer. He was really very good & understanding & rather profound about the H.G.W. aperçu of life – his passion for efficiency etc. the appeal made to him by a cork lino floor! his obtuseness about the finer emotions etc. After lunch I went out with the Mayor's wife, Mrs. MacKenzie & an amusing old boy called Dr. White. He took me first to the Carpenters Hall – a little old building – spoilt inside by painting & doing up, where the first Continental Congress was held in 1774 which decided on resistance.

We then went to the real old Independence Hall – as it is now called – it was the State House long before Independence came on the tapis. I was more moved & really thrilled by it than anything I have yet seen in America – I tried to analyse the ingredients of the strange emotion it gave me & came to the conclusion it must be partly because it was the very first old thing I have seen since I came to America. A lovely old Georgian building – in dark red brick – somehow redolent of Chelsea – & lime-trees & the river – with a clock tower rising at one end – & a little court behind. Steps lead one up into a high hall – with a polished floor – old oil-paintings hanging on the walls & all the dust & dignity of the Adams period. A big carved chair with a worn velvet seat stands on a dais at the end of it – roped off from the rest of the room – in front of it an old writing table & inkstand.

This is where the declaration of Independence was signed – I felt all the national glamour & romance of America – for the very first time when I saw this – & the Liberty bell – cast in Whitechapel – standing outside in a

---

[1] Courtfield Road, in London, is in the well-to-do district of South Kensington, where there are large town houses.

case – which first rang out the proclamation of Liberty to all America – & coupled with this a grudging blame of the bungling blundering statesmanship without which it might still have been as English & as loyal [and] as much ours as Canada is to this day.

We went upstairs to some jolly old galleries with polished floors & pictures – then up to the top of the clocktower where we looked down into the square where the declaration was first read.

I went rather tiredly but not boredly over the whole Curtis building – the biggest publishing firm in America. Three thousand 3 hundred women work there – & there were wonderful rest rooms & music rooms – hospital (where the nurse boasted to me she'd got 'the neatest-cutest new <u>nausea-basin!</u>') into all the board-rooms, show rooms, class-rooms etc. The taste was painstaking – no trouble or money had been spared – but it didn't seem to me to have <u>quite</u> come off somehow. Like everything in America it was too deliberate – there was nothing inspired or accidental – a striving after the objectively <u>correct</u> without any guiding inner sense of it. The panelled rooms & tapestry chairs & marble passages had all been taught not guessed.

The provisions for the comfort of the employees were – as always – wonderfully superior to ours in intelligence. Girls have to go on working in the classes & passing exams so as to keep their brains up to a good general standard – instead of allowing them to atrophy as a whole – & only preserving & cultivating the one highly specialized bump which their business brings into play.

Home & to rest – then a small dinner party at which I sat next to a <u>delightful</u> old man called Mr. Cadwalader with a nice explorer called Byron Gordon with the longest <u>waxed</u> moustache I have ever seen.[1] We had a piper & bouquets of heather & ivy with Forlina Sequatur on them – a delightful thought. Afterwards I talked about sculpture to a delightful old boy called Dana.[2]

Diary – Thursday 9 January – Train to New York

My Darling – We left Philadelphia an hour ago & I must write & tell thee about yesterday – I stayed in bed all the morning & then lunched with the Cadwaladers. Electric light in full glare as usual – I sat next to a

---

[1] Byron Gordon (1870–1927), lecturer in anthropology and museum director at the University of Pennsylvania; chief of the Harvard University expedition to Central America, 1894–1900.

[2] *Forlina Sequatur* is the Aberdeen motto, meaning 'Let fortune follow'. Charles Edmund Dana (1843–1914), art critic and lecturer at the University of Pennsylvania, 1904–14.

man – with whom I unexpectedly had the same kind of slum-outburst I
sometimes have with Hugh – I can never tell when it's coming! – &
discovered to my amusement that he was the Secretary of the Philadelphia
Charity Organization Society!...[1] Back to a large tea-drum – most people
in evening dress with hats – then more rest – & our dinner.

We arrived at the Hôtel & were ushered into a room full of men most
of whom I was told were of Irish extraction but none of whom betrayed
it by an inflection except perhaps our host – a papal Marquis.... After
dinner your Mother made the most excellent speech putting the thing
quite perfectly – I couldn't have changed a word. She spoke for almost an
hour & the most marvellous response followed – everyone rising & offering
everything they could give with the most extraordinary directness spontaneousness & lavishness. I have never seen such open handed &
ungrudging generosity – none of the reluctance, grumpiness & self consciousness which most people display when their pocket is attacked for
however near their heart a cause – 'How much do you want' was the note
they all struck – & your M. then sent round a little schedule of needs &
demands. Several really excellent speeches of different kinds were made
... & I expect a rich harvest from it.

We went on (though it was then about 15 to 7) to MacKenzie's studio &
there was what I had been rather dreading – his bust of you.

It did strike me as very bad I'm afraid – I cannot bear anything but the
most perfect – & this seemed so painful & wrong. It got a little better as
one looked at it & of course it must be impossibly difficult.

A strange thing happened that when I was just going away without
really having hardly seen a look of You – I caught sight of the profile
shadow thrown on the wall & was startled by its extraordinary likeness to
you. It made me almost look round to see where you were – & I couldn't
bear it when the lights were turned out – & we had to go. We got back at
15 to 3 – & went to bed & have a stiff day before us to-day.

Diary – Friday 10 January – New York

My Dear Love – We are back here again with the old Phippses – his wits
have gone utterly to bits since I saw him last – he is now quite gaga – &
almost repellently so at times poor old boy. His sickly amiability is the
note I can least bear – I could bear a vicious strain! or anything that gave
a little 'tang'. We had a full day yesterday – a very boring lunch at the

[1] What Violet regarded as Hugh Godley's apathy towards social issues occasionally elicited
from her angry protestations of the need for social reform; see below, pp. 386–7.

Colony Club with speeches[1] – followed by the most heavenly exhibition of dancing by 1800 children in the East Side – mostly little Polish Jewesses – most beautifully done – with wonderful sense of rhythm. One of them had real genius. They did Russian & Swedish dances – & lovely musical romps – I long to introduce it to Hoxton. . . .

To-day I have been too tired to do anything beyond rest with an unread Nation on my knee. Henry Wilson came in to see me after lunch – he is a real character part but I can't help loving him. He said of Barbara – 'God I am frightened of that woman'[2] – & 'There's no iniquity I haven't committed in this bally town!' – He has been gambling like fun but luckily winning.

Jewett brought Compton Mackenzie the author of Carnival to tea – rather a remarkable looking young man but suffering tortures from sciatica. . . .[3]

V.A. to M.B.C.   *Saturday 11 January*
                                              1063 Fifth Street, New York

One word to say I have at last heard from you – & now got 3 letters. This one of mine will I fear miss every mail but it is to say that instead of sailing for home to-day I am starting in half an hour for Canada! George Moore[4] has arranged (from California!) to have a private car provided for me – so I shall travel in great comfort – & my route is to arrive at Montreal to-morrow morning – spend Sunday there – then go on to Ottawa the next night – spend two days perhaps there – then to Toronto for the inside of a day to see Niagara & back here Thursday morning – sailing home by a North German Lloyd called Kaiser Wilhelm on Tuesday 21st – I believe its due at Plymouth on 27th. The only thing that will break my heart is if I miss the Suffrage debate.[5] Please – please struggle to have it postponed for me & keep me every word in the papers about it if I shld. miss it – I wish

---

[1] A prominent Manhattan ladies' club.

[2] 'Scatters' Wilson refers here to his wife, Barbara: see above, p. 357, n. 3.

[3] (Edward Morgan) Compton MacKenzie (1883–1972), author. Compton MacKenzie's reputation was established with *Carnival*, published in 1912, and was enhanced by *Sinister Street*, published in two volumes, 1913–14.

[4] George Gordon Moore, an American millionaire who was friendly with the Asquiths.

[5] Violet and Lady Aberdeen were originally due to leave for England on 11 January 1913, but they delayed their departure in order to visit Canada, where Lord Aberdeen had been governor-general. They eventually left on board the *Kaiser Wilhelm II* on Tuesday 21 January, arriving in England a week later. By this time it was known that the suffrage debate, which Violet feared that she would miss, would not be taking place: see above, p. 345.

I'd asked you to wire me the date out – I feel it's madness to risk missing it even for Canada – but perhaps it would be silly to come home for one afternoon – even of such vital & crucial moment. Pray God Lulu dishes them. One reason for our postponement is that Lady A. has become a little enmeshed – another that every good ship running between here & England has been taken off. The Lusitania broke down – then the Coronia was taken off – & the only possible thing to have gone by this next week was a Red Star called the Zealand which we thought sounded rather bad. The Minnewaska (our original plan which sailed to-day) carried cattle & was very smelly we were warned!

I got back here from Philadelphia on Thursday – <u>dog-tired</u>. We have had a pretty hard time between sights & people & the very fact of everyone being so kind & longing to talk to one took a good deal of electricity out of one. One was never allowed to lie fallow for one instant. When I got to Philadelphia after the most <u>glorious</u> 5 days at Washington I had to sit down immediately to a large lunch party & then be taken all over the town by the Mayor. Independence Hall (where the Declaration of Independence was signed) the biggest printing-establishment in America etc – till I really nearly <u>dropped</u> – I <u>had</u> to spend the next morning in bed & then every paper had huge headlines Miss Asquith RESTS – Miss A. overtired etc – it really is too impossible when the time one gets up is published. One is rather caught up & whirled round on a wheel of plans. I came back here Thursday & went to the most <u>wonderful</u> melodrama with Vincent [Astor] called 'Within the Law' – quite marvellous I nearly screamed aloud. Last night I dined with Bridget Guinness & the Troubetzkoys (she is Amélie Rives who wrote Virginia of Virginia) & Mr. Harry Higgins & went to another – <u>very</u> bad one.[1]

New York makes me feel more over-tired, over-excited, unstrung & homesick than any place I've ever been in – I feel as if I'd got the whole thickness of the world between me & everyone I love. Though my life is hourly padded with fun & comfort by friendly generous people I have never felt such desolateness of heart in my life. The hugeness & richness & hardness of everything – untempered by any saving <u>individual</u> grace simply kills me. I could cry at almost any moment of the day – & I do so long for someone who would understand it.

Perhaps I shall see Norton next week who will. I have had such divine letters from him, glittering with subtle, restrained – literary dew-drops – I should like you to have been here once just to realize this place's atmos-

---

[1] Prince Pierre Troubetskoy, a Russian portrait painter, emigrated to the United States and married, in 1896, the American author Amélie Rives (1863–1945), who had lived for some time in England; Violet probably first met her at the home of Lord and Lady Battersea. *Virginia of Virginia* was published in 1888.

phere. Apart from one's soul aching like a tooth – (I have never been so acutely aware of mine in my life) it is physically so over-exciting that I wouldn't give the <u>Heifer</u> 6 months sanity here. One wakes up early in the morning – however tired one is – restless & tingling all over with a quite causeless excitement – longing to get up & do something – no matter what. Bed is not a rest but a kind of electric cage on which one twitches & tosses & dreams strange American dreams – with no-one one knows in them. This reads like an overtired letter – but it is the calm objective truth – Barnie whom I saw to-day was in just the same condition. Just off – please give Father all my news – & love – I will write to him from Canada – Bless you – Yr V.

Diary – Sunday 12 January – Canada

… Barnie came to lunch which was a comfort & we walked together all the afternoon in Central Park; she was almost as miserable as me poor little thing & has an infinitely better right to be. Then after a last meal with those two poor old Phippses – whom it is heart-breaking to think of – sitting there rambling & wandering & maundering on together in their lovely marble shell – like two <u>very</u> old oysters dying of pearl – (he described his Sargent picture to-day as 'a good dividend') we went off & embarked in a carriage which George Moore has had specially reserved for me & after a terribly jolty & sleepless night – of constant collisions which shook every tooth in one's head – & a frantic hunt for my watch! which I lost between two & three & recovered in a fold of my mattress!! I got up to find myself in a vast white country under grey skies shedding gentle regular white flakes – I have never known any place give one such an indefinable sense of size – there were no features in the landscape to suggest it – only flat tracts of fields – but one somehow felt the scale – & I was only rather stunned when informed later on at lunch that I was nearer to Liverpool than to the other far side of Canada.

So that all the ocean I ploughed through for 10 long days is not big enough to hold this country. And over this vast area only 1,000,000 inhabitants are sparsely sprinkled – I suppose I ought to send all the Club boys out at <u>once</u>! We got out into a cold snowy station & packed into a landau-sledge which drove off jingling bells through a strange town – the newest Englishest sort of emergency sea-side place architecture – not as ambitious as Folkestone – more like Bournemouth – nowhere any <u>effort</u> at beauty or individual character – a brick church here & there & one or two – only 2 I think – large American looking hôtels – also the hydro-like Convent. Lots of the houses had largish gardens in front with railings round which accentuated the sea-side look. After a good deal of searching we found ours – in a wideish street called Sherbrooke – street doesn't really describe it – it shld. have been called Terrace – or 'Gardens' or 'Crescent' best of all though it was as straight as a dart – we went in – the sort of very best constituent's house I know so well – only better – with overcrowded pictures of all sorts – some rather good Turners & Corots.[1]

After a time Ly Drummond a rather fine featured woman in black with grey hair came in – I ached for breakfast & was finally given some by a very nice very tall 25 year old son called Guy – I dropped into bed & slept about two hours.... Down to a huge lunch – I sat between Guy Drummond & a young man called Barclay & had rather a good talk with them both about Canada – I can see all Canadians loathe America – their way of playing games, desire to win apart from the process of skill involved etc. & they rather dread their proximity from a point of view of infection. They say the French element in the population is the greatest buffer between them & becoming Americanized. It is marvellous how they have preserved their comparative likeness to us & unlikeness to them considering geographical conditions. Their sources of wealth are minerals, lumber & wheat. They ought to be as rich if not richer than the Americans in the future if they only husband their natural resources & develop their country....

I had the most heavenly drive all afternoon with Guy Drummond in a sleigh through the clearest cleanest most piercing air – under a pale yellow sky through snowbound woods & country – every tree's finest tracery delicately outlined in white – & all round on the slopes & fields delicious little woolly-clad boys rolling & tumbling in the snow – I thought how you must have loved it – & imagined you so well – on your skis & toboggan. How I wish we had had that week at Montana together. We wound uphill through a lovely cemetery scattered hap-hazard through a wood – one of the few beautiful burying places I have ever seen – up & up till we reached the top of what is called 'The Mountain' where the most glorious & dramatic view burst upon us.

A wide sweep of gigantic country through which the St Lawrence flowed in huge curves & curls – in the background some volcanic mountains & in the distance a blue blurred range the Lawrentian Hills. It gave me a real 'sense of Canada' – the space the scope & endless possibility & promise of it. A country where is room for all to breathe & move in & a chance –

---

[1] Violet stayed at 448 Sherbrooke Street West, Montreal, the home of Lady Drummond *née* Grace Parker. Lady Drummond was the widow of Sir George Alexander Drummond (1829–1910), senator in the Canadian parliament and president of the Bank of Montreal; they had two sons. Sir George had an extensive collection of fine art, including works by Constable, Corot, Velázquez, Rubens and Turner, and the collection was maintained for visitors to see after his death.

several chances even – for everyone. The St Lawrence was partly frozen & the ice covered with snow so that one could not very accurately follow its full course for far – but one caught glimpses of it winding away into the West – & Guy Drummond explained to me that the real raison d'être of Montreal was the fact that it was built at the last point possible for the great ocean ships to come up the river. It began to get dark as we went home – & a lovely little moon came out which made the snow sparkle like jewels. Our horse was a lovely little thoroughbred mare full of competitiveness & excitement – which G. D. drove very well. To my amusement we passed Miss MacNaughtan that rather dreary authoress whom I once met at the Hanburys' in another sledge – & felt the truth of all the platitudes about the world's smallness & roundness[1]....

Diary – Monday 13 January – Government House, Ottawa

Darling – I woke up this morning in Ottawa-station – thinking what a wonderfully smooth train we were in – having as a matter of fact been shunted off & standing still for hours – I got up & dressed & breakfasted & watched the furry-capped – gummi-schuhed porters fussing about on the snowy platform.

After the inevitable reporter & the railway manager – Sir Wilfrid Laurier[2] came up looking extraordinarily picturesque & attractive & sat & talked to us for a time & after this Captain Long, Walter Long's son & Sibell Johnstone's husband – who took us off to see Government House. I was thrilled darling at seeing where you lived – & a little surprised too at finding it painted the same colour as a greenish Dreadnought instead of red as I had expected.

We walked through long red-carpeted passages – & I saw your schoolroom – beloved & the view from its windows & thought of your eyes gazing out of them with a pencil in your mouth – through the hours of lessons with Miss Wattermann & Miss Wisdom! – & then I went off with Long to see the houses of Parliament & Library. They are built in real – elaborate Mid-Victorian Gothic – orange high-church Gothic wood inside the library – like the dining-room at Highfield. A dear old boy called Griffith took me round – the librarian – & insisted on my sitting for a moment in the Speaker's chair – a very comfy one....

---

[1] Sarah Broom MacNaughtan, a popular writer in the years before the Great War, whose publications included *Snow Upon the Desert* (1913).

[2] Sir Wilfrid Laurier (1841–1919), French Canadian statesman, Prime Minister 1896–1911. He married, in 1868, Zoë *née* Lafontaine.

I went on to a huge hen-lunch at Lady Laurier's – she is almost quite blind poor thing – I was waylaid & dogged upstairs by a female reporter disguised as a guest which made me rather angry! As usual the atmosphere was asphyxiating & all the gas on. I sat next to Mrs. Borden.

After lunch we all went on to a huge & suffocating meeting of the Ottawa Council of Women. There must have been over 1000 there & they produced that indescribable & inexplicable effect of slight <u>funniness</u> that vast conglomerations of women always do. Your Mother addressed them & was well under way with a very good speech when I had to leave them to go on to a tea-party at Sybil Long's – women again – & the inevitable Miss MacNaughtan first & foremost amongst them. She haunts & follows me like a ghost – I see her tiresome little face springing up before me framed in the strangest & newest of settings.

Back – through the coldest & cleanest & frostiest air to a rest in our luxurious little car in the railway side-ing – & then on to dinner with the Lauriers. . . . after dinner was drawn into a reluctant discussion of the Naval Situation with Sir Wilfrid.[1] It was rather a delicate position for me as I quite see that his idea is a more picturesque one from a <u>national</u> point of view – a Canadian built Canadian-manned fleet guarding their own shores & placed at our disposal in moments of stress etc – but as they have neither ports to build nor men to man it looks a little impracticable. I don't think Sir W. is much of an Imperialist even in the <u>least</u> offensive Liberal League sense of the term. . . .

Afterwards we went to the House to listen to the Naval Debate. It was an immense improvement on the House of Representatives. The inevitable desks were there & the little boys running about – but at least the Government & the Opposition sat opposite each other & the ball was tossed backwards & forwards as it is at home. After a few preliminary questions a man called Guthrie a supporter of Laurier's got up & made a very long speech against Borden's Naval Proposals – quoting several disconnected utterances of Father's plucked from the heart of their context – to prove that there was no real emergency & that no help was in fact needed.[2] As the Laurier faction are prepared to give 2 Dreadnoughts to head their two

---

[1] Laurier opposed Borden's proposal of a direct Canadian contribution towards imperial defence, and favoured instead the creation of a Canadian navy.

[2] Hugh Guthrie (1866–1939), Liberal representative in the Canadian House of Commons, 1900–17. The British government feared that the building of three Canadian Dreadnoughts, to be ready by 1915, and which it regarded as essential to the Mediterranean fleet, would lead to an escalation in the naval race with Germany. The ships were therefore presented as a welcome but not necessary addition to British strength. In March 1913, however, when the force of Canadian opposition to Borden's naval proposals became known, Churchill emphasized their importance (see Peter Rowland, *The Last Liberal Governments 1911–1914*, 249, 269–70).

fleet-units on the Atlantic & Pacific coast [and] Borden only suggests 3 there is not virtually much difference in this part of the conflicting policies – & it looks faintly as if the Liberals were anxious to get another election in whilst Laurier is still young enough to fight it. He (L.) is popularly supposed to be rather haunted by the pt. of view of the French Canadians of the Quebec province. People seem unanimous as to the enormous additional cost which building the Dreadnoughts in Canada would involve. We ought to be their ship shop whatever happens.

I was half-relieved & half-appalled to find that the standard length of speaking is even higher here than at home! I could not stay till the end of Guthrie's speech – nor hear a word of the reply – which I was particularly anxious to – but was obliged to hurry home rest & change in order to dine at 7 at the Chateau Laurier – the most wonderful new hôtel – like the mise en scène of the Merry Widow – with Mr. & Mrs. Rogers, the Longs – & many others all pleasant & interesting but not a single name of whom I can remember. I had a nice civil servant on one side & my host on the other.

Afterwards we went on to Hemmerde's old Butterfly on the Wheel[1] – vilely acted – & after the 2nd Act Captain Long took me up to the station & dropped me in my sleeper – a reserved 'drawing room' where I spent a shortish night – was woken before 7 by Coates & turned out into the grey early morning of Toronto station – where the poor little Governor's daughter Miss Gibson was waiting to meet me – a piece of heroic civility I thought. We got into a landau – & drove round a few of the Public Buildings – all uglyish & Mid-Victorian – standing in snowy streets – then on to the Governor's House where I had a bath & breakfast with the family – quite nice & amusable – then started off a little faint-heartedly for a long day at Niagara.

My companions were Dr & Mrs Vaux – an elderly couple the brother & sister-in-law of Ly A's friend Mrs. Sanford – rather strange boon-comrades for a day out. The Governor accompanied us some way – & at Hamilton I had a deputation of all the oldest & most influential citizens of the town – who brought me violets & a book of photographs – I shook hands & tried to pour as much stuff into 3 minutes hand-shaking as I could – then the train buzzed on through tracts of flat cultivated land – huge expanses of orchards – where peach-trees stood like soldiers in long marshalled rows – & here & there a little improvised village or practical town. There is no attempt or aspiration to beauty anywhere – everything is quite frankly made to be used not looked at – & though in a way the result is less painful than heavy & abortive aesthetic effort – it gives one a slight shock at first as if one of the decencies of life had been ignored.

[1] Edward George Hemmerde, *A Butterfly on the Wheel* (n.d.).

We finally crossed a huge bridge over a vast river – into the United States & found ourselves in Buffalo – a rather grim American business town. We went to the Iroquois hôtel & had lunch – then started off in an excellent motor on which I secured the box seat – which ensured me silence & air for an hour & a half.

The country was bleak & dreary I thought – covered with a thin layer of snow through which the grass pressed up brownly.... We reached the town of Niagara Falls about 3.30 whisked through it & came suddenly & startlingly in sight of the Falls themselves. There are two of them – one on the American the other on the Canadian side & this last one is incomparably the most beautiful. It is shaped like an inverted horse-shoe – & comes thundering down in a translucent green arch & sending up clouds of spray.

It is <u>stupendously</u> big – but like all things which have this reputation it does not surprise by size – one's imagination always figures something quite unrealizable – (still it doesn't disappoint either) – & like all waterfalls the volume is more wonderful than the height. The river is parted by an island & comes crashing down a terrific drop on each side of it.... One characteristic feature of the place very much to the credit of the Canadians is the way they have <u>deliberately</u> refrained from making any capital or taking any business advantage from the Fall. They have kept their side of the river quite unspoilt & lovely – whereas the Americans are busy on their side translating every drop of water into dollars in the filthiest way. Factories – chimneys – great blotches of sulphur – & every sort of disfigurement crowds together on the banks of this marvellous river – & 3 or 4 large jets of water come shooting out of the side of the rocks below the town like a horse's white tail – I went up to the top of the Power station & was amused by a strange device of electric writing they have got in process there – then put on oilskins – & plunged accompanied by the shivering & reluctant Dr. Vaux down the deepest darkest dankest lift – to <u>below</u> the Falls. We then walked in a cloud of spray under the thunderous green watery arch & saw the cataracts shooting over our heads. The rush of the water was deafening. We came up soaked & drove off with the Park Keeper a very nice little fellow called Jackson to see the Rapids – they are very wild & wonderful almost the best part of the river – no sea was ever more tempestuous & irresistible. We motored back in the darkness I sitting on the box of the car till the rain came on & I joined the Vauxs inside. We all felt very hungry when we got back to the Iroquois Hôtel & after tidying up on the 12th floor we ordered a strange meal at about 6.30 – dinner impending at 8 – I had poached eggs & chocolate & they went boldly in for steak.

After this I lay down exhaustedly on my bed & came down re-dressed & tidied & rather stimulated by the thought of the friendly covert of our beloved private car which was to receive me so soon – I waited in the hot-air of the hall fur-coated & veiled with some impatience for the C.P.R. man's arrival. He finally turned up with the dire news that there had been a derailment in front of our train on the line & the car had got to go all the way back & round by Hamilton & might very likely not be here till 10. Imagine my despair! A prolonged vigil then began. . . .

. . . Finally at 3 just as I had fallen asleep there was a loud knock at Dr. V's door which woke me & we were summoned to the station. I drove there too tired to speak or stand – & there we sat for an hour from 3 to 4 – in one of those cheerless pews – a few sleepy porters standing about & the wail of a child – the most desolate thing I ever heard occasionally sounding through the cold empty echoing asphalt spaces. I remember an Italian woman coming in with a bright handkerchief round her head carrying a baby & dragging a little boy by the wrist. At 4 the car came! Your Mother was still up isn't she <u>wonderful</u>? & I was put to bed & given hot milk by Coates & covered up with my blue eiderdown & have never felt so glad to be anywhere in my life. I slept till 10 next day – & we didn't reach New York till 4 or 5 – the Hudson ran along by the side of the train most of the last half of the way – what a <u>marvellous</u> river.

ELEVEN

The Sudan Revisited

1913–1914

V.A. to Venetia Stanley   *Monday 10 February 1913*
                                         Guildford Hôtel, Sandwich

My Darling – I really don't know where to begin – to give you even
the shortest & aridest résumé of the last two months – it has been the
<u>dismay</u> engendered by this impossibility that has kept me so long
dumb – but when your peremptory Edwinian tellie came this morning
I tremblingly ordered my Red Dwarf to be filled – & I now approach
you very penitently.

Cyril & I are at Sandwich where I brought him last Tuesday – a week to-
morrow. He has lost his sleep poor darling & is very overworked & anything
but well. Rest & air & exercise & lying mentally completely fallow would
soon put him right I think but with Greats impending these things are
difficult to attain – I feel really rather anxious & uncertain as to what I
ought to advise him to do – how far to let Greats & how far to let health
go to the wall.

We have spent a marvellously hygienic week here – it is a flat – wind-
swept – rather Littlestonian spot – all the regular Kent properties such as
larks & windmills – grey & yellow bents – muddy sea – a perpetual gale
difficult to stand up in – links etc. We battle round 18 holes twice a day –
with an interval of cold beef at 1.30 – & come back to tea with smarting
eyes & swollen faces. To put the coping-stone on I do Müller twice a day –
at Winston's behest. 'Trunk-twisting' makes me as sore & stiff as a day's
hunting. Father, Oc, Beb, Bongie & Hugh came for Sunday & we had a
rather delicious time, Auction & foursomes & the kind of meal-talk you
know so well – Father in very good form insisting on Müller exhibitions
at odd moments – & watching Hughley writhing & panting on the floor
in agonizing contortions with malignant joy – I go back Wed. for Club
etc. & Sat. we all go away somewhere for the Recess – where it is not yet
decided – as the prey from whom the requisite nest must be snatched has
not yet been marked down. I have only had <u>one night</u> in London since I
got back a fortnight ago – isn't it strange? I arrived at 2 o'clock in the
morning of Tuesday 30th – was greeted by the Suffrage bomb – really the

Speaker's <u>most</u> extraordinary performance[1] – went to the 2nd day's H.R.
debate in the H. of Lords – had rather an amusing tea in an interval with
Gosse[2] & the Archbishop of York – who after swallowing his last mouthful
of strawberry jam urbanely in my company – went off & spoke in the
most absurd way about Father never having mentioned H.R. at the last
election etc[3] – had Sympne & Norton (my new friend made on the White
Star) to dinner & went off the same night to Fife – where we had a <u>glorious</u>
meeting at Leven – Father in wonderful form.

We went on next day to Dundee – where a series of long but not
unamusing ceremonies took place in connection with the Freedom.[4] The
usual Suffragette interludes in the hall – the only new 'turn' being a fairly
cautious attempt on the part of one to leap over the edge of the Dress
Circle into the body of the hall. The meeting was followed by a lunch
lasting from 1 to 4 with 11 speeches! 2 being by Father & one by
Winston – & then we retired to the Enchantress – in the most uninviting
yachting weather you can imagine. Icy cold, heavy rain & so rough outside
that several ships had their bridges torn off – so we couldn't go up to
Cromarty but sailed rather tamely round to Rosyth – from where I did my
meeting at Ladybank. I spoke for $\frac{1}{2}$ an hour in quite tidy English – then
back the whole way by sea. Winston was in excellent form Father & I had
some very amusing Bridge against him & Masterton. You can imagine
what an absurd combination they made – Winston making & doubling
with insane recklessness – & Masterton watching every discard
religiously & building reasonable conjectures on W.'s play only to be
disillusioned again & again....

... Darling the dreariness of this letter simply makes me sick but I must
send it – such as it is. Isn't the Marconi enquiry going well. Let's hope
there'll be a Select Committee on Silver too – or best of all a libel action
when Ed. returns. I hear Bluey & Bongie are going out to you – which
sounds fun. <u>Love</u> & write to Yr. V.

[1] See above, p. 345.
[2] Sir Edmund Gosse (1849–1928), librarian of the House of Lords, 1904–14, and a trustee of
the National Portrait Gallery.
[3] In his comments the archbishop was reflecting Unionist feeling that the Liberals had
evaded the important question of Home Rule during the December 1910 election. Balfour
accused Asquith of suppressing it until late in the campaign, when it could do least damage.
The Liberals, however, pointed to Asquith's opening speech, at Hull on 25 November, in
which he had made clear that Home Rule was one of the government's ultimate objectives
(see above, pp. 229–30). There was considerable debate, though, as to whether or not the
election gave the government the necessary mandate for the proposed reform.
[4] Asquith was presented with the freedom of the city of Dundee in a special ceremony on
31 January 1913.

The 'Marconi Enquiry', 1912–1913

In March 1912 the government awarded the British Marconi Company a contract for the erection, operation and maintenance of an imperial wireless network. In March and April the share price of the company underwent a rapid rise, followed by a rapid fall. Rumours began to circulate that the attorney-general, Sir Rufus Isaacs, and the postmaster-general, Herbert Samuel, had used inside information to profit from speculation in the company's shares. Neither minister had in fact purchased stock in the British Marconi Company. In April, however, Isaacs, together with Lloyd George and the Master of Elibank, had bought shares in the American Marconi Company. The American company was independent of its British equivalent, but the three men chose not to make their involvement in it public, fearing that in the circumstances this might be open to misconstruction. In March 1913, though, they were forced to make public their dealings. The previous month Leo Maxse, editor of the *National Review*, had appeared before the Commons select committee which examined the allegations of corruption. There he questioned why those accused had not issued a categorical denial against any transaction 'in any shares in any Marconi company'. Believing that the facts were now bound to come out, Isaacs and Lloyd George sought a way of disclosing them with the least possible damage. An opportunity presented itself when the French newspaper *Le Matin* published falsehoods that were easily refuted in a libel action. In the ensuing court case Sir Edward Carson, counsel for Isaacs, set the record straight about the Marconi shares that *had* been purchased. Reactions to this were surprisingly muted, and Liberal fears about what might be revealed before the 'Marconi enquiry' appeared to be misplaced. At the end of the month, though, Isaacs was summoned to appear before it, and a number of disclosures followed that gave new impetus to the charges of corruption. It transpired that the American shares had been bought at a favourable price when they were not yet available to the general public, and that the Master of Elibank had used Liberal party funds to purchase shares. Unionists were convinced that there had been impropriety, if not in the purchases, then certainly in the way that information had been withheld from parliament. The culmination of the party controversy over the 'Marconi scandal' was a tense debate in the Commons on 18–19 June 1913. A Unionist motion of censure on Isaacs and Lloyd George was rejected by the government majority. Instead, the ministers' apology for their conduct was accepted, and no further action taken. Marconi damaged the standing of the government, and deprived it of the option of an early election. Asquith, though, took some consolation from the affair. Observing his chancellor in a debate in the Commons a few days later he remarked, with satisfaction, 'I think the idol's wings are a bit clipped.'[1]

V.A. to Hugh Godley   *Saturday 29 March*
                                    10 Downing Street, Whitehall,
                                                          S.W.

... We had an extraordinary scene in the House on Wednesday when a carefully laid Snap was only just foiled (on the Consolidated Fund Bill which has never been divided upon before in the memory of man).[2]

Moore was suspended.[3] Winston's estimates came on at 8 – he made a magnificent speech which as Father said no one but he in the world could have made. Marvellous wording, do read it. I missed it alas as I had to go off to my Club.

Yesterday Lloyd George's evidence came off before the Marconi committee.

I was shivering with anxiety as I felt sure he wld. be the worst possible witness. However everyone says – including the scum of the other side (Ian Malcolm whom I met last night at dinner) that it was almost the most wonderful thing in eloquence he's ever done.[4] He reduced his opponents to tears & himself too I believe. He's come out of it wonderfully. I must confess nothing has ever surprised me more.

[1] See Peter Rowland, *The Last Liberal Governments, 1911–1914*, 197–9, 203–10; also, Frances Donaldson, *The Marconi Scandal*.

[2] In fact the same tactic had been used by the Liberal opposition in 1905, when eleven divisions were taken on the Consolidated Fund bill of that year. There was an irony in the fact that Winston Churchill, whose naval estimates were delayed in 1913, had been a prime instigator of the events of 1905. Had a Liberal member not raised a point of order, thus delaying the division, and allowing Liberal MPs to return to the Commons to vote, the government might have been defeated by two or three votes, which would have had serious consequences (*The Times*, 27 March).

[3] William Moore (1864–1944), Unionist MP for North Armagh, 1906–17, and a founder of the Ulster Unionist Council, 1905. In a heated debate Moore described the parliamentary conduct of Charles Masterman as 'a piece of disgraceful trickery': he refused the speaker's request that he withdraw these words, and was asked to retire from the House for the rest of the day's proceedings. After he refused to do even this, he was suspended, and left amid loud cheering from the Unionist benches.

[4] Ian Malcolm (1868–1944), Unionist MP for Croydon, 1910–18.

I wonder so much what you are doing – whether working hard or having fun.

This goes to you in great haste with my love – Yr V

Rufus Isaacs to V.A.   *Tuesday 1 April*
                                                                House of Commons

Dear Miss Asquith

My warmest thanks to you. Your sensitive & sympathetic temperament found the words which would most comfort me. Your very partiality leading you to an over-favourable view of my part helps me. That I am causing bother to your father & to the Party gives me the acutest pain.

Still we shall emerge victorious out of this struggle – I have no fear so long as I retain the confidence of my friends –

Yours sincerely
                                        Rufus D. Isaacs

V.A. to Hugh Godley   *Monday 19 May*
                                                The Enchantress, *bound for Malta*

Beloved ὑ – We are having such a wonderful Odyssey-like journey; I don't know how to <u>begin</u> to tell you about it. So far as the inanimate & scenic part is concerned nothing cld. possibly have been more perfect – & the personnel have also been harmonious & sympathetic though two rather explosive elements (both singly & conjointly) no doubt exist in M. & Mrs. [Cornwallis-] West. They both illustrate the difficulties of growing-old-well – in very different ways. Both have rather thrown 'dignity' overboard & are clinging onto the skirts of youth by the teeth – Mrs. W. fatly good-humouredly, frankly vulgarly & faintly coarsely – M. emaciatedly curdlessly acidulatedly – dwelling morbidly on digestive problems, crabbing the food, the noise, the heat, the dust, in fact most of the fun of travelling. One longs for a little of her lemon in Mrs. W. & a little of Mrs. W's imperturbable, unoffendable treacly good nature in her. This reads spikily – but it is for you alone & you know how much to subtract. I have formed the firm resolve to go into a lace-cap & mittens at 35.

The rest of us are divinely happy day in day out – Clemmie is most smooth & serene & delicious to live with – & looking more beautiful than I have ever seen her. Winston an unfailing source to me of interest &

excitement – Eddie unintermittently sweet & keen & susceptibly reacting to every sunset, joke, sight, game, temple, gibbet, anagram, book etc. Masterton delightful – very sensitive & understanding – (though high shouldered & taking Bridge too seriously) Admiral Moore – nice, sound, easy & an admirable man to send out shopping with the older does – Father, bird-happy & as sunburnt as a large strawberry – pursuing the most childish occupations (such as drawing up lists of all the women's names beginning with 'P'!)

After a 24 hours journey across Europe (broken at Paris where I drank Vermouth at a table on the pavement –) we arrived at Venice in glorious heat – saw a few sights – embarked on the yacht for dinner & night & spent the next day there in social amenities with Louis Mallet, Lady Helen. It pelted with rain & I was quite glad to weigh anchor & sail off down the Adriatic. Our first stop was Spalato [Split] on the Dalmatian coast – where we saw glorious remains of palaces etc of the Emperor Diocletian who apparently retired there with an intestinal complaint after a gay life of Christian-bating. Then Ragusa [Dubrovnik] a heavenly place in Bosnia peopled by Croats – fierce-looking people with Turkish trousers & fiery eyes – & red sashes with daggers stuck into them. We motored to Trebinje & longed to go to Cetinje which was quite near. The war had been within 100 miles & the troops which had been hastily mobilised were just being disbanded. Admiral Burney who was in charge of the International Blockade came over to see us on a destroyer – he was to march into Scutari [Shkodër] the next day with 1000 troops – 2 or 300 from each power to establish martial law there – a very exciting experience – I never saw a wilder more desolate brigand-haunted looking country.[1] Our next stop was Cattaro – an Austrian port – one bay opens out of another like Russian toys & in the innermost of all is the town – then on to Valona [Vlorë] – a strip of solitary – unpeopled Albanian coast – where we spent a glorious Robinson Crusoe day – on the shore & in the woods – bathing in a tepid chrysoprase sea then picnicking near a trout-stream from which two or three brown & quite inarticulate natives extracted fish – then dozing with books on burning shingle – sun filtering pinkly through one's closed lids – then 'seining' or rather watching the sailors do it – dragging the bay for fish with a huge net – Winston superintending the operations in a boat – gesticulating – perorating – 50 men on each side drawing it in as hard as ever they could with meagreish results – though one or two huge silver wrigglers were netted. The sailors were too delicious playing football & catching tortoises on the sands – Winston stayed behind for a wild pig

[1] Admiral Cecil Burney (1858–1929), senior officer of the international fleet blockading the coasts of Montenegro and Albania, April to May 1913; senior officer and president of the international commission administering Scutari, May to November 1913.

hunt at 3 in the morning & caught us up next day at Corfu in a destroyer.

We had a marvellous reception there from the Greeks with whom we are apparently very popular – Rule Britannia & God save the King was played again & again & the musty old landaus were surrounded & pursued by large & cheering crowds – I saw & spoke to a good many soldiers recovering from their wounds in the old fortress.

I drove to the very spot where Ulysses swam ashore & met Nausicaa & saw his ship turned by Neptune into an island lying out in the sea.

Reaching real Greece was extraordinarily exciting – I <u>can't</u> tell you what it is like – it is impregnated with a quite indefinable & unanalysable glamour which may be in part provided by oneself. Low hills with wonderful outlines – intensely blue & violet – vines growing in little upright trees – not crawlers like in Italy – corn which one can almost see Ceres pushing up through the ground – thickly interspersed with poppies like drops of blood. We passed <u>Parnassus</u> – & sailed in the early morning into the Bay of Corinth – drove up to the site of old Corinth where a few old pillars are still standing – of the old temple of Apollo. It's so amusing to see the names written over the squalidest little shops in this cultured & precious calligraphy – Σωκρατης και ἑταιρια [Socrates and company].

We went to Athens by train – a very slow one – running along the edge of the sea past Eleusis & Megara – we passed Aegina & Salamis two large islands lying in the sun to our right.

The Acropolis was the first thing we saw – high up above the town from the train-windows – & we drove straight up there through a disappointingly crowded & modern town. It is a blow to find trams in Athens. We dined at the Embassy & went up there again by moonlight. There are no words to convey the miraculous wonder & beauty of the Parthenon – one can only say that it passes one's wildest dreams of it. It is the wisest serenest – most final thing I have ever seen – like the ultimate clinching conclusion of a great philosopher – or a perfectly satisfying harmony in music. Moonlight made the light & shade more dramatic – but one lost the golden mellowness of the stone – which one gets in the day. The Erechtheum, Propylaea, Nike-Apteros are up on the Acropolis – but the Parthenon absorbs & distracts one from all else.[1]

It was sad having to leave the very next day. We have since been to Cephalonia, & Taormina & I post this at Syracuse. We arrive at Malta tomorrow morning & I look forward with slight shrinking to three days of rather bleak official gaieties in tidy clothes.[2] <u>I haven't read much</u> you will be sorry to hear – as there has hardly been a chink of time. The Tariff

---

[1] The Erechtheum and Nike-Apteros are temples, and the Propylaea a gateway.

[2] The official purpose of the trip was an inspection of the naval establishment at Malta.

Reformers, Siri Ram a very clever Indian revolutionary story – given me
by Montagu[1]. . . .
. . . Are you missing me – Bless you – we get back late on Sat 31st Yr V.
I retract some of my adjectives applied to M. who is smoother to-day.

M.B.C. to V.A.   *Tuesday 10 June*
                                              5, Hyde Park Square, W.

Beloved. All your orders have I think been executed with promptness &
success I hope, though I have my doubts about the battledores reaching
you in time to give you much chance of more than a day's play.

I saw Viola last night, she is apparently paying [John Glover] 12/- a week
now, I told her that this was too much & it certainly is as it is more than
she is paying any of the other servants. . . . I had a very amusing lunch
where I sat next Barrie & talked to him about Ellen Terry whom he greatly
admires. He compared her to Pavlova for her art of fascination, & also to
Harry Lauder in that they both take their audience into their confidence.[2]

I asked him whom he would choose as Laureate, he said Hardy first as
the greatest literary figure & Kipling next as one whose poems would
outlast any others of his time. He thinks Bridges uninspired & the writer
of poems such as you expect to be produced by any cultured young man
in an ideal university.[3]

Then I had a talk with Lord Morley who was obviously pleased with
himself for having given L.G. what he said was as stiff a talking to for his
speech as he could give. He told him that he was disloyal to his party &
to the P.M. & thought only of himself. Thomas Hardy was also there & I
had a few words after lunch with him but mostly about the House. You
would have enjoyed them wouldn't you if you had been there. . . . God
keep you beloved one B.

[1] George Peel, *The Tariff Reformers* (1913); Edmund Candler, *Siri Ram* (1912).

[2] J. M. (James Matthew) Barrie (1860–1937), novelist and dramatist, author of the children's
play *Peter Pan* (first performed 1904, published 1911). Ellen Terry (1847–1928), actress, famed
for her Shakespearean roles, and for an artistic partnership with Sir Henry Irving. Anna
Pavlova (1885–1931), legendary Russian ballerina. Harry Lauder (1870–1950), star of British
music-hall, and the first to be knighted (1919).

[3] Violet later recalled, in a letter to Lord Baldwin, her father's decision to appoint Robert
Bridges Poet Laureate: 'The obvious choice was Rudyard Kipling. Bridges was the alternative
choice in my father's mind. What weighed with him was the very reason you give – that
Kipling was inspired and could not write to order. Bridges, with his classical chiselled gift
would be more likely to be able to do so. He wrote, offering it to Bridges . . .' (Charles
Carrington, *Rudyard Kipling*, 460). Kipling was, as Asquith knew, most unlikely to accept the
laureateship. Thomas Hardy's poetry, which has gained in reputation after his death, was not
widely acclaimed in his lifetime.

V.A. to Hugh Godley   *Friday 20 June*
                                              10 Downing Street, Whitehall,
                                                                      S.W.

20ᵗʰ June 1913

I can't bear to think I have hurt you – & of what separates us from each
other.

If only either of us had enough courage & conviction to sweep the other
along.

But whatever happens forgive me if I hurt you – I think what you don't
quite realize is how much these things mean to me.

I believe in them – as a means of changing the world – of making the
lives of <u>millions</u> – (which for a second I can imagine as my own) different –
of flooding them with ease enough to <u>think</u> – comfort & leisure enough
to feel the interest & joy of life. It is serious & <u>real</u> to me. And you think
it all just nonsense. That nothing can be done – & that our efforts to do it
are just cheap demagogy. A railway dividend is a sacred thing to you – a
porter's comfort is just not your business. So long as you earn your living &
do nothing wrong your moral ambition is satisfied.

And then as to Marconi – which has nothing to do with all this – I think
you forget that Rufus [Isaacs] & Lloyd George are my <u>friends</u> – that I care
for them – that it is pain to me to see them unjustly pilloried & going
through the fire for an error of judgement. Of course I am biassed in so
far as I care for them.[1]

And as you <u>don't</u> care & <u>don't</u> believe in any political creed wouldn't it
be easier for you not to bring us into conflict by saying what you do about
them?

My views can't hurt you – as you have no fixed beliefs to defend – in
this case you are the invulnerable agnostic & I am the stuffy sensitive
religious maniac.

But perhaps as you say the gulf is too wide to bridge. Only try &
understand me.

Your unhappy – V.

V.A. to Venetia Stanley   *Thursday 21 August*
                                                    Hopeman Lodge, Moray

My Darling – I send you my stocking & tweed & should like 2 pairs in this
colour if that were possible. I came up here Friday night – after a thrilling

[1] Raymond Asquith had been engaged as a junior counsel in the successful libel case against
Le Matin, in March 1913.

night with the Masefields & a day & night in London – everyone looking
very stale & tired at the House.[1] I saw Geoffrey – Illingworth, Tante, Bluey,
Jack Tennant etc – & Birrell Bluey & Tante lunched one day – & Nathan &
Davies the next.[2] The few plums left high & dry in the August sediment
seemed very desirable & precious.

This place is truly funny – in spite of being prepared for the worst it did
give me rather a turn driving up to the door. It is like a 3rd class carriage –
getting into it is the worst part – once in one feels all right. It is the most
uncompromising square you can imagine (the <u>wrong</u> yellow – with a
terrible porch & flight of steps) perched on a sandhill – no garden, no
blade of grass, no leaf of shade – but the sea at one's very feet – glorious
sunsets over it – & a lovely range of hills – rather like the coast of Greece –
at the other side of the Firth. The inside is hideous but comfy – <u>masses</u> of
bathrooms & hot water – & the whole thing only 18 months old. So far
no one is here but Donald Somervell one of Cys's nicest friends.[3] Tante
comes Friday. We bathe & golf at Lossie every day.

Yesterday we had a rather amusing foursome – Ramsay MacDonald
& I against Father & Somervell – they won by one putt.[4] Ramsay I fell
rather under the spell of; he is very goodlooking & fluent – rather
vain. . . .

I have masses of literary pabulum – so far unattacked as I have
been sweating under a slavery of letters – Let me know all your news &
plans

      Your lovingest V.
You owe me a letter – I wldn't have written if I'd remembered that.

V.A. to Venetia Stanley   *Friday 12 September*
                                                  Hopeman Lodge, Moray

My Darling – I loved getting your letter – but it was a rude shock to me
to find that it contained no reference to coming here. When are you
coming? . . .

---

[1] John Masefield (1878–1967), poet, novelist and playwright, who married, 1903, Constance
née Crommelin. 'Jan' and 'Con' Masefield became good friends of Violet, and were brought
closer through their shared friendship with Rupert Brooke, 1914–15.

[2] Lieutenant-Colonel Sir Matthew Nathan (1862–1939), GCMG 1908; under-secretary to
the lord-lieutenant of Ireland, 1914–16.

[3] Donald Bradley Somervell (1889–1960), educated at Harrow and Magdalen College,
Oxford.

[4] (James) Ramsay MacDonald (1866–1937), Labour MP for Leicester, 1906–18, and a leader
of the early Labour party.

To-day is Father's birthday & the usual ritual is being gone through – roly-poly is ordered for lunch – the breakfast table is littered with First Editions – a long & excellent letter from Frances Horner lies unopened – Pamela McKenna sends a bale of tweed – the Derenbergs a telegram signed 'Carlona'[1] – Puffin presents a piece of 'Arcadian china' bought at a Baptist sale at 'Duffus' – our neighbouring village. Father beams with pleasure & complacently rips up brown paper & string. Your present was a huge success & is I think very lovely. Cys & I gave him 2 volumes of Heraldry which is now his main interest. He only talks in terms of gules & pommes hinds trippant, & stags at gaze – the terminology is I must say very attractive & gets people like us who are always a prey to any verbal lure completely in chancery....

I have golfed once or twice more with Ramsay & yesterday played in a foursome with Sir George Abercromby, Beatrix Villiers & her husband. They are all staying at Rothes which has been taken this year by the Reginald Abel Smiths. The great new entertainment in our house is listening to Yeo the butler imitating animals – he is too marvellous – <u>much</u> better than Bongie almost a ventriloquist – he does lions, cats, cocks & hens, calves, wood being sawed etc. with the most extraordinary aplomb.[2] Are you having good political talks with Winston? I never in my life read anything so lamentably undignified as Lloyd George's correspondence with Wolmer – Wolmer scores heavily I think – & to achieve this result what depths must have been touched by the other side.[3] I am rapaciously

[1] 'Carlona' is perhaps a play on the Christian names of the Derenbergs, Charles and Eilona (d. 1967); he was a member of the stock exchange and she, born Eibenschutz, a distinguished professional pianist.

[2] Yeo's repertoire later extended to politicians. Cynthia Asquith recalled in her diary how, in September 1916, he was made to do 'his really excellent stunts' to an Asquith house party at Little Craigweil in Sussex, the home of Sir Arthur DuCros: 'He barked like a lion, made a noise like sawing wood ... but it was only the preface to – in my opinion – the greatest breach of taste I have ever witnessed. They made him do very good imitations of various prominent guests at Downing Street, their voices and walks – McKenna, Haldane, Lord Morley, and so on. It was a very pungent scene.... The funniest thing was the way Yeo – in his most professional, deprecating, butler voice – gave out the name (just as if he were announcing him) of his victim: "Lord Morley" and so on.... None of the family – except Beb, who was horrified – saw anything odd in it....' (Cynthia Asquith, *Diaries, 1915–1918*, 211).

[3] In the first week of September 1913 an exchange of letters between Lord Wolmer and Lloyd George appeared in *The Times*. In a public speech Lord Wolmer had denounced Lloyd George's role in the Marconi affair, and, though he later admitted to some small inaccuracy, he repeated in his letters to *The Times* his view that Lloyd George had acted improperly. The latter responded by attacking Wolmer personally, casting aspersions on the integrity of his father and grandfather, who had both been cabinet ministers. Wolmer consequently appears the more objective in this correspondence, which recalls Margot Asquith's opinion that Lloyd George 'could not see a belt without hitting below it'.

devouring all the King & Constitution letters – the Spectator & Times seem to be taking up a very sane line about it.[1] I am just going to read Loreburn's manifesto.[2]

... Tell me when you're coming too darling – I'm thirsting for the 'devil's garden' aren't you? When do you have to be at Penrhôs – Bluey tells me [he] is going sometime. Mind you are nice to the Baron – Love yr V.

My tussle with the Suffragettes was the longest & most violent ever indulged in & a <u>revelation</u> to me of my pugilistic capacity.[3]

Diary – Saturday 13 September – Hopeman Lodge, Moray

I drove back with Father from the links.

V. What a pity we can't couple Redistribution with Plural voting – we might oil them both through this year & go to the country on a new register – as it is we have to stay in till 1915.[4]

---

[1] The 'King and constitution' letters appeared in *The Times* in the first weeks of September 1913, when some Unionists were reinterpreting the King's constitutional position in the search for a way to defeat Home Rule. They argued that because the Parliament Act had deprived the Lords of their power of veto, the King should make use of his, and refuse to sign the Home Rule bill. This would bring about a dissolution of parliament, and a general election, which the Unionists who advocated this step expected to win. *The Times* editorial observed that the constitutional theory was flawed, and that it remained 'a first principle of our Constitution that the King acts solely on the advice of his ministers'.

[2] Loreburn's 'manifesto' took the form of a very long letter to the editor of *The Times*, 11 September 1913, appealing for an inter-party conference to settle the question of Home Rule. Asquith's experience of the failed conference on reform of the House of Lords, in 1910, made him sceptical of the merits of Loreburn's plan (J. A. Spender and C. Asquith, *Life of Lord Oxford and Asquith*, ii, 31–4).

[3] Violet had defended her father from a suffragette attack on the links at Lossiemouth, on 4 September, holding the attackers at bay until detectives arrived. She afterwards made light of the incident, which was reported in *The Times* the next day under the headline 'Miss Asquith and golf "hazards" ': 'Miss Asquith presented prizes to the winners in the Lossiemouth Golf Tournament yesterday, and, referring to the attack on Mr Asquith by suffragists, said their enjoyment of the links was in no wise over-clouded by any hazard appearing at the 17th green.' She recalled, many years later, that she had discarded her club 'to escape the temptation of using it' (*Observer*, 22 November 1969).

[4] According to electoral law that the Liberals sought to change, it was then possible for individuals who owned more than one property to record more than one vote at an election. Some businessmen might register as many as a dozen, in one or more constituencies. The practice of 'plural voting' gave undue electoral influence to wealth, and was especially significant in the smaller constituencies of the pre-1918 era (R. C. K. Ensor, *England 1870–1914*, 392–3). The government's 1906 bill to end the practice was abandoned when it became clear that it would not pass the House of Lords. The 'redistribution' of seats – effectively the redrawing of constituency boundaries – was an essential part of franchise reform, and a controversial issue.

F. Hmm – I think that rather unlikely.

V. That we shall be able to? then what a good thing it would be to get it through sooner. It wld. give us a much better chance of coming in again.

F. So people say – I am personally very much inclined to distrust such generalizations. The Borough Councils franchise which people hoped such great things from made not the slightest difference.[1]

V. Yes – Logically it ought to.

F. Yes – logically it ought but I doubt if it will. Besides Re-distribution can't possibly be settled till H.R. is dealt with – & ought really to be settled by consent.

V. Did Loreburn consult you as to the publication of his letter?

F. No.

V. Would a conference be any good?

F. Not at this stage – there is nothing to confer about – no common ground to meet on. It's no good all meeting round a tea-table.

V. It's the last thing <u>they</u> want!

F. The <u>very</u> last!

V. Is the King very funky about everything.

F. In an awful state! I get terrible bulletins of his state of mind from Crewe, Lulu etc from Balmoral – I've just written Simon a few instructions.

V. Has he always been against H.R.

F. No I think he realizes H.R. is inevitable. He is just in a blue funk. Poor little man he isn't up to his position.[2]

V. He's had a stiffer time than most kings. Two decisions of this kind to make in a year or two – I wonder what the old king wld. have done about the Parliament Act?

F. He was beginning to get very uncomfortable about it. Oh I think he'd have behaved in the same way as this one did.

V. Perhaps he could have done more through using personal pressure & leverage.

F. Oh no – I think not. He'd tried it before. He sent for Arthur Balfour & Lansdowne to ask them to pass the Budget – & absolutely failed.

V. Was he furious?

---

[1] Under the 1867 Reform Act all rate-paying householders living in boroughs were enfranchised; this franchise was in 1884 extended to those living in counties. In the four decades following the first of these democratic reforms the Liberals were in power for eighteen years, and the Conservatives/Unionists for twenty-two.

[2] By late 1913 King George V had come to realize that the Ulster Protestants would not submit peacefully to the terms of the Home Rule bill. Asquith, however, remained convinced until mid-1914 that the business community in Belfast would not risk its prosperity in resistance to the legislation. Ironically the 'poor little man' read the situation more correctly than the clever and experienced one.

F. Oh furious.

V. Amazing folly of AJB's.

F. Madness – sheer madness.

V. Surely he wldn't accede to this wild-cat scheme when it isn't even pressed upon him by the responsible men on the other side? If he did – we shld. romp next election just as we romped after the H. of L. rejection of the Budget – shouldn't we?

F. I don't know – it would be a very disagreeable election to fight – very disagreeable.

V. Yes it would be difficult. But what an awful hole they wld be in if we went out. Coming in with a smallish majority – the whole of the Irish against them in the House – & our men tearing them to shreds.

F. Yes imagine Winston & Lloyd George unmuzzled! & Montagu & Simon. Simon wld be very useful. They'd have an awful time. They don't know what obstruction means.

V. & The rest of Ireland!

F. Oh the rest of Ireland wld. give them hell.

V. I suppose they'd go to the country on repeal.

F. They might but their lives wldn't be worth living if they did. That wld. be the moment they'd try for a Conference.

V. Wld. Redmond ever accept anything they'd be prepared to concede.

F. Oh they'd have to offer a Parliament in Dublin – they can boggle over the finance as much as they like.

V.A. to Edwin Montagu   *Wednesday 8 October*
                                              Cloan, Perthshire

What a glorious letter you wrote me – one of your very best – I have been waiting for an oasis of solitude to answer it in – & I think this morning I have reached one – for there are relentless rods of rain coming down out of doors – & within – Haldane closeted with French & another General – Mrs Haldane – beautiful & bed-ridden upstairs – Elizabeth Haldane organizing the Auchterarder Red Cross at another writing-table – Professor Hume Brown writing Goethe's life in the hall.[1]

Your account of Arran was vivid almost to luridness! How well I can

---

[1] Field-Marshal Sir John French (1852–1925), chief of the Imperial General Staff, 1911–1914. Peter Hume Brown (1850–1918), professor of ancient (Scottish) history, Edinburgh University; *The Youth of Goethe* appeared in 1913, and his *Life of Goethe* posthumously, in 1920, partly revised by R. B. and Elizabeth Haldane.

imagine the Illingworth milieu & atmosphere.[1] The whole thing would have been better done with the Master still at the helm wouldn't it? – Father says that only an hour's business was talked all told – he seemed to think Runci[man] in quite a good frame of mind – & was more arrested by an epigram describing him as 'our alabaster colleague' than by any opinion he expressed! As you say he (Father) is far more engrossed in the H.R. than in the land situation. He says Loreburn's suggestions as to Ulster are quite unfeasible & absurd. I can't help hoping that we shall stay on until after the thing is <u>started</u> – I think it wld. be cowardly to go out after passing the Bill & leave the real solution to them.

I am sorry you didn't enjoy the Enchantress more – & I <u>wish</u> you got on better with Winston. I think one of your faults is to show very little stamina about an uphill social situation – & very little elasticity in an entourage which doesn't happen to exactly dovetail in with your moods.

Winston is disconcerting because he is so self-absorbed – & has very little loose, roving attention – but if you once manage to seize & rivet it you will find him amazingly appreciative. Poor Clemmie is the easiest, most automatically responsive woman I have ever met – I'm sorry Goonie's subtle – rather aromatic charm didn't penetrate you this time – but I expect you liked them all much better than you pretend. Father told me you left them for a Lloyd Georgian land breakfast – which sounded as if the whole thing had been not altogether barren in result. Father & I had a typical 3 days at Edinglassie. Bridge till 2.20 most nights – a brisk discharge of firearms during the day – & anecdotes about teal etc. all through meals....

Father comes on here to-morrow from Balmoral – I am longing to hear what news of the King's frame of mind he will bring – I suppose that old cuttle fish Stamfordham will have been flooding his mind with ink.[2] I heard from Bongie very happy with you at the Rutland Arms among the partridges. My plans are to go Friday to Beaufort Castle, Beauly for a few days then back to join Father at Hopeman for a fortnight. Do come up there again unless you are buried in constituency. <u>Be happy</u> – yrs V I broached yr. subject with Father he wasn't very favourable I will speak to him again.

---

[1] At the end of September leading members of the cabinet met at Brodick Castle on Arran, which had been taken as a holiday home by the chief whip, Percy Illingworth. The principal issues discussed at this 'council of war' were the possibility of an inter-party conference on Home Rule, and also the substance of a major speech on the question of land reform, which the chancellor was due to give at Bedford the following month.

[2] Arthur Bigge (1849–1931), 1st Baron Stamfordham, 1911; private secretary to Queen Victoria, 1895–1901, and to the future King George V from 1901.

V.A. to Edwin Montagu   *Friday 31 October*
                                                  Larbert House, Stirlingshire

I have been meaning to write to you my Collins every day – but time has
never seemed forthcoming. I went up Thursday night arriving Friday
afternoon & the whole of Saturday we motored south to Fife. Our Ladybank meeting happened about 6 – in a tiny little hall packed with delegates & press. Father spoke for a little over half an hour. I thought
extraordinarily wisely & well.[1] There was an amazingly strong anti-Ulster
feeling – all the 'firm' parts were cheered to the echo & the conciliatory
ones far more tepidly received. I think Carson has succeeded in interesting
the Scotch in Home Rule for the first time – Marie Corelli was our fellow-
guest at dinner – the most awful woman you ever saw![2] We motored back
the whole of Sunday – & on Wednesday went [for] another terrific drive
to Haddo & back to plant some trees. Then to-day down here leaving at
11 & arriving at 7.

Arthur Ponsonby is our fellow-guest – how clever he is. I had never met
him before.... Father tells me he has asked if he may stay with you again
for the inside of this week – he can bring servants if yours are away to
look after you both....

... Love & thanks – communicate with me next week

                                                              – Yrs Violet

V.A. to M.B.C.   *Thursday 11 December*
                                                           Train to Marseilles

One line to post at Dover – I can't write a cheque for what I owe you the
train shakes too much but will post one at Port Said. Bless & thank you
for all your grind – Have a good rest now I am gone.[3]

---

[1] Asquith addressed a meeting of the delegates of his constituency Liberal Association at
Ladybank, on Saturday 25 October 1913. Virtually the whole speech was devoted to the Ulster
crisis: the government would not accept the Unionists' offer of a formal conference on the
subject, but would give consideration to a frank, and informal, exchange of views (*The Times*,
27 October 1913).

[2] Marie Corelli (1855–1924), novelist whose *Sorrows of Satan* (1895) had an initial sale
exceeding that of any other English novel. Gladstone and Oscar Wilde were among her many
admirers, but her popularity declined after 1900.

[3] In the winter of 1913–14 Violet made a return visit to the Sudan, accompanied by her
younger brother Cys. She doubtless hoped that he would enjoy the experience as much as
she had done on her first visit, three years previously (see Chapter Seven, above). But Cys
became ill during their voyage out, and shortly after arriving in the Sudan he contracted
dysentery. Violet helped to nurse him to recovery, but his recuperation was slow, and they
were considerably delayed in their return to England. They eventually left Khartoum towards
the end of February, returning to England early in March.

I can't realize in the least yet that I shan't see you for 2 months – it is unimaginable. Please let me know <u>exactly</u> what I financially owe you for bag etc. & please ask <u>Father</u> what he thinks I ought to do about this thing of Uncle Norman [Wooding]'s & answer it for me.

Also don't forget about <u>Nellie Green</u> – & rake in the Club subscriptions. These are the only things I can think of I haven't done.

Send me any good cuttings or pictures – I have ordered a weekly Times – & Nation & daily Daily Mail to be sent us – keep the Wilmslow platform photograph for me – & Father's speeches & the Nat. Lib. Club menu.

Bless you my very dear – take great great care of yourself for my sake who couldn't do without you. I'll write again from Marseilles Yr V.

Have my little orange cup in your room brew potions of daily remembrance in it

M.B.C. to V.A.   ***Thursday 11 December***
                                      5 Hyde Park Square, W.

Beloved. It was glorious to get your letter written in the train, when I reached home tonight. It was not until I got back to Downing Street after dining with the Masefields that I really began to miss you. I have been fairly busy all day and I too cannot realise that it will be February before I see you again. Even now I only realise it with my head & not with my bones. It was quite unpleasant enough as it was to reach Downing St at about a quarter to twelve to find it all dark & friendless, Artie was out on some beano, and I felt entirely lonely and there is no one who will understand how much I am wanting you. I have been dining with Masefield where I met the Galsworthys.[1] Masefield was as delightful and as gentle as he always is. I did not have very much talk with him. You remember the description of Dauber's fall from the mast, how he feels that his companion has slipped & clutched at him as he is falling.[2] This is M's own experience – he said that he fell out of a tree when he was a boy & the impression left on his mind (which was certainly proved false by the evidence) was that it was the boy who was climbing with him who slipped & pulled him down. Mrs Galsworthy was very anxious to believe

---

[1] John Galsworthy (1867–1933), playwright and novelist, author of *The Forsyte Saga*; he married, 1905, Ada *née* Pearson.

[2] 'There came a gust, the sail leaped from his hands / So that he saw it high above him, grey, / And there his mate was falling ; quick he clutched / An arm in oilskins swiftly snatched away' : see above, p. 351, n. 2.

that you were at heart a Suffragist. I disillusioned her by saying that you felt more strongly about it than your Father and asked her what she would feel if she had seen her father covered by raving women with pepper & struck at with a whip. She expressed horror at militancy but as usual with suffragists thought that one's opinion of the cause should not be affected by their methods, which is not necessarily true & certainly not human. I was rather amused by her evident desire to write you down as one of her side....

I feel that you will have a glorious time with Cys & long to be with you, so as not to miss anything of your happiness. You must not forget to tell me everything that you have done & enjoyed, therefore God Bless & keep you. My other prayer I say silently, B.

M.B.C. to V.A.   *Friday 12 December*
                                          10 Downing Street, Whitehall,
                                                                  S.W.

Beloved. This you will understand is written at the same time as my Cairo letter, though you will get it four days or so later I suppose. The day you left we had a long Cabinet lasting till nearly two, all about navy estimates.[1] They all feel that this is the most serious fence which they have to face & I suppose are trying to make it as little formidable as possible with what success I cannot say yet. I think that they are faced with the difficulty that they cannot reduce enough effectively to quiet our economists & yet they may quite possibly do enough in that direction to cause the Tories to divide against us. Bonar Law has made what is I think rather a good speech for him, though I mean only from his party point of view because it certainly does not help agreement. I send it to you as you may perhaps miss it, also another cutting from the Times definitely announcing the fact that conversations have taken place.[2] I had some talk with Stamfordham about the situation this afternoon. He expressed himself strongly

[1] At the lord mayor's banquet at the Guildhall, on 10 November 1913, Churchill had given public warning that he would propose an increase in the naval estimates for 1914–15 'substantially greater than the enormous sum originally voted for the present year'. This was 'the curtain-raiser to a political crisis of the first magnitude'. Throughout December 1913 and January 1914 the 'economists' in the party, led by Lloyd George, battled in vain to reduce the estimates, which were eventually settled, effectively on Churchill's terms, in early February (Peter Rowland, *The Last Liberal Governments, 1911–1914*, 271–88).

[2] *The Times* of 12 December 1913 reported 'on the highest authority' that practical effect had been given to an offer, made by Asquith, for an exchange of views between the party leaders on the Irish crisis.

in favour of the economists in the matter of armaments & thought that the Big Navy people on the opposition side were digging a pit for themselves, as they would find it impossible to finance their programme if they were to come into power. I really think he is conscientiously trying to hold the balance between the parties but Knollys's judgement & far wider experience & outlook is a great loss to us. I like S. personally. I shall be glad when Honours are done with, I loathe the business from every point of view. I must own, that although your Father spoke without doubt of getting away in January, I cannot help feeling that it is very uncertain in the present situation.

If he stays I shall of course stay here too. . . .

Tell me how Cys gets on with his riding. I hope he will love it, it will make all the difference. My love to you, darling, be wonderfully happy & healthy & think of me from time to time. B.

V.A. to M.B.C. *Friday 12 December*
Train to Marseilles

We had a rather dank & chilly crossing – swarmed heavily laden through the Douane – & installed ourselves in one of those odd little slice-of-a-carriages very narrow – & a tight mosaic of kitbags – dispatch boxes etc on rack & floor. We had some lunch after which we both felt slightly less grey & wan – (though Cys is I can see in rather bad spirits about himself) – then an attempt at sleep repeatedly thwarted by the attendant yelling 'Tea is ready' at short intervals – a long & thorough perusal of yesterday's Times & to-day's Morning Post & now I write to you till dinner-time. I feel too tired to attack any – even the frothiest of my books – I shall hibernate like a dormouse on the P. & O. . . .

We are going the most <u>incredible</u> pace – it will be a very great wonder if we aren't killed – 80 miles an hour at <u>least</u> it feels like. We are just beginning to remember all the necessities we have left behind – the most important of mine is <u>cigarettes</u> & Cys's is pipe-cleaners – Cys says he wants 300 of the latter! . . . I long for my cigarettes – there are none to be got on the train.

<u>Fri-morning</u> – Marseilles.

A glorious still morning the sun not quite up. We have just come on board – hosts of Malays are padding up & down the gangways coaling – We start at 10.

It is nice to be out of the train – I lay with my shelf shaking beneath me like an earthquake all night. I thought of you – you are very near to me always – God bless & keep you & give you a little back of what you give to me. Always yr V.

Tell the boys to write & thank Venetia for the tree. Such a wonderful orange sky over the sea.

Diary – Saturday 13 December – P. & O. China, bound for Port Said

We left London on Thursday morning after a hellish week of rush – tryings on – Xmas presents – goodbyes – Club Xmas Tree – (& all broken into by a Thursday to Monday at Alderley & three meetings of Father's).

Bongie saw us off & Margot & Fräu & I felt a kind of nunc dimittis as we steamed out of the station armed with circular notes <u>&</u> itinerary & das Gepäckschein & French money – coupled with the faint misgiving that every leave-taking by train brings me as to whether I should ever see any of them again. . . .

[Marseilles] The ship was drawn up by the Quay – just where I found the Delhi 3 years ago – coaling in full process – & the Lascars & Malays running up & down the gangways. We bought 3 basket chairs & I posted two letters – & then went & sat on deck – & watched the harbour – the sun coming slowly up & the masts growing like trees out of blue mists & sea – I felt dazed with tiredness & lay down in Cys's cabin for an hour or two of coma – then lunch after which I went to bed solidly till just before dinner. . . .

Cys doesn't look or feel well – & went to bed almost immediately after dinner – I was in bed by 10. Too sleepy to read. To-day the sea is as calm as oil – not much sun. I have lain out on deck most of the morning. . . .

Diary – Tuesday 16 December – Port Said, Egypt

A rather rough night & a busy tipping bustling day – about 4 we stood out on deck in a perfect gale of wind – huge blue waves leaping & romping all round till the Nile flowed into them & turned them yellow – a little faint brown coastline began to appear – & at 4.30 we came alongside this extraordinary town – a little cleaner & gooder looking than when I was here last. The same howling inroad of browns & blacks with bags of merchandise on their backs & finally Cooks men appeared, & the Captain of the Port – one Trelawny, & gave me letters from Currie & the Sirdar & 2 wires from Bongie & Margot & we shuffled off in the Cooks launch to the station. As Cys says this place is extraordinarily like a grubby Earls Court & one would never be surprised at coming across a gigantic Flip Flop or suddenly emerging out of a turnstile into the Fulham Road – the stage-natives & painted cardboard houses. We are now sitting in the train waiting to start – our luggage is actually all there – it is quite dark outside, & the night-howling I remember so well of old is just beginning. We get to Cairo late to-night.

The Cairene Carter received us on the platform about 12.20.

Diary – Thursday 18 December – Train to Assouan

I spent the night under a very stuffy mosquito-net.... After the usual 20 minutes in the hall – while Cys shaved – we went out – bought cigarettes & sun helmets – saw Cook etc – & I bought little coloured leather-bags & various other nonsense purchases....

Ronald Storrs came to tea – he looked his vulgarest & most astrakhan-headed & was his nicest & most amusing ... we left in a whirl of tips & wires & thanks. Cook met us at the station with a letter from Bongie. We've lost South Lanark by 200 thanks to that damned split vote but there's nothing for the Opposition to be pleased about in that....[1]

It was <u>wonderful</u> seeing the desert again – that indescribable colour that is neither grey nor brown nor purple – more like a sort of peppered roseleaf – or a patch of pink sky reflected in a brown pool. Great ranges of maize coloured rock hills with violent volcanic peaks here & there – forlorn outlines of camels & old gnarled black men shading their eyes from the sun or crouching in a waste of dust – & from time to time a woolly wandering flock of goats or a domed mud tomb. This to our left – on our right luxuriant Zoo vegetation of palm trees, sugarcane plantations, a brilliant strip of green & the Nile flowing broadly – brownly – in magnificent rhythmic curves.

I began the 'Portrait of a Lady' but I couldn't keep my eyes off the window, that dazzling square – which framed it all in gold – – I think Cys liked it all – he was a good deal interested by the bright green birds that perched on the telegraph wires.[2] At Assouan we stopped – & at Shallaal we found the steamer waiting & plunged out of the sandy heat of our carriage up the little white gangway to the most delicious cabins. A marvellous orange & green sunset took place over the water, the first we have seen, & we drifted off about 7.30 – the 3rd class passengers huddled in a variegated mass in an odd pen-like craft we drag along by our side. The women are battened down in a hatch like chickens.... We have been going a week to-day – & not one stationary night except the Cairo one.

[1] See above, p. 289.
[2] Henry James, *The Portrait of a Lady* (1881).

Diary – Friday 19 December – On the Nile between [Wadi] Halfa & Shallaal

A voluptuously comfortable day – drifting up the Nile – I have never been more conscious of complete & positive physical well-being.

It was warm – really almost for the first time since we started – & we basked in chairs in the very front of the ship bathed in golden sunlight – the swish & glitter of the water in our eyes & ears – with this strange country – so varied & changing in spite of the immutable sameness of its character gradually unrolling itself before us. I wrote a letter or two & read a little Henry James – otherwise lay & gazed fairly passively & drank in all the warmth & beauty & deliciousness through my pores. How I wish I could imbibe some of these colours – & store them up in my mind – to dye my thoughts & then somehow like a cuttlefish shower them out into my life & other people's – Flood Hoxton with the orange of these skies – squeeze a little sunset into some of Simon's speeches. . . .

Diary – Saturday 20 December – Train to Khartoum

We are in the last lap of our journey now – installed in the comfiest train I have ever been in – I long to travel on it for weeks. It is a snow-white Galahad without – & within has berths of immense width & scope – table – chair etc – Cys & I & Coates have one each to ourselves. . . .

. . . We got there [Halfa] about lunch time – an odd little row of houses along the banks of the Nile. The Inspector of Railways a very efficient man called Mr Weeke came onto the steamer & took charge of our luggage – & we then went off for a little stroll in the town where we were abordée-d first by the incoming & then by the outgoing Governor – Lyall a fat rubicund soldier who said he had been at Winchester with Raymond – & Isles a very good-looking rather piano man – who one felt was having it taken out of him rather by the heat.[1] We are flying now through stretches & stretches of orange desert – with bright violet hills beyond. The sun has just dropped over the edge of the world like an orange – leaving a marvellous afterglow. We get to Khartoum at 3 to-morrow. It's odd how little one thinks of a 24 hours journey here – it's like running into London from Taplow – nothing approaching the seriousness of a journey to Scotland.

---

[1] Charles Elliott Lyall (b. 1877), educated at Winchester and Balliol. Joined the Sudan Civil Service, 1901; senior inspector, 1909.

Diary – Tuesday 23 December – The Palace, Khartoum

After a night spent breathing <u>lungfuls</u> of dust, & dressing in a railway carriage about as sandy as the average beach – & a last meal with little O'Farrell – we steamed into Khartoum station. The first face I descried was that of Captain Haddow – the Parlour Pet – then Currie's full cheese-moon – & lastly the Martian's sultry eye – veiled & hooded. He hardly dared go through the ordinary civilities of welcome for fear I shld. think he was breaking the letter or the spirit of his self-imposed ordinance.[1] We were spirited away by Haddow in a motor (no camel-cart this time) & whisked off to the Palace – where we found our hosts waiting to receive us on the steps that lead down into the garden....

Diary – Christmas Day – The Palace, Khartoum

We are just back from church. A blazing morning – & the Cathedral – much better inside than out – packed with strong good men with loud voices – Good King Wenceslas was sung – also Hark the Herald – Come All Ye Faithful etc. One wld. have had a really moved feeling at all this snow & holly fare presented to one in a faraway parched & sandy land if the Bishop had not so sickeningly emphasized the fact in his sermon.[2] Even he however didn't entirely dispel one's feeling about it – as they all filtered out into the sunlight – saluted the Sirdar – & lingered about wishing each other a Happy Xmas in stentorian tones. The Cathedral is a <u>very</u> odd building – not at all successful outside I think but this is partly because at present it has no spire or tower which gives it a rather squat appearance. Inside it has rather jolly brick arching – a strange wooden screen which looks like a game of single-sticks in full swing & odd triangular windows....

We had a delicious day at Omdurman yesterday. It gave me a great pang to see our dear little deserted messroom on the river – we trotted up to the Khalifa's house through the brown streets & cactuses – & lunched there with Cheeseman – Goldsmith – Purvis & Boyce – & they played the gramophone afterwards with pathetic pride 'We've got the Gaby Slide – Miss Asquith – wld. you like that or the Chocolate Soldier valse – oh isn't the Girl in the Taxi perfectly <u>ripping</u> – top hole what?' Boyce is a man of

---

[1] During her return to the Sudan in 1913, Violet occasionally referred to Edgar Bonham Carter as 'The Martian' in her diaries and correspondence. His 'self-imposed ordinance' was clearly meant to relieve Violet from any sense of pressure or obligation arising from his proposals of marriage, which she had not accepted.

[2] Llewellyn Henry Gwynne (1863–1957), bishop of Khartoum, 1908–20.

gold. He seemed not very well poor little thing & tells me he is too poor to go home this year.

We spent an afternoon in the Sukh, I didn't get anything worth possessing – an old brown coffee pot & some beads. Back by the launch & rather a quiet dinner with the Sirdar, Lady Wingate & Bigge – Stamfordham's only son – I had a glorious ride with Currie on Tuesday afternoon – we cantered along as far as the Blue Nile & back – I mounted on a heavenly pony of Haddow's which fizzed under me like Perrier water.

V.A. to M.B.C.   *Saturday 27 December*
                                                   The Palace, Khartoum

We got here on Sunday afternoon after our very last lap of journey – 24 hours across the desert.... We were snatched away however & borne off to the Palace by Captain Haddow – a frightfully social & unvirile ADC (a very odd feature in this country) – & here we have been ever since – it will be a week to-morrow. For comfort and beauty our quarters cldnt. be equalled. The Palace really is rather like one – huge & cool with steps down to the Nile in front & behind & all around a marvellous garden (rather like Eden) full of vast brilliant garish flowers – & palms & fountains & blossoming trees – & <u>lawns</u> – flooded daily with Nile water by a cohort of dark purple slaves who louse[1] under the trees all day – dappled with light & shade.

There are masses of loggias & broad white stone halls – half indoors & half out – with green sunblinds that let down – & bushes in pots standing about & birds flying through – & old flags furled in corners – & Arab tent-hangings & drums & weapons about the walls. The atmosphere however is heavy with officialdom – muffled meals – people standing about like badly placed furniture in the interstices between them & a general paralysis of natural instincts. This is largely if not entirely due to Lady Wingate who is a tiresome woman – bornée opinionated & incapable & even undesirous of establishing herself on any sort of personal basis with anyone whatsoever. She <u>can't</u> make friends & doesn't want to. He is <u>wonderfully</u> kind civil & charming – & at his best when one gets him to talk about this country & the fighting he has seen in it. He does this simply & well. It is extraordinary that this mild, fluffy little man shld have been the chosen instrument of God to destroy the Khalifa with – one of the cruellest men I suppose who has ever existed – Currie & yr brother are very hostile to

---

[1] By 'louse' Violet appears to mean 'lounge' or 'laze'.

him I can see – they say he has no courage or loyalty – I think he must be a coward to work with – & probably fussy & meticulous & with no discrimination between the trivial & the essential. It is much cooler than last year – so much so that I have been breakfasting quite late – about 8.30 so far & riding mostly in the evenings – about 15 to 4. I have been out once or twice before breakfast.

This morning I was up at 6 – & crossed the river with the Sirdar & headquarters staff to Khartoum North on the other side – feeling very much of an Elsa[1] – not only the only woman but the only civilian – amongst all these glittering men in clanking spurs – & swords – & bombées chests covered with ribbons & medals. We 'inspected' some mounted infantry on the other side – I riding critically (!) up & down the lines – & then proceeded to have a triumphal ride through the town (which is purely native on that bank). It was a most extraordinary sight – the whole population turned out beating tom-toms – waving banners – dancing – lulu-ing prostrating themselves in the dust – girls making the most extraordinary snakelike undulating movements wriggling up to the Sirdar's horse – I have never heard such a noise – or seen such a sight in my life as all the myriads of black faces crowding in around one, & the 1000 outstretched black arms as thin as pipe-clay. There is a terribly low Nile this year & greater famine & distress than there has been since the British re-occupation.

It was difficult to believe the day before yesterday was Xmas Day – though we went to the Cathedral in the morning & sang Good King Wenceslas & Hark the Herald Angels – & Come all ye Faithful. The church was full of the strongest & goodest men I've ever met with the loudest voices I've ever heard in my life.

As Cys says this is no place for the Oxford manner – even the most civil of civilians protrude their chests & click their heels together just a little. He (C) looks very odd amongst them – & oddest of all on horseback. He has only been out for one ride so far. He sat well forward in a rather loose limp grey flannel coat – looking at his horse interrogatively – with a pale puzzled face as though he were trying to fathom its psychology. The horse always stops absolutely dead – the moment he gets on. Cys remarks 'Curious' – just as he does when his luggage goes round by Spain – & as in that dilemma – remains completely passive. I am not really at all happy about him – he looks wretched – is in very low spirits & absorbed by his symptoms which apparently continue in some form or other almost unintermittently. He doesn't seem keen to ride – or do anything specially – doesn't say a word to his neighbours at meals – isn't amused by them – doesn't even turn them into food for imitations. I believe I could cheer

---

[1] Possibly an allusion to Elsa of Brabant, the bride of Lohengrin in Wagner's opera *Lohengrin*.

him up & interest him if anyone could & cater for his peculiar pleasures etc. but he doesn't seem to take any interest in anything – & feels I think really bitter & injured over his prolonged discomfort.

Currie suggested he shld. see Dr. Chalmers (Balfour's successor) at the Gordon College – whom he (Currie) has a very high opinion of.[1] He says they are at least 3 years in advance of British medicine here – but of course they go in mainly for bacteriology – Cys saw him for an hour in the morning & an hour in the afternoon yesterday – was completely sounded from top to toe & is I believe going to have his blood analysed. He has gone round again this morning. After this 48 hours of 'observation' I am going to see Chalmers about him & will write his opinion home....

One word for your own self quite alone to say I feel you very near me very often – & miss you – & want you to be with me in all this glory of sun & colour. Do all the things I want you to – like being marvellously competent & as keen as the blade of a knife – & as taut as a bow-string. That's how I want you to be – Yr V

V.A. to M.B.C. *Monday 29 December*
Civil Hospital, Khartoum

I sent yr. wire first & Father's later – as I thought perhaps he might mind a little less if you told him – but you are sure to have both been away in the country. I have written him full details – but you will only get these letters in 10 days time & by then they will be ancient history. I can't tell you what I feel about this but you will know – Cys has – thank God – been in the hands of Chalmers of the Gordon College a great bacteriologist & a really clever man ever since Wed. Chalmers has been analysing his blood etc. & thought certain percentages in his white corpuscles very fishy – Cys looked <u>ghastly</u> – but that he has done ever since we started – & his discomfort & pain remained of much the same nature – except that he complained to me of feeling something like a raw spot in his inside. On Sunday night he said he felt very ill & I took his temp. found it just under 101 – in half an hour it rose to 102 – I sent for the Dr. at once of course – he was very guarded in his diagnosis told him not to move or eat. He had a bad night – burning hot & headachy – I went in & out to him. Next day at 7 the Dr. came – & told me it was dysentery. He discovered the amoebae in what he analysed – I made up my mind after a momentary hesitation to have

[1] Dr Albert John Chalmers (1870–1920), director of the Wellcome Tropical Research Laboratories in Khartoum.

him moved to the Hospital & not to your brother's house which he
offered. He & Currie wld have been turned out because of the infection –
but it wld in a way have been more human & less black than the
Hospital. However Chalmers thought the treatment here wld. be more
scientific & he was moved at once in an ambulance – the Sirdar & Lady
Wingate were thank God out so it was all over by the time they
returned.

We are now here together – in this strange Civil Hospital (I have got a
room) full of people of every colour – black brown & orange – only 3
nurses – masses of little brown errand-boys. The nurses strike me as being
not particularly good – observant or intelligent – but I never leave him –
(except for half an hour after tea when Currie made me drive) I can sit
just outside his bedroom on a sort of loggia it opens onto. He is very
drowsy – dulled – & burning hot – asks no questions about himself or his
illness – he has no idea what it is & seems to have no curiosity. Not much
pain so far – but discomfort.

They say the dysentery is mild but it seems to me terrible – he is so
weak – & it is like physical death to see him being sapped. The Dr. says his
very high fever (he was just under 104 this morning) is not to be accounted
for by the dysentery – he is analysing his blood for some other symptom &
fears typhoid. He has so little resistance & reserve force – I daren't speak
or write of the thought that never leaves me – Oh Bongie I love him so.[1]
   Yr V.
I feel so far away – Pray for him.

V.A. to M.B.C.   *Thursday 1 January 1914*
        Civil Hospital, Khartoum

Thank God I feel that if things go on as they have done for the last 24
hours Cys will be all right now. He has no strength in hand for ups &
downs – he is very – very weak from the fever starvation & dysentery but
his temp is low – (between 99 & 100) he slept a little last night & he is
having a little less internal discomfort.

On Monday – when Chalmers told me the fever cldn't possibly be
accounted for by the dysentery & he was probably in for typhoid as well –
I felt sure that if this were so he couldn't possibly live. He was almost too
weak to speak & the fever & dysentery were sapping him more hourly. His
temp. was 103 Monday night at 9 (lower than in the day) 102 at 11.30 –

[1] Violet's mother had died of typhoid fever in 1891, and the disease held a special fear for
her.

101 at 2 Tuesday morning & just under 100 at 7. It seemed too wonderful to be true & at first Chalmers thought it might just be a flash in the pan – but it kept down all the next day & only went up a very little the following night.

He had 2 more terrific hypodermic injections of emmetine & Chalmers said considering all things his pulse was pretty good though it seemed weak to me. The typhoid danger is now absolutely excluded – & the dysentery is they say well in hand. Chalmers is a genius & I have had implicit confidence in him throughout – he has been absolutely frank with me & spared me nothing – concealed no possible contingency from me. He was very anxious <u>indeed</u> all Monday but is I think much happier now.... The nursing is <u>not</u> good I think – it is unobservant – & rather inaccurate in trifling matters which however make a great difference to comfort – I have to be always on the qui vive & it makes me terribly anxious & afraid of being away for a second. There are only 3 white nurses for the whole place. Little black boys – very silent & barefooted run in & out – but often when he has rung his bell I have been the only person to go & do what he needed – & it wld be <u>fatal</u> if he got out of bed. The Hospital is crammed with people of all colours – black orange brown & green – I sometimes go round in the night & peep into the wards. The native nurses – male & female lie like dogs curled up in black balls on the stone floor by the beds or outside the doors of their patients. The passages are full of these dark inchoate sleeping lumps.

It is such a strange life living up on this stone verandah – looking out on sand all day long – & mud houses & variegated people in their strange clothes – & the sun blazing down on it all out of an absolutely cloudless sky. It is much hotter – especially between 11.30 and 4 when the wind drops a little – luckily Cys's room faces north so we get what air there is to be had from the desert. A good many people ride round & ask after him & 3 or 4 times a day yr. brother drives up in a sparkling dog-cart accompanied by an orange-clad syce & brings me gifts such as roses – bottles of ink – wickerwork chairs – lime-juice – stamps – cigarettes – all very useful conveniences for a woman in my position! My meals are sent down from the Palace by a wonderful Arabian nights messenger on a donkey who unfolds them out of a dinner-napkin like a stone-breaker's lunch – piping hot & very complicated.

I don't think I have ever felt so tired in my life. Though I've hardly moved since Sunday except from one chair to another my limbs feel as if I'd walked 100 miles – & my head swims with giddiness when I stand up. To-night I shall feel better able to go to bed & sleep if things go on as they are doing. This has been the worst experience but one of my life[1] – I have

---

[1] Violet refers to her deathbed vigil over Archie Gordon in December 1909: see above, pp. 190–5.

lived through such possibilities so many times since Sunday – I <u>have</u> wanted you. You felt so very far away from me. Your brother & Currie have been <u>angels</u> – but I had to make every decision myself & there was no one I knew quite well enough to be a relief – I felt face to face with such <u>horror</u>. It wld. be resting to have you with me now & to sit quite silently beside you & know that everything was all right – that you were loving me <u>very</u> much yr V. Happy New Year

H.H.A. to V.A.   *Saturday 3 January*
                                                     Lympne Castle, Kent

My dearest Violet – I got your letter describing your journey to Khartoum & your first experiences of life at the Palace there. Then on Monday last I received your telegram about Cys's illness, and for two or three days was rather anxious. The D^r has been very good in telegraphing, and I gather that there were no serious complications. The latest report (last night, Friday) is very satisfactory. I am afraid you must have had a very trying time. It was a good thing that both the pseudo-Bongie & Currie were at hand. We shall of course get particulars in your letters wh. will arrive next week. We must make proper acknowledgements to the Dr & the nurses.

Margot has been worrying herself naturally, & all the more that she is so far away & in practical solitude.

I went from Lympne to Alderley on Tuesday & spent two days there, returning here Friday.... Venetia & Olive left at midnight on Thursday for Chamonix, Bongie joining them in London. Oc is going off to-day to Mürren with his friend Jameson, and Elizabeth, who is with me here, will join him there on Wed next week; so that I shall be quite deserted. I think of going about the 14th to Antibes, and bringing back Puffin whose school reopens on the 20th. There is no political news, as everybody is <u>en vacances</u>. I hope Cys is not very weak: he must take it extremely easy. Best love & every wish for '14. yr ever loving Father.

V.A. to Venetia Stanley   *Wednesday 14 January*
                                                     The Palace, Khartoum

My Darling – Thanks so much for your glorious long letter which reached me on Sunday – I haven't written to you yet because I have been so wretched & undergoing such horrors. As you will know Cys developed dysentery a week after we got here....

Lord K[itchener]. has been at the Palace for 3 nights (whilst I was at the Hospital) & I went up to dinner two or three times & saw a good deal of him. He was in very good & in extraordinarily mellow & placable form obsessed by India talking of nothing else & obviously (I thought) pining to go there – Storrs was in attendance looking very vulgar but great fun. We had a wonderful military review – camels mules etc – galloping past. A terrible series of closely packed gaieties is in process at this moment under the name of 'Joy-Week' – races – regattas – balls – gardenparties – Polo – Gymkhanas etc. every day. The only really exciting feature of it however was a quite unexpected one, the arrival of Poupre the airman from Cairo.[1] It was one of the most thrilling things I have ever seen. He sent a telegram in the morning to say he was coming at 2.10 – a white patch was drawn on the desert for him to come down on & I went up there with the Sirdar – thousands of natives were waiting – quite incredulous – & at 2.00 to the second we saw a black speck in this cloudless sky in the Atbara direction – & the brown monoplane like a great moth or dragonfly whirred over our heads – swooped round over the crowd & alighted – having come the whole way from Cairo. The crowd made <u>one</u> rush straight for him – to see if it was a bird – or a man or a god – I thought he was certainly going to be killed as indeed he wld. have been if it hadn't been for a few English officers – the Egyptian police were quite useless – I was very nearly killed myself in the crowd but saved by John Bigge, Stamfordham's son, who is out here & exactly what a soldier ought to be – young pink – good & stupid-ish.

... I have read practically nothing here. I was first too anxious & now feel too tired & lazy – Here are Ladies I loved[2] – also the Portrait of a Lady – by Henry James drawn in with tiny infinitely subtle strokes – it has to be sipped like liqueur.

I have ridden a certain amount but not yet slept out or done anything really jolly. How strange to think of you in Switzerland – Bongie is with you I believe – I wonder if Artie was able to get away? – Love & bless you my own Darling Yr V.

Plans uncertain as they depend on Cys's recovery.

---

[1] Poupre's exploit had been planned to mark the anniversary of King George V's visit to Egypt, and he had promised Lord Kitchener that he would arrive at Khartoum before 17 January. This he managed with several days to spare, despite being forced to make at least one unscheduled landing due to mechanical problems. He flew at around 1,500 feet, and navigated by following the railway tracks, which were sometimes hidden by the sand.

[2] James Stephens, *Here Are Ladies* (1913).

M.B.C. to V.A.   *Friday 16 January*
10 Downing Street, Whitehall,
S.W.

Beloved, I have just got back from Chamonix and find your letter waiting for me, written on New Year's day after Cys's condition had definitely begun to improve. You must have had a most horrible time, every letter which you write makes it appear worse and makes me more proud of what you did. . . .

. . . I also send you Bonar Law's speech, as it gives the first authoritative account of the conversations.[1] The Liberal Press, as far as I have read take his rhetoric very calmly & think him unduly pessimistic. All that seems clear is that officially the opposition do not mean to accept anything less than [Ulster] exclusion. I think that it is possible that when Parliament meets the position may become clearer & it certainly seems to me absurd to assert that the sands are running out & that unless the Government show their hand now, all will be lost. The weak part of the Tory case is that they know quite well that an Election would decide nothing.[2] I also send you L.G.'s interview which appeared in the Daily Chronicle. (You must not mind my sending you such things as these which you very likely have heard about or read elsewhere). The Tory papers all seized upon this interview as the first step in a campaign by L.G. against Winston.[3] Drummond says that your father minded it for purely diplomatic reasons in particular the part about Germany, but that he does not think that either he or Winston objected to it on the other ground. The real difficulty is as I said in my last letter the question of next year's programme. I suppose that Winston would feel bound to resign if he did not get his full programme of four ships. I cannot believe that it will come to such a crisis as this, as I think that your father will really settle it. I at present do not see how we can fail to build the four, granted that the figures given by the Admiralty are correct on which the programme was based, unless we came to some definite understanding with Germany. These four are necessary to give us the 60 per cent standard of superiority & I do not think that there is any real resistance even amongst Liberals to this standard.

[1] About the government's proposed Home Rule bill: see above, p. 396.

[2] Bongie means that no British administration, not even a Unionist government with an overall majority in the House of Commons, could now govern Ireland without granting some measure of Home Rule.

[3] In an effort to reduce the navy estimates for 1914–15, Lloyd George gave an interview to the *Daily Chronicle* in the New Year in which he decried 'the overwhelming extravagance of our expenditure on armaments'. He argued that conditions in Europe and at home were favourable for a significant reduction in naval and military spending (Peter Rowland, *The Last Liberal Governments, 1911–1914*, 271, 278–9).

I must send this off. I am glad to [be] back at Downing Street & a little nearer to you. I wish that I could do more for you.... All my love.

B

M.B.C. to V.A.   *Wednesday 28 January*
                                                 10 Downing Street, Whitehall,
                                                                        S.W.

Beloved. I have got your letter saying how much I have disappointed you by my letters about Cyril's illness.[1] It has made it difficult to write. When I look back I think it is true to say that I did not realise, not the anxiety which it would cause you, that I think I did, but the physical strain that was being imposed on you. I did feel & think of you & little else all those days, and mind bitterly that my letters were so disappointing to you. I think that my imagination is blunt, I have always said so & my powers of expression even blunter & that is what makes letter writing so difficult & hateful to me.

Try & forgive me for my failings I can only pray that some of my letters did make it more clear that I was in thought with you all that time. I hoped perhaps you would see that from my telegrams, which though meagre enough were the only means I had of showing my thought immediately to you. I have also been thinking of you lately for a very different reason, namely during what is described outside as the Cabinet crisis over Naval Estimates. It has really been a difficult time, though the controversy has not been carried on in the bitter personal spirit which the Tory papers would lead one to suppose.

Simon has I think been the real protagonist on the side of economy. I had some talk with him on Sunday about it. He thinks that not only is the actual programme extravagant, as being beyond the 60 per cent standard, but that also the whole administration could be easily reduced in cost. He says that the continuance of Winston's present scale of expenditure will hang a millstone round the necks of the younger members of the party such as will eventually submerge them. On the other hand he said that though feeling this, they would accept the Prime Minister's decision. After two Cabinets yesterday & today I think that things are settling down. The programme as I have told you was never seriously in question, though I think that the alternative to be taken to supply the

---

[1] Violet had written to Bongie on Monday 12 January: 'I have been so bitterly disappointed & hurt at getting no word from you.... I have had 3 letters from Margot since hearing of Cys's illness – which all arrived at the proper times.... I so wanted you to be the closest thing in the world to me – & so mind feeling others nearer in moments like these.'

absence of the Canadian ships may have been a source of trouble.[1] If L.G. had been a normal Chancellor of the Exchequer this fuss would either have come years ago or not at all, it is really do [due] to his own lack of economy that the present situation has become possible.

Simon said that naval expenditure was really a source of danger to the existence of the Government, far more so than the Cabinet really believed & it was this that led him to the course he has taken. He said that he feared the Tories would bring forward a motion in the House condemning the extravagance not of the programme but of the administration of the navy. This really is McKenna's point I think, and I cannot believe it likely to happen. If things are settled now as I think that there is every reason to believe that they are or will be, I think that not a little good has been done by this fuss. Winston's administration admirable as it is in many ways, has certainly not been directed to economy, & if he is to stay First Lord of the Admiralty in a Liberal Government it has got to be. I believe if he set his mind to it, he could cut down the expense of his administration enormously. I think that this has been brought home to him & though it is a thing that now he would never allow, I should not be at all surprised if his estimates in future years are not found to be considerably smaller than is now foreshadowed.

The other thing which I hope that he has learnt is that his future lies with the Liberal party, because at one time he really did have to face the possibility of resignation & that fact may have been brought home to him. I do not mean it actually came near that point in fact, as I do not think that the naval programme was ever seriously in question. I do not indeed see how that could have been, as it was indeed not his programme alone but your father's, Haldane's & in fact the whole Cabinet's. The sort of idea that I believe was in his mind, fostered by F.E., that it would be possible to form a party free from the old Tory mandarins & the Little England Radicals with a programme of Devolution, National Service & Social reform is the most futile dream & that if that has been expurgated from his mind I think a great service has been done....

... Margot is expected back on Monday. I am very glad she has not been here all this time. Your father has been marvellously placid & cheerful & has as far as I can see shown no signs of worry. She wrote some oddish letters I understand both to Simon & Winston. Think gently of me I do really need you ... & mind bitterly that I should not have come up to your hope of me. God keep you.

B.

[1] The inability of Canada to deliver three promised Dreadnoughts by 1915 (above, p. 347) forced upon Churchill an increase of £1,000,000 in the naval estimates for the year 1914–15, and an acceleration in the construction of two British ships.

V.A. to M.B.C.   ***Thursday 29 January***
                                                              Khartoum

Thanks for your Swiss letters which have been coming in throughout the
last fortnight....

Cys has seemed much better the last 2 or 3 days & the weather has
become much cooler which suits him.... We had rather an amusing
experience yesterday when we went over (to Omdurman) with your
brother & MacMichael (a nephew of George Curzon's who is now chief
inspector at Omdurman) to tea with the Mufti the native head of the
Church & law. We were ushered before him through innumerable daedal
mud-passages open air overhead all the time – to a kind of square court
where angaribs (native beds made of taut string – very comfy) were
prepared in a long row – covered with lovely carpets. The sand was also
covered with carpets.

We all sat in a long row like birds on a telegraph wire & drank – first
very sweet lemonade & then highly spiced coffee – finally we gathered
round a tea-table & had tea with native cakes – & to our amazement –
Albert biscuits! My whole conversation with the Mufti had to be interpreted which slightly took the bubble off it. He remembered hearing
Gordon's order of evacuation read & was tutor to the Khalifa's son. I
afterwards went in to see his wives who were all hideous but morbidly &
hysterically secluded – He introduced several of the more personable as
his sisters & daughters but I'm sure this was only the Abraham dodge.

I ride every morning at 15 to 7 & sleep on the roof. There is a distinct
lull in the social life of the place I am glad to say it was very feverish for a
time. I have made great & real friends with a young Ulsterman (only by
birth!) called Boyd – a contemporary of Oc's at Oxford though I don't
think he knew him.[1] He has had a very tragic experience as his wife died
last May quite suddenly of heart failure in the train between here & Halfa –
He has the best sense of humour here. Currie is <u>heavenly</u> to live with – I
feel slight compunction at staying so long with your brother – I didn't
mean my last letter to be unkind – only it is so difficult far away to know
what each other are feeling. I <u>loved</u> getting the cuttings. I will wire when
we leave here – probably in about a fortnight yr V. Love –

---

[1] Alexander ('Lex') Keown-Boyd (1884–1954), of Ballydugan, Co. Down. At St John's College,
Oxford; Sudan Civil Service, 1907–16.

H.H.A. to V.A.   *Friday 20 February*
                              10 Downing Street, Whitehall,
                                            S.W.

My dearest Violet – I have just been reading your letter to Margot of the 9, and yesterday we got your telegram saying you had put off your journey to next Monday. I think & hope it may be possible to find some temporary pied à terre for Cys in the Riviera, while you push on home. I have not written lately partly because I have been very busy, & as I knew that Margot was keeping you au courant with our affairs.

The Session so far has belied the predictions of the prophets of storm & stress, and we have got through the Address without anything in the nature of a row. The Tories are pressing for a disclosure of our 'suggestions', for which they will have to wait, & their latest move is to set up a House of Lords Marconi Committee, which is not likely to lead to much. We yesterday lost Masterman's seat by 24 in a 3 cornered contest to Harry Wilson of all people in the world. This is not exactly a blow – for there was a substantial Home Rule majority – but it is a bore, especially for Masterman who had just got into the Cabinet, and will have to find another seat.[1]

Cynthia is very anxious that Beb shd. become a candidate somewhere, & Illingworth is all for putting him into Peterborough, which is supposed to be a safe seat & is quite near London. I don't feel sure that this is wise, but I am not strong the other way.

There is no particular gossip here. Did you see that Venetia's late friend Grant had become engaged to a Scottish damsel. Eliza is still recruiting at Cannes with the Robsons. Margot got much good from her rest cure, and so far seems wonderfully well. Montagu is delighted to become Sect of Treasury. I am sending this for safety to Cairo.

                                Ever yr loving Father

M.B.C. to V.A.   *Wednesday 25 February*
                              10 Downing Street, Whitehall,
                                            S.W.

Beloved. Another small Home Rule Debate has come and gone. I enclose you the Times report of the speeches; you have not I feel missed anything

[1] Having been appointed chancellor of the duchy of Lancaster, Masterman was required to stand for re-election in his Bethnal Green South West constituency. In February 1914 he polled 2,824, just 24 votes short of the winning total of Sir Mathew Wilson, Unionist; 316 votes given to the Independent Labour candidate, J. Scurr, were decisive in Masterman's defeat.

really important by being away. There have been no scenes in the House &
on the whole not much feeling shown as one would expect. Your father
describes B.L's speech as that of a cad, as did old Algy West who met me
today. He makes one long for the opportunity & ability to answer him as
one is listening to his speeches. I get so angry with his debating society
tricks, especially his use of the false dilemma based on his misreading of
the facts. Your father was delighted last night over what he called the one
modest remark that he has heard Winston make. In the course of B.L's
speech he was bubbling over with irritation & said to your father how he
wished that he had the ability to answer him. It did give a golden opportunity which was lost in the mischievous mumblings of William O'Brien's
utterances.

You will see from your father's speech that he gives March 31st as the
date when the government will lay their proposals before the House, so
you will be in plenty of time for that occasion, which really will be worth
attending....

You have had a great number of invitations from various bodies to open
bazaars & to preside at functions in March, all of which I have refused for
you, thinking that you would not wish to have any engagements of such
a sort, so soon after your return. I have kept the letters for you of course....

I do hope that Cys has got through his journey comfortable. I wish that
you could be whizzed straight home. My love & constant thoughts are
with you B.

Epilogue

Violet made a belated return to London in March 1914. Waiting
for her in Downing Street on her arrival was a letter that had been
posted in Wellington, New Zealand, on 7 January. It was from the
poet Rupert Brooke, and had been written in mid-December, when
he was 'Somewhere in the mountains of Fiji' – and she on her way
to the Sudan.[1] They had first met in March 1913, at a dinner party
given by their mutual friend Eddie Marsh. The next month Brooke
was among the guests invited to a dinner to celebrate Violet's
twenty-sixth birthday, and before he left England for America, at
the end of May, they were already close friends. His letter from Fiji
told of his love of England, 'and all the people in it', but expressed
a longing, too, for the island life that he had discovered, and which
he was aware was already disappearing:

[1] This letter is published, almost complete, in Christopher Hassall's *Rupert Brooke*, 425–8.
Brooke, born in August 1887, was four months younger than Violet. He was educated at Rugby
and King's College, Cambridge, where he held a fellowship from 1913. He died in April 1915,
when on active service with the Royal Naval Division.

It's very perplexing. These people – Samoans & Fijians – are so much nicer, & so much better-mannered, than oneself. They are stronger, beautifuller, kindlier, more hospitable & courteous, greater lovers of beauty, & even wittier, than average Europeans. And they are – under our influence – a dying race. We gradually fill their lands with plantations & Indian coolies. The Hawaiians, up in the 'Sandwich Islands', have almost altogether gone, & their arts & music with them, & their islands are a replica of America. A cheerful thought, that all these places are to become indistinguishable from Denver & Birmingham & Stuttgart, & the people of dress & behaviour precisely like Herr Schmidt, & Mr Robinson & Hiram O. Guggenheim. And now they're so – – – It's impossible to describe how far nearer the Kingdom of Heaven – or the Garden of Eden – these good naked laughing people are than oneself or one's friends.

He teased Violet that she would be unsympathetic to his lament – 'But I forgot. You are an anti-socialist, & I mustn't say a word against our modern industrial system' – and concluded by inviting her to give up the bustle of London and join him in the tranquillity of the South Seas:

I suppose you're rushing from lunch party to lunch party, & dance to dance, & opera to political platform. Won't you come to learn how to make a hibiscus wreath for your hair, & sail a canoe, & swim two minutes under water catching turtles, & dive forty feet into a waterfall, & climb a cocoanut palm? It's more worthwhile.

It was an accurate depiction of a lifestyle that, before long, Brooke was himself leading. He returned to London in May, in time for the season, and for the next few months was rushing, like Violet, from one encounter to the next. Their paths must have crossed many times. On Thursday 30 July they were together for dinner at 10 Downing Street. Brooke sat between Violet and her father, and opposite Winston Churchill, to whom he was introduced for the first time.[1] Talk would naturally have centred on the events in the Balkans, and their far-reaching consequences. On Tuesday 28th the Austro-Hungarian government had declared war on Serbia, and on the Thursday, the Russian government resolved upon a general mobilization. The next day Brooke returned to Rugby, to spend

[1] Christopher Hassall, *Rupert Brooke: A Biography*, 454.

the weekend with his mother, apparently convinced that European war was now inevitable. His mother wrote to Violet in April 1915, shortly after his death:

> My Rupert hated the idea of war; I shall never forget his misery when he came home last July 31; he had been dining at your house the night before & had felt very strongly that war was on us; he wouldn't go anywhere & sat almost in silence.[1]

At the dinner on 30 July, Churchill had offered to assist Brooke with a commission, and within weeks of the outbreak of war he had volunteered to serve with the Royal Naval Division, a new military unit under the administration of the admiralty. Eddie Marsh used his influence as Churchill's private secretary to effect a short cut through the bureaucracy, and Brooke was soon in uniform. At the same time Oc Asquith was taking similar steps, and that autumn they found themselves comrades-in-arms in the Hood battalion of the Royal Naval Division. Oc's presence in the Division alone would have guaranteed Violet's loyalty to it, but the fact that Brooke was there also, and others of their friends, ensured that she would become as involved in its fate as if she had been serving in it herself. Her correspondence with Brooke, and with other members of the Division, in the first months of the war reveal their awareness, and their shared sense of excitement, at being participants in a great historical event.

---

[1] Mrs [W. P.] Brooke to VA, 28 April 1915: Bonham Carter *MSS.*

APPENDIX A : *Glossary*

An explanatory list of words, phrases and abbreviations appearing in the text. Foreign words, and notably French adjectives, are given as they appear in the original.

à contre-coeur – with reluctance

à tue-tête – at the top of one's voice

abasourdi – dumbfounded, stunned

abordée – the act of approaching or accosting someone

Academy – the Royal Academy in London

affiches – placards, bills, posters

ahuri – flustered, bewildered

Anglo-Indian – a member of the Indian Civil Service; in this period almost certain to be British

Aubrey – repetition, in particular the use of the same descriptive passage in correspondence to different people. The word, coined by Maurice Baring, was inspired by Aubrey Herbert, who was famously apt to use 'a choice phrase more than once' (Margaret Fitzherbert, *Greenmantle*, 2)

avenance – personableness (from the adjective avenant, meaning handsome, comely, agreeable)

barbe a l'Impériale – a small, short beard worn under the lower lip, and made fashionable by Napoleon III, Emperor of France 1852–70

bird – happy

bisk(s) – a sporting agreement; in golf, a player receiving three 'strokes' advantage must take each at pre-ordained holes, whereas a player receiving three 'bisks' may elect when to take them

blue/half-blue – a representative of Oxford or of Cambridge University at one of a number of designated sports: some sports were awarded a full 'blue', for example cricket, and others a 'half-blue', for example golf

Bluebook – official report of parliament or the privy council, identifiable by its blue cover

boil – to put off, or shorten, a meeting with one friend in order to spend time with another

bombé – with protruded chest; to stand proudly, as in a military parade

bornée – narrow (of opinions)

brougham – four-wheeled, box-like carriage for two passengers, drawn by a single horse

Buxton – letters, letter-writing, and the post: after Sydney Buxton, postmaster general, 1905–10

C.P.R. – Canadian Pacific Railway

cela va sans dire – 'it goes without saying'

Ceres – Roman corn-goddess

charmeuse – a soft, silken dress fabric

Charon – in Greek mythology, the aged ferryman who carried the shades of the dead across the rivers of the lower world

Chils – the children, i.e. Elizabeth and Puffin Asquith

chuck – to cancel a social engagement

Club, the – the Archie Gordon Club

clump – a small conversation group, usually in an after-dinner setting

Clumps – a parlour game, similar to 'twenty questions'

Collins – a letter of thanks for hospitality or entertainment: after the Reverend William Collins in Jane Austen's *Pride and Prejudice*

come out – to make one's début in society

Commem – short for 'Commemoration', the term applied to the balls held in Oxford colleges at the end of Trinity Term (May–June). The week in which the balls are staged was formerly known as 'commemoration' week, during which there was a special service to remember the University's various benefactors

Cook[s] – Cooks travel agents (or a representative of)

Cracknell – a light, crisp biscuit

crush – a social gathering, or party

D.M. – *The Daily Mail*

déménagement – moving house

démodé – old-fashioned

dentist – a tête-à-tête

dépit – pique, vexation

désoeuvré – idle

désorienté – confused, bewildered

dewdrop – a compliment on someone's character

Die-hard – the term is supposed to have derived from Colonel William Inglis's command of the 57th regiment at Albuera, in May 1811, a particularly bloody battle in the Peninsula War: 'Die hard! 57th, die hard'. It gained general usage long before, in 1911, it was applied to the hard-line Unionist opponents of the Parliament bill; see 'ditcher'

Disestablishment – see 'Welsh Disestablishment'

ditcher – Unionist prepared to 'die in the last ditch' fighting the Parliament bill, 1911

doe – a woman

Douane/douaniers – customs/customs officers

Dreadnought – a revolutionary new class of battleship: quicker, and with greater fire-power, it rendered all previous battleships technically obsolete. The prototype HMS *Dreadnought* was launched at Portsmouth on 10 February 1906, at a cost of £1,800,000

drimmy – vague, ethereal

drum – a large social gathering, either an afternoon tea-party or an evening assembly

Dumb crambo – the mime form of *crambo*, a word game in which a player has to guess a word after being given as clues other words that rhyme with it: in *dumb crambo* the answers must be mimed

E.G. – Easton Grey

Early Victorian – old-fashioned, conventional (of manners or dress)

Edwinian – of or like Edwin Montagu

eingelebt – settled in, mentally; content

élan vital, l' – life force, joy of life, spirit of enterprise

endimanché – Sunday best

epigrams – a parlour game in which the players have to devise epigrams for one another, and then guess which epigram is meant to describe which person

éreinté – exhausted

état-d'âme – state of mind

étape – stop; stopping place

étonnant – remarkable, in the sense of gifted, or talented

façon de parler – 'manner of speaking'

fiacre – a four-wheeled, box-like hire coach, named after the Hôtel Saint-Fiacre, in Paris, where it was introduced in the seventeenth century

fiscal question – the issue of tariff reform versus free trade

fishface – a nondescript

fleshly – detailed, often in a mundane way

floater – an embarrassing situation, or the cause of one

fly – a lightly built, fast-moving carriage, drawn by a single horse; it came to mean any single horse hire vehicle

frowst – the atmosphere of warmth in an over-crowded, or poorly ventilated, room

gaufres – waffles

Gepäckschein, das – luggage tickets

gibbets – (hangman), a word game in which part of a gibbet (gallows) is drawn every time a player fails at guessing a hidden quotation: after six failures the gibbet is completed, and the game ends in a 'hanging'. Cynthia Asquith recalled that it was extremely popular with her generation, and was played 'for hours on end … even sometimes to the general disapproval in the ballroom' (*Diaries*, 504)

Gigue Anglaise, La – the English Jig

gilets – waistcoats

glumse – depression, sadness

gouffre – abyss

Greats – the popular name given to *Literae Humaniores*, the school of Classics, philosophy and ancient history at Oxford University

groove – anything well-worn, such as a joke or topic of conversation

gummi-schuhed – rubber-shoed (an Anglicized rendering of the German)

Halma – chequer-board game involving two or four players; also known as 'hoppity'

H.G.W. – H. G. Wells

H.R. – Home Rule (see below)

Handgepäck – hand-luggage

hansom – a light two-wheeled carriage, drawn by a single-horse, and steered by one of the two passengers. They could be fitted with an additional seat, at the rear, for a professional driver, and in this form were popular hire vehicles

heap – a string of jade beads, given to Violet by Archie Gordon in July 1909, or a silk[?] scarf given to Violet by Bongie, probably some time in 1910

heygate – conventional (of manners, attitudes, etc.); the word carried a negative connotation, and was often applied to individuals ('a heygate') in a way similar to the use of 'square' by a later generation; after Maurice Baring's housemaster at Eton, Mr Heygate, though according to Violet this was an injustice 'because he wasn't one'

hinny – to neigh like a horse, to whinny

hobble-skirt – a highly restrictive article of late-Edwardian fashion 'in which one was encased like a banana and could barely step out of a brougham'

[Irish] Home Rule – the policy, favoured by the Liberals and opposed by the Unionists, of re-establishing in Dublin a parliament that would control the internal affairs of Ireland

hydro-like – a 'Hydro' was a type of hotel, with an emphasis on health and recuperation, and offering hydropathic treatment

Imperial Preference – system of trade tariffs by which countries within the British Empire would offer one another preferential terms of trade

Indian Civilian – a member of the Indian Civil Service

Indian judge – a member of the judiciary of the Indian Civil Service

Kavass – in Turkish lands, an armed state official

Khedive, the – the viceroy of Egypt

knurd – drunk (i.e. drunk spelt backwards)

L.S.C. – Liberal Social Council

landau – heavy carriage drawn by four horses, with room for four passengers and a driver

lasher – proposal of marriage

Lettergame – a parlour game

list-work – social engagements: either the planning or the fulfilment of

lord chamberlain – official in charge of the royal palaces, and in particular admission to court

Lossie – Lossiemouth, coastal town in Moray, Scotland, close to Elgin, and the site of golf links popular with the Asquiths

Mahdi – in Islamic tradition, a messiah whose coming is foretold by the prophet

Ministère des Affaires Étrangères – Ministry of Foreign Affairs

mise en scène – setting, background

navigate – to court; to approach with romantic intent

nespolis – medlars

nonconformist – a member of a non-Anglican Protestant church

Olivian – of or like Olive Macleod

P.S.A./P.S. – Personal Service Association

padlock – secret; used in letters to indicate something told in confidence

parti – a particularly eligible bachelor, typically a young aristocrat destined to inherit; from the French *parti*, meaning 'match'

pension – boarding-house

phantom – a late-stayer at a ball [?]

piano – 'down', 'off colour' or simply quiet

Pigeon – a simpleton

pie – a group of people at a social gathering

plait/platt – the early stages of a friendship

podere – farm

point d'appui – support, prop

pouding – pudding

provost – in Scotland, the head of a municipal corporation, or burgh; the equivalent of a mayor

raffinée – refined

réchauffés – rehashes

Reckitts – blue (of the sky)

relever – to raise, take note, or give an account of

Reuter – the telegraph

ridge – a mental barrier against someone, caused by anger or frustration at their behaviour

Rock, the – Gibraltar

rôdé-d – prowled

Roger de Coverley – an English country dance, often referred to as 'Sir Roger'

Runnymede – Charles Meade's motor car

saccadé – jerky

St John the Baptist – advance warning; a short message, in anticipation of a longer one

sans trêve – unceasingly

sathe – in a general sense used by Violet to describe sea fish

sauf – save, except for

schinken brötchen – ham bread roll

schools – at Oxford University, the final public examinations in the degree of Bachelor of Arts

season, the – the months of May, June and July, when fashionable society assembled in London

sehnsucht – longing

serrement de coeur – pang

shingly – of a woman's hair: cut very short; some suffragettes adopted a cropped hairstyle in obvious defiance of social norms

single-sticks – a game of fencing with stick-like swords

Sir Giles – overwhelming, extreme

Sirdar, the – the British commander-in-chief of the Egyptian army

soignée – dressed with care; well-groomed

souk/sukh – market-place in Muslim countries

'Souls, the' – a group of highly cultured friends in fashionable London society of the 1880s–1890s. Numbering around four dozen, they included many who were familiar to the Asquith children from their youth, through their step-mother Margot, a prominent member. Called the 'Souls' because their conversation was allegedly absorbed with spiritual matters

South African war – Boer War, 1899–1902

steerage – the part of a passenger ship accommodating those paying the cheapest fare

stylobate – in architecture, a continuous base supporting a row of columns

succès fou – tremendous success

Swift and Reliable – [probably] a hire carriage of some description

temperance – movement devoted to reducing the consumption of alcohol

tent – a word of Violet's invention, signifying anxiety, expectation: it merges 'tense' with 'taut'

Pole, the – Arnold Ward's name for the Asquiths' home: it plays on the remoteness of Cavendish Square from the fashionable residential areas of London, around Hyde Park

third, a – a third-class honours degree at Oxford

touch up – to arrange, to secure necessary permission

transformation scene – a theatrical technique involving an instantaneous, apparently magical, change of scenery: used in the annual pantomimes staged at the Drury Lane Theatre in London in these years

travailléd – finely wrought

trêve – break

Trinkgelds – tips

trottoir roulant – a moving walkway

U.P. – United Presbyterian, a Protestant sect that merged with the Free Church, to make the United Free Church

Unionists – opponents of the Home Rule legislation proposed by the Liberal party from 1886 onwards. Called 'Unionists' because they upheld the union of Great Britain with Ireland, enshrined in the 1800 Act of Union. The term embraces both members of the Conservative and Liberal Unionist parties, which officially merged in May 1912

Veto Bill – the Parliament bill of 1911

Victoria – a light, low four-wheeled carriage, renowned for its elegance

Watteauesque – suggestive of the style of Antoine Watteau, eighteenth-century French painter famous for his graceful depictions of female costume, and particularly the 'Watteau hat'

Welsh disestablishment – the severance, in Wales, of the close connection between the Anglican church and the state: Welsh bishops would be appointed by a synod of the church, and not by the prime minister

Whig element – the aristocratic and conservative wing of the Liberal party

Wykehamist – a pupil or former pupil of Winchester College: after William of Wykeham, founder of the College (1382)

APPENDIX B : *Biographical notes*

These biographical notes end in 1914, the terminal date of the present volume. Titles given are those held in the period; where a knighthood predates 1904, the title 'Sir' is included in the name; where it was awarded 1904–14, it is in brackets. Names enclosed in square brackets are commonly used nicknames, those in rounded brackets are unused given names. Unattributed quotations are from Violet Bonham Carter's unpublished papers. The following abbreviations are used:

> *Autobiography* – Mark Bonham Carter (ed.), *The Autobiography of Margot Asquith* (1995)
> *Edwardian Youth* – L. E. Jones, *An Edwardian Youth* (1956)
> *Raymond Asquith* – John Jolliffe (ed.), *Raymond Asquith: Life and Letters* (1980)
> Spender & Asquith – J. A. Spender & Cyril Asquith, *The Life of Herbert Henry Asquith, Lord Oxford and Asquith* (2 volumes, 1932)
> *Venetia Stanley* – M. & E. Brock (eds.), *H. H. Asquith: Letters to Venetia Stanley* (1985)

Aberdeen, Lady – Ishbel Maria Gordon *née* Marjoribanks (1857–1939). Youngest daughter of 1st Baron Tweedmouth. Married, 1877, John Campbell Gordon; four children: George (Lord Haddo), Dudley, Marjorie and Archie. Lady Aberdeen was active in public health and education, and in advancing the position of women in society: she was president of the International Council of Women from 1893, founded the Victorian Order of Nurses in 1898 and the Women's National Health Association (in Ireland) in 1907.

Aberdeen, Lord – **John Campbell Gordon** (1847–1934), 7th Earl of Aberdeen. Married, 1877, Ishbel *née* Marjoribanks. Governor-general of Canada, 1893–8, and lord-lieutenant of Ireland, 1886, and 1906–15. A diligent lord-lieutenant, he was nevertheless regarded with amiable derision in Ireland. Hugh Godley wrote to Violet from Cavan, in August 1912, where Lord Aberdeen had recently paid a state visit, 'He is apparently regarded by all classes as a complete fool & funny.'

Asquith, Anthony [Puffin] (1902–68). Violet's half-brother, Margot's youngest surviving child; universally known by his childhood name of 'Puffin', or 'Puff', an allusion to the hooked nose that he inherited from his grandfather, Sir Charles Tennant. Educated at Summer Fields preparatory school, at Winchester College, and at Balliol College, Oxford.

Asquith, Arthur Melland [Oc/Artie] (1883–1939). The third and favourite son of H. H. Asquith. Educated at Winchester and New College, Oxford, 1902–5; 'Oc' was the only one of Asquith's five sons not to go to Balliol. Went down without a degree in 1904 to enter business, but returned to New College in 1905 to read

Arabic. With the Sudan Civil Service, 1906–11. Left for employment with Franklin and Herrera, a London-based company with business interests in the Argentine, 1911–14. In his choice of career, as well as of Oxford college, Oc differed from his brothers. He was the most adventurous of Asquith's sons, resourceful and intelligent, though essentially non-academic, and although Cys was nearer to her in years, Violet looked to Oc as her 'equal'.

Asquith, Cynthia *née* **Charteris** (1887–1960). Eldest daughter of Lord Elcho, the future 11th Earl of Wemyss, and Lady Elcho (*née* Mary Wyndham), whose sons Ego and Guy were also friends and contemporaries of the Asquith children. Violet first met Cynthia when they were in Dresden together in 1903, and it was there, too, that Cynthia met her future husband, 'Beb' Asquith, who visited that winter; they were married in 1910.

Asquith, Cyril [Cys] (1890–1954). The youngest of the children of Asquith's first marriage. As gifted academically as his elder brother Raymond, 'Cys' won scholarships to Winchester and to Balliol, took the three top Classics scholarships at Oxford in 1911 (the Hertford, Craven and Ireland), and in 1913 a first in Greats, as well as the Eldon Law scholarship, and a fellowship at Magdalen. Sensitive and prone to ill health, Cys evoked in Violet a protectiveness that was intensified by the early death of their mother. She later wrote of their relationship: 'To me he was not only my brother but my child. I had to try and interpret life to him when I myself . . . was groping my way through it.'

Asquith, Elizabeth Charlotte Lucy [Eliza] (1897–1945). Violet's half-sister, and Margot's eldest surviving child. Despite a ten-year age difference, there was a competitiveness between Asquith's daughters that meant that Violet's feelings towards Elizabeth were cooler than those towards any of her other siblings.

Asquith, (Emma Alice Margaret) Margot *née* **Tennant** (1864–1945). Violet's stepmother, the sixth daughter of Sir Charles Tennant. Margot was a leading figure in fashionable late-Victorian society, having launched into it 'more like a rocket than a ship' (*Autobiography*, xx). She surprised many when, at the age of thirty, she married H. H. Asquith, and took on the responsibilities of a step-mother to his young family. Her health and emotional stability were weakened by five pregnancies, and the death of three of her children within hours of their birth; the children who survived were Elizabeth and Anthony. Margot contributed to her step-daughter's sense of taste and style, endowing her with social confidence, but their relations were fundamentally strained. In December 1909 Asquith lamented that the two women that he most cared for should be 'on terms of chronic misunderstanding', and three years later Margot wrote, with feeling, 'I always tell everyone of temperament *never* to be a step-mother' (*Venetia Stanley*, 10).

Asquith, Helen Kelsall *née* **Melland** (1854–91). Violet's mother, the daughter of Frederick Melland, a Manchester surgeon, and Anne *née* Kelsall. Helen married H. H. Asquith at the age of twenty-three, and died of typhoid fever fourteen years later, leaving a family of five children, the eldest of whom, Raymond, was twelve, and the youngest, Cys, barely eighteen months old. On the first anniversary of her death Asquith wrote to his friend Frances Horner: 'In the cant phrase our marriage was a "great success"; from first to last it was never clouded by any kind of sorrow or dissension; and when the sun went down it was in an unclouded sky' (Roy Jenkins, *Asquith*, 53).

Asquith, Herbert [Beb] (1881–1947). H. H. Asquith's second child. At Winchester and at Balliol 'Beb' followed in his elder brother's footsteps, though he could not repeat Raymond's academic success, taking a second in Greats in 1904. Like his brother and his father, he was president of the Oxford Union, and left Balliol for a career at the bar, to which he was called in 1907. He married, in 1910, Lady Cynthia Charteris, daughter of Lord Elcho. A prominent figure at Oxford in his day, Beb was perhaps the most original and idiosyncratic of Violet's brothers. She loved his 'peculiar qualities of thought and humour', but was aware that his subtle charm was not universally recognized.

Asquith, Herbert Henry (1852–1928). Violet's father. Born in Morley, Yorkshire, the youngest of two sons of Joseph Dixon Asquith, a cloth manufacturer, and Emily *née* Willans. Educated at the City of London School and Balliol, where he was a Classical scholar. In 1874 Asquith took a first in Greats, won the Craven scholarship, and was elected to a prize fellowship at Balliol. He left Oxford for the bar in 1875, and was called the following year. Married Helen *née* Melland, 1877; four sons and one daughter. Elected Liberal MP for East Fife, 1886 (held seat until 1918). Queen's Counsel, 1890. Home Secretary, 1892–5. After the death of Helen Asquith he married, 1894, Margot *née* Tennant; one daughter, one son. Chancellor of the exchequer, 1905–8; prime minister, 1908–16. Violet adored, and understood, her father: she had the ability to make him laugh, at times uncontrollably, but possessed also, 'where he was concerned, the gift of communicative silence' (Spender and Asquith, i, 225).

Asquith, Katharine *née* Horner (1885–1976). The younger daughter of Sir John and Lady Horner, Katharine married, in 1907, Raymond Asquith. They first met in the summer of 1901, at Clovelly in Devon, and while Raymond did not find her 'technically beautiful' he was impressed by her discovering 'two serious Homeric errors' in a friend's essay on 'the classical element in Tennyson'. They married after a three-year courtship, overcoming parental concern about her age and his prospects. In Margot Asquith they had a powerful ally: she thought them 'the most perfect combination of in-loveness and friendship marrying at the right age, with the right knowledge of each other, that I have ever known' (*Raymond Asquith*, 80, 94).

Asquith, Raymond (1878–1916). The eldest of H. H. Asquith's children by his first marriage. Raymond won scholarships to Winchester and to Balliol, where he gained the distinction of first-class honours in Greats (1901) and in Jurisprudence (1902), as well as the coveted Craven and Ireland scholarships, the Eldon Law scholarship, and an All Souls fellowship by examination. Following his father, he left Oxford and was called to the bar (1904). He married, 1907, Katharine Horner. Adopted Liberal candidate for Derby, 1913. Junior counsel to the Inland Revenue, 1914. Judged by the standards set by his father, and by his own record at Oxford, Raymond's career was one of unfulfilled potential. He was, nevertheless, a leading figure in his generation, famed for an iconoclastic and incisive wit: when asked the riddle 'what is it that God never sees, the King rarely sees, but that we see every day?', to which the expected response was 'an equal', Raymond answered 'a joke'. The most complex of all Violet's brothers, he was also the one most affected by their mother's early death.

Asquith, (Helen) Violet (1887–1969). The fourth child, and only daughter, of H. H. Asquith and his first wife, Helen. Born in Hampstead, London, 15 April 1887, and baptized 'Helen Violet' by Randall Davidson, bishop of Winchester, 1896. Two pivotal events of Violet's early life were the death of her mother in 1891, and her father's remarriage to Margot Tennant three years later: the first made her more dependent upon her father, while the second introduced a competitor for his affection, and both did much to mould her character. She was educated at home, but spent several months in Dresden in 1903 learning German, was 'finished' in Paris the following year, and 'came out' in 1905. She travelled widely, and read voraciously, though her greatest interest was in politics. By 1914 she had made a number of speeches in public, and was a Liberal activist in her own right. She possessed, in her father's opinion, 'a first-rate masculine mind of the same order as Raymond's' (Spender and Asquith, i, 225). L. E. Jones too saw a sharp intellect, but one 'veiled' in femininity, and he remembered 'her bright, fair hair, the chiaroscuro of her moods ... the quick impulses of feeling that had never to wait for the right, the inevitable, words' (*Edwardian Youth*, 216).

Baker, Harold Trevor [Bluetooth/Bluey] (1877–1960). A Winchester contemporary and lifelong friend of Raymond Asquith, whose Oxford success he rivalled when at New College, 1896–1900. Fellow of New College, 1900–7. Liberal MP for Accrington, Lancashire, 1910–18. Parliamentary private secretary at the war office, 1910–11, and financial secretary, 1912–15. Commonly known as 'Bluetooth', or 'Bluey', after an early king of Denmark, 'but for what precise reason both he and everyone else had forgotten' (Cynthia Asquith, *Diaries, 1915–18*, 486).

Balfour, Arthur James [A.J.B.] (1848–1930). The nephew of the Conservative statesman Lord Salisbury, whom he succeeded as premier: entered parliament 1874; Unionist leader in the Commons, 1891–1911; prime minister, 1902–5. Balfour, generally regarded as the 'high priest' of the 'Souls', enjoyed a long friendship with Margot Asquith, and cordial relations with her husband, his political adversary. Violet was captivated by his charm when they first met in 1906, but she was later warned by Edwin Montagu, in a letter written after her father had become premier, that Balfour was a 'professional charmer, [a] hater of the P.M's success, losing no opportunity now or ever to make trouble for him'.

Baring, Maurice (1874–1945). The fourth son of 1st Baron Revelstoke. Diplomatic service, 1898–1904. War correspondent for the *Morning Post* in Manchuria, 1904, and special correspondent in Russia, 1905–8; his many pre-war publications included *With the Russians in Manchuria* (1905). Violet knew Maurice Baring, a friend of her father's, from childhood, when much of their discussion was about books, and he remained throughout her life her literary 'confidant and confessor' (see V.A. to Venetia Stanley, 4 August 1910, above p. 214).

Battersea, Lord – Cyril Flower (1843–1907), 1st Baron Battersea, 1892. Married, 1877, Constance (1843–1931), daughter of Sir Anthony de Rothschild. A Liberal member of parliament, 1880–92, and a junior minister in Gladstone's last two administrations, Lord Battersea was also an enthusiastic huntsman, a keen photographer and the owner of a valuable picture collection, including works by da Vinci, Rubens and Whistler. Violet remembered childhood visits with her mother to his London home at Marble Arch: 'He was a flamboyant figure, exuberant, demonstrative, affluent and childless. He adored my father and my mother (the word is not too strong) and their family became the children he had longed to have.'

Belloc, (Joseph) Hilaire (1870–1953). Born in Paris, and educated at the catholic Oratory School in Edgbaston, and Balliol. Liberal MP for South Salford, 1906–10. Journalist, author, and founder-editor of the *Eye Witness*, 1911. Belloc's sharp criticisms of the Edwardian establishment, which extended to attacks on the leadership of his own party, had a strong anti-semitic taint.

Birrell, Augustine (1850–1933). Liberal MP for West Fife, 1889–1900; for North Bristol, 1906–18. President of the board of education, 1905–7; chief secretary for Ireland, 1907–16. Birrell was one of H. H. Asquith's oldest friends, and for more than a decade they represented neighbouring constituencies in parliament. They shared a love of literature and scholarship; Birrell was a successful author and literary reviewer. After the death of his first wife he married, in 1888, Eleanor Mary *née* Locker-Lampson.

Bonham Carter, Maurice [Bongie] (1880–1960). Violet's future husband, the youngest of the eleven sons of Henry Bonham Carter and Sibella Charlotte *née* Norman. 'Bongie', as he was universally known, was at Winchester with Violet's elder brothers, arriving the year after Raymond, and staying in the same House, 'Trant's', as Beb and Oc; he first met Violet when he used to visit Cavendish Square with them on their 'leave out' days from school. At Balliol, 1899–1903, he read chemistry, with the intention of pursuing a medical career, but instead went into industry. He was called to the bar in 1909, and became private secretary to H. H. Asquith the following year. Bongie was a popular figure at Oxford, a cricket blue, known for his musicality and athleticism, and revered in the undergraduate magazine *Isis* as in all things 'the apostle of variety': 'he will keep wicket one year, the next bat, the next bowl – the only monotonous thing about him is his good fielding.'

Bonham Carter, Edgar (1870–1956). The elder brother of Maurice, and the fifth son of Henry and Sibella Bonham Carter. Educated at Clifton College and New College, Oxford; a rugby blue, capped for England in 1891. Called to the bar in 1895; appointed judicial adviser to the governor-general of the Sudan in 1899. He devised, and set in place there, a complete system of civil and criminal law, and became the most prominent civilian in a military administration, serving from 1910 on the governor-general's council. On his forty-second birthday he wrote reflectively to his parents in England: 'Another year to one's total after forty is not a subject for congratulation for an unmarried man: but one has this advantage over youth that one is no longer troubled by such a strong anxiety as to the future.'[1]

Burns, John (1858–1943). Trade unionist, and member of the Social Democratic Federation, 1884–90. Represented Battersea as a London County Councillor, 1889–1907, and as a radical, later Liberal, member of parliament, 1892–1918. Burns became the first working man to enter the cabinet when appointed president of the local government board by Campbell-Bannerman in December 1905. He held this post until August 1914, when he resigned in opposition to British entry into the European war.

Campbell-Bannerman, Sir Henry [C.-B.] (1836–1908), GCB 1895. Educated at Glasgow University and Trinity College, Cambridge. Married, in 1860, Sarah *née* Bruce (d. 1906). Represented Stirling Burghs uninterruptedly from 1868 until his death. As leader of the Liberals in the Commons from February 1899, 'C.-B.' kept an uneasy peace over a party divided by the Boer War and Home Rule, and he led a united one into government in December 1905. Resigned as prime minister 4 April 1908, after a lengthy period of ill health, and died later that month. Margot Asquith remembered him as 'essentially a *bon vivant*, a *boulevardier*'. His political skill and toughness are easily underrated (*Autobiography*, 111).

Chamberlain, Joseph (1836–1914). A leading radical who left the Gladstonian Liberal party in opposition to Home Rule, 1886. Served as colonial secretary under Salisbury and Balfour, 1895–1903. His conversion to tariff reform in May 1903 broke the political mould, dividing the Unionist party, and unifying Liberals. He resigned from the cabinet in September 1903 to conduct a national campaign for tariff reform. A stroke, in July 1906, effectively ended his direct influence on British politics, and he died in July 1914.

Churchill, Clementine Ogilvy Spencer *née* Hozier (1885–1977). Second of four children of Sir Henry and Lady Hozier. Educated at Berkhamsted High School for Girls, 1901–4, and at the Sorbonne. Clementine's parents were separated early in her life, placing her mother in financial difficulty, and she 'came out' with the assistance of a benevolent relation. After a brief courtship she married, in September 1908, Winston Churchill.

Churchill, Winston Leonard Spencer (1874–1965). Eldest son of Lord Randolph Churchill and Jennie Jerome of New York. Educated at Harrow and Sandhurst.

---

[1] EBC to Henry and Sibella Charlotte Bonham Carter, 2 April 1912; Hants RO 38M49/86.

Served with the 21st Lancers on the Nile Expedition to retake the Sudan, 1898. *Morning Post* correspondent in South Africa, 1899–1900. Unionist MP for Oldham, 1900–6; broke with the party over tariff reform, and represented Manchester North West as a Liberal, 1906–8, and Dundee, 1908–18. Under-secretary of state for the colonies, 1906–8; president of the board of trade, 1908–10; home secretary, 1910–11; first lord of the admiralty, 1911–15. Married, 1908, Clementine *née* Hozier.

Crewe, Lord – Robert Crewe-Milnes (1858–1945), 1st Marquess of Crewe, 1911. Lord president of the council, 1905–8; colonial secretary, 1908–10; secretary of state for India, 1910–15. Asquith 'constantly sought Crewe's level-headed advice, called him the "most underrated man in England" and was always one of his most intimate friends and admirers' (James Pope-Hennessy, *Lord Crewe* (1955), 65).

Dunn, James (1875–1956). Canadian-born financier, educated at Bathurst public school and Dalhousie University, Canada. Married, 1901, Gertrude (*née* ?). Founded the merchant bank Dunn, Fischer & Co. in London, in 1907; survived in business, despite being liable for unknown debts when his partner, Louis Fischer, defaulted and absconded in 1913.

Edward VII (1841–1910). The eldest son of Queen Victoria, whom he succeeded in January 1901 at the age of fifty-nine; he married, in 1863, Princess Alexandra of Denmark. The King took a keen interest in European diplomacy, and in the early years of his reign helped bring about closer relations between Britain and France. His last years were troubled by bitter domestic disputes, and he was a reluctant arbitrator in the conflict between the Unionists and the Liberals over the veto power of the House of Lords. He died on 6 May 1910, during the parliamentary Easter recess.

George V (1865–1936). The eldest surviving son of King Edward VII; he married, in 1893, Princess Victoria Mary of Teck. Between his accession in May 1910 and his coronation in June 1911, the new King faced severe trials of statesmanship arising from the passage through the House of Lords of the Parliament bill. The stormy passage of the third Home Rule bill, 1912–14, represented a second great crisis, and it is an irony that peace came to his troubled realm only with the advent of European war, in August 1914. Asquith did not find George V easy to manage, and wrote to Margot, in September 1912: 'He is a nice little man with a good heart and tries hard to be just and open minded. It is a pity he was not better educated.' (*Venetia Stanley*, 43; see also Violet's diary entry of 13 September 1913, above p. 391).

Godley, Sir (John) Arthur (1847–1932), KCB 1893, GCB 1908, 1st Baron Kilbracken, 1909. Educated at Rugby and Balliol. Permanent under-secretary of state for India, 1883–1909: Godley was credited with virtually creating the India Office. Joined the Unionist party after retirement. He came to know Violet through her close friendship with his son, Hugh, and encouraged her study of the Classics.

Godley, Hugh John (1877–1950). Elder (and only surviving) son of 1st Baron Kilbracken. Educated at Eton, and at Balliol, where he was a friend and contemporary of Raymond Asquith, and of Bongie. Called to the bar, 1902; assistant parliamentary counsel to the treasury. Bongie wrote to Violet in February 1908 his perception of the importance to Hugh of marriage to her: 'I certainly think that he is the most sensitive of your friends and the most dependent on his main aim or – if it is better explained so – is less divided into compartments. So that I feel that his moodiness comes entirely from the jeopardy of his position in what he cares for most, and that security there would give him all that is needed to carry him happily through his life.'

Gordon, Archibald Ian [Archie] (1884–1909). Youngest son of 7th Earl of Aberdeen. Educated at Winchester and Balliol, where he was a contemporary of Violet's brothers. Worked for the Dresdner Bank in Berlin, 1907, and for Dunn, Fischer & Co., in London, from October 1908. Fatally injured in a motor car accident at the end of November 1909, Archie died in hospital in Winchester a fortnight later, at the age of twenty-five. He was an athletic and confident young Scot, high-minded and high-spirited. A half-blue at golf, he on one occasion risked sending a ball through the stained-glass window of the chapel at Hatfield House, where he was a guest, having entered into a bet that he could clear the wing from the gravel forecourt. When he failed, and the ball narrowly missed the window, hitting an upright mullion, 'he only grinned, and forked out half a crown'. He had, according to Evan Charteris, twenty years his senior, the ability to attach himself 'to anyone with whom he chose to make friends' (*Edwardian Youth*, 62–3; Nicholas Mosley, *Julian Grenfell* (1976), 127).

Grenfell, Ethel Priscilla *née* Fane [Ettie] (1867–1952), Lady Desborough. The granddaughter of two earls, 'Ettie' Grenfell was an orphan by the age of two, and married at the age of twenty, to 'Willy' Grenfell, the future 1st Baron Desborough. She was an old friend of Margot Asquith, a fellow 'Soul', and her sons Julian and Billy, both educated at Balliol, were friends of the young Asquiths. Ettie, however, developed a strong and enduring friendship with Violet in her own right.

Grey, (Sir) Edward (1862–1933), KG 1912, FRS 1914. Married, in 1885, Dorothy *née* Widdrington (d. 1906). Liberal MP for Berwick-on-Tweed, 1885–1916; undersecretary of state for foreign affairs, 1892–5; foreign secretary, 1905–16. Grey, Asquith and Haldane were an influential troika, on the imperialist 'right' wing of the Liberal party. Asquith rated him highly, placing him second in an imaginary class-list of the cabinet in February 1915 (*Venetia Stanley*, 452). 'He looked exactly what he was. Tall, square-shouldered, loose-limbed, with the head of an eagle and a schoolboy's laugh – there was an immediate sense of strength – strength in reserve.'

Haldane, Richard Burdon (1856–1928), 1st Viscount Haldane, 1911. Educated at Edinburgh and Göttingen Universities. Liberal MP for Haddingtonshire, 1885–1911. Secretary of state for war 1905–12; lord chancellor, 1912–15. Haldane and Asquith were friends and political allies from the days when both were struggling barristers in London: it was at Haldane's suggestion that Asquith first stood for East Fife, a constituency within sight of his own, in 1886. He had been devoted to

Asquith's first wife, and knew their children from infancy, and Violet recalled, 'In those days he was a constant presence in our home and life and seemed a natural part of both.'

Herbert, Aubrey (1880–1923). Eldest son of the 4th Earl of Carnarvon by his second marriage. Educated at Eton and Balliol. Served in the diplomatic service, 1903–5, after which he travelled widely in Ottoman lands. He married, 1910, Mary Vesey, only child of Viscount de Vesci. Unionist MP for South Somerset, 1911–18. Aubrey had been at Balliol with Raymond and Beb Asquith, and was a frequent visitor at Cavendish Square and, later, Downing Street.

Horner, (Lady) Frances *née* **Graham** (1858–1940). Daughter of William Graham, Liberal MP. Married, 1883, (Sir) John Francis Horner (1842–1927), KCVO 1907. Became friendly with H. H. Asquith shortly after the death of his first wife: her four children, Cicely, Katharine, Edward and Mark, were of similar age to his, and in 1907 her younger daughter married his eldest son. Through her father she had come to know the Pre-Raphaelites, and had been a close friend of Sir Edward Burne-Jones.

Kitchener, Lord – Horatio Herbert Kitchener (1850–1916). 1st Baron Kitchener of Khartoum, 1898; 1st Earl Kitchener, 1914. Educated at a French school, and the Royal Military Academy, Woolwich. Commissioned in the Royal Engineers, 1871. As sirdar of the Egyptian army, 1892, Kitchener planned and led the 'River War' to retake the Sudan, 1896–8, and was briefly governor-general there, before becoming Lord Roberts's chief of staff in the South African war, 1899–1902. Commander-in-chief of the Indian army, 1902–9. British agent and consul-general in Egypt, 1911–14.

Lansdowne, Lord – Henry Charles Petty-Fitzmaurice (1845–1927), 5th Marquess of Lansdowne. Lansdowne occupied minor posts in Gladstone's first two cabinets, but was in early disagreement with his chief's Irish policy, over which he resigned in 1880. He became Unionist leader in the Lords in 1903, and was foreign secretary, 1900–5. Following the 1906 Liberal landslide he led the Lords in using their veto power to obstruct government legislation emanating from the Commons, advising rejection of the 1909 budget and, initially, the 1911 Parliament bill. He owned land in England and in Ireland.

Lister, Charles Alfred (1887–1915). Eldest surviving son of 4th Baron Ribblesdale. Educated at Eton and Balliol. Charles Lister was the same age as Violet, and they were friends from childhood. L. E. Jones remembered him at Balliol as 'a creature all heart and mind': 'It was these sensibilities that led him when still an Eton boy to join the Labour party ... and to manage to combine, at Oxford, a first in Greats with sudden raids into anti-sweating, Fabianism and strikes' (*Edwardian Youth*, 57).

Lloyd George, David (1863–1945). Educated at Llanystumdwy Church School and at home. He married, 1888, Margaret *née* Owen; three daughters, two sons. Liberal MP for Carnarvon District uninterruptedly from 1890. President of the board of trade, 1905–8; chancellor of the exchequer, 1908–15. An anti-Boer War radical, who emerged as a central figure in the mainstream of Edwardian Liberalism.

Macleod, (Sir) Reginald [Waxworks] (1847–1935), KCB 1905; 27th chief of the Macleod clan. Under-secretary of state for Scotland, 1902–8. Married, 1877, Lady Agnes *née* Northcote: their daughter, Olive, was a close companion of Violet's in the years after 'coming out'. His nickname derived from his 'pink-and-white complexion and white cotton-wool side-whiskers' (Jones, *Edwardian Youth*, 217).

Marsh, Edward Howard [Eddie] (1872–1953). Clerk in the colonial office, 1896–1905, and a devoted private secretary to Winston Churchill from 1905. Using an inheritance, Marsh assembled a valuable collection of modern English paintings. He also edited, from 1912, *Georgian Poetry*, an anthology of modern verse whose early contributors included Rupert Brooke, John Masefield and D. H. Lawrence. Harold Nicolson's observation that Marsh 'was not the ordinary type of Civil Servant' was, Violet later remarked, a 'wild understatement of the truth'. He combined 'avid, all-embracing catholicity' with 'critical perception', so that he was 'not a patron only, but a pioneer and discoverer in the field of art and letters'.

McKenna, Reginald (1863–1943). Liberal MP for North Monmouthshire, 1895–1918. Financial secretary to the treasury, 1905–6; president of the board of education, 1907–8; first lord of the admiralty, 1908–11; home secretary, 1911–15. Married Pamela *née* Jekyll, 1908.

Meiklejohn, Roderick [Mikky] (1876–1962). Entered the war office 1899, transferring to the treasury in 1902. Private secretary to senior Liberals, 1903–5, and to H. H. Asquith, 1905–11. In constant attendance on Asquith for much of the period.

Montagu, Edwin Samuel (1879–1924). Second son of Samuel Montagu, 1st Baron Swaythling. Educated at Clifton College, the City of London School, and Trinity College, Cambridge. Liberal MP for Chesterton, Cambridgeshire, 1906–22. Parliamentary secretary to H. H. Asquith, 1906–10. Parliamentary under-secretary of state for India, 1910–14; financial secretary to the treasury from February 1914. Among Violet's close male friends Montagu stands out, both because he was a Jew and because he had been at Cambridge, and not at Oxford (still less at Balliol).

Morley, John (1838–1923), 1st Viscount Morley, 1908; Order of Merit, 1902. Journalist and barrister. Radical Liberal MP for Newcastle-upon-Tyne, 1883–95; for Montrose Burghs, 1896–1908. Chief secretary for Ireland, 1886, 1892–5; secretary of state for India, 1905–10; lord president of the council, 1910–14. Resigned in protest at British entry into the European war. Author of many biographical works, including the highly successful *Life of Gladstone* (1903).

Murray, Alexander [The Master] (1870–1920), 1st Baron Murray of Elibank, 1912. Liberal MP for Midlothian, 1900–5; Peebles and Selkirk, 1906–10; Midlothian, 1910–12. Under-secretary of state for India, 1909; parliamentary secretary to the treasury, 1910–12; chief Liberal whip, 1909–12. The 'Master of Elibank' was a trusted lieutenant in the early years of Asquith's premiership.

Raleigh, (Sir) Walter Alexander [The Professor] (1861–1922), Kt 1911. Educated at the City of London School, Edinburgh Academy, and King's College, Cambridge. Married, 1890, Lucie Gertrude *née* Jackson. Professor of English literature at Oxford from 1904, and fellow of Magdalen, 1904–14. Author of many studies in English literature, including *Wordsworth* (1903) and *Shakespeare* (1907).

Rosebery, Lord – Archibald Philip Primrose (1847–1929), 5th Earl of Rosebery. Married, in 1878, Hannah, eldest daughter and heiress of Baron Meyer de Rothschild; two daughters, one son (Lord Dalmeny). Former Liberal premier who remained an influential and often divisive presence in the Liberal party for a decade after he retired as its leader, in 1896. The leading Liberal imperialist, Lord Rosebery opposed the Gladstonian precept that Home Rule should dominate the party agenda. He was a substantial landowner, and the author of studies of Chatham, Napoleon, Peel and Lord Randolph Churchill.

Simon, (Sir) John Allsebrook (1873–1954), Kt 1910. Liberal MP for Walthamstow, Essex, 1906–18. One of the ablest advocates of the day, Simon was made King's Counsel within ten years of being called to the bar (1899), and was appointed solicitor-general in 1910 when only thirty-seven. He served as attorney-general, with a seat in the cabinet, 1913–15.

Smith, Frederick Edwin [F.E.] (1872–1930). Barrister and Unionist MP for Walton, Liverpool, 1906–18. A brilliant maiden speech in the Commons in March 1906 established 'F.E.'s' reputation and he took a seat on the opposition front bench when Bonar Law became Unionist leader, in 1911. He was deeply involved in the Die-hard resistance to the Parliament bill, 1911, and afterwards in Ulster resistance to Home Rule.

Stanley, (Beatrice) Venetia (1887–1948). Youngest child of the 4th Baron Stanley. To L. E. Jones, who knew her well, Venetia had 'dark-eyed, aquiline good looks and a masculine intellect ... but she permitted herself, in the morning of her youth, no recourse to her own femininity. She carried the Anthologies in her head, but rode like an Amazon, and walked the high garden walls of Alderley with the casual stride of a boy'. Venetia's famous correspondence with Violet's father, and the special relationship to which it bears witness, was in progress by the spring of 1914, when this volume ends.[1]

Tennant, Sir Charles (1823–1906), 1st Bt, 1885. Liberal MP for Glasgow, 1879–80; for Peebles and Selkirk, 1880–86. 'The Bart' was a Scots industrialist whose business investments made a large fortune, which he generously applied to supporting a family of twelve children by two marriages, the second of which he embarked

---

[1] *Edwardian Youth*, 214. For a detailed account of Asquith's relationship with Venetia Stanley, see the Brocks' *Letters to Venetia Stanley*.

upon at the age of seventy-five. An art collector, he possessed works by Reynolds and Raeburn.

Vincent, Sir Edgar [Sedgar] (1857–1941), KCMG 1887; 1st Baron d'Abernon, 1914. Governor of the Imperial Ottoman Bank in Constantinople, 1889–97. Married, 1890, Lady Helen Duncombe, daughter of 1st Earl of Feversham. Unionist MP for Exeter, 1899–1906. Broke with the Unionist party over tariff reform, and contested Colchester as a Liberal in December 1910. Of the same generation as Ettie Desborough and Frances Horner he became in due course, like them, a friend to Violet.

Ward, Arnold Sandwith (1876–1950). The only son of T. Humphry Ward, fellow of Brasenose, and Mrs Humphry Ward, novelist. Educated at Eton and Balliol. Special correspondent for *The Times* in Egypt, the Sudan and India, 1899–1902. Barrister, 1903. Contested Cricklade, Wiltshire, as a Unionist, 1906; Unionist MP for West Hertfordshire, 1910–18. Eleven years older than Violet, Arnold knew her brothers from Balliol, and was already acquainted with her before she 'came out' in 1905. A determined opponent of women's suffrage, and a strong advocate of tariff reform.

Ward, Mrs Humphry – **Mary Augusta** *née* **Arnold** (1851–1920). Famous late-Victorian novelist, best known for *Robert Elsmere* (1888), which dealt with religious and social issues that were prominent concerns of Mrs Ward herself. She led opposition to women's suffrage, founding the Women's Anti-Suffrage League in 1908. She married, in 1872, Thomas Humphry Ward, a journalist and fellow of Brasenose College, Oxford: they had three children, Arnold (above), Janet and Dorothy.

APPENDIX C : *Note on houses*

Unless otherwise indicated, quotations are from either i) Violet's unpublished diaries and letters or ii) the relevant edition in Nikolaus Pevsner's *The Buildings of England* series (which is arranged by county). Where a title and family name differ, the latter is given in brackets.

I. Houses outside London, and abroad

Abbey Leix (*Co. Waterford, Ireland*) – Home of Lord de Vesci.

Alderley Park (*Chelford, Cheshire*) – Home of Lord Stanley; the house, a large mansion, was built in the early nineteenth century; most of it was pulled down in 1934.

Archerfield House (*Dirleton, East Lothian*) – Lent to the Asquiths by Margot's elder brother, Frank Tennant, 1907–12. The house stood (only a shell remains) about a mile from the Firth of Forth, with a private nine-hole golf course. It was built by William Nisbet around 1700, and enlarged by Robert Adam in 1790.

Avon Tyrrell (*Hampshire*) – Home of Lord and Lady Manners; built in the New Forest by Lethaby in 1891, 'one of the finest houses of the date in England' (Pevsner).

Balmoral Castle (*Aberdeenshire*) – On the River Dee.

Barnbougle Castle (*West Lothian*) – Barnbougle, situated right on the Firth of Forth, was abandoned by the 3rd Earl of Rosebery in the early nineteenth century for more comfortable quarters at Dalmeny, half a mile further inland. It was rebuilt by the 5th Earl in 1881 as a private library, with modest living quarters.

Beaufort Castle (*Inverness-shire*) – Home of Lord Lovat. Built in 1880; designed by J. M. Wardrop. Violet found it 'a vast red house – very ugly bare & Hydro-like outside – green surroundings but with a wonderful river rushing through the Park'. Lutyens told his wife (1901): 'Architectural anachronisms at every corner'.

Belvoir Castle (*Leicestershire*) – The seat of the Duke of Rutland (Manners); a castle of eleventh-century origin, on the edge of the Vale of Belvoir.

Bywell Hall (*Stocksfield-on-Tyne, Northumberland*) – Home of Lord Allendale (Beaumont); a grand eighteenth-century villa.

Castle Ashby (*Northamptonshire*) – Seat of the Marquess of Northampton (Compton); an Elizabethan and Jacobean mansion on the site of an eleventh-century castle.

Castle, the (*Dublin*) – Centre of the British government's administration in Ireland.

Château de Laversine (*nr. Chantilly, France*) – House belonging to the Gustave Rothschilds, about twenty-five miles north of Paris.

Cloan (*Perthshire*) – Home of R. B. Haldane; a large country house in Scottish baronial style, set in a small estate.

Clovelly Court (*North Devon*) – Home of the Hamlyns, friends of Margot Asquith; originally an eighteenth-century construction, but extensively rebuilt in the twentieth, the house stands close to the deep cove that holds the fishing village of Clovelly. It was later inherited by Betty Asquith, *née* Manners, the future wife of Oc Asquith.

Dallas Lodge (*Forres*) – Described by Bongie as 'the best & most comfortable shooting lodge' he had seen in Scotland, 'lacking the castellated pitch pine Gothic character of the more pretentious & the dank horsehair discomfort of frankly makeshift. It is full of bathrooms and big chairs & looks as if it were lived in.' Situated close to the Moray Firth. The shooting lodge had been added to a late seventeenth-century 'round-square'.

Dalmeny House (*West Lothian*) – Seat of the Earl of Rosebery; built in Tudor Gothic style, 1814–17, 'a large cold, rather gloomy house with nice oak & fine pictures'.

Dalquharran Castle (*Ayrshire*) – Taken by the Asquiths in the autumn of 1904; Raymond described it as being large but uncomfortable, and wrote to Katharine Horner: 'Margot has put up a green tent of great architectural beauty . . . in the gardens, and there she sleeps at night, while the rest of us rough it in the Castle' (Jolliffe, *Raymond Asquith: Life and Letters*, 115).

Easton Grey (*Wiltshire*) – Home of Margot's sister, Lucy Graham Smith; a late-eighteenth-century manor house on the Avon, about four miles west of Malmesbury; 'a lovely house, grey like its name, standing among tall elm trees full of cawing rooks above a river [the Avon]'.

Ewelme Down (*Oxfordshire*) – Home of the Asquiths' friend Frank Lawson; built in Tudor style around 1910 by Walter Cave, 'on a high hill covered with Junipers' midway between Oxford and Henley.

Ewhurst Park (*Surrey*) – One of the seats of the Duke of Wellington (Wellesley); 'The house is really lovely full of nice things, pictures & furniture perfect, comfort & beauty combined. A big bath is the only thing lacking.'

Glen (*Peeblesshire*) – Designed in the 1850s in the Scottish baronial style by David Bryce for Margot Asquith's father, Sir Charles Tennant, and set in 4,000 acres.

Glen of Rothes (*Moray*) – Rented by the Asquiths 1905 and 1906; surrounded by 'very tame' Scottish countryside, it was like the set of 'a very, very sordid Bernard Shaw play': 'mustard coloured', devoid of comfortable chairs, useful tables and a library, though good points were 'two bathrooms, hot water and a kitchen garden with raspberries & peas'.

Gosford House (*East Lothian*) – Seat of the Earl of Weymss (Charteris), on the coast north of Edinburgh; built by Robert Adam in 1790, with additions by William Young, 1891; 'large labyrinthine & <u>most</u> beautiful . . . full of marble'.

Haddo House (*Aberdeenshire*) – Home of Lord and Lady Aberdeen. 'I had expected mist & turnip-fields – a kind of sea-less Slains & was amazed at the wet greenwoods with moss & lichen & roe-deer.'

Hartham Park (*near Chippenham, Wiltshire*) – Home of Sir John Dickson-Poynder.

Hatfield House (*Hertfordshire*) – Home of the Cecils; one of the most important Jacobean mansions in England, built 1607–12: 'The house is most beautiful . . . lattice windows & red brick seasoned into beauty by centuries of sun & rain & inside stone halls with men in armour & dangerous slippery oak galleries hung with Godfrey Knellers & other fine pictures.'

Highfield (*Muir of Ord, Ross*) – The Asquiths' base for the autumn of 1907; the house stood 'among peacocks & pinewoods', surpassing Glen of Rothes 'in things like grandeur, crenellation & size', but carrying on the 'suburban tradition' in the furniture: 'Gothic spires made of orange varnished wood all over the walls, brown velvet sofas – glass cases full of pampas grass, shells, fans, humming birds & other horrors'.

Hopeman Lodge (*Moray*) – Lent to the Asquiths by Thomas Gordon-Duff, Margot's brother-in-law; the house was eighteen months old when Violet stayed there in August 1913, and she found it 'truly funny': 'The most uncompromising villa you can imagine, painfully square & bare – dumped down in a welter of sandhills which produce not even an illusion of vegetation'. It was nevertheless comfortable, and Violet likened it to a third-class railway carriage: 'getting into it is the worst part – once in one feels all right.'

Hopetoun House (*Lothian*) – Ancestral home of the Marquess of Linlithgow; built in the eighteenth century, Hopetoun was a 'veritable palace' (Pevsner), the work of two generations of the Adam family.

Hutton Castle (*Berwick-on-Tweed*) – Home of Lord Tweedmouth (Marjoribanks); used as an electoral campaign base by Jack Tennant, who succeeded the 2nd Baron as the Liberal member for the surrounding constituency of Berwickshire.

Kiddington Hall (*Oxfordshire*) – A house in the Italianate style with terraces and formal gardens, remodelled in the mid-nineteenth century.

Killegar (*County Leitrim, Ireland*) – Home of the Godley family: built in 1813 by John Godley, and given in 1898 by Arthur Godley (Lord Kilbracken) to his son Hugh as a twenty-first birthday present. (The house was leased to an uncle, and Hugh did not live there until 1942.) It is a large and attractive Georgian villa.

Kilmaron Castle (*near Cupar, Fifeshire*) – Home of Sir James Low. Used by Asquith as an election campaign base.

Larbert House (*Stirlingshire*) – Just west of Falkirk.

Lympne Castle (*Lympne, Kent*) – Acquired for Frank Tennant in 1906, and restored by R. S. Lorimer. It stands on the edge of an escarpment above Romney Marsh.

Manor House, Mells, the (*Somerset*) – Home of the Horners; a beautiful Elizabethan manor house, extensively restored by Sir John and Lady Horner around 1900.

Minley Lodge (*Farnborough, Hampshire*) – Country home of Lord Kilbracken (Godley).

Munstead House (*Surrey*) – Home of the Jekyll family; built 1877–8 in a 'Scots vernacular' (Pevsner), the interior was remodelled by Lutyens *c*. 1900.

Palace, Khartoum, the (*Sudan*) – The official residence of the governor-general of Sudan; built on the site of the original palace destroyed by the Mahdists in 1885, and set in six acres of gardens, it stood at the centre of the two-mile river esplanade, which housed the principal buildings of the Sudan administration.

Panshanger (*Hertfordshire*) – Inherited by Ettie Desborough from her aunt Katie Cowper in 1913.

Pleasaunce, the (*Overstrand, Norfolk*) – Home of Lord Battersea (Flower); a large red-brick house, with cloisters and a clock tower, adapted from two existing houses by Lutyens, 1897–9.

Penrhôs (*Anglesey*) – Second country home of Lord Stanley; a Tudor foundation, with eighteenth- and nineteenth-century additions. Now ruined.

Pixton Park (*Dulverton, Somerset*) – Home of Aubrey and Mervyn Herbert's widowed mother, Lady Carnarvon; 'Pixton stands on a hill in a rolling wooded park near Dulverton in Somerset, in the midst of sharp valleys and hanging covers' (Jones, *Edwardian Youth*, 47).

Slains Castle (*Aberdeenshire*) – Let to the Asquiths in 1908 by the Earl of Erroll; the castle stands on a high cliff, at an especially rugged part of the Aberdeenshire coast, some twelve miles south-west of Peterhead. It had been rebuilt in 1836–7.

Stanway (*Winchcombe, Gloucestershire*) – Seat of the Earl of Wemyss (Charteris); built between 1580 and 1640, close to the North Cotswold village of the same name; its notable features include an impressive façade of mullioned windows. 'The house is a dream Elizabethan; grey stone covered with orange lichen & a porch one drives thro' like a thing of melting stone in a ghost story. Inside it is icy & comfortless but very attractive with stone floors & rush carpets, <u>most</u> beautiful windows of discoloured glass & a stage wind always whistling.' Extensions by William Burn, a noted Jacobean specialist, 1859–60: alterations by Detmar Blow, 1913.

Stocks House (*Tring, Hertfordshire*) – Home of the Ward family; a medium-size country house, built in the 1780s, and inherited by Sir Edward Grey, who let the property to the Wards in 1892.

Tain (*place*) – 6m east of Thurso, in Caithness

Taplow Court (*Buckinghamshire*) – Home of the Grenfell family; a large four-storey house of Tudor and French Gothic design, set in 3,000 acres, on the Thames just above Maidenhead.

Terling Place (*Witham, Essex*) – Home of Lord Rayleigh (Strutt); a large Georgian white-brick house, built 1772–80; 'very hideous & comfortless; no big bath, broken springed beds, hard pillows, tepid water, deal floors. At lunch a large soup-tureen of prunes is carried round & they are doled out impartially willy-nilly.'

Thurso Castle (*Caithness*) – Home of the Sinclair family; built in the Scottish baronial style for Sir John Sinclair, 3rd Bt, 1872–8.

Tomich (*Inverness-shire*) – Close to Beauly, at the head of the Beauly Firth.

Tulchan Lodge (*Moray*) – Shooting lodge where Lady Aline Sassoon entertained; Edward VII was among her guests there. Now demolished.

Vice Regal Lodge, the (*Dublin*) – Seat of the lord-lieutenant of Ireland.

Vinters (*Maidstone, Kent*) – Home of the Macleods; a derelict fragment of an eighteenth-century house restored, 1849–50, by C. J. Richardson, student of Jacobean and Elizabethan architecture.

Wharf, the (*Sutton Courtenay, Berkshire*) – Bought by the Asquiths in 1912; an eighteenth-century house on the Thames below Oxford, converted and enlarged for the Asquiths by Walter Cave.

Whittingehame (*East Lothian*) – Home of Arthur James Balfour; an early-nineteenth-century house, built in pale stone.

Windlestone Hall (*Ferryhill, Co. Durham*) – Home of the Edens; a large two-storey house, built in 1834.

II. Houses in London

Apsley House, Piccadilly – London residence of the Duke of Wellington (Wellesley); Cynthia Asquith remembered that it had no electricity, and when used for a ball during the season 'the vast rooms were entirely lit by great chandeliers of wax candles, greatly to the advantage of the guests, for that soft glimmering light was wonderfully kind to both old and young' (*Remember and Be Glad*, 61).

49 Bedford Square, W.C. – Home of Raymond and Katharine Asquith; their lease began in November 1907.

59 Bridge Street, Cambridge – Edwin Montagu's Cambridge address. Situated north of the city centre.

20 Cavendish Square, W. – The Asquiths' home from 1894 to May 1908, when the family moved into Downing Street, and the house was let. Violet remembered its 'symmetry and perfect proportions', 'the long, cool, spacious hall into the dining-room with its daffodil damask curtains, its great Adam chimney place supported by double eagles – a glowing Canaletto on the walls between two Scott riverscapes of London by the Thames'. The kitchen was located across the street in the adjacent Henrietta Place, and meals had to be transported to the dining room in Cavendish Square by means of an underground trolley and a lift; remarkably they arrived hot.

10 Downing Street, Whitehall, S.W. – The premier's official residence, and the Asquiths' home from May 1908 to December 1916; Violet lived there until her marriage in November 1915.

5 Hyde Park Square, W. – London home of the Bonham Carters, situated just north of Hyde Park.

25 Grosvenor Place, S.W. – The London residence of the Ward family, situated east of Hyde Park, in an area of 'aristocratic mansions, or rather palaces' (*Illustrated London News*, 1868).

18 Mansfield Street, W.1 – The London home of Lord Stanley; near Portland Place, part of a development by Robert and James Adam, 1770–5.

Office of the Parliamentary Counsel – The place where Hugh Godley worked as an assistant to the treasury; the full address was 18 Queen Anne's Gate, Whitehall, S.W.

29 Sloane Gardens, S.W. – London home of the Godley family (Lord Kilbracken).

Temple, E.C. – A number of Violet's correspondents wrote from addresses within the Temple, which houses two of the four Inns of Court that control admission to the English and Welsh bar: her father sometimes wrote from *1 Paper Buildings*; Arnold Ward from *1 Essex Court*; and Hugh Godley from *11 King's Bench Walk*.

SELECT BIBLIOGRAPHY :
a note on sources and further reading

I. Manuscript sources

The material presented in this volume mostly comes from the Violet Bonham Carter MSS (private papers, Oxford). This includes all diary references, and all correspondence except: i) Winston Churchill to Violet Asquith, which is to be found in the Chartwell Papers at the Churchill Archives Centre, Churchill College, Cambridge; ii) Violet Asquith to (Lady) 'Ettie' Desborough, which is to be found among the Desborough Papers at Hertfordshire Record Office (HRO D/ERv). The correspondence between Violet Asquith and her brother Arthur Melland ('Oc') Asquith is to be found both among the Violet Bonham Carter MSS and also his own papers, which form part of a private collection.

II. Printed sources

There is a voluminous literature on the Edwardian era, and it is only possible here to cite the historical works to which direct reference is made in the text. For the benefit of those interested in pursuing further reading on Violet and her times, a number of memoirs, autobiographies and biographies of special relevance has been included. In this respect, too, the list must not be thought to be comprehensive. Place of publication is London unless otherwise stated.

Asquith, Cynthia, *Haply I May Remember* (1950)
–*Remember and Be Glad* (1952)
–*Diaries, 1915–1918* (1968)
Asquith, Herbert, *Moments of Memory* (1937)
Asquith, H. H., *Memories and Reflections* (2 volumes, 1928)
Asquith, Margot, *Places and Persons* (1925)
–*Lay Sermons* (1927)
–*More Memories* (1933)
–*Myself When Young* (1938)
–*Off the Record* (1943)
Benckendorff, Constantine, *Half a Life* (1954)
Bennett, Daphne, *Margot: A Life of the Countess of Oxford and Asquith* (1984)
Blake, Robert, *The Unknown Prime Minister: The Life and Times of Andrew Bonar Law* (1955)
Blunt, Wilfrid Scawen, *My Diaries: A personal narrative of events 1888–1914* (1919)
Bonham Carter, Mark (ed.), *The Autobiography of Margot Asquith* (1995)
Bonham Carter, Violet, *Winston Churchill as I Knew Him* (1995)
Brock, M. 'The Eternal Lack of Motive: Raymond Asquith's Buried Talents', in R. Custance (ed.), *Winchester College: Sixth Centenary Essays* (Oxford, 1982)
Brock, M. and E. (eds.), *H. H. Asquith: Letters to Venetia Stanley* (Oxford, 1985)

Carrington, Charles, *Rudyard Kipling* (1978)

Charteris, Mary Constance (Countess of Wemyss), *A Family Record* (privately printed, 1932)

Churchill, Randolph, *Winston S. Churchill: Young Statesman, 1901–1914* (1967)

Churchill, Winston, *Great Contemporaries* (1942)

Clark, Kenneth, *Another Part of the Wood* (1974)

Clarke, P. F., *Lancashire and the New Liberalism* (Cambridge, 1971)

Cook, Chris, *A Short History of the Liberal Party* (1976)

Cooper, (Lady) Diana, *The Rainbow Comes and Goes* (1958)

Donaldson, Frances, *The Marconi Scandal* (1962)

Dugdale, Nancy (Baroness Crathorne), *Tennant's Stalk: The Story of the Tennants of the Glen* (1973)

Ensor, R. C. K., *England 1870–1914* (Oxford, 1936)

Fitzherbert, Margaret, *The Man Who Was Greenmantle* (1983)

Gilbert, Bentley Brinkerhoff, *David Lloyd George: A Political Life* (1987)

Grenfell, Ethel (Lady Desborough), *Pages from a Family Journal, 1888–1915* (privately printed, Eton College, 1916)

Grey of Fallodon, Viscount, *Twenty-Five Years* (2 volumes, 1925)

Haldane, R. B., *An Autobiography* (1929)

Hart-Davis, Duff (ed.), *End of an Era: Letters and Journals of Sir Alan Lascelles, 1887–1920* (1986)

Hassall, Christopher, *Rupert Brooke* (1964)

–*Edward Marsh: A Biography* (1959)

Hazlehurst, Cameron and Woodland, Christine (eds.), *A Liberal Chronicle: Journals of J. A. Pease, 1st Lord Gainford, 1908–1910* (1994)

Hollis, Christopher, *Along the Road to Frome* (1958)

Holmes, Colin, *Anti-Semitism in British Society, 1876–1939* (1979)

Horner, Frances, *Time Remembered* (1933)

Jenkins, Roy, *Mr Balfour's Poodle* (1954)

–*Asquith* (1964)

Jolliffe, John (ed.), *Raymond Asquith: Life and Letters* (1980)

Jones, L. E., *A Victorian Boyhood* (1956)

–*An Edwardian Youth* (1956)

–*Georgian Afternoon* (1958)

Koss, Stephen, *The Rise and Fall of the Political Press in Britain* (1990)

Levine, Naomi B., *Politics, Religion and Love* (New York, 1991)

MacCarthy, Desmond, *Portraits* (1949)

Mackenzie, Jeanne, *The Children of the Souls* (1986)

Magnus, Philip, *King Edward the Seventh* (1964)

Markham, Violet, *Return Passage* (Oxford, 1953)

Mosley, Nicholas, *Julian Grenfell: His Life and the Times of his Death 1888–1915* (1976)

Nevins, Allan, *Henry White* (New York, 1930)

Pevsner, Nikolaus, *The Buildings of England* (series, by county)

Ponsonby, F., *Recollections of Three Reigns* (1951)

Pope-Hennessy, James, *Lord Crewe* (1955)

Ridley, Jane and Percy, Clayre (eds.), *The Letters of Arthur Balfour and Lady Elcho 1885–1917* (1992)

Rose, Kenneth, *King George V* (1983)

Rowland, Peter, *The Last Liberal Governments: The Promised Land 1905–1910* (1968)

–*The Last Liberal Governments: Unfinished Business 1911–1914* (1971)

Seymour, Miranda, *Ottoline Morrell: Life on the Grand Scale* (1992)

Spender, J. A. and Asquith, Cyril, *Life of Herbert Henry Asquith, Lord Oxford and Asquith* (2 volumes, 1932)

Stewart, A. T. Q., *The Ulster Crisis* (1967)

Williams, Rhodri, *Defending the Empire: The Conservative Party and British Defence Policy 1899–1915* (1991)

Young, Kenneth, *Arthur James Balfour* (1963)

INDEX

An asterisk signifies those individuals who are listed in the appendix of 'Biographical notes'. An italicized page number indicates the location of a biographical footnote. Nicknames and aliases are cross-referenced. Those who ascended to a peerage pre-June 1914 are identified by title, not by surname. A cross signifies those houses listed in the appendix of 'Notes on houses'. The following abbreviations are used: AG = Archie Gordon; AGC = Archie Gordon Club; HG = Hugh Godley; HHA = H. H. Asquith; 'V' = Violet Asquith; WSC = Winston Churchill.

marriage to Katharine 132, 134–6; on
Shaw 46; V's relations with 55, 60,
141, 203, 225; mentioned 1, 22, 33,
36, 47, 71, 83, 84, 86, 143, 187, 286,
291, 306, 400; correspondence from
(1905–9) 33–6, 135, 141, 198
Asquith, Violet*:
accident at Slains 164–7; and American press 350, 353–4, 371; character
61, 65–6, 84–5, 101, 117, 124, 130,
133, 164–6, 181, 192–3, 199; on
'coming out' 26–7, 41–2, 36, 38, 66,
106 n. 1; and courtship 48–9, 50–1,
52, 54, 55, 56, 59, 61–2, 64, 70–1, 86–
7, 129, 257–61, 273, 276, 331–2; and
death of AG 191–7, 198–9, 203 n. 3,
266; and father 144, 150, 151, 153–4,
183, 184–5, 308, 327, 333, 338; health
146, 149, 170, 201; intelligence of
109, 286; and marriage 82, 86, 91–2,
105, 109, 132, 133, 146, 148, 181–6,
188–9, 219, 258, 270, 312, 327; on
men and women 116, 144, 213, 216,
375; philanthropic instincts of 45, 64,
78, 101, 106, 227–8, 298, 318, 369
(see also AGC); political involvement
145, 154–5, 166–9, 176–80, 220, 229,
266, 324–5, 393; as premier's daughter
156–60; and public speaking 168–9,
212, 284, 287, 291–2; and religion 18–
19, 74–5, 330; studies Greek 106, 138–
9, 142, 161–2, 170, 343 n. 1; on socialism 26, 415; on suffragettes 304, 390;
on women's suffrage 112–14, 291,
330, 354, 395–6; unconventionality
of 53 n. 1, 91, 96, 102, 239
Astor, Ava *357*
Astor, Vincent *329*-30, 371
Athens 385
Aubrey *see* Herbert, Aubrey
Austin, Alfred *208*
Austria-Hungary 169, 415
Auteuil 6–7
aviation 321, 408; V's flight in biplane
327
'A.W.' *see* Ward, Arnold

'B.' *see* Bonham Carter, Maurice

Bacon, Augustus *362*
Baedeker 29, 215, 296, 297
Baker, H. T.*:
AG's jealousy of 296; and general election (Dec. 1910) 230, 233; V's fond-
ness for 42, 56, 49; mentioned 39, 60,
68, 82, 117, 120, 161, 166, 174, 216,
224, 328, 380, 388, 390
Balfour, Alice *116*
Balfour, Arthur James*:
and general election (1906) 99; (1910)
230–2; and government (1905) 62–3,
88–9; and Lords' reform 271, 392; in
parliament 104, 131, 213, 268, 342;
V's impressions of 46–7, 77, 84, 116;
on WSC 45–6; mentioned 117, 169,
339 n.1, 340, 391–2
Balfour, Lady Betty *116*
Balfour, (Colonel) Eustace *116*
Balfour, Frances *116*
Balfour, Lt-Col. Francis *241*
Balfour, Gerald *364*
Ballinger, Richard *364*
Balliol College, Oxford 64, 88, 166
balls *see* Court; dances/dancing
Banbury, Sir Frederick *268*, 340, 342 n.1
Barbara *see* McLaren, Barbara
Baring, Maurice* 192, 213–4
Barker, Henry *247*, 287
Barnard, Emily *270*, 272, 286, 357, 372
Barnbougle Castle† 77
'Barnie' *see* Barnard, Emily
'Baronet, the' *see* Simpson, Sir Timothy
Barran, Sir John *230*, 273
Barrett, John *362*
Barrie, J. M. 51 n. 2, 271, *386*
Barrymore, Ethel *357*
Battenberg, Prince Louis *316*
Batterdogs *see* Battersea, Lord
Battersea, Lady 9, 94–5, 109
Battersea, Lord* 94–5, 104, 109
'B.C.'/'B-C' *see* Bonham Carter, Edgar
Beaconsfield, Lord *see* Disraeli, Benja-
min
Beatty, Rear-Admiral Sir David *313*, 316,
318
Beaufort Castle† 334
Beaumont, Admiral Sir Lewis *24*

Cambridge University 167

Cameron, Sir Ewen *59*, 61, 126, 224

Campbell, Beo 125

Campbell, Mrs Patrick *293*

Campbell-Bannerman, Sir Henry ('C.-B.')*:
and Liberal leadership 63, 88–91, 143; resignation of 143, 144, 145, 146, 149–50

Campbell-Bannerman, Lady 89–1

Camperdown, Earl of 277

Canada:
parliament of 374–6; and United States 373, 377; V's visit 1913, 350, 370–78; (*see also* Navy)

Canadian Born 219

Canterbury, archbishop of *see* Davidson, Randall

'Capable Scot, the' *see* Gordon, Archie

Carlisle, Alexander *312*

Carmichael, Alexander 225, *269*, 291; correspondence from 254–5

'Carrier, the' *see* Bonham Carter, Maurice

Carrington, Lord *211*

Carson, Sir Edward 271, *311*, 358, 381, 394

Casaubon, Madame 2–4, 27, 174

Casaubon, Monsieur 2–3

Cassel, Felix *43*, 47; proposes to V 121, 131, 166

Cassell, Sir Ernest *151*

Castle Ashby† 104 n. 3, 114

Castle, the, Dublin† 205, 209

Catholicism, V's attitude to 18–19

Cave, Mr *21*

Cave, Walter *128*

'C.B.' *see* Campbell-Bannerman, Sir Henry

Cecil, Lord Hugh 213 n.1, *268*, 271, 274, 278

Cecil, Lord Robert 271

Chalmers, Dr Albert *404*-6

Chamberlain, Austen *145*, 271, 326

Chamberlain, Joseph* 3, 20, 47, 85, 88, 131; and tariff reform 14–15

Chambry 8, 16

chaperones/chaperonage 51, 53, 55–6, 59–60, 103, 108, 117, 166

Charles *see* Lister, Charles

'Charlie' *see* Meade, Charles

Charteris, Evan *45*, 143, 188, 211

Charteris, Guy *40* n. 2, 60, 61, 62, 63, 93, 108, 125

Charteris, Hugo ('Ego') *63*, 93, 187, 305

Charteris, Mary *206*

Charteris, Lady V *125*, 305

'Charty' *see* Ribblesdale, Lady

'Cheeseman' *see* Currie, James

Cherbourg 33–36

Chesterton, Cecil 348 n. 2

Chesterton, G. K. *47*, 362

Chinese labour issue (1905–6) 76, 99, 101

Choate, Joseph *355*

Christian Science 79–80

church services 77, 143, 205, 239, 312, 316, 333, 363, 401

Churchill, Clementine*:
beauty of 40, 201–2; character 383, 393; engagement to WSC 162–3; V's friendship with 43, 171, 291; mentioned 227, 316, 326

Churchill, Lady Gwendeline *313*, 317, 318, 322, 394

Churchill, Winston S.*:
social: Balfour on 45–6; character 82, 146, 192, 221, 316–8, 338, 356, 380, 414; on Enchantress (1912) 317–21, 322–4; (1913) 383–5; engagement and marriage 162–3, 171; Montagu on 176–7; V's friendship with 178, 195, 286, 306, 393; V's impressions of 127, 162, 203
political: at admiralty 284–5, 304, 316–7, 319, 382, 396 n. 1, 409–11; Dundee election (1908) 157–8; foreign policy (navy estimates) (1908–9) 168–70; and general election (1910) 231; and Home Rule (1912) 298–300; and Lords reform 199, 266–7; in parliament 213, 342 n. 2; mentioned: 130, 227, 245, 274, 282, 379, 389, 392, 415; correspondence from 195